Mysticism and Morality

A New Look at Old Questions

Richard H. Jones

LEXINGTON BOOKS
Lanham • Boulder • New York • Toronto • Oxford

LEXINGTON BOOKS

Published in the United States of America
by Lexington Books
An imprint of The Rowman & Littlefield Publishing Group, Inc.
4501 Forbes Boulevard, Suite 200, Lanham, Maryland 20706

PO Box 317
Oxford
OX2 9RU, UK

British Library Cataloguing in Publication Information Available

Library of Congress Cataloging-in-Publication Data

Jones, Richard H., 1951–
    Mysticism and morality : a new look at old questions / Richard H. Jones.
        p. cm.
    Includes bibliographical references and index.
    ISBN 0-7391-0784-4 (alk. paper)
    1. Mysticism. 2. Ethics. I. Title.

    BL625.J635 2004
    204'.22—dc22

2003065679

Printed in the United States of America

♾™ The paper used in this publication meets the minimum requirements of American
National Standard for Information Sciences—Permanence of Paper for Printed Library
Materials, ANSI/NISO Z39.48–1992.

Mysticism and Morality

STUDIES IN COMPARATIVE PHILOSOPHY AND RELIGION

Series Editor: Douglas Allen, University of Maine

This series explores important intersections within and between the disciplines of religious studies and philosophy. These original studies will emphasize, in particular, aspects of contemporary and classical Asian philosophy and its relationship to Western thought. We welcome a wide variety of manuscript submissions, especially works exhibiting highly focused research and theoretical innovation.

Varieties of Ethical Reflection: New Directions for Ethics in a Global Context, by Michael Barnhart
Mysticism and Morality: A New Look at Old Questions, by Richard H. Jones

To

My Mother

Dorothy Hubert Jones

Contents

Part I
Framing the Issues

Part II
The Traditions

Part III
Analysis

Part I

Framing the Issues

1

Exploring Mysticism and Morality

The anthropologist Melford Spiro recounts the curious tale of an especially austere Buddhist monk living in the Sagaing hills west of Mandalay in Myanmar (formerly Burma). The monk was so pure in his renunciation that he abandoned living in a dormitory within his monastery and now lives in a cave. The local Buddhist laity believe there is great merit to be gained for themselves by giving, especially if the contributions are to a holy man. Thus, there is great merit to be acquired from contributions to such an obviously holy monk. And it turns out that building a dormitory for a monk is considered a very high form of giving. So over the years the faithful have constructed three new dormitories for the monk adjacent to the one he abandoned. Thus, there are now four uninhabited dormitories within the monastery, for the monk of course will not live in any of them. Indeed, it is precisely because he will not live in them that they were built. It is an instance of a paradox: the more a monk rejects worldly goods, the holier he is deemed to be; and the holier he is deemed to be, the more the laity lavish worldly goods upon him—dormitories, the finest food, and luxuries such as automobiles—since the amount of merit the giver receives depends on the holiness of the recipient.[1]

From a moral point of view, the actions of the Burmese laity are puzzling. The buildings given here do nothing for anyone but instead sit there unused—and the givers knew that was exactly what would happen. However, the givers are helped: by their giving they earn merit for themselves that helps them toward a propitious rebirth. In sum, no one is helped but the *givers* themselves. But are these acts of charity *moral* at all when the givers only help themselves? Does not the context of these acts actually invert the moral point of view? Apparently, in the world of religion even a seemingly simple act of charity may become morally problematic.

Extreme Positions

The problem only increases when we turn to one particular form of religiosity:

3

mysticism. The spectrum of views on the relation of mysticism to morality is broad. On the one end are scholars who deny mystics can be moral even in principle—mysticism and morality are in fact incompatible. One advocate of this view, Arthur Danto, claims classical Asian mystical traditions require beliefs about the nature of reality that do not permit the genuine concern for other people that is necessary to be moral: if all reality is really one, as advocates of mystical monistic metaphysics assert, love is impossible, since love requires a dualism of two persons (one to love and one to be loved).[2] Others argue that mystics are inherently selfish in their self-centered quest for their own enlightenment or that the values inculcated on the quest foreclose the possibility of concern for other people and thus accomplished mystics must be amoral. The inward orientation of mystical practices leads to a total disregard of all worldly affairs. All worldly concerns—including concern for other people—drop away as only the misguided delusions of the unenlightened. Mystics are "beyond good and evil" and all other worldly values. Having awakened from this "dream" world of ours, mystics are totally unconcerned with trying to improve the conditions within a dream by rearranging its parts. Like Plato's enlightened prisoner having left the cave, enlightened mystics do not deem the values of our shadow world to be of any significance—moral concern for others would be as much a product of our ignorance as is selfishness. Hence, the scandal: mystics, practitioners of what is usually taken to be the most advanced form of religion, are in fact not moral but coldly indifferent to the welfare of others.

On the other end of the spectrum are scholars who argue mysticism is either necessary for our concern for others or is in fact the very origin of it. Walter Stace was a strong advocate of mysticism as the justification of altruism.[3] The implosion of reality involved in a mystical experience releases an explosion of activity helping others. In fact, only mystics are truly compassionate and moral. Only mystical experiences permit a complete escape from the self-centeredness governing our normal lives, thereby freeing an outflow of selfless love. Only this total lack of personal attachment enables us to be deeply concerned with all people—otherwise we are merely imposing our own selfish desires upon others under the guise of "doing good." Plato's enlightened prisoner returning to the cave will ignore what the unenlightened prisoners take to be their vital concerns, but he will know what their true interests are and what will really help, and he will act accordingly. In fact, only enlightened mystics have the correct knowledge of reality and the proper motivation to apply it. They are not "world-denying" at all—they know what is truly real and the path to end our suffering. The rest of us are unknowingly operating out of ignorance and greed. Thus, mystics are not being selfish but are taking the steps necessary to become true vessels of concern for others.

In between these extremes, other scholars argue that mysticism either supports morality (or vice versa) to one degree or another or is in tension with it, if not a direct conflict. Thus, some argue that morality lessens a sense of self-centeredness and may thereby lead to mystical experiences. Or mystical experiences provide a sense of selflessness, and this may end up in some cases being expressed in a concern for others. Thus, some mystics may be moral and some not, depending on factors other than those experiences that earn them the label "mystics."

The Issues

Although most people probably think mysticism produces moral people, scholars have questioned this at least since Albert Schweitzer criticized Hinduism and wrestled with the issue of how to reconcile a monistic interpretation of mysticism with morality and life-affirmation.[4] Critics of the moral possibilities of mysticism are correct in insisting that mysticism is about an individual's inner development. But even if self-cultivation is the focus of a way of life, that fact alone does not determine the answer to the question of whether mysticism and morality are at odds—how mysticism intersects with our external actions toward others and our motives for acting still remain genuine issues. This leads to moral questions. Must a mystical sage be a saint? Or can a sage even be a saint? Are mystics beyond good and evil, having no interest in worldly values? In particular, are social concerns screened out of the mystical point of view? What is the relation of mystical experiences to values? Does mystical spontaneity or even-mindedness preclude the possibility of the mental reflection necessary for moral choice? Do mystical experiences in fact have no bearing on morality at all? Or are different mystical experiences related to morality in different ways? Do different mystical ways of life, rather than the experiences themselves, determine whether mystics are moral or not? Do all mystics in fact share just one set of values? Or do different mystics merely reflect the factual beliefs and values of the religions and cultures they find themselves in? And can mystics offer any guidance to the unenlightened with our ethical dilemmas today?

Before any of these questions can be addressed, certain preliminary questions must be dealt with. In this chapter, basic methodological issues will be addressed. In the next chapter, what exactly is meant by "morality" will be the issue. And in the final chapter of Part I, the importance for the issues at hand of religion as a way of life, types of mystical experiences, and aspects of mysticism related to the issue of morality will be discussed.

A Philosophical Project

The questions to be addressed here are philosophical.[5] The basic issues fall into two groups: whether mystical experiences or mystics' beliefs and values conflict with the presuppositions necessary to adopt a moral point of view, and whether mystics can be deemed to be moral because they act from a genuine concern for other people's welfare and fulfill the other requirements of morality discussed in the next chapter. The history of religions will supply the data in the form of a particular mystic's writings and actions or what the basic texts of a tradition state should be a mystic's motive and reason for his or her action.

Two preliminary points need to be noted about this approach. First, the moral status of various mystical traditions will be assessed here, and this involves more than merely listing their ethical precepts: the beliefs and values exhibited in mystics' writings and actions must be examined. The factual and evaluative claims involved in the mystics' ways of life—in particular, *why* they do what they do—will be central. Both the claims explicitly made by mystics and the beliefs logically entailed by a claim or act will be pertinent. The "why" question here will remain a matter of philosophical analysis related to concepts, doctrines, and justifications, not a matter of a psychological or sociological investigation into the sociopsychological conditions for why mystics do what they do—this is not a book on the "mystical mind." This does not mean a tradition can be reduced only to those aspects central to the issue of morality. Focusing on one issue obviously does not imply that there is nothing of philosophical or religious value in these traditions except what is relevant to this one issue or that other approaches to the traditions might not also be illuminating. In addition, philosophers focus on concepts and doctrines, but they cannot ignore all the other elements of a mystical tradition (e.g., meditative techniques and rituals) without distorting the subject under investigation. That is, just because philosophers focus on one element—the tradition's intellectual skeleton—does not mean this element can be understood independently of the interconnections with the rest of the elements that keep a way of life alive. Indeed, a skeleton only makes sense in the context of a whole body, and the same applies to the entailed claims of a way of life.

Second, this enterprise involves asking a question that mystics in earlier traditions may well not have asked themselves. Classical religious traditions do not have a distinct tradition of second-order philosophical reflection on value-issues and thus no separate discipline of "ethics." Ethics as a discipline did not develop within religious traditions until an encounter with Greek thought or until the modern era. In fact, the philosophical issues related to morality may be alien to the concerns of the mystics themselves. But the questions can still legitimately be asked, and the factual and evaluative claims of a particular tradition can provide answers to our modern Western questions. No answer is being imposed upon others simply by asking questions they have not explicitly asked themselves. It may still turn out that a particular mystical position is moral, immoral, or nonmoral, and the answer will be found only by examining the writings and actions of a mystic or the fundamental values and beliefs of a particular mystical tradition's basic texts. To defend this position, two more points must be addressed: the question of applying modern concepts to nonmodern cultures and the methodology used in answering these questions.

Modern Concepts and Classical Cultures

All the key concepts in this project—"ethics," "morality," "religion," "mysticism"—have long histories, but it is in their contemporary Western senses that they are being used here to aid in understanding traditional and non-Western cultures.[6] This opens up any study such as this to the charges of being anachronistic and of distorting the subjects being studied by imposing alien values and beliefs on other cultures. But no form of cultural imperialism is necessitated merely by using modern concepts. Concepts such as "religion" or "mysticism" can be useful for classifying nonmodern phenomena, even if other cultures never developed the terms. The fact that the concepts are relatively new does not mean that they distort what they purport to depict. No one says, "There was no gravity before modern scientists invented it" (except clumsily to make the point that the *concept* of "gravity" is a modern one). But academics say the same of religion and mysticism all the time. Nor does anyone say, "Gravity does not exist," simply because it does not exist apart from other physical phenomena and can only be studied by abstracting out aspects of a physical phenomenon for study. But again scholars frequently say that of religion and mysticism. Devising a descriptive category does not create the reality to be studied in any meaningful sense—a category, if it turns out to be useful, merely highlights aspects of existing phenomena.

In sum, common claims such as "Mysticism is an academic creation" are only confusing: it is true if we are only referring to the concept "mysticism," but it is false if we are referring to an historical phenomenon under study. In the study of other cultures, certain phenomena may fall into broader, more abstract categories such as "religion" or "mysticism" without the phenomena under study being forced to be modern or Western or anything else. Distinguishing "ethics" from "religion" or "mysticism" from "religion" may also prove helpful, even if doing so reflects only a modern concern. Scholars in the modern Christian West were the first to make a serious study of other religions, so of course concepts for cross-cultural study originally arose from Christianity. But just because our concept of "mysticism" developed in a Christian context does not make Jewish or Buddhist "mysticism" a Christian phenomenon. Nor does the use of the concept make a comparative philosophical enterprise into a theological one. In fact, the modern concept has *antitheological* ramifications when used in comparative studies: all mystical traditions are being treated equally; thus, if mystical experiences do involve genuine insights into reality, we cannot assert that the only "true" mystics come from one particular tradition without presenting an additional philosophical or theological argument. On the other hand, we cannot simply assume that the descriptive concepts must help in the analysis of non-Western and premodern contexts—practitioners in the traditions themselves will have to decide whether accounts in terms of these descriptive concepts distort their ways of life or not. As the historian of religions Wilfred Cantwell Smith stresses, no observer's descriptive statement about another's religion is valid unless it can be appropriated by members of that religion. (That contemporary practitioners would be asked to validate a claim about their classical tradition complicates the matter.) But explanations and evaluations of religious phenomena cannot be so restricted.

The concept of "morality" was also devised in a Christian, liberal, and individualistic culture. It involves a cluster of value-laden concepts—"ought," "freedom of choice," "individuality," "autonomy," "intentionality," "rights," "duty"—many of which have no counterparts in other cultures.[7] All cultures have terms for evaluating human actions as either "good" or "bad," "helpful" or "harmful," but they may not reflect our distinction between "moral" and "immoral." However, we need not search ancient Chinese for a concept corresponding to "ought" or Sanskrit for a term meaning "moral" to study other value-systems. As Hilary Putnam says of the problem of studying ethics of another era or culture, "the fact that a concept does not belong to some language does not show that statements in our language containing that concept cannot be entailed by statements in the other language."[8] He gives a simple illustration: the statement "I have one pear in each hand" entails "I have an even prime number of pears in my hands" whether or not the concepts "even" and "prime" belong to the language in which the first statement is made. This means we can ask whether other ways of life satisfy our requirements for morality by manifesting a real concern for other people's interests—our term "morality" may be a modern invention, but surely we should not assume that a concern for others is also only a modern Western creation. Answering this question does involve making an outsider's judgment, but the use of modern concepts from outside the traditions under study does not determine any answer in advance of actually examining those traditions. Our assessment remains a modern judgment, but it does not necessarily involve imposing any of the investigator's values on the traditions being examined.

The use of modern concepts, however, does raise two other concerns. First, the use of any term as a translation or a descriptive category must be sensitive to the context in which the original term appears. The danger here is that when we are brought up with a certain value-system it may unconsciously cause a particular translation. Not every general category used in connection with a way of life can be translated as "religion." For example, the Hindu ways of life have no concept corresponding to our concept "religion," although "*dharma*" is often so translated. Haphazardly translating any denotation of a code of conduct as "ethics" or "morality" also can lead to distortions. Simply translating the Buddhist term for their code of conduct— "*shila*"—as "morality" masks the very real issue of whether those who adopt the code are in fact moral, i.e., acting with a concern for others. Such a translation without a discussion of the philosophical issue is simply question-begging—or, as is more likely, shows that the translator is entirely oblivious to a very real issue. Scholars may well have their point of view fixed by their translation of another culture's value-term as "morality" and thereafter see other value-systems only in Western terms. Thus, scholars may be misled by their own translation at the beginning of their study and be screened from ever seeing any reason to question it.

This does not mean that all classical philosophical and religious terms must merely be transliterated. However, any translation of such terms as "*dharma*" and "*brahman*" will be loaded with modern Western philosophical and everyday connotations. There is a very real danger that a translation will supplant the original range of reference or the meaning of a term with modern distinctions.[9] But these terms can be *understood* in English even if there are no simple modern English equivalents for them. Benjamin Lee Whorf, while arguing that the Hopi and modern English speakers see the world quite differently because of the differences in the grammar and vocabulary of their languages, was still able to expound Hopi grammar and terminology in English.[10] The accounts of any such concepts in English may require a sentence or a brief paragraph, but they are still understandable by people outside the group in which they originate. The possibility of unwittingly reading in modern concepts is still there but is lessened by the interconnections of multiple concepts in the account of a tradition. Most importantly, non-Western concepts may still legitimately fall within a broader descriptive modern category without distortion and may also be used to answer the philosophical question of whether a doctrine fulfills the criteria of morality.

Second, using categories alien to the culture at the initial descriptive level does not impose anything at any stage of investigation. The modern concepts of "ethics," "ethical," "value-systems," and "codes of conduct" are used to represent a level of abstraction for categorizing phenomena. Believers may still accept the observer's abstract descriptive categories as capturing concepts within their faith. Such categories shape our understanding by determining what aspects of a culture we are going to study but do not distort the culture's ideas. Similarly, evaluative judgments of whether a mystic is moral or not are not determined in advance. Asking a question formulated in Western terms frames what will qualify as a possible answer, but it does not determine any actual answer that other cultures provide. If we study enough of their texts and actions, we are constrained in what answer we can give to the question of morality. Thus, other cultures supply the answers but only to questions we ask, and we decide what questions to ask. In sum, the moral assessment of other cultures involves our modern concepts, but the concepts do not predetermine the answers other cultures can supply—the cultures still speak for themselves.

A third problem is that any description can never be completely separated from the basic questions we frame. This does not mean that the description is in any sense wrong but only that it is limited by the underlying point of view. All scholars will have particular interests, and their questions will reflect what the investigators value or at least what they think illuminates the traditions being examined. Thus, scholars should make their frames of reference as explicit as possible for examination by others. For the project here, the very concepts of "mysticism" and "morality" set the questions to be asked and thus filter which features of each tradition are relevant. Certain features are placed as centrally important, and other features end up being omitted completely. Nevertheless, the most important point here is that, even if the framework for understanding selects and frames the features of a tradition, it still does not determine the substance of what is found. There are no neutral, value-free descriptions since the framework chosen reflects the interests of the investigator. But not all values are *moral* values, and a framework is not necessarily loaded with moral values. Thus, adopting a framework is not necessarily a moral prejudgment of another tradition. This project involves particular values, but it is not normative in the sense of advocating any set of ethical values explicitly or implicitly. (Similarly, a historian's "descriptive ethics" is "normative" in the sense of necessarily having a level of theory, but it is not "normative ethics" in the sense of advocating a particular set of ethical norms.) This philosophical study is normative in the sense that it is asking questions of the beliefs and values of different mystical traditions, but it is not normative in the sense of predetermining any answer prior to study.

A framework is also not carved in stone: the study of other value-systems can have a dialectical effect causing the investigator to modify his or her initial framework. Comparative studies may present value-options or ways of thinking not otherwise thought of and may expose some presuppositions in one's own point of view that are not apparent when the focus is upon one's own culture alone. The nature of our own factual and evaluative commitments at least become more apparent when we see a contrasting point of view.

The Need to Understand Mysticism in Context

It is true, however, that cultural bias can unconsciously affect the interpretation of what is found. If so, the phenomena then do not speak for themselves but are made into something they are not. This happens especially when scholars give answers on the relation of mysticism and morality based on generalizations about mysticism rather than looking at particular mystics in their cultural setting. For example, some scholars (such as Steven Katz) take the simplistic position that because mystical experiences involve a sense of selflessness, mystics by definition cannot act selfishly and hence must be moral.[11] What these scholars do not see is that if mystical experiences cause mystics to see reality as free of selves, then there also are no *other selves* for them to be morally concerned about—thus, they cannot be *moral* either. Instead, a *nonmoral* value-system, not morality, would have to follow for all mystics if mystical experiences dictated values so simply. (Conversely, if mystical experiences permit a metaphysics in which there is some reality in other people for mystics to be morally concerned about, then there is the same reality in themselves that they can act selfishly about.) Others may argue that merely because the language of some mystics have no term corresponding to our concept of "morality," the mystics by definition cannot be moral. That their value-systems may nevertheless conform to our sense of morality would thus be ruled out from the start.

In place of such simple *a priori* reasoning, the value-systems of mystics will have to be examined in the context of their ways of life. The method used by many scholars (e.g., Walter Stace)—quoting mystics totally out of context—is not adequate. The analysis connected to answering philosophical puzzles becomes inextricably tied up with history. (Of course, the *answers* reached by the simplistic approaches cannot be ruled out—investigation may in fact lead to one of those positions.) The intention of the claims and actions—the immediate objectives of an action—becomes clear only if the goals and purposes of actions within the tradition are studied. Intention is an internal state, but it can be studied by observing people's actions and asking them about their intended consequences and their reasons for their actions. This involves understanding mystics in their own terms and analyzing the interconnections of their ideas and actions. In addition, mysticism cannot be neatly compartmentalized apart from other cultural phenomena. Thus, to adapt Gilbert Ryle's image on the nature of the mind, ethical analysis requires a "thick" description of the mystic's writings and actions, not a "thin" description of merely recounting a particular tradition's code of conduct. Moreover, codes only make sense in the context of their own particular tradition, not in the abstract. For example, what beings may be killed varies from tradition to tradition, and thus the rule "do not kill" varies in its application.

This approach, however, presents difficulties. Mystical traditions with a well-defined mainstream have evolved and are undergoing major changes today. Even within the classical period, each tradition has different schools of practice and interpretation and also dissenters. Each religion cannot be treated as if it were one unified tradition on the issue of mysticism and morality unless the actual examination shows this to be so. That is, we may conclude there is one mainstream "Christian" or "Hindu" view on the matter but only after the examination of a great number of mystics in their particular settings. One must build from individual mystics and texts and not make blanket generalizations based on only a few examples or a normative view of what orthodoxy should be. But, even ignoring the antinomian traditions in both the West and East, any generalizations would have to cover the entire tradition and that means also having to account for the entire history of ethical developments within a tradition. As will be seen, many religions in fact have a variety of responses to the issues. We cannot claim "Buddhism says . . ." but at most only what the majority of Buddhists in a particular subtradition have advocated in their texts—there are exceptions to all points even in that more limited scope.

A related problem is that even among the more orthodox, not all members of any religion govern their lives by their tradition's normative principles—there are Buddhists who practice the condemned livelihoods (e.g., hunting and fishing), and there have been wars in which Jainas and even Buddhist monks have participated. In short, not everyone practices what their religion preaches. Indeed, there is often a great disparity between the values we claim to live by and those we actually live by. We only have to look at the history of "Christian civilization" to be reminded that people do not always live up to the ideals or the requirements of proper conduct espoused in the basic texts of their religious traditions. Any philosophical examination will focus on normative ideals and what the texts give as justifications for actions—that is the "official" doctrine and standards of a religion or subtradition. However, we also must look in some detail at how the religions are actually practiced. One can argue that since religions have *ideals* apart from actual *practices*, we should focus on those official doctrines alone, but this would not present a complete picture of any real tradition. Any religion is not just what the intellectuals of that tradition today think it should be. In the end, there is no Christianity apart from what Christians actually do, and the same is true of all traditions.[12]

A further problem is that mystics usually do not discuss their own experiences but instead discuss the nature of reality, meditative techniques, knowledge, goals, the path to enlightenment, and the appropriate way to live—indeed, mystics do not discuss "mysticism" as that modern category has developed. Moreover, they may not discuss what we consider ethics or be at all interested in the issue of the possible morality of their way of life. Typically they simply adopt the doctrines and ethical codes of their religious tradition as governing the mystical practitioners at least on the path to enlightenment; only sometimes do they further develop them. The sources of their ethics include not only the philosophical texts of usual interest to those investigating mysticism but other types of literature (e.g., in Hinduism the Dharmashastras, the Puranas, and the two great classical Indian epics). These sources contain stories and exemplars that can show the reasons many follow the action-guides, although they may not show why mystics follow a tradition's norms. The philosophical writings reveal more of the doctrines, goals, and purposes involved in a way of life, even if the fundamental moral issue is not addressed.

The differences between and within traditions make any grand cross-cultural theories of the nature of religion and morality, such as Ronald Green's,[13] highly problematic. We cannot assume there are any universal values to all human cultures or that a single structure must underlie all value-reasoning. If any cross-cultural theories are possible, they must be developed from studying a great many cultures. The anthropologist Clifford Geertz in fact denies the very possibility of any grand theories because all knowledge is "local."[14] But there is also danger in overemphasizing the cultural setting of mystical traditions. The position opposite to the grand theories is an extreme historicism which would render the very possibility of understanding other cultures or eras impossible even in principle.[15] A "holistic" understanding of the configurations of elements in each culture and the history of a tradition is necessary to understand any of its elements. But does the particularity of each culture mean that aspects of events also do not fall into some broader descriptive categories? Are all theories ruled out? Comparativists can argue that all historical and anthropological accounts of a culture by outsiders are by their very nature already comparative. To them, historians need not deny that comparison is possible; comparisons simply must begin from more nuanced accounts of each culture.

Postmodernists, however, go further and deny any understanding of other eras and cultures is even possible: context totally determines the meaning of terms and actions. Each culture is a self-contained whole that cannot be penetrated from without. Both the meaning and reference of the terms of any culture's language are totally determined by the other elements of the language—there is no way in or out of the interlocking whole. It makes no sense to try to take any part of the organic whole (e.g., a code of conduct) out of the whole to compare with parts of other wholes—that very process would destroy what is to be compared, and so the task is simply meaningless. Thus, not only would this position make any cross-cultural theories impossible, any sort of cross-cultural understanding would be ruled out from the start. This position, however, has problems. Leaving aside the philosophical issue of whether such postmodernism is self-contradictory, the fact remains that Western scholars have produced studies of other traditions that the participants themselves accept. Thus, even if context is essential for understanding the claims and actions within any way of life, cross-cultural understanding does appear possible, and this means context does not hermetically seal off meaning or reference in any sense detrimental to a study such as this. (It also should be noted that biologists routinely compare systems from different species, and doctors believe it is feasible to transplant organs from other species into human beings, even if they have not yet perfected the technique—postmodernists seem to think cultures are more "organic wholes" than organic bodies.)

Understanding cannot be "objective" in the sense of producing observable phenomena for others to inspect, since understanding involves discerning the intentions of actions and claims. Such intentions are internal and cannot be part of such observable elements of a mystical tradition as its texts' codes of conduct. (That faith and intentionality are inward does not mean they are *private* creations—they may be the products of social sources even if they operate internally in producing public actions.) But this does not mean understanding must be totally "subjective" (based on the scholar's personal beliefs and tastes) or involve the imposition of the scholar's own views. Discerning someone's intentions thousands of years after they lived is obviously difficult, but we can read what actions they advocated and the reasons the texts offer to justify them. All such writings and actions should be interpreted in light of what appears as the mystic's principal goal or purpose. This will affect such issues as whether mystics mean a statement literally or are using a morally startling claim (e.g., "If you meet the Buddha, kill him!") as hyperbole for teaching purposes. Similarly, a mystic may give assent to a tradition's basic textual authorities but give a symbolic interpretation of those texts—Meister Eckhart and Shankara are prominent instances of this. If so, their thought, not the ostensible authorities, is really controlling. Interpretation risks circularity in the scholar's account if the mystics are not explicit on what is centrally important to their way of life. The testing of any scholar's claim is whether a statement makes sense of the widest range of an individual mystic's writings and actions or the basic writings of a tradition or subtradition. Using a wide range of phenomena counters interpretations based on a few isolated references while missing the central intent of the whole. (Contemporary "socially engaged Buddhism" can be accused of the latter: as discussed in Chapter 15, it edits a religious tradition through modern Western values and ignores the central message of all classical Buddhist traditions.) Similarly with translations: texts are not totally amorphous, open to any meaning a translator may try to impose upon them—there is some "objective" substance to their content that scholars can discern, and thus acceptable translations do not reflect only the translator's culture or personal beliefs. The *Daodejing* is often cited as a text whose translation reflects more the translator's thought than Laozi's. But even that text is not open to any meaning an interpreter might want to impose but has an "objective" content.[16]

The Forgotten Philosophical Issue: Are Mystics in Fact Moral?

In the 1970s, scholars in comparative religion made some very promising advances in methodology of "comparative religious ethics."[17] But since then, scholars have mostly produced only narrow studies of different traditions of interest only to other specialists of those traditions. Most significantly, there has been very little on the philosophical issues involved in comparing value-systems and almost nothing on the philosophical issue of the relation of mysticism and morality.[18] The philosophical issue has typically been neglected or entirely screened out of the scholar's field of vision.[19] The level of much current analysis is that because Buddhists follow a code of conduct they obviously are moral or that anything connected with a religious *summum bonum* is by definition moral—scholars do not even see an issue there to discuss. Indeed, the fundamental moral question is now the forgotten issue in comparative religious ethics.

All mystical traditions of course have codes of conduct, rules, normative ideals, and exemplars of conduct that cover both actions toward other people and personal inner self-development. Creating such codes may be a universal feature of human cultures. But are we simply to *assume* both that the codes and ideals must reflect a moral concern for others and that the factual beliefs entailed by adherence to any code cannot conflict with the factual presuppositions necessary for moral conduct? Scholars routinely present the codes and ideals of religious ways of life, but surprisingly few scholars discuss the issue of *why* they are followed—in particular, whether the codes are followed out of a genuine concern for the welfare of the people whom the mystics interact with or for other reasons. Is there a genuine concern for other people for their own sake, or are people treated simply as means for the mystic's own spiritual advancement even if they are not actually mistreated? It is obviously easier to deal only with the codes recorded in a tradition than to look at the "inside" of mystical actions (the mystic's intentions and reasons), but it is the latter that reveals whether a particular mystic is moral. It is this issue that remains the most fundamental issue when value-systems are approached philosophically for a moral evaluation.

"Ethics" and "Morality"

Evidence that scholars simply miss the philosophical issue is that they routinely translate terms for codes of conduct (e.g., the Jewish *halakhah*) as "ethics" and state without discussion that the religious are moral. They assume that because such codes are "ethics" that they are "ethical" systems, and, since "ethical" is inter-changeable with "moral," the followers therefore must be moral, i.e., concerned for the welfare of others. In short, they go from "following a code of conduct" to "must be concerned with others' welfare" by nothing more than a simple translation. What is entirely missed is that there are two distinct concepts operating here: the notion of rules of interpersonal conduct ("ethics") and genuine concern for others as the reason for following those rules ("morality"). The substantive moral issue of whether a mystic is concerned for others is simply bypassed by substituting the modern term "morality" for a classical religious concept for a "code of conduct" and reading in all its modern connotations. But we cannot conclude by this sleight of hand that everyone following a code of conduct with rules against killing and stealing must be doing so out of concern for others (rather than some self-serving reason) and thus must be moral—the teachings and actions of the mystics must actually be examined closely.

"Ethics" can most broadly mean, as with Aristotle, the whole management of human life—what is the "good life" or whatever ends we should strive for—or it can mean only codes of conduct for actions affecting others. But "morality" involves another issue: do our actions exhibit a concern for other people's welfare? We cannot assume that any set of "ethics" must include a concern for other people—that is a substantive question of values that cannot be settled simply by definition but requires historical investigation. Thus, the concepts of "ethics" and "morality" each have different scopes.[20] The term *"ethics"* in this study will be limited to any code or value-system for actions impinging on other people. The term *"morality"* will refer to exhibiting a genuine concern for others. (Thus, "morality" will not refer to all of one's personal values or to all social values. The more limited sense of the term will also restrict the scope of inquiry here to more limited questions.) We can be "ethical" by conforming to the values of a society. It is a matter of behavior that has nothing to do with the question of whether our reason or motive is "moral," i.e., whether we are conforming to the code because of a real concern for others. (Thus, being "immoral" is deemed a moral wrong while being "unethical" may not be.)

In short, operating by some "ethical code" is not the same as "being moral." We can speak of "Nazi ethics" and still legitimately ask whether the Nazis were moral. Similarly, we can identify Buddhist ethics and still ask whether Buddhists are being moral in holding these ethics. If someone follows a cultural code—even a religious one—only for personal gain, he or she is not praiseworthy as being *moral*. That mystical actions are "selfless" does not by definition mean that the mystics then must be acting out of concern for others' welfare or that their actions always have positive consequences for others. In sum, mystics always have a set of ethics, but the question is: are the mystics morally concerned with others or only concerned with their own self-development?

Part of the reason for the confusion is that we use "ethical" and "moral" interchangeably in ordinary English. We speak of "sets of morals" (i.e., ethical codes) or "personal morals" (i.e., a set of values for oneself) or "moral develop-ment" (i.e., either the inner personal cultivation of specifically moral virtues or any personal cultivation of any set of values).[21] We speak of a "personal morality" (even though morality involves interpersonal action and has one universal value—a concern for others), and of "medical ethics" or "professional ethics" (but not of "professional morals"). Adding to the confusion, the term "value" in the context of what is worthwhile in one's life is also often uncritically equated with "moral" and "ethical." Thus, this confusion cannot be avoided by using "value-system" rather than "ethics." But this arbitrariness of everyday terminology means that rather than adopting "ethics" as the name for value-systems and "moral" to identify concern for others, one could just as easily call the former "morals" and the latter "ethical." But regardless of the labels, what is important is that the concept of "following a code of conduct" remains distinct from the concept of "acting out of a concern for others."

This raises the issue of whether any code of ethics can itself be called "moral." Morality involves the *intentions* of the actors or the consequence of their actions and hence has an inner aspect that purely external phenomena—such as a code of conduct—cannot capture. Thus, it may make sense to call persons (either individually or collectively) or an action "moral" but not a code. A code covering actions affecting other people (e.g., requiring us not to harm others or to provide aid to them) may have been constructed out of a concern for others. Or it may not: an ethical code may instead reflect only self-restraint from selfish behavior or some other value (e.g., just to maintain the social order). Moreover, even codes constructed out of a concern for others cannot require that we act out of concern for others rather than for some self-serving motive. That is, the codes themselves cannot compel the reasons and motives of those who adopt them—codes at best only control actions, not the reasons and motives for compliance. In sum, moral concern remains a matter of intention, and codes at best only indirectly reflect that. Some scholars may want to consider a code to be moral if a moral person can adopt it. But, as will be seen in Part II, action-guides that restrict selfish behavior can be incorporated into both moral and nonmoral ways of life. Thus, it is difficult to consider a code of ethics in itself to be moral or not. The real issue remains whether *the person* following the code is moral. So too *a mystical tradition* can be deemed moral if the reasons advanced in the basic writings indicate that a person should follow the codes out of a genuine concern for others and not merely to help oneself. To answer this, much more in mystical ways of life will need to be examined than merely noting that religious codes contain injunctions against killing, stealing, and so forth.

To most people, ethics infuse religion to the point that "religion" simply means "ethics," and thus the issue of the relation of religion to ethics does not arise. To many scholars too, religion simply *is* ethics, and thus they fail to differentiate "religion" and "ethics" at all. Or they assume the religious must be moral without seeing an issue at all. To cite a recent example: Joseph Runzo can say without further discussion that morality is an inextricable part of any religious meaning of life, that moral structures are a critical part of religious conceptions of the structure of reality, and hence "part of what it means to follow the religious life is to follow the moral life."[22] Books on the ethics of the world religions most commonly are merely introductions to the basic beliefs of a tradition with the adjectives "ethical" and "moral" thrown in profusely and with no discussions of the philosophical issues of "ethics" or "morality." Other books focus on basic beliefs and codes of conduct alone and not on all the aspects of a tradition related to the issue of morality. Either way, the philosophical issue of morality is missed entirely.

To keep the philosophical issue clearly presented in this study, terms related to religious and mystical interpersonal value-systems will not all be translated "morality" and automatically deemed "moral." They will be treated as instances of the other category—the descriptive category for rules of conduct, "ethics." Thus, the moral issue will not be surreptitiously finessed by slipping in the concept of morality through a coarse translation. Replacing historical examination with such an uncritical assumption would be an instance of unconscious cultural imperialism: if we label a practice "moral" before we actually examine it merely because we value morality, we will be looking at it through a modern Western perspective and not letting it speak in its own terms. Thus, calling a text in this study "ethical" or a work of "ethics" should not mean that it is necessarily advocating *moral* values but only that it is an axiological work related to a tradition's values and norms concerning actions that impinge on others. The moral issue must be dealt with explicitly before any conclusion can be reached as to the moral status of a particular mystic's ethics.

Dealing with the issue of values in other cultures does touch a nerve.[23] The modern concept of "morality" developed in the Christian West, but the idea of "concern for others" is not unique to the modern West, and it is not "bashing" other traditions to ask whether they advocate it too, especially when some will be shown to be clearly moral. Nevertheless, the reader should be warned that the politically incorrect conclusion will be reached that some of the non-Western traditions under consideration are not moral. But if the issues are seen clearly and if the traditions are approached without the preconception that all people must be moral, this is the conclusion that appears. Perhaps, then, another objective of this study should be a greater willingness on the part of modern Westerners to understand ways of life in their own terms rather than imposing our basic values on others.

Overview

In Chapter 2 the idea of morality will be examined, and in Chapter 3 concepts connected to mysticism will be clarified. In Part II, mystics from five religious traditions will be used to examine the issue of mysticism and morality. In Part III, the relation of types of mystical experience to morality will be discussed, as will the issue of social action. Finally, what impact classical mystics' ideas on values and morality can have on the contemporary world will be addressed. In Part II, the truth of the traditions' factual claims will not be questioned but simply accepted; the objective of this study is instead to examine the ethics of these traditions and to see how morality does or does not figure in them. Both values (in particular, the central issue of concern for others) and factual beliefs (whether they permit or foreclose morality) will be studied. The mystical path and the enlightened state will both be of interest. The amount of exposition will vary from tradition to tradition—Daoism requires more because it is open to so many varied interpretations, while Jainism requires very little because only a few points are of importance here.[24] But this a philosophical study of the moral status of mystical traditions, not a comprehensive survey of the ethical rules and norms of the different traditions. For the latter, the reader will have to look elsewhere.

Mystics have been chosen from around the world to illustrate the variety of positions and the issues involved. But this study is not a comprehensive survey of all mystics of the world or even of those within the traditions under study, even leaving aside the problem that no doubt most mystics have not left behind writings or identifiable teachings. First, the focus is upon "classical" mystics unaffected by modern Western scientific, philosophical, and ethical thought (although a few contemporary practitioners will also be noted). Second, even within the selected religious traditions the survey will not be exhaustive: only basic texts and representative mystics of selected subtraditions will be discussed. The foundational texts of a tradition or subtradition will be the focus for the Eastern traditions, but for Christianity the focus will be on the medieval period. The selection within Hinduism and Buddhism will also be limited but will be sufficient to show that there are different points of view within the same tradition.

Notes

1. Spiro 1982, pp. 413-14.
2. Danto 1987. His position will be discussed in Chapter 13.
3. Stace 1960. His position will be discussed in Chapter 13.

4. Schweitzer 1936.

5. More theologically inspired thinkers such as R. C. Zaehner will not be discussed in detail here, although their positions may be noted in passing.

6. For the history of the concept of "morality" and the modern approach, see MacIntyre 1984, pp. 35-48. The term "mysticism" has roots in the classical Greek word "*mūstikos*" meaning silence or secret. It was initially used in connection with the Greek mystery religions, whose essential rituals were kept hidden from all but the initiated. As adapted by early Christian theologians, it referred to the mystery of the divine and came to refer to certain scriptural and liturgical matters. Only in the modern era has the term come to refer exclusively to certain types of religious experiences and states of consciousness. (Indeed, the concept of "religious experience" is also modern.) For a history of the term, see Louis Bouyer, "Mysticism/An Essay on the History of the Word," in Richard Woods, ed., *Understanding Mysticism* (Garden City, N.Y.: Image Books, 1980), pp. 42-55. For a history of the term "religion," see Wilfred Cantwell Smith, *The Meaning and End of Religion: A New Approach to the Religious Traditions of Mankind* (New York: Macmillan, 1963).

7. See, e.g., Rosemont 1988, pp. 60-61 and 1991, pp. 239-40, on the Chinese language. In asking whether a person may be said to have a concept *x* if he or she has no term in his or her vocabulary for *x*, Rosemont notes that one can have concepts without having terms to express them, just as we attribute prelinguistic awareness to babies—they are aware of pain or hunger even though they have no terms for them (1991, pp. 238-39).

8. Putnam 1991, p. 306.

9. Another example is translating the Hindu term "*dharma*" as "duty" and then seeing the *Bhagavad-gītā* simply as a Kantian tract on "duty."

10. Benjamin Lee Whorf, *Language, Thought and Reality: Selected Writings of Benjamin Lee Whorf*, ed. John B. Carroll (Cambridge, Mass.: MIT Press, 1956), pp. 134-59, 207-19. Whorf argued that every language contains an "implicit metaphysics" in its syntax and vocabulary and hence any translation from one language into another language-group would distort meanings. The weakness of this claim will not be discussed here beyond noting that different metaphysics have been statable in the same language (e.g., Platonic and Aristotelian in Greek), as have radically different scientific views of reality (e.g., Newtonian and Einsteinian physics in English); thus, language does not control thought.

11. S. Katz 1983, 1992a, 1992b. Katz is a "contextualist" with regard to the history of religions, but apparently he finds the fundamental philosophical issue in comparative religious ethics simpler to answer.

12. If pushed to extremes, the subject of study could be each practitioner, since each person has his or her own particular interpretation of a tradition and own way of life. But focusing upon the doctrines advocated and defended in the core texts of different subtraditions is sufficient to understand the philosophical issues related to mysticism and morality.

13. Green 1978, 1988.

14. Clifford Geertz, *Local Knowledge: Further Essays in Interpretive Anthropology* (New York: Basic Books, 1983).

15. See the debate among Little 1981; Stout 1980, 1981, 1983, 1997; Levine 1995.

16. See Isabelle Robinet's discussion in "The Diverse Interpretations of the *Laozi*," in Csikszentmihalyi and Ivanhoe 1999, pp. 127-59.

17. Little and Twiss 1973, 1978; Green 1978, 1988.

18. Arthur Danto (1972, 1976, 1987) has raised one of the basic issues (whether mystical beliefs conflict with the beliefs necessary for morality) for Asian traditions. His work, however, has provoked only a limited amount of discussion (in particular, Proudfoot

1976; Wainwright 1976; Perrett 1998). For more general philosophical studies on mysticism and morality, see Stace 1960, pp. 323-41, Wainwright 1981, pp. 198-231, and Barnard and Kripal 2002.

19. Ronald Green's works (1978, 1988) are examples of how the fundamental philosophical issue can be missed even while discussing philosophical issues related to religious codes.

20. The conceptual distinction has been noted by some philosophers. See, e.g., B. Williams 1985, p. 6. But usually in philosophy, "ethics" is the study of reasoning about "morality." The further distinction within philosophical ethics is between normative ethics (evaluating specific norms) and meta-ethics (questions such as "what is morality?" or "why be moral?").

21. The plural "morals" will not be used here: there is only one moral point of view (a concern for others' welfare), even if it can be made operative by more than one set of ethics. There is more than one moral quality, virtue, or value, but the plural "morals" can be confused with any set of ethical values.

22. In Runzo and Martin 2001, p. 19.

23. See Reat 1980.

24. For an excellent introduction to each of the traditions covered here (except Jainism, which he omits), see Smith 1991.

2

Morality

The cornerstone of "morality" as the term is generally used today is this: taking the interests of other people into consideration when deciding how to act.[1] It contrasts with selfishness in one's actions. The terms "morality" and "ethics" have evolved from Latin and Greek terms for general social customs (*mores*, *ethos*), but by the seventeenth and eighteenth centuries morality came to be equated with altruism as opposed to the selfishness of egoism.[2] That is, morality concerns those actions that impinge on other people and requires that part of the consideration in choosing an action is the welfare of the people who may be affected. Morality in the modern sense is thus a matter of practical questions involving other people in particular situations. How should I treat other people? How should I weigh my interests against the interests of the people upon whom my actions impinge?

The *interpersonal* nature of morality should be emphasized: morality guides our interactions with other people, and thus is "social" in that sense, even if our actions do not involve institutions but only face-to-face relations. The cluster of concepts we connect with morality—"fairness," "justice," "loyalty," "trust," "honesty," "duty," and so forth—involve our relations with others. If a person were alone on an island he or she would not be harming anyone, but it would be odd to call the person "moral" since one cannot be moral or immoral unless there is someone with whom to interact (unless we expand the scope of morality to encompass animals or nature). Similarly, if a person were to cut off his or her toe for no reason, this action would not be immoral—the act may be stupid or even sinful, but since no other person is affected the person cannot be immoral. One may have a "personal morality" in the sense of having developed a particular ethical code for oneself unlike that in the culture at large, but to cover morality the code must involve interpersonal actions, not actions that are "private" or "individualistic" in the sense of not impinging on the welfare of others but only involving one's own self-development.

The second thing to notice is that the notion of morality requires a *valuation* of what is desirable, significant, good, advantageous, or important for us to pursue.

We must make an evaluation of something being good or bad, positive or negative, in determining what we ought to do. Not all values, however, are necessarily *moral* values since not all valuations relate to interpersonal relationships. "Beauty" and "truth" are certainly considered positive values, but whether they are related to a moral concern is not obvious. Values shoot through all activities, but they may not be moral values. Science has cognitive values (e.g., simplicity and accuracy), but whether moral values are implicit in it is a matter of debate. Something can be "good" in a *nonmoral* sense: it is simply something of value or worth to us (e.g., "good" health, a "good" pen, a "good" strategy to win at tennis). Similarly, not all "oughts" are moral "oughts" (e.g., "you ought to hang a picture there"). Moreover, the "good life"—the best life for us to lead for our well-being or flourishing (*eudaimonia*)—is not by definition the morally right one, and so its connection to morality requires argument.

"Morality" is often used very broadly to mean any basic values one lives by. Morality thereby becomes by definition whatever values are claimed to have overriding importance. Any values on how we ought to live (e.g., mystical or other personal self-cultivation) taken to be the supreme guides in one's life thereby become "moral." Religious values thus are routinely considered "moral." Plato's highest value—the goal most supremely worth pursuing—involved contemplating beauty. Similarly, Aristotle argued that the highest goal toward which all things aim is by definition "good." But the substantive issue in all these cases remains whether the values are indeed *moral* in the modern sense of manifesting a concern for others or are only selfish.

Emotion or Reason?

One central issue about the nature of morality is whether morality is basically a product of our emotional life or of reflection. Advocates of one position point to the sympathy exhibited by babies as the intuitive or even biological source of a full-blown moral concern in our later development. To them, this natural sense of sympathy is essential to morality. To the Confucian Mencius, whoever is not naturally moved to action from a heart of sympathy at the sight of a child about to fall into a well is not human. We might say afterward, "It was just the right thing to do," to explain an act of helping, but sympathy was its real source of the action, not reason. David Hume grounded the moral point of view in sympathy (and also subordinated reason as the slave of the passions). Contemporary advocates of this position argue that it is developing this disposition that is essential to the moral life: with sympathy, we do not need rules to tell us to help others; without sympathy, we would not follow the rules anyway.

But opponents point out that sympathy is not action, and action is necessary to be moral. We may be naturally sympathetic, but feeling concern for the suffering of others only shows that we are affected by the experiences and reactions of others. To be moral we must actually *act* for the sake of others, and once we decide to act, reason becomes central. Emotional states come and go, and we cannot morally condemn someone for not having an emotion. Moreover, emotion is not the only source of concern for others: reason can show that all people are entitled to moral treatment or that it is in our own "enlightened self-interest" to be concerned with others' welfare, and only reason can lead us to an impartial, universal concern for all people. Reason also becomes vital to morality through weighing competing interests and in devising the rules regulating our actions toward others. For example, how do we decide when sympathy for the person suffering in front of us has to give way to some good for a greater number? In addition, we cannot just feel sympathy and help whoever is in front of us—we need to know *how* to help and that requires factual knowledge and values worked out by reason. In sum, reason can lead us to morality, and only reason can show us how to act. Rule-following becomes the central moral activity, and for this any emotion is unneeded.

Some rule theorists—the deontologicalists—claim actions are right or wrong in themselves regardless of their good or bad consequences. Thus, moral goodness is determined by standards independent of an action's effects. That is, deontological requirements relate to motive and intention and so are agent-centered. Immanuel Kant adopted this approach: we are moral if and only if we follow a maxim because of its form and not for any other reason, let alone an emotion.[3] A sense of duty and principle is the only reason for moral action, regardless of whether any good is promoted. But for the other branch of the rule theorists—the consequentialists—no action is ever right or wrong in itself. The principal examples are the utilitarians, following Jeremy Bentham, who advocate measuring "the greatest good for the greatest number." The outcome of actions is all that matters: the moral rightness is measured in terms of actions' total good and bad results (defined in terms of a nonmoral good, such as the pleasure or happiness produced or lost) for all people. Any action is justified if the good of the larger number is better served.

For all rule theorists, morality is a matter of objective, dispassionate reason. Impartial reason must replace the vicissitudes of an individual's sympathy or ability to empathize. Indeed, some would argue that compassion or love is not even moral, since it is too partial. Kant would point out that if we act for our family out of love, we are not given *moral* credit, since no real sacrifice occurs. Only by following the rules set forth by reason are we truly impartial and thus morally concerned with others rather than just satisfying our own feelings. In short, emotions may not only be unnecessary for morality but in fact be incompatible with it.

But opponents reject this dichotomy in favor of a more "whole person" approach (as discussed below). The entire Kantian notion of morality in terms of acting only out of "duty" rather than "inclinations" (such as concern for others) is called into question. If morality were only a matter of reason, we could always find a rationale justifying an immoral act or for not acting—we would never *feel* we did wrong. Rule theorists, in short, make morality too intellectual.[4] Rule-following also makes morality too "legalistic" or "moralistic"—the focus is on trying to follow the letter of a code, not on the driving spirit (including any possible moral concern for others). Morality is above any rule, and so no rule is absolute. Rule theorists may reply that all rules of course have exceptions. But why should rules have exceptions if rules are the essence of morality? How could we see that the rules must be broken in some circumstance? Some rules should be devisable that capture morality without exception, if morality were indeed only a matter of rule-following. But any rule—even basic ones against lying, stealing, or killing—can be suspended in the name of morality if necessary to help others.[5] Most people would, contra Kant, value saving a life over a slavish adherence to telling the truth when a life is obviously at risk.[6] (Of course, rule theorists could advance the maxim "There is no rule but 'help others'" or "Break any rule when it is necessary to help someone," but this would be admitting that rules do not capture all the substance of morality and thus would refute their own position.) Moral deliberation always requires emotional monitoring and an interplay of affect and reason.[7]

Realism or Antirealism?

Divergence among philosophers also occurs when we look at theories of what grounds our sense of morality. What is the ultimate source of moral valuation? Is there something in reality that we can discover that grounds morality in the fabric of reality thereby justifying it, or do we simply invent ethical codes to control ourselves and societies? Value-realists (usually called "cognitivists") assert the former, while value-antirealists ("noncognitivists") assert the latter.

Realists believe morality makes little sense unless moral value is part of the fabric of reality. That is, reality is not value-free but contains a moral order. Plato grounded morality in the Good. For philosophical naturalists, our mental life is as much a part of nature as inanimate objects, and so human values and the process of valuation are fully real. Theists believe a transcendent source of the natural order is the ultimate source of value. But all realists believe that moral value is part of reality independent of us and thus is objective in that sense. Thus, something in reality fixes moral concepts—"good," "right," "just," "duty." There are moral facts for us to discover, and hence there are moral statements that are true, independently of what we may believe. That torturing babies is wrong is as much a part of reality as physical objects; it is a truth regardless of what we think or feel about it and even if people did not exist to make the precept against it applicable. We do not create moral value by our social codes of conduct, any more than we create the mathematical order to reality by our symbol systems. To naturalists, moral value is a nonphysical property that is part of the natural order and thus has as much right to be in our ontology as physical properties.[8] For some realists, value may involve mental states (e.g., hedonism) or interpersonal relations and activities. But morality for all realists is in some way ingrained in reality, and moral obligations and principles are therefore binding upon us.

Antirealists deny anything remotely like an objective moral order—reality is totally devoid of values. Since the heyday of the logical positivists, antirealists have argued that ethics are only our personal choices in the form of prescriptions. No values are part of the objective order of reality. We invent "right" and "wrong"—they are not part of the world independent of our creations. There are no "objective" values for us to know by some "moral intuition." Values are totally subjective, expressing no more than our opinions and tastes. For example, emotivists hold that moral statements only express our emotional reactions or preferences rather than report a truth about reality—"Do not kill" means only "I do not like murder." The emotional reaction we feel to a morally abhorrent act does not differ in type but only in degree from our reaction to a breach of etiquette or the breaking of a rule in a baseball game. For Marxists, the sense of objectivity that a society's ethics has is an illusion: ethics reflect only economic bases and serve only the interests of the ruling classes. For many anthropologists, ethical codes are no more than conventions reflecting the socially approved habits of a particular culture; this leads to the doctrine that values are relative to a particular background set of beliefs or cultural form of life.

At most, antirealists believe ethical codes are a social creation necessary to maintain societies, although the codes' strictly human origins may have to be hidden by a Platonic "good lie" to maintain their authority. Antirealists need not treat all ethics equally: some codes work for maintaining social order and some do not. That is, murder is wrong because society would not survive if we did not punish it—not because it violates some "moral order" to the universe. If so, the rule against murder need not be either arbitrary or a matter of personal taste. Antirealists thus need not be nihilists who deny any values or libertines who claim there is no god and so all things are permitted. They may hold strongly to their moral beliefs. But all antirealists assert that no values are grounded in a reality independent of us—some value-systems just happen to work better than others.

The antirealists' objection to moral realism may seem a bit odd: alleged moral "facts" are not the type of things natural scientists investigate and they do not play a role in scientific explanations, and so they do not exist. But it is not clear why the fundamental standard of reality must be what scientists need for their theories, especially if there is an area of reality (values) they do not investigate.[9] Realists reply that moral properties, like sensory properties, are real even if they are not part of a scientific explanation (although they do have trouble explaining how values are exactly fixed into the structure of reality).[10] In any case, antirealism in the form of emotivism appears to be the working hypothesis in American culture today.[11]

The Factual Presuppositions of Morality

Whether or not morality involves claims about reality, practicing morality does presuppose certain factual claims, i.e., claims about what is real that are either true or false. Morality is not reducible to these factual claims—it is a matter of imperatives, and imperatives are not true or false. But the practice of morality makes no sense unless certain factual conditions exist—in that sense, the practice "presupposes" the latter. This is true of any practice. For example, the request "Please open the window" presupposes that the person who makes the request believes there is a window, it is closed, it can be opened, and the person asked is able to open it.[12] The request is not reducible to those beliefs, but the request makes no sense unless the asker explicitly or implicitly holds them. If one or more of these factual claims are in fact false, the request is not *falsified* but is rendered groundless and thus *inoperative*. The same holds for the practice of morality: if its factual presuppositions do not obtain, morality is not coherent, and we are deluding ourselves in thinking it is. (As discussed below, factual knowledge also plays a second role in ethics: how we respond to others depends on what we take to be real and what goals we take to be real.) The logical relation between factual presuppositions and moral claims does not mean the latter must precede the former in our mind. For example, we may decide that morality cannot be justified because, some philosophers argue, scientists have demonstrated that the universe is physically deterministic and thus free will is an illusion, or we may reject determinism because we think morality is justifiable. All that is being asserted here is that morality cannot proceed unless certain factual claims are accepted. Thus, if the issue is presented to us, we must accept these conditions or admit we are behaving irrationally.

Morality has four presuppositions: consciousness, freedom of action, orderliness of actions, and real "persons." Moral realists might wish to add a fifth condition: God or another source of morality that grounds morality in the structure of reality. But since antirealists can also be moral, realism does not appear to be a necessary condition for morality, unlike the four presuppositions discussed here. The first two conditions are connected. First, a being without consciousness cannot value one thing over another and thus cannot make moral valuations. In this connection, morality also entails a minimal rationality: moral agents must have intentions and goals and be able to supply reasons for them if asked. Second, an agent must be autonomous and thus have freedom of choice—"freedom of will." We must be free to consider different courses of actions and able to act upon one of them. If we are biologically, psychologically, or culturally determined or if our actions are predestined by God, we cannot be a moral agent. That is, we cannot be held morally responsible for our actions if we have no control over them but are mindless puppets being completely pushed around by other forces. Nature and culture may limit the range of our choices and actions, but we must have freedom of action within that range.

The third condition is the opposite of determinism: our actions cannot be completely random, or we would not have the necessary control that makes genuine choice possible, and without such choice we cannot act morally. That is, if events are simply random and uncontrollable, then we would not be able to control our actions to any degree nor able to predict the general consequences of our actions. In short, a causal order permitting predictability and the effectiveness of our actions is necessary for free choice. We must have some real control over our bodies and actions through free will. Freedom of action thus requires a middle zone between a determinism by other forces and the chaos of no causal order—an "agent causation" in which we have at least some control over our actions.

The last factual condition has three parts. First is the ontological claim that moral agents are real. This does not require eternal "souls" or "selves" or any other particular entity, but there must be some reality that can reflect, choose, and act. Second, the "persons" the agents encounter are also real and are the type of realities entitled to our moral consideration—they also suffer, are conscious, or have whatever properties warrant the right to have their interests considered by a moral agent. Third, in addition to each being real, these two realities cannot be connected or identical. If they were, there would not be another "person" about whose interests a moral agent could be concerned but only something connected to or identical to our own reality—thus, there would be only self-interest in our actions. There could be no self-sacrificing concern for others, and thereby morality would be ruled out.

Are these factual conditions part of reality? In the modern West, the most common concern is free will versus determinism (although there are eliminationists who deny consciousness altogether). But, as will be seen in the following chapters, issues arise for each of the last three conditions in mystical ways of life.

The Requirements for Morality

If those are the factual preconditions, what are the requirements of morality? David Little and Sumner Twiss set forth five conditions for an "action-guide" to qualify as moral.[13] First, an action-guide must be intelligible to the actor and must direct our actions and attitudes. Second, it must be universalizable in the sense that the holder of the action-guide is willing that all other people in the same circumstances act by that guide. Third, it must be considered supreme among value-systems. Fourth, it must be justifiable: it must have *prima facie* priority over other values, and it needs no further nonmoral justification—we do what is moral simply because we morally ought to, not to attain some other goal.[14] And lastly, the action-guide must concern our actions impinging on others ("other-impinging" actions) and must reflect some consideration of the effect of those actions on the welfare of others ("other-regarding" concern). All religious traditions have codes and rules governing other-impinging actions, but a person is *moral* only if they follow those rules out of an other-regarding concern.

These five requirements are set up for whether a rule is moral or not, and thus they do not work as well for the "virtue ethics" approach discussed below, although exemplars of virtue can function as action-guides. Also, as noted in the last chapter, a code is hard to characterize as "other-regarding" since both the moral and nonmoral may be able to follow the same code; a tradition may be deemed moral if the official reasons advocated in the core texts for following its action-guides are moral, but a person or action are the prime instances of what is or is not moral. Nevertheless, discussing these requirements still exposes some of the philosophical issues concerning morality.

The Prescriptivity of Morality

The practicality of morality requires that a moral action-guide must provide at least some guidance on how to act in concrete situations. It can either prescribe or proscribe actions. A wide range of persuasive discourse may be employed both to make morality operative in different concrete action-guides and to convince someone to adopt the moral point of view. Action-guides themselves can come in many forms—e.g., simple commands and injunctions, detailed ethical codes, general principles, everyday rules of thumb, folk wisdom, stories reconstructing events to make a point, persons deemed to be exemplars of behavior or virtue. Ethical goals and ideals in the form of norms or exemplars can be targets toward which we strive even if we never attain them. The more authoritative action-guides are deeply embedded in a culture and thus appear explicitly or implicitly in diverse cultural expressions (including religious rituals) and are least open to change. But the moral point of view can be implemented by different action-guides. Indeed, action-guides can conflict over how to help others—e.g., showing mercy to all versus exacting justice, enforcing rights versus caring, individual versus communitarian rights. Deep divisions over what is the appropriate action typically exist in all areas of social activity within a society.

Action-guides are social institutions that impose themselves on us from the outside from birth. Even if we reject moral realism, action-guides are still objective cultural realities in that sense—we can alter them but they confront us first and shape our development. Indeed, our "private" ethical decisions may in fact be totally "public" products, shaped by social custom. Internal ethical states that function as sanctions for moral accountability—shame, guilt, conscience (i.e., the sense that we did something wrong or violated the moral order of things)—are also public creations in this sense. We may internalize a society's value-system so completely that we no longer need to reflect on particular options when confronting a choice of action. Indeed, we normally do not make formal "judgments"—we simply *see* what we ought to do without thinking.

Universalizability

The second condition for a moral action-guide is that it is universalizable in the sense that holders of the action-guide are willing that all other people in similar circumstances (including themselves at other times) act by that guide. Conversely, what we would require of everyone in a particular situation is also required of us in that situation. "Always tell the truth" is a guide we are all willing to universalize since we at least want others to be truthful to us. Kant formalized this requirement: to be moral, one must "act only according to that maxim by which you can at the same time will that it should become a universal law." Kant saw this as the only requirement for a maxim to be moral. But while it may be necessary for morality, it is not sufficient since we can universalize action-guides reflecting values other than other-regardingness. For example, we could universalize an in-group ethic. Thus, Christians who treat only other Christians fairly would be willing to universalize "Always treat Christians, but only Christians, fairly."[15] (If we accept the modern belief- and value-claims that people of all societies are equally real and valuable, universalizability would eliminate such in-group codes as moral. All people are entitled to moral consideration simply because they are people.) But universalizability does capture the idea that one's personal values or a society's customs cannot be moral if we have one rule for ourselves and another for all others to follow. An in-group ethics may in fact be socially very productive, but they cannot be *moral* unless they extend to all people similarly situated.

In the end, universalizability is simply a matter of *consistency* in the moral point of view: everyone must act the same way in relevantly similar circumstances all the time. What constitutes "relevantly similar circumstances" may not be apparent until an action-guide is worked out in practice. But to be moral, if we claim that it is morally right for us to do something in one situation and morally wrong for others to do it, we must be able to explain the relevant distinctions—and, to be moral, the explanation cannot simply be that the others are not ourselves or do not belong to our group.

Must Morality Be a Supreme Value?

The claim of morality upon us feels absolute, not subject to anything else or merely a matter of social convention. But must it be a supreme value, i.e, a value that can never be overridden? Many philosophers argue that if we take morality at all seriously we must always treat it as inviolate; some argue it must be our supreme and central value. The reasoning is that if we treat morality as other than supreme in itself, we are not genuinely other-regarding in our actions and so are not truly moral. In particular, being moral cannot merely be a means to an end—such as one's own religious salvation—since that would be using others for our own end and thus not really be morality. In sum, morality is either supreme and absolute or it is not really morality.

However, not all philosophers agree.[16] In the West since Aristotle, some have argued that nonmoral ends (such as the contemplative life) are higher than a commitment to morality. The rational way to live or the "good life" may not exemplify a moral concern in every circumstance. Whether religious values can override morality is also an issue. This is not to say that the nonmoral values must be immoral but only that other value-systems for how we should lead our life can supersede moral considerations at least some of the time. That is, in a *balanced* life, personal self-interest may legitimately prevail over concern for others in some circumstances. A person can still be deemed moral even if not every single one of his or her acts is an other-regarding action for others, and it is not clear why some other values cannot trump morality in some circumstances—for example, Beethoven is not usually deemed immoral for spending time composing music rather than devoting all his time to helping the poor. Nor need morality be the highest value in one's life. One can be genuinely other-regarding and not merely using others as a means to one's own end even if one places another value more centrally in one's life (as will be illustrated in Part II). To be moral the claim of others upon us must be accepted, even if we have other ends we value more highly. But as long as a genuine concern for others for their own sake is one component in one's decision-making, morality need not be one's supreme value to be moral.

The Problem of Justifying Morality

Justifying an absolute commitment to morality raises a basic question: why should I be moral? Egoists assert that we should be moral only if it increases our own welfare—which, of course, refutes the moral point of view. Nihilists and value-skeptics deny there is an answer: adopting the moral point of view is just an arbitrary personal taste, a rationalization of the underlying personal desires or social institutions really driving our actions, a social convention, or an illusion fobbed off on us by our genes to produce actions that maximize our genetic material. Moralists often believe that being moral is "self-evidently" the best course of action and that reason will inevitably lead anyone to that conclusion. But reason alone cannot compel us to sacrifice any self-interest to adopt a more encompassing point of view. To egoists, reason leads us only to maximizing self-interest. Such a position is not self-evidently irrational. As David Hume said, preferring the destruction of the universe to scratching one's finger is not contrary to reason.

The dispute is a matter of basic values, not rationality. Even if a form of value-realism is true, disputes still arise as to which one is correct, and we must then make a basic commitment. As Ludwig Wittgenstein argued, basic commitments are beyond the reach of a complete rational justification. This is not to say that such commitments cannot be examined and defended but only that reason cannot establish our most basic belief- and value-commitments. Our final values may be well considered, but they ultimately require us to make a real and important choice of basic values, and that choice lies beyond any further defense. It comes down to such things as what sort of person one wants to be or what sort of society one wants to live in. These commitments are not *irrational*—i.e., contrary to reason—since rationality only applies to how we handle our beliefs and values once we adopt basic commitments. The basic commitments are themselves beyond the dichotomy of rationality and irrationality and hence are nonrational.

Some moralists, however, advance a positive answer to the "Why be moral?" question. Some provide it in terms of the nature of reality or the nonmoral goal achieved by being moral, or they offer a religious justification (e.g., in terms of revelation or postmortem retribution). But the prevailing philosophical position today is that all attempts to ground morality on some irrefutable foundation based on reason or any other objective criterion have failed.[17] For example, theists can offer no convincing proof of the existence of God to ground a divine command theory of morality. No sustained skepticism concerning basic factual beliefs or values can be refuted. We cannot prove the first premises of any system of values (e.g., the hedonists' claim that our own personal pleasure is the only intrinsic good) from which ethical judgments are derived, and thus it is impossible to provide any complete proof of a value-system. The absence of a value-foundation does not mean that nihilists, who deny there are any values to reality, are therefore correct—the issue of foundations is an epistemological one, not an ontological claim about what exists in reality. The nihilists' denial is in the same boat as the moralists' affirmation.

But no such justification is needed to be moral: one can be other-regarding (and hence moral) without advancing a further nonmoral reason. Indeed, to be moral one must act at least in part out of concern for another's welfare and not for some other reason. If the nonmoral justification is the only real reason for an action, then that would in fact conflict with being moral—hence, a paradox of a nonmoral justification of morality. In any case, one's only answer to why one ought to be moral may be that people need the help. Similarly, hurting another for no reason but our own interests may be deemed morally wrong simply because another person is harmed for only a selfish reason. To moral realists, such acts are wrong regardless of what we might think. To others, the acts are wrong simply because of the harm or pain caused. Any such reasoning may ultimately be circular and so no justification at all, but in the end no nonmoral justification is needed to be moral. It is a basic value-commitment one adopts or does not adopt.

Justifying Ethical Codes and Actions

A related issue needs to be mentioned: those who have adopted the moral point of view can use moral reasons to justify performing specific actions or subscribing to a specific ethical code. Of course, such reasons will not convince those who reject morality, since this level of justification is only for those who share the basic value-commitment to morality. But moral reasons nevertheless can enter the process of justifying an ethical position for those who share the moral point of view. Other value-systems, such as religious ones, may also be involved. Moral concern will interact with other values. Thus, moral thinking will not be abstract or systematic but embedded in the person's total way of life. (The danger also cannot be ruled out that all the "moral" reasoning is simply a rationalization of some underlying psychological or social causes.)

It should also be noted that factual beliefs enter the process of justifying a decision. Facts are the application-conditions for values: how we see the facts of the situation determine how we act from a moral concern. But, as Hume pointed out, we cannot deduce an "ought" from an "is": an evaluative statement does not logically follow from any combination of factual statements, and so any argument in ethics must always contain an evaluative premise. (For moral realists, reality is not value-neutral, and so moral facts are still not deducible from purely nonmoral ones—i.e., an evaluative conclusion does not follow from a set of value-neutral factual premises.) Some factual claims may seem to dictate a specific action or value in a simple way. Plato saw immorality as a product of ignorance: if we knew the right, we would see that it is in our self-interest and do it. In short, we would always do the right if we only knew all the facts. But "is" does not entail "ought" here since the value-premise comes in through the idea of self-interest. Or consider the factual claim "This building is on fire." This would seem to dictate to anyone inside "I should get out now." But some implicit value-premise—such as "I should always act to preserve my life, at least as long as I do not hurt anyone"—is involved. This may seem perfectly obvious to most people, but it is no less an evaluative premise for being so. In classical China, women of a certain social rank were not supposed to leave a building unescorted by a man of a certain rank. And there were instances in which a palace caught fire and women refused to leave because no appropriate chaperon was around. Consequently they died. They valued the maxim "Preserve social customs" over the maxim "Preserve your own life."

For those who share a basic value, disputes may arise over the proper application of the value, and this may involve disputes over the factual nature of the situation. For example, the dispute over abortion rights is not be so much a dispute over *values* (although political beliefs may be in the mix) but over a *factual belief*: the disputants agree on the value and rights of human beings but disagree on the factual issue of whether a fetus is a human being, i.e., the factual issue of when life begins. Beliefs do not dictate values or vice versa: one may decide abortion is wrong because life begins at conception or vice versa. Thus, values may cause the beliefs we hold or vice versa, and either may cause our actions. If we make a mistake because our factual beliefs are incorrect, we are not usually deemed "immoral" since morality is a matter of values. But both factual beliefs and values are integral to the decision-making process—decisions are not based on values alone.

In the end, the appropriate course of action depends on how "things really are," as defined by a person's system of beliefs, and not just adopting the moral point of view. We live in accordance with reality, as we see it. For example, belief in life after death can alter what we would consider other-regarding: as discussed in Chapter 9, it is possible to argue that we can actually kill someone for his or her own good (in their future rebirths). The presence of such different beliefs in different cultures presents a hurdle for any "ideal observer" theory in ethics. An ideal observer must know all the facts and the future course of events and be disinterested in their outcome. A person may be able to attain a disinterested attitude, but he or she would also need a neutral, God's-eye point of view of the facts (in particular, whether there is life after death). Whether that is possible is open to question, and if there is no "perspective-free perspective," people must hold different points of view and will not be able to agree on what the facts are.

Concern for Others

What distinguishes moral action from other types of other-impinging action is that it involves a genuine consideration of the effects of our actions upon the welfare of others—i.e., one consideration for deciding what actions to take is the benefit or harm accruing to others without regard to possible advantages for ourselves. This claim's philosophical roots lie in Kant's requirement that we must always treat others also as ends in themselves and never merely as means to our own ends. Moral consideration, that is, represents a concern for others for their own sake and not only as instruments for our own betterment. It is the distinction between "altruism" and "egoism."[18] In everyday usage, we often equate altruism with acts of charitable giving, but philosophers use the term more broadly for actions and dispositions that promote the good of others independently of any good that might or might not accrue to ourselves. For example, Thomas Nagel defines "altruism" as any behavior motivated merely by the belief that someone else will benefit or avoid harm by it.[19] Morality, he adds, has its source in the claims of other people. In short, the moral point of view requires taking a wider perspective than the egoist's question "What's in it for me?" Often this involves no more than simply refraining from hurting others when it would be to our advantage to hurt them (e.g., not stealing their property for our own use). Most societies require no more than not interfering with others, and so laws are in negative form, specifying what we should not do. But sometimes morality requires something more positive—actually helping others. This can be as simple as lending a hand, or it can be as heroic as risking one's own life for the welfare of strangers. But sometimes self-sacrifice is required, not simply not harming or interfering with others.

In addition, the moral goodness of a person depends at least as much on the reason the action is done as the action itself. (As discussed above, consequentialists disagree.) If we see people convicted of crimes performing a sentence of community service, we may think, "Well, at least some good is coming from their crime," but we do not commend them for being moral. Or if the reason we are "doing good" is because we expect a reciprocal advantage, then we are not being moral—that is merely a straightforward self-interested bargain, not an act motivated by other-regardingness. Similarly, one may be a doctor or other service provider out of concern for others or only for the money and prestige. Or if one gives money to a charity solely because of a social custom or to advance one's social position or to save on taxes or only to make oneself feel good, it is hard to classify one's action as "moral"—the *action* is obviously not immoral and may have a positive effect, but earning the label "moral" for the *person* requires more. Consider Kant's example of a store clerk who is meticulously honest in his dealings with children, rather than pocketing some extra change for himself, but he does so only out of fear of losing customers if their parents found out. He would like to steal but fears being caught. The welfare of his customers is assured and his actions conform to ethical correctness, but he is not acting from a moral motive—his motive is not concern for his customers' welfare, and the benefit to others is merely a fortuitous effect. Such "enlightened self-interest"—i.e., our true interests are in fact advanced by our always acting for the welfare of others—may be a basis for socially advantageous value-systems and our own happiness may flow from it, but it cannot be a basis for *morality* since it is not based on a genuine concern for others but only on self-concern.[20] Doing good to others solely for ourselves is simply a socially beneficial form of selfishness. Morality requires something else.

Other-regardingness involves taking a wider perspective than one's own interests, and that means "taking another's point of view" in one sense. But this does not necessitate seeing from the perspective of the impinged-upon party: an action will be no less moral if what the actor considers the *real interests and needs* of others dictates his or her actions. And usually an actor's view of the true nature of reality and of what our goals should be will govern the actions, not what others may want. Thus, the issue of whether it is in fact possible to assume someone else's point of view through imagination or empathy need not arise—we can act for another's welfare without doing so. Imposing the actor's own perspective may seem paternalistic, and paternalism is normally morally condemned since it violates the autonomy of adults. But when it comes to issues of importance, doing what the other persons want when the actor thinks he or she knows better would not be truly looking out for their welfare for their own sake. Letting them persist in what is taken to be an illusion of profound importance to their lives is not looking out for their welfare. And morality only requires acting for the other people's welfare—that this is defined from the actor's frame of reference does not negate that.

The last point comes into play in the case of mystics who may take a very different view of what is real and valuable than that of the people they encounter. Mystics would be comparable to Plato's prisoner returning to the cave with a better view of what the imprisoned really need. They may not value "worldly welfare"—food, clothing, health, even life itself—as much as we unenlightened folk. To be moral, mystics must advance what from their point of view is people's "real" welfare or they would not be truly helping. Little and Twiss disqualify concern for such "real" welfare from the realm of morality: morality's only legitimate concern are worldly interests; "real" welfare belongs to the realm of religion.[21] But why this-worldly concerns must be the only morally proper ones is not at all clear—unless, of course, one wants to adopt the normative position of defining the concept of "morality" in terms of particular culturally accepted factual beliefs, values, and objectives and not in terms of "concern for others." Morality may have arisen out of family relations and a concern for physical well-being, but should moral concern be tied to that view? And even if we do define "morality" that way, the substantive question would still remain of whether those who operate by a concern for "real" welfare are *other-regarding* and thus are concerned with others' welfare, even though the label "morality" would now be refused for normative reasons.

Another issue is *whose* interests one must take into account. Usually we think simply in terms of the person in front of us, the person upon whom our actions impinge most directly. But we may gradually expand our point of view and not limit the issue to the interests of that one person or few persons. Psychologists see the development from childhood to adulthood as a process of less and less self-centeredness, and this may be the moral counterpart. People may consider the welfare of their own community, their own nation, or their own religious group in deciding how to act in a situation demanding a moral choice. Others may try to consider the welfare of all people or consider future generations. Still others may try to expand the scope of morality to include all sentient beings or all life or all of the planet, treating concern for people alone as merely an unfounded prejudice.

Of the five requirements set forth by Little and Twiss, other-regardingness is what is unique to morality. Morality does involve action-guides, but this requirement reduces to no more than the fact that morality does involve the regulation of our acts. The second requirement—universalizability—reduces to no more than consistency on the part of the actor. The third requirement—supremacy among values—was rejected as unnecessary. The fourth—justifiability of the moral point of view—presents problems and is also not necessary to the first-order activity of actually being moral. But concern for others' welfare, even if the interests are defined from one's own point of view, remains unique to morality. Thus, this requirement will be the central focus throughout this book, with only minimal discussions of the other requirements when pertinent.

Self-Interest and Selfishness

The natural enemy of other-regardingness (and hence morality) is selfishness. But not all acts to help oneself are selfish. Aristotle drew the distinction between self-interest (*philautia*) and selfishness. Some self-interest need not conflict with morality.[22] Selfishness involves a willingness to advance one's own interests at the expense of others in situations where others' welfare or the common good should be given weight and thus be a genuine concern. One's own well-being becomes the only real reason for action. But on the other hand, no one claims morality demands one be totally self-denying. One need not ruin one's own health in helping others to be considered moral. Getting enough sleep and food is not considered selfish. So also it is not selfish to expect to be paid fairly for one's labor or to expect equal shares for equal work. Placing ourselves in the center of our considerations is only natural: we naturally evaluate situations in terms of how an action would affect our own interests. Kant said any rational creature is self-interested and spoke of nonmoral duties to oneself. Normally it is not a moral issue if we act for our own interests—a moral dilemma arises only in those situations where there is a substantive clash between our own interests and those of others. (That at least some acts involve a conflict of interests is all that needs to be noted here. But it can be argued that *all interpersonal actions* are a conflict between self-interest and other-concern—in particular, American opulence in a world where so many millions are starving makes virtually every act a moral dilemma.) This may lead to total selfishness or to total sacrifice, but it can also lead to a self-interest compatible with an other-regardingness: one can weigh one's own interests against those of others and still have a genuine concern for others.

But this leads to another issue: are we moral if we consider others' welfare but always opt to enhance our own benefit more? We do not have to be totally self-denying, but we must not accord ourselves a highly privileged position either. How much weight to others' interests is enough? Giving ourselves some consideration or even a privileged position only means we are self-interested. But as long as a *genuine* concern for others' welfare is part of the consideration we are not proceeding from pure self-interest. After such consideration, we may still conclude it is best to act for our own interest, even if others are harmed to some degree. Of course, if we *always* conclude to advance our own welfare at the expense of others, then whether the other-regardingness is genuine is open to question—to be moral, some of our acts must cost us for the sake of others. Conversely, the side effects of our moral actions may benefit us: our welfare may coincide with the welfare of another, or our action may benefit all members of a group to which we belong, or helping others may make us feel good. But such personal repercussions of our actions are morally neutral. So too we may act with mixed intentions or motives. Consider the classic example of keeping clean a water hole you share with someone else. There may be three possible motives: you may be selfish, keeping the hole clean for yourself and not caring at all that another person benefits from your actions; you may keep it clean solely for the other person and thus be purely other-regarding; or you may be concerned both for yourself and the other person. Your actions and their effect—keeping the water hole clean—are the same regardless of which motive is involved, but only the last two motives are moral. Kant may require that we have a pure motive to be considered moral, but the issue for morality is whether we have taken into consideration the welfare of others for their own sake, regardless of whether our own welfare is enhanced.

Impartiality

Another aspect of the question of self-interest requires further comment: whether we should value our own self-interest as no more than one among equals against the interests of all other people. Every person has an equal claim, and so must we be totally impartial toward ourselves, our family, and total strangers? Morally speaking, every person is equivalent to me. Such impartiality is a possible interpretation of the "Golden Rule" to love one's neighbor as oneself. Kant also can easily be interpreted to be demanding the same, as can utilitarians. Each person counts for one only, including ourselves and all people important to us. All ethical reasons must be "neutral," "impersonal," and "objective" in that sense. To be moral, we must treat the universe as having no "I"—there are no subjective viewpoints but only objective ones. As William Godwin put it two hundred years ago, "What magic is there in the pronoun 'my' that should justify us in overturning the decisions of impartial truth?"

But this denial of self-interest leads to conclusions most people would find unsettling. For example, if you visit a hospital where there are six people who could be saved by organ transplants from you, are you morally required to sacrifice yourself? Are you *immoral* if you choose yourself over the six? Impartiality would require it. Or consider this: there is a house burning, and you can save either your own child or two babies of strangers but not all three. Are you immoral for choosing your own child? If you chose the other children and responded, "Well, I viewed the situation impartially and decided to do unto others as I would have them to do unto me, so I saved the two babies and not my own," most people would be shocked. The same dilemma also occurs on a less dramatic scale: how can we justify spending free time and extra money on a hobby or a luxury for ourselves or our family? How can be justify an expensive dinner when the same money could feed a small family in another country for months? Viewed impartially, any excess time and money should be used to help other people with their basic needs, and there are millions to help—if they can be helped more, are we not obligated to do so and immoral for indulging ourselves? The young man in the *Euthyphro* who was going to have his own father prosecuted for murder may have perplexed Socrates, but from the point of view of impartiality, what is the problem? No one is worthy of more concern than another.

Defenders of impartiality do see the harshness of the conclusions but reply that morality is a tough standard.[23] Critics, however, contend it is too utopian an ideal for society at large—it is attainable at best only by a few moral saints, who devote an extraordinary part of their time and resources in self-denying help of others, and heroes, who risk their lives for strangers. Indeed, saints go beyond impartiality to discounting any weight for themselves. They do not love their neighbors as themselves because they attach no significance to themselves at all. They act only for other people and have no regard for the consequences of their actions for themselves. Those deontologists who, following Kant, equate morality with doing one's duty have trouble considering such supererogatory actions even as *moral*, since saints and heroes go beyond the deontologists' requirements for moral concern.[24] Their actions are obviously not bad, but they are in some sense supramoral. Of course, many would reply so much the worst for Kant: making morality simply a matter of duty and having no place for greater concern for others cannot capture the nature of morality. Most people would be impressed on moral grounds with people who consistently acted only for others all the time. But some philosophers point out that anyone who acts with either pure impartiality or total self-denial will also appear flawed to most people.[25] To be a well-rounded human being, we cannot be totally other-regarding but must devote some time and resources to ourselves. Moral saints do not appear fully human to many people; they have lost a basic sense of our their own self and thus may have lost a sense of their own basic connectedness to other people in a society. Many would agree with George Orwell when he said of Gandhi that sainthood is a thing that human beings must avoid.

The coldness of the actions that impartiality requires has caused many philosophers to reject any deontological or consequentialist ethics based on it and to focus instead on questions of character and virtue. Any view of morality that would condemn someone who acts with some self-interest or other partiality as *immoral* is rejected as counterintuitive to our basic notion of "morality." Morality requires some self-transcendence but not total neutrality. Impartiality may be the requirement for government officials administering benefits to the public, but it leads to morally unacceptable results for private citizens in their interactions with each other.

If this is so, moral precepts must provide a place for asserting partiality. Part of the moral sense is that we should not be swayed by personal feelings but apply moral principles equally to everyone, and impartiality does highlight the concern that self-interest can cross the line into selfishness. But morality needs only a genuine other-regarding concern for the welfare of others, not necessarily giving it the same weight as concern for ourselves and our family. One can treat others as ends in themselves and not merely as means without valuing them equally with ourselves. Doctrines of the "good life" and the "mean" prevalent in the West since Aristotle limit the role of impartiality and balance the interests of oneself and others: all good things are to be held in moderation, including interest in others' welfare; thus, a commitment to other-regardingness would not be so all-consuming as to exclude all other commitments.

Actions and Persons

One source of the disagreement on the moral assessment is that scholars are not always clear on what is being judged—is it the persons themselves or just some particular action? More generally, philosophers split over "act-morality" and "agent-morality." The former approach treats our acts alone as the locus of moral praise or blame, while the latter sees the person and his or her character as the focus of the judgment. The distinction is revealed in saying that a person may be judged "morally good" and an act "morally right."[26] Theorists of agent-morality focus on motive and intent. For example, Kant looked for a morally good "will" as necessary. On the other hand, consequentialists focus on the action and its effects. Under act-morality, we can then judge by acts alone: actions that produce good are morally good regardless of motive, and acts that cause more suffering than good are evil regardless of motive.[27] Under this approach, for the moral assessment of a person we are simply the sum of our actions, and thus only our actions are of concern.

Yet we do allow for accidents—one is not deemed a "murderer" if a death is an accident. Moreover, if some good happens incidentally to result from an actor's evil intention, we do not let the results determine the moral worth of the action. This suggests we do not judge morality simply in terms of the externals of actions and consequences alone—what is going on in the actor's mind also counts. Things we normally consider morally good or bad include not just people and actions but motives, character traits, reasons and arguments, judgments, dispositions, attitudes, intentions, and desires. All have an inner mental dimension and are not simply external phenomena. Morality in this way has been interiorized in modern thought (under the influence of Christian thought).[28] Intention is a matter of the actor's purpose or planned consequences, and the reasons offered for the action can reveal it. Actions are tied to an inner dimension—indeed, some would argue that they are only the expression of inner personal states. And this inner dimension becomes central to our assessment, not just the externals. In a moral assessment of a person, one's motives and intentions count at least as much as the actions themselves and their foreseeable consequences. Often "actions speak louder than words" in revealing our real motives and intentions, but this does not mean that actions alone determine moral worth.

But morality also involves taking into consideration the impact of our actions upon the people whom our actions affect. Good intentions are not enough. Thus, actions remain an essential part of the picture under agent-morality: a good result combined with a good intention is moral, even if it is not the intended result or our knowledge is incorrect; a good result produced by a selfish intention may not be deemed moral;[29] harm resulting from a good intention is not morally condemned, even if it is a great amount of harm, but harm combined with a selfish intention is deemed immoral. The picture is further complicated by the fact that virtually all actions have good, bad, and unforeseen consequences. Act-morality, with a focus on the consequences alone, makes assessing the morality of acts easier, but when judging a person the focus has to be on the inner character manifested in action as well as the consequences.

Virtue Ethics

Agent-morality involves a judgment of the character of a person, and this is where "virtue ethics" enters the picture. This approach shifts attention away from the idea of rule-following and toward defining morality in terms of the way a virtuous person would act.[30] Morality becomes a matter of character traits and not just doing the right thing. The question is not "What should I do?" but "What kind of person should I be?" or "What kind of person would I be if I didn't do x?" That is, the concepts of duty and obligation—all ethical "oughts"—do not capture what is central in moral life, and we must instead return to examining moral character traits. An action is right only if it is what a virtuous person would do, not because it conforms to some rule or duty. The terms "virtue" and "virtuous" today sound outdated and carry connotations of prudishness, but they capture the notion going back to ancient Greece that excellence (*arete*) in character rather than some idea of "ethical duty" is the central feature in our moral life. As Alasdair MacIntyre puts it, virtue is an acquired human quality, the exercise of which tends to enable us to achieve certain ends that are good for us and the lack of which effectively prevents us from achieving those ends.[31] It is a disposition to act in certain ways and not a classification of a type of acts. (Thus, the term "supererogatory acts" is not part of the vocabulary in virtue ethics.) Plato advocated prudence (practical wisdom), courage (fortitude), temperance (self-control), and justice (including fairness, honesty, and keeping promises), arguing that ordering these different elements in a harmonious manner is necessary to happiness. Today we would consider other virtues as important—e.g., respect, tolerance, or loyalty. But the point of virtue ethics, as with agent-morality, is that a person's character is what qualifies as being moral or not, not individual acts.

Virtue theorists emphasize that moral decision-making is not a matter of disembodied reason. Theories that equate morality with rule-following—as do modern approaches from Kant to all forms of consequentialism—do not capture the fullness of a moral life and in fact make morality abstract, mechanical, impersonal, and even inhuman. Under this view, consequentialism treats people as mere quantities for calculation, not as whole beings. The Victorian wife who supposedly responded to the question of why she was taking care of her dying husband, "I'm only doing this out of a sense of duty," is not the paradigm of morality—hired help would do as much. An ethics of rule-following offers no more guidance in life than obeying the rules of chess tells us how to win a game. Equating morality with following a "categorical imperative" or "maximizing the greatest good for the greatest number" makes morality very different from the real moral life: it either permits too much (e.g., we can give to charity and do pretty much as we wish, as long as we do not harm others) or demands too much (all our lives must be devoted to helping others impartially). The true sources of morality are excluded in favor of the externals alone. These sources are logically prior to any good actions and cannot be excluded. We cannot reluctantly follow rules and be deemed moral—we must be the kind of person from whom the right acts flow immediately and naturally. We are defined by our character—the dispositions we have internalized. Our actions are expressions of this character.

The virtuous person is one who habitually does the right thing. Following rules may help, but imitating the exemplars of virtue in our community and practicing the virtues are more effective. As Aristotle said, a virtue is not just a technical craft learned simply by repeatedly doing good acts since the inner disposition to act morally is what is vital, not any behavioral skill. Nevertheless, habitual practice does work toward instilling the enduring dispositions that make us moral persons. Being moral is like becoming a skilled musician rather than someone who can only bang out notes following the musical score. With the skill internalized, conscious moral decision-making no longer is involved: we can see the right thing to do in any circumstance without considering how to follow some rule. In sum, morality is an acquired skill, but it can become second nature through practice.

Virtue ethics can accommodate all the roles of factual beliefs, goals, and different values in ethics and can provide action-guides through exemplars of virtuous action—it is merely the necessity of rule-following in a mature moral life that falls by the way. But rule theorists reply that what we consider a virtue is based on something more fundamental. How do we settle upon an exemplar whom we deem to be someone we should emulate? We choose what is a virtue only by standards determined by a moral sense that is logically prior to that determination, and that sense is expressible in moral principles. It is these principles that we internalize, and thus rule-following is vindicated. These principles tell us if we are making a mistake or are doing the right thing. But virtue theorists see principles of right and wrong as abstractions we glean from virtuous conduct; such principles at best offer limited aid in the process of becoming moral.

Some Christian theologians object to virtue ethics: our salvation depends on God's grace alone, not striving to become virtuous. Moreover, virtue ethics is too self-centered and individualistic: its focus is on changing our character, not on concern for others.[32] In addition, virtue ethics is justified in terms of cultivating our well-being or happiness or developing the whole person to the fullest, and it is not at all obvious that the dispositions we develop must involve sacrificing for others. We might like to think that the virtuous life is tied to morally good actions, but it depends on which virtues we choose. (Since Plato, some theorists have argued that all the virtues are tied together in a bundle, but most theorists today do not see it that way. If they were bundled together, then only one virtue would have to be moral to make a virtuous person moral.) After all, Aristotle tolerated slavery and did not live in a democracy. He was concerned with the good life and not necessarily the morally right one (although he thought action was a fruit of the contemplation of reason). Indeed, no school of ancient Greek thought had a concept of "moral obligation" as part of the "good life," although they did think of the individual as part of a community. And not all the classical virtues are concerned with the welfare of others—only justice (with fairness, honesty, and promise-keeping) clearly concerns other-impinging action. The others are self-centered.

But although virtue theorists focus on cultivating dispositions, it does not follow that they advocate cultivating only self-interest. Other-regardingness or compassion can be added as a separate virtue.[33] Dispositions related to a concern for others may in fact be valuable for our self-development. But if we want a moral virtue to be chosen, we would still need to show how developing our character in ways that are good for others is also good for ourselves. That is, we would have to show how cultivating a disposition that requires sacrificing some self-interest leads to our own well-being or our fullest potential. (How to keep genuine other-regardingness and not just "enlightened self-interest" would also be an issue.) But to make other-regarding virtues part of forming a full person, we would have to see ourselves as necessarily part of a group and not as isolated individuals.

This leads to the problem that which virtues are considered central has varied throughout history. For example, classical Greeks rejected compassion and humility as signs of weakness. There is no one timeless, cross-cultural set of virtues, any more than there is one full set of agreed-upon rules. Nevertheless, virtue ethics, with its focus on character development rather than on actions following rules, does appear to be a better approach for studying mystical ethics (as discussed in the next chapter). Rule-following theories may reflect philosophers' attraction to what can be reduced neatly to linguistic formulations, but they are not necessarily the best way to capture a subject.

Moral, Immoral, Nonmoral, Amoral

Finally, some terminology needs to be clarified: morality, immorality, nonmorality, and amorality. Each of these concepts is applied to value-systems related to our interactions with others. Granted, anything unrelated to morality can be called "nonmoral" or "amoral," but it is a little strange to call a flower, a car, or mathematics *amoral* just because it is not the sort of reality that cannot be moral or immoral. Morality and its negations relate to values for our interpersonal conduct, not to other types of evaluations. Thus, actions, such inner states as intentions, or persons can be called moral or immoral. Realities that can be related closely to our interpersonal values (e.g., experiences) are sometimes considered nonmoral, even though they cannot be other-regarding or selfish by themselves.

The concept of "morality" needs no further clarification. Being *unethical* means committing an action that violates a social code, but being *immoral* means consistently refusing to abide by moral demands for self-regarding reasons. We do not always consider immoral those who do an isolated act "out of character" or are weak-willed (i.e., who subscribe to the moral point of view but fail to follow it) or who commit a harmful act because of a mistaken knowledge of the facts of a situation (since immorality is a matter of values). Those who do not know moral right from moral wrong—the legally insane—are also not considered immoral. But the immoral reject any claim of morality upon us. Selfishness is their key value: if one acts selfishly and creates harm, one is immoral; if one acts selfishly and no harm results or in fact some good results for others, it may be hard to label the person "immoral," but he or she is not moral either. To the immoral, any results affecting others, whether good or bad, are irrelevant. They act out of self-interest in instances when the moral would be other-regarding. They do not feel bound by any code when it conflicts with their own interests. In sum, it is a callous indifference to the welfare of others in favor of themselves.

Many people mistakenly believe a value-system must be either moral (other-regarding) or antimoral (selfish): if one's acts are not based on selfishness, then it automatically follows that one must be moral—there is no third possibility. However, there is another possibility: a value-system that is neither moral nor selfish but *nonmoral*. The nonmoral have a set of values governing their lives that contains no concern for the welfare of others but is not self-interested either—it is a set of values not on the axis of immorality and morality. Any value-system based on self-development in keeping with a view of the way reality is deemed to be—as all mystical systems are—is open to the possibility that neither selfishness nor other-regardingness is the central value. Or, to be more exact, a nonmoral value-system may result in a benign type of selfishness since it does not involve intentionally disregarding the interests of others for one's own gain. That is, one can still be selfish without being hateful or vicious or even harming others. The only harm resulting from the nonmoral's lack of concern for others may be not actively helping others in situations where morality would require sacrificing for others. The nonmoral are not nihilists who deny all values. They have values—they simply justify their actions on grounds unrelated to self-regard or other-regard. The resulting actions under their value-system may in fact converge with those under a moral value-system, but the nonmoral would not care, since they are unconcerned with issues of morality. The nonmoral simply do not think in terms of "moral" or "immoral" but act only for other goals. If the resulting actions consistently harm others, we may want to judge their value-system as immoral—in effect, we impute selfishness to the person, even if that is not of concern to the nonmoral person. But as long as selfishness is a matter of motive and not just social effects, we cannot do that.

The term "amoral" has not developed any standard meaning in ethical discourse. Sometimes it is used interchangeably with "immoral," and sometimes it is used to describe those who do not hurt anyone but do not help anyone either. Some call "amoralists" those people who have one personal value-system for themselves and another for everyone else or who are in fact nihilists who deny all ethical values whatsoever. Sometimes the term is used to refer to someone who uses ruthless means to a socially desirable end—i.e., extreme (and harmful) measures to achieve an end we accept as moral. Other times the term is used for someone who actually should be judged moral: when morality is equated with duty, then someone who rejects such rule-following out of compassion for others' suffering is labeled "amoral."[34] These last amoralists are in fact other-regarding: even if they are not confined by the strictures of an ethical code, they are acting for others under a "higher morality" of other-regardingness that is "beyond morality" (i.e., beyond rule-following). Thus, saints appear amoral to rule-theorists.

Another use of the term "amoralist" is to describe those who advance a substantive value-system that is either immoral or nonmoral. Elitists who are not concerned with the welfare of all people but only for their own class advance such an ethical code. Friedrich Nietzsche is the classic example of an amoralist in this sense. He attacked morality as an unnatural evil sapping the strength of a society. He offered in its place a "revaluation of values" in which the natural forces driving our biological evolution—strength and aggression—replaced concern for others. Morality and compassion for the suffering of others are a "sickness" based on the weakness, fear, and resentment of weaklings who form the majority of humanity. The whole idea of equality is a triumph of the "herd morality." Moral good and evil are in fact illusions: "evil" is simply the word the weak use to refer to those who are strong and endowed with noble qualities. Thus, morality is actually an instinct against life. Our only task today is to aid in the evolution of future Supermen (*Übermenschen*). This strong nobility, freed from the "tyranny of the majority," will be "beyond good and evil." That is, the strong will be free of any authority based on the illusion of moral goodness and badness. This illusion constrains the "slave" ethics of lesser individuals, but it has no power over the Supermen who will have their own "master" ethics of cruel virtues. Nietzsche thus offered an alternative criterion of "good" and "bad" based on power. In his revaluation, "good" is simply the term the strong use to refer to themselves and "bad" their term for their inferiors. For Nietzsche, the Supermen will be solitary masters of themselves, without any social responsibility (including governing). But if put into political action, his value-system would be an antinomian ethics giving the strong the right to do whatever they wish, without concern for the ruled.[35]

Conclusion

All the points discussed above will appear again in the following chapters, but three points for the issue of mysticism and morality should be highlighted here. First, morality involves our interactions with each other, not self-development or any other activity. Second, morality involves one particular value for our other-impinging actions—concern for others' welfare—and not just any type of value we might place centrally in our own way of life. Third, the term "moral" should not be thrown around loosely. It should not be applied to all people, actions, or traditions automatically—being moral is a real accomplishment. We do not need to be a saint to be moral, but morality still involves a high standard: it demands restrictions on our behavior and sacrifice. Being ethical—i.e., having one's behavior conform to society's ethical standards—is itself an accomplishment, but being a moral person is a greater accomplishment. Even if we limit morality merely to self-restraints from harming others (rather than requiring some positive help for others), this still requires sacrifice. We may have a natural social sense, but our concern may only extend to ourselves, our family, and our friends—our restraints on behavior may not exhibit a genuine other-regarding concern for others. People may not be the selfish and aggressive animal, as some biologists believe, but acting on a concern for the welfare of others regardless of any possible benefit to oneself is not something all people automatically do. Thus, whether other-regardingness is a central value in all value-systems is a matter for empirical investigation, not something to be assumed in advance.

Notes

1. Frankena 1973, 1980.

2. See MacIntyre 1984, pp. 228-29.

3. Indeed, Kant presented the ultimate reduction of morality to pure rationality. He argued that self-interest is inconsistent: since I know I may need help from others at some point, I cannot universalize a maxim of self-interest ("Let each person pursue his or her own advantage"); thus, if I am to act only upon universalizable maxims, immoral action is irrational. However, selfish people see no reason to accept the "if" clause in this argument.

4. Scholars tend to overintellectualize the moral decision-making process—they substitute a positivist-like reconstruction of logical relationships between moral concepts for "practical reason." See, e.g., Little and Twiss 1978, pp. 96-119.

5. It can at least be argued that it is moral even to torture an innocent baby under extreme circumstances. Consider this scenario: the baby's parents are terrorists who have set up a nuclear bomb somewhere in Manhattan and you know it will go off in one hour killing millions unless you can find and disarm it; the terrorists have been caught but will not talk and are prepared to die for their cause, and you know that the only thing they value more than their political beliefs is their baby and that they are reconciled to the baby dying along with them in the explosion but that they could not stand to see their baby suffer. Is it then moral to torture the baby to get the terrorists to talk to save millions?

6. But see Sissela Bok, *Lying: Moral Choice in Public and Private Life* (New York: Pantheon Books, 1978) on Kant.

7. George Lakoff and Mark Johnson, *Philosophy in the Flesh: The Embodied Mind and its Challenge to Western Thought* (New York: Basic Books, 1999), pp. 326-27.

8. Although he is using "natural" in a different sense, G. E. Moore's argument against the "naturalistic fallacy" (that the moral sense of "good" can be analyzed without remainder into nonethical terms) fits easily with moral realism here: concepts such as "good" cannot mean "pleasurable" or "happiness" or any other nonmoral idea, since it will always be an open question whether pleasure or any other nonmoral value is *morally good*. Moral properties are simple properties, unanalyzable into any other properties. Most importantly, they remain irreducibly evaluative properties. They are nonnatural—i.e., not open to scientific study but still not supernatural—but are equally as real as material properties. Thus, they must be included in our ontology.

9. See R. H. Jones 2000, Chapters 4, 5, and 10.

10. Boyd 1995. See also Leslie 1979 and the essays by McDowell, Sturgeon, Sayre-McCord, and Platts in Sayre-McCord 1988.

11. MacIntyre 1984, pp. 6-35.

12. An elaboration on Danto's example in Danto 1987, p. 3.

13. Little and Twiss 1973, 1978.

14. Ladd 1957.

15. R. M. Hare dismissed counterexamples based an in-group value-system (such as a consistent Nazi who would accept death if it turns out that his parents were Jewish) as matters of fanaticism and not a serious challenge to Kant's position. But whether being willing to die for one's ethical beliefs is grounds to dismiss counterexamples in this area is far from obvious.

16. Foot 1978, pp. 181-88.

17. See MacIntyre 1984, 1995 on the failure of this modern Enlightenment project.

18. "Ethical egoism," it should be noted, is a form of ethics, but it is not moral: self-interest rules this value-system even if indirectly it might lead to some social benefits.

19. Nagel 1970, p. 16 n.1.

20. Nagel 1970, p. 79; Frankena 1973, pp. 17-20.

21. Little and Twiss 1973, pp. 73-74. They realize they are open to the charge of arbitrariness on this point (p. 74).

22. Cottingham 1983.

23. Some defenders of impartiality try to neutralize the harshness by arguing that concern for oneself and one's family should be part of the impartial point of view—i.e., all people should take themselves and their families into consideration. But how this differs from simply rejecting impartiality is not clear. Also see Wolf 1992 on a modified impartiality theory.

24. Urmson 1958; see also DeNicola 1983, Halberstam 1986.

25. Wolf 1983.

26. Frankena 1980, pp. 48-49.

27. Moral realists may argue that some types of acts are inherently wrong, regardless of motive or consequences. This might be argued on *religious* grounds—e.g., that the act violates the laws of God. But to argue this on *moral* grounds, they would have to appeal to other-regardingness—that is, that the act necessarily reveals selfishness. This may be hard to do, since as discussed in Chapter 9, it is possible even to kill someone for his or her own good. Thus, the precept "Do not kill" is not necessarily moral—indeed, not killing when killing would help the "victim" would not be other-regarding. (Of course, "Do not murder" may be necessarily moral since murder is defined as "intentionally killing a human being without justification." But then the substantive question is whether a particular killing is a murder or not. The label "murder" is simply the conclusion that an act was indeed the intentional killing of a human being without justification, and thus "Do not murder" is a truism: "Do not kill whom you shouldn't kill.")

28. MacIntyre 1984, p. 168.

29. Frankena (1980) deems as moral any act with good results or one done with good intentions or both. But to T. S. Eliot, the "greatest treason" is "to do the right deed for the wrong reason."

30. Anscombe 1958; Foot 1978, pp. 1-18; Slote 1992, 1997; Taylor 2002.

31. MacIntyre 1984, p. 191.

32. On the other side of the issue, Richard Taylor (2002) offers an interesting contrast. He discusses how Christianity altered the entire nature of Greek ethics, e.g., supplanting pride (the justified love for oneself) with the humility of a devout mind and supplanting the

merit of developing human worth with an equality of all persons before God. In general, religious "virtues" such as faith are the "corruption of noble ideals" with the "vulgar," the replacement of an ethics of aspiration with an ethics of duty—something with which Nietzsche, as discussed below, would no doubt agree.

33. See James Q. Wilson, *The Moral Sense* (New York: Free Press, 1993).

34. See Garner 1994 (although he does not judge any brand of amoralism to be moral).

35. Stack 1991. Nietzsche got the "dangerous slogan"—"beyond good and evil"—from Ralph Waldo Emerson. Stack argues that it is an esoteric religious doctrine only for the morally self-disciplined; thus, Nietzsche was not concerned with employing this principle in order to act upon others in an immoral way but with presenting a "stricter morality" (pp. 112, 121). Only in the hands of others were its antinomian possibilities brought out.

3

Religion and Mysticism

Religion as a Way of Life

Mysticism is usually introduced by discussing the experiences that are distinctive to mystics, but a better way is to start with mysticism as an encompassing way of life, one set within a religious context. From psychologists such as Viktor Frankl to physicists such as John Wheeler, many argue that the most important thing in life is the sense that we know how we fit into the scheme of things—to see the meaning of our life. In the words of Peter Berger, we cannot accept meaninglessness.[1] What separates religion from other human enterprises is that the search for this meaning is set in the context of supernatural realities.[2] That is, for the religious the meaning is grounded in realities transcending the natural order, not in the individual, a social group, or the natural world. Theists speak of hope, trust in the fundamental goodness of reality, and the purpose or goal we and the world have; but more neutrally, it is enough to speak of life having a transcendental meaning. All aspects of life—the problem of suffering, why we exist, our relations to others, and so forth—are interpreted in light of beliefs about transcendent realities. That is, just as we can know the meaning of a book only once we know the language it is written in, so too religious beliefs and values provide the knowledge to understand the meaning of life and the ultimate significance of this world. Life has meaning, and the *summum bonum* of the religious is to align their lives with the reality providing that meaning. Thus, those who suffer or feel out of step with reality now have a framework within which to live and to accept the suffering that living entails or have a way leading to the end of that suffering.

To the religious, the deepest reality transcends the natural order and the apparent diversity in which we live. The awe-inspiring power and authority of such a reality makes it considered sacred. In the traditional understanding of all the major religions of the world, there is more than one ontological level to reality: there is the world we inhabit (the natural order) and a reality that encompasses this world (God or a nontheistic counterpart) as its source. It can be experienced, however, either in religious experiences or by revelation. As the source, that level is more fundamental to our lives than this world. The natural universe also is in some way the creation, emanation, or appearance of that transcendent reality. Thus, the two orders are not unconnected. To mystics, the source is also immanent to our realm—paradoxically, a "transcendent ground." Reality is also multidimensional in two other ways: gods, angels, and demons are active in the world, and there are souls or other realities that survive the death of the body.

Religion, however, is not concerned only with a transcendent reality, life after death, or other such "otherworldly" matters. Indeed, what is most striking about religion is its *comprehensiveness* in human affairs—religion touches upon all aspects of our life here and now. It is not a private matter of experience or personal ethics. For many people, religious concerns may surface only during moments of crisis—death, birth, disease, or personal or group suffering. But the framework of meaning provided by religion shapes the whole life of those who take their religion seriously. Religion is an encompassing way of life consisting of (1) beliefs about the fundamental nature of things and what is real, (2) valuations and ethics, and (3) the goals of life. These three elements are oriented around a central meaning grounded in a reality encompassing both ourselves and the natural order. Not all religious ways of life successfully integrate all the elements into a systematic, consistent whole around transcendental realities, but all three elements are present. A tradition's rituals reinforce both the elements of the way of life and the practitioners' relation to their tradition. World religions are institutional, have a history, and involve communities. But religion can be individual in the sense that a particular religious person need not be tied to any organization. Religion, however, is not individual in another sense since it must cover those aspects of one's life involved in the interactions with others. Moreover, religious persons most usually simply belong to the religious tradition of their families and only rarely convert to another tradition or invent their own religion (although they may give their own interpretations to their tradition's beliefs and values).

Worldview and Ethos

Logically central to a way of life are one's beliefs about the fundamental makeup of reality, the nature of a person, our expectations upon death, and any goal we accept to life—whether we help others depends on our values, but *how* we help also depends on what we think is real. We strive to live in accordance with reality, as we see it—our worldview. We cannot help but live in accord with aspects of our environment, but the religious also think in terms of transcendental realities. We may never have the occasion to question such deeply rooted beliefs, but they operate as the background to our thought and actions. In traditional religions, ethical values depend on the worldview in the sense that the latter is believed to ground the former in the very structure of reality. As Clifford Geertz says, the most comprehensive ideas about the nature of reality (the worldview) are such that the most general values (the ethos) are appropriate.[3] The ethos is rendered reasonable by the worldview, and the worldview is rendered emotionally convincing by being presented as an image of an actual state of affairs peculiarly well arranged to accommodate the way of life.[4] Religious symbols and rituals combine the two in an emotionally effective way. The ethos, or "style of doing things" (e.g., nonviolence or individual freedom), gives a general orientation. It involves the value-principles underlying a culture's action-guides—and, it is important to note, it need not be moral. Indeed, *morality* as a basic concern for others can best be seen as a particular ethos rather than as an ethical code—it may inform the construction of a code, but it remains a distinct underlying value. An ethos does not determine one particular set of norms, as evidenced by how different Christian groups applying the principle of "loving one's neighbor" today come up with conflicting positions on social issues. But it nevertheless shapes the general character of a culture. In short, it sets the tone for a way of life.

The worldview's grounding of the ethos in the structure of reality is a form of value-realism. Thus, a religious ontology includes ethical values.[5] Values are part of the fabric of reality, but the is/ought dichotomy still holds: since different sets of values are compatible with one worldview and vice versa, the values are not deducible from the factual beliefs. The ethical code of a religious tradition may remain constant over the evolution of factual beliefs or in different subtraditions advocating different factual beliefs. For example, in India nonviolence as an ethos is grounded in radically different metaphysical systems. So too, the same biblical beliefs and values in the West have been used both to *justify* and *condemn* every social issue from slavery to capitalism to the death penalty to pacifism.[6] Thus, neither the factual nor the evaluative component is derivable from the other, and belief-claims by themselves cannot establish that one set of values or one way of life is in fact grounded in reality. The belief-claims validate or legitimate the value-system only in the sense that believers are convinced that the values are grounded in the final structure of reality.[7] In their minds, the values they hold are simply the way things are: no other values would be consistent with the structure of reality. (The religious thus have the same certainty about the values they hold as they have for their factual beliefs.) Central ontological concepts in religion (e.g., *dao*, *dharma*, God) have both factual and evaluative components—what is fundamentally real is *ipso facto* good, at least in the nonmoral sense of being valuable to us. (Thus, as noted in the last chapter, if religious persons deduce an ethical maxim from a factual statement about a sacred reality, an evaluative premise is already built in.) But the ethos of every religion is not necessarily moral.[8] For those religious persons whose basic values are moral, reality is not morally neutral but is morally good and also allegedly entails specific ethical precepts. In sum, religious symbols integrate the factual and evaluative into one order, thereby grounding basic values in the very structure of reality.

The Particularity of Religious Traditions

In relating religion and morality, we must realize that there is no generic "religion" but only particular concrete religions with concrete beliefs about realities and concrete value-systems. To invert a remark by George Santayana, any attempt to have a religion that is no religion in particular is as hopeless as any attempt to speak without speaking some particular language.[9] We can still speak of "religion," just as linguists speak of the nature of "language" in general, and we can discuss its general features (if any commonalities among different phenomena exist), but we must remember there are only specific concrete religions. To reduce religion to some "faith" devoid of specific belief- and value-content is impossible. No one has a contentless faith in some generic Ultimate Reality or a commitment to the ultimate meaningfulness of life in the abstract. Particular beliefs and values are not merely vehicles to an abstract, universal religion any more than specific languages are merely attempts to voice language in the abstract.

Moreover, the world's religious traditions are made up of multiple subtraditions that have evolved throughout history. No tradition is monolithic. The religious concepts and values—the conceptions of the transcendent, the rewards and punishments, the ethical norms—within these subtraditions do not remain constant but change throughout history. There are variations and exceptions in every religious tradition. Each tradition has different strands of religiosity, i.e., different ways of being religious (e.g., theistic mystics versus those theists who treat God as a distinct object of devotion). The focus here will be upon the mystical strand. But it is important to realize that no religion is a "mystical" religion as opposed to a "numinous" one. There are nonmystical Buddhists and mystical Jews. There is no simple contrast of Western and Eastern traditions or theistic and nontheistic traditions in terms of religiosity,[10] although mystical religiosity has certainly been more prominent in defining the official positions of some traditions than in others.[11] We cannot assume in advance of examining specific traditions that all religions or subtraditions speak with one voice on the issue of mysticism and morality.

Religious faith also cannot be reduced to a set of beliefs and values. The faithful are not speculative metaphysicians trying to construct a system for the intellectual comprehension of the universe but are dealing with the concrete problems of living. Theists do speak of "belief in" God, but commitment to a religious way of life entails more than merely giving assent to certain intellectual propositions—assenting to belief-claims abstracted into creeds may be deemed necessary to one's salvation, but it is not a substitute for living the way of life. But just as morality has its factual presuppositions, religious commitment also logically presupposes the acceptance of certain beliefs or the acknowledgment that one is acting irrationally and is out of step with reality. In other words, the practice of each particular religion has its own entailed belief-claims and value-claims. For example, if one participates in a theistic way of life and is not convinced of the reality of a supreme personal god, one is behaving irrationally or hypocritically. Or consider Theravāda Buddhism: the goal of this way of life is to end our suffering by escaping the cycle of rebirth. This presupposes there is a cycle of rebirth, that rebirth has a cause, that rebirth can be ended by ending its cause, and that we have the ability and control to end that cause. Without a commitment to these entailed beliefs, the Theravāda way of life makes no sense—without an acceptance of these belief-claims, the goal of ending suffering could be achieved simply by committing suicide. More generally, religious actions presuppose beliefs about the nature of a person, life after death, and so forth. This is simply an instance of how actions in general presuppose particular beliefs about the nature of things. To give an everyday example: if one takes a rope to be a snake, one's reaction will differ than if one thinks it is just a rope.

Such belief-claims, along with value-claims, are the focus of a philosophical study. However, although such claims can be abstracted from religious ways of life, this does not mean that the aim of religion is to advance disinterested beliefs about the nature of the world. No religion can be reduced to its intellectual content: they remain full, lived ways of life. Nor can all the different uses the religious make of language in prayers and worship be reduced to just making assertions. As noted in Chapter 1, we need to look at all aspects of a way of life to understand the intellectual skeleton. Focusing on the intellectual content without considering the rest would be like focusing on notes on a music sheet and forgetting the music.

Religion and Morality

As part of their comprehensiveness, all religions have action-guides, some of which cover other-impinging actions. Religious sets of action-guides have different degrees of specificity, from formal codes (the Jewish *halakhah* has 613 command-ments) to maxims to parables to exemplars of religious conduct held up for imitation. Action-guides are integral to each religion and cannot be eliminated. But what sets religious value-systems apart is not a concern for others but our relation to alleged transcendent realities. The objective is to lead a life in accordance with the way things really are, as defined by the religion's worldview. The *summum bonum* involves attaining some transcendental goal and does not necessarily involve other-regarding concern for others. Thus, religion and morality reflect different sets of concerns, and this raises a question: do "religion" and "morality" converge, or are they in fact not compatible at all? Are religious ethics necessarily moral, or do religious values always contradict and trump moral ones?

Modern intellectuals may wish to ignore such practices as rituals and the veneration of saints in order to reduce religion simply to ethics within a metaphysi-cal framework (which they would also jettison). Religion would thereby be reduced simply to a means to inculcate the moral point of view.[12] But traditional religious value-systems encompass all aspects of life. They distinguish "sacred" and "profane," "holy" and "sinful," "appropriate" and "inappropriate," or "pure" and "impure," as well as "right" and "wrong" as related to our other-impinging actions. But religiously proper behavior involves more than other-impinging conduct, and religious value-systems do not differentiate ethical from legal, ritual, or other concerns. As Joseph Dan says of the Jewish *halakhah*, it is impossible to draw distinctions between social, ritualistic, and ethical laws and reasons—they are all integrated into one system of laws that defines how we can conform to God's demands. All are to be obeyed only because this is God's demand, whether or not they benefit human beings.[13] Thus, Jewish law has dietary regulations alongside of other action-regulations. Indeed, only some of the Ten Commandments are what modern Westerners would consider "ethical" precepts—the rest are "religious." We can focus on certain beliefs and values to answer philosophical questions concerning whether a particular mystical tradition is moral or not, but we must remember that the context of the action-guides is one unified value-order.

We often equate religion with morality, but it is far from obvious that religious value-systems must be moral. The history of Christianity includes innumerable wars between Christian groups, crusades, inquisitions, torturing heretics, slavery, anti-Semitism, and the imposition of many unjust social systems—all with the backing of the church in power in the society at the time. The history of other religions once they gain political power is not much better.[14] But even ignoring what actually has occurred and focusing on the ideals based on fundamental religious texts, problems still remain. Religious value-systems are legitimated by appeal to a religious authority and not by other-regardingness. Soteriological goals are not by definition other-regarding. The potential conflict between morality and religion is seen in Søren Kierkegaard's discussion of Abraham's near sacrifice of his son Isaac under the command of Yahweh: Abraham's immoral act would have been justified by a "teleological suspension of the ethical" in light of an overriding duty to obey Yahweh's will.[15] Theists, concerned that a god could command an immoral act, argue that Yahweh was merely testing Abraham and called off the sacrifice of his son. But the point here is that Abraham was willing to do a morally reprehensible act for a religious end. It would have been sinful but clearly not immoral to disobey. A moral person would have dissented. Many religious actions may end up helping other people, but the justification for them is the reward or punishment in this life or a future life or some other religious reason, not that they help. Basing one's actions on personal consequences is by definition not other-regarding, and thus a person acting only out of religious obligation is not being moral, regardless of the positive consequences to others, but nonmoral or even immoral.

Thus, acting out of a sense of religious duty need not be other-regarding and hence is not necessarily moral. The problem is not that religions involve exclusively "otherworldly" matters, but that the framework for "this-worldly" interpersonal concerns is a transcendental worldview. Within that framework, religious norms are justified on religious, not moral, grounds. The theists' claim that we ought to obey God does not involve a moral "ought" but only looking out for what is best for us. God is *nonmorally* good in that he is the source of our being and obeying him is a value to ourselves—in fact, the greatest value since our eternal fate depends upon him—but whether he is *morally* good is a separate issue. The world of nature is a good (valuable for us), but that does not make it moral, and the same point applies to the source of our reality. The converse of this point is that morality is nonreligious—it is a distinct value-system. Some actions and character traits under religious and moral value-systems may converge, but they remain distinct types of value-systems because the justifications of action-guides and the intent of the participants differ.[16] For example, murder is morally condemned because it harms another person, but it is religiously condemned because it interferes with God's purpose for that person, upsets the murderer's state of mind, or for some other soteriological (and hence nonmoral) reason.

In short, religious and moral evaluations remain separate. The autonomy of religious and moral values can be seen by a simple argument. Either one's reasons for following a religious ethic are moral or not: if they are moral, then the role of a transcendent reality as justification is not needed; if they are not moral, then any justification will not make our reasons for adopting the religious value-system moral. Either way, religion adds nothing to the reasons for being moral.

Divine Command Theory

Philosophers have argued for the autonomy of morality from religion since Plato first posed the problem in the *Euthyphro*: "Do the gods approve the holy because it is *holy*, or is it holy because the gods *approve* it?"[17] Theists put it in theistic and moral terms: "Does God command acts because they are *moral*, or are they moral because God *commands* them?"[18] Either way, theists, who believe God's commands must be moral, have a problem: if God commands acts because they are moral, then there must be a standard of morality independent of God's sovereignty, freedom, and power; on the other hand, if the acts are moral merely because God commands them, then whatever God commands must by definition be good. Under the first horn of the dilemma, God's will is not the source of morality, and thus God is not omnipotent and not sovereign in all matters, even if he freely chooses only to will morally just acts; that is, God is bound by morality and thus there is something real that is independent of God. Under the second horn, theists must hold that if God commanded the gratuitous torture of babies, then it would be good to torture babies—the acts would still be "immoral" (hurting others for no other-regarding reason) but religiously "good" nonetheless. This would make ethical precepts as totally arbitrary as they are supposed to be under moral relativism. Thus, under the second horn, there could be no moral justification to worship such a reality, although such a powerful reality would still be feared and dreaded. Theists cannot be comfortable with either horn, and the dilemma leads the nonreligious to believe not that morality does not depend on religious beliefs. To counter the second horn, some recent Christian thinkers have advanced a modified divine command theory: a *loving* god could not command an immoral act, and, since God by his nature is all good, God's commands are necessarily moral.[19] This may satisfy theists (assuming they can argue to a loving god in a noncircular way), but this still leaves morality independent of God's control. That a loving god would not command an immoral deed simply does not address the *Euthyphro* dilemma.

Divine command theorists also encounter practical difficulties in the relation of morality and religion. The problem is determining *what are* God's values. We must reply upon revelations to know God's plan, since we cannot know the ultimate nature of reality through ordinary experiences and reason. But theists disagree among themselves about the content of the value-system supposedly revealed by God. One fundamental problem is the lack of one ethical code across different religious traditions (i.e., ethical pluralism): if there is a god revealing divine commands, to which group has he revealed his commands? Why is there not one uniform set of basic action-guides? Why are there differing commands reflecting the interests and values of different societies and ages? Second, religious codes also contain ritual and other prescriptions that lie outside of ethics. How can Christians, for example, exclude all Old Testament dietary regulations as not required and yet retain the authority of the Ten Commandments without admitting that some nonbiblical standard is being invoked? The entire value-order has the imprimatur of being God's divine decree—how can they justify picking only the ethical rules as binding?

These points show that the religious and ethical precepts still require interpretation, and these theorists must admit that religious communities use the same texts and yet split on important social issues (e.g., segregation, abortion, divorce, and euthanasia). According to the Bible, God grants us dominion over nature (Gen. 1:28; Heb. 2:8), but does this mean that nature is simply there for our benefit and exploitation or, as many have started to advocate today, does it mean stewardship? Religions supposedly of love (Christianity and Buddhism) have been easily adapted by those who favor war. Moreover, both sides of any war or other dispute always think "God is on our side"—their "revelations" merely reinforce the positions taken for other reasons. Groups may well think they and they alone know "God's will," and some are willing to kill those who disagree. Also note that, once a theism is in power, alleged revelations challenging the political power of a ruling class seldom get accepted as legitimate. Instead, religious institutions support the elite, with the religious authorities devising myths and theories that reinforce their power. Religion will remain the broadest level for the legitimation of values, but the issue is where our real values come from—is it God, or our selfish economic interests, or where?

The converse of this is also problematic: would theists not reject any alleged revelation that conflicts with their own moral sense as obviously not really from God? Are they not judging the authenticity of any alleged revelation by an independent moral standard? How do divine command theorists justify moral actions any more than "the divine right of kings"? How do they differ from the antebellum Southerners using the Bible to justify slavery? Or how do divine command theorists justify discounting everything they currently do not like in the Bible and claiming what is leftover is the word of God? For example, liberal Christians want to dismiss passages in the Bible condemning homosexuality, but then what becomes of the "divine command theory" if we can pick which ethical precepts we will accept?[20] In the end, do *we* decide what is a "true" revelation and what is God's will? It is hard not to conclude that what we consider good for our group just happens to be what God commands. This circularity suggests that values and interests outside of the religious texts themselves determine the content of the supposedly revealed "divine commands." We become the measure of all things under the guise of a "divine command."

Another problem for divine command theorists is that, as religions evolve, there often have been *moral advances* over earlier stages of each tradition. A prime example is that slavery was acceptable throughout Christendom for over a millennium but is condemned today. Christians were instrumental in the change, but the change came from moral reflection by Enlightenment thinkers (many of whom were at best nominal Christians), not new revelations or biblical exegesis. More generally, the god of the Christian New Testament does not command immoral acts, as did the savage Lord of Hosts of the Old Testament (e.g., Num. 31:14-18, 50-53),[21] although the book of Revelation reveals a bloody and vengeful god. Prophets and reformers challenge aspects of religious ways of life in all traditions, even if they rarely prevail. Are they judging what the authorities in power take to be God's commandments by some independent moral standard? The only alternative is that God's standards are themselves changing as societies change and thus not permanent—something most theists are disinclined to accept, since it would mean that there are no fixed moral standards and that God's will may in fact be arbitrary. To assert that moral standards are evolving or that God is giving different standards as needed at each stage of our cultural evolution would mean that the action-guides of the foundational texts do not necessarily apply today. Again, some standards independent of any alleged ethical revelations must be at work. These new ethical values and the moral point of view itself are not given by the religious traditions themselves but remain an independent perspective on the earlier tradition.

Also consider this problem. Yahweh tells the Israelites to plunder Egypt (Exod. 11:2) and tells the prophet Hosea to have sex with an adulteress (Hos. 1:2, 3:1). Christian theologians such as Thomas Aquinas and Bernard of Clairvaux who see the chief virtue as acting in conformity to God's will conclude these acts are not "immoral" because God ordains everything and commanded them. Thus, the plundering was not "theft" and the marriage of the adulteress was not "adultery" because God commanded these acts. In effect, God sets the rules of what is and is not "moral" and can change the rules at will. Such acts would then be religiously justified, but a moral appraisal of this situation must be that if acts are immoral they still are immoral even if God commanded them (and even if it is in our interest to obey God's will). The acts are immoral—not other-regarding—and cannot be made moral by fiat or by playing with the word "moral." Even God cannot make something moral by declaring something not to be immoral when it clearly is.

Yet another problem for divine command theorists is that there are nonreligious people who are without question moral. Dietrich Bonhoeffer's observation of total self-sacrifice on the behalf of strangers in World War II by people who rejected all religion is evidence enough. They can be genuinely other-regarding and not simply advancing their own self-interest through helping others. The adamant atheist Bertrand Russell can say that our most urgent need for today's problems is not new technology but love and compassion. The nonreligious may accept that religion historically was the social origin of our moral beliefs. Their logical point is that what makes a thing moral is not God's will and thus we do not need to be religious to be moral. They may also ask what is the real source of religious ethics—is it truly a revelation from God, or did ethical precepts arise from purely natural sources and then get placed in a religious context? They would argue the latter and thus see no problems with the "religious origins" of a culture's ethics. Thus, even if the nonreligious learned their values by growing up in cultures informed by religious beliefs, the logical independence of morality from religious value-systems remains. We may develop a conscience—the inner sense that we have violated a moral universe—not from some act of God but merely from internalizing a set of purely natural social values. In sum, the sense of moral obligation, as well as the content of an ethical code, may well come from exclusively natural sources.

The religious may reply that of course the nonreligious can be moral but the nonreligious cannot *justify* being moral and are in fact living a life inconsistent with their naturalistic beliefs. An answer to "Why be moral?" can only be supplied by the transcendental framework of religion—as Dostoyevsky said in *The Brothers Karamazov*, without God all is permitted. That is, if naturalism is true, we are accountable to no one but ourselves, and so why not be selfish? To theists, morality may seem odd in a naturalistic worldview—a world in which persons are the accidental collections of atoms and there is no purpose to the universe. But to naturalists it is the idea that morality must be commanded from another realm that seems odd: we are at home in a realm where concern for others is more natural than selfishness since we need others to survive and we are all produced together as parts of a greater whole. We do not need a divine command to know that it is morally wrong to torture babies gratuitously. So too needing to threaten human beings with hell to make them ethical renders ethics and morality utterly alien to this world (since it means theists have no this-worldly reason to be moral). Moral realists in general may argue that a baby's need for adults to survive or the cooperation needed for the evolution of species is evidence of a natural moral structure to natural reality and thus to act selfishly is simply to be out of step with nature. That is, a moral concern for others is simply an ultimate fact of the natural universe—a nonmaterial part of an objective order to reality—and no appeal to the will of God or anything else transcendental is needed. On the other hand, antirealists may argue that genuine other-regarding concern, although a purely human phenomenon, may still be necessary for any society to survive because self-interest is not enough to motivate compliance to the self-restraints of laws. Indeed, to naturalists the fact that theists within the same religion split on the meaning of alleged divine commands shows that the transcendent actually plays no role in morality.

In sum, there is nothing *religious* about the moral point of view. Morality remains autonomous, and no nonmoral justification is needed. There is no need to invoke God or any other religious premise, even if a religious justification of the moral point of view were possible. A religious command remains a religious command, and morality something else.[22]

Is Religion Compatible with Morality?

The problems just discussed can be extended to argue that religion, far from being identical to morality, in fact conflicts with it. "Religious ethics" are never moral because a moral concern is always overridden by an alternative, nonmoral value-system of a particular religious tradition. That is, appealing to a religious authority or sanction to justify helping others is incompatible with holding a moral point of view. Again, the problem is that the religious act out of a sense of obedience to a god's will, hope of reward or fear of punishment, or some other religious end, while morality requires that we act out of a genuine concern for another's welfare and not any other reason. In short, if theists answer the question "Why be moral?" by saying it is God's will, they are actually not being moral. So too if we want to steal or murder but do not only out of a fear of hell, our behavior will be ethical (conforming our actions to the social standards), but we are not being moral. Even if God fortunately only commands morally good deeds, theists are still acting out of a religious imperative, not out of a concern for others. Helping others may be what God commands, but to be *moral* we must actually be concerned with the welfare of others. God may command us to respect and value others, but that is not the same as being genuinely concerned with others for their own sake.[23] Abraham would have been rewarded for his actions, not because they were moral, but because he was obedient to Yahweh. Even if religious actions converge with moral ones and are extremely beneficial to other people, adopting a religious value-system still means one is not truly moral. In sum, we can be moral only if we reject the religious point of view.

This argument, however, has a flaw. As noted in the last chapter, people can act out of more than one concern at the same time: they can act both out of concern for themselves and out of a genuine concern for others. Thus, they can act both out of a religious concern for themselves and a moral concern for others at the same time. If they did act only out of any selfish concern (such as their own salvation) or only to fulfill a religious duty, they are not being moral, but as long as one of the concerns driving their actions is in fact a genuine concern for others' welfare, they are being moral. Nothing about a religious point of view forecloses this possibility. Religious personal cultivation and moral concern are not either/or. Moreover, morality need not be one's supreme value to be moral: one can place one's own religious concerns above moral ones and still be genuinely concerned with the welfare of others for their own sake. Thus, a moral point of view can in principle be incorporated into a religious way of life. Such value-systems should be judged moral if they in fact reflect a genuine other-regardingness. Similarly, religious concepts—"sin," "holy," "sacrifice," "*dharma*," "*nibbāna*"—may in fact carry two levels of significance if they reflect a concern for others.

In sum, the religious may be moral, but we should not assume in advance that they must be. A religious value-system must be deemed nonmoral unless it can be shown to be otherwise. If it is moral, it will add a religious dimension to the concern for others—a transcendent reality will become the source of morality's claim on us. Values become grounded in reality by a transcendent source and thus are objective and unchanging. Indeed, as traditional believers see it, a transcendental reality is the only way to ground morality in the structure of things. Religious worldviews, as part of their function of legitimizing the value-system of a culture, can provide a framework in which morality makes sense and is the highest social vision. This makes the context of religious other-impinging action-guides different from that of nonreligious ones: the action-guides become part of the religious demands on a person. In sum, a religion can provide reasons and motives for being moral, even if morality is logically autonomous.[24]

But if the moral point of view is integrated into a religious value-system, more is still needed to implement it in one's life. We need more concrete guidance. The factual claims and values of a specific faith will still be needed to complete a religious set of ethics. Other religious values will provide substance to the abstract moral point of view in guiding how we should act toward others. The religious are not forced to use only nonreligious concepts in their value-system—morality is logically autonomous, but the full religious ethics of a moral tradition will include a moral claim. In other words, if one were to construct a formal syllogism about an ethical issue, the value of being moral will remain a separate premise but will be included along with religious premises in the argument. Religious ethical arguments thereby differ in style and substance from secular ones but are no less moral. However, uncritically speaking of a "moral order" or the "moral authority" of religion can lead to a distorted picture of religions. The concepts of "morality" and "ethics" once again must be distinguished. This is no "religious morality" as opposed to "secular morality," but there are "religious ethics" and not all religious ethics are necessarily moral.

Religion and Virtue Ethics

Viewing mystical actions in terms of deontology and consequentialism is not very illuminating. Mystics are not deontologists who think an act is good in itself—a higher good (liberation or salvation) is always valued more, and an action is (nonmorally) good only if it leads to that end. Similarly, mystics are, of course, concerned with the consequences of their actions, since they have a goal to reach (enlightenment) and they expect that their actions will have lawful consequences leading them in that direction. But they are not "consequentialists" in the technical sense of measuring or calculating the "goodness" of an action solely in terms of the outcome to themselves or others, without regard to the intentions and motives driving actions. Nor do mystics choose whatever actions just happen to lead to the best mystical result. They do not think in terms of "whatever works": what works works because of the structure of reality—we have to follow the nature of reality in order to gain enlightenment. Thus, all classical mystical ethics are forms of value-realism. The enlightened may dismiss the unenlightened's values as products of emotion or delusion or as only a cultural convention, but they see their own values as ingrained in reality.

Religion has an analog to the distinction of "act-morality" and "agent-morality." Scholars can view the religious life simply in terms of whether someone follows a set of rules laid down by their religious leaders. Some practitioners may well only follow a list of rules mechanically. But for practitioners who take their religious life more seriously, external conformity to a code is not enough. For them, religion involves the development of the whole person—not just one's actions, but one's inner life (attitudes, dispositions, desires, and so forth)—and in the higher stages of development this means attaining a purity of heart that the idea of simply following rules does not capture. Thus, it may be possible to view religion in terms of "act-religiosity," but viewing serious religious practitioners in terms of "agent-religiosity" is a better approach. Actions will still remain necessary, but it is not only a matter of *what* they do but of *why* they do it. Act-appraisal may reflect a modern Western prejudice toward action over the inner life, but since religion is comprehensive, it, even more so than morality, is a matter of what sort of person we should *be* rather than simply what we should *do*. Religion is a matter of how we live, and this means shaping the inner person, not only our actions. Cultivating religious excellence includes shaping our desires and emotions so that we instinctively conform to God's will or the *dao* or the *dharma*, not just feeling obligated to follow a list of duties or other rules. In sum, for the highly committed, virtue ethics is a better framework than the rule-following alternatives.[25] Certainly the mystics within each tradition, with their focus on self-development, can best be seen in terms of virtue ethics. Their lives reveal their commitment. Mystical virtues may not be the classical Greek virtues, but mystics cultivate virtues connected to what they see as the highest state of a person. The state of a person, not conduct alone, is central.

Religion both gives meaning to a life of virtue and shows how to lead a virtuous life. Different religious traditions identify different virtues as good or valuable to us. Even within one religious tradition, there may not be uniformity on virtues. For example, within medieval Western Christianity it is impossible to find a single list of virtues exemplified by all of the canonized saints.[26] Religious virtues may not be moral, nor may mystics be "prudent" by ordinary social standards. Religious virtues cannot foster immorality (since the virtuosi are motivated by their religion's reality-centered value-system and not selfishness), but they may be nonmoral since the religious value-system's underlying values may not include other-regardingness. For example, the basic vices of medieval Christianity—the "deadly sins" of pride, greed, lust, anger, gluttony, envy, and sloth—do not all relate to interpersonal actions, but they all relate to our personal welfare.[27] Thomas Aquinas added three religious virtues to the classical Greek list—faith, hope, charity. For him, the reward for virtue is our happiness in the form of a vision of God. But the religious virtues differ from "natural" virtues: they are "infused" in us by God, not merely cultivated by our own efforts. (Protestant reformers were also influenced by this position.) The first two of these religious virtues do not necessarily make us moral and the third only covers part of morality. The religious framework also transforms the place of natural virtues in our lives: they are still to be valued, but they by themselves no longer lead to our happiness. Even suffering martyrdom or giving all of one's property to the poor is not meritorious unless it is done for the fulfillment of God's will. As Augustine put it, being morally good in itself is simply a "splendid vice." Conformity to God's will supplants even morality as a virtue to be cultivated in itself.[28]

That is the basis for some Christians objecting to the idea that virtue ethics is applicable to their religion. Virtue ethics switches the focus from God to an individual's self-development, but self-development is of no concern to a truly Christian way of life—only God and other people are. No self-development is needed: God's grace alone is involved in salvation, and our response is a matter only of doing our duty to God. Some Christians even charge that virtue ethics is immoral: it is only about oneself (one's own virtuous life) and not a matter of how one deals with others. Nevertheless, even though inner attitudes rather than other-impinging actions may be the focus, cultivating virtues does not mean one is necessarily being selfish—it can in fact be the way to become more other-regarding. That is, just because one is cultivating certain virtues does not mean one is concerned only with one's own welfare—the focus can be on developing character traits needed to be more concerned with others. Nor need there be fewer other-impinging actions. Nor does focusing on virtues mean that other people are merely being used for one's own end. (Nor, conversely, need a moral concern negate a focus on the transcendent reality.) In sum, the focus can be inward (developing certain traits) for an outward moral application (others' welfare) and not only for the selfish end of concern with one's own life. Indeed, it is hard to see how cultivating moral virtues such as giving or justice can be seen as *selfish* just because one is trying to develop them.

Observers may still be able to glean rules that describe how a virtuous person acts, even if rules are not the central focus in how the latter lives. Virtue theorists would also note that there may be exceptions to any ethical rule: the only absolute in morality is concern for others, not any particular rule trying to implement that concern. Similarly, in religion: a religious end may involve ignoring a religious precept in some circumstances. The conduct of exemplars of the religious virtues of a given tradition becomes a more valuable guide than any particular set of rules. In addition, virtue theorists can emphasize the development of a person within any religion. Thus, one may begin a religious life out of a fear of hell or other punishment or a hope for a reward. Such self-serving reasons cannot be moral, but they can be reasons for being religious. However, as we develop our religious life, our religious sensibility deepens and our reasons and motives change. We can move from concern with personal repercussions to following a set of rules or commands solely out of a sense of religious duty.[29] The intention for following the rules would thereby change to the religious analog of Kant's idea that acting only out of a sense of duty is essential to being moral. The chances that one will follow the rules are greater, but such actions are still not the acts of a religiously virtuous person. One can achieve a greater depth of religious sensibility than simply trying to follow a rule, in parallel to a deepening of moral sensibility, through the cultivation of character traits and the development of habits.

Higher stages of religious cultivation are usually engaged in only by people who dedicate their lives to the pursuit—the mendicants, monks, and nuns of all traditions. The highest stage goes beyond obeying rules out of a sense of duty to totally internalizing a religious worldview and ethos. An image applied to both the Christian Francis of Assisi and the Japanese Buddhist Bashō contrasts the ease and steadiness with which they walked in the exact footsteps of the founder of their respective religions—precisely because of their lack of effort to do so—with the faulty and clumsy efforts of the learned who try to put their feet in the footsteps but with thought and hesitation. Without being aware of them, the virtuosi are effortlessly following what others see as rules. Moral religious virtuosi then act with a disinterested impartiality toward all. Acting merely out of obedience to a command of God is then seen, as many ethicists assert, as immature.[30] The final goal is to lose all sense of self and to align oneself completely with reality (as defined by one's religious tradition). Thereby not only one's actions but also one's inner mental states are correct. One acts spontaneously "for the sake of God alone" or for an analog in nontheistic traditions. This obviously is getting into the area of mystical enlightenment, although the higher stages of religious virtue may well also be attainable in the other strands of religiosity.

The upshot of this is that intentions and beliefs, not just actions themselves, will be central in assessing the moral status of mystics. That is, the focus of the moral appraisal must be the mystics' intentions in following religious action-guides or otherwise cultivating religious virtues—are they other-regarding, or are they acting for another reason? As long as a tradition's religious action-guides covering other-impinging actions—the tradition's ethics—can be followed by a moral person, the specific content of the action-guides is of no further concern for the issue of a moral assessment. Morality is one possible inner side of such a way of life, and the question is whether moral reasoning and motivation, as revealed in the mystics' writings and actions and the fundamental texts of a particular mystical tradition, constitute one driving force in the life of a mystic. In short, do the writings and actions of a given mystic or the normative mainstream doctrine of a particular tradition entail that a moral ethos should be informing the life of a practitioner?

Mysticism

Religious ways of life include more than just ethical practice and tradition. They cannot be reduced to ethics, but neither can they be reduced to experiences. Mysticism is the same. Indeed, it is a subcategory of religion; thus, what has been said above about religion applies. It is a form of religiosity present in all religious traditions, but it is not, as is often claimed, the "essence" or "core" of all religion: there are other ways of being religious (e.g., the devotional) and other types of religious experience (e.g., numinous experiences of revelation), even if mystics have been a shaping force in every religion. "Mysticism" is not simply the name for the experiential component of all religious ways of life or for the inner life of the intensely pious or scrupulously observant of any strand of religiosity. It is tied to specific types of altered states of consciousness. Mystical ways of life, in the words of Ninian Smart, consist primarily of "an interior or introvertive quest, culminating in certain interior experiences which are not described in terms of sense-experience or of mental images."[31] The objective is to correct the way we live by overcoming our basic misconception of reality and to experience the fundamental reality as it really is, to the extent it is humanly possible. Through the mystical quest, we come to realize the reality present when all the conceptual and emotional content (including all background structuring to our awareness) is removed. With our knowledge and will corrected, we can align our life with the way reality truly is and thereby end the mental suffering that results from trying to manipulate reality to fit our own desires and images. Mysticism thus is, to use a term common to many traditions, a "way" (*dao, yāna*), both in the sense of a path and the resulting way of life.

A distinction must be drawn between "mystical experiences" and "mysticism." Cultivating certain experiences is central to mysticism, but mysticism is a matter of an entire way of life, not just those experiences. Isolated mystical experiences may occur without cultivating them and without having a religious worldview or way of life. They may also not transform one's life—the experiences may seem powerful, but they may only be ends in themselves and thus not affect the rest of one's life. But when the experiences have a transforming effect on one's character, the mystic believes he or she is aware of a transcendental reality and his or her life is reoriented around that reality. When that occurs, mysticism will be a form of a religious way of life, whether the mystic belongs to an established religious tradition or not. Certain experiences play a more important role here than in other forms of religiosity, but mysticism is no more personal, private, or asocial than other religious ways of life. In sum, mysticism cannot be reduced to mystical experiences—doctrines (both factual and ethical) and the other elements of a way of life matter.

Although certain types of experience are central to their ways of life, classical mystics actually discuss experiences very little. Only modern thinkers make mysticism a matter of experiences alone. Instead, mystics discuss reality, knowledge, values, how to live, and the path to enlightenment. Even when discussing inner states, mystics refer more to a transformation of character or the state of enlightenment than types of experiences (including "enlightenment experiences"). Most mystics do not justify their claims by reference to their own experiences but rather by the authoritative texts of their tradition. Thus, it is often hard to tell if certain thinkers (including Shankara, Meister Eckhart, and Plotinus) are mystics who have undergone mystical experiences or are nonmystical philosophers or theologians (like Rāmānuja) whose systems are not informed by personal mystical experiences but are merely the working out of the logic of some religious or philosophical ideas. Their writings, however, usually make it clear if they centrally value the direct personal awareness of the transcendent by way of mystical experiences rather than just the acceptance of religious doctrine.

It is also important to realize that there are more types of religious experiences than just mystical ones. Religious experiences can be broadly classified as those experiences imbued with such a strong sense of reality and meaning that experiencers believe they have been in contact with the transcendent source of the natural realm or some other supernatural reality. These experiences allegedly produce a genuine insight into the fundamental nature of reality. Such experiences are what separate religion from simply holding historical or metaphysical beliefs and following a prescribed code of conduct. They involve transforming our cognitive and emotional programming away from a concern with ourselves to a life centered on reality, as defined by the practitioner's tradition, and a life suffused with religious virtues. Thus, undergoing a religious experience will transform our dispositions, even if the beliefs we accept after the experience are the same ones as we held before.

There is a great variety of such religious experiences, e.g., prayers, alleged public revelations, conversion-experiences, and trances or other altered states of consciousness that the experiencers take as having profound significance concerning the meaning of life. There are also other types of experiences and mental states often associated with mysticism, such as alleged parapsychological powers, auditions, and visions. But the inner quest central to mysticism involves a process of "forgetting" (to use a Daoist and medieval Christian term) or "fasting of the mind" (to use a phrase common to many traditions) of all cognitive and emotional content, including even the sense of an individual self. It involves a calming or stilling of the mind—an "unknowing" of objects or a "withdrawal" of all powers of the mind from all objects. (Such negative terminology emphasizes that the mystic is getting away from the world of differentiated objects, not to deny that there is a ground of reality.) And yet throughout the process one remains awake—indeed, mystics would argue that only then are we fully conscious.

Mindfulness and the Depth-Mystical Experience

The inward mystical process can take two different tracks.[32] Thus, there is not one "mystical experience" but two significantly different types: the mindfulness state and the depth-mystical experience. Both types are allegedly cognitive. The quest may lead to sensing a simplicity and unity to the differentiated flux of experienced phenomena free of our normal conceptual distinctions (the "mindfulness" state) or to an awareness of an identity transcending all subjective phenomena and, under some interpretations, all objective phenomena (the "depth" experience). Mindfulness thus is not simply a low-level, failed, or partial experience of the depth-mystical reality but a distinct type of mystical experience—in this state, there is a sense of "beingness" but the mind still has sensory content or other differentiations. The meditative techniques and the resulting physiological effects differ for the two types: mindfulness involves a passive receptivity and attentiveness in observing the content of the mind during our experiences (as with Theravāda *vipāssana* techniques), while the depth-mystical experience involves focusing attention and concentration (as with *samādhi* techniques). Meditators may practice both techniques, each supplying some mental effects the other does not. But meditators cannot force the mind to become still by following a series of steps. As long as one is still trying to "get" enlightened, one is still in an acquisitive state of mind and thus cannot succeed. Once meditators stop trying to force it, however, the mind stills itself and the mystical experiences automatically occur. Thus, in the depth-experience, the transcendent ground appears active and the meditator passive; in mindfulness, the same holds for the natural world.

Mindfulness involves loosening the grip that our mental concepts normally have on our sense-experiences and inner experiences.[33] It may involve incorporating the inner stillness of the depth-experience into a permanent change in consciousness once the mental content returns. Mindfulness exercises in working, walking, or just sitting attempt to destructure the conceptual frameworks normally structuring our perceptions. The process produces a clarity missing when our mind is cluttered with the concepts and emotions of everyday life. In the resulting state, an experience of the uniformity and connectedness of all we experience comes through—the simplicity of the "suchness" or "beingness" or "thatness" of all reality—along with more intensity to sensory input. We witness whatever arises in our consciousness without judging and without a sense of possession. We no longer identify with our thoughts and emotions but simply observe them free of a sense of self, as if seeing events from a third-person point of view. Awareness is no longer tied exclusively to the images we manufacture—consciousness is no longer just the reaction of our mind to its own creations.[34] Awareness is freed from the dominance of our habitual anticipations and categorizations, and our mind becomes tranquil and lucid. The mind then mirrors only what is there, without adding or distorting whatever is presented.[35] The false world we create of distinct, self-contained entities is seen through, and reality appears as it actually is. Mental categories no longer fix our mind, and attention shifts to the underlying beingness (although structures still remain present in most mindful states). Mystics give special attention to language: naming fixes the flux of reality into distinct units—separating phenomena from their surroundings—when reality in fact is continuous. That is, reality is not illusory—only the conceptual constraints we impose on it, thereby generating a false world of multiple real entities, are. In sum, the conceptualizations and images we create—in particular, the sense of a self separated from the rest of reality—become a barrier between us and the fluid, continuous reality we are part of. Freed by the realization that that is so, the enlightened give up self-will and any attempts at manipulating reality to satisfy what they now know is an illusory self. They simply let things be, and with that perspective comes an inner calm and serenity of being free of the burden of personal concerns and attachments—and the humor resulting from being hit with the unexpected.

Mystical serenity is often described as "joy," but it is not the ecstatic exuberance usually connected with that concept. The experiences may be "ecstatic" in the literal sense of "being outside of oneself" but not in the sense of being incapable of action or coherent thought. Nor is it the happiness of hedonistic fulfillment of personal desires. "Bliss" may be connected with the temporary depth-mystical experience, but the inner calm or coolness of not being troubled by the vicissitudes of life (through detachment or even-mindedness) is the principal emotion connected with living a mystical life aligned with reality "as it really is." There is a sense of peace and well-being not connected to any object as with hedonistic pleasures. Strong emotional responses (e.g., rage, anxiety, or passion) are squelched. But not all emotions may be deadened: temporary joys and sorrows may still occur (and physical pleasures and pain still occur), but they are now greeted with equanimity and so can no longer dominate the inner life. Thus, mystical joy and even-mindedness are in fact compatible. But mystics neither grieve nor celebrate: they have an inner stillness free of the storms of experiences still swirling around them.

With the depth-experience, attention shifts from the realm of change to the still center of being. The mind is stilled completely, thereby allegedly permitting the awareness of a dimension of reality not known through sense-experience and ordinary self-awareness. One is free of all mental content and yet still awake. In the total stillness, an implosion of a transcendent reality allegedly occurs, with a resulting sense of reality, certitude, and usually finality. Mindfulness may be a permanent transformation of one's mental state, but the depth-experience lasts only a limited period of time. Because it lasts only a comparatively short time, it can be called an experience. But even calling it an "experience" is problematic since there is no experiencer separate from what is realized—there is no experience *of* reality, since there is no duality of an experiencer and what is experienced. It is a contentless awareness, a light not illuminating any object. Thus, it is a state of consciousness free of any intentional object. Indeed, the state is sometimes characterized as "unconscious" or "nonconscious" to distinguish it from our ordinary object-driven consciousness. But that characterization misses the fact that one is awake and aware during the experience, even if the conceptualization and understanding of what has occurred comes only after the experience is over.

The depth-mystical experience arguably must always be the same for all experiencers since there is no mental structuring occurring during the experience that would differentiate one experience from another in different people. (Experiences in the state of mindfulness will differ from experiencer to experiencer since, except in the possible case of a "pure" structureless state, the state of mindfulness involves structuring sensations in ways developed from the experiencers' religious traditions prior to their experiences.) It is not that theists experience a loving reality and nontheists experience something else—they all experience the same transcendent reality. The three basic epistemological issues involved in this claim—that no structuring occurs during the depth-experience, that the same reality is involved in all cases, and that a transcendent reality rather than merely some depth to the human psyche is experienced—will not be entered into here. But it should be noted that these assumptions give prominence to the elements of a mystical way of life outside the experiences themselves (e.g., in explaining why some mystics see the same transcendent reality as moral and some do not).

In the classical traditions, mystical experiences are cultivated, not as pleasurable ends in themselves, but for their alleged insights into the fundamental nature of reality. Mystical experiences allegedly give us the ability to know reality free of our culturally created images, thus enabling us to align our lives in accord with the way reality truly is. We are, in Evelyn Underhill's phrase, no longer united to our images and notions but to reality.[36] Both types of mystical experience allegedly have cognitive import, although specific claims depend on how experiencers and their community interpret the significance and nature of these experiences. Mindfulness may lead to a sense of the unity in which all things are part of one whole, or at least to a sense of a fundamental uniformity and connectedness of all internal and external reality. The depth-mystical experience may lead to an undifferentiated oneness or identity of all apparent subjective and objective reality. (Seeing the phenomenal realm as a glowing manifestation of an underlying reality may involve mindfulness, but it can be connected to both the depth-mystical experience and numinous experiences.)

The resulting sense of oneness tends naturally toward a monistic ontology. Advaita Vedānta is the classic instance of a metaphysical system based on overcoming the duality of subject and object. Not all mystical systems, however, involve a nonduality in which all apparent diversity is in the final analysis unreal. The two types of mystical experiences have been fitted into radically different ontological schemes. Sāmkhya-Yogins interpret the depth-experience as the isolation of a self from all matter; within this fundamental dualism of matter and consciousness, they also accept a plurality of selves. Theists in Judaism, Christianity, Islam, and Hinduism have also accommodated the depth-experience in different ways—union with God's will or a sense of experiencing the ground of the self—while retaining the reality of persons. Contrary to popular opinion, most classical mystics do not speak in terms of a "union" of two substances—the experiencer with another reality. Mystics with an emanationist metaphysics such as in the Upanishads and Neoplatonism can speak of "merging" and "absorption," other mystics do not. No mystical tradition has adopted a pantheism equating the transcendental realm with the natural world, creator with creation. For Advaita Vedānta, there is only the transcendent and so no union; for Buddhism, there is nothing to unite; for Daoists, the *dao* is already "in" us; for theists, our creaturehood always remains a distinct reality. Things remain ontologically unchanged: the experiencer, by losing a sense of "I," now simply knows what has always been the case. Of the traditions covered here, Buddhists deal least with the relation of the natural world to any purported transcendent reality. They value mindfulness over the depth-mystical experience in their view of reality and give a pluralistic interpretation of the ontological nature of our experienced reality.

Mystical Enlightenment

Mystical enlightenment can be defined as ending a sense of an individual self by means of mystical cultivation. It involves knowledge of the fundamental nature of reality (as defined by each religious tradition) and subsequently living a life in accordance with it (again, as defined by each tradition). It is not the goal of all religions since salvation may be defined in other terms, but it does make possible the perfection of a tradition's religious virtues. The state of enlightenment may be a permanent state of consciousness produced through a gradual series of events or one sudden event. The enlightenment-event may be the depth-experience, followed by a change in knowledge and dispositions. More depth-mystical experiences may occur, and enlightenment may be further deepened by these experiences or by mindfulness. Indeed, mystics often attach little significance to an event inaugurating the enlightened state since it is the latter state that matters.

But the enlightened have not escaped the world into a trance. They now live in the world in a state of freedom from the attachments and concerns generated by a false sense of an individual self—they act literally selflessly, i.e., free of a sense of self. Evidence that the enlightened still live in a world of distinctions, rather than being absorbed into a oneness, is that they teach others and leave writings. Any language necessarily makes distinctions, and while the enlightened's ability to use language may be in abeyance during certain mystical experiences, their ability to use language in the enlightened state shows that they do in fact make distinctions. However, the enlightened, unlike the unenlightened, do not project the distinctions languages make onto reality and reify them into a false pluralistic world of ontologically distinct entities.

Enlightenment involves a transformation of the whole inner life of a person—cognition, motivations, desires, emotions, dispositions. Only with this complete reorganization of our inner life can we accept the vicissitudes of life without sorrow. The mere intellectual acceptance of a proposition is not enough—we do not need to be mystical to accept that we are all tiny parts of one interconnected natural whole with no ontologically distinct entities, or to follow the analogy of a dream and its dreamer to envision there being a reality underlying all of this world. Only with a mystical experience can we *experience* what is true. Even if the beliefs and values that are mentally internalized in the enlightened state are those of the religious tradition the enlightened grew up in, they now know them to be true in a way they did not before. In the Theravāda analogy, it is the difference between an intellectual acceptance of the idea that water will relieve thirst and actually drinking water. Such a reconstruction of a person, not any esoteric experiences for their own sake, is the concern of mystical ways of life. Enlightenment does result in the internalization of a new point of view, but it is related to living in the awareness of the ground of reality, not merely to the intellectual grasp of an idea or the logical inference to an intellectual conclusion. To emphasize the difference in the knowledge allegedly given in these experiences from that given in sense-experience and reasoning, mystics often use terms such as "contemplation" or "spiritual gnosis" (to distinguish this knowledge from everyday knowledge) or "intellect" (to distinguish the mental function involved in the depth-mystical experience from sense-experience and reasoning). To stress the transcendent's otherness, mystics claim that the reality experienced in mystical experiences is ineffable, although this is either a case of hyperbole for the sake of making a point or a mistake about the relation of language to reality.[37]

Is Mysticism Compatible with Morality?

The role of meditation and mystical experiences in mystical ways of life raises problems for the issue of morality not present in other forms of religiosity. For example, do the beliefs and values of mystical ways of life come from the mystical experiences themselves or from the mystics' particular religious environment? Are all mystical experiences morally neutral? Do mystical and nonmystical sources interact in a religious tradition's beliefs and values? If the depth-mystical experience is in fact ineffable, there can be no sense of love conveyed, or indeed any content at all, and so how could a mystic get any beliefs, values, or action-guides from it? The emphasis on individual experiences itself presents an issue: is mysticism necessarily asocial and apolitical? Must mystics be antinomian with respect to social rules of conduct? Or, even when their acts have positive social effects, does their inner focus change their moral status? What are we to make of Mahatma Gandhi's answer when asked why he was helping some poor villagers: "I am here to serve no one else but myself, to find my own self-realisation through the service of these village-folks."[38] (The Christian Mother Teresa said essentially the same thing about her work among the poor of Calcutta.) Gandhi added: "My national service is part of my training for freeing my soul from the bondage of flesh. Thus considered, my service may be regarded as purely selfish."

The role in mysticism of a reality transcending the worldly order also presents problems. If the transcendent is in fact beyond all natural attributes including values—"beyond good and evil"—how are action-guides such as "love your neighbor as yourself" grounded in reality? Mysticism involves attaining certain experiences related to the ontological depth of reality, so is a mystical way of life totally unrelated to any worldly concerns, including morality? That is, morality involves "horizontal" relationships between people while mysticism involves a "vertical" orientation to being—so how can the two intersect?[39] How can a temporal good relate to the atemporal good? Desiring the good and abhorring evil would be an attachment, but mystics are now free of all attachments, and are they thus indifferent to worldly values? Giving up the entire world is no sacrifice, since they have found something of infinitely greater value. Mystics now know a good that all other goods can be sacrificed for. The only this-worldly change that matters is the inner remaking of an experiencer—does that not mean that the rest of the world must be ignored? Would not rearranging the exterior world be irrelevant? Thus, do mystics remain "otherworldly" and "world-denying," ignoring all "this-worldly" concerns and values such as morality as irrelevant? Can mystics possibly value the realm of multiplicity at all?

Looking at mystical cultivation and the enlightened state yet other issues arise. The virtues to be cultivated are those that aid a practitioner in reaching enlightenment, not necessarily those connected to morality. Enlightenment is the determining value. Thus, mystics cannot be deemed moral simply because they are on the path to enlightenment—only their being other-regarding, not their being mystical, establishes that. What is mystically "good" is what leads to selflessness, not necessarily a concern for others. This reduces "good" and "bad" to nonmoral senses only: what is "good" is what is advantageous to us in a quest for enlightenment, and what is "bad" is what hinders us. Hence, selfishness is mystically "bad" because it is the opposite of the selflessness we should be cultivating. Thus, we should not be immoral only because selfishness does not help us—other people have no claim, as morality requires.

The stages of the mystical life can be divided into the preparatory, the path, enlightenment-experiences, and the enlightened state. The first order of business is reorienting one's actions away from selfishness; this involves both cutting down on desires and self-restraint in actions toward others. Developing skill in following a tradition's religious ethics is part of the preparatory stage; following any such rules involves a detachment from self-centeredness and thus helps in the mystical quest. It forms the base for further cultivation. The path is a more concerted effort toward enlightenment; it involves rigorous training in both the regular virtues of the religious tradition and more specialized practices leading toward the tradition's mystical goal. The path combines contemplation and action as the practitioner moves away from a self-centered point of view to a reality-centered one (as defined by each tradition). Employed in conjunction with other exercises, self-restraint in other-impinging actions or positive help to others provides an outlet for expressing virtues connected to non-self-centeredness. The moral issue is whether this path is essentially selfish, since the mystics focus only on their own self-development.

The path successfully followed leads to enlightenment. (Again, the mystic cannot force enlightenment by means of any exercise or action since reality is now doing the work.) Any enlightenment-experience itself cannot be moral or immoral—no experience in itself is either selfish or other-regarding. (The sense of selflessness resulting from mystical experiences will require further discussion in Chapter 13.) In addition, if the depth-mystical experience is in fact free of all content, one cannot act during the experience itself and thus cannot act either selfishly or morally during such experiences. (Some receptive and concentrative meditative exercises on the path may also present the same problem of nonaction.)

The resulting enlightenment-state presents another set of issues. Even if practitioners are moral on the path, need they be moral in the enlightened state? Is the ethos of morality internalized and thus informing their actions? Or is morality part of the unenlightened point of view to be jettisoned once one has attained enlightenment? Conversely, if mystics are nonmoral on the path, how can they be moral in the enlightened state? There are four possibilities: (1) mystics on the path are immoral or nonmoral, cultivating their own self-development, but the resulting selflessness in the enlightened state produces a burst of concern for others and thus a life of moral activity; (2) mystics are immoral or nonmoral on the path, but the enlightened cannot act selfishly (since they have no sense of self) and instead merely internalize whatever nonenlightened value-system they happen to have been following, whether it is moral or not; (3) mystics are moral on the path, but morality is only a part of the illusory multiple world that is transcended, and thus its value and its factual presuppositions are transcended in enlightenment; or (4) morality is part of the way reality truly is, and so it is cultivated on the path and is internalized in the enlightened life so that the enlightened are completely and spontaneously moral. The danger modern Westerners face is that since we value morality so highly either we can see only the fourth (and perhaps the first) possibility and therefore conclude without any discussion that the enlightened too must be moral or we dismiss mysticism out of hand as scandalous.

Both factual and evaluative issues arise: do the enlightened have the factual presuppositions that make morality possible, and are they other-regarding? It is not obvious that either condition is fulfilled. For example, if all of this world is in any sense unreal, why do any actions matter? Or, if all that is real is God or *brahman*, again why do any actions matter? We could not hurt or help a real individual "person" even if we wanted to since there are none. Or, if the enlightened have no sense of any self, how can they be concerned with other "selves"? And why act out of a concern for others, even if such a concern were possible? If the enlightened simply let things be, being neither attracted nor repelled by anything, how can they show moral concern for the state of others? If the enlightened are not driven by any purpose but act spontaneously without attachments, how could they be moral?

In sum, we cannot simply conclude that being enlightened or being on the way to enlightenment must by itself makes a person moral. But the possible compatibility of mysticism and morality cannot be ruled out in advance. Operating by a mystical value-system does not mean one must be nonmoral or immoral. As with the issue of religion and morality discussed above, one can be both mystical and moral at the same time. Mystics on the path need not treat others merely as means for their own mystical advancement—a genuine sense of the worth of others would work to weaken one's self-centeredness and thus could be incorporated into a mystical way of life. And in the enlightened state, a sense of selflessness is compatible with a concern for others. Whether mystical belief-systems in the enlightened state in fact conflict with the presuppositions of morality is an issue for investigation, as is the status of the enlightened value-systems, and cannot be settled by a matter of formal definitions. Instead we need to examine the mystics of specific traditions in context. Thus, the central questions in the following chapters will be (1) whether the enlightened's factual beliefs conflict with the presuppositions for the practice of morality and (2) whether the value-systems of a mystical tradition (both for those on the path and for those in the enlightened state) are in fact other-regarding. The best place to begin this is with a set of religious subtraditions normally cited as the paradigm of the conflict of mysticism and morality—Hinduism.

Notes

1. Peter L. Berger, *The Sacred Canopy: Elements of a Sociological Theory of Religion* (Garden City, N.Y.: Doubleday, 1967), p. 56.

2. Liberal Christian theologians deny all this and embrace a form of naturalism that reduces the sacred to something natural. Such theology will not be considered here since it lets modernity control what is deemed real and basically denies all traditional religiosity.

3. Clifford Geertz, *The Interpretation of Cultures* (New York: Basic Books, 1973), p. 127.

4. Ibid., pp. 89-90. Also see Clifford Geertz, *Islam Observed: Religious Development in Morocco and Indonesia* (Chicago: University of Chicago Press, 1971), pp. 97-117.

5. Moore 1951.

6. This raises the issue of whether religious beliefs and values are merely used to rationalize a decision made on other grounds. It occurs in all religious traditions. For example, Buddhists justify killing rats for disease control on the grounds that their deaths are only the result of the rats' own past *karma* and we are merely helping them along. This in turn raises the issue of where our fundamental values really come from.

7. G. E. Moore's prohibition against the "naturalistic fallacy" in ethics can also be applied to religious values. That is, a religious "good" is never definable in nonreligious terms: one can always ask of any value, including moral ones, the further question of whether it is religiously "good."

8. Rodney Stark (2001) makes the point that religion does not create morality and a religion's worldview sustains a moral order only if the gods of a society are already moral. He concludes that the vast majority of premodern societies do not link religion and morality and that the moral function of religion requires a particular conception of supernatural beings as deeply concerned about the behavior of human beings toward one another. In sum, the effects of religion on morality are contingent on the images of the gods as conscious, morally concerned beings; thus, religions based on impersonal or nonmoral gods will not influence moral choices.

9. George Santayana, *Reason in Religion* (New York: Charles Scribner, 1905), p. 5.

10. Theists often lump all non-Western religions together in one pile labeled, for example, "monism" when trying to show the moral superiority of theism (and Christianity in particular). See Part I of Barnard and Kripal 2002 for a recent example of this approach.

11. For example, mysticism came to influence mainstream Judaism fairly late. See Dan 1996 on Judaism's discovery of the inner spiritual side (as opposed to the external side of following ethical codes).

12. For example, Ronald Green (1978, 1988) sees all religions merely as means to lead their adherents to a spontaneous and selfless but reasonable commitment to the moral point of view. Whether any moral religious way of life, let alone all religions, can be reduced to just that is open to question. Even within moral religions, whether that is the central focus is also open to question.

13. Dan 1996, pp. 119-20.

14. See Hick 1989, pp. 326-27.

15. Gen. 22:1-19; Kierkegaard 1983, pp. 54-67.

16. See Frankena 1986.

17. See Frankena 1973.

18. It should be noted that not all theists subscribe to the "divine command" explanation of morality. For example, according to Louis Jacobs, in Judaism both biblical and rabbinical literature assume the autonomy of morality. See Jacobs 1973. The Muʿtazilites in Islam sparked a similar controversy. (Al-Ashʿarī and al-Ghazālī upheld the orthodox "divine command" position.) In general, it is tied to the devotional strand of religiosity in theism, not the mystical.

19. Adams 1973; see also Quinn 1978. William Alston argues that a more plausible form of the divine command theory is one in which moral *obligation* but not moral *goodness* is dependent on God. Richard Taylor (2002) argues that the entire idea of "moral obligation" and "ethical duty" makes no sense independent of a religious framework. This highlights the issue of whether the divine command theory leads to *moral* obligation or merely *religious* obligation.

20. Old Testament passages speak of God visiting the sins of the parents on their children up to ten generations (Exod. 20:5, 34:7; Num. 14:18; Deut. 5:9, 23:2; Isa. 14:21-2). How can divine command theorists dismiss these today without admitting an independent moral judgment?

21. If a modern army were to do what Yahweh commanded there—to kill every citizen (man, woman, and child), except the young virgins whom the soldiers are to keep for themselves—we would morally condemn the act even if the leaders claimed to following a divine command.

22. Not only need one not be religious to be moral, but not all members of an ostensibly moral religious tradition are especially moral. In a Good Samaritan-type experiment conducted at a liberal Christian seminary, only 40 percent of the students stopped to help a person who was apparently poor and sick (Batson, Schoenrade, and Ventis 1993, p. 346). If only 40 percent of young ministers-in-training stopped to help, it is unlikely that a higher percentage of Christians in general would.

23. The command "I command you to be moral" leads to an apparent paradox: to obey, we must be other-regarding; but to be other-regarding, we must act only for the sake of others and not act out of a sense of duty to God (i.e., not follow a precept just because God commands it); therefore, if we follow the command, we cannot follow the command. But as discussed in the next paragraph, we can act out of both a religious duty and a moral point of view at the same time; so in fact the second prong of the alleged paradox does not hold.

24. Kant, in his later *Critique of Practical Reason*, argued that we must postulate both (1) a transcendental moral rewarder and punisher as the source and foundation of morality and (2) a life after death in which we are rewarded or punished to remedy the obvious injustices of this life. He accepted these as two factual presuppositions of a moral way of life, since the sense of our obligation to others as absolute and as a supreme value must be grounded in a reality in which goodness is in fact rewarded and badness punished. Morality would then be necessary to the highest way of life (i.e., a life that reflects this reality), and our happiness would be proportional to our moral goodness. But his argument at best leads to a moral realism compatible with both nontheistic and naturalistic worldviews—e.g., *karma* as a natural but moral force would fulfill the same function as a rewarder—and not to the personal, omnipotent, self-existent, loving, creator god of theism. So too theists cannot argue from moral realism to God by simply equating God with "goodness itself" or with whatever it is in reality that would make morality an obligatory value, since a theistic god is a personal agent and the source of the rest of reality and "goodness itself" is not necessarily either of these things (again *karma* supplies the natural counterpart). Similarly, it is not obvious that rewards or punishments in a future life are needed to make morality a supreme value—indeed, if we only act for possible gain or retribution, then we are not being moral at all.

25. Without distinguishing between general religious practitioners within a tradition and only those practitioners who take their tradition very seriously, Donald Swearer (1998) and Damien Keown (1992, 1996) show how virtue ethics is an illuminating way to approach Buddhism. Lee Yearley (1990, 1997) does the same for Confucianism.

26. John Coleman, "Conclusion: After Sainthood?" in Hawley 1987, p. 220.

27. Note that the deadly sins are matter of character, not specific acts such as murder. They are antivirtues. Thus, virtue ethics is appropriate when approaching them.

28. Plotinus exemplified the problem. His contemplation, reflecting his Roman and Greek ethos, was self-centered—concern for others for their own sake was absent (Dillon 1996, pp. 319, 332-33). But his practice did not always conform to his theory—e.g., he was a kind and caring guardian of the orphans in his charge (ibid., p. 323).

29. Just because a religious tradition has a precept in its fundamental texts does not mean all members always follow it. Religious "duties" can be seen as ideals that are not always fulfilled by the majority of practitioners. People also apply the precepts differently in their lives. To cite an extreme example: one hit man for Al Capone's mob considered himself an especially devote Catholic—he would not kill anyone on a Sunday. Obviously not everyone who considers themselves religious distorts a religion's commands that badly, but it should also be noted that a religious tradition having a basic precept of "Do not kill" has never prevented religious authorities from justifying some killing.

30. The "religious duty" theory of religious conduct parallels the "strict father" theory of raising a child. Research on the latter shows that it tends to produce children who are dependent on the authority of others, cannot chart their own moral course very well, have less of a conscience, are less respectful of others, and have no greater ability to resist temptations than children who are raised in a "father as nurturer" environment. George Lakoff and Mark Johnson, *Philosophy in the Flesh: The Embodied Mind and its Challenge to Western Thought* (New York: Basic Books, 1999), p. 327.

31. Ninian Smart, "Interpretation and Mystical Experience," in his *Concept and Empathy: Essays in the Study of Religion* (New York: New York University Press, 1986), p. 98.

32. See Ralph W. Hood, Jr., "The Empirical Study of Mysticism," in Bernard Spilka and Daniel N. McIntosh, eds., *The Psychology of Religion: Theoretical Approaches* (Boulder, Colo.: Westview Press, 1997), pp. 222-32.

33. Today another sense of "mindfulness" has gained attention in academia. See, e.g., Ellen J. Langer, *Mindfulness* (Reading, Mass.: Addison-Wesley, 1989). With its emphasis on attention to the present, this overlaps the mystical sense of mindfulness to some extent. However, it does not emphasize emptying the mind of conceptual and emotional structures but instead involves being mindful of certain facts about one's situation when one acts.

34. See Willard Van Orman Quine, *The Ways of Paradox and Other Essays* (New York: Random House, 1966), p. 211. (Needless to say, Quine was not discussing mysticism.) The psychologist Jerome Bruner would agree: we represent the world to ourselves and act in reaciton to our representation.

35. Richard Rorty uses the phrase "the mirror of nature" to mean that we take the categories of language that we ourselves create as mirroring the objective structure of reality. Wittgenstein's early "picture theory of meaning" is a refined version of this. To prevent confusing this theory with the mystical idea of the mind mirroring nature, it is better to call the philosophical idea that we reify the categories of language into absolute ontological features "grammatical realism" (to use Arthur Danto's phrase) or some other phrase referring explicitly to the role of language in the process.

36. Underhill 1915, p. 5.

37. See R. H. Jones 1993, pp. 103-4.

38. Jag Parvesh Chander, ed., *Teachings of Mahatma Gandhi* (Lahore, India: Indian Printing Works, 1947), p. 375.

39. This distinction is from Paul Tillich's image of two dimensions to religious experience: the "vertical" (referring to "personal union with the Ground of Being") and the "horizontal" (moral obligation, social justice, and other worldly interests). See Tillich 1945-1946.

Part II

The Traditions

4

The Upanishads

Before proceeding, it should be pointed out that the very concept "Hinduism" is only a modern invention, appearing alongside the rise of a sense of Indian nationalism under British colonial rule in the eighteenth and nineteenth centuries. "Hinduism" can refer to anything Indian—indeed, the modern Indian constitution officially included Buddhists, Sikhs, and Jainas as "Hindus." But "Hinduism" will be used here to refer to the various classical theistic and nontheistic subtraditions evolving out of the idea of the Vedas as at least titular authorities and the orthopraxis of the class system and stages of life, even though not all Hindus accept them (e.g., some theistic traditions and Tantrism do not accept the Vedas as the supreme revealed authority and reject the class system, and there are secular Hindus who accept only the social system).

But the important point is that all these various religious subtraditions cannot be amalgamated into anything like one unified system, and this prevents any tidy generalizations about Hinduism and morality. However, most defenders of the thesis that Hinduism is either moral or immoral routinely use the tactic of treating all the various Hindu subtraditions as one (e.g., Sarvepalli Radhakrishnan speaking of generalities about the "spirit of Hinduism"). They see one unified system where there is none and use part of it to speak for all of Hinduism—in particular, the *Bhagavad-gītā*, usually under an interpretation influenced by modern Western moral thought. Instead, specific subtraditions have to be looked at individually. Two of Hinduism's many texts and subtraditions—the Advaita Vedānta of the nontheist Shankara and the theistic *Bhagavad-gītā*—have been chosen here to show the very deep contrasts within Hinduism on the position of mysticism and morality. But the place to start the examination is with the Upanishads since they are the foundation for India's later philosophical thought.

Brahman and *Ātman*

The Upanishads arose out of the Vedic speculation that had begun unifying the

79

powers behind phenomena through connections and correspondences (e.g, the microcosmic/macrocosmic identification of the eye with the sun). Eventually, the power of ritual utterances—*brahman*—was identified as the power behind all phenomena and thus as the source of all things. Its main descriptions emphasize its permanence: it is eternal, unchanging, unborn, constant, without impurities, and imperishable. In the ultimate unification, this power was identified with the power behind a person: the self (*ātman*)—the changeless, the immortal, the inner controller, the inner light, the "unseen seer" that cannot be sensed but is residing in the space within the heart (BU II.5.1, CU III.14).[1] *Ātman* is simply what is vital and permanent in us. It is the "subject" that is never an "object" (BU III.4.2, III.7.23). As some of the oft-cited sayings put it: "I am *brahman*" (BU I.4.10); "you are that [*brahman*]"[2] (CU VI.8.7); "this self is *brahman*" (MaU 2).

The objective and subjective are thereby united in one fundamental reality. The move is away from a sense of an individual self toward realizing the reality underlying all phenomena. It is a form of realism, even if the reality is not an object open to sense-experience. The phenomena of the world are usually treated as real but dependent on an underlying source—they are like sparks from a fire or the web spun by a spider (BU II.1.20; MU I.1.7; SU VI.10), woven on *brahman* (BU III.6), strung on the string of *brahman* (BU II.7.1), or they are like the many colors produced by a prism from a colorless light (SU IV.1). *Brahman* is the root of the world (KU II.3.1). Thus, it is "the reality of the real (*satyasya satya*)" (BU II.1.20), but the phenomena are also deemed real. This doctrine is emanationist rather than illusionist (as with Advaita). *Brahman* is an immanent, if still transcendent, reality grounding our world rather than the creator god of Western theism set off from his creation.

The classic early Upanishads are not entirely consistent on these ideas, both because of the difficulty of formulating new ideas and because significantly different conceptions are in play. Most remain nontheistic, but the Shvetāshvatara and parts of the Katha and Īshā clearly envision the fundamental reality theistically as a person. The Chāndogya and Brihadāranyaka both assert that the *ātman* and *brahman* are identical (e.g., CU III.14; BU I.5.1), but they differ in their focus. The Chāndogya in general deals more with the *beingness* of the world itself and the Brihadāranyaka with the *source* of the world's being. Thus, the Chāndogya focuses on the sensed realm: just as once we understand clayness all clay objects are understood, so too once we understand *brahman*—the common reality to everything—all things are understood (CU VI.1.4). The Brihadāranyaka deals more with the reality behind all objects—the unmanifest behind the manifest, the reality of the real, the inner controller, the unseen seer (BU II.1.20, II.3.6, III.9.26, IV.2.4, IV.4.22, IV.5.15). For the latter text, there are two forms of *brahman*, one of which is not understandable by the mind—for how can one know the knower (BU II.3)? A knife cannot cut itself, and a light cannot be turned back on itself to illuminate its source; so too the undecaying, imperishable, immortal *brahman* is not an object that can be sensed or grasped intellectually by the mind. The roots of the later doctrine of phenomena as "illusion" (*māyā*) are found here—e.g., "lead me from the unreal (*asat*) to the real (*sat*)" (BU I.3.28). The Brihadāranyaka thus deals more with negatives than does the Chāndogya—e.g., *ātman* is "not this, not that (*neti neti*)," thereby negating all predicates to the transcendent (BU II.3.6, III.9.26, IV.2.4, IV.4.22, IV.5.15). It also deals with the apparent duality of this realm and the source, while the Chāndogya emphasizes the positive nature of reality. The Brihadāranyaka bifurcates the inner controller and the outer person, the lute and the sound it makes, and presents images of emergence from a root source (e.g., the spider and its web). The knower in the Brihadāranyaka is a silent one who does not speak at all (*muni*, IV.4.22). The analogy of the enlightened person as a drop of water merging in the sea is more in keeping with the Chāndogya, while the analogy of the dreamer and the dream reflects the approach of the Brihadāranyaka. (But it should be noted that the analogy of the dreamer and the dream does not occur in the Upanishads.)[3]

These differences within the Upanishads themselves allowed later thinkers to advance fundamentally different understandings of the most basic nature of reality under the guise of interpreting these authoritative texts. To mention two: according to the nondualism of Advaita, *brahman/ātman* is the only reality; according to Rāmānuja's qualified nondual interpretation, *brahman/ātman* is the ground of all phenomena, but the latter are also real in the final analysis. (The latter interpretation appears more in keeping with the Upanishads overall.)

Rebirth and Liberation

The Indians' interest in the *brahman/ātman* doctrine was not an intellectual search for a neat explanation of the world. Instead, it is related to two belief-claims with religious import: rebirth and "becoming what we know." The former idea was being introduced in the Upanishads, representing a secret doctrine to be given only to those properly prepared (BU III.2). The idea of "re-death"—i.e., dying in the afterlife—as "the way of the fathers" seems to be older than the switch to emphasizing re-birth. The earliest version of rebirth was based on actions: "as one acts, so one becomes—the doer of good becomes good; the doer of evil becomes evil."[4] The ideas that desire (*kāma*), rather than the resulting action (*karma*) itself, might be the cause of rebirth and that knowledge is the way to end rebirth were also slowly developing (BU IV.4.5, VI.2.16). The concept of a series of rebirths—an ongoing cycle of birth, death, and rebirth (*samsāra*)—had also not yet been fully articulated. The earliest mention of a series of rebirths is in Katha III.7. Understanding (*vijñāna*) is the means to the goal of not being born again (KU III.8). *Karma* at that time still meant *ritual* actions as much as any actions by thought, word, or deed. Only later did the soteriological significance of *all* actions emerge.

Early on, two paths were commended: better rebirths in the realms of the gods, and getting out of the chain of rebirths completely (e.g., CU IV.15.5).[5] Why liberation from the chain is desirable is not always made explicit in the Upanishads. One early reason given for knowledge is that it is a means to control, and so knowledge of *brahman* is the practical means to satisfy every desire.[6] The Vedic ethos is that life is good, and so obtaining desires was considered positive. But there also begins to appear in the Upanishads the idea that this world should be escaped—that it is better to escape rebirth completely than to be reborn even in the heavens—although terms for release (*mukti*, *moksha*) were not yet introduced.[7] A quest for immortality was advanced over possessing even the entire world filled with wealth (BU II.4.3), especially in the more dualistic Brihadāranyaka. As the hymn of Brihadāranyaka I.3.28 puts it: "From the unreal, lead me to the real! From darkness, lead me to the light! From death, lead me to immortality!" The idea of human existence as suffering (*duhkha*) is thus developing, although concepts of immortality could at this stage still share the Vedic ethos and be only the highest form of satisfaction.

The way to escape rebirth developed through the idea that "who knows x, becomes x" (*ya evam veda . . . bhavati . . .*) (e.g., BU IV.4.25). This is true in the matter of fulfilling more mundane desires (as in the Chāndogya). But who knows *brahman* also obtains the whole world (BU I.4.17). Most importantly, one obtains release from rebirth, for who knows *brahman* becomes *brahman* (BU IV.4.13, 17, 25; MU III.2.9). Who sees diversity goes from death to death (BU IV.4.19; KU IV.10-11), but knowers of *brahman* are not reborn (BU IV.4.8-14). Under the Advaita interpretation, it is wrong to say that by knowing one *becomes brahman* because we already *are brahman*. But such Upanishads as the Katha are more easily interpreted dualistically: the self is freed from the series of reembodiments into new bodies and is returned to *brahman* after death, like rivers merging into the sea (MU III.2.8; see also BU IV.3.32). With knowledge of *brahman*, one becomes the reality known, and the chain of rebirths is ended. The knowers of *brahman* are freed of both their good and their bad deeds and go to *brahman* (KsU I.4). They become immortal, while only suffering and destruction awaits the rest of us (BU IV.4.14; KeU II.5).

It is important to note that it is only by *knowledge* that one becomes *brahman*. No other path leads there (SU III.8). This places mystical knowledge centrally in Upanishadic soteriology. The idea of nescience (*avidyā*) as the error to be overcome by knowledge (*vidyā, brahmavidyā*) is also developing.[8] Becoming *brahman* cannot be achieved by rituals, austerities, or any other acts. Nor can any learning or the intellectual grasp of an idea achieve the necessary knowledge (MU III.2.3). Such learning is a lower knowledge, in contrast with the higher knowledge by which one grasps the imperishable (MU I.1.5). This requires an awakening (KeU II.3, 4), an experiential insight in which one becomes what ones knows. Thus, a mystical insight into the nature of the reality is needed to attain release. As noted above, the Chāndogya gives the analogy of knowing everything made of clay by knowing just one lump of clay: all the objects are just names—the reality is the clay (CU VI.1; see also MU I.1.3). So too all of reality is known by knowing the common core of being shared by consciousness and all objective and subjective realities.

The Upanishads turn the quest inward to find this identity—to know the reality common to all of reality by knowing the knower of knowing, the *ātman*. For example, the passage in the Chāndogya beginning with the analogy of the clay ends with the quest for the reality within the listener (VI.12). For the Brihadāranyaka too, by knowing the self one knows the whole world (IV.5.6). The latter text, with its emphasis on the reality behind phenomena, has more in this regard. This process involves "unknowing" sense-objects and all other mental content, thereby stilling the mind. The Kena emphasizes that *brahman* is not open to sense-experience (KeU I). Later Upanishads are more explicit on the topic of mystical practices. For the Katha, *brahman* cannot be grasped by the senses or reason, and so realizing *brahman* requires an experience when the mind has been prepared by meditative practices: the self cannot be grasped by the senses, and so the wise turn inward (IV.1); yoga is the control of the senses (VI.11); one must quit evil ways and become calm with a stilled mind (II.24); the mind and senses must be tranquil (II.20); the wise control speech and mind within the tranquil self (III.13); one can see diversity but by the mind alone can the seer be attained (IV.10-1). The theistic Shvetāshvatara also requires yogic practices related to concentrating the mind and to breathing exercises (II.1-10). Both the Katha (II.23) and Mundaka (III.2.3) state the self cannot be attained by instruction, learning, or intelligence but only by those whom the self chooses (i.e., no practices can force the experience but a mystical "grace" by the transcendent is required). The earliest Upanishads, still making the transition from Vedic speculation to later mysticism, reveal the beginning of such yogic practices. The Brihadāranyaka emphasizes that one cannot see the seer because there is no object to be seen (IV.3.31-32); thus, we need to be tranquil, self-controlled, withdrawn, patient, and collected to "see" the self (BU IV.4.23).[9] So too we need to banish all desires (BU IV.4.6-7). The Chāndogya too speaks of the necessity of tranquility and of concentrating all the senses within oneself (III.14.1, VIII.15.1). But the Brihadāranyaka, with its emphasis on negatives and the underlying reality, entails that a depth-mystical experience free of all sensory content is required for the enlightening knowledge.

The state of consciousness in this knowledge was hard for the Upanishadic thinkers to describe, since when one is embraced by the *ātman* one is oblivious to everything within and without (BU IV.3.21). It is like merging with *brahman* in deep, dreamless sleep and after death (e.g., BU II.1.17; CU VI.8.6, VIII.11.1; BU II.4.12, IV.5.13)—states where the awareness of objects, or indeed where all duality of knower and known, vanishes. We all merge into *brahman* in those states, but the unenlightened reemerge because they have nescience and desires. The Māndūkya Upanishad (III-VII) advances a state of consciousness beyond even dreamless sleep. That state is simply called the *turiya* (the "fourth" state) because it cannot be otherwise characterized. Modern Westerners do not take dreamless sleep to be a state of consciousness in any sense, but under the *brahman/ātman* doctrine consciousness is always present, even if we are not using it—thus, even dreamless sleep is a state of consciousness. Consciousness is present in all mental states and only needs to be focused. The state beyond dreamless sleep is when consciousness is completely focused—that pure consciousness is *brahman/ātman*.

Conduct on the Path to Enlightenment

As with other topics, the Upanishads do not systematically set out all that a student on the path to liberation from rebirth must do in order to advance toward this knowledge. In particular, there is very little on the ethics of the preparatory stage or path, since these texts focus on new doctrines related to the enlightening knowledge. Scholars commonly claim that the Upanishads presuppose the moral excellence of anyone seeking this knowledge. But this ignores the fact that there are in fact a few sections on proper conduct and the issue of morality (i.e., other-regardingness) does not figure prominently in any of them. The early Upanishads exhort its students to recite the Vedas, give gifts to their teachers, honor their parents, have children and perform other householder duties, follow the code of social conduct (*dharma*), tend to their health, perform the rituals, and follow other matters that relate to the way of life evolving out of Vedism into Hinduism (TU I.9, I.11). Teachers pray for their own prosperity, students, and fame (TU I.4.2-3). Virtues related to meditation and asceticism (*tapas*)—self-control, tranquility, self-denial or renunciation (*nyāsa*), desirelessness, fasting—also figure in these lists (TU I.9; BU IV.4.6-7, IV.4.22, VI.2.16; CU II.23; KeU IV.8).[10] Celibacy figures in later Upanishads' precepts (MU III.1.5; PU I.2, 10, 13, and 15). Noninjury (*ahimsā*) was not yet established as a major precept: it is mentioned rarely, and an exception is made for killing an animal needed for a sacrifice (CU III.17.4, VIII.15). But two moral virtues are important: truthfulness (*satya-vācana*), both because of the belief in the magical power of truth over physical events and because the term "*satya*" does not distinguish "truth" and "reality";[11] and alms-giving (*dāna*), although in the early period this was probably limited just to giving to teachers and the Brahmins (BU V.2; CU II.23).

Needless to say, not all the virtues of a path need to deal explicitly with morality for the path to be moral—the questions are whether morality is among the underlying values and whether the virtues and norms are consistent with morality. But nowhere in the Upanishads is there an endorsement of the value and importance of other-regardingness or indeed any discussion of it. Commentators often cite the rule "by good acts, one attains a good rebirth, and by bad acts, one attains a bad rebirth" (e.g., in BU IV.4.5) as evidence that the Upanishads require good acts for enlightenment. But this rule relates to how rebirth works and not to enlightenment. The Upanishads insist that we cannot escape the chain of rebirth by any acts, including good ones, but only by knowledge. This includes actions cultivated on the path, such as austerities and almsgiving—the former help concentrate the mind, and the latter lessens a sense of self-centeredness—but actions do not lead to knowledge (e.g., BU III.8.10). Something else is needed to escape rebirth. Giving still leads to rebirth (BU VI.2.16). Nothing in the texts suggests using others for one's own spiritual advancement, but there is also nothing about the value of others for their own sake or working to help them as morality requires.

Nor is "good" ever defined in terms of other-regardingness. The closest the Upanishads come to suggesting that morality is required on the path to liberation from rebirth is in the Katha: the self is not grasped by a man who has not quit misbehavior (*dushcarita*), is not tranquil, and is without a stilled mind (II.24). The passage does not specify what constitutes "bad" or "good" acts—must they be morally good or simply conform to a given code or fulfil some other criterion? (In the medieval *Mahābhārata*, the term "*dushcarita*" means bad or wrong behavior or wickedness and refers to what is considered the chief forms of misbehavior—murder, theft, lying, covetousness, envy, and so forth.) The action-guide is given in the context of personal cultivation and does not suggest an other-regarding concern. That is, we need to cease committing selfish acts in order to make progress toward attaining knowledge of *brahman*—such a change in conduct would orient us away from self-centeredness and toward the reality underlying everything—but the passage in context does not indicate that we must be concerned with *others' welfare*. Self-control, not other beings, remains the center of concern. Even assuming morally good acts are required, this passage also involves only reordering conduct and not the inner transformation of character necessary for becoming a morally virtuous person. An other-regarding inner character is not part of the inner transformation needed for enlightenment and thus is not a subject of the Upanishads. The turn inward described in these texts involves only a matter of meditative techniques and mystical virtues such as desirelessness. Conduct remains only a first step on the path of cultivation and does not make us a person either moral or enlightened.

In sum, morality is not an important matter for the path to enlightenment. The criterion of "goodness" is what leads the experiencer toward the release from the chain of rebirths. But the moral status of the path can be salvaged if the goal of this mystical self-cultivation—the enlightened state—is itself a moral state. That is, the path may temporally require a person to be exclusively self-concerned, but if the state resulting from these practices is other-regarding then a person is morally justified in undertaking the quest (unless the path takes all of one's life). This leads to the issue of whether a person in the enlightened state must be moral.

The Enlightened State

The principle "who knows x, becomes x" applies both to rebirth and to enlightenment: who knows diversity is reborn in the realm of diversity, but who knows *brahman* becomes *brahman* and takes on all its features. Of particular importance, one becomes, like *brahman*, immortal (e.g., BU V.14.8; KU VI.14).[12] (Or, to be more precise, when the body dies, one returns to *brahman*, one's individual "self" ceases, and one is no longer reborn.) The Upanishads do not discuss any experience initiating the enlightened state, but the idea was developing that when one's mind becomes tranquil, one "sees" the reality common to all subjective and objective phenomena (e.g., BU IV.4.23). The ground of the world is beyond pleasure and pain and untouched by evil (e.g., BU IV.3.21; CU VIII.4.1; IU VIII; MU III.1.1), and since one who knows thus becomes thus, the enlightened is in exactly the same situation. The Upanishads do not discuss ontological issues related to how a person can exist in the enlightened state: if *brahman* is changeless and we become *brahman*, why is our personal existence not immediately annulled? Why is the emanated reality not immediately reabsorbed? How can we continue to experience diversity, and indeed how can we act at all? The images are given of two birds nestled in the same tree, one active and one watching (MU III.1.1.4; SU IV.6-7), and of a charioteer and a chariot (KU III.3) to try to explain how the unmoving self and the active person can be the same reality. These analogies may not satisfy our understanding, but, in any case, the enlightened do live in a world of multiplicity and do act. They perform works (*karma*), although the works do not smear off (*lipyate*) on them, i.e., no merit or demerit leading to new rebirths is produced (IU II). Just as a mirror stained with dust shines brilliantly when it is well cleaned, so the embodied person, seeing the nature of the self, becomes concentrated (*eka*, "one") and free from sorrow (SU VI.8).

The Upanishads deal more with the emotional issues of the enlightened state. The key idea is that this state is beyond our unenlightened state in every regard. The knower of *brahman* is emotionally still—free from joy and sorrow, pleasure and pain, delusion and fear, and all passions (BU IV.4.25; CU VIII.12.1; MU III.2.5; IU VII). The Upanishads, however, are not uniform on the status of desires in the enlightened state. Many early texts, perhaps still under the Vedic life-affirming ethos, see the knowledge of *brahman* as the magical power for obtaining all worldly desires—kingship, cattle, wealth, fame (CU VI.25.2; TU I.3.1, I.4).[13] The Chāndogya in particular emphasizes the fulfillment of all desires in this world (e.g., CU V.1.4, VII.26.2, VIII.1.4-6). Those who desire the real (*satyakāma*) obtain all desires and all worlds (CU VIII.7.1-2). Indeed, it describes an enlightened state that may not seem very spiritual: the enlightened sage "roams about, laughing, playing, and enjoying himself with women, carriages, or relatives, without remembering the appendage that is this body" (CU VIII.12.3). That the enlightened can eat whatever they like and assume whatever appearance they like (TU III.10.5) may involve a similar sentiment. (Also see Chapter 10 on Tantrism.) Passages in other early Upanishads follow the Chāndogya on fulfilling desires, including some in the Brihadāranyaka (BU I.4.7, IV.4.22-24, VI.1.4; TU II.1). But the Brihadāranyaka also emphasizes the other position: the enlightened, like *brahman*, are free of all desires.[14] Becoming free of desires is the path to enlightenment, and the resulting desirelessness is incorporated into the enlightened state (BU III.5.1, IV.4.6-7, IV.4.12; CU III.17.6). Desire for hedonistic pleasure is eclipsed by a state desiring nothing. In fact, desire, not external actions, begins to be seen as the engine driving rebirth. A person becomes seen as being made only of desires: "as we desire, so we will; as we will, so we act; as we act, so we reap" (BU IV.4.5-7). In short, desire drives the actions causing future rebirths. Thus, knowledge of *brahman* shows there is in fact nothing to desire; thereby desire ends, and that in turn ends the chain of rebirth. The later Mundaka states both that the wise obtain whatever they desire (III.1.10) and that they are free from desires (III.2.1). That is, whoever still has desires is reborn, but the enlightened now have all their desires satisfied and so all their desires have vanished (III.2.2).

Whatever their position on desires, the most important consequence in the Upanishads is that the enlightened are out of the cycle of birth and death. Brahman is untouched by evil and is not increased by good acts nor decreased by evil ones (e.g., CU VIII.4.1; IU VIII; BU IV.4.22),[15] and so those who know *brahman* are in the same position. In terms of later Indian philosophy, the enlightened are beyond the sanction of *karma*: their actions have no karmic repercussions in this life and do not produce a future reembodiment. Such consequences have permanently ceased, and thus the enlightened is unaffected by any action. This leads commentators from Paul Deussen to Albert Schweitzer to Robert Zaehner to claim that the enlightened are "beyond good and evil." Many of the passages cited for this proposition can more easily be interpreted merely as referring to getting out of the chain of rebirths. That is, the enlightened are not beyond *moral* good and evil but are beyond *karmic* good and evil—i.e., beyond the merit (*punya*) and demerit (*pāpa*) that produces rebirths. "Merit" and "demerit" are nonmoral concepts related to actions having consequences for rebirth, not moral concepts related to other-regarding or selfish actions. Thus, the knower of *brahman* is free of stain, having "shaken off" merit and demerit (MU III.1.3; see also KsU I.4).[16] Just as water does not cling to a lotus leaf, so demerit does not cling to one who knows *brahman* (CU IV.14.3). Thus, they are free from demerit (CU VIII.4.1). The enlightened have burned up all merit and demerit and no longer think about the past (e.g., BU IV.4.22-3; CU V.24.3). The knower of *brahman* is not troubled by thoughts like "Why didn't I do the right thing (*sādhu*)?" and "Why did I do the wrong thing (*pāpa*)?" (TU II.9). In sum, the enlightened are beyond the sanction of *karma*, which applies only to the path. But the issue of whether the knower of *brahman* in the enlightened state have also "shaken off" *moral* good and evil is not raised.

The Moral Status of the Enlightened

Thus, the issue remains of whether the enlightened are beyond moral good and evil. But a basic problem here is that *brahman/ātman* is not just beyond merit and demerit but is unaffected by any action (e.g., BU IV.4.22; CU VIII.4.1; IU VIII), and, since knowers become what they know, the knowers of *brahman* are also unaffected. All of this world is a dependent "dream" realm, and the underlying "dreamer" is unaffected by any action within it. Nothing that happens in the dream is ultimately real and thus is no longer of concern to the enlightened—including any moral or immoral actions of the dream-characters. In short, the enlightened are beyond all moral concern. All matters of proper social actions (*dharma*) or improper social actions (*adharma*), right (*sādhu*) and wrong (*asādhu*), are merely the product of speech and do not reach the reality of *brahman* (CU VII.2.1). Proper social action (*dharma*) is contrasted with knowledge of *brahman*: all the things connected to *dharma*—sacrifices, vedic recitation, almsgiving, austerities, and the student stage of life—produce only merit, while one steadfast in *brahman* reaches immortality (CU II.23.1). That is, almsgiving and austerities are part of the path leading to rebirth but not the path to *brahman* (BU VI.2.15-16; CU V.10.1-3). *Brahman* is beyond proper action (*dharma*) and improper action (*adharma*), beyond what is done or not done (KU II.14). Even if moral action is required on the path (and, as discussed above, that is far from certain), in the enlightened state the knower of *brahman* is beyond such matters.

Thus, everything is permitted to the enlightened, and there are examples in the early Upanishads of how the enlightened can engage in *immoral* acts harming others. The Kaushītaki Upanishad III.1 states that one who knows is not injured by any deed whatsoever—even stealing, procuring an abortion, or killing one's own father or mother. An enlightened's face glows (BU IV.14.2), and when he commits an evil (*pāpa*) his face does not lose its color (KsU III.1). "One who knows" is not stained by evil (*pāpa*) even if he associates with people who commit any of five deadly acts—stealing gold, drinking liquor, killing a Brahmin, having sex with the wife of one's teacher, and associating with people who do any of these—and instead becomes pure and clean and attains a good world (*punyā-loka*) (CU V.10.9-10).[17] The Brihadāranyka V.14.8 adds that however many evil acts (*pāpa*) the enlightened commit they burn them up and emerge clean and pure—in the highest state, a thief is not a thief and a murderer is not a murderer (IV.3.22). And there is an incantation to kill one's rivals and foes (TU III.10.4). What motive the enlightened would have for any of these actions is not clear if they are desireless; but if they are to obtain all desires in the enlightened state, no actions would be proscribed.

These passages are not advocating that the enlightened should commit such harmful actions, but the texts are doing more than simply stating by hyperbole that the enlightened's actions carry no karmic consequences leading to rebirth, i.e., that the enlightened are beyond the sanction of merit and demerit. For once the Upanishads are explicit about moral matters and do not condemn immoral action. The passages make clear that the enlightened could in fact engage in such actions, and there is no moral condemnation if they do. (Also see Chāndogya VIII.12.3 quoted above concerning the enlightened satisfying their very worldly desires.) It is clear the knowers of *brahman* can behave anyway they want—they remain

Brahmins, no matter how they act (BU III.5.1). The enlightened thus do not simply automatically follow the rules of proper social conduct (*dharma*) or any other-regarding precepts. They are beyond morality: any rules of morality have no role in their lives. *Brahman* is not constrained by morality, and thus neither is one "who knows thus."

The characterization of *brahman* is a basic problem for anyone claiming the enlightened state is moral: there is nothing in the Upanishads portraying *brahman/ātman* as concerned with people, with moral good and evil, or with any moral issue. Even the theistic portions of the Upanishads do not portray *brahman* as a concerned or loving god. Nothing portrays *brahman/ātman* as even active within this realm (rather than being its underlying source).[18] No moral attributes are ever ascribed—all that is important is that *brahman* is the immutable, immortal reality underlying all phenomena and is beyond our comprehension. In addition to the passages cited above, *brahman* is described as having no obligation to act nor any means to act (SU VI.8). It does not speak and has no care (CU III.14.3). Even if it could be described as aware of the content of the "dream," it is still totally indifferent to anything in the world of multiplicity. The real self is not an actor, and no reason is suggested for how (or why) it could help one part of the dream over another. *Brahman* may be deemed "good" in the nonmoral sense that it is of value to us as the source of our existence and the *summum bonum* of our life, but there can be no grounding of moral values in this underlying reality.[19] And since the enlightened become what they know, the moral consequence of this doctrine is that the enlightened too will be morally indifferent. The enlightened will be at peace, perhaps indulging their desires, but nothing in the Upanishads suggests they will be loving or concerned with the welfare of others.

Despite Shankara's best efforts, it is difficult to interpret the Upanishads as advancing the belief-claim that is most damaging to a moral way of life: absolute nonduality. Instead, our world is seen as emerging from *brahman/ātman*, with the objects of this realm having some reality. An emanationist metaphysics can certainly ground a moral way of life: the emanations simply need to be considered real and a concern for them needs to be expressed. However, this is not the case here. The Upanishads emphasize only the reality common to all of the objective and subjective realities of this realm, not any individuality or otherness. In addition, the texts themselves do not suggest any concern for other parts of the emanated realm. The underlying reality, not any concern for the parts of the realm of manyness, is the only focus of concern.

The Katha brings out the implications of this: the wise know that they are unborn and eternal and that that reality is not killed when the body is killed, and so they have no sorrow; thus, if the killer thinks that he kills or if the killed thinks that he is killed, he fails to understand what is real (II.18-19). We could not actually kill someone even if we tried: there are no real "individuals" to kill—the only reality is *brahman*, and it cannot be affected. (If this passage is given a Sāmkhya dualistic interpretation, still the self [*purusha*] is unaffectable and the matter cannot be hurt.)

Thus, we cannot but practice noninjury (*ahimsā*) no matter what we want to do. Even if we went through the apparent act of killing (and the passage presupposes that this is possible), there is nothing real to kill and no reality that can be a killer. Nor can this doctrine support the idea that we can adjust our actions to help others if we elect to be moral—there are no *others* to help. In the end, the immutable *brahman/ātman* trumps the surface diversity, and morality is ruled out.

In sum, the Upanishads' metaphysics conflicts with a presupposition of moral practice—the reality of others to be concerned about—and thus the enlightened of the Upanishads cannot be moral. This belief-claim also rules out being selfish: the quest for enlightenment may be individualistic from our unenlightened point of view, but there is no individual self to be selfish about. Thus, this value-system must be deemed neither moral nor immoral but nonmoral. Its values relate to the mystical matter of awakening to the true nature of reality and not to ethical matters about conduct within what is actually a "dream" realm, including any concern for the welfare of others. Moreover, even if the factual beliefs did not render morality impossible, the ethos of the Upanishads presents a problem: as just discussed, the enlightened state is never characterized as morally virtuous. Nothing suggests a concern for others, either leading them to enlightenment or helping them with their problems within the realm of multiplicity. To use Robert Hume's extreme characterization of the situation: unlike for the Greek sages for whom knowledge leads to a virtuous character and a virtuous life, here possession of knowledge of *brahman* "cancels all past sins and even permits the knower unblushingly to continue in 'what seems to be much evil,' with perfect impunity, although such acts are heinous crimes and are disastrous in their effects for others who lack that kind of knowledge."[20]

Possible Objections

Some scholars have defended the position that the Upanishads are in fact moral. Franklin Edgerton believed noninjury (*ahimsā*) is logically deducible from the nondualistic doctrine of the *brahman/ātman* identity: "we injure ourselves when we injure others since the Self in each of us is identical."[21] Paul Deussen saw this identity as grounding the Golden Rule: you should love your neighbor as yourself because you *are* your neighbor.[22] This position, however, badly misconstrues the *brahman/ātman* identity even under Shankara's interpretation in two ways. First, that "*brahman* is *ātman*" do not mean that people are identical *to each other*. There is no identity of the surface phenomena within the realm of multiplicity. The differences within the dream remain intact—if you have a headache, it does not mean I have one. (And of course the true reality "in" us—*brahman/ātman*—cannot have a headache.) Different people and objects are not one in that sense. I am not you, but we emerge from, or are identical to, one unchanging underlying reality. The separate "self" within the "dream" realm we normally identify with is not the reality behind all phenomena. In sum, the underlying reality is one, but the emanations dependent upon it remain distinct from each other. Second, what is in fact real (*brahman/ātman*) is unharmable no matter what we do (KU II.18-19). In no way do you harm the real "you" by harming another "person." Conversely, non-injury or compassion is equally groundless: what is real about other "individuals" cannot be helped or otherwise affected, and they have no individual interests to take into account. Nothing the "dream" self does could even in principle affect what is actually real, since nothing phenomenal "reaches" *brahman/ātman*. (And even if we could help or hurt *brahman/ātman*, there is still no reality separate from ourselves whose interests we can take into account because we *are* it; thus, there would still be no other-regardingness but only the self-interest of helping our true reality.) The moral consequence of this is that how we treat other parts within the "dream" realm is irrelevant. In the end, no actions within the "dream" are any better or worse than any others. This can only lead to moral indifference. As Deussen was forced to conclude, when the knowledge of *ātman* has been gained, "every action and therefore every moral action has been deprived of meaning."[23]

Sarvepalli Radhakrishnan and others have defended the morality thesis in other ways. First, some argue that morality is a necessary prerequisite in the Upanishads to the mystical knowledge—i.e., one cannot be enlightened without being moral—and this moral way of life is implicitly carried over into the enlightened life. Thus, the enlightened life presupposes morality, even if it is not explicitly discussed.[24] But whether the path is necessarily moral in the strict sense of being *other-regarding* was questioned earlier. Moreover, even if morality is necessary on the path, the Upanishads stress the total discontinuity of the values in the unenlightened and enlightened ways of life—*brahman* is beyond the social rules of proper conduct (*dharma*), and so forth. Any preenlightenment morality would be something jettisoned upon enlightenment. We therefore cannot simply assume the enlightened must be moral, especially when the texts explicitly present contrary evidence. Thus, this response will not succeed.

A second response is that the passages conflicting with morality are only meant to deny that the enlightened consciously consider alternatives or follow rules; instead, the enlightened have internalized moral values completely, and thus they instinctively and spontaneously act only morally.[25] Therefore, the only way the enlightened can act is for the good of the world—they cannot even consider another way of acting. In particular, they cannot conceive of acting selfishly. They are thus beyond concepts and rules but not beyond morality itself. However, once again nothing in the texts support this position. Not only is there nothing explicitly stating this, there is nothing in the texts suggesting that the ethos of the enlightened state is other-regarding. And the passages discussed above in fact explicitly indicate otherwise. Thus, this response also fails.

A third strategy is to note that the Upanishads focus more on the inner life (e.g., self-denial and renunciation) than on external acts and their results or on conformity to rules imposed from the outside—an inner transformation, rather than any external change in conduct, is central.[26] But, while this is undoubtably true, it does not follow that the Upanishads' values therefore must be *moral* ones. And, as discussed above, a concern for others' welfare is not part of their ethos. Nothing in the descriptions of the enlightened state suggest anything but indifference to the entire "dream" realm (or, even worse, indulging in one's own desires). *Brahman*, not the phenomena dependent upon it, is the only good, and it is beyond all our values.

Conclusion

The enlightened state is a spiritual state and is the supreme value and goal of self-development, but in the Upanishads it is not necessarily moral. Thus, the path to enlightenment cannot be indirectly justified as moral by being the means to a necessarily moral life. Later Hindus may have moralized the enlightened state—value-systems, after all, like all cultural phenomena, have a history. But we should not read later values back into the Upanishads. The Upanishadic sages may have been struggling to give voice to a new mystical tradition, but they show that a nonmoral value-system is one option in mystical ways of life.

Notes

1. The abbreviations for the Upanishads will be as follows: BU = Brihadāranyaka, CU = Chāndogya, IU = Īshā , KU = Katha, KeU = Kena, KsU = Kaushītaki, MU = Mundaka, MaU = Māndūkya, PU = Prashna, SU = Shvetāshvatara, TU = Taittirīya.

2. A more literal translation of "*tat tvam asi*" would be "You exist in that way (*tad*)," referring to existing by reason of *brahman*.

3. The closest to the dream analogy is found in the Chāndogya VIII.10.1: the one who goes happily about in a dream is *brahman*. Shankara, however, did use it (e.g., *Brahma-sūtra-bhāshya* III.2.1-6), and the Buddha's title means he is the one who has awakened from the sleep of nescience. The analogy does not strictly apply since in the enlightened state—after one is "awakened" with mystical knowledge—the dream still occurs. But the analogy is as good as any: all analogies and images will have to come from our ordinary dualistic experience and thus will never strictly apply to what is beyond that experience.

4. BU IV.4.5; BU III.2.3 on *karma*; PU III.6. See also CU V.10.7: Those whose conduct here has been good (*ramanīya*, "pleasant") will quickly attain a good birth—the birth of a Brahmin, Kshatriya, or Vaishya. But those whose conduct here has been evil (*kapūya*, "foul") will quickly attain an evil birth—the birth of a dog, a pig, or an outcaste.

5. The Katha distinguishes the path of the pleasant (*shreya*) and the path of the good (*preya*), with the wise choosing the latter (II.2).

6. Edgerton 1929, p. 118.

7. The term "*mukti*" does occur in BU III.1.3-4 but not explicitly in the sense of release from the chain of rebirths. Only in the relatively late Maitri Upanishad (I.3) are the ideas made explicit that the body is unsubstantial and foul, that all in *samsāra* is decaying, and that

there is no good in enjoying desire. This text may have been devised under Buddhist influence.

8. The term "*avidyā*" occurs only rarely in the Upanishads, usually in contrast with "*vidyā*" (CU I.1.10; KU II.4-5; IU 9-12; SU I.9, V.1). But it also occurs on its own (MU I.2.8-9, II.1.10; PU VI.8). But, like all the other doctrines in the Upanishads, this one is also developing and no set meaning was established in this period. See R. H. Jones 1993, pp. 47-55.

9. The Brihadāranyaka does speak of "seeing" *brahman* (e.g., II.4.5), but this is more a problem of developing new terminology for mysticism. It does not mean that the unmanifest *brahman* is open to sense-experience but only that we can "experience" or "grasp" or "become aware" of it in some sense. However, the problem is also present with these terms: all our experiential terms have been developed in the context of an observer experiencing a distinct object, so how do we speak of an "experience" when there is no object to be experienced (since we are one with the source)?

10. Some passages suggest that austerities lead to knowledge of *brahman* (e.g., MU III.2.5; SU I.15-16; PU I.10), but the position more in keeping with the rest of the texts is that such practices cannot lead to such knowledge (e.g., BU III.8.10; MU III.2.8).

11. E.g., the story of Satyakāma Jābāla (CU IV.4). See also CU VI.16 (a trial by fire by holding a hot axe).

12. BU IV.4.7 states that one can be liberated in this life (the state of *jīvan-mukta*) and not have to wait until death to attain enlightenment (*videha-mukta*). Not all upanishadic passages suggest this, although Shankara agreed (as discussed in the next chapter).

13. See Edgerton 1929, p. 104.

14. Two possible reasons for this are: one is free of all desires because desires simply no longer arise or because all of one's desires are satisfied. The second reason would fit better with the Chāndogya.

15. The Kaushītaki III.8 gives a theistic and predestination-like twist to this doctrine: the *ātman* is not increased by any good actions nor decreased by any bad ones (see BU IV.4.22), but as the lord of the worlds it makes those people perform good actions whom it wants to lead up from these worlds and makes those people perform bad actions whom it wants to push down from these worlds.

16. The Upanishads here are once again not always consistent as they develop these new doctrines: one passage states that a knower of *brahman* is still a maker of merit (*punyākrit*), although this passage is about the path rather than the enlightened state (BU IV.4.9).

17. This passage involves the merit/demerit of a rebirth rather than liberation, but it suggests the development of the position stated explicitly in the other early Upanishads. Some scholars cite this passage for the claim that the Chāndogya does not advocate non-injury (*ahimsā*) in general but only prohibits killing Brahmins—i.e., the authors of the text were protecting themselves but no one else. A more generous interpretation, however, is that this passage is about the *power of knowledge* and that these five acts are cited as examples of extremely bad acts, not as an exhaustive list of what is prohibited.

18. The one exception is Kaushītaki III.8. See note 15 above.

19. At best, one verse could be interpreted as grounding a moral order in *brahman*. Shvetāshvatara VI.6 refers to the lord of prosperity, the immortal reality residing in ourselves and in all beings, as the bringer of rules of social conduct (*dharma*) and the remover of demerit (*pāpa*), since this entire world emanates from him. Thus, if *dharma* is moral, so is *brahman*. But see the discussion of *dharma* in Chapter 6.

20. Hume 1931, p. 60.

21. Edgerton 1942, p. 155; see also Radhakrishnan 1948a, pp. 208-9.

22. Deussen 1966, p. 49. Ralph Waldo Emerson and Arthur Schopenhauer made similar claims. Another interpretation of the Golden Rule also has problems. If you should love your neighbor as yourself because you are thereby loving *brahman* in another body, there are two problems: first, you are not being other-regarding but simply loving the same reality that is in you; second, you are not treating the other person as real but only loving the underlying reality.

23. Ibid., p. 362.

24. E.g., Radhakrishnan 1948a, p. 230.

25. E.g., ibid., pp. 229-30.

26. E.g., Deussen 1966, p. 364.

5

Shankara's Advaita Vedānta

Even after more than a century of serious Asian studies in the West, it still has to be pointed out to philosophers and theologians that Advaita Vedānta is not the "official" philosophy of Hinduism. Too many Western scholars writing on mysticism and morality think Advaita is the only school of Vedānta or in fact the only philosophical system in Hinduism. (Many also mistakenly believe that all Hindu traditions are exclusively mystical.) But there are theistic schools of Vedānta and also other philosophical schools that have always been more popular in India than Advaita. Only in the last two centuries has Advaita come into prominence, especially in a form heavily influenced by Western thought, Neo-Vedānta.

Brahman

The metaphysics of Shankara's early form of Advaita Vedānta conflicts with the presuppositions of morality. The earlier Upanishads took the phenomena of the world to be real—*brahman* is merely the root (KU II.3.1), "the real of the real" (*satyasya satya*) (BU II.1.20), the fire producing equally real sparks or the spider spinning the equally real web (BU II.1.20; MU I.1.7; SU VI.10), the colorless light refracted into the equally real colored lights through a prism (SU IV.1). But to Shankara only *brahman* is real (*sat*)—everything else is *unreal* (*asat*). This caused Shankara sometimes to give quite forced interpretations to parts of the Upanishads, which he takes to be part of the supreme religious authority, as well as to the *Bhagavad-gītā* and even the *Brahma-sūtras*.[1] His focus remained firmly fixed on what he took to be real and on how to attain our realization that we are that reality and nothing else. This means that he did not discuss many philosophical topics that would help us today to understand him. He also did not challenge the Hindu religious way of life and did not produce anything like a detailed discussion of ethics.

Add to this another problem: virtually every philosophical term Shankara used presents confusions in English translations. Any translation of "*brahman*" other than the very abstract "the Real" is misleading. *Brahman* is not merely the source of reality—it is the only reality. *Brahman* is not the sum total of all things in the universe—one big object with parts—but is a reality "behind" the appearance of objects. Technically, *brahman* is not even a "source" at all, since no reality is "created" or "caused." Any pluralism, dualism, or even monism is denied because *brahman* has no diversity or parts, and thus no number—including one—can apply. (Hence, the name "nondualism" [*a-dvaita*] to stress the absence of any other reality rather than "monism" [perhaps "*ekaita*"], which might be interpreted as denoting an object.) Since *brahman* cannot be sensed, we cannot explain its nature (KUB I.4). Indeed, *brahman* is not an instance of any category, and so no descriptive or explanatory terms can apply. Any noun, and thus any pronoun, would imply *brahman* is an object, and so all are denied. "Being" or "nonbeing" or "is" or "is not" do not apply (BGB XIII.12). *Brahman* is beyond our intelligibility. Thus, to the extent *brahman* is an object of desire or thought, it is not real—even thinking "*brahman*" superimposes an unreal mental object upon it. *Brahman* is not an entity among entities but a nonobjective reality that from our unenlightened point of view can be characterized only as beingness itself (*sat*), consciousness (*cit*) without a thinker, and the bliss of being at peace (*ānanda*). Beyond that, there is nothing to say about "it."

For Shankara, however, something must be real or there would be nothing upon which to superimpose our errors. *Brahman* is considered ultimately real because no form of experience can, even in principle, contradict its existence: dreams seem real, but the dream world is sublated (*bādha*) when we wake up; illusions seem real until they are sublated by other sense-experiences; the waking world as a whole seems real but is sublated when we realize we are identical to the one true reality; and nothing can sublate that mystical experience. Indeed, *brahman* cannot be sublatable since it is present in all experience. To Shankara, it is impossible to claim the *ātman* is not experienced, for who would the denier be (BSB I.1.4, I.1.17)? René Descartes took the one unchallengeable reality to be the individual consciousness experienced in self-consciousness, but Advaitins take the same experience to be awareness of the one reality underlying all of what we take to be everyone's subjectivity and also all objective realities in the universe (BSB I.1.1).

Ātman is the reality "in" us that is identical to *brahman*. It is not, as naturalists might suppose, that we are merely made of the same substance as everything else in the universe or that we are all parts of one big naturalistic whole—all that is actually real is paradoxically contained in each part. Contrary to a popular mystical image, each drop of water does not merge into one ocean—all of the "ocean" is contained in each "drop." To use an Advaita analogy: just as the entire moon is fully reflected in each drop of water in a pool, so too all of reality is entirely contained in each part of the universe.[2] Each of us is identical to the consciousness that is *brahman*. That is, *ātman* is merely *brahman* "in" us. But translating "*ātman*" as "self" is misleading: *ātman* is not an individual entity (either body, mind, or both), and the "self-knowledge" needed for enlightenment is not the type we would get from learning more about our individual self (*jīva*) in this realm through biology or psychology. It has no connotations of individuality, individual selfhood, or self-consciousness but only of an impersonal *consciousness*—a colorless beam of light illuminating no object, not even itself. What we take to be objects is merely the rainbow of lights produced by the prism of our own nescience (*avidyā*). In sum, *brahman*, the reality of all objective and subjective phenomena, remains a nonindividual, nonpersonal consciousness.

The Realm of Illusion

Thus, all phenomena of our world are identical to *brahman*—that they appear distinct and independently real is the illusion. But translating "*māyā*," a term Shankara used relatively little, as "illusion" can mislead: phenomena are not totally nonexistent—we simply misread their reality by making them into objective, individual realities.[3] The realm of illusion is not *dependent* on *brahman* (as in the Upanishads) but simply *is brahman* improperly experienced. Thus, our world is neither real (*sat*), since it is sublatable by enlightening knowledge (*vidyā*), nor unreal (*asat*), since it is not totally nonexistent (like a married bachelor), but has an indefinable status (*anirvacanīya*). Like a dream, there is something there (the consciousness constituting the dream), but we misread its status while dreaming (BSB III.2.1-6). Nescience (*avidyā*) is taking the surface diversity of multiple objects and individual selves as ultimately real and thus misreading *brahman*. It is not merely a lack of knowledge but a positive error—the active falsification of true knowledge—that causes rebirth. The unenlightened create a world of multiplicity by superimposing objectness and division on the nondual *brahman*. Once we start to differentiate reality into distinct entities according to "name and form" (*nāma-rūpa*), we enter the realm of illusion. Thus, language plays a basic role in this process: since nescience is the distinctions made by names and forms, it arises from speech alone (BSB II.1.27). The same applies equally to the concept of "*brahman*": *brahman* is unreal to the extent it is distinguished as an entity by its name.

Within the realm of illusion, we image *brahman* in two forms—the higher (without any attributes, *brahman*-in-itself) and the lower seen as the creator of the world and as a theistic object of worship (with attributes, *brahman*-in-relation-to-the-world-of-illusion). Of course, *brahman* itself is neither form—both forms ("with attributes" and its negation) are just our ideas in this realm. We see *brahman* as creating, sustaining, and destroying this realm. *Brahman* does so for no purpose other than to create: it proceeds from his nature as mere sport (*līlā*) and has no more reason to it than does our breathing in and out (BSB II.1.33). It is just what *brahman* does. Here there is a duality of *ātman* and the individual self (*jīva*), the latter being an illusory reflection of the *ātman* produced by nescience (BSB II.3.49-

50). Consciousness is the only reality, not the "objects" apparently experienced, just as in dreams the dreaming itself is real but the content (the characters and events occurring within the dream) are not. The whole process of rebirths is a product of our nescience—*ātman* is not reborn but is eternally free of the rebirth/liberated dichotomy. The chain of rebirths is beginningless, and will continue as long as nescience continues.

The illusory realm does occur, so we might think the realm itself must also be real in some sense—after all, dreams do occur and are not identical to the dreamer. But despite appearances, ultimately there is no "we," no "realm of multiplicity," or the prism of "nescience" but only *brahman*. *Brahman* appears plural to the unenlightened but remains one, just as the one moon is not really multiplied by appearing double to a person with defective vision (BSB II.1.27; TUB II.4.1; Upad I.40). How this illusion could arise and the whole metaphysics of this process—where our error can come from, where "we" came from, how rebirth began, who or what is reborn, who has nescience, what is blinded by nescience, why the prism of nescience is not just as real as the light it refracts, and so forth—are basic philosophical issues that Shankara and later Advaitins have never adequately answered. The problem is on the same order as the theists' mystery of how God creates and interacts with the world. But such philosophical matters are not Advaitins' chief concern—becoming enlightened is.

Vidyā and *Moksha*

"*Avidyā*" has been translated here as "nescience" rather than "ignorance" to prevent confusing it with simple, everyday lack of knowledge or error. This nescience is the fundamental error that takes reality to be multiple. It is the superimposition (*adhyāsa*) of objectness and its attributes upon *brahman*. Similarly, the idea of *brahman* as an entity is superimposed on the word "*brahman*" (BSB III.3.9). *Brahman* is open to such an error because it is open to being realized in the depth-mystical experience. We misidentify our true reality with part of the plurality within the realm of illusion. We couple the real and unreal when we say "That's me" or "That's mine" or "I am acting." Actually, all we ever "see" is *brahman*—we simply mistake its nature, like seeing a rope but taking it for a snake. Such an error has no beginning and comes to an end only with the enlightening knowledge. It is what propels us through a chain of rebirths (Upad I.1.5, II.2.10), although all this is happening in a realm of illusion and does not apply to what is in the final analysis real. Thus, cognition rather than our will is the root problem for Advaita: it leads to desires (*kāma*) which leads to action (*karma*) which leads to consequences requiring rebirth.

So what is the knowledge (*vidyā, jñāna*) that will correct this error of cosmic proportions? Knowledge is simply realizing what has always been the case: that we are *brahman* and nothing else. It is seeing through the veil of nescience and seeing the dream is just a dream. It is like simply realizing that the morning star is the evening star—and that neither is in fact a star. Nothing is created or destroyed; no state is "attained" or "gone to" (BSB IV.3.14). We do not "gain" something we did not previously possess (BSB III.2.21). Release is not "brought about" or "achieved"—it is eternally *brahman* all along (BSB III.4.52). We do not "become" something we previously were not. There is no "union" or "merging" with *brahman*—we have been that reality all along. *Brahman* is "separated" from us only by nescience, and knowledge is simply the removal of nescience (MUB I.5). Because nescience is the root cause, only knowledge can "effect" release. Our understanding alone is transformed.

Thus, the "end" of nescience and the "arising" of knowledge are the same "event." *Avidyā* is dissolved, and therefore rebirth comes to an end. From our unenlightened point of view, it appears we will have "attained" release (*moksha*). The "subtle body" involved with karmic retribution in future lives is dissolved upon enlightenment, not death (BS IV.1.13-14), although the karmic effects of acts committed prior to enlightenment must come to fruition before we die one last time. But in fact this is an illusory change: knowledge does not "produce" any change. All the distinctions we make—knower, act of knowing, objects of knowledge, knowledge versus nescience, *brahman* versus the realm of illusion, release versus rebirth—are illusory distinctions we make within the dream (BSB Intro., I.2.6, I.1.4). With the end of nescience, only a change within the dream seems to occur—the actual reality involved in rebirth and immortality remains eternally unchanged. There is no one who is reborn (Upad I.18.44), and there is no "self" to free (BS II.32). What is real has always been "liberated." Nothing is accomplished; nothing real changes. "Liberation" consists simply in realizing what has always been the case.

Of particular importance to Shankara, enlightening knowledge is not an *action*—we do not *do* anything but simply *realize* what has always been the case. Realizing what is real is simply seeing that the rope is a rope and not a snake (BSB II.1.14)—no action is involved. Thus, no amount of action in the state of nescience can produce knowledge. Nescience cannot remove nescience. To realize we are dreaming we must wake up—nothing done by a character in the dream will work. Deeds are events in the dream accomplished by an actor in the dream; they have their origin in the error that one is a doer and the desire of having the results of what one does; thus, deeds and knowledge are completely separate (Upad I.1.6). Action cannot "cause" enlightenment, both because actions are caused by nescience and because there is no real cause/effect relation connected to *vidyā*—it is eternal and therefore cannot be the result of an action. For Shankara, knowledge is itself the reality realized, since the consciousness constituting the experience is also the consciousness constituting *brahman*. Knowledge cannot change (since it is *brahman*) but is eternal, and thus it cannot be affected by anything within the dream.

Brahman is not open to sense-experience or thought and thus is not open to "experience" within the dream. Hence, Shankara did not emphasize meditation or "mystical experiences," since the insight is not any experience or other action or an event within the dream. Nevertheless, such an awakening is not merely the intellectual adoption of some proposition—what is needed is a direct realization of nonduality, and that is the depth-mystical experience. The insight (*anubhava*) is the final result of the inquiry into *brahman* (BSB I.1.2). It is immediate and certain (BSB III.4.15) and does not admit of degrees (BUB III.4.52). Once we are enlightened, enlightenment cannot be lost. Thus, there is no backsliding into the chain of rebirths. Knowledge transforms the whole person, since the desires, dispositions, and other mental phenomena depending on nescience now vanish. One has awakened from a dream and cannot but be totally transformed—what was previously taken to be real is now seen to be unreal, and true reality has taken over. One sees there are no individual selves and no objects to be manipulated for "our" advantage.

The Advaita Path

Shankara made a distinction between transcendent truth (*pāramārthika satya*) and truth within the realm of nescience (*vyāvahārika satya*); this permitted him to accept the law of *karma* as operating within the dream-realm. He also accepted the revealed Vedas as the only source that defines which actions are required (*dharma*) and which are prohibited (*adharma*) (BSB III.1.25). Thus, he accepted the conventional ethics of the Hindu religious way of life of his day, as contained in the ritual part of the Vedas (*karmakānda*) and the Dharmashāstras. The rituals and other orthodox injunctions and prohibitions thus were obligatory for the unenlightened on the path (BUB IV.5.15). But this has a morally very negative consequence: Shankara denied that the lowest class of workers (*shūdras*) and non-Hindus were entitled to study the Vedas, which he accepted as a prerequisite to enlightenment, and hence they cannot become enlightened (BSB I.3.34).[4] He even accepted the cruel physical punishment recommended for *shūdras* who hear or study the Vedas (BSB I.3.38). (He did, however, concede that *shūdras* could study the necessary knowledge through the nonsacred literature and that some *shūdras* did in fact become enlightened based on events in their former lives [BSB I.3.38], which later Advaitins interpreted as meaning that they had studied the Vedas in a previous life.)

There is a little in Shankara's writings on the training of the seeker of enlightenment. The *Upadeshasāhasrī*, a work probably by him, contains passages on it. The means to liberation are to be explained only to an aspirant who must: (1) be dispassionate toward all things noneternal (since those are attainable by means other than knowledge); (2) have abandoned the desire for sons, wealth, and worlds; (3) have entered the state of a wandering ascetic (*sannyāsin*) endowed with tranquility of mind (*shama*) and self-control (*dama*); (4) possess the qualities of a student as defined in the Vedas; (5) be a Brahmin who is both internally and externally pure; (6) be of a suitable caste, profession, behavior, knowledge, and family; and (7) approach his teacher in the prescribed manner (Upad II.1.2). Following the personal stage-of-life (*āshrama*) and class (*varna*) duties would also be assumed prior to this instruction, although one must give up these duties and become a wandering ascetic who abandons all family and social ties as a prerequisite to enlightenment (BSB III.4.20). Once initiated to the path, there are five prescriptions: (1) abstaining from injury, lying, theft, sex, and possessions; (2) austerities (*tapas*); (3) concentration of the mind (*samādhāna*); (4) emaciation of the body; and (5) performance of the obligatory rituals and sacrifices (*nityakarma*) to remove past hindrances (Upad I.17.21-23). Elsewhere, Shankara set forth a fourfold discipline (*sādhana*) for qualifying to inquire into *brahman*. The aspirant must: (1) possess the ability to discriminate between what is real and what is only apparently real; (2) have renounced all desire to enjoy the present and future fruits of his actions; (3) have acquired tranquility of mind, self-control, dispassion (*uparati*), endurance (*titikshā*), concentration of mind, and faith (*shaddhā*); and (4) yearn for release (BSB I.1.1).[5] Shankara also noted the need for yogic meditation to calm the mind and to subdue the senses as a prerequisite for knowledge (e.g., BSB I.4.1, III.4.26-27, 47-51; BUB III.2.22-30; BGB IV.38-39). The state of extreme concentration (*samādhi*) is also valued (BSB II.3.39). But since nescience cannot be removed by any experience, duality reappears after any concentration experience. Purifying the mind, however, is necessary since knowledge appears only when the mind becomes as clean as a mirror (Upad I.17.22). This prepares the mind so that when one hears the knowledge portion of the Vedic scriptures (i.e., the Upanishads), the insight of enlightenment arises.

These virtues are to be cultivated on the path as a prerequisite for the enlightening knowledge, but Shankara insisted they are only "actions" and cannot themselves produce the insight itself (e.g., BSB III.4.52; BUB I.4.7). Enlightenment follows automatically only from knowledge, not from ceasing to commit prohibited acts or observing the obligatory rituals (TUB I.1.1). However, this presents a problem: if the enlightening knowledge and actions in the dream-realm are in fact incompatible, how are any actions better than others in leading us to knowledge? Why are some prescribed in the dream and not others? Why are some proscribed? Indeed, if actions cannot produce knowledge, why do any actions matter? Shankara's only response is rather weak: worldly activity should be regarded as real prior to the realization of enlightenment, just as dream activity is taken as real as long as the dream continues (BSB II.1.14). But as he stressed, the enlightenment insight is of an entirely different order from any action in the unenlightened state—what we need to do is wake up, and no actions within the dream will cause that.[6] Thus, there is a total discontinuity of the realm of action and the realm of knowledge. Waking up is not something the character in the dream does, and thus no actions within the dream can effect the insight and therefore none are of value. So why are some actions "better" or "more helpful" or "more useful" than others? If all are only part of the dream, why are some preparation for the insight and not others? If the insight is distinct from the dream-realm, why are any virtues or character development within the dream of value? That is, if waking up is just an insight, why do we have to change the character in the dream at all?

Shankara argued that actions, which are unreal, can nevertheless assist in liberation, which is real, just as "unreal" events can have "real" effects (e.g., dreaming of being attacked by a tiger can cause the dreamer to sweat) (BSB II.1.14). Thus, not all unreal acts are equal—some unreal actions are better than others for preparing the mind. Within the dream, even unreal actions have (equally unreal) effects, as defined by the law of *karma*. Seeking enlightenment is one activity, and actions that tend to calm the mind (e.g., meditation or automatically adhering to the social code of the culture) thus help prepare the mind for the insight-event, even though they cannot individually or cumulatively force the necessary insight. Complete actionlessness (*naiskarmya*)—abstaining from all proper (*dharma*) and improper (*adharma*) action—may be a stage on the path (see BGB XVIII.55, XVIII.66), but even renouncing all actions and no longer acting at all is itself an action in the dream and will not produce enlightenment.

Still, the basic inconsistency remains: according to Shankara no action can produce enlightenment, so why are some actions prescribed? It does not help to invoke the "two realms" or "two levels of truth" argument that until one awakens the dream seems real and so some acts are better than others (BSB II.1.14). If no action in the dream will produce enlightenment, then all actions remain valueless no matter what we think while we are still in the realm of illusion. Only if the realm of illusion is in some final sense real would any action be "better" than another. Only then can some act be valuable for the effect it produces. All the yogic preparation, the conformity to dharmic practices, listening repeatedly to Vedic utterances, and contemplating the analogies advanced to explain the identity of *brahman* and *ātman* until we grasp it would make sense only if that were so. Shankara would be forced to give an antirealist interpretation of all value. He could not give a realist view of what is good in terms of what leads to enlightenment without accepting the realm of illusion as real. Only by accepting this realm as real could we talk about acts causing or preparing for the enlightenment event, like doing something to pinch the character in the dream to cause the dreamer to wake up. But that would require accepting the enlightening insight to be an event in the dream, which Shankara rejected. As things stand, Shankara's metaphysics and his theory of action on the path are inconsistent.

Moreover, even if we could get past that inconsistency, the Advaita discipline has a virtual lack of moral virtues. Many scholars label the whole course of training as "moral prerequisites" or "ethical discipline" without addressing the moral issue of whether the aspirant shows other-regardingness or not. Only one of the prerequisites noted above involves actions toward other people—abstaining from injury, lying, theft, sex, and possessions—and since its context is as part of an aspirant's training in self-development, one must ask whether a genuine concern for others is the intent of that practice. That is, do we abstain from killing and stealing because such acts of selfishness would show that we take the dream-realm to be real, or because of concern for the effect on (unreal) others? The main concern seems to be only that selfish acts would further lock us into an unreal worldview. As Saral Jhingran says, even the interpersonal virtues like noninjury and forgiveness are valued mostly as a means of protecting the self from passions and involvements in the world.[7] Thus, it seems these requirements are mystical virtues for self-discipline and "purifying" one's own character, not for helping others. What is "good" is what aids an aspirant in gaining enlightenment, and what is "bad"is what harms the quest.[8] What is moral or immoral is not the determining value. Indeed, enlightenment is the only value on the path, not other people or anything else within this realm of illusion.

The mystical values on this path are self-centered, but they are not moral (other-regarding) nor immoral and thus are nonmoral. Not harming other beings, not lying, and so forth may have the effect of helping others, but the focus is only on how these actions help the aspirant overcome an error (the sense of individuality and multiple realities), not on a concern for others. Shankara's is an ethics of self-cultivation, and other-regardingness is not a prerequisite to enlightenment. Morality cannot produce enlightenment and thus is not an Advaita value. In fact, any concern by the unenlightened for other characters in the dream—as morality must be—would only be a reflection of their nescience.

The Enlightened State

Shankara accepted the idea that one can be enlightened while still alive (*jīvan-mukta*) (e.g., BGB VI.27). The enlightened are wandering ascetics who have renounced all actions (BGB V.2). But the same two problems discussed concerning the path—the inconsistency of his metaphysics with any action and the values espoused—reappear here in a new way. The enlightened have destroyed all nescience and so all sense of "I" or "mine." They no longer have a sense of any individual "actor" (*kartritva*). They have realized they are *brahman*, and since *brahman* does not act (e.g., BSB Intro.; BGB IV.13, 18; BUB II.1.20) neither do they. And yet they—the characters (the *jīvas*) in the dream—are still alive and do "act." How, consistent with his metaphysics, is this possible at all? Why does the "dream" realm not disappear? Shankara recognized the problem and dealt both with how enlightened action is possible and its nature.

First of all, why are the enlightened alive at all? Nescience disappears when the enlightening knowledge appears, so should not the individual self and body disappear? According to Shankara, the enlightening knowledge burns all actions (*karma*) that have not yet begun to produce fruit (*phala*), but it cannot stop the fruit of past actions that has begun to take effect (*prārabdha-karma*).[9] That is, all past merit and demerit that would cause a future rebirth is destroyed (BSB III.3.27), but just as a potter's wheel will continue to spin by its own momentum after the potter stops pushing it or an arrow once shot will continue to fly until it lands, so too the body will continue until the undestroyed fruit works itself out (BSB III.3.32, IV.1.15, 19; BUB I.4.7, 10; see also CU VI.14.2; KU VI.14-15; MU III.2.9). When that fruit is exhausted, the body falls away and one achieves isolation (*kaivalya*) or rest (*kshema*) from all matters of the realm of illusion (BSB III.3.32; BGB IV.37). Until then, one continues to see apparent diversity (BSB IV.1.19), except in the state of objectless nondual concentration (*nirvikalpa-samādhi*).

But this means that the dream-realm still continues, even though the enlightened have now awakened from the dream. How can the enlightened see diversity when they know there is in fact none but only one reality? Shankara's response was that the bondage of the *karma* coming to fruition affects the enlightened while they are embodied. Wrong knowledge (*mithyajñāna*) lasts even after it has been refuted by enlightenment owing to the impression it made, just as a person with an eye defect will continue to see two moons even though he knows better (BSB IV.1.15; but see BGB XVIII.48). Knowing the true facts does not cause the second moon to vanish, and the enlightened mystics' experience is the same—only their knowledge has changed. The content of their waking state is never negated (BSB II.2.29), even though the enlightened now see correctly. (This is the inverse of the fact that knowledge is not an action: knowledge does not affect the content of the dream.) The enlightened are not disturbed by any pleasure or pain caused as fruit of past acts, but the apparent diversity remains. Thus, even the enlightened will see apparent diversity, although they will not project this perception into a world of multiple real objects (Upad I.10.13). In short, the world of appearances continues, but the enlightened do not see any real duality or multiplicity there, only a dream they know is a dream. They must act because they still are "in" the dream world, even though they know they are not "of" it. They will be able to discriminate between actions, even though they know the actions are only in a dream. In sum, the enlightened know this realm is just a play, but they must go on playing characters in it until the fruit of their past *karma* works itself out and the play finally disappears. (Again, why the realm of illusion is not considered *real* is not satisfactorily answered when it is admitted that knowledge can destroy neither the illusion nor all fruit of actions from coming to fruition and that false knowledge still has force in the enlightened state.)

The next question that arises, however, is how the enlightened can do any acts at all. According to Shankara, enlightenment (*moksha*) is not possible if there is a perception of difference, and action (*karma*) is not possible without it (KeUB Intro.). The enlightened have no nescience or desires driving actions and so do not *act* at all (BSB II.3.48, III.4.20, IV.1.14; Upad I.1.15, I.17.48). Actions proceed on the basis of erroneously seeing a difference between actor and action, action and result, and so forth (BSB I.1.4), or misidentifying the true reality with objects (the body or mind) (Upad I.10.14), and thus the enlightened who know what is real cannot act (BSB II.14.20; BUB IV.4.14). All actions also have motives, but the enlightened have no desires, and a person who has nothing to desire cannot perform action (BUB IV.4.6, I.5.2). Thus, their apparent actions in the enlightened state have no karmic repercussions (BGB II.10), and they will have no future rebirths nor will their actions extend their last life by means of generating new karmic fruit that have to come to fruition.

Shankara's use of the concept "*karma*" may seem paradoxical: our actions are not really actions at all. But he is using "*karma*" to mean only a specific type of act—action driven by nescience or desire—and not *all* acts by a person. "*Karma*" becomes a term of art for only "action with karmic consequences" and not for all action. (Thus, translating "*karma*" as "action" without qualification in Shankara's work introduces a needless confusion.) Only karmic action generates karmic effects, and the enlightened no longer have the dispositions necessary to commit such acts. Thus, Shankara can explain the *Bhagavad-gītā*'s phrases of "inaction in action" (*karmany-akarma*) and "action in inaction" (*akarmani-karma*) by claiming that the enlightened have no sense of "I" or "mine"—hence no "actor"—to propel any karmic actions (BGB IV.18-20). Enlightened action is not nescience-driven karmic action. The enlightened have no nescience or desires and therefore cannot commit karmic acts, but they can perform (nonkarmic) acts for their entire enlightened life and have no karmic effects (BSB III.4.14). They have withdrawn inwardly from action (since they have no desires) but not externally—the actions in the dream still occur. Any intentions producing actions are dictated by something other than personal desires. Thus, the body moves, but there is no misguided personal willing that moves it. Moreover, even that action is not real: to the unenlightened and even to the enlightened, there appears to be action, but to the enlightened there is no real action, just as trees appear to move as we sail pass them although we know they really are not moving (BGB IV.18).

Thus, the enlightened characters play a role in the play but have no sense of personal agency, knowing that they are only in a play having no further purpose—*brahman*'s "creation" (*līlā*). But just as *brahman* is not "active" in the play and yet the realm of illusion is still here (Upad II.17.80), so too the enlightened can "act" in this realm. In sum, the play continues after enlightenment, and so the character (*jīva*) still "acts" but now free of any sense of being an "actor." But since *brahman/ātman* does not act and is not "in" the play, the character that "acts" is reduced to a nonreality in an unreal play doing unreal actions.[10]

Four Options for the Enlightened

In any case, the enlightened can act in the realm of illusion. How do they choose what actions to take? *Brahman* cannot dictate actions (since it is not a god who acts or has a will), nor can the karmic residue of past actions dictate all actions. Nor is it clear why the enlightened would have any intentions at all: the enlightened person has no purposes—there is no "actor" and thus no intentions for actions either. Why the enlightened should have *options* on how to act in the dream is also not clear, but Shankara made clear that they had them. (Thus, Shankara would accept one presupposition of morality: the enlightened, as well as the unenlightened, somehow have free choice.) They cannot act selfishly (since they have no sense of an individual self) and thus cannot be immoral. But beyond that, the enlightened have four options. First is total passive *inaction*—not just renouncing the fruit of action but renouncing the actions themselves. Since *brahman* is inactive (BGB V.13) and the enlightened know they are *brahman*, the only position consistent with Shankara's metaphysics is for the enlightened to renounce the whole world of actions and to become literally *inactive*. Indeed, Shankara said precisely that: the enlightened should stop all movements and sit quietly (BGB IV.13; see also BGB II.21, III.17-18, IV.19-20, XVIII.48).[11] How one could do this if past karmic fruit has to work itself out is not clear, and the fact remains that sitting doing nothing is still as much an *action* within the dream as engaging the world in other ways. The second option is just to beg for food and do the other things that are the bare minimum necessary to maintain the body until the fruit of past *karma* is exhausted (BGB IV.20-21). An enlightened person would then be little more than a zombie controlled by past *karma*, but not much.

In his commentary on the *Bhagavad-gītā*, Shankara allowed a third option: in the event the enlightened are not able to renounce action for whatever reason, they should engage in the same action as before enlightenment but now for the benefit of the world (*lokasamgrahārtham*) (BGB IV.19-20; see also BGB III.16, 24-28, IV.13, 20, XVIII.16).[12] The enlightened have nothing to gain and no desires, but they can act for the guidance of the world. They need not become recluses in the mountains, since the wilderness is as much a part of the dream as society. They can lead an unassuming, even childlike, life modestly and quietly conforming to social norms by performing the social duties expected of everyone, passing their lives unknown (BSB III.4.50; see also BUB III.5.1). They thus can remain in society and become exemplars of proper conduct for the unenlightened by disinterestedly carrying out the prescribed rules and injunctions of the Hindu way of life (BGB III.21-25). Shankara said very little about the mental state of the enlightened in general. He merely adopted the standard Upanishadic virtues: tranquility, self-control, even-mindedness to pleasure and sorrow, and so forth (e.g., BSB III.4.27; BUB IV.4.23).

A fourth option is that the enlightened can change their preenlightenment actions and become teachers (BGB IV.34; CUB VI.14.2). Such teachers are endowed with understanding, memory, tranquility (*shama*), self-control (*dama*), compassion (*dayā*), and concern (*anugraha*), versed in traditional doctrine, not attached to any enjoyments, having abandoned all the rituals and their requisites, a knower of *brahman*, steadfast in *brahman*, leading a blameless life, and free of the faults of deceit, pride, trickery, evildoing, fraud (*māyā*), jealousy, falsehood, and a sense of self or self-interest, and so forth; with such characteristics, their sole concern then is to help others (Upad II.1.6). This would be a more active way of helping others than merely being an exemplar of social duties. Advaita works directed to the lay public, such as the *Crest-Jewel of Discrimination*, also speak of being engaged in helping others. Shankara also accepted that, while the enlightened cannot perform merit- or demerit-producing actions that cause rebirth (BSB III.4.40-43), they may return after death for one or two more embodiments to help mankind (BSB III.3.32, IV.4.51).[13]

The Moral Status of the Enlightened State

While the last two options involve helping the world and would be moral, they are not consistent with either Shankara's metaphysics or the prevailing set of values he set forth for the enlightened state. That there is a problem is apparent in his comments on the *Bhagavad-gītā*: he made clear that the *primary option* was total inaction and that engaging in action for the sake of the world was only for those who could not accept it (BGB IV.19). He may have felt constrained to accept the *Bhagavad-gītā's* position on an active life as one possibility for the enlightened, but he set forth the other options in a way that accented his primary position of inaction. Indeed, given Shankara's framework, why the enlightened should act for the welfare of the world is not at all clear. First, Shankara made clear the enlightened are beyond all the obligatory acts of the ritual rules and injunctions of the Hindu way of life—the *dharma* (BSB I.1.4, II.3.48; BGB IV.10; CUB II.23.1; Upad II.1.30-32). All such obligations are consumed by the fire of knowledge (BGB IV.42). The required religious duties are based on the false view that there are actors and fruit of actions (BGB II.21, XVIII.48; IUB Intro.) and thus have no meaning for the enlightened who see what is real. Not performing the duties has no repercussions for the enlightened, just as it has no effect on *brahman*. They are wandering ascetics who, even if they were not enlightened, would still be beyond the *dharma* governing the prior stages of life (BGB IV.10, XVIII.48). Thus, the enlightened have no obligation to engage in any of the recitations, charity, or austerities of the path. In sum, they have no obligation to the world and can see no significance to dharmic activity.

One can respond that it does not matter what the enlightened do in the dream, so the enlightened can give up being a wandering ascetic—i.e., renounce renouncing—and quietly do what they did before they reached that stage in performing the social duties or can become a teacher. But that response leads to a second problem: the enlightened know the realm of illusion for what it is—there are no real selves to help by adhering to the class and life-stage obligations or any other actions. It is all a dream, and so why should those who know this take it seriously? They know *brahman* to be the only reality, and thus showing a concern for other people would be a sign of nescience. But a presupposition of morality is that there are *other people* who are real. Otherwise, we cannot be other-regarding: we cannot love or care about characters within a play or dream—we have to take the characters to be *real* in some sense of the word or a moral concern for them makes no sense. A related problem is that must also be a real moral *actor*, but it is not at all clear what could be a moral agent in this metaphysics: the reality *brahman*/*ātman* does not act and the "person" within the dream is not real. In sum, the realm of illusion and its occupants must in the final analysis be real or morality makes no sense, and that is precisely what Shankara will not admit.

Morality requires that we are concerned for others for their own sake. But our illusory world is devoid of value, and any concern for the welfare of other "people" is an emotional attachment without a basis in reality. Love and hate are equally groundless, and there can be no reason to choose one over the other. Morality, in short, is part of the realm of nescience, and the enlightened are beyond it. Attaching any value to interpersonal relationships within the realm of illusion—wanting to help other characters in the play—would only reveal our fundamental nescience regarding what is real at both an epistemological and emotional level. Thus, Shankara advanced no moral virtues as essential to the enlightened way of life. Nor are the enlightened obligated to do anything, let alone help "others." Action is inevitable in the enlightened state (since the illusion still remains after enlightenment), but the enlightened may come as close to inaction as is possible in this world. Even if they quietly return to their old dharmic way of life for the welfare of the world by being an exemplar to the unenlightened, there is nothing about "social action" in the sense of changing the material conditions of the realm of nescience to help others.[14] On the other hand, there is no reason to advance antinomian values; that would reveal as much attachment to the realm of nescience as positive social ones. Enlightenment remains the only good. The social system with any inequities is simply accepted (e.g., *shūdras* not being eligible to study the Vedas)—the enlightened know the distinctions do not apply to what is real.

The enlightened can also become teachers. This last option involves the "real" interests of the students—i.e., it is exclusively focused on attaining enlightenment, not their "worldly" interests—but is no less other-regarding. It would be moral if it were consistent with Shankara's metaphysics. But the characters in the dream-realm are not real, and so there is no one to teach—there is nothing real to remove from the dream. Similarly, why act to maintain society by fulfilling one's dharmic duties? So what if the society in the play collapses into chaos? Nothing real is affected. The enlightened could not harm the realm of nescience even if they wanted to. Thus, doing good within the realm of nescience is a value that simply conflicts with Shankara's metaphysics. Indeed, ultimately all actions are the same—equally valueless.

In sum, indifference to other "people" is all that can be justified within this metaphysical framework. There are no other "people" or other reality that we could help or whose interests could be considered. Once we see that a rope is just a rope and not a snake, questions about what to do about the snake evaporate, and the same is true of "other people." Desire, including feeling the concern to help others, only reflects nescience. All reality is absolutely one and beyond the reach of action.

No actions in the dream matter. None are better or worse than others to choose or to avoid. Thus, to realize *brahman* is to know there is nothing worth doing in the dream world. Nothing one could do affects reality—nothing is accomplished, and nothing changes. There are no individuals to lead anywhere since the reality in each of them has always been identical to *brahman*. All individuality has the status of characters in a dream, and a moral concern for the characters in the dream would reveal a misunderstanding of the nature of reality. In short, other-regardingness is rendered impossible because there is no other to regard. Nothing in the dream is of significance, and therefore how can any action matter to the enlightened? Total inaction would be the appropriate choice, but that is impossible since the dream-realm continues even after we awaken from the dream. However, indifference remains the only appropriate value.

Possible Objections

Some scholars reject this morally negative conclusion and argue that the oneness of *brahman* in fact grounds morality. (Similar arguments were addressed in the last chapter concerning the Upanishads.) For example: I should love you because you are me, or I should not hurt you because I would only be hurting myself.[15] Spontaneous universal love should be the result. But as Karl Potter points out, love is not required under this interpretation: one need not love any other manifestation of the "self" even if we know we are all identical to the underlying reality.[16] Love still has to be opted for—it is not compelled by enlightenment. Modern Neo-Vedāntins, heavily influenced by Western humanist and Christian thought, see Shankara's nondualism as the ground for social works, especially helping the poor. But as Andrew Fort notes, this tactic reinterprets and even distorts Shankara's doctrine of nonduality.[17] It confuses the identity of *brahman* with the surface diversity of persons: *brahman* is the one reality everything in this realm "has," but the individual persons (*jīvas*) within the dream remain multiple and unreal. Again, *ātman* is merely the impersonal consciousness of *brahman* "in" a person. Translating "*ātman*" as "self" may lead to seeing a moral possibility where there is none—there are no "selves" in the makeup of reality. And nothing we can do to individual persons affects *ātman*. Hurting another *jīva* in no way hurts what is actually real (*ātman*)—we can do whatever we want to the characters in the dream, and the dreamer will remain unaffected. Killing another *jīva* does not affect either anything real or the killer's own (unreal) individual self within the dream.

Similarly, there is no reality to love. Love requires two realities—a lover and a beloved—but *brahman* is not a distinct object (it is the only reality that we already are), and there are no real individuals (including oneself). Thus, there is no reality to hate (IUB 5-6), but conversely there is no reality to love. Love and hate are equally groundless. Even if one loves oneself (either *brahman/ātman* or erroneously the *jīva*), this still has no bearing on how one treats other individuals (the *jīvas*) in the dream of nescience. Any moral or immoral action is simply without effect, and thinking otherwise is a sign of nescience. In other words, showing a genuine concern for another's welfare—being moral—is a sign of nescience. Invoking a doctrine of "two levels of truth" or "two realms" at this point again does not help: some actions in the realm of illusion can be moral only if the characters in this realm are in some final sense real. But the enlightened know the status of the realm of illusion, and the issue is how they could take any actions seriously once they know that the characters in *brahman*'s play are not real. In sum, morality is a matter of the relations of the *jīvas*, and they are not real. Thus, if only *brahman* is real, the realities needed for morality are not present.

Two other common responses warrant comment. First, it is often claimed that the enlightened are "beyond good and evil" only in the sense that they have completely internalized a moral set of values and virtues and so no longer need to follow rules but still spontaneously perform only good deeds.[18] For Sarvepalli Radhakrishnan, the metaphysical truth of the oneness of *brahman* in no way prejudices the validity of the moral distinctions within the realm of nescience: as the rules against murder, theft, and the like do not worry the civilized person, so the spiritual person is not concerned with the conventional rules of morality.[19] The enlightened are no longer affected by the consideration of "good" or "bad," but by their very nature they always respond by helping. Mystical freedom is only freedom from the formality of following rules, not their content, and so the enlightened work tirelessly for others in helping action—indeed, all they can do is act for others. The path is the "breathing in" phase, and enlightened moral action is the natural "breathing out" phase. However, as appealing as this may sound to modern readers, nothing in Shankara's writings supports it. The enlightened are not spontaneously anything—they have to choose. They cannot be immoral (since selfishness is rendered groundless), but the options Shankara saw as the primary ones do not involve any other-regardingness. Nor does anything in Shankara's works suggest that the enlightened have internalized moral virtues that they must express in action. Like *brahman*, the enlightened are beyond all obligation and beyond all sense of otherness. But morality is always a matter of distinctions. Thus, all questions of good or evil remain part of the realm of nescience, having no application to reality.

A second response is to argue that Shankara was only interested in knowledge and not matters of morality: his interest was overwhelmingly on enlightening knowledge, and he simply assumed the necessity of being moral while discussing that one issue. He was only interested in the worldview of a way of life, not its values; so he omitted talk of morality but never meant to deny it. He simply left the matter of ethics to the Dharmashāstras. His lack of discussion of issues related to the conflict of morality with his one topic of interest only reflects the general lack of any critical reflection on the issue of morality in any traditional Indian philosophical school. However, the texts once again do not support this claim. Shankara certainly dealt mostly with knowledge, but he also dealt explicitly with the nature of action, both on the path and in the enlightened state, as they relate to knowledge. He also dealt with values, and he advanced nonmoral ones: they are the values and virtues related to an individual escaping the realm of illusion and attaining the bliss of *brahman*. Moreover, his concepts of knowledge (*vidyā*), enlightenment (*moksha*), and reality (*brahman*) are value-laden and have direct implications for how we should live. In particular, *brahman* is the only good and hence enlightenment is the only goal. *Brahman*, like many religious concepts, combines ontological and evaluative dimensions. In this way, values pervade his work.[20] Treating *brahman* as the only reality and enlightenment as our ultimate goal does not merely ignore the issue of morality but negates moral concern for "other people" as a value at all. His talk of inaction and of being beyond social obligations was not merely hyperbole to shock students into the enlightenment insight[21]—they were the only value-position consistent with his metaphysics. Indeed, not even enlightenment can be valued since nothing a character in the dream does ultimately matters. In sum, we are left with a value-system ultimately free of values.

Conclusion

From the above discussion it is clear that there are good reasons for the familiar position that Shankara's Advaita Vedānta does not present a moral value-system but a nonmoral one for aligning ourselves with the true nature of reality.[22] Neo-Vedāntins and others who dispute this have to impose the ideas of later thinkers and not analyze Shankara's writings in any detail. In effect, they make postclassical thought the context for the earlier mystics. But in analyzing the texts themselves, both evaluative and factual problems are found for both the path to enlightenment and the enlightened state. The values center on an individual's own quest for enlightenment, not concern for others' welfare. And the metaphysics conflicts with the presupposition of morality that there is a reality toward which one can be other-regarding. Nor can his metaphysics account for why some actions lead toward enlightenment and some do not, since that realm is not real. Indeed, from a moral point of view, Shankara's nondualistic metaphysics brings out the worst option possible. Inaction is the logical conclusion of a position that denies any value to this world. Since the enlightened still see the illusion after enlightenment they must act, but indifference to the welfare of the characters in the dream is the only consistent response—otherwise the enlightened would be exhibiting an unenlightened point of view or value. The enlightened cannot consistently commit a selfish act (since any sense of "I" or "mine" is out of the picture), but conversely they see no "others" to be concerned about. The value of all human action is explained away.

It is, however, hard to maintain Shankara's position in light of the fact that the dream-realm continues after enlightenment. As Rāmānuja asked, what is the difference between the realm of illusion's status as "indefinable" (*anirvacanīya*) and it actually being real? It is a feature of reality that in the final analysis we cannot get around—and Shankara conceded as much when he admitted the "illusion" remains even for the enlightened. One can argue that Shankara advanced his extreme and uncompromising nondualism only for soteriological reasons and was no more interested in speculative explanations of this or other problems than was the Buddha—getting out of the realm of illusion was his only concern. But such problems caused Rāmānuja and other theists to accept the realm of nescience as *real* and to reject the possibility of being liberated while still alive in this realm. Indeed, Shankara himself was quite active in the realm of illusion, presumably after he was enlightened, in teaching, setting up centers for monks, and writing—if only half of the works attributed to him were actually written by him, he was a very prolific writer for someone who supposedly died at age thirty-two. Even if he merely wandered over into the forests at that age, he previously showed a real concern for the "realm of nescience." In short, the most that can be said is that Shankara's practice did not conform to his theories.[23]

Notes

1. Like most mystics, Shankara did not see himself as an innovator but merely as expounding the true meaning of the texts he accepted as sacred. The abbreviations for his works to be relied upon here are: BS = his *Brahma-sūtra-bhāshya*, BGB = his *Bhagavad-gītā-bhāshya*, Upad = *Upadeshasāhasrī*, and "B" for his "*bhāshya*" added to the abbreviations for the Upanishads. The authorship of the other works attributed to him is more open to dispute.

2. The analogy does show that what is real (the moon) is not the union of all that is unreal (the drops of water reflecting it)—the total reality is reflected in each drop and not made up of those drops. But this analogy, like all analogies since they come from the realm of multiplicity, is limited: the drops of water are also real, and Shankara has no explanation for why they are there. As discussed below, nothing we can do to the "drops" affects what is real (the moon), and the moral problem is that the one reality is contained totally in "my" drop and all drops (mine and others) are ultimately unreal, and thus there is no reason to be morally concerned about the other "drops."

3. The concept *māyā* appears once in the late Upanishads (SU IV.9-10), meaning a trick of a magician (the Lord). In the rest of the Vedas, it refers to the craftiness of Varuna and not to a cosmic creation.

4. Another socially discriminatory distinction made within the realm of illusion is that only Brahmins, not members of other classes, can become wandering ascetics, a prerequisite to enlightenment (BUB III.5.1, IV.5.15; but see BSB III.4.36-39). Women also are not mentioned.

5. The last requirement is still a form of desire—"true" or "real" desires replacing the desire for worldly matters. But it too must be overcome on the path.

6. What "wakes up" is not clear in Shankara's metaphysics. It is not the individual illusory self (*jīva*) since it is not real but only a character in the dream, nor *brahman* since it does not change and is not a character in the dream.

7. Jhingran 1989, p. 137. Even Radhakrishnan, the most adamant defender of the morality thesis, conceded that "Hindu ethics treat inner perfection and inward calm as of more importance than outer activity. . . . The motive behind ethical practices is that of purging the soul of selfish impulses so that it may be fitted to receive the beatific vision" (Radhakrishnan 1940, p. 105). But, again, "ethics" is not the same as "morality."

8. Deutsch 1969, pp. 100-101; see also Bauer 1987, p. 37.

9. How the enlightening knowledge does this and why it cannot destroy all fruit is not explained. But *prārabdha-karma* can even prevent knowledge from arising in one's current embodiment, thereby preventing one's enlightenment until the next life (BSB III.4.51). None of this fits with a strict nondualistic metaphysics, since it makes *karma* real in some sense.

10. Sāmkhya-Yogins resolve the issue of who acts by claiming matter (*prakriti*) alone acts, not the unmoving and blissful self (*purusha*). But Shankara cannot resort to such an ontological dualism. For him, one reality "underlies" both the objective and subjective.

11. Also see Chapter 7 on the enlightened Jainas' inaction.

12. In his *Brahma-sūtra-bhāshya*, Shankara stated that, although the enlightened have no obligations, they cannot do whatever they want (*yatheshtācarana*) in the enlightened state, since it is only falsely identifying the *ātman* with the body that causes action (II.3.48). This may mean simply that they cannot be selfish (since they no longer have a sense of an individual self) but should be totally inactive. However, in the context of the passage as a whole, it can also be interpreted to mean that if the enlightened "act," they will conform to the duties. That is, if they do "act," they will not violate the *dharma*, no matter what they do.

13. This differs from the Mahāyāna Bodhisattvas to be discussed in Chapter 9 in that the latter return after enlightenment voluntarily, while for Shankara such a "commission" (*adhikāra*) is merely the result of preenlightenment *karma* that had not yet come to fruition in the enlightened state (*prārabdha-karma*). See Fort 1998, pp. 39-40.

14. Fort 1998, p. 174.

15. E.g., Pandeya 1966; Hiriyanna 1975.

16. Potter 1981, p. 37. Potter argues that the enlightened Advaitin will be moral: the mental impressions (*vāsanās*) in the enlightened state will be the result of a life of training in the Advaita path; since there is no evil karmic residue interfering with the moral residue, the enlightened Advaitin's life will be moral (pp. 36-38). However, this is open to question. The path is a matter of self-development with little other-regardingness (as discussed above), and thus it would not produce a switch to moral action in the enlightened state. The enlightened must still opt even to act, let alone to engage in moral action. Potter acknowledges that the enlightened have no obligation to act, either to perform acts enjoined by scriptures or any other acts. This means that the enlightened do have a choice, but even if to the contrary their prior training produced automatic actions in the enlightened state—the body merely moving to the command of past unexpired karma (*prārabdha-karma*)—the actions would not necessarily be moral but would merely follow the restraints observed while on the path. Nor in that case could the enlightened be deemed moral, even if they were good, since their actions would be totally determined and thus would invalidate the requirement of "free will" presupposed in morality.

17. Fort 1998, p. 173. See generally Fort 1998, pp. 172-85, for the Neo-Vedāntins' emphasis on a compassionate need to provide for the physical needs of the poor. However, Neo-Vedānta is an instance of reading back modern Western values into an earlier work. It should also be noted that even the grandfather of Neo-Vedānta, the guru Ramakrishna, frowned upon social activism and favored Advaita's traditional emphasis on mysticism.

18. E.g., Warrior 1975.

19. Radhakrishnan 1948b, pp. 620-21. According to Radhakrishnan, the enlightened remain concerned with the welfare of the realm of nescience: "The normal mystic has a burning passion for social righteousness" (Radhakrishnan 1940, p. 109).

20. As Eliot Deutsch says, "Value questions do enter, however implicitly, into every ontological and epistemological analysis" (Deutsch 1969, p. 99).

21. Mayeda 1976, 1979. Mayeda realizes that Shankara's treatment of action contradicts his metaphysics and thus that he was "self-contradictory" (1979, p. 89).

22. The value-systems for the other classical schools of Indian philosophy are very similar to Advaita's, despite very different sets of factual claims. See Jhingran 1989, p. 137. For example, Sāmkhya-Yoga distinguishes "good" and "bad" in terms of what leads to enlightenment, not in terms of moral "right" and "wrong" (Furtado 1992, p. 122). Thus, if it is one error to suppose that all Hindu traditions must have only one value-system, it is also an error to conclude that differences in the metaphysics of each philosophical tradition requires that their value-systems must be different. (This issue will return in Chapter 14 on the relation of beliefs and values.)

23. Warrior 1975, p. 505; Mayeda 1979, p. 89.

6

The *Bhagavad-gītā*

Before anyone overgeneralizes from the conclusions concerning the Upanishads and Shankara to all of Hinduism, it should be noted that, contrary to popular Western opinion, the majority of Hindus from the classical period to today have been theistic. Moreover, they have not been followers of the philosophical systems but have instead followed less rigorous traditions and texts—in particular, the *Bhagavad-gītā*. To understand this work, three basic concepts from traditional Hindu religion must first be discussed: *karma*, rebirth, and *dharma*.

Karma and Rebirth

The belief-claim of *karma* developed in the Upanishadic period and became so pervasive in Hinduism that it was simply assumed in the classical era and not argued for.[1] It evolved out of the Vedic idea that ritual action (*karma*) has good or bad effects into the idea that any action (done by the body, voice, or mind) driven by a sense of an individual self has personal repercussions. Thus, our action has a second part: the "fruit" (*phala*) that shapes our existence later in this life or in a future one. The fruit occurs automatically by a law of nature. These repercussions are not visited upon us by a personal god, and thus to speak in theistic terms of "reward" and "punishment" for our actions distorts the concept. If you stick your hand in a fire, you are not "punished" by having it burned; the forces at work in nature simply cause it to burn. Similarly, with *karma*: an impersonal mechanism in nature causes our actions to have lawful repercussions. Actions are simply part of the structure of the universe and are as governed by laws as inanimate objects. (*Dharma*, as discussed below, is the set of rules telling us what we should do and what we should avoid in order to have only good repercussions.)

There is nothing fatalistic about *karma*. The lawfulness of action and its natural repercussion permits us to control our future. Past events do not force our present choices in a deterministic fashion. (Nor, as is sometimes asserted, is the freedom to choose our action—"free will"—something earned only by enlightenment: according to most traditions, *karma* cannot produce enlightenment, and if we did not have freedom while still within the realm of rebirths, the chain of actions would be deterministic and we would never be able to get out of being reborn.) However, our past deeds have set the stage for our actions: our dispositions toward actions, the family and class we are born into, and our physical makeup are all determined by our own past actions. There are no accidents of birth. For example, one is blind in this life because of having blinded someone in a past life.[2] Fate in that sense plays a major role in the epic the *Rāmāyana*—all the characters' apparent choices dovetail with the gods' plan. But the actors can still control their actions. Release from the chain of rebirths is not the product of *karma*, but at least the doctrine of *karma* does show an orderliness to actions that makes control of our actions possible. Thus, we can engage in practices that cannot force enlightenment but which even Shankara would accept as preparation. In effect, we are dealt the hand of cards we must play based on our own past actions, but we have the freedom now to play them as we wish. Thus, *karma* is ultimately an optimistic doctrine: even if we are pessimistic about our current state, we can control our future in this realm.

A connected belief-claim, also arising in the Upanisadic period, is that of rebirth: the fruit of our actions may not come to fruition in this life but in future lives. This notion developed into the idea that each being, not just human beings, is in a chain of rebirths having no beginning. Human existence is pivotal in that only here can we actually control our fate—animals, gods, and demons do not have the freedom to choose actions but are controlled by past actions until their merit or demerit is exhausted and they become human beings. (Thus, animals can kill without karmic repercussions because they are acting naturally; killing in itself is karmically neutral.) While the thought of being reborn (especially in a pleasure heaven) may seem wonderful at first, the feeling of despair can also set in as we realize all the suffering we will have to endure if we remain trapped in a chain of rebirths forever. Those who weary of this "fleeting and joyless world" (BG IX.33), the home of misery (BG VIII.15), are led to the idea that we should get out of the process of dying and being reborn, i.e., release (*moksha, murti*).

However, if actions always produce repercussions, then once we are in the chain we cannot get out. Actionlessness is impossible, but the idea developed, perhaps in an interaction with Buddhism, that actions are not the problem—it is the personal drives behind them that cause rebirth. Only actions driven by the error of an independently existing self or by desires for personal gain produce karmic fruit—if we act in accord with the way reality actually is, our actions have no future repercussions. Every act with an "ought" or "ought not" attached to it becomes a concern. But it is the interior of an action—the actor's intention—that matters. The external actions are not objectively good or bad. If, for example, one could kill for a nonselfish motive, the action would not be karmically bad. As a corollary of this, no amount of karmic actions can produce this desireless state (since such actions always have only karmic fruit as their result). In sum, we pay for selfish acts (since such acts go against the grain of reality), but we do not get any credit for selfless acts (going with the grain of reality is simply the way we are supposed to be), and so no amount of acts can produce enlightenment. Thus, some other type of event is needed to achieve release, as with knowledge in Advaita correcting our misconception.

This doctrine has the effect of producing an ethos of individualism. That is, each of us is solely responsible for our own present condition, and only we can improve our own future state. Some doctrines do mitigate against individual responsibility—"group *karma*" (family, racial, or national), demerit falling on one's sons and grandsons, "transfer of merit"—but these are later epicycles of the fundamental doctrine emphasizing individuality. This leads to an indifference to the plight of others who are suffering: they have to help themselves—nothing we can do will help them in the larger picture of their chain of lives. We can only focus on our own karmic welfare. The poor, the sick, and the homeless are getting only what they deserve for their own past deeds. They have no one to blame but themselves. Even today the suffering of elderly widows in India is often ignored, because—as most of them would agree—they are personally responsible for their own situation. Indeed, under this view, helping them produces merit for us, but it is actually *wrong* for them—it is trying to interfere with cosmic justice. Instead, each of us should focus on our own future. Thus, the concept of *karma*, which began as affirming our own responsibility for our actions, ended up with a selfish concern for only ourselves and a lack of social interest.

This leads to the question of the moral status of the doctrine. Many scholars refer to *karma* as "moral reward and punishment" or as a "moral order of the universe." Indeed, this doctrine is often cited as proof that Hinduism is moral. But while there may be a natural lawful order to our actions and their personal repercussions, to refer to this as *moral* without further argument obscures the substantive issue of whether in fact other-regardingness is involved in this theory of action. The karmic order may represent "cosmic justice" in the sense that we get what we deserve, but the moral issue involves the standards for determining what we deserve. It would be proper to refer to a "moral order" only if the criterion for good repercussions for our other-impinging actions was an other-regarding intention and the criterion for bad ones was harm to others. But the criterion for "goodness" and "badness" in Indian mystical traditions is whether the action leads the actor toward escape from the chain of rebirths or whether it increases the chain (i.e., decreases or increases of sense of self). Thus, it is not at all obvious that *karma* represents a *moral* order at all. As will be discussed later, the factual beliefs of *karma* and rebirth can be incorporated into a moral way of life expressing concern for others. But, as just noted, they can have the effect of leading people to a selfish concern with only their own welfare. Thus, *karma* and rebirth certainly need not lead to a moral point of view, and hence they are not themselves moral concepts. *Karma* may mean that actions in our universe are causally ordered, but such a law of actions does not mean there is a *moral* order to the universe. In itself, *karma* is no more moral than gravity or any other natural force.

Thus, referring to *karma* as a moral order, let alone as proof that all Indian traditions are moral, is wrong. It may be argued that killing or stealing produces demeritorious *karma* precisely because they harm other beings, and it is for that reason these acts go against nature—in short, *karma* is a natural force enforcing a moral order to reality. Even if this were true, the issue still remains why those who believe in *karma* practice what they do: if their focus is upon their own enlightenment or other reward or punishment, they are not being moral. The issue is not whether nature is moral but whether we are.

Dharma

Western scholars have translated the term "*dharma*" as "law," "duty," "custom," "good conduct," "morality," "social ethics," "righteousness," "justice," "virtue," and "religion." This variety shows that the term is best left untranslated. In Hinduism it refers to the value-system and codes of proper conduct shaping the way of life common to virtually all the various Hindu subtraditions. In addition to sets of virtues, it consists of sets of rules of conduct. There are no individual rights but only responsibilities and obligations we must fulfill to maintain society. In theory, it answers what a Hindu of a particular class and stage of life should do with regard to all basic social problems. *Dharma* specifies the appropriate conduct we must follow toward our family, our ancestors, other people, animals, and the gods. It is an all-embracing set of social regulations, encompassing not only rituals but all other-impinging actions. Only within its framework does one pursue the other two aims of the ordinary Hindu life—material well-being (*artha*) and sense-pleasure (*kāma*). (That the Hindu way of life has a life-affirming ethos for the householder should be noted.) All three of these aims of life are to be developed in unison. For example, *dharma* cannot be developed without a material base in one's life (and wealth also provides the opportunity for the virtue of giving); and producing sons (and hence sex) is part of one's duty. *Dharma* may be different in nature in that it is the proper framework for developing the other two values, but the total way of life is encompassed by this value-system.

Dharma is an eternal structure of the universe, not created or enforced by a god.[3] It is said to have been revealed to the Vedic seers, although, in practice, most of the literature on it is the later nonsacred Dharmashāstras, such as the *Laws of Manu*. Behind it is the idea that the entire universe, including human society, is an integral whole, and we must each play our part correctly in order that the world will continue to function properly. Thus, violations of *dharma* can disrupt the course of nature—e.g., a king's violations can cause famine and drought.[4] Just as birds must fly and fish must swim, young adult male members of the warrior class must fight in a prescribed war—not to do so is to go against their nature. That is, there is a natural order to society and nature, and *dharma* sets forth the order of things on the social level, i.e., the rules we need to observe and the virtues we need to develop. In this way, our *dharma* "supports" or "maintains" (from the root "*dhri*" meaning to sustain or nourish) the social/natural order of the universe, and the observance of one's *dharma* leads to heaven. But human beings can go against their *dharma*, even though adharmic conduct produces demerit (*pāpa*) leading to inauspicious rebirths. Thus, each person's individual *karma* is the sanction enforcing the social system of *dharma*. In short, the two concepts interlock: karmic harm is the sanction for violating *dharma*, or, viewed the other way, *dharma* describes the propitious conduct under the law of *karma*.

However, determining what one's *dharma* is is not as easy as looking at a list. There is always a complex interaction of types of *dharma*—one's class, one's stage of life and gender,[5] and universal virtues. In addition, there are also other considerations: the world-age (*yuga*), times of distress (*āpadharma*), and the possibility of suspending a rule in order to help another. Thus, one's *dharma* is not constant throughout one's life but varies according to time and circumstance. The class system is central. There are four classes (*varna*, meaning "color"): the Brahmins, warriors, farmers and tradesmen, and servants and slaves, with everyone else in the world being outcastes. Members of different classes are in effect members of different species, with very few duties or virtues common to all. Any attempt to fulfill the duties of another's class leads to severe karmic consequences. (Thus, Rāma killed a servant, rightfully according to this theory, for fulfilling the duties of a Brahmin.) This classification is religious, not based on econom-ics—there are poor Brahmins and rich members of the servant class, but their religious status and dharmic duties remain unaffected. Originally, one's class was based on one's natural inclinations (BG IV.13); for example, some Brahmins by birth were prominent warriors in the *Mahābhārata*. This permits the *Bhagavad-gītā* to treat *sva-dharma*—one's own *dharma*—as converging with a class *dharma*. That is, Arjuna's *dharma* is that of a warrior because of his nature, not because of his birth. Thus, it is argued that the class system represented the natural stratifica-tion of any society (as with Plato), and according to the *Laws of Manu* the purpose of the system was to encourage social harmony for the common good. But the class system devolved into merely a ritual status, being replaced in practice by thousands of castes (*jāti*) based rigidly on birth, with no social mobility between ritual classes being permitted. The justification for such rigidity is the doctrine of *karma*: we get the station in life we deserve based on our own past actions. We can improve our lot only by fulfilling our class duties and thereby obtaining a better rebirth. Thus, the focus should be on our own future rebirths.

There are four stages of life: student, householder, forest-dweller, and wandering ascetic. After their initiation, male members of the first three classes spend a period of time studying the Vedas and related subjects. After that, they become householders, in which stage they marry, have at least one son, and carry out prescribed rituals. To Manu, this stage is the highest because householders produce the wealth that supports a society. At this stage, the practice of *dharma* and attaining heaven is the soteriological focus; considerations of release from the chain of rebirths do not apply to one's life and values. Most Hindus do not proceed beyond the householder's stage, but the dharmic system did institutionalize something beyond itself—release from the cycle of rebirths—that in principle is expected of every initiated male. Thus, within a life-affirming ethos the Hindus' system of values created a place for a mystical quest, even if it restricted it to the later stages of life. In the last two stages, the male becomes celibate and gives up possessions. Thus, what is required at one stage is prohibited at another. In the third stage, the man who has completed his householder duties begins to move away from his earlier obligations. He may live alone, with his wife if she so desires, or in a group. He studies the Upanishads, still takes part in rituals, and fulfills *dharma* through acts of friendship, giving, and compassion toward all living creatures; he is to be a vegetarian and to begin more extreme asceticism. (The hermits in the *Rāmāyana* do not come close to fulfilling the ideals of the *Laws of Manu*—among other things, they leave before completing the householder stage, have children, eat meat, and use their power to curse to kill.)

The last stage is basically only for Brahmins. The ascetic wanders alone, living only on offerings. He adopts ascetic practices as means to release from the cycle of rebirths. He is free from desires and thus indifferent to everything, including life and death. His actions reflect the universal *dharma* (*sādhārana-dharma*)—e.g., truthfulness, patience, and noninjury (*ahimsā*). Most importantly, he has renounced all dharmic class and stage-of-life responsibilities and virtues in favor of the quest for escape. He has fulfilled all his social obligations and no longer performs rituals. (Certain *bhakti* traditions go beyond Manu and elevate the householder life to an equal religious status with that of a wandering ascetic: the duties of a householder are considered higher than renunciation, since householders maintain society, and in each a beatific vision is possible.)

In the classical Hindu view, the world has declined from a golden age in which *dharma* was automatically and effortlessly fulfilled to our present dark age (*kali-yuga*) in which *dharma* is forgotten and misunderstood as we have gradually fallen prey to delusion and desire. Most schools say enlightenment is not possible during this age; all we can do is lay the foundations for our enlightenment in a future age. This decline also affects our physical nature; for example, we are not as tall nor live as long today as people in past ages. The reason for the decline is in fact the decline in *dharma*, starting when the first innocent bird was killed. We have now reached a stage when the classes mix and we need governments to enforce the rules of *dharma* and teachers to explain it. The god Krishna had to take human form to help (BG IV.7). Different dharmic virtues are prominent in different ages: in the golden age, austerities (*tapas*) were primary; today, giving (*dāna*). The rules of *dharma* also change from age to age.

In most discussions of Hindu ethics, much is made of the universal or "eternal *dharma*" (*sādhārana-dharma*) that in theory is binding on all classes and stages of life. These are the major virtues within Hindu ways of life. There is no one list. Various lists in the *Laws of Manu* include abstaining from injuring living creatures (*ahimsā*),[6] truthfulness, nonmalicious speech, abstaining from theft, sexual purity, helping the distressed, cleanliness, steadfastness, forgiveness, intelligence and knowledge, restraint of anger, and self-restraint (control of the mind and the senses). The *Mahābhārata* contains similar lists, usually out of any meaningful context. For example, Yudhishthira says "truth, giving, steadfastness, proper conduct, noninjury, austerities, and compassion—he who observes these is a Brahmin." Giving (*dāna*) is also sometimes recommended; for example, Manu says a householder should place some food (but not enough to harm one's own interests) outdoors every day for dogs, outcastes, and the sick.

However, there are exceptions to the universal *dharma*. Personal survival is valued over nontheft; so a starving person can steal food as a last resort. Truthfulness is considered the foundation of the world, but we can lie within a marriage, in defense of Brahmins, and to save an innocent life. (Krishna also got Yudhihthira, the "king of *dharma*," to make a key lie in the *Mahābhārata*, for which Yudhishthira had to pay karmically.) The *Mahābhārata* recounts the story of the ascetic Kaushika who had undertaken the vow always to tell the truth. One day a group of travelers fleeing a band of bandits passed by a crossroad where he was sitting. One of them pleaded with him not to tell the bandits which way they were going. But when the bandits showed up and asked, he told the truth, and the bandits found and slaughtered the travelers. Kant would have recommended Kaushika's course of action and have said that no blame falls upon Kaushika for the consequences of others' actions, but in the *Mahābhārata* Kaushika is said to have lost all of his accumulated merit for this one act of selfishness and not to have attained the heaven he hoped for upon his death. Thus, in the conflict of universal dharmic precepts of truth-telling and noninjury, Kaushika misvalued telling the truth over saving innocent lives.

What is most important to note, however, is that whenever there is a conflict between a universal *dharma* and a class *dharma*, the latter always prevails. Thus, the universal *dharma* is not the highest value but has only a *prima facie* authority for those still in the first three stages of life. Noninjury (*ahimsā*) is often cited as a universal value that proves Hinduism is moral, but it is open to so many qualifications that it actually seems out of place in classical Hinduism. (Gandhi said he got the idea from Jainism and Buddhism.) One can kill animals for ritual sacrifices or to protect another animal. One can kill people in self-defense or to save an innocent life. Even capital punishment is permitted. Members of the warrior class must kill as part of their *dharma*, and India's history has not been free of violence.[7] In the *Arthashāstra*, the rules for kings include killing, going back on their word, and breaking the peace. And as the *Gītā* states, "there is no greater good for a warrior than a war enjoined by *dharma*" (II.31). Also remember that the objective of the *Gītā* is for the god Krishna to convince the reluctant warrior Arjuna to participate in a war. Perhaps this is why the *Gītā* does not contain any mention of a universal *dharma*. Some of the explanations of violence sound like the rationalizations of divine command theorists; for example, ritual sacrifices according to Manu are not really "killing" because *dharma* requires it and the offerings go to heaven. Hinduism accepts that one cannot be a farmer without killing, and the *Mahābhārata* states that one cannot even drink water without killing the entities living in it but it better to do so than to die of thirst.[8] In the evolution of Hindu ethics, noninjury did come to be seen (under the influence of the devotional *bhakti* tradition) as an ideal for all to try to follow, but it was originally incorporated into Hinduism as a virtue only for Brahmins and wandering ascetics who could more easier practice it.

This last point brings up the question of the fourth aim of life—liberation from the cycle of rebirths (*moksha*). In the final stage of life, the wandering ascetic renounces his class and all else in the dharmic order. The observance of *dharma* leads only to accumulating the merit that leads to a heaven, not to the escape from the cycle of rebirth. No amount of merit can produce the latter; one thus cannot gain release by any amount of the practice of dharmic duties. The practice of *dharma* comes to be seen as at best preparation for the full-time quest for release and so must be superseded. That is, the wandering ascetics are beyond *dharma* and its sanction, *karma*. Thus, their actions are beyond all karmic good and evil for themselves. All this creates a tension between *dharma* and *moksha*. Whether on the path or enlightened, the wandering ascetics, having renounced the dharmic values, are now operating with a different set of values.

Do the "extraordinary norms" of the renouncer completely negate the "ordinary norms" of the dharmic life?[9] Dharmic values cannot be deduced from mokshic ones—indeed, it is hard to see any logical connection between the two. *Dharma* is not, as is often alleged, the foundation upon which *moksha* is built: *dharma* would be necessary for *moksha* only if *moksha* is a further development of the dharmic life (i.e., of good *karma*), which it is not—the total break between the two aims of life makes whatever went before irrelevant. (The complete discontinuity between the two sets of values brings up the issue, discussed in the last chapter, of how the former is *preparation* for an enlightenment-experience.) Conversely, *moksha* has no relevance for *dharma*, since knowledge of the eternal does not give guidance for the life within time.[10] Each value-system is simply irrelevant to the other. At best, the dharmic system leads to the rebirth in which *moksha* can finally be pursued but has no further significance for the mystical quest.

This raises the question of the relation of *dharma* to the content of the enlightened state. Are the enlightened mystics constrained by any particular value-system, since they previously left *dharma* behind?[11] Does the universal *dharma* now rule their life, since they no longer have class or other *dharma*s to interfere with it? Depictions of the enlightened state in the *Mahābhārata* suggest as much: the enlightened are freed from attachment and desire, tranquil, and content; they are truthful and forgiving; and they practice noninjury—in general, the very embodiment of the universal *dharma*. Or, on the other hand, do the enlightened transcend even that, and thus become totally nondharmic or even antidharmic? That is, is *moksha* a quantum leap in values that actually negates *dharma*, so that *dharma* no longer has any positive value? The enlightened cannot commit a selfish act (since they no longer have a sense of a physical self in the world), but beyond that are they restricted? As discussed below, the *Bhagavad-gītā* offers another solution: one's class *dharma* defines one's conduct in the enlightened state.

Dharma and Morality

All of this raises the issue of the relation of *dharma*, *moksha*, and morality. More will be said on this below, but enough has been said already to see why the term "*dharma*" should not be translated as "morality." *Dharma* is a religious value-system for regulating society, and its criterion for "right conduct" is not other-regardingness but simply conformity to certain duties.[12] *Karma* is the only sanction. An other-regarding concern for maintaining society or a concern for other individuals' welfare is problematic under the individualist ethos of *karma*. There are a few instances of a moral concern being reflected in the rules (e.g., exceptions to the rule of telling the truth are permitted in order to help others), but there is no systematic moral critique of the rules. Indeed, the presence of moral *exceptions* only shows that the dharmic system is different from a moral one. Conduct that is dharmic is not necessarily moral, and conduct that is adharmic is not necessarily immoral. This system of ethics simply involves a different set of categories. That *dharma* and merit are not moral categories can be seen by the type of practices involved. For example, some of the rules of *dharma* relate to pollution (by other class members and outcastes) and the preparation of food. Merit can be gained through touching or even just seeing holy men—one does not even have to listen to the teachings, let alone be moral in conduct.

The universal *dharma* certainly contains values—e.g., truthfulness and non-injury—that a moral person can live by, but class duties always override these values when a conflict arises. And, as Yudhishthira says in the *Mahābhārata*, "There is nothing more evil than the warrior's *dharma*." The lying and the killing that the warrior's *dharma* entails are prime examples of how this *dharma* negates the universal one. (Also, the villain in the *Mahābhārata* who starts the trouble by cheating at gambling ends up in a heaven, since he faithfully fulfilled his warrior *dharma*, while the family of the heroes end up temporally in a hell for their conduct.) Rāma in the *Rāmāyana* treats his faithful wife Sītā unfairly (or, to be more exact, it seems unjust to those of us who do not know the gods' eternal plan), and he chooses to obey his father even though he knows the people of his kingdom will suffer for it—his dharmic duties outweigh any moral concerns. Indeed, Rāma is portrayed as performing *dharma* perfectly. He is loyal, slow to anger, truthful, firm in his vows, free of envy, grateful, benevolent, even-minded to all his misfortunes, and an ideal son, husband, and brother. But his *dharma* remains a nonmoral absolute that must be rigidly obeyed regardless of the consequences to the people involved. Throughout Indian history, many social practices that appear to moderns to be many unjust have flourished under the dharmic system, but there can be no incentive to reform society to help others—in fact, it would be (karmically) wrong to try to do so, since the existing *dharma* spells out the eternal and immutable way a society should be run. The only legitimate reason under the dharmic system that one can have for any political action is to revolt against a king if he is not performing his warrior class duties properly.

In sum, *dharma* is a "duty," not in the sense of performing an act out of a sense of justice or other-regardingness, but in the sense of having a cosmically defined role to fulfill within society. The dharmic system regulates the acts of all members of society except wandering ascetics and remains a matter of external compliance to a code of ethics. The more mystically advanced Hindus concentrate more on the inner motivation for compliance. But again the quest for *moksha*, not other-regardingness, is the value. Renunciation, not other-regardingness, is the central ethos of mokshic values. The focus is on developing oneself, not on social concerns. As Saral Jhingran points out, the universal *dharma* is a matter of inner development: even the apparently other-regarding universal virtues—the interpersonal ones like truthfulness, kindness, forgiveness, and noninjury—are practiced for an individual's own self-cultivation. They become passive qualities nurtured for the sake of self-purification, not active ones to help others.[13] In short, these virtues are not pursued for other-regarding reasons. Therefore, it is hard to agree with Karl Potter when he says that the attitude of *dharma* is an attitude of concern for others as a fundamental extension of oneself.[14] And this conclusion follows even if we ignore the issue of whether *moksha* entirely transcends or negates the dharmic values—i.e., whether the enlightened, in severing their ties to society, leave behind any latent other-regardingness in the dharmic values.

The Metaphysics of the *Bhagavad-gītā*

The conclusion from the above is that the *dharma* is a nonmoral value-system. But the *Bhagavad-gītā* has a unique perspective to add to the issue. It is the first full text of the emerging tradition of devotion to God (*bhakti*). It has always been highly popular because it brings together many different philosophical ideas and grounds them in a theism. Unfortunately, in finding a place for many competing ideas, the text is not always clear on its basic ideas (and perhaps is not entirely consistent).[15] From the dharmic tradition, it adopts a life-affirming ethos and the need of *dharma* for the maintenance of society. From the Upanishads, it adopts *brahman* and *ātman* and the importance of *karma* for rebirth. From Sāmkhya, the most prominent of India's philosophical schools, it adopts the dualism of self and matter and various ontological categories. From the yogic tradition, it adopts meditative practices. All of this is placed in a theistic framework from the *bhakti* tradition. Krishna is a monotheistic god: he is the one ultimate source of the world (and paradoxically one being incarnated within it) and is personally concerned with it. (Whether he is ultimately personal or nonpersonal is not clear, e.g., compare XIV.27 with VIII.21. No passages suggest pantheism, but some suggest an encompassing panentheistic god, e.g., VII.7.)

One possible reconstruction of the *Gītā's* metaphysics is that Krishna is the "highest person" (*purushottama*), who, contrary to most Hindu traditions, underlies *brahman* (X.15, XIV. 3, XIV.27, XV.17-18), and out of *brahman* emerge both matter (*prakriti*, and its subsequent evolutes) and individual selves. Whether ultimately there is a plurality of individual selves as in Sāmkhya-Yoga or whether they dissolve in Krishna is not clear. But the religious goal is a return to Krishna, not rebirth in heaven, so that one is not reborn (IV.9-10, VII.19, VIII.15-16, X.3). "*Moksha*" and "*mukti*" are not terms in the text, although the Buddhist term "*nirvāna*" does occur once (VI.15). Still the idea is familiar: one who knows the true nature of God or of the self and matter, or is free of any desire or personal attachment, is out of the cycle of rebirths (e.g., IV.23, XIV.2, XIV.20, XV.4). Such a person has attained an eternal peace and a sorrowless state (e.g., II.71).

Part of the *Gītā's* synthesis is to affirm different paths or disciplines (*yogas*) leading to enlightenment. Traditionally, scholars delineate three: the way of knowledge (*jñāna-yoga*), the way of devotion (*bhakti-yoga*), and the way of works (*karma-yoga*). The way of knowledge involves the Sāmkhya discrimination of self from matter—that "I" am not an actor in "my" actions, and in fact only matter acts (V.8). The way of devotion involves fixing one's mind on Krishna and making offerings to him, in particular offering all of one's works as sacrifices (III.9, IV.23, IX.27). The way of works involves a renunciation of the fruit of one's actions: there is no personal investment in the outcome of one's actions but an even-mindedness to both good and bad personal repercussions as one carries out one's *dharma*-prescribed actions. This also applies to performing religious rituals (VI.1, XVIII.9). All paths lead to the same result—Krishna—and one should choose whichever path fits one's nature (e.g., III.3). However, the text does not support this three-part division. First, the text does not state how many paths there are, and one more can be found—the way of meditation (*dhyāna*).[16] This involves withdrawing the senses from their objects and a general calming and concentrating of the mind (II.44, II.58, VI.10-32, VIII.12). Second, the text does not always distinguish the different paths neatly (e.g., XVIII.51-63). All involve knowledge (either of Krishna or discrimination of the self and nonself) and desirelessness. In addition, meditation is best when the meditative object is Krishna (VI.46-47, VII.1, XII.2), and it prepares the mind for knowledge. Knowledge in turn is necessary for the even-mindedness of the way of works. And devotion involves concentration and offering one's works to Krishna. Nevertheless, all paths lead to the "supreme secret" or "secret wisdom" that Krishna is the supreme reality (IV.3, IX.1-3, X.1, XIV.1, 19, XVIII.63-64), and he draws to himself those who know thus.

Arjuna's Dilemma

The most original contribution of the *Gītā* for the issue of morality is how it combines *dharma* and *moksha* through the idea of disinterested action (*naishkāma-karma*). To see this, consider first the archer Arjuna's predicament at the beginning of the battle central to the *Mahābhārata*. Arjuna saw huge armies on both sides of the field, his brothers and their forces lined up facing his other relatives and their forces. Seeing this, he was struck with deep pity (*kripayā*) and did not want to participate in the upcoming slaughter. In despair, he threw down his bow and refuses to fight, wanting to renounce the entire warrior way of life. He argued out of a concern for all the others in terms of the harm that the battle would cause: the battle would result in everyone ending up in the hells—*dharma* would be destroyed, the classes would intermarry, all of society would be destroyed, the ancestors would not be fed, and so all would end up in a hell (I.28-46).

Modern commentators see Arjuna's dilemma in terms of a conflict of *dharma*s—his class *dharma* as a warrior, his clan *dharma* (*kula-dharma*) to preserve his family, and the universal *dharma* of noninjury. But Arjuna did not frame the problem that way, nor did Krishna respond in that way. Instead, the problem is simply how Krishna can convince Arjuna to fulfill his class *dharma*. Krishna in fact wanted to eliminate the warrior class—over a billion souls strong—because of the decline in their *dharma* and overpopulation. And he knew that if Arjuna was not to incur severe karmic damage he must fulfill his part in the divine plan for the ultimate maintenance of the world by fulfilling his class *dharma* and not letting his limited personal point of view interfere. Thus, Krishna offered a number of arguments. First, he informed Arjuna of the ultimate truth: the eternal selves are unkillable, so Arjuna would not be actually killing anyone by "killing" their bodies (II.19). (Later he said that they are all already dead or that he, Krishna, is in fact the slayer and Arjuna is only his instrument [XI.33]—these claims are not consistent with the first claim and also raise the specter of a determinism. More on this below.) Next he appealed to Arjuna's class *dharma*: "there is no greater good for a warrior than a war enjoined by *dharma*" (II.31, III.35, XVIII.47), and thus great demerit accrues if he does not fight. Arjuna would gain a heaven if he died in such a war (II.32-33), and he would also be doing any soldiers he killed a favor since they will gain the same. Lastly, Krishna appealed to Arjuna's emotions: he would be labeled a coward and gain ill fame if he left the battlefield (II.34-36).

But the bulk of the *Gītā* espouses another argument: if only Arjuna will play his role in the cosmic plan by following the *dharma* of the warrior class, his actions will produce no karmic effects and he will not be reborn at all but will return to Krishna. If Arjuna's actions were free of personal (and hence unenlightened) intentions, if he would simply perform the required acts without any desires, Arjuna's actions would finally be aligned with the ultimate structure of reality and he would be free of the chain of rebirths. Thinking "I will not fight" only shows that Arjuna is clinging to egotism (XVIII.59). The rest of the *Gītā* tries to correct

Arjuna's view of action and to convince him to fight. This leads to the central concept of "desireless action."

Desireless Action

The basic idea of desireless action (*naishkāma-karma*) is that the actor's attention should be focused exclusively on performing the action itself, not on the personal "fruit" (i.e., the positive or negative karmic consequences for the actor) (II.47, III.7, III.19, IV.14-15, IV.20-23).[17] Such action can also be called "without attachment," "nonattached," "detached," "dispassionate," or "disinterested" since its personal effects are no longer of concern. The theory of action behind this is that personal desire (*kāma*) is the root of all karmic effects, not the actions themselves (II.55, IV.2, IV.19-23).[18] Thus, if one acts according to the dharmic precepts without concern for the consequences to oneself, no karmic effects accrue. The same holds for Krishna's own actions (IV.14, IX.9). Thus, actions are neutral in themselves, and if one commits them without any personal intentions and desires—i.e., without desiring any outcome for oneself—no karmic repercussions will occur in the future.[19] With such an understanding and with skill in performing action, we are freed from rebirth and reach the sorrowless state (II.50-53). The enlightened's actions will have no karmic repercussions, since they are done desirelessly. The *Gītā* suggests that total inaction is a possibility in this world (V.2, contra III.5, III.8, XVIII.11). But, even if that were possible, it may still involve a personal desire, and instead the inner renunciation of the personal fruit rather than the action itself is deemed superior (V.2). Like Shankara, the *Gītā* sometimes equates action with karmic action (produced by desire) and so says that the enlightened both act and do not act (e.g., IV.18-20, IV.33, XVIII.17) and also that Krishna does not act (IV.13) when it means they do in fact act but not through personal (and hence unenlightened) desires. Thus, the enlightened still act, but their acts now are clear, not black (with bad karmic effects) or white (with good karmic effects).[20] In this way, renunciation of personal repercussions, not renouncing actions themselves, becomes central. Thus, the intentions behind actions become important.

But if personal desires are not driving enlightened actions, how do such actions occur? Sāmkhya belief-claims entailed by the *Gītā* come into play here: no "I" acts; only strands of matter (*prakriti*) do (III.27-28, XIII.29). The real self—the *purusha*—never acts. It is pure consciousness, devoid of intentional states; thus, it is not an agent, and no consequences accrue to it. The *Gītā*, following the Sāmkhya metaphysics, does not deny an agent—either Arjuna or Krishna—but simply affirms that only matter actually moves ("acts") and is affected. One possible misunderstanding is that much of what we consider mental (thinking, feeling, and so forth) is considered *material* in Sāmkhya theory. Only the beacon of consciousness is attributed to the *purusha*; all other mental activity is "material." This mitigates the idea that "unconscious matter"—the complex "material" body—can still think, feel, and act. Thus, when the *Gītā* states, "I do not act at all" but only the strands of matter work (V.8-10), what it means is that the true self (the *purusha*) does not act nor is affected by acts, not that bodily motions occur only mechanically through nonconscious natural forces. The error is to identify the self (*purusha*) with matter, which interacts only with itself, not to affirm an agent. The self is not reduced to matter controlled by socially defined roles. Thus, Arjuna should conclude that the true "I"—consciousness—does not act and only unconscious matter acts "through" him (and consequently he should act desirelessly).

The *Gītā's* objective in claiming that only matter acts is to get Arjuna to see that any personal desires he might have are out of step with the way reality truly is and thus that he ought to adopt the *dharma* as his action-guide—that what happens to the matter (*prakriti*) is of no concern to the true self, and so he should have no attachments. That Arjuna is free to act otherwise is accepted in other passages—e.g., he is free to do another's *dharma* imperfectly (XVIII.47). These passages presuppose a "free will" agent and that Arjuna in the end has a choice to make (XVIII.63), even if the choice is only to do what his unenlightened ego wants. There is no deterministic chain of material events, even if only matter acts since "matter" includes thinking and feeling—only pure consciousness (the *purusha*) is excluded. In the enlightened state, "matter" is still all that acts, even though the enlightened are no longer bound by matter (XIV.20).[21] (The *Gītā* may not have discussed free will because there is no concept of "will" in Sāmkhya.[22] Moreover, free will is not a major topic in Asian religions.) There are also, however, passages to the effect that only Krishna or *brahman* is the real actor (XI.33, XVIII.46, 61) and that Arjuna is not really free to choose his actions (XVIII.59)—Arjuna is merely the instrument, and Krishna pulls the trigger. This suggests that ultimately there are no selves and only a *determinism* of actions by the one real actor, Krishna. But the *Gītā's* focus remains firmly on the issue of choosing to follow one's *dharma*-defined role or not, not on the metaphysics of how agents cause actions to occur.

So how does Arjuna discover what his dharmic actions are? The *dharma* of his nature—his *sva-dharma*—is his natural course. In the *Gītā*, one's class is not determined by birth but by one's natural disposition (IV.13). (Later the standard position became that under the law of *karma* our past actions determine our birth into a particular class, and thus our class necessarily reflects our own nature.) Thus, Krishna might have given different advice to another warrior by birth but not by nature. The *Gītā* outlines the sva-dharmic actions and virtues of each class: the Brahmins' are calmness (*shama*), control of the mind (*dama*), austerities, purity, patience, uprightness, knowledge (*jñana*) and understanding (*vijñana*), and orthodoxy; the warriors' are heroism, vigor, firmness, skill (*dākshya*), not fleeing a battle, gift-giving (*dāna*), and a lordly nature; the workers are to till the fields, tend the cattle, and engage in trade; the servants and slaves are to serve (XVIII.42-44). Arjuna was by nature a warrior: he enjoyed being a warrior prior to this battle, and his dejection at seeing his family arrayed to die was not characteristic of his feelings. Krishna knew Arjuna's reaction was not in tune with his real nature and that his *sva-dharma* in fact converged with a warrior's class *dharma*; thus, Arjuna should perform the social role of the class in which by his nature he belonged. He had "free will"—he was free to leave the battlefield and go off into the Himalayas to meditate, but that would have been against his nature and frustration would ensue. *Sva-dharma* is the psychological equivalent of one's physical abilities. Going against one's own *sva-dharma* would be like a person who could not swim trying to save a drowning person—no good would come of it, and only more trouble would result.

Thus, it is better to perform one's own *dharma* imperfectly than to perform another's well (III.35, XVIII.47). This presupposes that any act other than those that *dharma* determines by one's own nature cannot be performed with complete detachment. We can choose how to develop ourselves, but we will incur karmic repercussions in struggling to perform what we cannot, while no effects accrue if we act according to our *sva-dharma*. We then move effortlessly within reality, and thus no repercussions are possible. Karmic action, in short, is acting unnaturally. Karmic reactions are the friction generated from going against the grain of reality, fighting our own nature rather than performing our natural, *dharma*-guided actions. Arjuna, clinging to a sense of ego—i.e., erroneously identifying his self with his material body—had desires that remained out of sync with reality. His real nature converged with a particular role in the social world, and it is unenlightened not to act according to one's *sva-dharma*. He must see how things really are to choose the proper course of action. Only then could he either attain heaven or become unattached to the fruit of actions and attain enlightenment.

There is a problem, however: our true self (the *purusha*) is a consciousness with no "personality," and so how can we act according to our true nature? Why is one code of conduct in keeping with our true nature when the *purusha* has none? Why must one do what one's present life's *dharma* dictates to become liberated when it is irrelevant to the true self? The *Gītā*'s answer is that our place in the scheme of things (and thus our *sva-dharma*) is determined by our *material base*—the strands of *prakriti*. The material strands of our this-worldly "self" of course have no "personal" desires either, and so our acting with disinterest according to what *dharma* requires is acting in keeping with reality. Acting according to one's nature thus means acting according to one's material base (III.33), and in the end matter will determine our apparent choice (XVIII.59)—although the *Gītā* immediately turns around and says Arjuna has to choose (XVIII.63). Thus, when we selflessly and effortlessly fulfill whatever *dharma* is dictated by our material nature, we see that only matter is really acting and that the true self is silent and inactive. We escape the grip of identifying our true self with our material body and are enlightened. Thereby, the self, which was never in fact reborn, is no longer reembodied and the chain of material rebirths ends.

The Enlightened State

Being enlightened is doing the works required by *dharma* desirelessly (XVIII.45-48). The standard social *dharma* is thus transformed into a way of personal salvation: one can realize mystical freedom by fulfilling one's class *dharma* without attachment to the fruits of one's actions. Thus, instead of an ascetic renunciation of the world, there is a way of enlightenment through everyday social activity. The renouncer is no longer a wandering ascetic—it is anyone who renounces the fruit of action but not *dharma* (XVIII.2-7). The *Gītā* thereby unites the enlightened state with socially defined actions—*moksha* with *dharma*. The dharmic state is no longer something that must be transcended, as with Shankara.[23] Rather, *dharma* outlines both the means to enlightenment and the content of the enlightened state. The *Gītā* requires following one's *dharma* and rejects both the renunciation of all actions or the adoption of any other actions. Instead, there is an inner renunciation through desireless action, while outwardly one's material nature conforms to social requirements. With no personal desires, the material body continues to act (IV.21)—the action is dictated solely by one's *dharma*, not by any personal (and hence unenlightened) desires or intentions. Thus, the body continues to act, while the true self (*purusha*) looks on unaffected, as it always has.

The enlightened have no personal desires, but they act with the purpose of maintaining the world (*lokasamgraha*, i.e., keeping the world "hanging together") by fulfilling their dharmic duties (III.20, 25). They have nothing to gain or lose thereby—indeed, they have no interest in any action done or not done in this world (III.18)—but their actions have the effect of helping to maintain the social/natural structure that holds the universe together. Arjuna would harm this order if he did not participate in the *dharma*-required war, both by not fulfilling his *dharma* and by setting an example of improper conduct for others (III.21, 26). Without the dharmic work of each person, the world would fall into chaos. In this regard, the enlightened follow the example of Krishna's own *yoga*: Krishna has no need to do anything, nor do his acts affect him (IV.14, IX.9), but he continues to act to maintain society (III.22-24). He created the class system (IV.13) and even became embodied in this world (IV.6) in order that people not all fall into the hells.

The *Gītā* does not emphasize getting out of the chain of rebirths as much as the philosophical schools, although it certainly accepts that is the result of enlightenment (e.g., IV.9-10, V.12, VII.9). Rather, it focuses more on the enlightened state of mind and on how actions are performed in the enlightened state. Those who see God in all and all in God (VI.29-31), who are fixed in wisdom (*sthitaprajñā*) (II.54), are in a state of mindfulness.[24] Being free of attachment to the fruit of their action, they are content with whatever comes their way, calm, and unshakable, since they have no personal investment in the outcome of any action. They are not attached to the world nor to solitude and the renunciation of action. They would suffer no grief for killing in battle, since they know no one is really a killer or killed

(II.19). They are free of all desires and personal purposes (II.55, II.57, II.71, IV.19, IV.21, XII.16-17, XVIII.23-26) and thus are disinterested in their actions. They have a sameness or even-mindedness (*samatva*) to pleasure and pain, gain and loss, success and failure, honor and disgrace (II.15, II.38, II.56, IV.22-23, V.3, VI.7, XII.13, XII.17-19, XIV.25). Indeed, discipline (*yoga*) is defined as even-mindedness (II.48) and thus skill-in-action (*karmasu-kaushala*) (II.50). (Translating "*samatva*" as "indifference" or "insensitivity" is misleading since this suggests an indifference to the effect of one's actions on *others*, which, as discussed below, is not the case. *Samatva* refers to the emotional effects of actions on *the actor*.)[25] They see with an equal eye both Brahmins and outcastes, elephants and dogs (V.18), and thus do not adopt the traditional valuing of one as better than the other. The masters of their senses are alike to a clod of dirt, a stone, and a piece of gold (VI.8, XIV.24). They are even-minded to the loved and unloved, friend and foe (VI.9, XIV.24-25). Krishna too is alike to all beings, none being hateful or dear (IX.29, contra XII.13-20, XVIII.64-65). Those who are fixed in sameness are out of the chain of rebirths, for *brahman* too is even-minded (V.19-20).

Sameness in one's emotional state does not mean that the enlightened cannot act. All personal desires and objectives have vanished, but *dharma* has replaced them and now provides the direction for actions. Thus, the enlightened have a purpose and can act—the purpose now is simply Krishna's and not their own. Moreover, actions are not carried out without regard to consequences. The enlightened are now disinterested in the fruit of their actions (II.47), but this only means they are not concerned with the effect of their actions on themselves; thus, the issue of the effect of those actions on others remains. (Whether the enlightened should also be uninterested in the effects on others—since that is a concern for Krishna alone—will be discussed below.) Nor does it mean that they will treat a Brahmin and an outcaste exactly alike: they will treat each person as their *dharma* dictates. Their actions will be the same socially defined ones that the unenlightened do; the enlightened mystics' even-mindedness toward themselves is all that is new.

The only change in the dharmic actions would be in *how* they are carried out: the enlightened will do these acts more effortlessly, efficiently, and spontaneously, since they have completely internalized a worldview and value-system and so no longer have any confusion as to what they should do, and since their focus is now fixed exclusively on performing the action itself without concern for the consequences to themselves. It is a state of mindfulness, with the mind concentrated on the act itself, responding to the moment without a thought to the past or future. In the state of even-mindedness the actions would be carried out without any emotions that normally accompany our actions. The actions may be performed well, but with the absence of normal human feelings there would be a coldness to them. The enlightened remain serene and emotionally uninvolved with the world.

Even-mindedness is the principle virtue of the *Gītā*'s way of life. It overcomes the three vices connected to desire—lust, anger, and greed (XVI.21; see also III.34, III.37, XVIII.53). The *Gītā* contains a number of general lists of other virtues—e.g., noninjury, truth, angerlessness, renunciation, calmness, freedom from backbiting, compassion to all beings, freedom from greed, gentleness, modesty, no fickleness, majesty, patience, fortitude, purity, freedom from treachery and pride, worship, giving, and austerities (XVI.2-5).[26] Some lip service is paid to noninjury (*ahimsā*) as one item in lists (X.5, XIII.7, XVI.2, XVII.14), but it is difficult to get around the fact that the objective of the *Gītā* is to get Arjuna to fight in a war—indeed, violence is the norm for society in classical Indian literature—and so this virtue is far from central. Indeed, the universal *dharma* is not mentioned at all, since class *dharma*s always prevail. Similarly, other-regarding virtues, such as compassion, are rarely mentioned and never prominent. Thus, while alike to good and evil persons (VI.9), the enlightened are friendly and compassionate to all (XII.13-14), are free of hatred toward any being (XI.55), and take pleasure in the welfare of all beings (*sarvabhūtahita*) (V.25, XII.4); seeing all beings in themselves and themselves in all beings, they regard others' pleasure and pain as their own (VI.29-32). But enlightened warriors are still warriors. As Surendranath Dasgupta said, the *Gītā* does not advocate the active performance of acts of friendliness: the positive friendly state of mind is just the mental correlate of the practice of non-injury.[27] In short, self-cultivation and its virtues remain central.

Universalizability

Before proceeding, one issue should be addressed that arises for any traditional cultural ethics: universalizability. The *dharma* of each of the various classes in traditional Hindu ethics is universalizable in the primary sense of holding for anyone similarly situated. That is, the rules for Arjuna would hold for any member of the Hindu warrior class. However, the *dharma* is not universalizable in the stronger sense that one set of rules holds for all people, regardless of station or culture, and that all people are to be treated equally regardless of social status unless there are some distinctions that can be defended on moral grounds. Different classes are in effect different species, and outcastes are literally outcastes. The *dharma* is designed to preserve one particular traditional society. Each class within the society has its own in-group ethics, and few of these rules and virtues apply across the board to all groups. Many scholars make much of the ideals of the universal *dharma* in attempts to show that Hindu ethics are a universalizable morality.[28] But the fact remains that the *Gītā* makes no reference to the universal *dharma*, and even Manu strongly qualifies the virtues and holds that class *dharma* trumps the universal every time (e.g., a warrior's duty to kill overrules noninjury to living beings). Thus, there is no basis for treating the universal *dharma* as a code of ethics that would be universalizable.

We might be able to get out of the confinement of orthodox Hindu culture by allowing each person in each culture to find the appropriate social role in his or her culture and fulfilling it disinterestedly. *Dharma* would then become a form of life, rather than the content of a particular culture's ethics. But then any social code, no matter how immoral (e.g., Nazism), would do. Nor would it avoid the problem of each *dharma* being an in-group action-guide. But this does reflect modern liberal Hindus, e.g., Radhakrishnan, who argue that, while *dharma* is absolute in some sense, the content of specific codes is not timeless and cultureless but only reflects specific traditions and not revealed sources. This issue may be sufficient to eliminate the *Gītā*'s *dharma* as moral in the modern sense, but we can still ask whether Arjuna was other-regarding.

Is Arjuna Other-Regarding?

At the end of the *Gītā*, Arjuna is enlightened—his confusion is destroyed and his doubts dispelled, and thus he will do what Krishna says (XVIII.73).[29] He has the serenity of someone who knows what he must do. Krishna has declared this war to be *dharma*-required, and so Krishna and he, with a "semblance of a smile," proceed to cut a human swath across the battlefield. Is Arjuna being moral? That is, is he choosing to perform disinterestedly his class duties out of concern for the others? The *Gītā* does not present his dilemma as a moral one, nor does it resolve it in moral terms. But the moral question can be answered by looking at the values and beliefs entailed by its arguments. The issues break down into two steps: (1) Is at least one of Arjuna's motives a concern for others? (2) Does Krishna's dharmic plan also help others (or at least is it reasonable for Arjuna to believe so)? Unless both of these questions can be answered affirmatively, Arjuna is not being moral. In addition, there are questions concerning the presuppositions of morality to consider.

Consider the first question first. Arjuna begins the *Gītā* with an other-regarding concern for others. He explains how he believes his fighting will help lead many people to hell (I.28-46). By the end, he is ready to fight, but did his motives or his factual beliefs change? It may be his motives: he might now be concerned with himself getting into heaven or out of the chain of rebirths, or only with consigning his actions to Krishna, so that he is totally unconcerned with the consequences to others and the content of *dharma*. He then could not care less about whether the *dharma* he is following is moral or not. This would be mystical, but it would also be nonmoral. However, it is also possible that what has changed is only Arjuna's *factual beliefs*: Krishna has corrected Arjuna's view of the consequences of his fighting and shown how society and the world will in fact be helped by Arjuna fighting. Now Arjuna can manifest his other-regarding concern by fighting. It is important to note that according to Krishna it is a proper for Arjuna to be concerned with maintaining society (III.20, 25) and Arjuna can delight in the welfare of all beings (V.25, XII.4). (Again, concern for the welfare of others is consistent with Arjuna's disinterest in the consequences for himself.)

How can this be reconciled with the prevailing theme that Arjuna should focus on his actions alone (*naishkāma-karma*)? Can other-regardingness and disinterest both be maintained at the same time? Karl Potter's comment on nonattachment (*vairagya*) in Hinduism addresses this: giving up actions prompted by personal desires and overcoming the personal emotions connected to our actions means only that we are no longer personally attached to the outcome (the success or failure, the pleasure or pain), not that we cannot predict an action's outcome.[30] Potter contrasts "renunciation of the fruit of an action" with "resignation," which is blind to the outcome of deeds. Renunciation involves how we view the effects of actions on ourselves and may produce a difference in how we execute our actions, but it is not a disregard of the consequences for oneself or others.

In this way, Arjuna can accept both other-regardingness and disinterest if he accepts that Krishna's system will take care of others—he then no longer has to concern himself with the consequences of his actions to himself (since he is desireless) or to others (since Krishna's dharmic plan will provide for their welfare). Thus, Arjuna's actions are still driven by a purpose—it is just that the purpose is now Krishna's and not Arjuna's personal unenlightened one. He no longer has a will of his own—it is surrendered to Krishna. He is no longer interested in what actions are done or not done in the world (III.17-18). Even-mindedness toward the effects of actions upon oneself does not wipe out all other-directed emotions (such as compassion) and thus does not interfere with a warrior's dharmic actions.[31] But even-mindedness will wipe out any self-directed moral emotions (such as remorse or guilt), and his final adoption of the dharmic value-system will replace a moral conscience with an automatic dharmic determination of action. Arjuna would have the inner security and freedom that comes with simply fulfilling a role in the social hierarchy of a traditional culture and not having to make moral choices. His last moral decision is whether to follow his *dharma* or to follow his personal desires (which he now sees to be misguided).[32] Once he has internalized the dharmic point of view, he is no longer concerned with his actions' effects on others because, if he is moral, he believes the dharmic plan is moral. He must do whatever the ethical code of *dharma* dictates: having decided to act according to his own *dharma*, any moral crises are replaced with fulfilling the requirements of his class.[33] This will involve all warrior duties from fighting a dharmic war to gift-giving (XVIII.43). Killing the soldiers in a *dharma*-required war is the right thing to do: according to the *Mahābhārata*, over a billion soldiers died (and ended up in heaven), but Arjuna's actions helped to sustain the world and thus were other-regarding overall, even if he does not know the details of how his actions fit into the cosmic picture. If the dharmic plan is moral, Arjuna is not pursuing his own *dharma* at the expense of others because all will be helped.[34]

Thus, it is possible that Arjuna's original other-regardingness was in fact one motive for his finally adopting Krishna's dharmic system in the first place. That is, after his enlightenment his attention may be directed toward his actions alone, but Arjuna had first to decide to accept a life in which he consigns his decision-making over to Krishna's plan. The *Gītā* unfortunately does not state why Arjuna decided to accept Krishna's arguments, and it must be admitted that there are only a few verses about concern for others and thus that other-regardingness does not figure prominently in Krishna's arguments. But nothing in the *Gītā* refutes the possibility that Arjuna was convinced at least partially out of his original concern for others. And having other-regardingness as at least part of one's motivation for actions is sufficient to consider someone moral. Thus, this possibility is enough to answer "yes" to the first question.

The interaction of Arjuna's disinterested working and Krishna's dharmic plan also helps to clarify a confusing point: we can conclude from the *Gītā* both that only actions themselves matter and that actions themselves are totally irrelevant. These conclusions depend on different points of view. From Arjuna's point of view, the actions are irrelevant (III.1)—only *how* he acts matters. His "material self" can just follow its *dharma*. Actions in themselves—even killing—are neutral in themselves. How he acts is a matter of his character. The inner attitude is everything: he has no karmic repercussions if he does his dharmic actions disinterestedly but has such consequences if he follows personal (and hence unenlightened) desires—what exactly the actions are does not matter. The actions are not judged "good" or "bad" but are ends in themselves.[35] No longer identifying his self with matter, he can kill in the battle without incurring any karmic effects (XVIII.17). But the perspective changes for Krishna. From his point of view, only the actions themselves matter—i.e, how they further or hinder his dharmic system. What Arjuna does is important to Krishna because it will or will not help to maintain the world. Once enlightened, Arjuna will do his dharmic duty simply because it is *dharma*, while Krishna is concerned with consequences.

Is Krishna's *Dharma* Moral?

However, to be moral, Arjuna must also be concerned with the consequences of his actions upon others—his disinterested performance of actions may take care of himself, but to be moral the action's effect must also be a concern. This leads to the second moral issue: whether the *dharma* can in fact make Arjuna's other-regardingness operative. Arjuna has cast all responsibility for the consequences of his actions onto Krishna (III.30, V.10-11). The soldiers are already slain, and Arjuna is merely Krishna's instrument for carrying out his dharmic plan (XI.33). Krishna is the real killer—Arjuna is no more morally responsible than any other tool. Arjuna is not responsible for his assigned role—that is created by Krishna and dictated by Arjuna's own nature—but he is morally responsible for deciding to follow it and not to resist it if it is immoral. Thus, unless the *dharma* is itself moral (or at least that it is reasonable for Arjuna to believe so) Arjuna cannot be deemed moral. If the *dharma* is moral, then Arjuna's enlightened life has converged with a life of selfless service for others. But if the *dharma* is not a moral social system, Arjuna is in no better position than a Nazi officer who claims, "I was only following orders." He is not absolved from moral responsibility simply by claiming he is the agent of someone else: he cannot claim he is a good little trooper with no personal desires if he freely chose to be a trooper in an immoral campaign in the first place. That is, it may only matter to Arjuna *how* he plays the game, but whether the game he has chosen to play is moral is still an issue. If Arjuna is indifferent to the issue of whether the way of life he has adopted is moral, he himself is not moral.

So does Arjuna have grounds to think that Krishna's scheme of things is moral? As discussed above, the concept of *dharma* is a religious concept of a value-order to the universe and is not necessarily moral. The *Gītā* does state that Krishna needs to do nothing but continues to work, for otherwise his creatures would be destroyed (III.22-24; IV.6).[36] This suggests a moral concern.[37] But the picture is complicated by verses reflecting *bhakti* devotionalism: even very evil persons go to Krishna if they perform even one act of devotion (IX.30; see also IV.36, VII.15). This can mean both that morality is not a religious criterion within this way of life and that Krishna has a moral concern for every being (see IV.9, IX.29). It can also point to Krishna being beyond not only dharmic and adharmic concerns but also beyond moral good and evil—i.e., morality, as well as *dharma*, is a matter of regulating society and not a concern of the ground of that reality. Krishna is the basis underlying all that happens here, good and bad, but moral concepts do not apply to him.[38] The fire of knowledge reduces even the worst acts to ashes (IV.36-37), and so the enlightened are beyond the sanction of *karma*, but the whole point of the *Gītā* is that Arjuna is not beyond fulfilling his *dharma*. In short, the issue is whether Krishna's dharmic scheme is moral in revealing a concern for beings. Arjuna may not know Krishna's plan. He does know not all actions are acceptable, but he need not know Krishna's criterion of "good" and "bad" or whether it is arbitrary—to him, all of *dharma* may be a type of divine command theory of ethics. He knows his *dharma* will involve a lot of killing but killing is not itself bad. Krishna also tells him that he himself is concerned with the welfare of his beings, and Arjuna has no reason to doubt it, even if he does not know the whole picture. Arjuna accepts that Krishna has created and is maintaining the world. Thus, Arjuna can conclude that Krishna's *dharma* is moral. Therefore, Arjuna is moral in adopting the dharmic way of life.[39]

The Unaffectability of the Selves

However, a factual belief presents problems for the presuppositions of a moral way of life. Morality requires real people whose interests we can take into account when we decide how to act, but the *Gītā* claims that no one kills or can be killed. The *Gītā* (II.17-25) quotes the Katha Upanishad (II.18-19): the wise know that they are unborn and eternal and that that reality (*ātman/brahman*) is not killed when the body is killed, and so they have no sorrow; thus, if the killer thinks that he kills or if the killed thinks that he is killed, he fails to understand what is real. The problem with the Upanishads' metaphysics was discussed in Chapter 4. The *Gītā*'s Sāmkhya metaphysics presents the same problem: no one kills or can be killed. The self (*purusha*) is eternal, never being born and never dying (XIII.31). Thus, we cannot but practice noninjury (*ahimsā*) in the ultimate sense toward selves no matter what we do to the material (*prakriti*) bodies of "people."[40] Arjuna can do whatever he wants in the battle, but he knows no one is really killed—even if he were to slay every world, he slays nothing (XVIII.17). More generally, how can we hurt or help anyone? Advocating what appears to the unenlightened to be noninjury—here, not killing the soldiers—is due as much to our nescience as thinking that we can kill, and seeing one as better is likewise a product of nescience. No actions appear to matter, and so how can Arjuna be anything but indifferent? It is easy to act in a detached manner if we believe no one is really affected. Even-mindedness is the obvious personal reaction if nothing matters but so is indifference to others.

In addition, why does Krishna care what Arjuna does? It is hard to argue that Krishna cares about how the piles of matter (*prakriti*) interact, but the real selves (the *purushas*) do not act and cannot be acted upon. Who or what is Krishna really helping? The real selves have nothing to do with the realm of actions. So how is one action any better than another? How does doing *dharma* help others? How does maintaining the world and social order help others? Any deviation from *dharma* leads to the degeneration of the world, but so what? Why work to maintain this "impermanent and joyless world" (IX.33)? Why would Krishna be concerned with helping different piles of matter (the bodies of different embodied "persons")? Matter is real but cannot be hurt in whatever state it is in (or at least the *Gītā* expresses no concern for matter), and the real selves are unaffectable and so cannot be hurt. How can the *Gītā* affirm actions at all when the beings are not really affected? And how can any actions reveal a concern for others in such circumstances? Morality presupposes a reality that can be helped or hurt, and the *Gītā* ultimately rejects precisely that. There is no ontological basis for a choice between values. In the end, moral questions involve a choice among intrinsically worthless options.[41]

This point has a wider implication. The *Gītā* is usually contrasted with Shankara in its life- and world-affirming ethos and its clarion call to action.[42] Despite its mixture of detachment and killing, it also has an emphasis on maintaining society as part of the enlightened way of life that should put to rest the idea that all mysticism is "quietistic."[43] But in light of its belief in the unaffectability of the selves, the call to action is, in the final analysis, not justifiable. The best one can say is that the *Gītā* is not consistent with its own factual belief-claims. There may be nothing in the *Gītā* about the world being merely Krishna's purposeless play (*līlā*) or of *māyā* in the Advaita sense, but it is hard to see how else the world and its beings can be treated. It is not that Krishna has some inscrutable purpose we human beings cannot possibly fathom. Rather, how could there be any purpose at all? All social systems are equally valueless. The *Gītā* is most naturally seen as cementing one social system for all time as a reflection of an eternal order—in particular, its class system—and so there would be no impetus for a moral critique of the system or for any social reform rather than very conservatively maintaining the status quo.[44] But the objection here is that all social systems are simply meaningless games. Arjuna may be a serene player, scything his way across the field with a "holy indifference," but what is the point?

Only if we can get passed this presuppositional problem can we conclude that in the final analysis the *Gītā* advocates a moral way of life. As it stands, the values it advocates for the worldly realm are arguably moral, but its metaphysics makes it hard to ground any values at all. Its metaphysics concerning the self may be the direct opposite of Shankara's—a dualism rather than a nondualism—but the ethical consequences are the same and cannot be reconciled with the *Gītā*'s arguably moral concern.

Notes

1. It should be noted, however, that not all classical Indians accepted the ideas of *karma* and rebirth: there were materialists who denied both belief-claims. The Ājīvakins argued that our future lives are controlled by the determinism of fate (*niyati*). The Cārvākins (Lokāyatins) insisted we should eat, drink, and make merry because there is no soul, no life after death, no reward for our good actions, and no punishment for any suffering we cause. There is no fault in killing since striking a body is the same as striking the ground. The *Gītā* (II.17-25) agrees with the last point but on other grounds.

2. That one's *karma* must be completed in this way leads to bizarre complications if specific events and not just a general outline of one's life (in terms of one's dispositions) must be played out. For example, the enlightened Buddhist Moggallāna had committed murder in a past life and so had to die by a similar murder in his last life; he postponed it by his magical powers a few times but finally died that way. But whoever killed Moggallāna in turn had to be murdered. Did the murderer kill Moggallāna freely, or was it the result of his own past *karma*? If it was done by free will (which must be the case if there is no determinism), problems arise: a chain of future murders would have to occur. According to idea of *karma* from the medieval period, if some one kills a goat then he or she has to be reborn five hundred times as a goat and die by decapitation each time. So there have to be five hundred new human beings who each kill a goat who in turn will have to pay for their karmic crime by being reborn as a goat, and so on and so on. See Humphreys 1976, pp. 65-66.

3. In the earlier Vedic tradition, the god Varuna administered the natural/social order of *rita*.

4. Such a concept also goes against the individualism of *karma*, but this only shows that other forces are also karmically at work in our state. The Theravāda Buddhist canon has an example (with a Laozi's Daoism-like flavor): when kings are virtuous, their ministers are virtuous; then the Brahmins and householders are virtuous; then the townspeople are virtuous; this being so, the moon and sun go right in their course, and the rest of nature follows; thus, the *deva*s are not annoyed and the sky-*deva* bestows sufficient rain for the crops to ripen; people then live long and healthy lives on the crops (Anguttara Nikāya II.85).

5. As with most of classical Hindu culture, the *dharma* system is male-oriented. The basic duty of a woman is to become a wife, have children, and serve her husband.

6. The prohibition against killing includes suicide and abortion. In classical Hinduism, abortion is strongly condemned (except in cases to save the life of the mother) because a fetus is considered a reborn person and so abortion interferes with his or her karmic destiny. Killing a pregnant woman is considered as bad as killing a Brahmin. However, abortions are common in India today—indeed, it has been called a "hushed epidemic"—which raises the issue of the superficiality of ethical commitment or at least the problem of the relation of belief-commitments to people's actual practices. Suicide is also condemned, although it is distinguished from heroically giving one's life to save others. Also an exception was made for a death motivated by *dharma*, such as a wife jumping on a funeral pyre (*sati*) and, as with Jainism, the enlightened who have renounced everything (death being the supreme act of renunciation). See Coward, Lipner, and Young 1989.

7. Commenting on Jainism, A. L. Basham points out that warfare was considered legitimate in Indian thought, often even a religious duty. Manu viewed it as a sort of "grim sport." See his "Jain Philosophy and Political Thought," in *Sources of Indian Tradition*, vol. 1, ed. William Theodore de Bary (New York: Columbia University Press, 1958), p. 86.

8. Noninjury does not mean vegetarianism. According to Manu, even a renouncer could eat meat if the animal was killed by another animal. But, also according to Manu, one who eats meat in one life is eaten by whom one eats in another.

9. Edgerton 1942, p. 151.

10. Creel 1972, p. 164.

11. See Larson 1972 on the possible relations of *dharma* and *moksha*.

12. That the *Laws of Manu* judge the severity of an improper act in terms of how it affects the favored class—Brahmins—rather than people in general, also shows that a universalizable other-regardingness is not at work here. (Universalizability will be discussed below.)

13. Jhingran 1989, pp. 175, 181. Seeing the universal *dharma* as a matter of cultivation for those advanced on the mystical path brings it into line with the personal cultivation of the philosophical schools. For example, *Yoga-sūtras* II.30-31 states as the second limb of yoga: "Non-injury, truthfulness, not stealing, celibacy, and non-covetousness are the restraints (*yama*). They are the great vow, universal, applying irrespective of class, place, time, or circumstance." These are meant absolutely for the advanced practitioners, but commentators give them interpretations that render them innocuous for the general practitioner (e.g., Vyāsa qualifies the precept against noninjury to permit fisherman to kill fish).

14. Potter 1963, p. 8.

15. Some scholars suggest that the *Gītā* originally ended with the grand theophany of Chapter 11: the first six chapters discuss different paths; Chapters 7 to 11 discuss the nature of God; Chapters 12 to 18 are later miscellaneous add-ons (hence the possibility of inconsistencies).

16. BG XIII.24-25. *Dhyāna* cannot be interpreted to mean *jñāna-yoga* since the passage also mentions *yoga* and *sāmkhya* (the way of discrimination).

17. Some commentators equate *naishkāma-karma* with *karma-yoga*, but desireless action is the theory of action for all the paths to enlightenment in the *Gītā*, however many there are. For example, under *bhakti-yoga*, we dedicate all actions to God and perform them in this same selfless manner. All actions become literally sacrifices (i.e., "made sacred") (III.9, IV.23, V.10, IX.27-28). Thus, this is another instance of the difficulty of trying neatly to distinguish different paths in the *Gītā*.

18. The *Gītā* never states that nescience (*avidyā, ajñāna*) is the root of the problem, as with Shankara. The *Gītā* (II.61-71) has its own version of what in Buddhism is called "dependent arising": when one senses the sense-objects, attachments arise; upon attachment, desires arises; this leads to bewilderment and loss of memory; this leads to the destruction of understanding; and this leads to perishing and rebirth. Ending desires leads to mental calmness and the end of rebirths. That is, the law of karmic causation would not apply to the enlightened because one of the antecedent condition in the chain of conditionals—attachment or desire—no longer exists. Buddhist see the process differently, starting it with nescience.

19. Manu denies desireless action is possible.

20. *Yoga-sūtras* IV.7.

21. Eliot Deutsch sees the *Gītā* as advocating a determinism of matter, but he concedes that *karma* allows freedom of action (Deutsch 1968, pp. 181-88). Thus, verses such as III.5 are better interpreted as conveying only the idea that matter does the actions and actions continue in the enlightened state. But as Deutsch also notes, some passages suggest a determinism by Krishna.

22. Furtado 1992, p. 118.

23. At the very end of the *Gītā*, Krishna's highest secret is that Arjuna should abandon all *dharma* and go to Krishna as his refuge (XVIII.66). This contradicts the general theme of the *Gītā* and is perhaps related to the *bhakti* tradition. But elsewhere the *Gītā* also states that one must go beyond the Vedas, which in theory are the source of dharmic precepts (VI.44, VIII.28; see also II.45). These may all relate to getting beyond merit and attaining the escape from rebirth, but how they fit into the *Gītā* as a whole is not obvious.

24. The basic passage on sameness in Chapter 2 also contains a verse with an image associated with depth-mysticism and concentration: the person whose wisdom is firmly established withdraws his senses from sense-objects, as a tortoise withdraws its limbs from all sides (II.58). Other passages in the *Gītā* relate to yogic practices (V.27-28, VI.11-17, VIII.10-13), but any depth-mystical experience is subordinated to the enlightened state of mindfulness.

25. This mistranslation may also be done intentionally for normative reasons. Robert Zaehner may have connected the word "indifference" to *samatva* for theological reasons as part of his campaign to show Christianity is morally superior to Hinduism.

26. The *Gītā* correlates vices and virtues with the three strands of matter—goodness, passion, and darkness—of the Sāmkhya system (XVIII.23-28). Work done from goodness is the work required by *dharma* by one who seeks no fruit from it (and thus done free from attachment, desire, or loathing); the actor is free from attachment, steadfast and resolute, and unchanged in failure and success; and he never speaks of himself. Work done from passion is by one who seeks desires and thinks, "It is I who do it," and requires much effort; the actor pursues the fruit of actions and is passionate, greedy, intent on doing harm, impure, and full of joy and grief. Work done from darkness is by one who disregards the consequences, the loss, the harm, and his own role; the actor is undisciplined, vulgar, arrogant, a cheat, dishonest, lazy, despondent, and procrastinating.

27. Surendranath Dasgupta, *A History of Indian Philosophy*, vol. 2 (Cambridge: Cambridge University Press, 1922), p. 511.

28. E.g., Hindery 1978.

29. The *Gītā* does not state how Arjuna became enlightened, or indeed even if he is—at the end, he is merely ready to do what Krishna says. According to the *Mahābhārata*, he may not have been enlightened (i.e., have internalized the enlightened point of view), since later in the story Arjuna is said to have backslided, i.e., to have forgotten his knowledge and to

have suffered karmic repercussions for his actions in later life. But for the issue at hand, it can be assumed his actions at the end of the *Gītā* are those of an enlightened person.

30. Potter 1963, p. 39.

31. Prior to enlightenment, giving (*dāna*) produces merit leading to a heaven (VIII.28). After enlightenment, it would produce no karmic effects.

32. It is possible to see each decision in the enlightened state as a fresh moral crisis—i.e., at each encounter with others, Arjuna can ask himself whether to accept or reject the dharmic plan. But if he has internalized his position, this will not occur. See Chapter 13 on enlightened decision-making.

33. This is not as simple as it sounds since there still are conflicts of dharmic requirements (as seen in the *Rāmāyana*), but this is an issue that can be bracketed for philosophical purposes. Whether there are conflicts and whether *dharma* consists of broad principles or a list of detailed precepts, the point is that *dharma* will guide Arjuna's decision-making.

34. *Karma* also plays a role here: each person gets what he or she deserves. Each soldier in this battle who dies does so because of his own past acts. Arjuna is freely choosing to be merely the impersonal instrument of cosmic justice.

35. But this does not mean work is an end in itself rather than an exercise in mystical mindfulness. The focus is on Arjuna's inner life in his acting. From his point of view, mystical freedom, not an act, is the objective—it is just expressed through performing the act perfectly.

36. Whether Krishna is interested in seeing all beings attain enlightenment or only in maintaining the world is not clear. One may argue that Krishna's concern in getting one being enlightened—here, Arjuna—is immoral since this values the enlightenment of one being over the lives of a billion soldiers. But if Krishna does have a concern for all, then getting one of the chain of rebirths is valuable, since the others have an indefinite number of rebirths anyway. That selves are unaffectable, however, again complicates the picture (as discussed below).

37. A passage that states that Krishna is the gambling of rogues and the violence of kings (X.36-38) is sometimes taken to mean that he is beyond *dharma* and *adharma*, but these are dharmic activities and Krishna is desire to the extent it is dharmic (VII.11). No dharmic activity in the *Gītā* is clearly immoral, although Yudhishthira says in the *Mahābhārata*, "There is nothing more evil than the warrior's *dharma*." Also, other Indian stories depict, for example, thieves as simply following their own dharma (*sva-dharma*). This again points to the fact that the concept of *dharma* is not closely tied to that of morality.

38. Robert Zaehner has to distort badly the concept of being "beyond good and evil" in the *Gītā* to see Charles Manson as in any way connected to the concept (Zaehner 1974a). The quotations from Manson he cites certainly do not fit the presuppositional problem discussed below or anything evidencing depth-mystical experiences.

39. Arjuna is not killing the soldiers for their own good (although they do go to heaven for dying fighting in a *dharma*-required war) but to maintain the world. Thus, his motive is other-regarding: the welfare of all beings is advanced by obeying Krishna. Krishna's justification for the war—to decrease the overpopulation of the world by removing the arrogant warrior class—may seem morally questionable, but Arjuna believes Krishna has created and maintains the world and so Arjuna can accept that Krishna knows what he is doing. (How society was to survive with the warrior class decimated is not clear, since it was needed to maintain the world.)

40. "Killing" is not simply separating the true self (*purusha*) from the matter (*prakriti*), as Rāmānuja claimed, since there is a karmic residue that is reborn and that is part of the matter. If "killing" did separate the true self, we would be helping others by "killing" them and thus freeing them from the chain of rebirths.

41. See Goodwin 1955, 1956.

42. It should be noted that the *Gītā* is not a "moral advance" on Shankara's position, since Shankara lived at least five hundred years *after* the *Gītā* took its final form. Indeed, the *Gītā*, despite its setting in a battle, is merely offering a mystical justification for quietly carrying on one's normal dharmic life—one of the options Shankara would later also advocate for the enlightened state.

43. It is important to note for Chapter 15 that for all its talk of social classes and action, action in the *Gītā* remains a matter of individual decisions—what should Arjuna do?—not a call for group action or for social reform. Thus, his action is "social" in that it maintains society but not "social" in the sense of being part of a group effort. He may be part of an army, but it is still his individual choice to participate that is the issue. The army is, in the end, just a collection of individuals each having to decide to follow his *dharma* or not.

44. It was *bhakti* devotees, coming mostly from lower classes, who advocated social reform and the abolition of the class system. Gandhi also appealed to the universal *dharma* in his opposition to untouchability. The point here is that they cannot rely on the *Gītā* for justification.

7

Jainism

The Jainas' ethical doctrines warrant a brief discussion because they put more emphasis on the *externals* of actions (as opposed to the inner drive of intention and motive) than do Hindus and Buddhists. Their belief in an infinite number of independent souls animating all of reality produces a harsh and relentless asceticism that is also illuminating for the issue of morality in its own right and is useful for understanding, by contrast, both Hinduism and Buddhism.

Souls and Matter

Jainism is a product of an early non-Vedic Indian ascetic tradition and presents a philosophy older than Buddhism. In its ontology, all of reality is divided into two categories: the infinite number of conscious souls (*jīvas*) and the nonliving matter (*ajīva*) they inhabit. The souls are finite in size and all bodies have them. They are eternal but are trapped in the chain of births and deaths of bodies. In their pure state, they are pure consciousness and knowledge; they shine forth and are omniscient. Souls are a light substance, and the objective of this religious way of life is to free each person's own particular soul from the karmic matter accumulated on it and to let it float to the top of the universe where it will remain forever in an omniscient but inactive bliss. This ontology is materialistic and also an ancient form of hylozoism: all of material reality is alive with souls—not only in what we consider "living" beings but in rocks and all other "inanimate" objects, down to each atom. Thus, when a blacksmith hits an iron rod with a hammer, souls in both the hammer and the rod are hurt. Or when we pour water on a campfire, we "kill" souls both in the fire and in the water. Of course, these souls do not actually die—they are eternal—but they are returned to the cycle of rebirths. They are simpler than our souls but are nevertheless in the same chain of rebirth as we are.

The most important type of matter for the issues at hand is the sticky *karma* in which unenlightened souls are completely enmeshed. That *karma* is seen as material is important: it is a substance that flows in through the senses and gets stuck on our soul. Every action produces an influx of this substance. The more selfish the deed the more karmic substance produced, but even unselfish acts produce some—"merit" (*punyā*) is a category of karmic matter. Killing a higher type of soul (e.g., one in a human) produces more *karma* than killing a simpler one (e.g., one in a plant). But all killing, either direct or indirect, produces *karma* that sticks to the soul. Intention affects the amount of *karma* produced: an intentional murder produces more than an accidental killing, but even the latter produces *karma*. Thus, action itself (*kiriya*) is the problem, but our unenlightened knowledge and desires remain in the picture.

Vows and Virtues

The Jainas' hylozoistic view of nature and materialistic view of *karma* alter the process of liberation from the chain of rebirths from the process in Hinduism and Buddhism: we have to physically scrape off all the past *karma* accumulated on our soul and to limit the production of more by limiting actions. Since every thought, word, and deed produces some *karma*, this is not easy. Accumulated *karma* can be removed by voluntarily undertaking renunciation and suffering.[1] The Jaina tradition has a laity of householders in addition to the orders of ascetics (*sangha*), but only the ascetics will be discussed here. The laity can at least begin to cut down on the *karma* being produced, but the ascetics (or "renouncers"), both male and female, work on eliminating accumulated *karma*. As part of a way of life that includes rituals and meditation, the ascetics undertake five great vows (*mahāvratas*): noninjury (*ahimsā*), truthfulness, not taking what is not freely given, celibacy, and not possessing any property. Noninjury is the central virtue and the others support it; for example, lying is a form of verbal violence, since the lie will lead to physically or psychologically hurting another person. The Jaina standard of what is good (*subha*) is the degree to which an act is in keeping with noninjury; the more in tune with that principle the act is, the less *karma* produced. Noninjury encompasses more than not killing a being—any ill-treatment such as overloading a pack animal or even breaking a spider's cobweb is condemned. Noninjury is extended to make tolerance in general a virtue.

The ascetics take on an extreme life of deprivations that dissipates accumulated *karma*. The theory is that *karma* naturally wears itself out—we do not pay for a murder forever—but austerities can speed up the process. The five vows are rigorously observed. They give up all attachments including family and originally even clothing. They begin the quest by renouncing all their former social obligations and ties, renouncing their possessions, pulling out their hair by the roots, and giving up their former name.[2] Under the guidance of a monastic teacher, the ascetics practice right conduct, austerities (*tapas*), and different types of meditation (*dhyānas*), calmly or cheerfully enduring all hardships. The ten virtues to be cultivated on the path are: patience, humility, uprightness, absolute truthfulness, purity, absolute self-restraint, austerity, complete renunciation, voluntary poverty, and celibacy. The models to be emulated are the twenty-four conquerors of passion (*jinas, tīrthankaras*), of whom Mahāvīra, an older contemporary of the Buddha, was the last.

Absolute *Ahimsā*

With the factual belief that nature is alive with souls, Jainas see every act as causing death. As with Advaita Vedānta and the *Bhagavad-gītā*, nothing we can do could ultimately constitute violence against the real souls, but in this tradition every act is still seen as constituting violence. The world is seen as a theater of pain and death. This leads to a bleak and dreary ethos emphasizing the depth and pervasiveness of suffering, death, and the need for total renunciation. Their accounts dwell on the torments on earth and in the hells, and not even the bliss of the enlightened state seems to be a major motive for adopting their path. (Ironically, the ascetics are usually portrayed as cheerful, knowing that they are on the way out of rebirth.) Add to this the factual belief that *karma* is a type of matter that accrues from every action and must be removed by actions to gain enlightenment, and the result is a focus on trying to control actions. This is not to deny that correct knowledge is still needed, but ending the *acts themselves* becomes more important than in Hinduism and Buddhism. The focus on action is not, as in the *Bhagavad-gītā*, on detached performance but on completely eliminating the action itself (and thus the material *karma* it generates). In addition, the category of "actions" include, as with Hinduism and Buddhism, not only those acts committed by means of the body but also thoughts and words. Indirect actions (such as hiring someone else to kill an animal for us) are equally condemned.

It is not hard to see that anyone who takes such beliefs seriously will end up practicing a radical and unqualified type of nonviolence. Jaina ascetics carry noninjury to extraordinary extremes. They have to be concerned about not harming an infinite number of souls in animals, plants, the earth, water, fire, and the air. Not only intentional violence but accidental injury must be avoided. Thus, the ascetics have to be concerned about potential damage from walking, eating, breathing, and every other conceivable act by mind, speech, or body. They cannot eat vegetables and fruits that have been cultivated and harvested but only fruit that has fallen from trees. Milk and honey are also possibilities. Drinking water requires a filter. Breathing requires a mask to protect the airborne beings. One cannot light a fire. One cannot wash since that may injure beings living in the water and on one's body. Brushes have to be used to clear insects and eggs from one's path. Walking has to be done gingerly, treading in the footsteps of the person in front of you, to avoid injuring any more of the souls embedded in the earth. There can be no sudden movements because they may harm a being. This leads to not moving at all—hence, the pictures of ascetics standing motionlessly for so long that vines are growing on their legs. But for all of this, we cannot but still "kill" an incredible number of souls everyday just by being alive.

The Enlightened State and *Sallekhanā*

Freedom from rebirths (*moksha, nirvāna*) is achieved when the soul is totally separated from matter, allowing it to float freely to the top of the universe. That only occurs at death, but if one has conducted the austerities and other practices that scrap the encrusted *karma* off a soul, one can attain a state of living liberation in this life (*arhant, jīvan-mukta, sayoga-kevalin*).[3] That this state may be achieved while still alive may seem surprising, given the Jaina belief that all actions *per se* produce *karma* and thus, unlike in the Hindu traditions covered earlier and in Buddhism, *karma* is still produced in the enlightened state. But the *karma* capable of producing a new rebirth has been destroyed. In the enlightened state, only enough *karma* remains to maintain the body, and if all actions are mindfully carried out with fully concentrated awareness so as to minimize unintentional injuries to beings, the amount of new *karma* produced in the enlightened state is very small and dissipates almost immediately. The *karma* blinding the soul has been removed and thus the soul now has the same omniscience, perfect perception, and bliss it will have after the final death.

Thus, the enlightened live a life as completely in tune with noninjury as is humanly possible. However, the problem that as long as we are alive we still must be continuously killing souls is not lost on Jainas. This leads with ruthless logic to their final solution: sitting down and starving to death (*sellekhanā, itvara*).[4] For the fast to be effective, one must be free of five factors: the desire to live future lives, the desire to avoid suffering, the longing for friends, memory of past happiness, and the desire for future happiness. It is not so much that the Jainas are intentionally killing themselves but only that they have come to realize that action equals death—so they stop all movement, including eating, and this has the consequence of dying. Jainas thus distinguish this from suicide, which is uniformly condemned, since this is not done out of any selfish desire or attachment.[5] In sum, the proper response to enlightenment is to not harm any creatures, which can only be done by not moving, which leads to death. It is passivity and renunciation of action to the maximum degree.

The final fast may also be other-regarding, even if this concern is shown only by ending all other-impinging action through complete inaction. The motive may be concern for other beings impinged upon, rather than simply stopping the accrual of one's own *karma*. The enlightened no longer have any concerns for themselves, since they have attained the omniscience and bliss of the final enlightened state, and the amount of *karma* they produce in the enlightened state of mindfulness is too minimal to cause a rebirth. However, the enlightened cannot be attached to whether they live or die, and so the final fast may simply reflect their final lack of any attachments and hence of any motives. Thus, the issue of whether this practice is moral must be examined.

The Moral Status of the Path and the Enlightened Way of Life

The Jaina factual beliefs and resulting ethos of asceticism produce a way of life that centers only on self-cultivation. *Moksha* is the only aim. Asceticism is never an end in itself—renunciation and the deprivations are always only a means to achieve some further end—but the only focus of concern is on the practitioners themselves. This is more than the pervasive Indian individualism entailed by the doctrine of *karma*, which entails that we can only help ourselves and not others, although Jainas do subscribe to such karmic individualism. In the words of the *Uttaradhyānasūtra*: "My own self is the doer and undoer of misery and happiness; my own self is friend and foe, as I act well or badly." Precepts specifying what produces meritorious (*punyā*) or demeritorious (*pāpa*) *karma* are negative, not just in form, but also in substance: only the effect on the practitioner in avoiding his or her own accumulation of *karma* is of concern.

Compassionate acts reveal our nescience and are limited to the laity and less advanced ascetics—advanced ascetics are not to be compassionate or otherwise involved in the lives of others. The Jainas' counterpart to the story of the ascetic Kaushika in the *Mahābhārata* and his act of truthfulness is a Jaina being asked by a hunter where a deer is: a lay Jaina can lie to help another being (but never to help him- or herself), but an ascetic can never lie. For the ascetics, there is no expedient lying—they cannot even remain silent to save a life. Their focus is on their own *karma* and enlightenment, and thus lying to help another being is not accepted. Even the central virtue of noninjury is cultivated, not because of the possible positive impact on others, but to help the practitioner end his or her own *karma*. As A. L. Basham puts it, killing or violence "is chiefly to be avoided not so much because it harms other beings as because it harms the individual who commits it."[6] In short, one practices noninjury, not so much out of altruistic concern, but to avoid injury to *oneself.*[7] A concern for others may be part of the motivation of the Jaina laity and ascetics on the path (since the unenlightened are never unified in their motivation), and noninjury would certainly be of benefit to the others impinged upon. But the only consideration recognized for following the Jaina path is one's own enlightenment. Thus, the path must be deemed selfish and hence not moral. Since it is a path pursued only out of self-concern but does not involve harming others—indeed, it is noninjurious to the extreme—it is not immoral but must be deemed nonmoral.

The enlightened are focused only on curtailing their own *karma*. The final fast to the death may arguably be undertaken out of a sense of other-regardingness, but it is a passive sort of other-regardingness: the ascetics are "helping" in the only way they can—by not interacting with others at all. But helping others is not a motive for the enlightened. Passive other-regardingness—not harming by complete inaction (*akarana*)—cannot morally salvage the self-centeredness of a life devoted solely to enlightening oneself. This self-centeredness is not an unenlightened selfish desire or attachment for anything in this world, but it is a concern only for the state of one's real self. Thus, the verdict must be that the Jaina path and resulting enlightened state are forms of benign nonmoral selfishness, regardless of any positive social side effects.

Notes

1. Hinduism also has the idea that austerities remove *karma* and observance of obligatory rituals prevents further accumulation, although it is not explained in physical terms.

2. Adopting a new name is common in monastic orders in different religions, signifying the renunciation of all of one's old life and social status.

3. Mahāvīra appeared just before the beginning of the dark age (*kali-yuga*). Times are now too evil for another savior to appear, or, according to most Jainas, for anyone to gain liberation.

4. Both Hindu and Buddhist traditions recognize a similar practice for the elderly. (Some unenlightened Jainas also partake of this practice.) But since detachment rather than acts themselves are emphasized in those traditions, this practice is not prominent there.

5. One can argue that by being alive we are killing innumerable souls, and thus merely by being alive we are being immoral. All souls are equal, and so to be moral we ought to kill ourselves out of concern for other beings and end the massive killing we are committing daily. But suicide will not help since we will be reborn as long as we are unenlightened, and if anything we will be reborn more often because of the karmic fallout from our suicide. Thus, the only way for the unenlightened to be other-regarding is to try to minimize the harm we inevitably do or to become enlightened and thus stop all harming by getting out of the chain of rebirths.

6. "The Basic Doctrines of Jainism," in *Sources of Indian Tradition*, vol. 1, ed. William Theodore de Bary (New York: Columbia University Press, 1958), p. 50.

7. Purusottama Bilimoria, "Indian Ethics," in Singer, ed., 1991, pp. 52-53.

8

Theravāda Buddhism

The Theravādins, like the Jaina mystics, also have an ethos of self-interest, but the Buddha developed a "middle path" between the extreme asceticism of the Jainas on the one hand and self-indulgence on the other. To see how ethics fits into this path, the place to begin is not with the basic Buddhist code of conduct but with its context—the Buddhist soteriological way of life. And that means starting with the Buddhists' religious concern—suffering.

Suffering and its Cure

The Buddha's teaching has only one flavor: how to end suffering permanently (M I.22).[1] Suffering (*dukkha*) does not mean that all experiences are painful but that even pleasurable experiences are only temporary, and, if we add to this the belief in rebirth, then we realize that even the most pleasurable and privileged lives are only temporary and ultimately frustrating and disappointing. Such unsatisfaction is ingrained into the very fabric of life. The only way to end suffering completely is to get out of the chain of rebirth that keeps us in the realm of suffering. The Buddha's analysis of the problem parallels ancient Indian medical practice: the disease is diagnosed as suffering; its cause is identified as desire (*tanhā*); the cure is indicated (ending desire); and the treatment is set forth—the "noble eightfold path." The eight parts of this path are divided into three groups:

> right conduct (*sīla*)—right speech, action, and livelihood;
> right mental discipline (*samādhi*)—right effort to eliminate the unwholesome states of
>   mind and to cultivate the wholesome ones, mindfulness, and concentration;
> insight (*paññā*)—right views and thought. (M I.301)

"Right" (*sammā*) does not mean morally correct but "complete," "comprehensive," or "perfect." Right conduct is not merely a preliminary step to be completed and then abandoned when meditation is finally taken up. Instead, all the components are to be developed together: right conduct alters the unproductive dispositions driving our actions, while meditation works on deeper levels of the mind, and insight works on our cognitive structure that informs the other two. Insight and right conduct are like two hands washing each other: from the observance of right conduct, insight arises, and vice versa (D I.124). The Buddha's teachings contains both a fact- and a value-component, prescribing both an analysis of reality and a course of conduct to achieve an objective. The result of internalizing the teachings is a state in which ego-centered desire is ended—*nibbāna*.[2] A person in such a state is able to live out this life free of mental suffering and will not be reborn.[3] Thereby, the religious disease is cured.

Buddhists thus emphasize suffering, while offering a way out of all suffering. Because the Buddha's concern is only with ending suffering, many philosophical questions are dismissed unanswered (M I.140, IV.431), just as if we were shot with a poisoned arrow we would want an antidote and not answers to who made the arrow, its composition, and so forth (M I.63). Hence, the Buddha did not discuss what happens to the enlightened after death, both because that is not our present concern and because any answer would create a mental image we could become attached to and thus would be a hindrance to the quest. This would also account for the lack of any philosophical ethics in the Buddha's teachings. But the Buddha did set forth an analysis of reality that made his religious prescription appear plausible. According to this analysis, our suffering results from misperceiving the nature of the world: we cut the world up into distinct entities and attempt to manipulate the rest of the world for the advantage of what we take to be our separate self (*attan*)—i.e., we attempt to appropriate nonexistent "things" for a nonexistent "self." But because reality is not so constructed, we inevitably suffer. The elaborate twelve-step scheme of "dependent arising" (*paticcasamuppāda*) shows how this fundamental nescience (*avijjā*) is the root upon which desire (craving and clutching) depends and how this leads to future rebirths. Thus, if we uproot nescience, the entire process of rebirth collapses. No further effort is needed, since it is the nature of things (*dhammatā*) that a person "who knows and sees" becomes free of craving (A V.313).

Nescience is mistaking what is intrinsically impermanent as permanent, what can only bring suffering as pleasurable, what is repulsive as fair, and what is without a self as having a self (A IV.52). Of particular importance is the lack of any self (*anattā*). There is the matter, the feelings, the thought, and the suffering we associate with a "person," but there is no "self" in addition to them to be experienced. In the place of a permanent self, there is a connected stream of impermanent and conditioned elements (*dhammas*) in a continuous chain of rebirths. A rope is made of intertwining short threads, with no one thread extending the whole length. The same holds for a person: the elements are real but no one element lasts a lifetime, let alone through all lifetimes. When we are reborn, there is no soul that passes to a new body but only a karmic residue from our present and past lives that conditions what comes later. We are a functioning whole made of changing parts, like a chariot—the parts are real but there is no "chariot" in addition to them (Mlp 27-28). A "person" becomes no longer a "who" but a "what"—a collection of impermanent things. Such impermanent elements constitute the ultimate components of our experienced world, and thus terms such as "self" and "rebirth" do not refer to any entity in reality. Nevertheless, there is an impermanent reality behind the concepts, and in principle the concepts can be restated in terms of what is actually real (i.e., the streams of *dhammas*).[4] Thus, saying an enlightened person is not reborn means a "stream of elements" is terminated. (This also means that the terms "selfish" and "other-regarding" can be reformulated to reflect what the Buddhists deem real, although the conventional terms suffice to address the moral issues.)

"Right views" are seeing things as they are (*yathābhutam*)—impermanent, selfless, and leading inevitably to suffering (D II.311). By experiencing in this manner, we see persons and objects as no more than the rising and falling flux of substanceless elements, and we overcome the egocentric attitude that gives rise to the craving that in turn would start a new rebirth. Thus, with the fundamental nescience ended, the process of rebirth ends, and "the stopping of becoming is *nibbāna*" (S II.117). Thus, our fundamental misalignment with reality is a matter of cognition and not our will. *Nibbāna* results from an experiential insight (*paññā*) into the impermanent nature of reality—no accumulation of merit nor any meditative experience nor discursive knowledge (*ñāna*) can force the transformation of our cognitive state needed to end suffering. The conceit of "I am" is uprooted only by insight (S III.83-84). With the cognitive basis of unenlightened action destroyed, all the intentions and cravings based upon the error are ended; thereby the chain of rebirths is terminated, and thus the quest to end suffering is accomplished.

Thus, *nibbāna* is not a thing to be attained nor a place gone to nor a transcendental reality—rather, it is simply the state of a person in which the fires of hatred, greed, and delusion are extinguished (A I.38; S III.251). A person who has accomplished this "has done what was to be done, has laid his burden down" (M I.4) and thus there is nothing else to accomplish. Nibbanized persons (*nibbuto*) have internalized the way of seeing informed by the Buddhist metaphysical system. They see that there is nothing to crave and no center of a "person" around which to orient their lives. Sensations still occur, but the enlightened in their state of mindfulness see the factors of the experienced world as they really are—free of any permanence or "self."

Buddhist Metaphysics and Morality

This view of reality as selfless is the fundamental worldview grounding the values and action-guides of the Buddhist way of life. The no-self doctrine, however, has presented some problems for the issue of morality that should be cleared up before proceeding. First, the lack of a core to a person does not mean that there is no actor who acts. Theravāda Buddhism is a form of realism: things exist, just not the way we unenlightened people think they do. A functioning whole person is there, even if there is no real substratum or entity called a "self." All the factors necessary for moral agency are present, and no additional element—the self—is needed. That is, no "being" exist which "has" feelings or discrimination or suffers, but there are the feelings (*vedanās*) and acts of discrimination (*viññāna*) and suffering (*dukkha*) within a constantly flowing chain of elements. This permits the agency needed for the "actor." Second, this doctrine does not mean that there is no reality—another "person"—that the enlightened may be concerned about. Rather, it merely means that there is no permanent, independent, and self-sustaining center to what we conventionally call a "person"—the various series (*santāna*) of impermanent elements that constitute "persons" can still be guided to enlightenment or otherwise helped.

Thus, two important presuppositions of a moral way of life that presented problems for the Hindu traditions previously discussed are satisfied here: there is a moral agent and others to be concerned about. But concern for others does not immediately follow from the no-self doctrine. Nothing in the no-self doctrine or the metaphysics of dependent arising entails that we must be concerned with any other part of reality than our own stream of becoming. The metaphysics does not entail that it is detrimental to ignore other streams of becoming. We can still act "selfishly" (i.e., ignore the other streams of impermanent elements) even if there is no abiding core to anything. (There will be more on this in the next chapter.)

An Ethics of Intention

According to the Buddha, *kamma* (Sanskrit, *karma*) is equated with the motive or disposition (*cetanā*) behind acts done through body, speech, or mind (A III.207, A III.415).[5] We are made up of how our mind directs actions: if an act is committed when one's consciousness is polluted (*paduttena*) suffering follows; if one acts with a calm mind, happiness (*sukha*) follows (Dhp 1-2). This does not mean that the thought of killing is the same as actually carrying out the deed (although the thought itself is also a deed in this view). Rather, if we do kill someone, the degree of karmic damage depends on the intentions and motive behind it—the act itself is karmically neutral. Here, unlike in Jainism, the focus is on the inner dimension—*the intent and motive*.[6] Thus, if the killing is an accident, there is no karmic fruit (*vipāka*) produced that would perpetuate the chain of rebirths (VP III.78, IV.125).[7] Similarly, unwittingly saying something in error is not karmically equivalent to lying. Thus, the more our mind is aligned with nibbanic attitudes—the more "wholesome" (*kusala*) it is—the less karmic damage we do to ourselves. Unwholesome acts (*akusala*) are produced by greed, hatred, or delusion (M I.47) and will always have bad karmic consequences for the actor, regardless of the effect on others. Most importantly, any act committed free of all desire produces no karmic fruit. Thus, mindfulness in actions also becomes important.

The interiorization of *kamma* makes intentions and motives central to the Theravāda value-system, not actions alone. It is an ethics of intention. This makes an inner transformation of the person central. Thus, for serious Buddhists, Buddhism is a matter of character change, not of changing actions alone.

The Quest for Merit and the Quest for *Nibbāna*

An important distinction among the unenlightened is between those who focus directly on attaining *nibbāna* and those who focus on acquiring merit (*puñña*) for their material well-being in this life and a more auspicious rebirth (A IV.34, IV.57). The realm of rebirth (*samsāra*) and *nibbāna* are completely distinct in Theravāda Buddhism, but most practitioners still focus on the former and not on their direct release from rebirth. Thus, happiness (*sukha*) is the accumulation of merit (Dhp 118), although no amount of merit will effect the inner transformation needed for attaining enlightenment. Melford Spiro draws the distinction between "kammatic Buddhism" and the radical "nibbanic Buddhism."[8] The distinction, as Spiro realizes, is not absolute. First, it is not the distinction between the Buddhism of the laity and of the order of monks and nuns (*sangha*). According to anthropologists, even most members of the monastic order today focus on acquiring merit: they realize that the quest for *nibbāna* takes more than one lifetime and do not expect to be enlightened in their present life. Conversely, there are also practitioners among the laity who focus on the quest for *nibbāna*. The accumulation of merit is a step in the direction of the ultimate goal: more propitious rebirths for the long course leading to *nibbāna* are possible by meritorious acts even if merit cannot produce enlightenment. Second, some practices such as giving (*dāna*) may be prominent only in the quest for merit, but many Buddhist practices are common to both quests. In particular, the practice of right conduct (following the *sīla*) and meditation (such as the "sublime attitudes") are common to both, even if those on the serious quest for *nibbāna* do not practice them to acquire merit. Right conduct is not relegated to the first quest and insight to the second. Thus, no absolute dichotomy of paths can be drawn—both groups are heading toward *nibbāna*, even if one is taking the scenic route and one the more arduous direct route.

The distinction is sometimes drawn in terms of actions that produce merit (*puñña*) and those that are "wholesome" (*kusula*), i.e., leading to *nibbāna*. But this distinction too is not absolute. Unwholesome acts are the product of greed, hatred, or delusion (M I.47), while wholesome acts are the opposite (M II.114-15). Unwholesome acts (*pāpa, akusala*) produce demerit (*apuñña*) leading to bad rebirths, while wholesome acts by the unenlightened produce merit. But the acts of the enlightened are also wholesome—indeed, the definition of enlightened actions are those completely free from greed, hatred, and delusion. Thus, the categories of merit and wholesomeness overlap to that extent. However, it must be noted that the criterion for both *kusula* and *puñña* is not moral goodness but what leads to *nibbāna*. The focus of what is "good" remains on the *summum bonum* of *nibbāna* in all key evaluative terms. In fact, "*kusala*" literally means "skillful"—the performance of actions in tune with an enlightened mind. Those are the acts that are "effective" or "productive" in the quest for ending suffering and so should be cultivated. Thus, the *Dhammapada* can state that the essence of the Buddha's teaching is to avoid demerit (*pāpa*), to cultivate the wholesome (*kusala*), and to purify the mind (Dhp 183).

It can be argued that, although merit and demerit are not defined in terms of conduct motivated by other-regardingness or selfishness, they are still ultimately moral concepts because we only get merit for deeds that help others and demerit for deeds that harm others. Thus, "making merit" ultimately means "doing good." Similarly, what is karmically harmful is harmful because it disturbs the mind of the actor (and thus leads away from *nibbāna*), but the mind is disturbed because of the harm one's actions have done to others. Also, the karmically worst actions—killing the enlightened, and so forth—mostly relate to what hurts the greatest number of people in the most important area of ending suffering. Thus, it can be argued that an other-regardingness is ultimately built into the concept of "merit" below the surface. However, even if "merit" and "demerit" could be redefined in these terms rather than in nonmoral terms of what increases or decreases a sense of selflessness (and thus what leads toward *nibbāna*), the problem about to be discussed of the selfish *motive* for acquiring merit would still apply. As Winston King says, combined with the individualism of *kamma* and the doctrine that one must help oneself before one can help others, "the merit doctrine has tended to keep the eye of the ordinary Buddhist fixed on the main chance [to make more merit for oneself] and sharpened to a careful calculation of the merit potentiality of each deed."[9] As he adds, the alternative of the ideal of good-for-itself and love for others has been missing on the practical and ethical plane in Buddhism.

The Code of Conduct

The basic code of conduct (*sīla*) regulating other-impinging actions is in principle followed by all lay and ordained Buddhists. Adhering to it both produces merit and leads the practitioner toward *nibbāna*. These five precepts commend abstaining from (1) directly or indirectly taking the life of any human or other sentient being (i.e., any being that can feel pain), including abortions; (2) directly or indirectly taking what is not freely given or by deception; (3) adultery, homosexuality, and certain other sexual practices (for monks and nuns, all sexual activity is to be abstained); (4) false, malicious, harsh, frivolous, or misleading speech; and (5) consuming any intoxicants. Monks and nuns, more rigorous lay persons, and all of the laity on certain auspicious days also hold various combinations of more precepts—indeed, the basic code of the monastic order has 227 rules.[10]

Buddhists, especially those on the quest for merit, may treat these action-guides as commands that must be obeyed to get merit and to avoid karmic repercussions if they are violated. Or they may treat them as ideals only—there are, for example, Buddhist hunters who know they will incur karmic damage from their livelihood but go on hunting.[11] Similarly, Buddhists, like all other people around the world, often pay more lip service to the value of truth than actually practice it.[12] But for those seriously on the path to *nibbāna*, the fivefold code is a voluntarily adopted set of rules of training encompassing the first division of the eightfold path: right action, right speech, and right livelihood. Thus, occupations that directly or indirectly harm sentient beings—e.g., dealing in arms, slaves, or intoxicants—are condemned. The precepts are the various means by which the unenlightened, who are internalizing the prescribed analysis of reality, can enact this attitude at the level of action and thus help to develop wholesome mental states. Developed in conjunction with the mental exercises and insight, the practice of these virtues aids in rectifying our views and intentions. By restricting actions based on unwholesome attitudes, we begin to weaken greed, hatred, and delusion and consequently to weaken both the sense of a "self" whose interests need to be enhanced and our attachment to sense-objects. Conversely, any self-enhancement feeds self-centeredness, and thus the first step toward any further training is to alter our behavior by not appropriating people and objects for our own interest. Hence, this irony: only by renouncing what appears to be our advantage (killing, stealing, and so forth, to increase the well-being of the "self") is our real welfare advanced.

Thus, the code in context is part of Buddhists' self-development. In itself, it is neutral to the issue of morality: it can be incorporated into a moral or nonmoral way of life since the precepts are matters of abstentions from certain acts—the issue for morality is the motives and intentions for which a person adheres to it. The first four precepts cover other-impinging actions, but the precept against intoxicants (to keep the mind clear) shows that the positive effect on the practitioner is the focus of the code. The longer lists of eight or ten precepts utilized in addition to the initial five—not eating after midday, and so forth—do not contain anything concerning other-impinging action either and thus also show that the intent of the code is to develop a practitioner's state of mind. In short, they are only forms of self-restraint, and the concern is the effect on the practitioner, not on helping others. Thus, if we are abstaining from killing for the wrong reasons (e.g., just to conform to societal rules) rather than to end attachments, then we may gain some merit but we are missing the point of the precept as a means of mystical development. The precepts are of the same nature as "Don't smoke" or "Don't stick your hand in a fire"—they are not divine commands that must be obeyed or the morally right thing to do, but advice on what how to help ourselves, and harm to ourselves will naturally ensue if we do not follow the advice. In sum, following each abstention may well also have positive effects on others, but the central consideration is only the practitioner's own welfare.

But just because this code of conduct is used for self-cultivation does not mean Buddhists cannot also be moral when following it. (That we may have more than one motive in our actions was discussed in Chapter 2.) That is, an other-regarding concern for the people affected by one's action may still be one motive for adopting the rules of conduct, even if the primary consideration is the advantage to oneself. However, the texts of the Theravāda canon make only one's own welfare the reason to adopt the code. The effects of one's actions upon others are of concern only to the extent they adversely affect the practitioner's own mental equilibrium and thus affect one's own quest for *nibbāna*. Consider Winston King's observations on contemporary Burmese Buddhists:

> To kill another being is "bad," *not* because it destroys another living being or disrupts social order, but because it may destroy and disrupt the peace of mind of the killer and cause his rebirth in one of the hells. . . . Evil is evil, bad dispositions are bad, not primarily because of their social effects, but because they disturb and moil the perfect purity and peace of their subject's mind. And a muddled mind cannot achieve Nibbāna. . . . [I]f one can remain neutral in feeling toward the drowning man, neither rejoicing nor sorrowing in the slightest over that man's death agonies, there is nothing *karmically* evil in letting him drown. That is, no evil rebirth will result from refusing to save his life.[13]

Killing may disturb the killer's mind because of the suffering of the victims, but choosing a course of action ends with only the consideration of the effect upon the killer's calmness of mind necessary for his or her own enlightenment. That is, not killing leads toward *nibbāna* because it calms the mind. Why? Because we are not acting selfishly in a situation where another course of action would cement a sense of self—the idea "Because it helps another being" does not enter the picture. Thus, killing is bad only in a nonmoral sense because of its consequences for the killer.

In sum, abstaining from killing and following the other basic action-guides may maximize the welfare of all sentient beings, but in the Theravāda's soteriological way of life the practitioner's suffering is the only relevant concern. If it were the case (which it is not) that killing and stealing could help in one's spiritual advancement, the Theravāda would recommend it. Of course, concern for the victim may not be totally absent from a particular unenlightened practitioner's motivation, but the important point is that the Pāli canon tells a Theravāda Buddhist to subscribe to this code of conduct because it is profitable for the practitioner. The practitioner's own advancement is the only justification offered for an action.

A Buddhist "Just War" Doctrine

Before proceeding, it should be noted that the concern with propagating the Buddhist doctrine leads to a Buddhist justification for killing. The *Mahāvamsa* relates how King Duttagāmani of Sri Lanka undertook a war against the Tamils to spread Buddhism throughout the land and, once victorious, grieved over all the killing he had done. The Arahants assured him that he had been responsible for the death of only one and a half people—one Buddhist and one person who kept the fivefold code of conduct but had not formally become a Buddhist. The rest could be considered demons or beasts and not really human. According to these Arahants, there was nothing negative in killing nonbelievers since the king's *intention* was not to kill but to save Buddhism. In fact, since the war was undertaken for a good cause—a Buddhist "holy war" fought for the sake of preserving the teaching—the killing and other acts of harming were justified and so no demerit at all was produced. Indeed, the monks predicted the king would be reborn as the chief disciple of the next Buddha. (The monks could have argued from a moral point of view that more good was created on balance for all beings by preserving Buddhism, but instead a religious value trumped the moral one. Also notice that the concern expressed in conversations with the king is only with the killer's own karmic fate, not for the victims of the war.) Some Buddhists in Sri Lanka and other countries today hold a similar "just war" view.[14] But this has not been the majority opinion in the history of Theravāda Buddhism, although there have been other wars fought to defend the Buddha's teaching.[15]

Possible Counterexamples

Scholars rely on a handful of passages in the canon to argue that the path is in fact moral. For example, the Theravāda "Golden Rule": refrain from harming others, since you would not want others to harm you (S I.75, V.354). Another passage states that in helping oneself one helps others and vice versa (S V.169). Another states that if an action is harmful to oneself, others, or both, do not do it (M I.415-16; see also A IV.134-35). Or, monks should be constantly intent on accomplishing their own good as well as others' (A II.104, IV.125; S II.29). The canon also states that by mindfulness (*sati*) we protect ourselves and thereby protect others. In addition, it should be noted that today Buddhists in Theravāda countries are typically described as gentle and self-sacrificing.

But the point of such passages is that favoring one's own interests in circumstances where one could help equally both oneself and another would be a case of self-centeredness and thus would not help the practitioner. Treating others equally in those particular circumstances lessens a sense of self. But the benefits to others are not the reason for the practitioner's actions—the practitioner's own welfare remains the operative consideration. That is, one is karmically harmed by favoring one's own interests (*attadattha*) over others' (*parattha*) in circumstances where one can advance both one's own and others' interests (*ubhayattha*) (A IV.134-35, IV.216; M I.415-16). But the Theravāda canon never states that one should put others' interest *over one's own*, as morality would sometimes require.

One never foregoes one's own advantage for another (see Dhp 166 again).[16] Looking after one's own welfare does have the effect of helping others (through not killing, and so forth), but this is only offered as a reason to pursue one's own interests (S V.169)—it does not suggest that one should value others' interests on a par with one's own. Similarly, the rationale for the Golden Rule—that others feel the same way you do—is offered only as a rationale for adhering to the precept against harming others, not for actually helping others or being concerned about them.

If we are looking out for others only as a means to advance our own welfare and are not genuinely concerned for others for their own sake, we are not being moral, no matter how helpful our acts might turn out to be. Any benefits accruing to others when we are pursuing our own welfare are not relevant but are merely a fortuitous side effect. At best, it can be said that it does not hurt to take others' interests into account as long as they do not jeopardize one's own welfare but not that it is necessary (as morality would require). The overriding self-concern is made clear by the vast majority of the relevant Theravāda texts and practices.[17]

The Buddha's Social Teachings

There is more to Buddhist ethics than the basic code of conduct, and these aspects of the Theravāda way of life must also be examined for evidence of other-regardingness. A good place to start is to note that the Theravāda ethos entails an individualism that has an adverse affect on social concerns. All interpersonal activity is, of course, "social" in the sense that more than one person is involved, but there is no emphasis on social concerns in the sense of collective group actions or effects. The canon states four bases for social harmony: giving, kindly and beneficial words, helpful acts, and impartiality (A II.32, IV.218; D III.152). None of these requires more than face-to-face interactions. More importantly, the radical end of suffering can only be accomplished on an individual basis: one can purify only oneself; no one can purify another (Dhp 165). All unwholesomeness (*pāpa*) is produced only by oneself (Dhp 161, 165). Part of this is simply the individualism resulting from the factual belief of *kamma* common also to Hinduism and Jainism: each person is responsible for his or her own condition in the world as a natural product of his or her own past conduct and each person is solely responsible for doing whatever is necessary to improve his or her condition in future rebirths. Each of us is on our own in the quest for merit or for *nibbāna* (with the later qualification of "transfer of merit," as discussed below).

In short, the Buddha's interest was only in the religious interests of the individual (A IV.203). But there are instances recorded in the canon of the Buddha advising the laity on matters unrelated to the radical end of suffering. Most prominent is the Discourse to Sigāla (D III.180-93; see also A III.29-30, IV.56-58), in which the Buddha gave a householder advice on how to use his wealth to maintain his business, to save for an emergency, how to deal with servants and slaves, and so forth. Scholars have questioned the authenticity of these few passages, since the trite recital of bourgeois values is totally out of character with the rest of the canon and the goal central to the Buddha's teachings. Of course, it is possible that these discourses are authentic—they merely reflect a different set of values and interests for those followers who are not seriously set on the path to *nibbāna*. For them, the best the Buddha could say is "save your money and be diligent."[18] But such passages cannot seriously be taken as relevant to the central values of the Buddha's teachings. Spiro notes that the vast majority of Burmese monks consider social service *an obstacle* to the quest for their own salvation.[19] The Buddha recommended avoiding some socially valuable livelihoods, such as being a doctor (D I.12, I.67-69; although Buddhists later ignored that), as interfering with the practitioner's own quest for enlightenment. On the other extreme, any occupations connected to the world of entertainment are also condemned as diverting our attention to a world that fosters fantasies and desires. Worldly values, in sum, simply do not figure in the Buddhist ethos.

There are also instances recorded in the canon of the Buddha advising kings or describing the effect rulers may have on their kingdom (e.g., A II.85). However, social reform was not the intention of the Buddha's teachings on these matters. As Joseph Kitagawa says:

> It was taken for granted by [the Buddha] that the transformation of 'society', which significantly included all living beings, would come only as a by-product of the religious transformation of individual beings in this world. . . . [C]ontrary to the popular notion that the Buddha was a crusading social reformer for the common man against the establishment of his time, there is no evidence that he attempted, directly at any rate, to change society. He seems to have accepted the various forms of socio-political order known to him.[20]

Trevor Ling is mistaken in representing a reorganization of society as one of the Theravāda Buddhist objectives (alongside a reorganization of each individual person's inner and outer life to end suffering). No "strongly developed sense of a need for a Buddhist state"[21] is even indirectly implied in the Theravāda canon. Nor did the Buddha suggest that the kings impose laws or other force on the populace to change their direction toward *nibbāna*. As Richard Gombrich points out, the Buddha in these discourses was not seriously interested in politics but in *the kings'* own self-development and liberation.[22] In the words of Winston King, concerns with political struggles are "the very quintessence of samsāric delusion and its un-Buddhistic pursuit."[23]

The Buddha was not a social reformer but was concerned with reforming the individual.[24] Our calling is to save ourselves, not the world. For instance, the Buddha did not teach against social inequalities, such as the class system and slavery, because it was irrelevant to individuals attaining *nibbāna*. Throughout history, Buddhists in different cultures simply adapted to whatever social conditions they found themselves in. Indeed, the first move of many Buddhist missionaries was to secure their place in the royal courts. This has the effect of legitimating whatever the powers that be. Social harmony, justice, or any other end other than *nibbāna* is not seen as a value and so is not worth devoting energy to. No improvement is worth pursuing in this realm of impermanence and suffering other than redirecting each person toward *nibbāna*. Winston King notes the Buddhist "passive accommodative acceptance" of the traditional cultural patterns and dominant forms of social organization in the countries it has penetrated and adds that "concern for individual and depressed-group freedoms and rights has been almost totally missing from the Buddhist message."[25] As he says: "The Buddhist mandate is not to 'save' the world by 'reforming' it but to enable the individual 'self' to overcome it from within—for the world order is fundamentally unsav-able."[26] What the Buddhists require is "an inner awakening" that can be done "without lifting a finger to change historical-social conditions."[27] There have been a few anomalies in the premodern period—most notably, Emperor Asoka—but a more accurate description of the tradition as a whole comes from Edward Conze: "To reform the outside world is regarded as a waste of time. Once we have reformed our own minds, nothing can harm us any longer."[28] All our energies should be devoted to attaining our own enlightenment, not to rearranging the deck chairs on the Titanic, as it were. In short, the *summum bonum* of Theravāda Buddhism—*nibbāna*—renders social concerns meaningless.

Within the Buddhist monastic order, there are no Hindu classes. (But there is some discrimination: a hierarchy based on age, and ranking all women below all men.) So too the Buddhist laity are outcastes with no classes, but no effort was made to reform the social norms of the world at large. Indeed, the order itself soon ended up owning slaves. Most monks and nuns are not cloistered away in the woods, but they remain detached from the social and political matters of society at large. Even within the order individualism reigns, with each working at his or her own enlightenment. Each monk and nun is to "wander alone like a rhinoceros." In the final words of the Buddha, the monastics are to be "lamps unto yourselves. Take on no external refuge, but hold fast to the teaching as a refuge. Work out your own salvation with diligence."

No matter how social persons are in some respects, from the point of view of the Theravāda worldview, ethos, and religious goal, society is merely an aggregate of individuals, each looking out for his or her own interests. Any benefits for "society" in general would be no more than a secondary by-product gained in the aggregate from each person advancing for his or her own interests. And getting oneself out of the social realm is in principle always the ultimate objective of all of one's actions, even if more mundane matters usually enter the picture. Helping each other in this world is simply not a proper consideration. Nor is there any notion of fulfilling one's role in society as an expression of enlightenment, as in the *Bhagavad-gītā*. In sum, individual self-concern prevails.

Giving

An activity regularly cited as evidence of a moral concern is giving (*dāna*). It, along with practicing the basic code of conduct and some mental development (*bhāvanā*), is the way most lay Buddhists gain merit (see D I.110). It adds a positive activity to supplement the abstentions of the fivefold code, and, like following the code, it provides a means through action by which the laity can reduce a sense of selfishness and attachment. Giving may reveal a freedom from attachment to our possession or even to our body and life, as in the Jātaka Tales.[29]

However, the moral problem is that the central consideration is the accumulation of merit for *the giver* (Dhp 118). Our normal expectation is that giving should be deemed meritorious only if it is done out of real concern for the welfare of the recipient or produces benefits to the recipient regardless of the consequences for the giver. But the Theravāda value-system dictates otherwise. The canon delineates seven motives for giving, the lowest being expectation of rebirth in a heaven (A IV.60-63; see also A III.39-41, IV.236; D III.258). The possible motives include thinking, "It is good to give," and simply following custom. The motives may change as the practitioner develops. The two highest motives are giving alms to calm the giver's mind and to adorn the giver's mind. Each, including the first, leads to a heaven. But none of the motives are other-regarding. None say, "Because the recipient needs it"—only self-serving benefits are recognized.

Among contemporary Burmese Buddhists, Spiro finds giving not to be selfless but to have a soteriological value for the giver.[30] The amount of merit acquired depends upon what is given, how it is given, and especially upon the sanctity of the recipient. Thus, although there are such socially worthy concerns as supporting widows and orphans or building hospitals, they are often slighted in favor of giving to monks engaged in attaining enlightenment, regardless of their material needs. In effect, the Buddhist "begging" becomes an exchange system: the monks and nuns get food and other material support, and the lay giver gets merit for the giving. Some Buddhists also feed secular beggars—indeed, most Buddhist societies are known for friendliness and generosity—but, as Spiro notes, this is *despite* their religious framework.[31] As he says, Buddhists differ very little from people in general, but he must add that many "do not subscribe to all the doctrines of normative Buddhism"—many Buddhist "doctrines are only rarely internalized by the members of these societies, because they are ignored or rejected by the faithful."[32] Since widows and orphans are not auspicious and thus giving to them would not produce much merit, they are of no real value to potential givers. Even the monks themselves can be ignored: any goods given to a monk who is actually impious are still seen as expressions of reverence, not for the monk himself, but for the robe and the monastic order and hence merit still accrues.[33] Spiro notes the irony of this arrangement: the more a monk renounces material goods, the more worthy he is and therefore the more material goods he is given.[34] This can lead to absurd results. (Recall the story beginning Chapter 1.) The monastic order has itself also become a supreme object of giving. Hence, this order of "beggars" has become a wealthy institution, and the members of the laity still thank the monks for accepting their gifts.

It can be argued that giving material objects to people who do not need them shows even greater nonattachment to material things than giving to those who do. Or, it can be argued that from the Theravāda point of view the most effective type of giving for society is donating to the monastic order: since the order preserves and teaches the doctrine of the end of suffering, and, since each person is responsible for him- or herself because of *kamma*, the only way to really help other people is to help the order. A similar rationale can be made for the major donations made to images and relics of the Buddha. In sum, giving to the order helps spread the teaching and thus is more beneficial to more beings that any other kind of giving. But the moral point is that the *motive* of the giver remains the giver's own interests, not the gift's effects (if any). Any concern for the material or spiritual welfare of the recipient, or that of anyone but the giver alone, is not a recognized consideration in such giving. At best, this giving is a simple business transaction in an established exchange system, not an instance of charity or moral concern for the recipient. At worst, it has the effect of using other people as merely the occasions for the giver's merit-gaining—obviously not a moral approach to others. In the words of Spiro, giving "to be sure, has beneficial consequences for its recipient, but it is motivated primarily by the self-interest of the donor."[35] The self-interest central to the unenlightened Theravāda ethos is once again apparent.

The Transfer of Merit

Another practice often cited as an instance of selfless giving is the "transfer of merit" (*patti*): the dedication (*parināmana*) of one's accumulated merit to the welfare of another person. The act of dedication does no harm to its practitioner—in fact, it *increases* merit for the giver since the act of dedication is itself considered a good (i.e., advantageous) deed. Similarly, rejoicing in the merit of another (*pattānumodanā*) produces merit in the rejoicer because of the wholesome mental state—indeed, it produces *greater merit* for the *rejoicer* than the original merit-producing act did for the doer. This is so since it reveals the practitioner's own selflessness. Rejoicing in another's good fortune obviously does not help the other person, but that is not the criterion—acting in one's own interest is.

This practice was not part of early Buddhism, and there is no denying the impossibility of reconciling it with the harsh factual foundations of karmic individualism. This practice represents, in the words of Spiro, a blatant "inconsistency with the entire structure of Buddhism."[36] That is, any actual *transfer* of merit from one person to another would conflict with the absoluteness of individual responsibility for one's own progress caused by *kamma*. Some Buddhists try to reconcile the doctrine with *kamma* by claiming that the merit-donors only *wish* that other people could reap the benefits of their actions—hence the phrase "dedication" of merit—or that the donees *empathize* in the donor's merit.[37] It is the intention of the mental act that counts, not the possibility of a material transfer of merit. In effect, thinking, "It would be nice if I could share my good fortune with others," is itself a good act, since it points the thinker away from selfishness and toward *nibbāna*, and thus itself earns merit for the practitioner even though no others are actually helped. Spiro suggests that the practice may have become popular because the "faithful are incapable of following the inexorability of the karmic doctrine to its logical conclusion."[38] The "more sophisticated" monks realize that such a transfer is impossible, and the "very sophisticated" monks practice the ritual for accomplishing the transfer only as a means of spiritual discipline for themselves.[39]

But despite its conflict with the Buddha's doctrine, the practice has entered Buddhism. And it presents yet another moral problem: acquiring merit for oneself is again the focus of action. The act of dedication may be done to show the practitioner's detachment from merit, to cultivate a productive (*kusala*) state of mind, or some other motive unrelated to benevolence. Spiro provides instances of merit-transfer that are motivated exclusively by self-interest—what clearly is driving the practice is that the donor gains merit by the intention to help others.[40] Thus, even such an apparently generous practice as dedicating one's own merit to others becomes absorbed into the self-interest characterizing the rest of unenlightened Theravāda practice. Spiro mentions this practice as an instance of the larger paradox of giving: a virtue (generosity) comes to exhibit the same properties as the vice it was intended to combat (selfishness).[41]

The Sublime Attitudes

The five self-restraints (*sīla*) and giving (*dāna*) are the first two of a standardized list in Theravāda ethics of ten virtues to be cultivated by habitual action, the others being renunciation, insight, exertion, patience, truthfulness, persistence, friendliness, and even-mindedness. There are other lists of skillful actions (*kusalakamma*), but the role of self-development is prominent in all. The Jātaka Tales illustrate the virtues in action. But meditation is also a virtue, as can be seen by looking at the practice of the four "sublime attitudes" (*brahmavihārās*, "divine abodes"): friendliness (*mettā*), compassion (*karunā*), sympathetic joy (*muditā*), and even-mindedness (*upekkhā*).[42] Each attitude is radiated outward in all directions to all sentient beings. They are not part of the eightfold path. Instead, they are auxiliary meditative exercises primarily for the monastics for concentrating the mind (*samatha-bhāvanā*), not the insight-meditation (*vipassanā-bhāvanā*) essential for enlightenment. But practicing the sublime attitudes may lead to rebirth in the highest heaven (D II.251; M II.76; A II.129). They are also practiced in the enlightened state. The Buddha supposedly stopped a charging elephant by radiating friendliness, but such alleged paranormal powers do not figure prominently in the canonical texts.

However, for those on the path the practitioner's own mental cultivation, not the effect on others, is once again the center of attention. These practices break down a meditator's sense of separation from other beings, but the purpose for doing so is not other-regarding—e.g., compassion toward all beings lessens a sense of self and thus calms the practitioner's own mind. The expressed objective of these exercises is to overcome the practitioner's particular untoward mental states: friendliness is to be practiced by the ill-willed, compassion by those with evil thoughts, sympathetic joy by those who are jealous of others, and even-mindedness by those who lust. That is, the purpose for these exercises is conquering certain unwholesome states of mind and replacing them with ones that lead the practitioner toward *nibbāna*.

But sympathy and other such attitudes are not actions, and other-regarding actions are necessary to be moral. These exercises are not even preparation for other-regarding acts. In the words of Harvey Aronson, in the Buddha's discourses "compassion is never described or prescribed as the motive for social activity."[43] As he says, each practice consists of *wishes* rather than any necessary commitment to actual *action*.[44] There is no impulse to actual moral action. Once again, the concern is the inner development of people. Cultivating such positive attitudes is an "action" under the Theravāda worldview (since all thoughts are actions with karmic effects) but one that only benefits the practitioner. The exercise of compassion consists only of wishing that others be free from suffering; friendliness is merely wishing, "May all beings be happy"; and sympathetic joy is merely taking joy in others' success.[45] But mere identification with the suffering of another is not moral action. Thinking, "We should help the homeless," is not action to help them and thus is not moral action. Even-mindedness is the "complete evenness of mind in perceiving others' happiness or suffering."[46] Such an attitude toward criminals and their victims may help the practitioner, but it may well lead to apathy. As Conze said of the sublime attitudes in general, "on reaching its perfection the social attitude . . . seems to become distinctly asocial."[47]

These attitudes extend the positive feelings that meditators have toward themselves and people close to them to all sentient beings. For example, one begins by directing the same compassion a mother has for her only child first toward oneself and slowly expands until it embraces all beings. But in the movement from emotional attachment to calmness, each person is reduced to, in King's words, "a formless depersonalized 'someone'" toward whom compassion is to be radiated.[48] King concludes that, despite the personal terminology, the practice is impersonal: "these seemingly ethical and personal attitudes, in the process of their universaliza-tion, have almost totally lost their ethical-personal quality."[49] The practices are merely a matter of attitudes, and "persons" are reduced to objects toward which no moral action is exhibited. Thus, these attitudes, as meditative practices, do not contribute to a general cultural atmosphere of concern for others that is ultimately expressed in moral action. Indeed, Aronson, who considers these attitudes moral (without discussing the concept), has to admit that the objects of the sublime attitudes are not affected but the mind of the meditator is protected from anger, cruelty, and displeasure toward others.[50]

The practitioner, as with the other Theravāda practices, is the only beneficiary of concern here. These practices weaken the meditator's entrenched and mistaken view of distinct beings that should be valued differently, and more generally of the values of "better" and "worse." Since these meditative practices work inwardly on our dispositions, it is natural to suppose that they will be expressed in actions outside of meditation in right action.[51] However, since the practice's only purpose is to help the meditator break down a sense of self, the texts do not even bother to state this potential other-regarding effect.[52] Thus, this practice is no more other-regarding than any other meditative technique that is unattached to external actions.

The Monastic Order

The order of monks and nuns has an ample opportunity to help the laity. It is in constant contact with society at large (although some monks are more forest-dwelling ascetics). The order, along with the Buddha and the doctrine, is a refuge for the lay community. Indeed, the purpose of the order is often said to be to advance the happiness of all beings. And the monastics do fulfill a vital role for the lay community: passively as the most effective field of merit (*puññakkheta*) (A I.208) and the exemplars of both proper conduct and the satisfaction of the monastic life (A I.211), and actively as preaching and teaching and as "spiritual friends" (*kalyānamittas*). In fact, teaching and preaching, being a spiritual friend, and preserving the teaching are the most fundamental aid any person can offer another, since ultimately each person must accomplish the end of suffering for him- or herself—you must strive yourself; the enlightened only point the way (Dhp 276). Thus, within this framework of factual beliefs, instructing others is the highest manifestation of other-regardingness. Conversely, the karmically worst actions (along with killing one's parents) are any actions that hurt the propagation of the teaching, i.e., killing an enlightened person, even hurting a Buddha, and causing a schism in the order. The order also involves the practice of giving: the monastics give both their presence to receive gifts and the Buddha's teachings—the greatest gift possible (Dhp 354), since it leads to the end of suffering—in the reciprocal relation with the laity, who gives food to begging monks and nuns and material to the monasteries. In some cases, the monasteries are quite luxurious—hence, the paradox of renouncers living in luxury.

Throughout the order's history, monastics have also performed nonreligious functions for the laity—i.e., services not closely related to leading the laity toward *nibbāna*—often in direct conflict with the precepts of the monastic code governing their conduct. It is not recommended that they engage in this-worldly good works—even an occupation as morally commendable (from our point of view) as being a doctor (D I.12)—because such deeds may become objects of attachment (D II.3). These actions may karmically damage the impinged-upon parties by making them more comfortable in the realm of nescience, thereby rendering them less inclined to take up the religious quest. And since the actions are done by the unenlightened, they may not be effective and only hurt the actor. At best, these acts do no harm and no (real) good.

It can be argued that the monks and nuns should not teach until they are enlightened, since one cannot pull another person out of the mud until one has first pulled oneself out (M I.45). But in practice, unenlightened monks teach the doctrine since the order in general is commended to advise the laity against doing "unwholesome" courses of action, to exhort them to do the propitious, to cultivate the sublime attitudes, to deal with the laity's misunderstandings, and to show the laity the way to the heavens (D III.183). But only the enlightened Buddhists have the proper worldview and dispositions that enable them to help others without attachment. If persons along the path have the desire to teach, their concern is misguided at least insofar as it is directed toward an inappropriate object since there is no real "being." Teaching could therefore be detrimental karmically to themselves and misleading to others in the guidance given. Only the enlightened have totally replaced mistaken views and selfish ends with benevolence and compassion, enabling them to help without any consequences for themselves and others. Enlightenment also enhances the monks' and nuns' merit-value for the giving by the laity.

Thus, it is often argued that gaining enlightenment first is of supreme benefit to others, and therefore the monks and nuns should be focused on their own development. On the path, they are to be "islands to themselves, their own resort" (D II.100) for their own development. Not all monastics are seriously on the quest for *nibbāna*, but for those who are the quest only exacerbates the moral problem. Ironically, the intense quest for freedom from a sense of self heightens the self-centeredness of the person on the quest.

An illustration of the central concern is the disturbing story of a precept of the Buddha frequently cited as evidence of moral concern: "Whoever wishes to care for me, let him look after the sick ones" (VP I.302). This precept was spoken to the monks in response to their actions toward some monks. The latter monks were sick and had been ignored, being left to lie in their own filth in their cells. In one instance, a monk's condition became so bad that the monks carried him out of the monastery and dumped him by the side of the road. The Buddha had to institute the special rule to alter this appalling lack of caring by the monks for their fellow monks. It was *ad hoc*, not following from their basic Buddhist values and goals. The problem was that each monk's concern extended only to himself and to the Buddha (whose teaching was of direct importance to himself) but no further—the sick monks were of no value to the other monks and thus of no concern. Their actions toward the sick monks must be considered immoral. (One can argue that dumping the sick monk on the road was actually helping him because he then could be picked up by others and might receive medical attention. But if that is so, then the monks should have placed all the sick monks outside the monastery. Either way, some of their conduct was not moral in situations where morality would require other-regarding action.) They literally stepped over the sick to get to what they valued.

The Verdict for the Path

Thus, the conclusion for the Buddhists on the path to enlightenment is that the advocated way of life is not other-regarding. Instead, selfishness in the form of looking out for their own religious welfare is the only motive recognized by the tradition, and thus this way of life is not moral. Most Buddhists are not harmful to others or as negative in their actions toward others as the monks just noted. Indeed, most Buddhists' actions of self-restraint and giving may in fact have the effect of being quite beneficial to others, but the Buddhists' indifference to the welfare of others for their own sake requires the conclusion that they are nonmoral.

Only a nonmoral sense of "good" or "bad" is appropriate in describing these action-guides. Actions are "wholesome" or "skillful" (*kusala*) if and only if they lead the practitioner to enlightenment. The values of the path leading to enlightenment are considered supreme and justifiable solely because of that: what is good is what leads to *nibbāna* (i.e., those actions which weaken the sense of "I" and the accompanying cravings), and what is bad is what hinders the quest. No other criterion is deemed relevant—there are no crimes against humanity nor sins against God but only errors that are unproductive or harmful to oneself. In particular, the action-guides are not defended on moral grounds, as would be required if following a code of conduct is to be considered moral.

But it should be noted that just because "good" is defined in terms of what calms the mind or otherwise leads an individual to the end of suffering does not mean that the Buddhist theory of value is merely instrumental or pragmatic. There is a standard of nonmoral goodness grounded in reality: the doctrines that work do so because they are in accord with reality (*dhammatā*); not just anything will do. Thus, the Buddhist value-theory is a form of realism.

A verse from the *Dhammapada* summarizes the Theravāda position: "Let no one neglect his own welfare for the sake of another's, however great" (Dhp 166). Just as no actions may be prompted by purely other-regarding motives (although this will be questioned later concerning the enlightened), so also no self-centered actions may be totally selfish. But the only consideration the Theravāda tradition recognizes for the unenlightened is the practitioner's own welfare. Sally Wang, while reflecting the Mahayāna and Tantric perspectives, gives a fair summary of the Theravāda way of life: "Win Enlightenment for yourself and, while not harming others, do not concern yourself with them."[53] This way of life involves aligning oneself with the way reality actually is, but, again, no harmful results normally accrue to impinged-upon parties—and thus the verdict is that it is the soft sort of selfishness of nonmorality.

Nibbāna and Morality

However, the moral status of *enlightened* Buddhists' actions may fare differently. The enlightened have awakened from the dream of nescience. In the enlightened state, they have reached a state of mindfulness in which they move free of projecting our linguistic concepts unto reality, and thus they no longer create an artificial world of distinct entities. Thereby, all nonexistent "realities" to which they could become attached have disappeared, and the sensory world remains "as it really is" (*yathābhutam*). The enlightened are freed from a sense of "I" and all the motives of greed, hatred, and delusion accompanying it (S III.127-28). All greed and hatred are ended, since these motives rest upon the delusion that there is a distinct self whose interests take priority; and with all attachments ended, suffering ends. Just as the enlightened eat whatever is offered in their begging bowls, not judging its worth or taste, so too do they accept all experiences. The nibbanized person seeks nothing and thus is free. One is permanently in a state of calm even-mindedness, both concerning whatever happens to oneself and in seeing all beings impartially.

Is there anything about such a state of a person that rules it out as being moral? A few objections can be dismissed easily. First, it is often objected that the mystical point of view is monistic and therefore there is no room for moral reflection.[54] It is true that during the trances (*jhānas*) that prepare the mind for the enlightenment-insight there is no mental space differentiating oneself from other realities, and thus there is no mental space available for moral or any other type of reflection. But the enlightenment-experience in Buddhism is not of that nature: it is a mindful insight into the nature of reality made while the mind's sensory and conceptual activity is occurring. In the subsequent enlightened state, reflection and the consideration of alternatives are possible. The Buddha's ability to use language is evidence of this. Also, his ability to adjust his teachings according to the capacity of his listeners (A I.10) entails that he was not an automatic machine spewing out at random words and phrases memorized before his enlightenment. This means there is also the mental space necessary for moral reflection.

A second objection is that the enlightened are "beyond good and evil" and thus not interested in the welfare of others. An enlightened Buddhist is beyond the sanction of *kamma*, freed from merit and demerit (S II.82; Dhp 39). The enlightened can, without any karmic repercussions, do any deed that for the unenlightened would produce the merit or demerit that perpetuates rebirths—their acts are neither "black" nor "white" (A III.384; M I.389-91), i.e., free of karmic bad or good fruit. Therefore, they can undertake any action. No course of action is binding. No act is bad *per se*—only the motivations for doing it are good or bad. And the personal intention (*cetanā*) that is *kamma* has been replaced with even-mindedness. This can lead to indifference to others. The enlightened have internalized a perspective from which deeds motivated by personal concerns are impossible—i.e., they do not have the factual beliefs permitting an evil (selfish) act—but beyond that they have no restrictions but only freedom and so are beyond moral good and evil. They may be moral or nonmoral, however they choose.

To reply to this requires two steps. First, as discussed in Chapter 6, we can maintain both other-regardingness and disinterest at the same time. Thus, we can combine compassion (*karunā*) toward *others* with even-mindedness (*upekkhā*) toward *ourselves*. Personal detachment need not involve an indifference to the needs and concerns of others but instead may involve a truly impartial concern for all (S I.206). For the unenlightened, complete impartiality is impossible, since without even-mindedness being completely internalized some people are valued more than others. But the enlightened can be totally impartial. Impartiality is compatible with compassion since it is only a matter of treating all people equally. That is, being personally detached, and thus not treating some people with favoritism, does not mean being unconcerned for people. In short, the enlightened can have a dispassionate inner life and yet still perform moral actions.

Second, if we equate "good and evil" with merit and demerit, then the enlightened are obviously "beyond good and evil," since they are beyond the sanction of *kamma*. But this still leaves the *moral* issue, since morally "good" does not equal "merit" and morally "bad" does not equal "demerit." They cannot act selfishly (since the factual beliefs for that have been ended), but the enlightened still act and thus will have some specific value-system. Some argue that the absolute ontological gap between the world of rebirth (*samsāra*) and *nibbāna* leads to a break with all worldly values.[55] The Buddha presented his teaching as a raft to be jettisoned once we have attained enlightenment (M I.134-35). He presented a type of prescriptive metaphysics, a way of looking at reality to achieve a certain end—here, to end suffering—and was not interested in an intellectual account of reality independent of the religious objective to be achieved.[56] In addition, the Buddha was willing to teach conflicting doctrines to different listeners, depending on their stage of development. For example, he told some that there is no mental development and others that there is (A I.10). Thus, the beliefs and code of proper conduct and other action-guides of the unenlightened life are merely a means to an end—*nibbāna*—and are of instrumental value only. Hence, they are totally superseded in the enlightened state. The unenlightened action-guides are not ultimate, nor ends in themselves, but merely the means to transform the practitioner to a new state and then to be discarded. Indeed, the values of the unenlightened state are an obstacle to be overcome by insight and the deconditioning of meditation.[57] *Nibbāna* is beyond this world (*lokuttara*) and so are its values.

To the opponents of this "transcendency" thesis, there is a continuity of values from the unenlightened to the enlightened state, and thus at least the code of proper conduct will govern the enlightened Buddhists' actions, even if merit no longer accrues for following it.[58] Right conduct alone does not bring enlightenment, but this does not mean the enlightened state is beyond its precepts. Enlightenment is the final, complete internalization of Buddhist beliefs and values. Thus, the code of proper conduct and insight still remain inseparable (see D I.124). The enlightened still hold to the eightfold way—indeed, only they really fulfill it.

However one wants to interpret the parable of the raft—do the enlighten jettison all the *factual beliefs* held on the path, or some of them, or do they just hold the standard Buddhist beliefs in a new way?—nothing in the Pāli canon suggests that the *values* and the *code of right conduct* are jettisoned. Instead, it states that the enlightened cannot violate the code or do any act based on greed, hatred, delusion, or fear (A IV.370, V.232; D III.133; M I.256). They are incapable of killing (D III.235) and in general have the highest degree of virtue (D I.174, II.217; Dhp 217). Thus, the most natural interpretation is that the enlightened have internalized the values they have been cultivating on the path and thus that these values now form the value-framework for their enlightened lives. That is, the enlightened would then follow the precepts naturally and automatically, without consideration of whether an action is good (productive) or bad (harmful) for themselves (see M II.25-27). They are beyond any conflict of proper and improper conduct and beyond rule-following, and thus they are beyond the rules of ethics in that sense but not beyond the content of the rules. The only difference would be an effortlessness and spontaneity in action acquired from fully internalizing a point of view and a set of action-guides.

However, even if the unenlightened values of Buddhism still reign in the enlightened state, this does not end the issue of whether the enlightened are *moral*, as critics of the transcendency thesis think. It only means that we have identified *the action-guides* followed in the enlightened state. As should be clear by now, simply having action-guides does not make a person moral. The issue is why a person follows those action-guides. Thus, we still must examine the motives and intentions of the enlightened to see if they are other-regarding and hence moral.

The Fully and Completely Enlightened Buddhas

There are three categories of enlightened beings: "fully and completely enlightened Buddhas" (*sammāsambuddhas*), who enlighten themselves without teachers of the complete path and who show others the path; Solitary Buddhas (*paccekabuddhas*), who also enlighten themselves without teachers but who do not show others the path; and Arahants ("worthies"), who enlighten themselves by following those who teach the entire path. Each has escaped the chain of rebirths, as the basic formula for Arahants states: "Destroyed is rebirth; destroyed are the influxes from attachment (*āsavās*); lived is the highest life; done is what was to be done; laid down is the burden; and there is no future existence" (e.g., M I.184). Because each has "done what was to be done," they now do not have to do anything. They cannot act selfishly (since the cognitive basis of selfishness is destroyed), but do they have to be other-regarding rather than indifference to others? Consider first the fully and completely enlightened Buddhas.

In the Pāli versions of his enlightenment, Gotama the Buddha is portrayed as having doubts about the value of teaching the doctrine that leads to the radical end of suffering because he worried that people would not understand. But, after being entreated by the *deva* Brahma to lead others to enlightenment, he finally decided to take up the life of a teacher out of compassion for the unenlightened (D II.36-39; M I.13, I.21, I.168-69; S I.136-38; VP I.5). The Buddha's course of action was freely chosen—he had "done what was to be done" in attaining enlightenment, and there is nothing in any way that he had to do. He was beyond the sanction of *kamma* and therefore could have elected not to help others without incurring any karmic harm in any manner. But out of his great compassion (*mahākaruna*) for other beings, he elected to help. Other-regarding dispositions had replaced any unenlightened self-centered ones. He voluntarily undertook a restriction on his actions for the sake of others, a restriction which he could also have renounced at any point since he was free. This led, according to the Buddhist tradition, to forty-five years of nothing but totally selfless activity helping others.

The important point of these accounts for the issue of morality is that the Buddha's enlightenment did not automatically produce a life of other-regarding action.[59] That is, becoming selfless does not necessarily give rise to a concern for others. Instead, Gotama had *to choose* to be actively concerned with others' welfare. Thus, at the end of the Buddhist path, there remains a choice—neither the path of the unenlightened way of life nor the enlightenment-experience compels the enlightened to adopt a moral way of life. The enlightened have to choose, and Gotama's decision to teach and his subsequent actions were clearly moral. He choose to teach, not out of a sense of duty, but out of compassion and sympathy (S I.206). He focused on only religious matters rather than material needs (since, from his point of view, that is all that really matters), but he was nonetheless other-regarding. In fact, his course of action appears to be totally altruistic since, from his point of view, he had absolutely nothing to gain by following it or to lose by refraining from teaching and yet he engaged exclusively in helping others. In contrast to his followers on the path, the Buddha was genuinely compassionate, not someone who used compassionate states of mind merely as a means to further his own ends. Such actions also showed a much more active concern for others than merely remaining an example for others to follow or receiving alms. He acted solely for other people's sake (or, more accurately, for the sake of other streams of conditioned elements). Granted, he was being moral in teaching a selfish way of life, but based on his beliefs this way of life was in the best interests of his listeners.

The Solitary Buddhas

Scholars often attempt to justify the unenlightened Theravāda way of life as a selfish means to a moral end—i.e., after one's own enlightenment, one can lead others to the end of suffering.[60] Thus, the moral thing to do is to devote yourself exclusively to enlightening yourself first and then to help others—thus, the self-centeredness of the path is morally justified. However, the problem with this position is that, while enlightened Buddhists may opt for a moral way of life, they need not: the path and enlightenment do not guarantee the enlightened must adopt a moral way of life.[61] All enlightened Buddhists have the option to do nothing for others. This can be seen in the lives of the Solitary Buddhas. They epitomize the "self-interested ascetic."[62] The epithet of the Arahants—"wandering lonely as a rhinoceros"—is better applied to the Solitary Buddhas, since they live separately from society (although some are said to live together in their own communities). They will follow the abstentions and restrictions on their conduct of the code of conduct (*sīla*). They will refrain from harming other sentient beings, but they do not perform any positive other-regarding actions. Thus, when it comes to the crucial fork in the road of whether to teach the way to enlightenment or not, fully and completely enlightened Buddhas take the moral fork and the Solitary Buddhas take the other.

Commentators centuries after Gotama, perhaps seeing the moral problem, did modify the doctrine of the Solitary Buddhas. They ascribed certain minimal moral practices to these Buddhas. Thus, in order to remove suffering, some Solitary Buddhas may beg for alms, thereby permitting the exchange arrangement involving merit. Or some may also teach elementary aspects of the doctrine (perhaps by example or gesture only, not by word), although they do not teach the entire path to enlightenment. However, the significant point is that the option remains for these enlightened Buddhists not to engage in any other-regarding action. There is nothing inherent in the Theravāda way of life or enlightenment-experience that requires the enlightened to be moral. The Solitary Buddhas may not have plumbed the deepest depth of the doctrine (as have the fully and completely enlightened Buddhas), but they have "done what was to be done"—they have escaped the chain of rebirths, and that is all that matters. They may remain in the forests doing nothing to aid others. Since according to the tradition Solitary Buddhas only exist when there are no fully and completely enlightened Buddhas in the world, they would be opting for a course of action that is not other-regarding at a time when their teaching would be especially valuable.

Thus, the Solitary Buddhas reveal that the Theravāda tradition provides a nonmoral option for the enlightened. They may remain indifferent to the welfare of others, and thus the self-centeredness of the path to enlightenment cannot be indirectly justified as leading to a necessarily moral way of life. However, the option of becoming a Solitary Buddha highlights the morality of the choice Gotama and the other fully and completely enlightened Buddhas made to help others.

The Arahants

The goal of the Theravāda way of life is not to become a Buddha but for a follower to become enlightened following the Buddha's teaching—an Arahant.[63] There are both lay and monastic Arahants (A III.451; M I.490), but lay Arahants must then join the order (VP I.15-20). Once they are enlightened, they too have "done what was to be done," but the Buddha exhorted them to go forth and lead others to deliverance by teaching the path, for the benefit of the world, out of compassion for the world (A I.167-68; D II.119; M I.45, I.167-68; S I.38, I.105, I.131-32; VP I.21; see also Dhp 158). Their welfare is secure, not varying with the reactions of the persons upon whom their actions impinge. But if compassion moves them, their teaching will not bind them (S I.206). In the Theravāda tradition, the Buddha is the one person who came to be for the welfare of the world (A I.22; M I.21), who out of compassion helps beings to the "other shore." But the Arahants can opt to help too, and those who do are moral. Their actions, as with the Buddha's, would be done solely for the benefit of others. Thus, the Arahants who choose to redirect "people" (i.e., streams of becoming) toward enlightenment by teaching and advice, by example, and by making themselves available for the laity for merit-making gifts are engaging in other-regarding actions and thus are moral. Again, this is not the objective—ending the practitioner's own suffering is. They have accomplished that and now must decide how to spend the rest of their last life. But the actions of the Arhants who opt to teach are, like those of the fully and completely enlightened Buddhas, clear instances of wholly other-regarding actions. They choose to do more than simply following the restraints of the code of proper conduct—they are doing positive acts for others.

But the Buddha's recommendation to help the unenlightened was only a recommendation—the Arahants do not have to do so. The majority may well have chosen to help, but one example of an alternative will suffice: suicide. There is an recorded incident of a mass suicide of monks during the Buddha's life.[64] (Some Solitary Buddhas, including Matanga, the last one before Gotama, are also said to have committed suicide.) The Buddha criticized the unenlightened who committed suicide, for it revealed disgust with their present body and an attachment to another (M III.266; S IV.59). Such an act produces negative karmic consequences. Thus, there is a precept against the unenlightened committing suicide (VP III.82; see also Mlp 195-96). The situation, however, is different in the case of the enlightened. For example, Godhika committed suicide when, due to a painful disease, he was unable to maintain the calmness and concentration necessary to maintain the enlightened state.[65] (Two other monks who also suffered from painful diseases, Channa [M III.262; S IV.55] and Vakkali [S III.119], became Arahants at their death from suicide.) But he had no attachments to his life or to a future life. Thus, his suicide was not condemned by the Buddha, although it took the life of a sentient being, because it was done with no craving and so was karmically neutral (S I.21). He was not trying to escape pain; that would have been a desire. Instead, killing himself was the only way to end the interference to maintaining his enlightened state. The act of killing is itself neutral if done without (unenlightened) personal desire, and thus his suicide is completely consistent with the Theravāda doctrine.

These suicides cannot be taken to be other-regarding actions in any manner. Because of the physical condition of these suffering monks, no doubt they could not have taught the laity, but if they had chosen to live they could have been exemplars of enduring pain for the monks and laity on the path to enlightenment. Thus, enduring the suffering would have been other-regarding. Moreover, if they were not yet enlightened, they will have laid the foundations for becoming enlightened in the next life and thus would then have led a life of great value for others. But such other-regardingness is not a consideration in the Theravāda tradition. The monks would have had to go on living in an unenlightened state, and that is rejected. If they were enlightened, they were not acting "selfishly" (since that was no longer an option), but they were not acting other-regardingly either. They were simply indifferent to everyone, including themselves.

Conclusion

The conclusions are that the Theravāda path to enlightenment is pursued for selfish reasons unjustified by a concern about the effect of one's actions upon others, and the enlightened may or may not choose a moral way of life. Because the enlightened have the option not to be concerned with the welfare of others, the enlightenment-experience and subsequent state cannot be deemed necessarily moral.[66] Consequently, the path to the enlightened state cannot be indirectly justified as moral by arguing that it leads to a necessarily moral way of life. Therefore, the way of life of self-cultivation commended by the Theravāda remains essentially selfish and thus not moral. The self-centeredness of the path may occasionally produce immoral actions (as with the monks' indifference to the welfare of the sick monks), little effect for others (as with Solitary Buddhas walking away), or beneficial effects for others (from the absence of harming when following the code of right conduct to giving for making merit), with also some bizarre results (building dormitories for monks precisely because they will not live in them). Thus, the final verdict has to be that the prescribed Theravāda way of life is basically nonmoral, with being moral a very real option available in the enlightened state after a life of self-concern on the path.

The problem is not, as in Advaita Vedānta and the *Bhagavad-gītā*, with the factual beliefs but with the *central values*. The Buddha's first sermon after his enlightenment reveals the problem: there is no mention of compassion but only of self-cultivation to end one's own suffering. The majority of the enlightened may in fact opt for a moral way of life, but the logical significance of the opportunity not to do so cannot be denied. Similarly, the majority of the unenlightened

Buddhists may be warm and giving, but the only doctrinal reason for being so is self-service. They paradoxically combine an ethos of generosity with one of concern only for oneself. (Some contemporary Burmese Buddhists note the selfishness of their fellow believers, attributing it to the Arahant ideal.)[67] Some scholars may wish to bypass the logical point and argue that since becoming an Arahant is the Theravāda ideal goal and since the Buddha *commended* the Arhants to be moral that the Theravāda way of life is therefore moral. But the fact remains that some enlightened ones who are nonmoral—at least the Solitary Buddhas—are part of the Theravāda tradition. It is not as if these Solitary Buddhas are a few rogue antinomians who are misbehaving by disobeying the required norms—they are as much a part of the tradition as the fully and completely enlightened Buddhas. They reflect core beliefs and values. Some critics may wish to play down the significance of the Solitary Buddhas, but the danger with such a maneuver is that of imposing modern values onto a classical tradition. That is, we may wish to dismiss those elements of a religion that conflict with our sense of morality and then conclude that the tradition is in fact moral. Obviously, such reasoning is blatantly circular. Instead, we should accept the tradition as it is, not pick and choose elements based on a preconceived Western view of what must be the case.

However, for the fully and completely enlightened Buddhas and those Arahants who opt for a moral way of life, the completeness of their moral actions should be emphasized. Their acts of compassion for the unenlightened can be called acts of love, not in the sense of being attached to another's happiness in any way, but in the sense of giving oneself completely to others without regard to possible personal consequences. The only philosophical issue in such circumstances is whether the concept of "morality" can even apply when *all* their actions are *purely* moral. (This will be discussed in Chapter 13.) But the important point is that their acts are still purely other-regarding, regardless of whether the concept of "morality" is applicable.

Notes

1. The abbreviations for Theravāda Buddhism will be: A = *Anguttara Nikāya*, D = *Dīgha Nikāya*, Dhp = *Dhammapada*, M = *Majjhima Nikāya*, Mlp = *Milandapañha*, S = *Samyutta Nikāya*, and VP = *Vinaya Pitaka*.

2. Two types of desire must be distinguished: ego-centered (*tanhā*) and wholesome (*kusala-chanda*) (A III.440). The latter includes the desire for enlightenment. (Thus, one begins the quest for enlightenment by *adding* a desire.) Even the enlightened can have wholesome desires. (Other-regardingness should be classified as "wholesome," since it is not self-centered.)

3. Feelings from physical pain still occur in the lives of the enlightened (S II.82)—the Buddha himself experienced pain (A I.27; S I.174). But for them the craving or other emotional reactions are no longer generated because of the change in their way of viewing the world.

4. Restating everyday statements into statements about what is actually real may not be as easy as this, if the logical positivists' failure at trying to restate scientific statements in terms of only sense-experience is any indication. But this problem can be bracketed for the issues at hand.

5. The concept of *"cetanā"* is connected to the concept of a person's dispositions (*sankhāras*). See Keown 1992, pp. 213-21 (although his translation of *"cetanā"* as "choice" may be too oriented toward a discrete event rather than, as he says, the total posture of the personality, both cognitive and affective).

6. Other factors also figure in the karmic evaluation of an act. For example, killing an enlightened person or a parent is worse than killing someone not as worthy (D I.85), and killing a human being still brings worse karmic consequences than killing another sentient being.

7. See W. King 1964, p. 120, for all the necessary conditions for an act to be considered a "killing" in the karmic sense.

8. Spiro 1982; see also W. King 1964. For criticism, see Aronson 1979, Keown 1992, pp. 83-105.

9. W. King 1964, p. 56.

10. The rules of training for the order have been as many as 250 for monks and 348 for nuns, but the standard regulations number 227. These differ in character from the fivefold code of conduct in that they are enforced by the monastic order to keep the order pure while the only sanction for not fulfilling the *sīla* is *kamma*.

11. Hunters often give heavily to earn merit to counteract this demerit. Buddhists, like all religious people, also have rationalizations for their killing. For example, fishermen argue that they are not killing the fish—they are just taking them out of the water, and the fish die on their own. When killing rats or mosquitoes for health projects, Buddhists often claim the animals earned their fate by their past karmic deeds and so the Buddhists are not doing anything wrong. Some Theravādins justify killing animals by arguing that they are actually helping them along to their next rebirth and thus shortening their time until they are enlightened.

12. Gombrich 1991, pp. 307-8. It should also be noted that the homicide rate in Sri Lanka is one of the highest in the world.

13. W. King 1964, pp. 72, 127, 159.

14. See Bartholomeusz 1999.

15. The more standard Theravāda position is that a soldier who is killed in battle will be reborn in a hell or as an animal (S IV.308-9), and a killer gets killed in turn and a conqueror gets conquered (S I.185). Victory breeds hatred, and the defeated live in pain, while the peaceful who give up victory and defeat live happily (Dhp 201).

16. An act which benefits others but causes one *material* harm is not unwholesome (M I.342). That is, if one puts one's own material welfare above others, one will be karmically harming oneself and thus not looking out for one's own real welfare.

17. A common position is that the dichotomy between self-regard and other-regard does not exist and that it is a "constant theme" of the Theravāda texts that "he who protects himself protects others; he who protects others protects himself" (Reynolds and Campany 1975, p. 500). But that is difficult to support from these few passages, especially when they can so easily be interpreted to fit with the overwhelming thrust of self-centeredness in the Pāli canon. Similarly, a later Theravāda text, Buddhaghosa's *Vissudhimagga* (I.34), discusses different foci of attention that a practitioner of the code of conduct may have—focusing on oneself, others, or the Buddhist doctrine. But these foci are not the motives for the actions—one does not follow the code for the sake of others, any more than

for the sake of the Buddhist doctrine. Concern for one's own welfare remains central.

18. The canon also records worldly reasons for the laity to follow Buddhist practices, such as the five benefits from practicing the code of conduct—wealth, good reputation, self-confidence in public, a peaceful death, and a rebirth in a heaven (D II.85-86). But it is hard to argue that these are the point of the Buddha's teaching.

19. Spiro 1982, pp. 289-90.

20. Kitagawa 1980, p. 87.

21. Trevor Oswald Ling, *The Buddha* (Baltimore, Md.: Penguin Books, 1976), p. 20. Ling's interest in Marxism may have colored his perception here.

22. Gombrich 1988, p. 81. He realizes that some scholars disagree with him (ibid.).

23. W. King 1989a, p. 25.

24. Gombrich 1988, p. 30.

25. W. King 1989a, pp. 24-25.

26. Ibid., pp. 25, 26.

27. Ibid.

28. Edward Conze, *Buddhist Thought in India* (Ann Arbor: University of Michigan Press, 1967), p. 110. See also Saddhatissa 1970, p. 149.

29. The Pāli Jātaka Tales portray the Buddha in his previous lives as a Bodhisatta as giving up everything—including all his possessions, his limbs, his body, and his wife and children—out of compassion for the well-being of all beings and for the attainment of enlightenment. (The texts carefully avoid saying that he was doing this to accumulate *merit*.) For example, in one tale he offers his body to a hungry tigress out of compassion for her, for the good of the world, and for his own attainment of Buddhahood—not a standard phrase in the Pāli canon for acts of giving by the followers. In addition, the tales involve only worldly aid, such as food, which is of only temporary help under the Buddhist worldview. Thus, the tigress would be hungry again, but the Buddha-to-be advanced toward enlightenment. These tales may reflect genuine other-regardingness. Reasons are given for why even giving his wife and children to an ogre helped *them*. (Otherwise, giving away another person could not possibly be moral.) But these moralizing folk tales are not in keeping with the goal of the unenlightened in the Theravāda tradition, i.e., becoming an enlightened follower (i.e., an Arahant) rather than a full Buddha. They conform more with the ethos of Mahāyāna Buddhism, where the Bodhisattva emerged as an goal for practitioners and where these tales have remained more popular.

30. Spiro 1982, p. 411.

31. In India, hospitals (including those for animals and birds) that would appear to be built for quite other-regarding concerns are called "places of merit" (*punya-shālā*).

32. Spiro 1982, pp. 10, 11. The difference between "normative" and "actual" religion may be no greater than in Theravāda countries than in Christian or other countries but is nonetheless real.

33. Ibid., p. 410.

34. Ibid., pp. 413-14.

35. Ibid., p. 106. He adds the example that, when he was attending a monk's funeral, he was passed a bottle of soda water. Since he was not thirsty, he did not drink. But his companion asked if he would nevertheless drink so that the sponsor might acquire merit. He states, "The water was not so much intended to quench the thirst of the participants as to provide merit for their benefactor."

36. Ibid., p. 127.

37. See the comments in Gombrich 1988, pp. 125-26.

38. Spiro 1982, p. 127.

39. Ibid., p. 125.

40. Ibid., p. 106.

41. Ibid., p. 105.

42. These four practices also appear in *Yoga Sūtras* I.33. However, as in Buddhism, they are "generally valued as aids to self-discipline and do not provide a motive for acts of mercy or active help of others. What is more, these positive feelings are to be transcended, along with all the negative or impure tendencies or feelings, in the state of *samādhi* [one-pointed concentration], which is the culmination of the yogic discipline" (Jhingran 1989, pp. 132-33, 177). (The last sentence reflects the fact that the Sāmkhya-Yogins focus on the depth-experience of enlightenment.)

43. Aronson 1980b.

44. Aronson 1980a, p. 64.

45. Ibid., pp. 64-65.

46. Ibid., p. 65.

47. Edward Conze, *Buddhist Thought in India* (Ann Arbor: University of Michigan Press, 1967), p. 90.

48. W. King 1980, p. 60.

49. Ibid., p. 64.

50. Aronson 1980a, p. 54.

51. There are passages in the Buddha's discourses on "simple compassion" (*kāruñña*) unconnected to meditation (A III.192-96, IV.186-90; M I.167-69; S I.136-38, II.199-200), but these remain separate from the passages about the sublime attitudes and thus cannot be used to justify their moral standing—in fact, there absence only reinforces the conclusion that these meditations are not related to action. Aronson does use these passages as justification for social action (1980b, pp. 3-4). But this everyday reaction to others does not seem to have had the effect on the Theravāda laity and monastic order that it had in the Mahāyāna tradition (as discussed in the next chapter). Genuine compassion is central to the Buddha's enlightened life, but self-cultivation is central to the followers'.

52. See Aronson 1980a, pp. 51, 54, 57, 64. Aronson adds that there is no instance in the Pāli discourses where a practitioner is stated to affect another person's *attitude* beneficially (p. 51).

53. Wang 1975, p. 145.

54. For the most developed version of this objection, see Danto 1987.

55. See Tachibana 1926; Bastow 1969.

56. See R. H. Jones 1986, pp. 56-58, 84-88.

57. The Mahāyānists and Tāntrikas also raise the issue of whether rigidly holding on to a set of action-guides designed for those still in the realm of nescience might be taken as absolutizing that realm. In support, it can be noted that in the Jātaka Tales, the Buddha-to-be is portrayed as breaking all the five precepts except lying, as he used his skillful means to lead the unenlightened toward *nibbāna*. More on this in the next chapter.

58. See Gudmunsen 1971; Keown 1992, pp. 83-105.

59. The flowering of the Buddha's compassion in the enlightened state may be caused by the preenlightened moral vow he had undertaken many lives before to help others. That would not bode well for the moral status of the Solitary Buddhas and Arahants who did not take that vow.

60. E.g., P. D. Premasiri, "Ethics of the Theravada Buddhist Tradition," in Crawford, ed., 1989, p. 47.

61. The fact that the process of enlightenment may take up many lives is also a moral problem: one spends a long series of lives in selfish self-development and is left with comparatively little time in one last life to help others. There is a problem even if the process only takes up most of one life: one is still being selfish with little time left to be other-regarding. There is what is derisively called "*mañana* Buddhism" (K. Jones 1989, pp. 201-5)—that first we should heal ourselves and put off any work to help others only to after our own enlightenment. That is, first devote one's life (or lives) entirely to one's own enlightenment—no matter how long it takes—because only then will one have the proper point of view to help others effectively, even if there is only a little time left actually to help.

62. Kloppenborg 1974; Wiltshire 1983.

63. Today some Theravāda monks have opted for the path of becoming a Buddha and thus to remain in the chain of rebirths to help others rather than to aim for becoming an Arahant. See W. King 1964, pp. 234-35. This is no doubt under the influence of Mahāyāna Buddhism, and it remains totally out of character with the worldview and ethos of classical Theravāda Buddhism.

64. See Wiltshire 1983, p. 124.

65. Some later commentators try to get around the idea that an enlightened being—an Arahant—could actually take a life by saying that Godhika attained arahantship just *after* he began cutting his throat. But if Godhika did not have the desirelessness needed to be an Arahant, what would be the difference between his act (whenever it began) and an ordinary unenlightened suicide? The act itself is neutral only if the actor is free of personal desires (*tanhā*).

66. The basic Theravāda precepts do appear to be universalizable since they are not tied to one group—they can apply to conduct toward, and by, non-Buddhists. However, a few problems do arise. First, the precepts are meant to be advice for our own well-being, like "Don't smoke," and not absolute rules. This in itself does not mean they are not universalizable, but as discussed in the next chapter some Buddhists may make exceptions out of other-regarding concern for others. Second, the "deadly sins" of Buddhism tie more demerit to deeds harming the propagation of the Buddhist doctrine (e.g., killing the enlightened or even harming a Buddha) and one's own parents and thus do not value all people equally. The story of King Duttagamini of Sri Lanka discussed above also suggests that Buddhists do not always value all people equally.

67. Spiro 1982, p. 63. King notes the "ethic of aloofness," while noting that Buddhists may be loving, gentle, and helpful (King 1989b, p. 143).

9

Mahāyāna Buddhism

The moral criticism leveled against the Theravāda tradition in the last chapter is nothing new. Buddhists of the Mahāyāna tradition (the "Great Way" or "Greater Vehicle") labeled the Theravāda, along with certain other schools that now are extinct, "Hīnayāna" (the "Small Way" or "Lesser Vehicle") precisely because of its emphasis on a self-centered concern with one's own spiritual advancement. The last chapter merely confirms their judgment. The Mahāyāna schools instead place Bodhisattvas, with their concern for others, centrally in their religious ways of life. The different Mahāyāna schools, however, are not uniform on the Bodhisattva doctrine, and the discussion here will be based mostly on the early Perfection of Insight (*Prajñāpāramitā*) school of India, Shāntideva, and the Zen/Chan schools of East Asia, with a few asides to other schools.[1]

The Bodhisattva

The Bodhisattvas are beings set on becoming Buddhas.[2] The Theravāda tradition recognizes them, but its goal is to become an enlightened follower—an Arhat—not to become another Buddha. The Mahāyānists, however, produced a new ideal by valuing a genuine concern for the welfare of others in their quest for enlightenment. Indeed, the Mahāyāna ethos is a 180-degree shift in moral orientation. One objective is still to end our own suffering by attaining *nirvāna* for ourselves, as with the Hīnayānists, but a new concern has been added: to go further and become a Buddha to help others end their suffering too. Thus, they make the great vow of a Buddha-to-be who through many lives helps others attain enlightenment. To quote the standard fourfold version:

> However innumerable sentient beings are, I vow to save them;
> However inexhaustible the binding passions are, I vow to extinguish them;
> However immeasurable the Buddha's Dharma is, I vow to master it;
> However unsurpassable the Buddha-way, I vow to attain it.

(By "saving beings" is meant that the Bodhisattva establishes them on a path to the end of rebirths.) A simpler formulation reveals the centrality of both their own goal and their compassion for others: "I surrender my all to promote the welfare of others and to attain complete and perfect wisdom." Bodhisattvas commence their careers with the sincere determination during meditation to attain Buddha-wisdom (*bodhicitta*), thus fixing both a concern for others and the attainment of a Buddha's knowledge in their way of life. Both ends are achieved at once: the Bodhisattvas' own welfare is not neglected, but they place a concern for all other sentient beings as centrally in their way of life as their own welfare. They will become enlightened (i.e., attain *nirvāna*) first but will forego their own private postmortem *parinirvāna* in order that they may be reborn again and again to save other beings and to attain the "complete and perfect wisdom" (*bodhi*) of a full and complete Buddha.

The distinctions between *nirvāna*, *parinirvāna* (the enlightened's state after death), and *bodhi* are important. The Bodhisattvas first attain their own enlightenment (*nirvāna*), thus enabling them to attain release (*parinirvāna*) if they so elect. Only after that enlightenment do they take the great vow to renounce release in order to help others by teaching or in other ways and to attain *bodhi*. Bodhisattvas thus have not yet attained the *bodhi* of a Buddha. But they are not disturbed by the mental fluxes caused by hatred, greed, and delusions—they have attained the tranquility, concentration, and even-mindedness of a nirvanized state of mind.[3] When Bodhisattvas attain *nirvāna* and consider the depth of the Buddha's wisdom, they may be inclined toward carefree inaction and not to demonstrating the Buddhist doctrine—after all, to use a Mahāyāna metaphor, a Bodhisattva is to a fully enlightened Buddha what a grain of sand is to the earth—but they elect to persevere (8PP 304). Moreover, while they could remain delighting in the bliss of the "blessed rest," free from rebirths, they would still bear in mind all suffering beings (8PP, p. 47). But the Bodhisattvas vow that when they attain *nirvāna* (and thus could be released from the chain of rebirths) they will forego their own release and remain in the realm of rebirths for the sake of other sentient beings.[4] This reaction is totally at variance with the value-system of the Hīnayāna schools—indeed, there even the Buddha was not reborn but entered *parinirvāna*.

Freed from suffering themselves, the Bodhisattvas will remain in the realm of suffering for countless eons solely to help others. The earliest strata of Mahāyāna texts restricts the help to establishing beings in one of three paths to the end of suffering—the Buddha's, the Solitary Buddha's, or the Arhat's—and to "maturing" them by means of positive acts (such as examples of selfless action) once they are on the paths. The four means of conversion (*samgraha-vastu*) are giving (especially the gift of religious teaching), kind words, helpfulness, and consistency between their words and deeds. Bodhisattvas will instigate others to observe the wholesome (*kushala*) types of actions (8PP 325). Bodhisattvas will become a shelter, refuge, and place of rest to all sentient beings trapped in the realm of suffering (8PP 294). In some schools, they vicariously take on the suffering of other beings upon themselves, or create heavens (Buddha-fields or "pure lands") for others, or use their merit to help others attain release. All of this reveals an evolving shift in beliefs away from one's own effort in attaining release ("self-help") toward the help of others ("other-power"), eventually in quite theistic terms.[5] The Mahāyāna texts do not discuss suffering to the extent that the Pāli texts do, but its presence is just as keenly felt (e.g., 8PP 28)—that is what produces the Bodhisattvas' compassion.

The roots of all the major Mahāyāna doctrines can be found in earlier schools and there remain major points of continuity between the two sets of schools, but Mahāyānists elevated compassion (*karunā*) to an equal status with insight (*prajñā*) as the two chief virtues. This infuses a moral concern into their way of life. The shift in ethos from the Hīnayānists' self-interest to the Mahāyānists' compassion is epitomized in a revision to the *Dhammapada*. The Theravāda version states that the essence of the Buddha's teaching is to avoid demerit (*pāpa*), to cultivate the wholesome (*kushala*), and to purify the mind (Dhp 183). Mahāyānists replaced the last phrase with "to save many beings." They also always group the Hīnayānists' Solitary Buddhas and Arhats together as being selfish. Mahāyānists fault them for focusing on their own salvation—getting themselves out of the realm of suffering—while the whole world suffers. Early Mahāyānists did accept that the Solitary Buddhas and Arhats were enlightened and out of the realm of rebirth, but the doctrine did develop that *all* sentient beings would eventually become full and complete Buddhas, and thus Solitary Buddhas and Arhats were not in fact out of their chain of rebirths but only in a temporary repose.[6] (The idea of universal salvation does not arise for Hīnayānists, since the focus was only on oneself.)

In sum, there is a reorientation of values away from exclusive self-concern to at least an equal concern for others. This compassion is enough to conclude that this way of life is moral. Granted, the Bodhisattvas are helping themselves in their own quest for a Buddha's supreme wisdom, but one need not be solely other-regarding to be moral. Nothing in these texts suggests that the Bodhisattvas are merely using others for their own end—they must help others to attain their goal, but they are also genuinely concerned with the welfare of others (as discussed below).

A New View of *Karma*

Besides the shift in ethos, a major innovation in factual beliefs permits a revolutionary new way to implement other-regardingness: the enlightened after *nirvāna* can opt to remain in the realm of suffering and even control where they are reborn. The enlightened Bodhisattvas can truly be in the world but not of it, since they are beyond the sanction of *karma* and so can control their rebirths to choose ones that are most helpful to others. Under the standard law of *karma*, such control is not possible: the law of *karma* dictates where one is reborn, and once a person has ended desires or nescience he or she is no longer reborn. Thus, those who achieve *nirvāna* are not reborn at death but achieve *parinirvāna*, and there is nothing they can do about it. If that doctrine is true, Solitary Buddhas and Arhats cannot be morally faulted for not doing the impossible. (Of course, the unenlightened could *renounce* attaining *nirvāna* for themselves and thus remain unenlightened, suffering through rebirths for the sake of others, but that would blatantly conflict with the Hīnayāna value-system.) Arhats do not have the vestige of a sense of self, as Mahāyānists accuse them of, by making a distinction between their own salvation and that of others—that is just the way reality is according to the standard doctrine of *karma*. But Mahāyānists modify the *karma* doctrine: they now claim control over their rebirths once they are beyond the sanction of *karma*.[7]

This new factual belief irrevocably distinguishes the Mahāyānists from the Hīnayānists: Bodhisattvas now opt not only for a new goal (attaining the Buddha's wisdom) but expand their capacity to help. The Hīnayānists' ideal—the Arhats—now seem unnecessarily selfish: the Arhats actually *opt* for the personal serenity of freedom from rebirth when they could have opted to remain in the realm of suffering for the sake of others. Their choice reveals both an attachment to a personal state (or alternatively "clinging to the Void"), and, more importantly, a lack of compassion for others. Thus, within this worldview the Mahāyānists rightly see the Hīnayānists as selfish.

Compassion and Insight

Compassion (*karunā*) and insight (*prajñā*) become the two bases supporting the Bodhisattva's quest for a Buddha's wisdom. They are the twin foci informing the value- and belief-components of the Bodhisattva's way of life.[8] They are interlocked in the Bodhisattva's development: insight internalizes a worldview that reinforces the disposition of compassion, and compassion gives expression to the worldview through action. Compassion is both the beginning of insight and its highest expression. Compassion, in short, is insight in action. In the words of Nāgārjuna, great compassion (*mahākarunā*) is the instantiation of wisdom (*bodhisādhana*). Enlightened Bodhisattvas are not attached to the defiled world because of their insight, nor to *nirvāna* because of their compassion. They thus dwell unattached in the world doing acts that help others.

Bodhisattvas begin with a sense of compassion for all beings as victims being led to slaughter. They wish that the pain of every living being be completely cleared away (BCA III.7). From Shāntideva: "Whatever happiness there is in the world arises from the wish for others' happiness; whatever suffering there is in the world arises from the wish for one's own happiness" (BCA VIII.129). Shāntideva also advanced a version of the Golden Rule: "When fear and suffering are hateful to myself as well as to my fellow beings, what justification is there that I should protect my own self and not others?"[9] The Bodhisattvas equate themselves with others (*parātmasamatā*) or exchange themselves with others (*parātmaparivartanā*). (See BCA VIII.95-96, 120, 129-30.) But for Mahāyānists this thought prompts actions for other beings, not merely abstentions from harming them. The Bodhisattvas' meditation expands from themselves to their loved ones, to neutral people, to enemies, and finally all beings, identifying each as having once been their mother in a previous life. But compassion is not merely a meditative exercise for self-cultivation, as with the Theravādins—it manifests itself as actual action helping others. Bodhisattvas perform acts as a mother loves her children. But this compassion for others is free of attachments and thus is combined with impartiality and even-mindedness—it is not a matter of emotional identification of the suffering of others through pity but of an emotionless, active concern for the welfare of all. The ideal compassionate person is like a skilled physician rather than a fellow mourner.[10] In short, the result is nondiscriminating compassionate action for all.

Does this impartiality involve treating oneself as one among equals or disregarding one's own welfare completely? The unenlightened would start with a sense of self and (as with the Golden Rule) with how they would want themselves to be treated. Only later would a sense of self drop out of the picture. Later Mahāyāna texts, unlike the early *Prajñāpāramitā*, also dropped all reference to oneself, and thus any self-regarding motives (*svārtha*), in formulating reasons to be compassionate—only another's welfare (*parārtha*) remained as a concern. Indeed, in the words of Shāntideva, "no other activity is fitting for Bodhisattvas except working for another's interest." (Even though they are thinking only of others, this nevertheless advances the Bodhisattvas' own welfare.)

How do the Bodhisattvas help? They are interested in relieving all suffering, so the unenlightened ones give material aid (i.e., this-worldly help rather than leading beings to *nirvāna*). For example, Buddhist monasteries in China had hospitals, orphanages, and homes for the elderly. They did everything from feeding the poor to building roads and digging wells. (But as noted below under "Social Action," Buddhist teachers do point out dangers when the unenlightened provide such help.) Once Bodhisattvas are enlightened, they are incapable of doing any acts that would harm their quest for a Buddha's wisdom and are only concerned with helping others. They thereafter focus on religious matters since the best way to end others' suffering is to end it completely through their becoming enlightened. This involves teaching the path, being an exemplar for the unenlightened to emulate, and establishing beings in one of the ways to the end of rebirths (e.g., 8PP 300, 322, 325, 333). The enlightened will have perfected insight and thus be able to see what people really need and how best to achieve it. Thus, only they should teach; otherwise, it is a case of the blind leading the blind. That is, prior to enlightenment, unenlightened (selfish) desires—including desires for one's own enlightenment and to help other "beings"—would taint their teachings and so only after enlightenment should Bodhisattvas concentrate on teaching. Then they can even-mindedly educate an infinite number of beings, expounding both the letter and meaning of the doctrine (8PP 105).

The insight (*prajñā*) that is the other base of a Buddha's wisdom is, as with the Theravāda, seeing the three characteristics of reality: that constructed things are impermanent, that there is no self, and that everything inevitably involves suffering. But while Theravādins emphasize the impermanence of constructed things, Mahāyānists shift the focus to the no-self doctrine. That is, even the parts of constructed things have no "essence" or "substance"—no "self-existence" (*svabhāva*). Just as a person has no "self" or "soul" but is only an ever-changing collection of parts (a body, feelings, and so on), so too all the parts are void of any "own-being"—i.e., they are empty (*shūnya*) of self-existence.[11] Nothing has its own independent "nature" or "support." Nothing exists by reason of itself. Nothing is "real" or "objective" in the sense of having its own permanent, independent source—everything arises and falls based on conditions, and thus there is no multiplicity of self-contained "real" things. In some Mahāyāna schools, emptiness was raised into an ontological ground like *brahman* in Advaita Vedānta—the Void (*shūnyatā*)—but in the early *Prajñāpāramitā* literature all that emptiness means is the absence of any reality differentiating one thing from the rest of reality. Things have no "mark" or "sign" (*nimitta*) that sets them apart from the rest of reality. There is no thing to attach a name to. Words—"there is," "there is not," "a being," "a *dharma*," "*nirvāna*"—do not denote any independently existing entity.[12] (To treat the concept of "emptiness" as itself a "sign" of something real would only reveal our lack of understanding.) As the *Prajñāpāramitā* literature puts it, who sees reality correctly does not "course in signs" (*nimitta-carati*) but "courses in the signless." Thus, a Bodhisattva realizes that thinking, "I am a Bodhisattva," is coursing in signs: no entity is denoted by the word "Bodhisattva" (8PP 11-18), only a stream of selfless, conditioned elements (the *dharma*s).

Insight is merely seeing reality that way, i.e., seeing reality free of separate "real" entities (and thus seeing the ultimate unreality of our conceptualized entities) and seeing the presence of the rising and falling of conditions as described in the Buddhist formula of "dependent arising." Insight penetrates the elements of reality (the *dharma*s) as they really are. With the insight-experience, nothing has changed: ontologically, reality is as it always has been. Insight thus is simply seeing the flux of reality as it really is, free of our conceptual boxing of what is there into a plurality of distinct and independent entities. It involves a state of mindfulness in which sense-experience is freed from the normal confines of conceptualization. It is directly experiencing reality free of the discrimination (*vikalpa*, *samjñā*) caused when we reify our mental images and concepts into distinct entities and project them onto reality. In sum, it is the mind functioning as a mirror of what is really there, not adding to, distorting, or judging what is in fact real. In this state, one does not value any person—including oneself—more than any other. With insight, we see that reality does not consist of a set of objects to which attachments can be formed. With no fixed points for attachment, the mind becomes calm. Sense-experiences still occur, but we react only to what is really there. Without the idea of independently existing "things," no acts of will (*cetanā*) arise (8PP 358). Thus, emptiness ends all the mental processes that give rise to *karma*. In short, the enlightened still think, feel, speak, and act but without "discriminating" separate self-contained entities. They now can act with compassion free of the idea of independent realities.

It is important to note that the Mahayāna metaphysics is realistic: it does not deny that there is a reality independent of the experiencer but only that there is no set of ontologically distinct *entities* to apprehend or "settle down" in—no kind of multiplicity of existing or nonexisting things to grasp or desire. (As discussed in the last chapter, the Theravāda's metaphysics is also realistic, but it stresses the reality of the *dharma*s.) The configuration of things we call "a chair" is real and still supports us even though it is empty of any permanent core—it exists, just not in the manner we unenlightened folk think. Of most importance, such emptiness includes any independently existing experiencer. Those who have perfected insight see that there is no basis for treating the elements of reality as "real" entities—thus there is no idea, name, conception, or conventional expression connected to them (8PP 177).

In sum, that things are empty of anything giving them self-existence does not mean that they are literally *unreal*. Emptiness stands in the middle between permanence and nonexistence—there is a "no-thingness" to reality (no separate, self-contained entities), but not "nothingness" (lack of existence). Reality is just such as it is (*tathatā*), void of differentiating substances. There is no "thing" for the mind to grasp hold of. What is real is likened, as in Advaita, to a dream, a magician's illusion, a mirage, clouds constantly forming and reforming in the air, foam, or an echo: something real is there but we mistake it for something it is not—an entity existing in its own right, independent of the rest of reality (e.g., 8PP 38-39, 512-13). Mahāyānists sometimes describe reality as "nondual" (e.g., 8PP 265) because of the lack of substances that could differentiate one thing from another. But this term might be confused with the nonduality in Advaita Vedānta. The distinction in Advaita is between the depth-mystical reality (*brahman/ātman*) and the "dream" realm, while in Buddhism the distinction is between parts of the "dream." Any possible "depth-reality" does not play a role in the *Prajñāpāramitā*.

Language and Paradox

Thus, the emptiness of reality must be understood properly. If a "person" is standing in the middle of a "road" with a "car" bearing down on "him" or "her," the "person," "road," and "car" may all be empty of their own substances, but what is there will still have a terrible (but equally empty) "collision" if the "person" does not move. There is "suffering" even if there is no "sufferer" or a real thing called "suffering." These quotation marks indicate the problem any language presents: our concepts do not correspond to anything real (i.e., a self-existent entity). What happens, however, is that the unenlightened get caught up in their web: we divide the world up into distinct entities designated by words, and end up grasping for the words' nonexistent independent, permanent designations. In short, we respond to the mental images we ourselves create rather than to what is real.

Naming thus has a central role in the problem of desire. But this also presents a problem for teaching the path to the end of desire. If all naming "marks" off objects but reality has no "marks," then all of language is fundamentally misguided. All terms for "beings" and "objects" only designate dreams and illusions—mere words that designate nothing "real" (8PP 475). Thus, the *Prajñāpāramitā* literature repeatedly states that the Buddha's doctrine cannot be talked about, or that we cannot properly express the emptiness of all the elements of reality, or that it is not possible to write down the perfection of insight (e.g., 8PP 240-41, 348; DS, p. 36). The texts do reconcile the fact that so many thousands of words are said about the perfection of insight by arguing that the enlightened do not "course in signs." That is, words designate impermanent configurations of elements or selfless elements and not anything permanent. Thus, the enlightened know that the words do not denote any distinct and independent realities, but they can still use any conventional terms to discuss matters with the unenlightened. Enlightened Bodhisattvas thus can speak without discriminating realities, i.e., without projecting categories onto what is real to create an unreal world of multiple entities. Emptiness, in short, ends the reification of concepts (*prapañca*). Thus, the enlightened can speak of the great way without transgressing against perfect insight (8PP 25). They can also use language to get around in the world in general without thinking in terms of existent referent.

This theory of language leads to paradoxes: on the one hand, the Mahāyānists want to deny anything is real (when "real" means "independently existing entity"), but on the other hand they want to admit that there is some reality there (when "real" means a conditionally arising, empty reality). Thus, the texts deny that anything real is designated by the word "Bodhisattva" and then blithely turn around in the next sentence and talk about what a Bodhisattva does (e.g., 8PP 18). It is a common formula in the *Prajñāpāramitā* literature that Bodhisattvas do *x* while stating that they have no idea or conception of *x*. Conversely, if they think, "I am enlightened," then they are not enlightened. The literature goes so far as to say that the Buddha was silent (because nothing real in the first sense is designated by his words) although he obviously spoke. Or, there is nothing to understand in the Buddhist doctrine (because there is nothing real in the first sense to be grasped) (8PP 38). Thus, the enlightened can say, "I am enlightened, and yet it does not occur to me 'I am enlightened'" (because there is nothing real in the first sense that is enlightened) (see DS, pp. 43-44). Or, *nirvāna* is not different from *samsāra*: since neither term designates anything real (in the first sense) they cannot be either different from each other or the same.[13] These paradoxes would evaporate if the Mahāyānists rejected the first prong of the dilemma and simply denied a theory of language that requires that referents of terms must be independent, permanent, self-contained realities rather than impermanent, temporary configurations.[14] They could then simply stick with the second prong and restate all the alleged paradoxes in consistent, if complicated, terms. But the texts do delight in paradoxes, perhaps for their soteriological shock value for getting us out of our routine frame of mind.

Metaphysics and Morality

Such paradoxes also raise an issue for whether Mahāyānists are moral. The problem is: how can one be genuinely other-regarding if there is no *being* to be compassionate toward? If everything has no substance and is no more than an illusion, what is there to be moral about? How then can Bodhisattvas, with their insight perfected, both see there are no persons and yet with their compassion still not abandon them? To quote the paradox from the *Prajñāpāramitā*: "Countless beings should I lead to *nirvāna* and yet there are none who lead to *nirvāna*, or who should be led to it" (8PP 20). Or from the *Diamond Sūtra*: "All beings must I lead to *nirvāna* . . ., and yet, after beings have thus been led to *nirvāna*, no being at all has been led to *nirvāna*" (DS, p. 25). Conversely, how is murder even conceivable when there is no *person* to murder or to be a murderer? Āryadeva, a Mādhyamika Buddhist, argued precisely that while holding his bleeding stomach as he was dying from an assassin's stab wound.[15] Indeed, Shāntideva realized the problem: there is no demerit in killing a phantom; and, if there are no beings, for whom shall we feel compassion?[16]

How can the paradox of seeing no beings and yet not abandoning them be resolved? The problem would vanish if we again reject the prong of the dilemma that equates "real" with "an independently existing, permanent entity." There is something not totally unreal that arises conditionally and that can be directed to the end of suffering.[17] There may be no self-existent centers of suffering (no "beings"), but there is something (streams of conditioned elements) toward which compassion is possible. Thus, the "beings" are there, just not as we "foolish common folk" imagine. Moreover, these realities also have the nature of a "person." That is, we may love (in a nonmoral sense) objects, but we can have *compassion* only toward a reality having the nature of a person. But the impersonal elements constituting a "person" have the interior life (including suffering) that make other-regardingness an appropriate response. Thus, Bodhisattvas can internalize compassion without a sense of permanent, independent entities—precisely as the rest of the passages from the *Prajñāpāramitā* texts quoted in the last paragraph state (8PP 20-21; DS, pp. 25, 57-58). Therefore, Buddhist metaphysics concerning the reality of a "person" does not present a presuppositional problem for the practice of morality: there is in fact a reality to what we conventionally call a "person" whose interests and feelings can be taken into account when "we" decide how to act.

Thus, Bodhisattvas can develop their compassion, directing it first toward beings in the unenlightened sense, then toward impersonal events, and finally (when enlightened) toward empty realities and thus no "object" at all. They are then compassionate without "coursing in signs" and not conscious of any "beings." It does not occur to a man conjured up by a magician when looking at an audience to think, "I will please these people," but nevertheless he performs his work; just so, it never occurs to a Bodhisattva who courses in insight to think, "Having known enlightenment, I will set free the world!" but nevertheless he works in various rebirths to save beings (8PP 439-43, pp. 57-58). Similarly, giving is perfected when Bodhisattvas see there is no "giver," "recipient," "act of giving," "gift," or "reward"—the reality of what happens does not involve any self-contained realities but only realities that arise and fall conditionally. Terms such as "I," "beings," and "*nirvāna*" become mere conveniences that can be reformulated in principle more accurately in terms of the empty, impersonal elements of the experienced world (the *dharma*s).

A similar problem arises with respect to values. "Goodness" too is not "real" but "empty" (not self-existent). All valuations of "good" or "bad," "pure" or "defiled," are equally empty. They are not just terms defined relative to each other (as Nāgārjuna argued) but are groundless. Free from "dualistic" ideas of independent entities, the enlightened have no likes or dislikes but are even-minded toward all. Nothing is "dear" or "not dear." They see all beings the same (*samatā*). A mass murderer and a saint both arise the same way and are equally unreal. But if all is "unreal," then so is "compassion"—so why be compassionate? Indeed, "suffering" and "*nirvāna*" are unreal, so why act in any particular way at all? And how do we decide what to do? If a Bodhisattva makes a distinction between observers of the code of right conduct (*shīla*) and those who are not—or between the enlightened (who do not need help) and the unenlightened (who do)—he or she is "coursing in signs," seeing multiplicity where there is none (8PP, p. 69). If all "discriminations" of value are foreclosed, is not all ethics impossible?[18]

But again things are not as bad as they seem. Even if all values are empty of their own self-existence, because of the nature of reality some values still work for getting to *nirvāna* and some do not. That is, values are real in the second sense discussed above even if there are no independent, permanent realities. So too Bodhisattvas do make "discriminations" in the usual sense—they simply do not project them onto reality into distinct, self-existent realities. Seeing the suchness (*tathatā*) of reality does not mean that Bodhisattvas as a rule drink poison rather than water—they see what is really there and act accordingly. Similarly, they make value-distinctions in the usual sense without reifying concepts into substantive entities. Compassion remains the master value; Bodhisattvas merely do not discriminate it as a distinct entity. They do not try to advance "the good" as if it were a distinct reality that must be addressed. Instead, they see reality as it really is, see what people's real interests are, and act in ways that really help them (as defined by the Buddhist belief-claims).

One discrimination enlightened Bodhisattvas do not make is to value themselves more than others. They have no reason to treat themselves differently from how they treat others. Their suffering is not morally distinguishable from any one else's (see BCA VIII.90). They think of others in the same way they think of themselves, and thus self-interest (svārtha) and other-interest (parātha) become synonymous.[19] They need not deny themselves: helping others here, unlike in the Hīnayāna, is helping oneself (since a Buddha's wisdom [bodhi], not just their own release through parinirvāna, is their goal), and that requires a genuine concern for others. Thus, they work for the welfare of all, not just themselves. Upon completing the cultivation of insight, the focus of self-interest is gone, and the last vestiges of selfishness disappear. But this does not mean that Bodhisattvas then believe others are "real" and they themselves are not—they see all beings, including themselves, as equally empty of self-existence.

Most importantly, Bodhisattvas can still "discriminate" different empty "persons," even though they now do not see any self-existence. Thus, a type of holism often attributed to all Mahāyānists—"self = others = universe"—does not hold. Bodhisattvas do not see a "gift," a "giver," and a "recipient" all as one thing, but only as all equally empty of self-existence. The nonduality of emptiness simply means there is no plurality of self-existent entities, not that the universe is a monistic whole or even interconnected in an organic way. Each series of elements (santāna) constituting a "person" is conditioned and empty of anything permanent, but it is still not identical to any other series. Bodhisattvas can "discriminate" individuals for other-regarding attention without coursing in signs and without treating persons as impersonal parts of some cosmic whole. Most importantly, one's welfare is not interdependent with another's. Salvation remains individual: Bodhisattvas can lead some people to nirvāna before others—not everyone must be enlightened all at once or none can be. (If self = others, only one Bodhisattva would ever need to get enlightened, since that would automatically enlighten everyone; or, conversely, the unenlightenment of one would keep anyone from ever becoming enlightened.)

Many scholars jump from the doctrine of emptiness and the doctrine of dependent arising to a holism without realizing that the former does not entail the latter.[20] That is, they jump from the dependence of elements within a stream of becoming to the conclusion that there are no streams at all but only an interdependent whole and that our existence is dependent upon, or identical to, that whole. Just because everything arises dependently (i.e., nothing exists independently) does not mean everything is dependent upon everything else—distinct streams of becoming are still possible. The Hwa-Yen school does advocate a holism. The central image of its Avatamsaka Sūtra is Indra's net: a net of jewels in which each gem reflects every other gem—thus, all the jewels are "in" each jewel, and each jewel is "in" every other one. However, not all Mahāyāna schools have such a holism. Moreover, even if there were such a holism, morality—a concern for the other parts—would still not be entailed. Any actions for preserving the other parts may only be enlightened self-interest. For example, killing could still be justified: just as we may cut off a cancerous leg (a part) to save the body (a whole), so too we may need to kill a person (e.g., Hitler) to save the rest of a larger social or natural whole. That the leg is "not different" from the whole does not save it—indeed, it is precisely because it is integrated into that particular whole that it must be cut off—and the same could equally apply to that person within society. Thus, choices of what to do still remain, and a moral concern is not dictated by the holism.

Shāntideva argued that it is just as reasonable to be concerned for other "persons" now as it is to be concerned for the welfare of one's own "self" in the future since there are no real "persons" at all (BCA VIII.98). So too there is no "owner" of suffering but only the suffering, so why should we not be working to eliminate the suffering of others (BCA VIII.102)? But by that reasoning we might as well focus only on our own suffering—all suffering is the same, after all, and there is nothing magical about the word "theirs." Morally, however, there is a big distinction. Even if there are no self-existent selves, there are different conditioned "persons," i.e., different series of becoming (santānas). Shāntideva did accept that we can distinguish "beings," and thus the future "me" and the present "others" are distinguishable, even though none have a "self." And the concern for one's own stream of conditioned elements is not "other-regarding"—i.e., the suffering in one's own stream is not morally the same as the suffering in another's. Thus, the difference between our series of conditioned elements and those of others is morally significant: concern only for "our" future suffering over that of other present "beings" remains "selfish." In short, one must still choose to be other-regarding even if there are no selves.

Deducing Value-Systems from Factual Claims

The last point highlights the problem of trying to deduce a value-system from a set of factual beliefs: compassion does not necessarily follow from the doctrine of emptiness.[21] There may be no self-existent selves, but an "actor" can still look out for the interest of his or her particular stream of dependently arising and falling elements (santāna) and thus be "selfish." Seeing everything "as it really is" does not mean that concern for our own stream of becoming must melt away or that we automatically become concerned for other streams of becoming. We can still opt to maximize our own pleasure in the realm of suffering as much as we can—that there is no independently existing entity called a "self" to satisfy and no permanent "things" to crave does not change this. Similarly, we can still be simply indifferent to the welfare of the other streams. Thus, we cannot go directly from the doctrine of emptiness to the conclusion that we must be compassionate. As Paul Williams says, if we can distinguish at all between ourselves and others—and Mahāyānists accept this, even if there are no real "selves"—then we can give priority to ourselves.[22] He adds: "there is no contradiction whatsoever in accepting as true a teaching of no Self (anātman)—even seeing it directly in the fullest possible way—and being selfish."[23] In short, why I should not be selfish is simply not answered by the no-self doctrine.[24] Mahāyānists accept different persons—different streams of becoming—even if there are no permanent cores to reality, and that is enough to permit either selfishness or other-regardingness. Neither selfishness nor morality is required. After enlightenment, the moral choice remains open. This leads most Mahāyānists (unlike the Hīnayānists) to emphasize that each enlightened person must decide, like the Buddha did, to act upon their newfound insight and actually help others. (The Yogācāra believe that compassion flows automatically from enlightenment, but they have to explain away the Solitary Buddhas' nonmoral choice.)

The problem can be illustrated by a thought Bodhisattvas cultivate on the path: "Each and every being, throughout the beginningless series of their lives, has at some point protected me with kindness, just like my mother in this lifetime, and will do so again in the future." Kindness toward all beings is supposedly to follow from this thought. But by the same logic, each and every being has killed you or tortured a loved one or done some other harm to you over the infinite course of your rebirths. This may generate hatred and revenge. Only by making the separate value-choice to forgive and help does the moral conclusion actually follow from the factual statement. In short, a value-choice is not dictated by metaphysics.[25]

But emptiness can ground compassion: seeing everything as equally impermanent and transitory (and subject to suffering) can lead to detachment and can let an impartial concern for all flow forth. But that separate value-choice still must be made if we are to be morally concerned with others. If the simplistic approach to the issue of the relation of morality to factual beliefs were correct, it would follow from the emptiness doctrine that there is no reality that can be harmed or killed and so we could not but follow the precept against killing no matter what we did. Indeed, nothing we could do would in principle violate any of the Buddhist precepts. But then again the argument cuts both ways: there would also be no "selves" to help either, and so we could not be other-regarding either. A variant argument is that under the Buddhist analysis of reality there is no person to hate or with whom to be angry. That is, what exactly do you hate—the hairs, the skin, or what? All that is there are the impersonal elements of reality. Thus, we should only be compassionate toward others. But the problem with that conclusion is again that by the same logic there is nothing to be compassionate toward. What are we to be compassionate toward—the hair, the skin? Loving-kindness thus is as groundless as hatred. And if we accept that there is a reality (some configuration free of permanent realities) toward which we should be compassionate, then by the same reasoning there is a reality we might hate.

In sum, selfishness and other-regardingness are simply two sides of the same coin: if one is not possible, neither is the other; if one is possible, so is the other. A *nonmoral* value-system would follow from Buddhist metaphysics, if value-systems could be deduced from metaphysics. Emotional detachment and indifference is all that would follow from these factual beliefs, not any compassion, let alone compassionate action. But values are not deducible from facts, and a value-choice still must be made. And Mahāyānists made a moral choice.

Virtues

The virtues Bodhisattvas cultivate must be seen in light of both insight and compassion. Insight explicitly governs the virtues and compassion implicitly does. The six basic virtues are: giving (*dāna*), proper conduct (*shīla*), patience (*kshānti*), vigor (*vīrya*), concentrative meditation (*dhyāna*), and insight (*prajñā*).[26] Giving includes both material gifts (e.g., food to the poor and medicine to the sick) and the supreme gift—religious teaching and guidance to individuals or groups.[27] It is any giving to help end the suffering of others. (Many Mahāyāna texts praise giving by the laity to monks and the order, but the latter in turn are to give material aid to others; Bodhisattvas are to give to the needy first.) This means that for eons Bodhisattvas, who see everything as having the nature of a magical illusion, make heroic sacrifices (including life and limb) motivated only by compassion (8PP 481-511).[28] But the highest giving is the thought of becoming a Buddha for the sake of all sentient beings with which Bodhisattvas begin their career (*bodhicitta*). Following the code of proper conduct is a matter of abstention and self-restraint; it preserves oneself for the benefit of others by making sure of rebirths where one can help others. (An other-regarding modification to the enlightened Bodhisattvas' practice of the code will be discussed below.) Giving and proper conduct are the main sources of the laity's merit. Patience is the forbearance of our own suffering, the forgiveness of others for the harm they do us, tolerance of others' actions, and faith. One accepts harm by others without anger or resentment, knowing that we are only suffering the karmic consequences of our own past deeds and that there is no "reality" harming us or being harmed. It produces merit, and its opposite—impatience, resentment, and anger—destroys merit. Vigor is energy and courage, sustaining the quest to benefit others and to attain a Buddha's wisdom. Concentrative meditation involves both focusing attention and mastering mindfulness; thus, practices designed for stabilizing and calming the mind (*shamatha*) and for insight-meditation (*vipashyanā*) are involved.

The first three virtues express compassion in action, and the last three develop the Bodhisattva to do the first three. Some schools hold that a Bodhisattva must master one virtue before moving on to the next on the list. But his or her level of insight informs all the virtues as the Bodhisattva advances. Thus, each of the other virtues go through three stages of insight: first, seeing persons (both onself and others); second, seeing only elements of reality (the *dharma*s), and thus no sense of "I" enters the picture; third, seeing the emptiness of the elements. The first is the way ordinary people practice; the second, the way Solitary Buddhas and Arhats practice; the third, the way of the Buddha. When insight is perfected, the other virtues are also perfected (8PP 172-73). In that way the other five virtues are contained in insight, and the perfection of insight thus is merely a synonym for the fulfillment of all six virtues (8PP 81-82). Thus, after eons of practice, each virtue is perfected or complete (*pāramitā*) when the Bodhisattva sees that all phenomena are empty of self-existence and are "illusions" in that sense—there is no distinct being to hate, forgive, or be compassionate toward.

The change occurring in enlightenment thus is in the factual component of the way of life—the nature of the reality helping and being helped—not values. The basic value (compassion) remains the same: it is "purified" only in that the enlightened Bodhisattva no longer has a sense of self. In the enlightened state, Bodhisattvas embody a state of mindfulness. Having perfected *dhyāna*, they are permanently in a tranquil, concentrative meditation, even while teaching or otherwise helping others. They practice the other-impinging virtues through skillful means (*upāya-kaushalya*), as governed by a compassionate concern for others. They initially have desires (*kleshas*) for a Buddha's wisdom and the salvation of all sentient beings. But when their insight is perfected, they are free of any sense of self-existent realities; hence their practice of the other virtues is also perfected. All sense of self and other is gone, and yet they carry on, even-mindedly helping all. Still practicing the virtues—giving, proper conduct, patience in the face of adversity—Bodhisattvas both help others and advance themselves toward *bodhi*.

Compassion is notable by its absence from the list of virtues. Nevertheless, the master value affects each virtue. Virtues of self-cultivation directly help only the Bodhisattvas, but the Bodhisattvas are committed to helping others, and thus these virtues indirectly aid other beings. Compassion can also turn the entire nature of an apparently self-serving virtue upside down. Patience becomes a type of other-regarding action: enemies, by providing an opportunity for us to practice patience, become an instrument for our own enlightenment, and thus *they themselves* also gain merit (BCA V.107). And Shāntideva points out a strange consequence: the enemies go to hell for harming us, and so *we* are injuring *them* while they are *helping* us (BCA V.47-49)—hence, the bizarre circumstance of thanking the people beating us for giving us an opportunity to practice patience while we feel sorry for them.[29] After all, the enemy is only there because both their past actions and our own (by the law of *karma*) require it. (It is their own new freely chosen act to harm us that causes them to go to a hell.) We should therefore give some of the merit we gain by this instance of patience to the person creating the opportunity (BCA V.108). Thus, this virtue is a means to an end for the Bodhisattvas themselves (to attain enlightenment and a Buddha's *bodhi*), but it also has a direct other-regarding component (others gain merit despite their own actions or are helped by being taught or established in a way to the end of suffering).

Violating the Code of Conduct

Even the code of conduct (*shīla*)—designed for self-cultivation as discussed in the last chapter—becomes a vehicle for other-regardingness under the Mahāyāna ethos of compassion. Mahāyānists accept the same basic code of conduct as Hīnayānists, although they expand the fifth precept to explicitly include abstention from trafficking in intoxicants. They also expand the practice of noninjury in ways to help animals. The five additional precepts are different than those of the Hīnayāna: not discussing the faults of others, not praising oneself and reviling others, not withholding any spiritual or material aid, not indulging in anger, and not defaming the Buddha, his teachings, or the order. (Note that some of these latter five also cover other-impinging acts, unlike in the Hīnayāna.) These are the ten wholesome actions (*kushala-karma*). Those on the path, both in the laity and in the order, also should abstain from the ten unwholesome (*akushala*) acts: injury, taking what is not freely given, sexual misconduct, lying, divisive speech, offensive speech, senseless prattling, greed, ill will, and wrong views. Rigorous observance of these precepts is necessary for the unenlightened on the path to enlightenment (BCA IV.1), as in the Hīnayāna, since they relate to personal development. In addition, since Bodhisattvas are out to help other beings, they would delay their own enlightenment by any transgression and thus would be hurting the welfare of other beings (BCA IV.8-10).

However, the Bodhisattvas' other-regarding concern manifests itself in an interesting way once they are enlightened: they no longer have any need to follow the code itself, and so they can violate it if necessary to help other beings.[30] "Even what is forbidden is allowable for one who seeks the welfare of others with compassion" (BCA V.84). Their actions are for the welfare of the world, and this trumps any rules of self-cultivation. This does not mean any libertine violation for their own benefit is possible (since they have no sense of self) or any arbitrary violation that might mislead or hurt the welfare of others. Nor are they breaking the precepts just to show that they are liberated from them. However, the precepts are not absolute. In the Hīnayāna, the precepts are are a matter of self-restraint and so it is natural that they would be internalized in the Hīnayāna enlightened state.

But to Bodhisattvas, compassion cannot be restricted by any rules. Precepts are no more sources of attachment than is a "being," and so Bodhisattvas can respond in any way to help what is really there. What counts is the Bodhisattvas' intention and the final results accomplished, not the actions that accomplish the results and thus not the rules governing actions. In sum, Bodhisattvas can violate any rule if it is done solely out of compassion for the beings being affected.[31] (Since the enlightened are beyond the sanction of *karma*, they need not consider that these actions, if committed by the unenlightened, would produce demerit.)[32] In effect, the objective—ending another's suffering—justifies any means necessary. This means that the enlightened in Buddhism do not automatically or necessarily follow the rules of *shīla*, contrary to critics of the "transcendency" thesis (as discussed in the last chapter). In the Mahāyāna, with the prevailing value of compassion, these rules may be contravened. It is only when the rules of conduct are combined with the Hīnayāna ethos of self-centeredness that the control of these rules in the enlightened state seems natural.

Thus, enlightened Bodhisattvas can use their skillful means to help others, even if it involves violating the precepts, free of any personal consequences. This "holy cunning" may involve adopting objectionable modes of livelihood, lying and harsh speech, stealing (to deprive robbers and kings of ill-gotten gains that would lead them to their own ruin), having sex with an unmarried woman (to prevent her from harboring thoughts of hatred and ill will), and even killing a person who intends to murder a Buddhist monk or his own parents.[33] Skillful lying (i.e., telling what the Bodhisattva knows is not actually true to lead the listener to the end of suffering) may be better than a rigid adherence to truth.[34] The same holds for the other precepts related to speech (e.g., using harsh speech to warn or chastise). Similarly, Mahāyānists praise the value of monastic celibacy, but lay Bodhisattvas may use sex to help others. For example, the Buddha in a previous life is said to have lived with a woman for twelve years to prevent her suicide. A female Bodhisattvas practiced as a prostitute to get men's attention and then taught the doctrine to them. There are also married Bodhisattvas.[35]

The most extreme instance is killing others for their own good. The precept against killing sentient beings is scrupulously held in ordinary circumstances (e.g., BCA V.11). But in some cases compassion for someone requires killing them. (Obviously, this only holds if one accepts the belief-claim of a future rebirth and that actions in one life have consequences in a future life or lives.) For example, the *Mahāparinirvāna Sūtra* states that the Buddha himself in a former life killed some Brahmins, both to protect the Buddhist teaching and to save them from the negative karmic consequences of continuing to attack it. Asanga, a Yogācāra Buddhist, offered another justification for some killings: if a Bodhisattva sees a bandit about to kill many hundreds of people, he should kill the bandit before he commits the dreadful act. The Bodhisattva's intention is central: he wants to protect the innocent (just as we would kill a wild animal if we see it about to attack a group of children), but he also thinks that if he kills the bandit he himself will go to a hell but he will be saving the bandit from a worse fate; so out of compassion for all concerned except himself and with a tranquil mind, he should kill. Thus, only one life is lost, and only the Bodhisattva suffers karmically. (Hīnayānists would not jeopardize their own destiny by intervening—the fate of all the others is governed by their own *karma* and their own choices.) Ironically, the true consequence is that the Bodhisattva commits no fault whatsoever and in fact gains much merit from his act of compassion. Asanga added that this justified assassinating government officials who are excessively cruel and have no compassion. This political policy was put into practice in the ninth century when a monk in Tibet assassinated King Glan-dar-ma who was harming himself karmically by persecuting Buddhists. While the monk thought he had committed a fault, he was in fact reborn in a heaven for his willingness to violate—solely for the sake of others—the precept against killing.[36] Thus, according to Asanga, as long as the intent is purely other-regarding, no karmic harm befalls even the unenlightened.

The metaphysics of emptiness is sometimes advanced as a justification for this change in attitude toward the precepts: killing is impossible since there is no real killing—there is no real "self" to be killed or to be a killer, and thus there is no real "murder" (see BCA IX.11). That is, since there are no real beings—no "thing" to kill—the precept against killing is inoperative. (The Upanishads and the *Bhagavad-gītā* offer the same justification for the *opposite* factual belief—because there is an unkillable self.) But the early *Prajñāpāramitā* Buddhists would not accept such a claim: although there is no self, there is still a conditioned "person" empty of self-existence who can be "killed." Thus, "killing" is possible. But no indiscriminate killing would be justified; only "killing" to help "people" would be.

Not holding rigidly to any rules in order to help others reflects the Mahāyāna ethos. That is, guiding what really exists may be best accomplished by means other than rigidly following the precepts. Violations of the code redefine a Bodhisattva as an exemplar of Buddhist virtue, but their concern is still moral. The code of conduct designed for self-cultivation simply becomes less important when the concern shifts from only helping oneself to a genuine interest in the welfare of others. In the Hīnayāna, where one's own salvation is the central concern, the idea of violating the precepts solely for another's benefit would not occur, but it became justified in the Mahāyāna when compassion for others for their own sake entered into consideration and protecting the Buddhist teaching was given a higher priority than self-cultivation alone. This relativizes ethics only in that compassion is now the master value that prevails in all situations: the rules still have *prima facie* priority for the enlightened (and are governing for the unenlightened) and can be abrogated only when a moral concern requires it. Things such as thoughts of pride may be considered a more serious fault for Bodhisattvas than violating the fivefold code of conduct (8PP 390-91). The master other-regarding value cannot be captured by a set of rules, let alone a set of rules for self-restraint such as the *shīla*. Indeed, this means the enlightened Bodhisattvas have an *obligation* to violate the precepts when others can be helped. Thus, the strangeness of the mystical outcome in those circumstances: one must kill the "victim" to be other-regarding—not killing would reflect not caring. Once again, it is the intent and result, not the act itself, that matters.

Skillful Means

Violating the code of conduct is an instance of the Bodhisattvas' skillful means (*upāya-kaushalya*) that they employ to help others along the path to enlightenment. Skillful means is born from an enlightened Bodhisattva's insight—indeed, in the *Prajñāpāramitā* it was all but equated with insight itself (e.g., 8PP 427). Other schools place it as the first stage after the perfection of insight. Early on, it was treated as the means by which a Bodhisattva with perfected insight could remain in the realm of rebirth and choose a helpful rebirth. For example, Bodhisattvas can perfect forms of concentrative meditation (*dhyāna*) that would usually cause rebirth in certain heavens, but they forego that effect to be reborn in a realm where they can help others (8PP 427). In general, it means that they can recognize signs, both their marks and causes, and yet surrender themselves completely to the signless and thus not course in unreal discriminations (8PP 355-57). Through skillful means, a Bodhisattva can abide in emptiness and still demonstrate the doctrine. Thus, perfect insight and skillful means are the Bodhisattvas' two "wings" or "parachutes" (8PP, p. 47) whereby they can remain on the path to a Buddha's wisdom benefitting all sentient beings and not prematurely escape the chain of rebirths by falling into Solitary Buddhahood or Arhatship. Whatever wholesome life comes forth from a Bodhisattva comes from skillful means (8PP 75). Insight itself is powerless to act, since no "doer" is distinguished (8PP 205). It is inoperative without some mechanism to apply it to the world, and skillful means is that vehicle. Thus, Mahāyānists describe insight as the Bodhisattvas' mother and skillfulness in means as their father. Their offspring are beings established on the path to the end of suffering.

In later *Prajñāpāramitā* thought and in the *Bodhisattvabhūmi*, a second focus was made explicit: skillful means is not only what helps the Bodhisattvas themselves stay on the path to a Buddha's wisdom but is also the means the Bodhisattvas employ to help others. That is, skillful means has a double role: it brings about the welfare of both the Bodhisattva and others. This is a natural extension of the original concept since compassion for others is necessary to attain a Buddha's wisdom—"skillful means" is simply the term denoting any methods employed to achieve that end. In other texts, this second focus came to dominate. Skillful means then came to mean any technique enlightened Bodhisattvas employ to implement their compassion and their insight into the emptiness of phenomena in order actually to help others. In short, it is the application of their insight to the spiritual advantage of others. It is any means that convert the Bodhisattva's insight and moral concern into action. This can be both words (such as utilizing heretical views) and also actions. Bodhisattvas adopt whatever method is appropriate for the particular needs and ability to understand of the person they encounter (e.g., they may speak only of a pleasure heaven to those who would not understand *nirvāna*). Thus, as noted, Bodhisattvas will violate the code of conduct if that is necessary and can choose an appropriate place to be reborn (including heavens and hells). Through paranormal powers, they appear, like magical illusions, in different forms to help (e.g., a beggar, an animal, or the king of demons). With the merit they have made, they set up Buddha-fields for others to be reborn into (e.g., 8PP 361-65). (Skillful means enable enlightened Bodhisattvas to perform acts that produce huge heaps of merit, even if they do not apprehend merit as "real," that they of course no longer need and so use to help others.)[37] Indeed, some Mahāyānists came to see the historical Buddha himself simply as a skillful manifestation of the true cosmic Buddha, i.e., merely a device used to lead others to enlightenment.

The Bodhisattva Vimalakīrti is considered the very embodiment of such expedient means. Like many Bodhisattvas, he is portrayed as rich and powerful, living in luxury, well educated and eloquent.[38] He was a householder, with a wife, a son, and concubines, but he was considered to be free of passions, following full monastic discipline, since he was in the married state merely as means to aid others. All his lavish eating and drinking were only to create opportunities to convert others; he himself remained pure and dispassionate throughout it all. He mixed with all classes of people and participated in government. He wore ornate clothes and attended sports and gambling houses to help "mature" those attending. He frequented brothels, but only to convert the prostitutes and patrons within. He was a landlord and engaged in business endeavors, yet he had no interest in profit or possessions. (He spent his wealth to help the poor.) He met with teachers of other religions. Always in a concentrative state of mind, he would talk to people on the street, and he feigned illness in order to lure monks and others to come inquiring about his health, thereby giving him the opportunity to teach for their benefit. He was said to be second only to the Buddha in the depth of his understanding of the Buddhist teachings.

The roots of the concept of skillful means lie in earlier schools in the actions of the Buddha. The Pāli canon portrays the Buddha as having the knowledge of the capacity of his listeners to understand and adjusting his teachings accordingly (e.g., AN I.10; MN I.483-88). (Some see the Buddha's entire teaching as skillful means, since we would not understand the actual truth.) Another type of skillful means is the story of the Buddha taking the monk Nanda to a heaven filled with nymphs to break his lingering attraction to his former wife; Nanda thereafter renewed his meditation in order to be reborn with the nymphs but instead ends up heading for a better goal, *nirvāna*. This does not involve lying for another's good (as does the parable in the *Lotus Sūtra* of the father luring his preoccupied sons out of their burning house by claiming he had more toys for them), but it is a similar example of skillful means. In the Jātaka Tales, the Buddha-to-be is portrayed as breaking all the five precepts except lying, as he used his skillful means to lead the unenlightened toward enlightenment. Some tales involve giving up his limbs and even his life, all out of compassion to help others. Thus, suicide, like killing in violation of the code of conduct, can be permitted as long as the intention is solely to help others.

Such skillful means fit naturally with the metaphysics of emptiness, since all beings are considered as having the nature of a magician's trick. Deceptions on the phenomenal level thus seem less significant. (But, again, there is a reality empty of self-existence to lead toward enlightenment and so not all conduct is acceptable.) However, the most important point is that these practices are moral. Bodhisattvas are merely readjusting their teachings, both doctrinal and ethical, to the overarching value of compassion.

Zen

The Meditation (Zen/Chan) schools of China and Japan are often considered to be amoral or antinomian or "beyond good and evil"—burning texts, smashing icons, advising students to kill the Buddha, shouting or looking fierce, hitting students, and killing cats. The problem is not the Bodhisattva goal of Mahāyāna in general, but the techniques of the Zen schools. The Sōtō school's emphasis on sitting meditation is said to lead to moral quietism. And the shock tactics of the Rinzai school are said to show that enlightenment has nothing to do with morality. The state of mind resulting from these practices is said to be such that the discriminations necessary for morality are impossible. However, these conclusions badly misrepresent classical Zen.

Sōtō Zen places less emphasis on any breakthrough experiences (*satori*, *kenshō*) occurring upon the "death of the self" than on applying the ever-deepening enlightened state of mind to everyday events. The *zazen* sitting meditation of breathing mindfulness is central, but meditation is not limited to that setting. Instead, concrete action in the world in a state of mindfulness, free of mental images and emotions intervening between us and what is really there, is equally central. Free of the mind being fixed on nonexistent self-existent objects and yet focused by meditation, one can let the mind and body take their course in the immediacy of the present moment. In this state of "no mind" or "no thing" where we have quieted the inner turmoil of our "monkey mind," we respond spontaneously without reflection and without hesitation to what is present.[39] This state leads to very practical conduct—when hungry, we eat; when tired, we sleep. No more thought is involved than with a child playing with a toy. There is no longer a duality of the actor and the act. The tea ceremony and archery are famous exercises in focusing on the task at hand with the concept-driven mind turned off. This approach is applied to work, art, and all other activities. The issue becomes *how* we do something, not *what* we do. (It is said, "If you can serve a cup of tea properly, you can do anything.") Thereby, all of life becomes a meditative exercise.

But, contrary to a popular belief, this does not reduce Zen merely to a meditative technique. With its focus on living in the present, Zen teachers may not discuss the nature of reality as much as teachers in other Buddhist schools, but classical Zen was a way of life with classical Mahāyāna belief-claims adopted from the Mādhyamika school. Teachers may have burned *sūtra*s, but this was only a teaching technique to make a point—it was never intended that the Buddhist teachings should disappear from the planet. Instead, in monasteries the study of Buddhist texts was stressed. We need words to get beyond words (i.e., to a state where self-contained entities designated by words are no longer discerned). Other Zen doctrines also deemphasize words: the direct mind-to-mind transmission of doctrine from teacher to disciple without words, or the more extreme antirealistic interpretation of language under which denotative language is merely the finger pointing at the reflection of the moon and not a mirror of what is real. But these doctrines still do not negate the need for words.

The same situation applies to values. The great Sōtō teacher Dōgen held a very conventional view of Buddhist values, while emphasizing *zazen*. In the *Shōbō-genzō*, Dōgen advocated three basic Mahāyāna precepts: "Cease from doing evil.

Do only good. Do good for others." These and the code of conduct were to be rigorously followed by all, including advanced monks.[40] He also advocated a set of monastic rules to regulate the behavior of the monks. He could reject as Hīnayānist any discrimination of "good" and "evil" while still insisting on following Buddhist rules.[41] So although he was free from discriminations, he could still state that it is a grave error for Zen monks to prefer evil acts or to say there is no need to practice good or to accumulate merit.[42] Once we have thoroughly realized the nature of reality, we know that evil is always evil and good is always good.[43] Following the precepts may be a matter of self-cultivation, but by following the Buddha's way we see our own nature—the "Buddha-nature" or "original-mind"—and we will be naturally compassionate. (Zen adopted the Chinese belief that we are naturally compassionate: to paraphrase the Confucian Mencius, if we are human and we see a child about to fall into a well, we naturally try to help.) Compassion, as with the rest of the Mahāyāna, is expressed mainly in guiding others in the Buddha's way. Thus, if we get beyond discriminating different value-concepts, we will spontaneously be other-regarding and hence moral.

This means the phrase "beyond good and evil," common in D. T. Suzuki's works, can be easily misunderstood when applied to Zen. Only discriminating the concepts of "good" and "evil" as eternal, self-existent principles is attacked as interfering with a more spontaneously compassionate mind. It does not mean that Zen Buddhists ultimately devalue compassion. It is our unenlightened division of reality into "good" and "bad" that is the problem. We apply values to reality and end up clutching at our own judgments. Our mind gets fixated in unnecessary dualisms of values—we set a goal of trying to "do good" rather than emptying our mind of unenlightened ideas and letting our natural compassion flow. But values, like descriptive concepts, are all empty of self-existence. This does not mean there is nothing to them but only that we are imposing values and not seeing what is really there when we think in terms of a dualism of "good" and "evil." There is a Zen saying: "Before my training, there were mountains and rivers; in the middle, there were no mountains and rivers; after completion, there were mountains and rivers again"—i.e., first the unenlightened think there is a mountain in our unenlightened way; practitioners next see the unreality (emptiness) of anything denoted by language; and finally in the enlightened state they see what is really there and can use our conventional terms once again without thinking in terms of self-existent entities. Thus, language is not to be abandoned but seen in a new light. This applies equally to values. Just as there is a reality behind the concept of a "person" but no self-existent referent, so too there is no independent things called "good" and "evil" but reality nevertheless involves compassion. (Zen also adopts the idea of the interconnectivity of terms from Daoism discussed in Chapter 11.)

Dōgen thus could still speak in terms of "good" and "evil" without "coursing in signs." He made clear that, even if "good" may be a term empty of a self-existent referent, not all acts are acceptable. Most importantly, he still valued compassion. The enlightened do not act selfishly or randomly but have internalized a set of values and a goal that give direction to their actions—in this case, the standard Mahāyāna Bodhisattva's virtues and the goal of leading others to the end of rebirth, even if there are no eternally existing beings. Zen meditation itself cannot be the source of these values and goals; it is only a mental exercise, even if it gives a sense of selflessness enabling us to express compassion more spontaneously. In short, enlightened Zen Buddhists do not see eternal qualities of "goodness" or "badness" but are nonetheless compassionate. The state of living fully in the present is beyond consciously analyzing reality in terms of our concepts but is not beyond compassion, and in this way of life a state of other-regardingness prevails.[44]

Zen masters often use bizarre techniques to try to induce enlightenment. Dōgen struck meditators who were falling asleep rather than gently admonishing them, but his aim was to help the students. The Rinzai school takes a different approach to breaking the hold of conceptual thought on our mind. Its most famous technique is an active type of meditation on a *kōan/gong-an*. This is a mental puzzle designed to force the disciple to see the way concepts control our mental life and thus to attain a sudden breakthrough to our true selfless nature, free of the grip of conceptual thinking. An example is Hakuin's famous question "What is the sound of one hand clapping?" Any answer disciples give is not so important as what they do and how they do it, thereby revealing their attitude toward concepts. Also consider Rinzai's call to commit the cardinal sins of Buddhism: "If you meet the Buddha on the road, kill him! If you meet the Patriarchs, kill them; if you meet Arhats, kill them; if you meet your parents, kill them. Then for the first time you will see clearly." This teaching is meant to help disciples with its shock value—not something meant literally as an action-guide. The objective is to remove any mental idols we might have, not to go around killing people. But violating the precept against killing is possible. Consider the *kōan* of Nanquan killing the cat. He found his disciples arguing about a cat. He grabbed it, held it up, and said, "Everyone! If you can say something rightly, I will spare this cat. If you cannot, I will cut off its head." No one spoke—thus showing their lack of enlightenment—and so he cut the cat in two. Most Buddhists, including Dōgen, took this to be an acceptable violation of the precept, since it was done to evoke enlightenment in the students. But a sentient being was dead and in no way helped. Inducing enlightenment in others by harming a being was placed over compassion for that being, and thus this act is anomalous for the tradition as a whole.

A more fitting image of the role of other-regarding action for Zen as a whole is the ox-herding pictures.[45] They present an allegory of the Zen quest, beginning with a man seeking a lost ox (i.e., enlightenment) and ending with him entering the marketplace riding the ox with helping hands. That is, the quest ends with the now-enlightened seeker ready to help others. (It should be noted, however, that the earliest versions of the series of pictures do not end with the man entering the marketplace to help but with him lost in the realm of contemplation.)

The state of "no mind" does not mean "mindless"—the agency needed to be moral is present, and the enlightened have internalized the moral point of view.

Zen's iconoclasm toward our intellectual creations makes devising any elaborate set of ethical precepts totally out of character. Adding anything that might be the source of further discriminations—such as any intellectualization concerning values—would be discouraged. But this does not mean Zen is amoral. Compassion was valued supremely from the founder Bodhidharma on. There may be no prescribed course of action for the enlightened, and cultural conventions may come to be seen as a form of legalism standing in the way of true compassionate action, but a moral concern for others is always present. Other aspects of the highly disciplined and ritualized classical Zen way of life could be discussed, but the important moral point would remain that meditative calm does not entail moral quietism or indifference. Indeed, Zen is a mainstream Mahāyāna tradition in this regard.

Social Action

Another aspect of Zen has also raised questions about whether it is moral or not. Throughout its history, it has been readily adaptable to whatever political setting it happens to find itself in. Moreover, there have been Zen temples with armies of warring monks, Zen was adopted by the warrior class of medieval Japan (the samurai), it influenced the martial arts, and in the early and middle twentieth century it adopted a nationalist and imperialistic stance in Japan—Zen temples in fact prepared soldiers for World War II.[46] Why have the majority of Zen Buddhists always supported the status quo and been aligned with the conservative elements in whatever society it is in? For all their iconoclasm, why have Zen Buddhists not regularly attacked political structures? Is Zen, and, more generally all of Mahāyāna, free of any social values? Is it nihilistic on at least a social level? Are Buddhist masters merely spiritual technicians concerned with curing spiritual illness and unconcerned with any matter unrelated to that? (That Zen has strict discipline and is extremely authoritarian, requiring the student's complete submission to the will of the master, warrants notice here.) Is Buddhism merely a matter of mystical self-development that can be adopted by anyone, regardless of one's walk of life or political beliefs, without affecting them? Does *what* someone does not matter, but only *how* he or she does it? That the German author of the popular *Zen in the Art of Archery* became a Nazi after his Zen training in Japan has to be at least disquieting for a religion supposedly of compassion.

The history of Mahāyāna Buddhism does support the conclusion that it has no political values. The virtues to be cultivated are individual in nature, not political. "Injustice" and "rights" are political concepts that simply have no place in the Mahāyāna ethos. Political concerns, as with the Theravādins, are irrelevant to classical Buddhist interests in ending individual suffering. As D. T. Suzuki noted of Zen, all Buddhism can be wedded to anarchism, fascism, communism, democracy, or any political or economic dogmatism.[47] From the Buddhist of view, no system is intrinsically better than another, nor is there a need to abolish all of them. Buddhism can also accommodate differing economic and social settings. Inner liberation and not any transformation of the external world is what matters.

This does not mean, however, that Mahāyāna Buddhists are totally bereft of all social concerns. All suffering—both "worldly" and "religious"—is their central concern. Unenlightened Bodhisattvas are urged to provide help of a material kind—caring for the sick, feeding the poor, guiding the blind, educating the young. (No special rule would have to be instituted to prevent Mahāyāna monks from stepping over the sick.) As the saying goes, one cannot understand the Buddha's teachings on an empty stomach. The work is usually in face-to-face interactions, but there are instances of Buddhists collectively helping on a societywide scale. Nāgārjuna commended rulers to engage in social projects related to health, the water supply, food for the poor and for animals, and other social projects. The Zen master Hakuin wrote to the ruling class on behalf of the oppressed farmers and peasants in Japan. Nichiren's less mystical Pure Land school was also socially oriented. In Vietnam, some Zen monks during the Diem regime in the 1960s set themselves on fire to bring the world's attention to Vietnam's plight and to move the hearts of those involved in the war by their intense suffering.[48] Some illustrations of skillful means also involve political acts: killing oppressive kings, or taking ill-gotten wealth from the rulers à la Robin Hood.

However, most Buddhist masters see a danger in "worldly" acts (i.e., help not directly related to spiritual advancement). There is a spiritual danger both to the worker and to the recipient. The Tibetan master Milarepa, when asked if monks could perform works that were in a small way beneficial to others, answered: "If there be not the least self-interest attached to such duties, it is permissible. But such detachment is indeed rare; and works performed for the good of others seldom succeed, if not wholly freed from self-interest. . . . It is as if a man hopelessly drowning were to try to save another man in the same predicament."[49] He recommended instead resolving to attain Buddhahood for the good of all living beings. Before that, the monks do not know the true nature of reality and thus may in fact be inadvertently hurting both themselves and those they are trying to help. And, even if the others are materially helped, they may be spiritually hurt—they may become comfortable enough in the realm of suffering not to seek *nirvāna*. They may also end up attaching too much significance to what is only one life in a huge chain of rebirths. Both the helper and the helped may become attached to the impermanent and not really helped at all. Thus, getting enlightened first is the best way to help others as well as oneself.

Enlightened Bodhisattvas focus exclusively on the religious help. Only such soteriological help is of concern to them, not anything related to reorganizing society. Ending all poverty, war, and illness would still not end the fundamental suffering of decay, death, and rebirth and thus is not an enlightened Bodhisattva's concern. Nor is there anything like utilitarian thinking in which the greatest good for the greatest number is most highly valued, where "good" is anything other than *nirvāna*. The spiritual advancement of a single person is valued more than any amount of good for any number of other people measured in other terms. Social action would be an instance of *bad* means (*anupāya*), not skillful means. Thus, when faced with an epidemic, an enlightened Bodhisattva thinks only, "There is no element of reality (*dharma*) which sickness could oppress, nor is that which is called 'sickness' an element of reality," and then thinks about creating a Buddha-field free of sickness (8PP 364-65).[50] They would no doubt show compassion to anyone they encounter, but making people comfortable in the realm of suffering would only militate against them wanting to end suffering and thus would make suffering continue through more lives—doing anything that establishes them in a path to *nirvāna* helps more in the long run. Thus, helping to free people completely from suffering by demonstrating the Buddha's teachings is the greatest aid possible, and the only aid on which the enlightened focus. Indeed, the brevity of one tiny slice of the immense stream of karmic becoming that constitutes each "person" is insignificant compared to their big picture—not intervening at all might be more positive help by indicating the ultimate unimportance of all worldly comfort. (Another reason under the Buddhist worldview not to intervene is that the illness of each person is seen as the karmic fruit of that person's own past actions working itself out.[51] Many Japanese Buddhists saw their defeat in World War II as an instance of this as retribution on a social scale for the past actions of each individual.)

Acceptance of the doctrine of *karma* here, as with the other traditions so far covered in this book, causes an individualist interpretation of social phenomena. "Society" is merely a collection of individuals, and thus "society" can only be changed by transforming people individually. There is no "group salvation" but only each person working out his or her own salvation. The coercive nature of laws will not effect the radical transformation of the person necessary to end suffering but at best alters only our behavior, and thus Mahāyāna Buddhists, like their Hīnayāna counterparts, are not interested in reforming laws. And the same holds for society in general. They can accept the status quo and focus on the inner transformation of individuals.[52] (This would have the side effect of supporting the status quo.) At least the enlightened Bodhisattvas would be interested only in helping people toward the religious goal. Their concern would still be other-regarding, even if their interests do not reflect our modern Western ones. They would be critical of a person's attachment to any political system, and they could not favor one political system over another since they do not value worldly distinctions.

However, since compassion is the central value to this way of life, Mahāyāna Buddhism arguably could not be wedded in full to every possible value-system—in particular, compassion would mean these Buddhists could not fulfill all the social obligations of highly oppressive regimes. Some Mahāyāna values and meditative exercises may help soldiers face death, but this would be abstracting out only part of its total way of life. (The purpose of the meditative exercises may become inverted: practicing archery may no longer be an exercise in Zen but practicing Zen may become just a way to make a better archer.) The comprehensive transformation of a person to a life centered on compassion would have to be ignored, and thus Mahāyāna Buddhism would be reduced to something other than what it is.

Conclusion

The Bodhisattva's career begins with unenlightened self-interest, but from the start it also incorporates other-regardingness in the form of compassion expressed in action. And the particular course Bodhisattvas take makes differentiating the two ends impossible, since the same actions fulfill both. Nevertheless, genuine other-regardingness remains one component: concern for others must remain genuine, for if they thought to use others for their own interests their insight would not be perfected. Paradoxically, they promote their own welfare by promoting others' and vice versa. Their goal—a Buddha's full wisdom—requires acting for the welfare of others. Bodhisattvas thus seem to be using others for their own end, but choosing to pursue that goal rather than opting out of the chain of rebirths (as Arhats do) is itself other-regarding precisely because they remain in the realm of rebirth to help.[53] Thus, their goal helps both themselves and others. In the enlightened state, they even move beyond impartiality: others' welfare is always valued over their own. In sum, Mahāyānists, unlike Hīnayānists, are other-regarding since a concern for others is built into both the path and the enlightened state. There is also no presuppositional problem concerning agency or realities to be helped. Thus, the conclusion must be that the Mahāyāna Bodhisattvas are a clear instance of morality in mysticism.

It is often claimed that the Mahāyānists changed their evaluation of the world from that of the Hīnayānists: the world no longer needed to be escaped because everything is empty, or because *nirvāna* is not different from *samsāra*, or because Mahāyānists are willing to live in the world by accepting rebirth when they could opt to get out. Thus, they are "this-worldly" while Hīnayānists are "otherworldly." The Mahāyānists are positive and world-affirming—just wanting to reorient how we live in this realm—while the Hīnayānists are negative and world-denying. However, this contrast cannot be supported: the objective in the Mahāyāna is still to get out of the realm of rebirths. The change is a moral one: the Bodhisattvas no longer strive to get out of the realm of rebirths alone but now want to help others get out too. They make the supreme sacrifice of staying in the realm of suffering solely for the sake of others. This highlights the morality of their choice.

The switch from the Hīnayāna is partially a change in factual beliefs, but it is more importantly a radical change in values. Mahāyānists accepted essentially the same metaphysical beliefs as Hīnayānists but placed them in a moral framework. The only important factual change is that the idea that the enlightened do not automatically leave the realm of rebirths but can choose to be reborn and can choose particular rebirths in order to help others. (Whether this belief was in fact the result of the change of values is also an issue.) Mahāyānists also accepted essentially the same virtues and codes of conduct but placed them into a moral framework where compassion is the master virtue. Helping others then became the central focus, and the centrality of this focus is completely absent in the Hīnayāna. This shows how morality is an ethos independent from religious codes and how the same belief-claims and codes of conduct can be fitted into either moral or nonmoral ways of life.[54]

Such a fundamental revolution in orientation means that the two traditions should not be amalgamated into one on the issue of morality. However, scholars often claim that the Theravāda merely accents insight while the Mahāyāna accents compassion, or that the latter gives a more complete account of the Pan-Buddhist value-system, and so in the end each tradition is the same on ethical matters. Such a unifying approach misses entirely the radical difference in the central ethical values and moral thrust of the two traditions. Mahāyānists rightly criticize Hīnayānists as being selfish in their core values. The moral status of the Theravāda cannot be finessed merely by claiming that Mahāyānists give the real "essence" of all Buddhists' ethics. What is absolutely central to the Mahāyāna value-system is totally missing in the Theravāda's ethos of self-cultivation. From the moral point of view, Theravādins are indeed "Hīnayānists"—followers of the "Small Way"—since they are concerned only with their own interests.

Generalizations about all of Buddhist ethics are further weakened by the antinomianism of Tantrism to be considered in the next chapter. Mahāyānists are sometimes considered antinomian because they permit the enlightened to violate various precepts when compassion requires it. Such violations are alien to the Hīnayāna, where the action-guides serve only one's own self-development and the lack of other-regarding concern means that the rules are more likely to be held rigidly even in the enlightened state. But since the violations are in order to help others, this does not make the Mahāyānists immoral—if such violations are "antinomian," it is still done only for moral purposes. Indeed, it does not even mean that Buddhist norms are not universalizable. Laws can be suspended "in the interest of justice," but this does not make the laws unenforceable in general. The same applies to Buddhist norms: they can be suspended by enlightened Bodhisattvas "in the interest of compassion" to help others, but they still are general action-guides for the rest of us. That is, the general ethos is more important in an ethics of intention than any set of rules, but the rules still may be universalizable. Either way, the important conclusion remains that the Bodhisattva's is a moral mystical way of life.

Notes

1. The abbreviations for this chapter will be: 8PP=*Ashtasāhasrikāprajñāpāramitā* (*The Perfection of Insight in Eight Thousand Lines*) (page citations to the verse section are to Conze 1973); BCA = Shāntideva's *Bodhicaryāvatāra*; DS = *Vajracchedika* (*Diamond Sūtra*) (citations are to pages of Conze 1958). The work of Shāntideva, a later Prāsangika Mādhyamika Buddhist, is the most important Mahāyāna work on the Bodhisattva's path.

2. The general Mahāyāna laity will not be discussed here. It is the switch in ultimate goals from the Theravāda's that is morally significant. This is not to say that are no self-centered laity in the Mahāyāna, as in any religion—indeed, the early *Prajñāpāramitā* admitted some Buddhists were self-centered and had a place for the self-centered Solitary Buddhas and Arhats.

3. Bodhisattvas also continue to deepen insight (*prajñā*) after enlightenment. (The Hīnayānists reject that idea, as illustrated in the *Lotus Sūtra* when the Arhats walked out angry and puzzled by the Buddha's claim that Buddhas had a deeper insight than they did.) This shows that insight and meditation continues after enlightenment. Meditation is also necessary because the tranquility of mind necessary to maintain the nirvanized state of mind can be lost (as illustrated in Godhika's problem discussed in the last chapter).

4. The early doctrine was that a Bodhisattva would cause only a *great many* beings to achieve release (8PP 18), not that they had to save *all* beings. But most Mahāyāna schools accepted that all beings will eventually be released from the chain of rebirths (*parinirvāna*), if not become full Buddhas. (Shankara, perhaps under the influence of Mahāyāna Buddhism, also accepted "universal release" [*sarva-mukti*] and also accepted the idea of the possibility of a few rebirths after enlightenment to help others.) Thus, nothing Bodhisattvas do could stop everyone from ultimately being saved, but their help shortens the time and thus relieves some suffering of others.

5. Some Mahāyāna schools made the Buddha into a savior god and equated him with ultimate reality, all in contrast with the Theravāda tradition. These schools also expanded the ceremonial and devotional elements present in earlier traditions.

6. The Solitary Buddhas and Arhats have overcome the defilements (*kleshas*), but they have not attained the Buddha's knowledge (*jñeya, sarvajñata*). As a corollary of this, the *Prajñāpāramitā* tradition accepts three ways—the Bodhisattva's, the Solitary Buddha's, and the Arhat's—as all leading to the end of rebirth. But later Mahāyāna schools accept that ultimately all will become Buddhas—in the words of Shāntideva, even flies and earthworms will attain the Buddha's wisdom (BCA VII.18). Thus, there is really only one vehicle (*eka-yāna*)—the Bodhisattva's—and, as the *Lotus Sūtra* states, the other paths the Buddha described are only his skillful means to lead his disciples to the true path.

7. This also affects the morality of dedicating one's life to meditation. (The "*mañana* Buddhism" problem was noted in the last chapter.) If one spends most of one's life in meditation and other forms of self-cultivation without any moral action, then the fact that in one's life after enlightenment one can spend what little time is left engaged in moral conduct may not salvage the moral status of the total life. But if the enlightened can choose eons and eons of rebirths in the realm of suffering engaged in moral conduct, then dedicating one entire life to meditation is not so long a period. Thus, Milarepa spending twelve years in a cave, dedicating every moment to the welfare of all beings, is not that long a time compared to the eons of selfless service he believed were to come.

8. In East Asia, insight became personified as the Bodhisattva Mañjurshrī and compassion as the Bodhisattva Avalokiteshvara, who became the most popular among the laity.

9. Shāntideva, *Shikshāmuccaya* 1; see also BCA VIII.95-96. Similarly, from the *Prajñā-pāramitā*: "As I myself want to be quite free from all sufferings, just so all beings want to be quite free from all sufferings" (8PP 28).

10. W. King 1964, p. 159.

11. The Mahāyānists' emphasis on emptiness is a reaction to Hīnayāna Abhidharmists' obsession with analyzing countless categories of the elements of reality (*dharma*s), which they treated as constituting ultimate reality.

12. E.g., 8PP 5-6, 39, 47. Some texts (especially the *Diamond Sūtra*) state this in a confusing way when they speak of there being no "self" or no "no-self." What is meant is that there is nothing of the nature of a self to reality—there is no self nor the absence of a self nor anything related to a self. That is, since there is no real self, the absence of one is not possible either; similarly, with anything even indirectly related to a self. Even if we think of the *unreality* of the self, we are still thinking in terms of a "self." In short, thinking of reality in any terms generated by the notion of a "self" is wrong.

13. In the words of the *Heart Sūtra*, form (*rūpa*) is emptiness (*shūnyata*) and emptiness is form, since all the elements of reality have the nature of emptiness. In the *Prajñāpāramitā* literature this claim is based on emptiness. In Nāgārjuna's thought, it also involves the interconnection of concepts (see R. H. Jones 1993, p. 87). In some other Mahāyāna schools, it is based on the idea that this world is the ultimate reality: being subject to nescience (and thus in *samsāra*) is merely misseeing ultimate reality; with insight, ultimate reality is seen as it really is (and thus we are in *nirvāna*). That is, *nirvāna* is not another realm to escape to or to become attached to, nor (as with the Theravāda) a state after death (*parinirvāna*).

14. See R. H. Jones 1993, pp. 94-95, 104-11, for a discussion of problems with such "grammatical realism" in mysticism. Reconciling an "antirealist" theory of language with a metaphysical reality about the world independent of us would be along those lines: language refers to impermanent, temporary configurations of elements but is still useful for getting around in the world and making knowledge-claims.

15. S. N. Dasgupta, *Hindu Mysticism* (New York: Frederick Ungar Publishing, 1959), p. 103. Āryadeva also showed concern for his murder. He told him to take his clothes and begging bowl and escape over the mountains in monk's garb so that others might not capture and punish him (thereby extending the cycle of violence and karmic damage). He added that he was very sorry for him because of the karmic consequences he would suffer (ibid.).

16. BCA IX.11, IX.76. Shāntideva tried to resolve the paradox by arguing that we feel compassion for an illusory being that is accepted as real for the sake of the goal to be attained (BCA IX.76-78; see also VIII.100-3). But the goal (*bodhi*) and suffering are no less an illusion, and thus this argument cannot succeed.

17. Contra Wainwright 1976, p. 31.

18. Stauffer 1989.

19. Dayal 1970, p. 181.

20. E.g., Macy 1979, 1991.

21. Contra 8PP 75. Nāgārjuna also said that emptiness is pregnant with compassion (*shūnyatākarunāgarbham*).

22. P. Williams 1998, p. 111.

23. Ibid., p. 110.

24. Ibid., p. 111.

25. To take a contemporary example: Jeffrey Hopkins (2001) argues that compassion follows from internalizing the insight that "Everyone wants happiness and doesn't want suffering, just as I want happiness and don't want suffering." But again the value does not follow automatically from the factual claim: we may realize that everyone is alike with

regard to happiness and suffering and still see no reason not to maximize our own happiness at their expense. We may feel sorry for others as we act totally selfishly. Moreover, just because we are all alike does not meant that I must value all impartially (see Chapter 2).

26. Later, four more virtues were added: skillful means (which will be discussed below), resolve (*pranidhāna*), strength (*bala*), and knowledge (*jñāna*).

27. The reciprocal exchange discussed in the last chapter occurs here too: the order receives material goods and the laity receives teaching and guidance in exchange. But the moral picture is more complicated here since the Bodhisattvas are on a genuinely other-regarding quest. Helping them will help *others*, since the Bodhisattvas will help others. This gives the lay givers more merit for their gifts, but it also adds the possibility of an other-regarding motive to their giving.

28. "Even-mindedness" does not mean "indiscriminate" but giving the appropriate aid. Shāntideva points out that Bodhisattvas owe a duty to all sentient beings and so should not wantonly give up their own lives just to make a sacrifice but only when it will help those who are compassionate (BCA V.87). They must use their powers to see into the person's state of mind and not waste their gifts on the unworthy.

29. In the Pāli canon, a similar story is of a monk asked if people were to kill him how he would respond. He answered that he would think them to be good and gentle folk, as they are releasing him from the rotten carcass of the body without much difficulty (MN III.267; SN IV.60; see also 8PP 361-22). (Note that the focus there is again on oneself and not on helping the attackers, unlike in the Mahāyāna.)

30. The minority opinion in the Mahāyāna is that the precepts and monastic code must always be strictly observed, even if violating it might help others, or to permit only certain limited types of violations. Some texts restrict some types of violations only to lay Bodhisattvas (e.g., only they can have sex). Some say only a Bodhisattva at a *lower* stage of development may kill to help others; others say only a Bodhisattva of an *advanced* stage may.

31. Bodhisattvas cannot perform any of the last three unwholesome acts—greed, ill will, and wrong views—since these can only enhance a sense of self. But the other seven unwholesome acts in fact become wholesome if the Bodhisattva's motives are totally other-regarding.

32. If an act should earn the Bodhisattvas rebirths in hells for 100,000 eons for transgressing the precepts but establishes one being on the path to the end of rebirth, they should commit it and not forsake others (*Shikshāmuccaya* XCIII.20-22). This is not to say that they will actually end up in the hells but only that that should not be a consideration. As Asanga said in the *Bodhisattvabhūmi*, those who work with insight and compassion through their skillful means are not harmed and in fact earn merit and can control their rebirths.

33. Dayal 1970, p. 208.

34. Skillful lying is a good illustration of skillful means. Since all words are "false" (in the sense that there are no real entities to designate), truthfulness is literally impossible, and so lying is not seen as a major transgression. All words are "empty," but some expressions work better than others in leading people toward enlightenment. Why, if language does not mark what is real? Because there are real states of affairs (although they are empty of self-existence), and language, even if it is only a "convenient fiction," helps us maneuver around—in particular, it helps ontologically empty "Bodhisattvas" lead empty "persons" toward an equally empty "*nirvāna*."

35. Some texts state that married Bodhisattvas only appear to be married. They are actually celibate, although having sex, because they have no defiled intentions, no feelings, and no pleasure—thus, the act of sexual intercourse itself is irrelevant. Their marriages are

another instance of skillful means to convert others. See Dayal 1970, p. 222.

36. Some Buddhists advance the justification that the person doing the killing is not responsible and so no karmic harm befalls them. The victims are merely reaping the karmic consequences of their own past deeds—their *karma* put them into the position of being killed, and so the killer is not doing anything wrong. In effect, their destiny predetermined their own death. Buddhist-trained samurai warriors believed their sword itself did the killing—they themselves desired no harm to anyone, but the enemy appeared (due to their own *karma*) and the sword automatically performed its function of justice, which is also a function of mercy (Suzuki 1970, p. 145). Christmas Humphreys, who was a judge in the English criminal courts, also said he would have no problem with sentencing a murderer to death because the defendant would just be getting what his own *karma* required. No karmic repercussions would befall Humphreys or an executioner since he would just be the tool of the law of *karma*.

37. Merit (*punya*) does not help enlightened Bodhisattvas on their quest for the Buddha's *bodhi*. But from the beginning of their quest, unenlightened Bodhisattvas dedicate their merit to the enlightenment of all beings and rejoice in the merit of others (8PP 138). In the earliest strata of the *Prajñāpāramitā*, the dedication is solely for the unenlightened Bodhisattvas themselves to gain full enlightenment for the benefit of all; later the idea was introduced of dedicating their merit directly to the welfare of all, thereby providing the unenlightened Bodhisattvas another way to help prior to enlightenment (e.g, 8PP 139-40). (The issue of "merit transfer" was discussed in the last chapter.) Following the code of proper conduct and giving are the main ways to produce merit (especially after the Bodhisattva is enlightened), but Mahāyānists value the religious teachings more. According to the *Prajñāpāramitā*, there is infinitely more merit to be gained (even though Bodhisattvas know it is not "real") by teaching even one stanza on the perfection of insight than in all the merit gained worshiping the Buddha or in all the merit accumulated by Arhats (e.g., 8PP 344-45; DS pp. 55 and 62). Similarly, even the thought of dedicating a Bodhisattva's own merit is infinitely more valuable than the merit accumulated by others (8PP 135-38).

38. The Bodhisattvas of the *Prajñāpāramitā* "are usually rich and powerful men who live in splendid mansions in the cities, are models of education, virtue, and eloquence, respected and loved by everybody, handsome and surrounded by female admirers, and, as occasion demands, energetic and heroic" (Kajiyama Yūichi, "*Prajñāpāramitā* and the Rise of Mahāyāna," in *Buddhist Spirituality: Indian, Southeast Asian, Tibetan, and Early Chinese*, ed. Takeuchi Yoshinori et al. [New York: Crossroad, 1997], p. 139).

39. This claim is often overstated in works on Zen since even the enlightened may need to reflect on alternative courses of action. They cannot respond selfishly, but what the right course of action is (i.e., the most helpful or best for the other person) may not be obvious even to the enlightened. Compassion and a set of Buddhist beliefs will have been completely internalized, but they may not entail one course of action. Of course, habit may simply replace reflection, but moral dilemmas may still remain, even if considering one's own advantage is not an option. (This will be discussed in Chapter 13.)

40. The basic Bodhisattva precepts are: (1) faith in the Buddha, (2) faith in the Buddhist doctrine, (3) faith in the monastic order, (4) eradicating all evils, (5) exerting oneself for all things good, (6) liberating all sentient beings, and (7) following the ten Mahāyāna precepts (*shīla*) listed earlier. Dōgen also recognized that Bodhisattvas can suspend the precepts when compassion requires it.

41. Masunaga 1971, pp. 29-30, 37.

42. Ibid., p. 55.

43. Ibid., p. 56.

44. This is not to deny that the unenlightened often feel "beyond good and evil," with antinomian actions resulting. (Whether the enlightened may do the same will be discussed in Chapter 13.) The monastic order had to be periodically reformed, and part of Dōgen's insistence on following the precepts and avoiding "evil" was because of the state of the monasteries in his time. Today, there are sex and money scandals in Zen Buddhism too.

45. For the pictures and a commentary, see Roshi Philip Kapleau, ed., *The Three Pillars of Zen* (Garden City, N.Y.: Anchor Press, 1980), pp. 313-25.

46. See Victoria 1997. See also David Loy, "The Lack of Ethics and the Ethics of Lack in Buddhism," in Barnard and Kripal 2002, pp. 279-80. The Mahāyāna has a long history of militant monks. Such texts as the *Mahāparinirvāna Sūtra* state that monks can kill to protect the Buddha's doctrine and that kings can go to war to protect his subjects. This has led to monasteries of monks warring with each other (over who has the correct interpretation of the doctrine) and aiding their government. Needless to say, this is moving the justification for killing more and more outside of the mystical context of helping the person with whom a Bodhisattva is interacting along the path to enlightenment.

47. Suzuki 1970, p. 63. He qualifies the remark by adding that Buddhism is animated with a certain revolutionary spirit that comes to the fore when things become deadlocked.

48. Most Vietnamese Buddhists at the time frowned upon these acts. (And the motives of the unenlightened by definition are never only other-regarding but mixed.) These acts are distinguished from suicide in Buddhism since they, like the Buddha-to-be's acts in the Jātaka Tales, were done for the benefit of others and not for any self-serving purpose, although they did expect merit to accrue to acts of self-sacrifice. The objective was to show their suffering. They were giving their lives for others, not taking their own. Any resulting merit was dedicated to the welfare of the others in the worldly form of bringing peace to the world.

49. W. Y. Evans-Wentz, *Tibet's Great Yogi, Milarepa* (New York: Oxford University Press, 1958), pp. 271.

50. Buddha-fields can be seen as a type of social action, since people will be comforted and the aim is to help their religious advancement toward *nirvāna*—Buddha-fields have ideal conditions for attaining Buddhahood. Whether Bodhisattvas in meditation are connected to all beings and "radiate" compassion is also a possibility, but that will not be discussed here.

51. Many Buddhists are more concerned with the karmic consequences to themselves of killing disease-carrying insects or animals then in helping end an epidemic. These beings are also in the realm of rebirth, and thus another issue is whether killing millions of them to save a number of humans that is few by comparison is not an instance of selfishness. Thus, these belief-claims can render social health care action in Buddhist countries more difficult than as we might think.

52. It is not just theists who assert a "divine right of kings." See the *Sūtra of the Excellent Golden Light*, one of the few Mahāyāna texts on government in *Sources of Indian Tradition*, vol. 1, ed. William Theodore de Bary (New York: Columbia University Press, 1958), 182-85.

53. There may be a moral problem if *all* beings must gain Buddhahood (as with the *Lotus Sūtra*) before a Bodhisattva could gain Buddhahood: a Bodhisattva may still be other-regarding, but he or she may also need to use others to get his or her own release. See Dayal 1970, pp. 179-81.

54. The historical issue of whether this revolution in values in Buddhism resulted from a conscious moral critique of the earlier beliefs or from some other cause will not be addressed here. Whether there is a natural evolution away from self-centeredness toward morality present in all religious traditions or whether there is a moral alternative found from the beginning of any tradition will also not be addressed.

10

Left-Handed Tantrism

Tantrism warrants mention, not primarily for its enlightened state, but for its means to enlightenment. Hinduism, Buddhism, and Jainism all have tantric subtraditions. "Right-handed" Tantrism (such as the Dalai Lama's tradition) is comparatively orthodox in its method of yoga and devotion, giving symbolic interpretations to any extreme teachings.[1] But "left-handed" Tantrism *inverts* the orthodox values and rules of conduct—*desire* (*kāma*) becomes the means to enlightenment. It is the opposite extreme from any ascetic form of mysticism. It is an attempt to place desire, in every sense of the word, in the service of religious liberation—not to sacrifice the world for liberation's sake, but to reinstate it in various ways within the perspective of salvation.[2] Right-handed Tāntrikas use desire (including sex) as a starting point for universal compassion on the path to enlightenment, but it is the left-handed Tāntrikas who cultivate unabashed desire as a direct means to enlightenment.

Thus, the most morally interesting point here is not the claim that the enlightened are beyond the restriction of rules and so can do anything—"to the pure everything is pure"—but that the unenlightened Tāntrikas on the path in fact utilize desires to advance their own spiritual careers. It is a case of transmuting poison into medicine: the passions are a poison for most people, but they can be used as an antidote by those who know how to counteract the poison itself and thus to produce a healthy state. Desire, something very dangerous in itself, becomes, to those who know how, a way to release from rebirth. As the Buddhist *Hevajra Tantra* puts it: "By desire this world is bound, and by desire it may be released."

The Path and the Enlightened State

The tantric path is considered the quick path to enlightenment—possibly in this very lifetime and not only after the eons of rebirths it takes a Bodhisattva or a follower of the Hīnayāna paths.[3] Thus, in Buddhism it is called the Vajrayāna—the "path of the thunderbolt." Some in fact consider it the only means to enlightenment possible in our spiritually degenerate age (the *kali-yuga*). It is considered more effective than traditional forms of Indian mystical religiosity because it works on both the mind and the body, not just on the mind. Everything in life is employed to gain enlightenment. This is also considered easier than the arduous work of traditional forms of yogic discipline—in this dark age, austerities and self-denial will only get us so far, not to enlightenment. In the words of the Buddhist *Guhyasamāja Tantra*, "no one succeeds in gaining perfection by means of difficult and wearying exercise, but perfection can be easily won by satisfying all of one's desires."

The tantric enlightened state of one liberated in life (*jīvan-mukta*) differs from that in other Indian traditions in that the state is much more worldly—satisfying desires figures more prominently, even if, as discussed below, only through highly stylized rituals. (As discussed in Chapter 4, the idea that the enlightened satisfy their desires goes back to the Upanishads.)[4] No longer defiled by the world (because of desires), they can enjoy the world. As discussed below, Tāntrikas may share the metaphysics of illusionism with Advaita Vedānta and emptiness with Mahāyāna Buddhism, but they have a different *evaluation* of the world: the world is not to be escaped but comprehended as it really is and lived in fully. We are part of the world, and so the body is not considered foul and disgusting, as in much Indian and Western mysticism—instead, all the pleasures of the world are to be enjoyed. Indeed, Tāntrikas do not differentiate using the energies of the universe for manipulative "magical" ends for their own advantages from the "religious" end of enlightenment: all energy is the same in a world of illusion or where *nirvāna* is not different from the realm of rebirth (*samsāra*). The cosmic energy of the universe is neutral—energy is energy, however we choose to use it. Thus, Tāntrikas have many magical formulas (*mantras*) to develop paranormal powers (*siddhis*) for mundane matters of wealth, pleasure, and power over others, as well as for the supramundane matter of enlightenment.

Metaphysics

The metaphysics of tantric religiosity is fairly orthodox. As with the Mahāyāna, all sense of duality within the phenomenal world is considered unreal. All "discrimination" of distinct and independent entities is unreal and is in fact the cause of our suffering and rebirth. The world itself is pure. It is our discriminations that make it seem "impure." The objective is to return to the pure mind prior to such discriminations. For this, all sense of duality must be abolished. In both Hindu and Buddhist Tantrism, the metaphysics grounding this belief is a monism based on a union of principles. In Hinduism, this is derived from Sāmkhya-Yoga dualism set within a nondualistic Advaita Vedānta framework, although the emphasis is shifted to the illusoriness within the phenomenal world rather than the depth-reality. (Some

Hindu tantric schools have remained more dualistic.) In Buddhism, the metaphysics comes from Mahāyāna schools (the Mādhyamika and Yogācāra) with a nondualistic ground considered basic—i.e., emptiness (that all entities are empty of self-existence) becomes the Void out of which all empty entities arise, with our mind alone creating the objectness of the "entities." There is no realm of *nirvāna* distinct from the world. (Not all Mahāyāna schools subscribe to this.) The only innovation is that the basic principles are personified into active gods and goddesses uniting all forces into a unity. This gives Tantrism a theistic element not present in all philosophical schools of Hinduism and Buddhism. However, these deities are seen as merely projections of powerful positive and negative forces within our minds—but then again all objectness is only our mental creation, and thus the deities are as real as "tables" and "chairs."

The body is seen as a microcosm—a place where all the forces of the macrocosmic universe operate—and thus the locus where the truth of the universe can be found. Sexual intercourse is then seen as the union in our body of male and female principles at work in the universe. The universe works by the passive and active principles coming together—so, Tāntrikas conclude, we should duplicate this cosmic process in ourselves, free of any social conventions (since our conventions are not part of the real forces). In Buddhism, the male is active ("means," *upāya*) and the female inactive ("insight," *prajñā*). In Hinduism, the roles are reversed: the male (Shiva) is passive and the female power (Shakti) is active. With sexual intercourse, the cosmic duality is overcome with the body.[5] The thunderbolt symbolizes the union. All sense of duality is lost in the union. The basic union of the forces of the universe is thereby recreated in our body. This action is the paradigm of how the ultimate forces of reality interact. By this act, a Tāntrika comes to see that all duality—most importantly, ultimate reality and the phenomenal world, *nirvāna* and *samsāra*—is an unreal creation of our minds.

What is new is not so much the metaphysics but the yogic techniques and also the ethical implications Tāntrikas derive from the metaphysics. Advaitins and Mahāyānists have the same metaphysics but do not embrace any antinomian conclusions. As discussed in the last chapter, Bodhisattvas can accept nonduality and the emptiness of all entities—and thus that all of the phenomenal world is an "illusion" in that sense—while still espousing a moral concern for others. (In Advaita, as discussed in Chapter 5, inaction is the primary option, but actions harmful to others is not considered an option.) Immorality is not even a stage of training to be passed through on the path in order to show nonattachment. But Tāntrikas ask why, if all duality is an illusion, if the mind is pure and all objectness is caused by the mind but is empty of any reality, and if everything is in fact pure, then why can we not do anything? Indeed, they argue that the quick way to learn that all dualities are not real is by actually doing all things. Any restrictions (including morality) must be ignored in order to see reality as it really is. In particular, this means no restrictions on the passions nature gave us. Pleasure is release (*moksha*), to one who knows.

Turning Poison into Medicine

Oscar Wilde said, "There is only one way to get rid of a temptation—that is to yield to it."[6] But in Tantrism, passions are transformed into the means to a religious end—to get beyond the process of attachment to enlightenment. The desires are yielded to, but only with sustained attention paid to each act of desire, its causes, and its consequences and with the object of desire transformed into a deity. There is no need to destroy sexual impulses, which would be unnatural and impossible in any case. This involves indulging in everything deemed repugnant in nontantric Indian religiosity. Thus, Tāntrikas intentionally do everything the orthodox condemn. (Their sects and the rituals were kept secret to avoid persecution by the orthodox and to protect the uninitiated from the powers supposedly released.) For example, their central ritual (*cakra-pūjā*), set in cremation grounds or other places considered extremely unclean by orthodox Hindu standards, begins with the master (*guru*) and his consort (the Shakti) seated in the center of a circle of initiated students (with women to the left of their partner).[7] They all then drink wine (*madya*) from the same cup and eat meat (*māmsa*; preferably beef) and fish (*matsya*) from the same plate. To make matters even more disgusting, excrement, urine, blood, or vomit is mixed in with the food and wine, since all things are "pure." Just the presence of lower class women and servants (*shūdras*)—for the class system is intentionally ignored—is enough to offend Brahmins. But the females may be young girls of low class. Adultery and incest are also suggested. If the women are menstruating, so much the better, since that is considered impure. The females are then made into vehicles of the divine energy ("goddesses," *devīs*) by means of incantations (*mantras*). All then take aphrodisiacs, such as parched grain (*mudrā*), and have sexual intercourse (*maithunā*) in a ritualized way such as mentally reciting verses during intercourse.

Outside this ritual, Tāntrikas have other rituals—some involving sex with corpses or cannibalism. Other rituals involve Tāntrikas' own form of ritual dance and music. Like ascetics, they may flaunt the laws of pollution by living in graveyards or using human skulls as cups. Most significantly, the rules of proper conduct, such as those against murder and stealing, are also broken (again in a highly ritualized fashion). What is "evil" becomes "good." Thus, the dichotomy of proper conduct (*dharma*) and improper conduct (*adharma*) is completely broken down. Indeed, *adharma* now becomes, by definition, the path to enlightenment. If one is attached to a value—e.g., labeling something as "evil" if it makes another being suffer—then one has not transcended the duality of our concepts. Violence and "evil" are as much a part of reality as what we label "good." One must perform acts—including rape and murder—to see the emptiness of our dichotomies. Thus, the Tāntrika finds *nirvāna* in the embrace of a young girl—or with her murdered body.

But the Tāntrika is not indulging a passion simply to burn it out. They are not trying to remove a desire by overdosing on it and thus becoming weary of it or revolted by it. The "path of excess" does not lead to the "palace of wisdom" in that sense. The point is to do what is prohibited precisely because it is prohibited, since to abhor something is as much an attachment as valuing something. All shame, disgust, and fear must be overcome. We can then observe the desires at work and see that everything is pure in itself. Thereby, we can see the desires for what they are, free of socially defined evaluations—the very energies of the universe at work in us, and nothing "evil." Tāntrikas are gaining mastery over desires, not eliminating them. Thus, when they internalize the enlightening knowledge, their inner dispositions are not altered the way most mystics' are (i.e., by the elimination of all desires). But the Tāntrikas now see the desires differently: they see the desires operating in themselves as the energies of reality and use them accordingly. The enlightened no longer have the disposition of an ordinary person (*pashu*, an "animal") or even a hero (*vīra*) but of a deity (*divya*).

And considering both the amount of work required even before one can enter into the complex rituals and the mindfulness that is to be employed during the rituals, Tantrism should not be seen as libertine. The highly ritualized life keeps this from being a life of pure lust.[8] One only gets to the tantric rituals after initiation and a long period of training in the traditional forms of yoga (in Buddhism, the exercises for mindfulness and calming the mind), study of the orthodox texts, and following the standard ethics of the tradition. (For Buddhists, this includes the compassion of the Mahāyāna way of life.) Tibetan Gelugpa lamas are said to study twenty years before they are initiated. There are strict vows governing all aspects of one's life. One must engage in complicated meditations involving visualizations of deities and *mandalas* (two-dimensional reconstructions of a deity's palace).[9] One's daily life is a long stream of *mantras* and rituals—starting the day with worship of the guru, bathing in the prescribed manner, rituals for selecting the place to meditate, and so on.[10] Taking drugs such as hemp requires another ritual. Sex is restricted to the rituals and there strictly governed by rules. It is an elaborately and carefully choreographed event. Far from being an orgy, one is to observe soberly the actions going on in order to see the energies actually at work in reality. No hedonistic enjoyment of any part of the rituals is to be involved. The sex is an act of worshiping a goddess. If one does not recognize the deity or otherwise loses focus on observing the energies at work and becomes attached to the act, one has not converted the poison into medicine—one is no more than an animal (*pashu*) committing an impure act that will hurt one's karmic destiny. Buddhist Tāntrikas bring this point home by insisting that no ejaculation of sperm occur during the sex. In sum, the objective is to use desires to get beyond attachments, including any attachment to desires.

Freedom from Value-Attachments

Tantric religiosity is a reaction to the standard codes of conduct in Indian religiosity: not killing, not eating meat, and the other codified abstentions can
themselves become sources of attachment and thus obstacles to enlightenment.
Suffering is caused by the nescience of seeing the dualities in the phenomenal
world as ultimately real. Evaluations are not real—only the energies of the world
are. Discriminating "pure" from "impure" becomes a dualism keeping us from
enlightenment, which simply is the nondiscrimination of what the unenlightened
take to be separately existing "real" entities. Repulsion is as much an attachment
as attraction. Nothing is "unclean," and Tāntrikas are to see this directly with the
experiences occurring within their own bodies. Thus, they act on that principle,
showing no attachments. That compassion and hatred are simply two sides of the
same coin takes on a new meaning. Any precepts of conduct (e.g., the Buddhist
shīla) designed to lessen attachments become objects of attachment. Nothing
distinguishes such precepts from any other object of attachment that must be
broken—they are a mental box confining us in the realm of nescience. Thus, a rule
against harming others, if obeyed rigidly, would tend to absolutize the realm of
nescience. Why obey the conventions of the unenlightened, even those rules
designed to lead to enlightenment? Indeed, an attachment to a moral concern for
others is as much an attachment as any other. What is wrong with killing or stealing
if all phenomena are ultimately illusions? The problem is one of points of view:
only a belief separates the unenlightened from the enlightened, not any type of
action. Thus, in a revaluation of values, Tāntrikas transform what was used by the
orthodox as an ethical criticism of both Advaita and Buddhism into a way to cut
through the illusion.

In sum, any mental objects—including values—can become objects of
attachment and hence a hindrance to enlightenment that must be overcome by
shattering them. Seen in this light, Tantrism is not, as is often claimed, a "degeneration" of Hindu and Buddhist traditions but is simply a mystical response to
something that may tend to absolutize a realm without substance. As a reaction to
earlier schools, it is a continuation of the tradition. Thus, the tantric approach is
extending the tradition (one possible meaning of the word "*tantra*"). Such an
approach is especially valuable when formalism has replaced a living religion—i.e.,
when the previous forms of a religion have become ossified into a set of rules that
are no longer working as means to enlightenment but are followed only *pro forma*
as ends in themselves. And within a monistic metaphysical framework in which the
phenomenal realm is seen as becoming ossified into illusions, this approach is
ruthlessly logical: no values of the illusory realm are grounded in reality, and in
fact there are no "beings" to be concerned about.

In short, Indian mysticism started by attacking attachments but its practices
became themselves a source of attachment, and thus Tantrism attacked them.[11]
Rules of unenlightened social conduct are then no more than idols to be smashed

and obstacles that must be overcome. Each new set of values—including those designed to lead toward enlightenment—creates a new possible source of attachment, and Tantrism is merely attacking each new progression. This carries on the Advaita and Buddhist approach of preventing anything from becoming a possible attachment. If we had different values, Tantrism would involve different actions. But whenever the means to breaking down obstacles of attachment itself becomes another object of attachment, one must break down the means. The tantric turn simply moves in the opposite direction of any given set of values, including those of Hindu and Buddhist mystics.

In sum, Tāntrikas are being antinomian toward any set of values without advancing any new set of their own. This is logically the last possible position in this mysticism: Tāntrikas are not advancing a new set of evaluations but reacting to there being any set of values at all. (One might argue that, since Tantrism still involves a highly ritualized practice, the next logical step would be to do away with all such restrictions—abolishing all rules altogether. But that step can only be to indulge in the desires merely as an end in itself and thus to abolish the quest for enlightenment entirely.) Again, this is because overcoming attachment, not any rules to gain this end, is the objective in the mystical quest.

Is Left-Handed Tantrism Moral?

On mystical grounds, one can object that left-handed Tāntrikas, by deliberately breaking the rules of conduct just because they are norms, have made a mental object of orthodox values. *Adharma* rather than *dharma* becomes the object of attachment. Unless adharmic behavior is merely a step on the path which also has to be overcome in the enlightened state, Tāntrikas are "coursing in signs." As things stand, it is the Mahāyāna Bodhisattvas, who obey the rules or disregard them as compassion requires, who are truly free of the mental obstacle of rules. (Valuing compassion over selfishness can be neutral and not an attachment only if compassion, like the energies of desire, is considered somehow grounded in reality.) On moral grounds, there is a different problem: Tāntrikas differ from Bodhisattvas in that the violations of the precepts are for their own benefit, not to help others to enlightenment. Both see the precepts as "empty," but for Bodhisattvas this lets their spontaneous compassion flow, while for Tāntrikas this merely creates another means to their own enlightenment. For them, violating the precepts is an instance of a selfish means to a religious end. Thus, the Buddhist Tāntrikas' prior long training in the Mahāyāna's other-regarding ethics cannot change the fact that once they enter the tantric path their moral status changes.

In addition, this end cannot be judged moral even if the tantric path is considered the quick way to enlightenment. If the tantric path is merely considered the quick path to ending one's own suffering by ending one's own rebirth, the immorality is clear: the Tāntrikas are using other people only for their own selfish end. But there is a moral problem even if the path leads left-handed Tāntrikas in both Buddhism and Hinduism to an enlightened life in which they engage constantly in compassionate action toward others in this life and in eons of freely elected future rebirths. The problem is that Tāntrikas use other people to attain this end. With their ethos of desire, they remove any concern for others. It can be assumed here that all who participate in the central ritual are doing so of their own free will (leaving aside the issue of minors), but it is the Tāntrikas' actions outside this ritual that is the problem. The Theravādins use others for their own ends, but they abstain from actually harming them and in fact often help others. Tāntrikas have no such restrictions. People are deliberately hurt on the path (to show the Tāntrikas' own freedom from attachments), and hurting some people to help oneself cannot be considered moral. Even if it leads indirectly to helping third parties, it is still immoral: intentionally hurting an innocent person even to help many more later on cannot be deemed moral when the motive to help oneself is also present. Unless an argument can be made that they are sacrificing one person in danger to help many others and that only an other-regarding concern is present, Tantrism must be deemed immoral. To be moral, we must exhibit some concern for the people impinged-upon, even if this represents an attachment. (Right-handed Tāntrikas recognize that at least enlightened Bodhisattvas can be compassionate without compassion becoming an object of attachment.) But the tantric approach involves attacking any standards, including moral ones. Thus, the extreme case of breaking all attachments goes beyond morality into immorality.

Notes

1. The left-handed branch probably predates the right-handed, since left-handed tantric texts were later given symbolic and innocuous interpretations as Tāntrikas adopted ethical codes that were conventional by Hindu and Buddhist standards. For example, in the central tantric ritual coconut milk was substituted for wine, curd cheese for meat, ginger for fish, rice for any aphrodisiacs, and a simple kiss for sexual intercourse—it is doubtful such a substitution would have occurred the other way around. But how the ritual could achieve the desired end with such substitutions is not clear.

2. Madeleine Biardeau, quoted in André Padoux, "Tantrism," in *The Encyclopedia of Religion*, vol. 13, ed. Mircea Eliade (New York: Macmillan, 1975), p. 273.

3. According to the Theravāda tradition, many of the Buddha's followers attained enlightenment very quickly after taking up his teaching—in as little as seven days. (Of course, it can be argued that in previous lives, these people had advanced along the Buddhist path for many eons, so that it only looked like quick enlightenment to us.) But those days quickly disappeared.

4. The Tāntrikas' interests seem to reflect more the interests of the laity than those of the monks. The unorthodoxy of Tantrism and the fact that it arose in areas of India that were not yet fully Brahmanized has caused many scholars to see it as a form of indigenous religiosity present before the arrival of the Indo-Europeans. The elements of goddess worship, yogic practices, medicine, and magic all suggest this. (Some practices, such as

*mantra*s, also have roots in the Vedas.) While this is certainly possible, Tantrism may also be simply the natural evolution within a form of religiosity that is constantly breaking down new obstacles of possible attachment. Or both factors could be involved: the indigenous religiosity emerged as a part of the dominant traditions when the historical conditions of those traditions made its forms of breaking obstacles appropriate (i.e., when the dominant tradition's teaching begin to ossify and not to lead to enlightenment).

5. The energy involved is not limited to sex. It is the cosmic energy in the *kundalinī* system within the human body, but the details of tantric physiology need not be discussed here.

6. Or, in *The Portrait of Dorian Grey*, Wilde has a character say that to realize one's nature perfectly one must give form to every feeling, express every thought, and not suppress any emotion.

7. The role of gurus for initiation and oral teaching is central to all tantric sects. They also are said to transfer energy mentally to their students. Some Tāntrikas are initiated into the mysteries by sex with special women, *dakinis*, who are also said to have paranormal powers and who pass their powers to the initiated through the sex. The highest of the four classes of tantric texts are encoded in a "twilight language" (*sandhyā-bhāshā*) that is made deliberately unintelligible to the uninitiated. It is said that this is done both to protect the ordinary person, who may be harmed by mishandling the powerful and potentially dangerous mystical knowledge, and to transport the initiated into a new world of knowledge. One needs the oral teachings of a master to understand them. This makes the tradition properly labeled "esoteric." Even today many tantric texts have not been translated because of problems with the language (and because the way of life is considered degenerate).

8. Of course, not all Tāntrikas perform up to the specified goal. Today many Neo-Tantric groups treat Tantrism merely as a license for sex with a very thin veneer of religiosity.

9. As in the Upanishads, one becomes what one knows. Whether projecting oneself onto an image or internalizing an image, one becomes the deity upon whom one meditates. In *mandala* meditations, one mentally transports the body into the center of the deity's palace, thereby both identifying with the deity and placing oneself at the center of the universe.

10. This total ritualization of life separates Tantrism as much from earlier Buddhism as the inversion of values. The Buddha rejected all rituals, even though the laity and the order adopted more and more over time.

11. One might ask why Tāntrikas attack practices and not the basic metaphysical beliefs of Advaita and Buddhism. After all, Mahāyānists such as Nāgārjuna showed how to put a new spin on them. Arguably, since their emphasis is on experiments within the body and actions, any focus on ideas is not as important as focusing on action-guides for behavior. Nevertheless, they did advance a belief-framework for their attack on the conventional mystical values.

11

Daoism

The subject of this chapter will be the two main texts of early Daoism[1]—the *Daodejing*, attributed to Laozi (the "Old Master"), and Master Zhuang's *Zhuangzi*.[2] The *Daodejing* is a book of sayings and does not form a systematic, coherent whole from one thinker. There are passages on politics, mystical techniques, and military defense. The stories in the inner chapters of the *Zhuangzi* may be the product of Zhuangzi, but the book also contains chapters of later miscellaneous material. The two texts differ enough that whether Zhuangzi thought of himself as a "Daoist" in the sense Laozi was one is not clear. Thus, while they share many points, each will also require some separate treatment.

The atmosphere of the Chinese thought of the pre-Qin period is very different from that of classical India. There was a focus in religious and philosophical thought on such social realities as the family and government that was absent even from the *Bhagavad-gītā*, let alone the rest of the Indian religiosity discussed earlier. Nature is seen as an dynamic whole exhibiting patterns of interlocking natural forces, the most famous of which are the *yang* (masculine) and the *yin* (feminine). The harmony of all things is central, but there is no sense of a monism to reality that obliterates the individuality of each thing and each person. Indeed, whether the traditional Chinese conception of reality was of a unified "universe" is open to question: nature is simply the myriad of beings—the "ten thousand things" (*wanwu*)—operating in conformity with the Way (*dao*).[3] Nor is there a major division between the natural and social orders: people and the rest of reality are part of one order. Our happiness is to be found in living in conformity with the Way—thus, most early classical Chinese thinkers were "daoists" in the broadest sense. But we human beings do not automatically conform to the natural flow of the Way. We need a form of self-cultivation in order to achieve a return to it. Thus, the focus of classical Chinese thought is a "this-worldly" concern for cultivating oneself to conform to the Way in a social setting. Any postmortem reward or punishment for our actions in this world is not the central concern.[4] Instead, our life in this world should be fully developed (along the different lines set forth by each philosophy).

Reacting to Confucius

As Tantrism was a reaction to earlier Buddhist and Hindu religiosity, so too Daoism was a reaction to the dominant Confucian culture of its period. Confucius was concerned with human affairs and the Way as manifest in a harmonious society (*ren dao*). Harmony in the world was a matter of our proper place in the scheme of things seen in social and political terms.[5] The rules of appropriate social behavior (*li*), as set forth in the Confucian classics, outline our roles and relationships within the hierarchy of society, from the relation of ruler and ruled to family relations (parent and child, husband and wife, older and younger brothers) to elder and junior friends. These rules cover many situations, but they do not cover all situations. To know how to act in the situations that are not covered, we need a sense of reciprocity (*shu*), summarized in a negatively stated Golden Rule: "Never do to others what you would not like them to do to you" (*Analects* V.11, XII.2, XV.23). In addition, a limitation on the *li* rules is that, as Confucius realized, social conventions evolve and vary. But what always informs any set of rules is our sense of common humaneness (*ren*).[6] This reflects the inner side of our social behavior: our underlying sense of what is appropriate (*yi*).[7] Once we can carry out the appropriate behavior without effort or having to think of what is right (i.e., with *cheng*—"sincerity" or "integrity"), our actions are those of a person in whom the Way of humaneness is manifest.

The entire Confucian life is ordered by social convention. Central to this project is the cultivation of certain virtues—especially humaneness—by practicing the rules of appropriate behavior (*li*) and following exemplars of proper conduct, such as the legendary emperors from the golden age. Such self-cultivation is a matter of education in social etiquette and status and of internalizing social conventions. Thus, the social sphere is where we fully develop into human beings. We are not born human—we are social beings and only become fully realized human beings by our own inner transformation (*xin*). Humaneness is defined relationally rather than individualistically—the symbol for "*ren*" combines the symbols for "human being" and "two." Each person is not a self-contained atom but a separate node in a web of relationships. No one has value in themselves but only in their social role and obligations to others. Thus, it is only through developing interpersonal virtues (e.g., loyalty, courage, considerateness) that we become fully human. Until we have internalized the sense of what behavior is called for in each situation, we need external rules (*li*) to follow. But Confucians disagreed with the Legalists (*fa-jia*) over the need for laws: regulations can force changes in behavior by means of reward and punishment, but they cannot cause the inner transformation needed for one to become a fully realized human being. Confucius' own life reflects the difficulty in attaining this sense: at fifteen, he set his heart on learning the classics; at thirty, he established himself in that pursuit;

at forty, he no longer had any perplexities; at fifty, he knew the will of Heaven; at sixty, his ear was attuned to Heaven's will; only at age seventy could he follow his heart's desire without transgressing the boundaries of appropriate conduct (*Analects* II.4). His heart and mind were then aligned with the Way of humaneness, and so he could do whatever he wished. Only at that age was he truly an exemplary person (*junzi*).

Self-cultivation is the basis for reforming society into a more harmonious whole. For Confucius, there is a hierarchy of social roles, with the family being the foundation. The rival thinker Mozi rejected the rules of *li* as the prerogative of the elite in favor of an "all-embracing love" free of any hierarchical relations. But Confucians dismissed such impartial universal love as utopian—it does not reflect the reality that we live in a hierarchy of different social relationships and that we are rightly partial toward family and friends. One is being selfish to think of oneself as independent of familial and social relations or to refuse serving in government, let alone to withdraw from society—we *are* our social roles. Once we align our inner dispositions with humaneness, our families will be transformed; with each family transformed, the society as a whole will be well run; and finally, with each country well run, there will be peace in the world. This is a bottom-up reform rather than a top-down one in which the ruler first rectifies himself and society transforms itself by the power of the ethical example, although the ruler remains the most important instance of change in the society. An instance of the change is to reorder government by the "rectification of names" (*zhengming*) so that each government official fulfills his duties properly. That is, only when a government official speaks only of what is proper for him to carry out and accurately expresses what he means can governmental action be effectively carried out (*Analects* XIII.3). Actions tally with words, and language encodes the important social distinctions and properly guides action.

The Daoist Approach

It is precisely such distinctions and rules that Daoists object to. Confucius realized that the rules of *li* do not supply an answer in all situations, but such rules were firmly embedded in his view of things, along with the accompanying hierarchy of social roles and statuses. They define what it is to be human. Learning such matters is the central task of Confucian cultivation, but to Daoists, social embellishments are exactly what we must *unlearn* to allow the Way governing reality to operate in us unimpeded by personal desires. Zhuangzi's parable of people boring seven holes into Chaos (*hun-dun*) to make it like us—thereby killing it—illustrates their attitude to all things cultural (Z 7). It is imposing a human order on the naturalness of reality. In sum, if Confucian cultivation is a matter of learning more social distinctions, then Daoism is a matter of uncultivation. To Confucius, we become fully realized only by internalizing a set of names and rules.[8] But to Daoists, we need to unlearn precisely those distinctions vital to the Confucian way of life to become aligned with the Way. To Confucius, Laozi understood how to look inward but knew nothing of looking outward—if the Way prevailed in the world as Laozi thought, Confucius would not have needed to try to alter things. To Xunzi, Zhuangzi was blinded by nature and did not know the human experience. But to Daoists, Confucians are only aggravating the problem: what they value most is exactly what interferes with the action of the Way and thus must be removed. Any names, rules, or rituals are imposed on us externally and only interfere with our natural actions. We must eliminate the layers of artificiality added to us from the outside to let our *de* (the Way as it operates in us) manifest itself. How nature acts is the model for how we should act (D 25), not the artificial inventions of culture, since the various parts of nature follow the Way spontaneously. Confucians go against the grain of reality by developing culture, and the objective of Daoism is to return to what we really are.

Daoism is sometimes said to complement Confucianism—the *yin* to Confucius' *yang*. The two traditions do share much of the common Chinese worldview, but philosophical Daoism cannot be seen as complementing Confucianism: Laozi and Zhuangzi are not adding something Confucius missed to complete a way of life. They saw no need for Confucianism.[9] Rather, they are offering an alternative. Zhuangzi's reaction when his wife died—singing and banging on a tub (Z 18)—was a complete rejection of Confucian ritual. It was not merely a different attitude toward the funeral rituals: it reflects a totally negative judgment of the artificiality of Confucian ritual requirements. Antonio Cua, who defends the complementary thesis, realizes that Confucian and Daoist attitudes cannot be maintained concurrently.[10] However, this is because they are incompatible in principle. To speak of them as complements rather than contradictories may reflect the later selective Neo-Confucian synthesis, but it goes against the spirit of philosophical Daoism. Daoists certainly reacted to the prevailing cultural force of their day, but they did not supplement it—they reacted against it. The entire thrust of Daoism is toward fewer and fewer rules and less social cultivation in order to allow the Way to flow spontaneously through us.

The Daoist way of life involves a yielding approach to all events, an absence of coercion, naturalness, and a spontaneity to action. The objective is to live as long a life as possible (e.g., D 50, 52, 55), and not being in accord with the Way leads to an early demise (D 30).[11] Violent and fierce people do not come to a natural end (D 42).[12] Being content and knowing when to stop striving leads to a long life (D 33, 44, 46). But all cultural enterprises involve such striving. The twisted, gnarly tree is valued more than the cultivated trees, since the latter end up being cut down for lumber while the former is ignored (Z 1). This is very much a life-affirming ethos of being at home in the world. No renunciation of the world or society is recommended. Nothing about this life is disparaged (except the cultural accretions we impose on it), and no goal outside this life is suggested. Zhuangzi did make death a major topic—although not suffering, as with the Buddhists—but there is no great fear of it.[13] He was lighthearted even about that. Death is merely part of the transformation of things—a return to the natural forces at work in reality. He was even-minded toward death, since from the point of view of the "equality of all things," whether he is alive or dead makes no difference—there is no individual to consider. What is real remains what it always was. Moreover, Daoists ask, how do we know that love of life is not a delusion and that those who fear death are not like a child who is lost and cannot find his way home?

The strategies for attaining a long life differ for Laozi and Zhuangzi. As discussed below, Laozi emphasized a depth-mysticism—discovering the Way by emptying the mind of all content. Zhuangzi emphasized a mindfulness that also involved stilling the mind; he also added more philosophical arguments to try to crack the rigidity of thinking that our own point of view is somehow founded in reality in a way that others' are not. His most famous parable is of his dream in which he dreamed he was a butterfly and had no idea he had ever been anything else; when he awoke, he asked himself, "Did Zhuangzi dream he was a butterfly, or is the butterfly now dreaming he is Zhuangzi?" (Z 2). The point is not the Advaita conclusion that we should awaken to the true reality behind the "dream" realm but our inability to know what is the correct point of view. From the "point of view of heaven," all our limited points of view reduce what is real to what is valuable for us and do not let reality be as it truly is. What one animal considers beautiful, another considers ugly—there is no one standard for all nor a fixed, universal point of view. Believing our point of view is superior is like a frog in a well seeing only a small sliver of the sky and thinking it sees all of it.

Laozi and Zhuangzi also differ in the basic application to life of their mysticisms. Laozi was interested in the political life, while Zhuangzi wanted to wander free and easy, living quietly, unimpeded by such concerns. For the former, being without personal desires is the way to gain the things one desires (D 7, 28, 48, 66, 67). Herrlee Creel draws this distinction as between "purposive" and "contemplative" Daoism, the former being mostly in the *Daodejing*.[14] These are probably not the best terms, however, since even Zhuangzi's examples of skilled individuals who had a mirrorlike mind from following the Way still had goals—the cook, after all, wanted to cut up the ox, the swimmer wanted to survive, and so forth. They were not literally "wandering" (which implies no destination) but had a "purpose." Both types of Daoism involve a mystical cultivation, and neither is unconnected to this-worldly, practical applications in life.

The Daoist Way

What exactly Laozi and Zhuangzi meant by "the Way" (*dao*) has been open to widely varying interpretations. But the basic idea seems to be that it is both the underlying source of the world and also a structure guiding phenomena within the world. Laozi set forth a cosmogony: the constant Way (*chang-dao*) that cannot be named is the source of heaven and earth (*tian-di*); the nameable Way is the mother of everything in the world—the "ten thousand things" (*wan-wu*) (D 1, 40, 42).[15] All things emerge from this great mysterious "root" or "womb" and return to it (D 6, 16, 40; Z 18).[16] The Way creates and sustains everything (D 51). The unnameable Way is not dependent on anything, formless, unchanging, all-pervading, never-failing, and soundless; it is the nonbeing (*wu*) that is the source of being (D 40); it is not caused by an external agent and thus is its own cause ("self-so," *ziran*) (D 4, 11, 25, 40; Z 6, 12).[17] The emphasis in both the *Daodejing* and *Zhuangzi*, however, is on the Way as the *source of change* rather than, as in the West and Advaita, as the *source of being*. Nor is there any questioning of the phenomenal realm (*you*) as unreal in any sense. This gives Daoism a much more positive "this-worldly" feel than the Indian traditions covered earlier. Zhuangzi emphasized the constant transformation of things (*wuhua*) in nature and never elevated the permanence of the Way over the perpetual change, while Laozi emphasized things' inevitable reversion to the root (*fan*).

The Way has nothing to do with a theistic god intervening in nature but is more like the space-time continuum in Einstein's theory of gravity: natural objects moving under the "force" of gravity are actually guided by the curvature of space-time. Similarly with the nameable Way: it is the organizing structure that gives order to the flux of change in the world. It is unchanging, as Zhuangzi emphasized (Z 1, 6, 7; D 1). It operates impartially in all things (Z 2, 6, 18). Thus, the Way both transcends the world (since it is the inexhaustible source of everything and in that sense is the sum total of all things) and operates within the world as the structure of order. The manifestation of the Way in a particular thing is that thing's potency (*de*).[18] Although the Way is constant, *de* varies from thing to thing, reflecting what each individual thing receives from the Way and thereby determining what its natural activity is. While the Way can be thought of in the singular as an organizing principle, still there are many ways ("*dao's*") to nature and not only one master "Way" to which all the various patterns can be reduced. Zhuangzi emphasized this variety and particularity more than did Laozi. It is these ways, not the underlying source (the unnameable Way), that can be followed. All of nature automatically follows the way of its particular type, thereby producing a harmonious order. Thus, despite its profundity (*xuan*), the Way has an order, an order we can discern and follow.

Language and the Way

We human beings, however, have fallen out of step with our way. We do not spontaneously move with our *de*.[19] The culprit according to Laozi is our habit of living according to the conceptual distinctions we ourselves devise. We reason what is right or wrong, and we accept our concepts as reflecting the nature of reality, but concepts are in fact only a reflection of our preferences and needs.

Nevertheless, our own creations fix our attention, and we respond to our concepts rather than to reality. Under this view, all of language is the central problem: it does not capture natural distinctions but creates artificial ones. This is an antirealist theory of language: words reflect our interests and not real distinctions in the world. Indeed, there are no distinct entities. Language carves the "uncarved block" (*po*) of nature into differentiated entities (D 19, 28) reflecting our interests. Concepts arise by differentiating: we call something "beautiful" only when we have something "ugly" to contrast with it (D 2, 38)—if everything were beautiful, we would have nothing to contrast beauty with, and so we would have no term "ugly" and hence no term "beautiful." Not all concepts arise in pairs, but all set off part of reality into something distinct from the rest. If all the world were red in color, we would have no concept of "redness" (or of "color") because we would have nothing with which to contrast it. Or, to use a Daoist image, fish have no concept of "water," because it is a constant in their experience and thus they never have anything with which to contrast it and thus are not even aware of it (unless they are removed from it). The same occurs with values: concepts of humaneness (*ren*) and appropriateness (*yi*) arose only when the great Way declined (D 18)—when all the world conformed to those standards, there were no standards to state (because we were not aware of another condition). The man of superior power (*de*) is not conscious of his power (because he has nothing to contrast with it) and thereby truly possesses power (D 38). That is, we have the concept of "power" only when we are aware of it, i.e., only when we are not one with the Way and are aware of a distinction between it and something else. When we are aware of discriminations, we live in a world of discriminations, not in accordance with the Way. The use of names is the first step in converting the world into what is apprehensible and a source of desire. Once we have such desires and preferences, our actions are artificial (*wei*) rather than a natural response to the situation (*wu wei*). In short, language codifies our differentiations and thereby artificially guides our actions. A proscription of names, not a Confucian rectification of names, is thus necessary (D 32, 37). Returning to the unnameable uncarved block frees us from desire, and the world will become peaceful of its own accord (D 37).

This attack on language is a direct rejection of the Confucian point of view. Names and rules are central to the Confucian ethical program: all cultivation of potency (*de*) is a matter of mastering a system of differentiations and conforming our actions to them. The rectification of names is part of this, but more generally our social discriminations guide actions, and thus social categories (names and rules) are ingrained in that way of life. But while Confucius' way is language-guided, the Daoists' is reality-guided, free of the artifices of culture embodied in a language's distinctions. We need to turn from our cultivated self and allow our natural prelinguistic capacities (*de*) to flow forth. That is how we become properly human, not by dwelling in the discriminations. To Daoists, Confucians are painting by numbers, while Daoists are creating natural landscape paintings.

Zhuangzi continued Laozi's attack. He too noted how language generates discriminations. Thus, the concept of "this" produces the concept of "that" and vice versa (Z 4). The very concept of "to divide" means there is something to divide (i.e., something undivided) that is missed by the division—thus, to discriminate between alternatives is to fail to see something (Z 5). The world is a whole and does not come precut for our distinctions. Reality is free of all of our points of view. All our words draw boundaries between things, but these boundaries are constantly shifting as our interests and preferences change while reality remains the same. The parable of the monkeys and the nuts illustrates the point: the monkeys complained about getting only three nuts to eat in the morning but four in the evening, so their keeper placated them by giving them four in the morning but only three in the evening—the substance of what they got was exactly the same as the day before, and yet the monkeys were now happy because they were caught up in the labels (Z 5). Adopting a set of names means adopting a point of view. Nevertheless, in the Daoist view, if we realize that the substance discussed remains the same, our minds do not become fixed by whatever set of words we adopt. But people who are still within the borders of knowing and not knowing, of right and wrong, cannot see through Zhuangzi's words (Z 17). Words exist because of their meaning; once we have gotten the meaning, we can forget the words—where, he asked, can he find someone who has forgotten words so he can have a word with him (Z 26)?

Laozi had more trouble reconciling his theory of language with the fact that he used language at all (D 2, 23, 25, 43, 70, 73, 78). The enlightened are to reflect the Way but the Way is silent, and so one who knows does not speak and one who speaks does not know (D 56)—and yet Laozi spoke. Indeed, he said his words were easy to understand and to practice (D 70). The *Daodejing* begins with the problem that the constant Way (*changdao*) cannot be dao'ed (walked or spoken) and that there is a nameless Way (D 1, 14, 20, 25, 32, 37, 41). If names distinguish, how can we name the undifferentiated reality from which all else emerges? That is, all names function by setting off part of reality as distinct from the rest, so how can we designate the whole?[20] What can we contrast it with? Nevertheless, Laozi obviously did speak, even if he claimed a "doctrine with no words" (D 2, 43; see Z 5). He also spoke of the nameable Way (D 1), even if he never reconciled this claim with his theory of naming. But this does mean that for him not all language is foreign to the Way: there is the nameable Way (or, better, ways) that can be discerned or conformed to in some manner and thereby followed. Thus, the human way, unlike the rest of nature, does involve a role for language, even if the Confucian approach of conforming to categories is rejected. Language at least leads us to following the Way properly.

The Way and Mystical Experiences

The point that Daoists made about the relation of language to reality can be seen as simply a logical one that we all could hold on philosophical grounds: language cannot mirror reality because language divides while reality is contiuous and because words are static while phenomena are impermanent and constantly changing. But the impetus for the theory may also be an extralinguistic experience of reality in the form of a depth-mystical experience or mindfulness. That claim is controversial, since some scholars see the *Daodejing* simply as a matter of political and other types of strategies and the *Zhuangzi* as linguistic philosophy. And it must be admitted that there is nothing like a systematic treatment of meditative techniques in either book. Nor do Daoists see any need for a mystical "union" since we are already a product of the unnameable Way and are as substantively at one with it as we are ever going to get. There is also less on the loss of a sense of an individual self in Daoism than in most mystical traditions.[21] But Daoists stress that we are out of alignment with the Way and need to get back in step. And there are many passages in both texts whose least-forced interpretation is that mystical cultivation and an inner transformation is how this realignment is accomplished. That is, we need a cultivation that is a decultivation by Confucian standards to enable the Way to manifest itself in us. It is by cultivating an inner stillness (*jing*) that we are able to follow the human way. And this would mean that there is a mystical dimension at the core of all the activities discussed in the texts.

Laozi's mysticism appears to be a form of depth-mysticism and Zhuangzi's a form of mindfulness.[22] Laozi referred to concentrating our breath and sweeping clean the profound mirror (*xuan-jian*) of our mind (D 10). Other passages are more cryptic but also suggest mysticism. For example, the "profound merging" (*xuan-tong*): we should close our mouth and shut our doors (the sense organs), blunt the sharpness (of perception and reasoning), untangle the knots (of conceptualizations and attachments), soften the light and become one with the dusty world (D 4, 52, 56).[23] *Daodejing* 47 states that we can know (*zhi*) the world without stepping out of the door and see the Way of heaven without looking out windows; the farther we go the less we know. This may refer simply to not getting caught up in worldly matters, or it may be a symbolic statement for stopping sense-experience during concentrative meditation, since to know the mother (the Way) is to know the sons (all things) (D 52). Other passages suggest a mystical quest. For example: by learning one increases everyday while by practicing the Way one decreases (indicating as a goal the total end of conceptual discrimination) (D 48); we thus need to decrease desires and abolish learning (D 3, 19, 37, 46, 64); the sage has learned to "unlearn" (D 64) and has no extensive knowledge (D 81) and so is ignorant (D 20). Instead, we should embrace the undifferentiated (D 10, 22). Thus, Laozi is not against mystical knowledge of the root (the Way) but only against learning (*xue*), which is an obstruction to realizing the Way (D 52, 57). The Way is accessible, but not as an object of knowledge: we need to unlearn the content of our mind; with the mind empty, nothing more needs to be done, and the depth-mystical experience of the Way occurs automatically. The central practice thus is embracing the one and attaining the complete emptiness (*xu*) and the calmness (*jing*) of realizing the eternal (D 15, 16, 39). We need to reduce selfishness and desires because the Way is without desires (D 1, 3, 7, 19, 37, 46, 57, 64).[24] We need to return to the simplicity of the "uncarved block" (reality prior to differentiations) (D 28). The sage returns to the uncarved block and the root (D 1, 16), since the Way is invisible, inaudible, and without form (D 14, 25, 35). Only by the inward vision (*ming*) do we know the everlasting (D 10, 16, 22, 24, 41, 52, 55). All of this suggests that Laozi's distrust of the intellect and language is based squarely on mystical experiences.

Zhuangzi also emphasized emptying the mind of sensory and conceptual content—"sitting and forgetting" (*zuo-wang*) and "fasting of the mind" (*xin-zhai*) (Z 4). There are also passages that suggest controlled breathing (e.g., Z 4). The doctrines that scholars meticulously learn and memorize cramp their vision as much as the limited point of view of a frog in a well (Z 17) and thus must be forgotten. Zhuangzi's philosophical arguments fit naturally here: there can never be any fixed knowledge of reality because reality is constantly changing—there is nothing constant for our words or statements to correspond to, and thus reality will never remain contained in the conceptual boxes we create. Forgetting and fasting the mind is to lose all the conventions and distinctions associated with a Confucian sense of self.[25] It is totally forgetting oneself: "I drop away my limbs and body, drive out perception and intellect, cast off the body and do away with knowledge, and merge with the Great Thoroughfare" (Z 6). Such cultivation involves discarding little and great knowledge to become clear (Z 26) and wandering outside the realm of forms and bodies (Z 5). Only by such unknowing of what others take to be knowledge can we hope to know the Way (Z 24), since nonmystical knowledge obscures the Way. Emptiness is the knowledge that does not know (Z 4). Such emptiness is where the Way settles in (Z 4).

But, while Zhuangzi saw Laozi as going for a stroll at the origin of things, he himself remained with the myriad of the ten thousand things and the power of the Way in everything. Thus, while Laozi saw the depth-mystical experience as the route to the Way, Zhuangzi remained with a mindfulness of the everyday realm. Zhuangzi spoke of seeing things as equal: "the sage leans on the sun and moon, tucks the cosmos under his arm, merges himself with things, leaves the confusion and muddle as it is, and looks on slaves as exalted. Ordinary men strain and struggle; the sage is stupid and blockish. He takes part in the ten thousand things and achieves simplicity in oneness" (Z 2). If we perceive things with attention to differentiating factors, then our own liver and bladder are as different as different countries; yet from the point of view of their sameness, "the ten thousand things" are one (Z 5, 17) since they are all equally products of the Way. The "axis of the Way" indicates that what is high from one point of view (e.g., the value we attach to our own well-being) is low from another (the value others attach to our well-being). What is death from one point of view is a return to the process of change—a birth of sorts—from another. From the point of view of the Way, there is nothing greater in all the world than the smallest item (Z 2, 17)—all things are the same from the Way's point of view. From this point of view, one can "embrace the ten thousand things and roll them into one" (Z 1).

This evenness is not a mystical unity (absolute oneness) but rather the claim that all things share the same nature—being a product of the Way. Western philosophical naturalists accept a similar uniformity—that everything is made of the same material—although they deny any transcendental elements to reality. But in Daoism, there is an experiential change rather than merely the adoption of a philosophical point about the "thatness" of reality apart from the "howness" of things: the enlightened approach the world without differentiating concepts being involved. This affects perceptions. Such a way of seeing levels out "this" and "that" (*qiwu*) (Z 2), and thus we do not become attached to any particular feature. This includes ourselves: with our death, nothing real is lost—whatever is real remains what it always was, one with the Way. More generally, all passion and desire, all likes and dislikes, are foreign to the Way (Z 2, 6). Having relegated all to the constant, all chaos and doubt can be steered around (Z 2). Using the constant is using the clarity or illumination of the still mind (*ming*). This does not blur out differences in perception—indeed, variety and individuality can be celebrated—but all particular things are seen as equal in the Way. Only then do we reach the impartiality of the Great Understanding (Z 26). We have leaped into the Boundless (Z 2), free of emotions and of attachment to conceptual differentiations.

The Enlightened State and Enlightened Action

We cannot see the Way but we can get at it (Z 6), since we are already its product and it is always sustaining us. It is a path that can be followed (D 14, 21, 24). All that is required is the inner cultivation of the Daoist point of view to remove the encrustation of the cultural realm. In Zhuangzi's terminology, the "untrammeled man" (*zhenren*) is completely in harmony with the natural curvature of the Way. Thus, the enlightened embody the human way fully—their potency (*de*) is fully active—and they mesh seamlessly with the ways of the rest of nature. Thereby, they move frictionlessly through life. They are at ease (*shi*) in all situations. The enlightened thrive in the Way like fish in water. In the enlightened state, one is conforming fully with the Way (D 55). This mystical knowledge is not intellectual: one is not understanding the Way as one would an object of study but is participating in it. The enlightened sages are not just philosophers who know ideas but are mystics who have experiences. The contemplative approach (*guan*) of the enlightened state is a state of mindfulness. One is calm, receptive, free of attachments, even-minded (*ping*), and emotionally unaffected by both disasters and the ordinary everyday concerns.[26] The enlightened are mindful of all that occurs. Any conceptual elements from culture that remain in the mind do not fix the mind, but instead the mind's focus goes with the flow of experience. Nothing attracts attention more than anything else. Free of desires, the mind (*xin*, literally, the heart) makes no interpretations or judgments. It is empty and still, letting reality fill it. The mind becomes an unclouded mirror, fully attentive but merely reflecting what is really there—seeking nothing, welcoming nothing, responding but storing nothing (Z 7). Small things mean as much as great things. Thus, one remains dispassionate and quiet even at the sight of magnificent scenes (D 26). One goes from moment to moment, letting events come and go and forgetting what went before.

In the enlightened state, the sage is still and nothing disturbs him, but he is not inactive. Instead, the enlightened respond immediately to what is before them. Enlightened action can be called simple, natural, and spontaneous, since no artificiality of cultural conventions or personal desires interferes with the flow of the Way. It is free of self-consciousness and deliberation, and thus it is a self-generated (*ziran*) action. Mindful knowledge mirrors what is there, and the enlightened act mirrors that knowledge by responding to what is there. The enlightened in effect float on the waves of the Way. Zhuangzi referred to this as "wandering free and easy, tending to nothing" (Z 19). But, as noted above, that is not strictly accurate: enlightened action is not purposeless—there are objectives to be attained—and thus it is not mindless wandering without a destination or goal. Nor is the action simply an involuntary muscular reflex or some other physically determined chain of events: our choices and intentions enter the picture. The manner of action has changed but not its objectives. The point is that the enlightened stay centered, focus on what is really there before them, and respond immediately, free of deliberation but not literally "mindlessly."

Zhuangzi gave examples of enlightened action. (It is worth noting that the examples all come from lower-class artisans—cooks, wood-carvers, cicada catchers, wheelwrights—i.e., activities that Confucians looked down upon.) In each case, an artisan is totally absorbed in the object he is dealing with. He spreads his attention over the whole situation, lets his mind's focus roam freely, and forgets himself in a total absorption in the object; then his hand reacts spontaneously with a confidence and precision impossible to anyone who is applying rules and thinking out moves.[27] Before picking a piece of wood to carve into a bell stand, Qing the wood-carver fasted for seven days in order to forget everything—his rewards and salary, any blame or praise, his skill or clumsiness, even his body and limbs (Z 19).[28] He then went into the forest with his skill concentrated, and all outside distractions faded away. He remained open and flexible. If he did not find a superlative piece of wood, he left. If he did, he saw a bell stand, and his hand then spontaneously followed the natural patterns and carved it. He was simply matching up his "heavenly nature" with that of the wood. Or consider the swimmer: he stayed afloat, not by fighting the currents, but by forgetting everything, including himself, and moving with the flow of the swirls and eddies in the whirlpool; thereby, he did not drown in a river even fish could not swim in (Z 19). Similarly, Ding the cook carving up an ox: early in his career, he saw the whole carcass; after three years, he saw no more whole animals; finally, he worked only with his spirit, not with his eyes and understanding; thereupon, in carving an ox his hand moved his cleaver smoothly through the hollows and openings of the ox, missing all ligaments, tendons, and joints, and thus his blade was never dull again (Z 3; see also D 28). Perception and understanding had come to a stop, and his spirit moved where it wanted, since it no longer needed the control of his senses. His final skill did not involve scientific knowledge of the anatomy of an ox—instead, he followed the structure immediately before him without applying external knowledge of the nature and location of the ox's parts. He responded with a still mind to whatever was there, not with imposing a preconceived notion of what he would find or what he would do. Only by unknowing all discursive knowledge, such as anatomy, did he achieve his spontaneous skill. Any intellectual knowledge would go against the grain—it is "underbrush" (Z 1) filling the mind, cluttering up the person, and interfering with what he is doing. More generally, the enlightened apply such mystical skill to life: they move effortlessly through the currents and empty spaces of the world and do not perish.

Western scholars routinely distort the nature of this action. Philosophers since Gilbert Ryle have made a distinction between propositional knowledge ("knowing that") and acquired skill ("knowing how"). Scholars see Zhuangzi's artisans in terms of the latter, and then use examples of skills acquired through practice (playing tennis, typing) to make the point that we respond automatically when a skill is finally perfected. But Zhuangzi mentioned nothing about repeated practice, either out of habit (e.g., walking) or to acquire a special skill. (Moreover, since the artisans have an objective to attain, they are not perspective-free but have some "knowledge that" implicit in what they are doing.) Ding the cook did not become an expert carver just by years of practice but by being able to empty his mind of preconceptions and responding to what was before him without deliberations. It is not a matter of internalizing propositional knowledge of the nature of an ox, nor a skill acquired through repetition of certain strokes, but an ability to follow the natural patterns of the Way by an inner emptying of the mind. In short, it is a mystical knowledge by participation in the Way, not knowing that or knowing how. Daoist action is the self-expression of the Way, not the product of training in an activity. The enlightened share with supremely skilled athletes or musicians being lost in the moment and responding automatically (and also the ineffability involved in trying to express clearly any type of expertise), but that is all. The point of the stories is not how to train better wood-carvers and cooks but how to conform to the Way. Scholars miss all this by imposing something familiar (our distinctions) on the unfamiliar—something Zhuangzi would no doubt have found amusing.

Wu-wei

Laozi took a different approach to action than did Zhuangzi. He emphasized taking the yielding tack in any situation. He employed a number of symbols to describe the Way: the weak over the strong (D 30, 36, 76); softness over hardness (D 43, 78); the soft, flexible, supple, and yielding as the principle of life (D 76, 78); water that conforms to the space available but wears down even the hardest rock (D 78); water that nourishes all and does not compete (D 8); children and infants rather than adults (D 10, 20, 28, 49, 55); the feminine rather than the aggressive masculine (D 6, 25, 28); the mother of heaven and earth rather than the father (D 1, 3, 20, 25, 52, 59); the womb that pours out and receives back all beings (D 6); the root rather than the trunk and branches (D 16); the empty vessel (D 4); the vacuous bellows that produce without fail (D 5); the valley that receives the rivers (D 6, 15, 28, 32, 39, 41); the empty hub of the wheel where the spokes meet (D 11); silence and emptiness (D 4, 25, 33); the dark and mysterious rather than brightness and the known (D 1, 4). The Way—the vague and elusive receptive source of everything—operates by weakness (D 40), noncontention (D 8), and by receiving back beings (D 40).[29] When its work is done, it withdraws (D 9). Thus, the virtues we are to cultivate are similar: taking the passive role, humility, stillness, simplicity, emptiness of any self-assertion. The depth-mystical techniques discussed above also could also be cited here. One becomes more like a child, with their genuineness and spontaneity, than a learned person of high social standing. In short, one knows the *yang* but adheres to the *yin* (D 28). By such cultivation of the negative, the sage operates in conformity with the Way, and one's potency (*de*) is maximized.

The enlightened's action is "*wei wu-wei*," literally "acting without acting" (D 63). The phrase has led to many misleading translations—"inaction," "passivity," "no action," "not doing," "doing nothing," "taking no action," "unintentional action," "directionless action," "purposeless action." Some of these phrases capture the contradiction in the Chinese phrase, and there are justifications for translations suggesting "no action." The *Daodejing* states that the Way takes no action (D 37; see also Z 6), and, since the actions of the enlightened mirror that of the Way, they do not act either. That is, any personal actions impede the unfolding of the Way; so we take no action and the Way then simply acts through us. In short, we should stop planning and pushing and just let the Way operate. But the concept of *wu-wei* in no way suggests *inaction* or the *lack of a goal* but only action free from personal desires and all sense of self. (Hence, there are similarities to the distinction drawn above in Chapters 5 and 6 between "action" and "karmic action.") Thus, "nonassertive action," "action free from striving," or "yielding action" would be a better translation. It is not sitting and forgetting, nor is it giving in to defeat and helplessness. The idea is that if we remove all the artifices of Confucian cultivation of humaneness (*ren*) and all other self-assertion from our actions, the Way will act spontaneously (*ziran*) through us and thus accomplish our goal. It is like gravity: instead of fighting to defy it, and losing, we should use it to accomplish a goal and live easily within it. Zhuangzi's artisans are good examples of *wu-wei*, although he rarely used the term. For Laozi, the term is most often associated with the sageruler, whose purpose is to govern. However, with *wu-wei*, we are not trying to bend a situation either for personal profit or in reaction either to preconceived ideas of the nature of reality or to what we judge to be good or bad—it is the way to bring about objectives in keeping with reality.

In short, "*wu-wei*" is another label for "*yin*-action," i.e., taking the yielding position to accomplish an objective. It is any action that does not interfere with the Way's power (*de*). It is not resisting but letting the flow of the Way work through us to accomplish something. Thus, the Way takes "no (assertive) action" and yet nothing is left undone (D 37; also Z 18). *Wu-wei* is part of a family of *wu's* in the *Daodojing*, all indicating the absence of something: *wu-yu* (the absence of desire) and *wu-zhi* (the absence of knowledge). But just as nonbeing (*wu*) is the positive source of being (D 40), so too each absence is filled by something positive: the absence of desire with enjoyment without attachment to objects; the absence of learning with direct, nonconceptual knowledge of the Way; and the "absence of action" with the power of the Way. Our *yin*-actions are noncontentious, noninterfering, free of deliberation, conforming to the path of least resistance. We have no partiality-laden personal motives and so do not impose ourselves on the world. Even our conceptualizations create obstacles to the Way and thus friction. All personal motivations and attachments—such as the emotions of joy and anger, delight and worry, sadness (Z 2, 4)—go against the grain of the Way. Thus, we "do nothing (through personal striving) and everything will be done (naturally, by the Way)" (D 48; Z 18). By yielding, we tap into an inexhaustible reserve of power, and all is accomplished: events occur of their own accord ("self-so," *ziran*). We become empty of a sense of self through uncultivation and consequently harmonize with the natural course of the Way. The totality of our inner character is aligned with the Way, and thus its power (*de*) shines forth. With our being firmly rooted in the Way, our actions then express our being—a state where actions flow effortlessly and naturally—rather than our struggling to implement some plan or desire. In this manner, we live a long life free from strife.

Governing by *Wu-wei* and the Ideal Society

But, again, *wu-wei* involves actions that are "intentional" and "purposeful." Zhuangzi's artisans had goals they wanted to achieve through their actions, and Laozi's sage had tasks that he wanted to accomplish (D 2, 3, 9, 17, 30, 34, 37)—they did not simply let things evolve naturally without intervention. That is, through *wu-wei* they utilized the Way's power as the means to achieve their goals most effectively and efficiently (D 47).[30] For Laozi, chief among the goals is governing society. The *Daodejing* also contains passages on defensive war (D 30, 31, 68, 69). Laozi apparently accepted the inevitability of war and indicated that the Way-inspired response is to try to avoid it in the first place (D 68), to fight only when compelled to, to retreat (D 69), and to mourn even in victory (D 31). No passages are on a strategy for fighting a war, such as using our opponents' power against them (as in *jūdō*) as a means to win, although other passages provide the theory of taking the yielding *yin*-action as the way for the soft to overcome the hard (D 36, 43, 61, 76, 78). But to Laozi war is an evil to be avoided if at all possible and never used to gain any type of power. Nevertheless, the Daoists, taking a yielding *yin*-action, will strike if necessary and use sharp weapons (D 30, 31). But all aggression is the epitome of the assertive *yang*-action that goes against the Way. The sage wins because he never competes, i.e., takes no *yang*-action (D 3, 8, 66, 68, 81), as the Way does not compete and yet achieves victory (D 73).

Zhuangzi, on the other hand, appeared to be thoroughly uninterested in governing. He did not abandon society, but he was indifferent to political affairs or to reforming society, and thus he did not object to the existing political or social structure. The remedy for our condition lies not in changing the social structures but only in the mystical inner transformation of an individual's mind. The vicissitudes of social life can no longer affect the enlightened. He did not want his mind disturbed with talk of governing the world, but he did say that if an untrammeled man could not avoid governing, he should do it through a *wu-wei*-like manner—letting his mind wander in simplicity, blending his spirit with the vastness, following along things the way they are, and making no room for personal views. He himself preferred simply to drag his tail in the mud (Z 7, 17).[31]

However, central to the *Daodejing* is the role of the ruler in the operation of a society.[32] The Daoist sage is an ideal ruler, and much of the book is about actualizing the Way in human affairs. The sage-ruler is to his people what the Way is to all of reality. To Laozi, anyone who acts assertively will harm others and will fail (D 29, 48, 64). The more a ruler acts assertively, the more difficult the people are to rule (D 75). Thus, the sage-ruler keeps actions to a minimum, as with cooking a small fish (D 60). To be qualified to rule, one must be tranquil (D 45, 58). Using *wu-wei* is the ideal (D 63). That is, the sage-ruler does act (D 2, 10, 51, 77, 81) but takes no assertive actions. He has no mind of his own but considers the minds of the common people to be his mind (D 49). To lead, he must put himself below and behind the people (D 66). Like the Way, he leads but does not master (D 10, 30, 51). He never strives to do what is great and thus he achieves great things (D 63). He does not rely upon himself but takes only yielding actions (D 61). Thereby, he is no longer part of the picture—perfectly following the Way leaves no trace (D 27; see also Z 2)—and yet his goal is achieved. Hence, if the country is being run properly, the ruler will be barely known (D 15, 17, 22, 24). We praise the loyal ministers only when the country is in disorder, when the Way has declined (D 18). Thus, the problem of the awareness of distinctions returns: as soon as there were regulations and institutions, there were names—thus, as soon as there are names, we have drifted from the Way and it is time to stop (D 32).[33] Instead when the Way acts effortlessly through the ruler (D 2, 29, 30, 32, 34), all things return to their natural state (D 2, 64). All happens of its own accord (*ziran*) (D 17). Thus, the Way takes no action, but all is accomplished (D 37, 48). The Way's natural pattern of governing takes over.[34] Through *wu-wei*, all is duly administered (D 3).

By never striving for self-assertion, the sage-ruler's task is accomplished. The people are clothed and fed (D 2, 34). He does not dominate with force nor oppress (D 30, 72) and does not attempt to be the people's master (D 2, 10). There is no need for capital punishment (D 74). The ruler need not impose order on things since under the influence of the Way the people transform themselves. Conversely, the more laws there are, the more robbers there are (D 57). Thus, without laws or compulsion, the people dwell in harmony (D 32). When the people are not contending, the spontaneity of the Way prevails (D 46) in the society.

In sum, when the ruler achieves a noncoercive and nonauthoritarian government through *wu-wei*, the people spontaneously transform themselves (D 37, 50, 57), all things return to their original state of harmony (D 48, 54, 65), and the country will be at peace (D 37). How exactly the people automatically transform themselves is not clear. The state described by Laozi may be the natural state of things, but how does just one person—the ruler—transforming himself through cultivating an inner stillness and practicing *wu-wei* bring that about? Why are the ruler's *yin*-actions all that is needed? Do his actions enlighten others? That is, does the Way now take over and the people do not have to do anything themselves? Or do they also have to do something? If they do not, this would mean ordinary people are controlled by the Way in a manner the ruler is not—only his actions matter. But otherwise, how does the ruler being free of assertive actions, not interfering with the people, and being without desires (D 57) *cause* other people to change? On the political scale, how does a state taking a yielding position cause other states to become allies (D 61)? How does one person simply acting nonassertively cause everything to be ordered properly (D 3)? It cannot be simply by force of example or moral persuasion, as with Confucianism.[35] Embracing the Way may be a model for the world (D 22), but being a model of inner cultivation or conduct to emulate does not guarantee anyone will change. Also, unlike exemplars of conduct who inspire people to change simply by their example, the ruler is not self-assertive and is barely known by the people—indeed, the people think all these things happen naturally (*ziran*) (D 17). How could their simply knowing that somewhere the ruler is sitting serenely on a throne, facing south in the ritual way, cause people naturally to gravitate to nonassertive actions or effect any other transformation? The ruler's most active role is that he keeps the people uneducated and lessens their desires (D 2, 3, 19, 20, 65). This, under Daoist theory, would lead to less interference with the Way, but it is hard to find any other type of action that the ruler uses to guide the people in any way (see D 10, 64). The theory may be that of inverting the problem of discriminations: by doing away with laws ("discrimination"), people will automatically revert to the state prior to the distinctions (see D 19).

This problem has led some scholars (such as Arthur Waley) to suggest that the ruler's inner power (*de*) is magical. That is, through fasting his mind and *wu-wei*, the ruler cultivates a force of the Way's power that can radiate outwardly and transform other people, causing them to conform to the natural patterns of the Way (D 32, 35). There is also a passage suggesting that sitting and meditating is enough

(D 62). Thus, his change alone would be enough to effect change throughout the country. And there are passages that strongly suggest a magical dimension to the *de*: one who possesses *de* in abundance will not be stung by poisonous insects, mauled by beasts, or attacked by predatory birds (D 55), and has no place for death (D 50). The *Zhuangzi* also states something similar: when a man has perfect *de*, fire cannot burn him, water cannot drown him, cold and heat cannot afflict him, birds and beasts cannot injure him (Z 17). These passages may refer simply to fitting smoothly into nature and thus avoiding dangers, thereby enabling us to live a long life (D 16, 44, 52), or to being unconcerned about death, or they may in fact indicate some paranormal power.

But regardless of how the transformation of society occurs, according to Laozi the society that will automatically arise under the sway of the Way is one of small nonassertive agrarian groups. The Way will shape society as it does the rest of nature, if only we end our artificiality. In the Way's natural society, utensils, boats, carriages, and weapons would not be used; records would be kept by knotted cords, not writing; people would not have the urge to travel or even visit others (D 53, 80). Carriage horses would only be used to make fertilizer (D 46). It would be a land of uncultivated fields, rather than the cultivated fields of Confucian society. All machines and other contrivances of an industrial society would fall into disuse. All social hierarchy and status would disappear. Natural action is not defined in terms of being in tune with any social role (as with the *Bhagavad-gītā*). Nothing that could increase the people's learning or personal desires would be present. People would be content, living together peacefully, free of coercion or any other self-assertion that would impede the Way, and the Way then feeds and clothes them (D 34, 58). Freed from artificiality, we would then be what we are truly meant to be by the human way. This envisions a primitive form of society, but it does not abolish society, nor does it see people as something other than social beings. It is our natural social state free of the artificiality of Confucian culture—and free of all negatives (and advantages) of technology and medicine.

Social reform held no interest for Zhuangzi, and his mystical way of life is not tied to Laozi's political vision. But there are passages in the *Zhuangzi* that suggest his opposition to technology and a return to the natural. For him, any artificial means is a torture. What is natural for an ox is having four feet and what is of man is being yoked and having a rope through its nose. A hermit chided a ruler who wanted to use the Way to make more grain grow for feeding the people and to direct *yin* and *yang* to secure the comfort of all; the hermit felt the ruler was concerned only with the material—his only desire was to control scattered fragments of things (Z 11). To Zhuangzi, the objective is to live in keeping with the Way, not adding to our material well-being. What also illustrates the point is the story of the farmer who refused to employ a device to irrigate his field in less time and with less energy than he used now because it would introduce him to a competitive way of life disrupting the "pristine purity of his nature" (for in the disquieted state, the Way would not dwell in him).[36]

We may wonder why anyone would think the natural state of society under the Way is one of peace and harmony, since nature under the sway of the Way involves great deal of competition, not to mention "nature, red in tooth and claw" with animals killing and eating other animals. Moreover, we do not have to think in these terms to realize that water comes naturally in the form of floods and hurricanes in addition to its yielding and nourishing forms. In general, the social vision of simple rural communities may seem no longer possible, even if there were an enlightened Daoist sage around today to test whether it could in fact be created.

However, the important point for the issues at hand is that mystical experience is tied closely to social concerns: a mystic (the sage-ruler) is given an essential role in reforming society. Even the *Bhagavad-gītā*, which defined enlightened action in terms of social roles, accepted the social structure of the day and did not advocate reform. But here is an example of a mysticism in which the state of mystical enlightenment is valued for its social impact (even if it is not clear exactly how this works). Thus, mysticism is not necessarily asocial or inactive. Mysticism and politics can in fact be related, even though mystical experience involves the "vertical" dimension of the depth of being and politics is a matter of the "horizontal" relationship among people.

Laozi's Values

Many scholars claim that all values under the Daoist analysis are merely human conventions, and thus they conclude that Laozi and Zhuangzi are nonmoral. These scholars start with *Daodejing* 2: all concepts arise only because we are aware of a contrast (as discussed above)—the concept "good" arises only when we are aware of "bad." We would not have the concept of "north" without the concept of "south," and the same applies to all evaluative terms. Thus, to get to the Way we need to eliminate our artificial rules and standards. Plagues and earthquakes are not "evil" in themselves but only seem so from the point of view of our selfish interests—from the point of view of the whole, they are just natural. So, these scholars conclude, we should not reify our concepts of "good" and "evil" into separate entities or try to eliminate "evil" and develop "good" but simply accept without emotional reaction that there cannot be "good" without "evil." In short, we should accept things as they are, the bad along with the good—the Way is both good and bad (and thus nonmoral), and we therefore should be the same.[37] Heaven and earth (and hence the enlightened sage) are not humane (*ren*) but ruthless, treating all of reality like the ritual straw dogs that are treated with great respect until they are used and then are just thrown away (D 5).

This conclusion, however, misses Laozi's central point. He does claim that our evaluative concepts, like our factual concepts, introduce artificiality into the situation—they carve the "uncarved block" into dichotomies. Our evaluations, which will have to be based only on our interests and desires, impede the Way, and thus we should do away with evaluations (D 20). But Laozi's point is about doing away with artificiality and not any claim about the moral status of the Way. That is, we become aware of "goodness" as "goodness" only when there is something to contrast with "goodness" (i.e., "badness"), but that does not necessarily mean that the Way is not *good*—it simply means that the Way no longer prevails in the world and so we are now able to see the contrast of good and bad. Whether the Way is in fact moral, immoral, or nonmoral is another question—one that would not arise if the Way prevailed, but nevertheless one that we can still ask in our present unenlightened situation.

The same problem arises with interpretations of Laozi's remark that the Way is not humane (*ren*) (D 5). Scholars translate this negation of "*ren*" as "ruthless," "inhumane," "unkind," "nonbenevolent," or "amoral" and thus conclude that the Way is not moral. But all Laozi is saying is that the Way does not follow the artificiality of Confucian evaluations.[38] The Way is not "humane" in that it does not follow our standards. Our moral categories do not govern the Way, but this says nothing about its own moral status. Laozi's point is that we should not strive to orient our lives around our socially approved standards. The doctrines of humaneness (*ren*) and appropriateness (*yi*) only arose when the Way declined (D 18). Only with the decline of the Way in society do we have evaluations in general (D 18, 38). Striving to "do good" is forcing the Way and only leads to harm by imposing our values on things. Instead, we should act without self-assertion (*wu-wei*), and the Way will prevail on its own. When the Way prevails, we will have no other situations to contrast with it, and so we will have no evaluative terms. Thus, if we conform to the Way, we will no longer need any evaluative terms. Laozi also suggested the opposite: if we simply stop seeing things in terms of "humaneness" and "appropriateness," people will automatically return to filial piety and compassion (D 19).

In sum, Laozi was again discussing the Way being free of human standards, not the question of whether the Way is in fact moral or not. And Laozi was certainly not neutral on values: he advocated the naturalness of the Way, and he condemned actions that are contrary to the Way (D 53). His is a realist theory of values: Daoist values are grounded in reality (the Way), and we reflect them when we conform our actions to the Way. Thus, we should model ourselves on the Way (D 25), and anything leading to that end is valued—stillness, lessening desires, lessening learning, and so forth. In all situations, the yielding position of holding to the *yin* is to be valued over the *yang* (D 28)—e.g., we should repay injury with kindness (D 63). The highest value is represented by water—something that benefits all and does not compete but takes places that people treat with disdain (D 8, 81). The basic action-guide is simply to act non-self-assertively. If we do not act selfishly, we will not impede the Way, and the Way will act through us. Our resulting *yin*-actions of *wu-wei* will benefit all.

Thus, the Way is not a value-free order of reality. Its two central values are impartiality and compassion. The Way is alike to the good and the bad and has no favorites but benefits all (D 5, 8, 16, 34, 79). It supports good and bad people (D 62). As impartial and disinterested, the sage too has no desires and makes no personal judgments. Emotions revealing partiality—love and hate, joy and sadness—are contrary to the Way. Thus, the sage too should be free of these emotions and all partiality. He treats good people with goodness and bad people with goodness (contra *Analects* XIV.36), and so his actions produce goodness (D 49). He promotes the good of everyone and does not select some for favor over others. The Way's beneficial treatment of all is compassion, and the sage reflects that. If the sage discards learning and desires, the people naturally return to filial piety and compassion (D 19).[39]

What exactly Laozi meant by compassion (*ci*) is not clear (D 8, 31, 67), but Laozi considered it basic. The standard edition of the *Daodejing* ends by saying that the Way of Heaven benefits others and does not harm, and the Way of the sage is to act for others and not to compete (D 81). The Way is self-emptying and so is the sage, although he benefits too since the more he bestows on others the more he has and having given away everything he is richer still (D 81). Thus, Daoist compassion apparently represents a positive sympathetic attitude and the resulting action toward others, like a parent's love for his or her child (D 18, 19). (The concepts of "filial piety" and "parental kindness" only arose, of course, when familial relations no longer held their natural harmony [D 18].) Filial piety and love for children normally conflict with impartiality, but they need not: they reveal the type of concern for others that should now be extended to all. If so, each person receives what he or she needs regardless of his or her social status. This does not mean everyone—each adult and infant, criminal and victim—is treated exactly the same but only that they each receive what he or she needs.

Enlightened sages will act spontaneously, free of any conceptions of "good" and "bad," but their actions will reflect these values of impartiality and compassion (D 2). If they are aware of doing "good" or avoiding "bad," they will not be completely aligned with the Way and thus not enlightened. Or, as Laozi said, the man who truly possesses the power (*de*) of the Way is not conscious of his power (because he has nothing to contrast with it) (D 38). But even though they are not intentionally doing "good" in response to our labels, they are not operating free of all values: what Laozi took to be the Way's values—including impartiality and compassion—will have been internalized.

Zhuangzi on Values

Zhuangzi agreed with Laozi that the concepts of "good" and "bad" produce each other: just as the recognition of "this" requires recognition of "that," so too where there is recognition of "right" there must be recognition of "wrong" (Z 2)—we cannot have one without the other. It is only when the Way declined that the distinction of "right" and "wrong" appeared, and individual bias was formed (Z 2).

Zhuangzi, however, concentrated more on the fact that there are no fixed standards of rightness and wrongness—what is right from one point of view is wrong from another (Z 2). No line can be drawn between right and wrong (Z 17). Small robbers are put in prison; great robbers become feudal lords (Z 10). But with the "axis of the Way," we see that each "this" is a "that," each "right" is a "wrong" (Z 2). Just as there are no fixed standards of beauty for all beings, so too the rules of humaneness (*ren*) and appropriateness (*yi*), the paths of right and wrong for Confucian culture, are hopelessly snarled and jumbled (Z 2). All are learned cultural distinctions—there are no natural distinctions of right and wrong grounded in reality that fix our varying evaluations in aesthetics and ethics as universally applicable. We cannot apply one standard to all of reality without killing it (Z 7). From the point of view of the Way, all things are the same, all are equal in worth (Z 2)—there is no nobility or lowness (Z 17). Any cultural point of view will make value-distinctions, which then are internalized as our personal interests and desires. But from the point of view of the Way, there is no reason to prefer one's own interests over another's or to make any value-judgments at all. Judging "right" and "wrong" are human activities, not activities of the Way. In addition, what seems "good" for us now may in fact turn out to be "bad" later and vice versa. Only the impartiality of the Way (Z 2, 6, 18) reflects how things really are, independent of our interests.

Thus, we should forget all human conventions and partial perspectives. They are merely forms of self-assertion, and thus they inhibit the Way. We should forget humaneness (*ren*), appropriateness (*yi*), and rules of proper behavior (*li*) as part of our "fasting of the mind" (Z 6). If right were really right, it would differ so clearly from what is not right that there would be no need for argument, but since that is not so we should forget all distinctions and simply leap into the boundless (Z 2). All valuations warp the Way, and thus all must be forgotten. The idea of "forgetting right and wrong" has led many scholars to conclude that Zhuangzi was either amoral, totally free of any values, or a radical relativist.[40] However, his writings do not support either conclusion. Being free of rules and ethical reflection is one thing; having no internalized values is another. To use his analogy: when our shoes are comfortable our feet forget about them, and when our mind is comfortable our understanding forgets about right and wrong (Z 19). But that does not mean we are not wearing shoes, and it does not mean our mind is not "wearing" right and wrong. Merely because we are to forget all evaluative categories along with factual ones does not mean no values are operating when we act. Just as the Ding the cook had implicit objectives and knowledge operating in him when he effortlessly carved an ox, although he was not consciously following any plan, so too enlightened untrammeled persons have implicit beliefs and values operating when they "respond with awareness."[41] We always have some belief- and value-perspective; otherwise, our actions would be totally directionless, and the enlightened Daoists' actions are not that. Thus, forgetting our own biased conventions means the automatic infusion of the Way's own impartial perspective and values, not valuelessness.

Thus, Zhuangzi agreed with Laozi on the Way's impartiality. And he stated another of the Way's values that also has major moral significance: humaneness (*ren*). Again, this is not a rule-driven behavior, since the category of "humaneness" is to be forgotten (Z 6). But for Zhuangzi, there is the Great Humaneness that is not humaneness (Z 2, 12) that will shine forth when we get beyond the category. As Antonio Cua says, for Zhuangzi "forgetting" moral distinctions does not mean denying morality—it permits us to regain the morality of the Way.[42] Again, once we truly embody something, there is nothing in us to contrast with it, and so we are not aware of the category (see also D 5, 19). For example, we cannot have "peace" without "war": if we lived in a world that had never had war, we would not have the concept "peace" but a Great Peace would prevail, even though we would have no concept to describe it. Similarly, "hate" causes (the concept of) "love." Or, as Zhuangzi said, discard (the concept of) "goodness," and goodness will come of itself (Z 26). Thus, the enlightened forget all recognition of "right" and "wrong" and illuminate everything in the light of Heaven (Z 2). Their actions will then mirror the Great Humaneness of the Way.

This too is a form of moral realism: the Way's values are part of the objective order of reality. The Way is real and can be relied upon (Z 6). Zhuangzi's position also presupposes that there is in fact a state of reality prior to "good" and "bad" and that it is good. This means the fundamental Great Humaneness of the Way is above any relativism of basic values in his thought. More generally, all virtues that conform to the Way are affirmed over living in conflict with the Way. Chief among these are emptiness, tranquility, even-mindedness, and acting without assertion (*wu-wei*) (Z 6, 13). The myriad of things do not distract the sage, and in his tranquility his actions succeed (Z 13). He has the impartiality of the Way: he has no delight in bringing success, has no affections for particular people, can withstand profit and loss, does not calculate the right time to act, and does not think of fame (Z 6). He is lofty, dignified in correctness but not insistent,[43] vast in his emptiness but not ostentatious, mild and cheerful, reluctant but acting, relaxed in his potency (*de*), tolerant, towering alone, withdrawn unto himself, and bemused; he appears to lack but accepts nothing, and when annoyed he lets it show in his face (Z 6). His mind is still and mirrors what is there, free of desires and preconceptions. Thus, his actions, imbued with the Way, respond in the most beneficial way (i.e., with Great Humaneness) to what is before him.

Does Daoism Reject Personal Agency?

Whether what Laozi meant by "compassion" is the same as what Zhuangzi meant by "Great Humaneness" is not clear—neither text has anything like a systematic discussion of these values, or of values and doctrines in general. Neither Daoist discussed the moral question of other-regarding concern—indeed, there is no ancient Chinese word corresponding to "morality" in the modern Western sense.[44] But if both Laozi and Zhuangzi did see values operating in the Way (and thus in the enlightened sages), two questions arise: are the Way's values moral, and if so, do the sages adopt the values for other-regarding reasons? If the Way's values are moral, we can conclude the sages' resulting actions are moral; and if the sages lead their Daoist way of life at least in part out of concern for others, then the sages themselves are also moral.

But one of the presuppositions of morality must first be addressed: personal agency. Neither Laozi nor Zhuangzi, nor any other Chinese philosopher of the time, presented a theory of the self, individual choice, or responsibility. But the Daoists believe that we have somehow fallen out of step with the Way and that we can get back in step. This entails the belief that we have the ability to do so and the ability to choose our actions. That is sufficient to conclude that both Daoists presuppose the freedom of choice necessary to morality in the unenlightened state. But the issue for the enlightened state remains: in "forgetting" or "unlearning" all cultural categories and aligning ourselves with the Way, have we given up free will and consigned ourselves to some nonhuman control? Do we not need to retain some personal intentions and some personal choice in choosing actions to be moral? Is our last act of personal agency simply to step out of the way of the Way and let it take over? If *wu-wei* means stopping all personal assertion, does reality then merely evolve of its own accord through us and without our control? Can this be reconciled with the idea that we are a real causal part of the world? That is, the Way may have a pattern of governing programmed into the world that will occur automatically if we simply remove ourselves through *wu-wei*, but does this mean we have no role to play in reality? Are we empty ciphers and the Way alone real, or do our actions still play a role in reality?

Laozi held up infants as exemplars of the Way (D 10, 49) because they naturally follow the Way, due to their total lack of enculturation. But this does not necessarily mean that Laozi thought we should be, in effect, animals having no connection to the past by memories or to the future by imagination, and in no way human. A Daoist sage was not the anti-intellectual Cynic of ancient Greek culture who rejected all cultural customs to live doglike (hence the name) in accordance with nature. However, Laozi did not agree with the Confucian view that we are not born human but made human by culture. For Laozi, human nature is part of nature, and so the human way is part of nature. If we fulfilled the human *dao*, we would then return to our proper niche in the natural order of things. It is a matter of finding the natural human way, not reducing us to something we are not—animals. That he wrote or taught at all and held political ideas suggests that there is some role for language and some culture in his view of the human way. The conscious-ness necessary to use language may be foreign to the depth-mystical consciousness for aligning ourselves to the Way, but it is not foreign to the mindfulness of the enlightened state. Thus, the enlightened can speak about the Way without falling out of sync with it. Despite their claims to have problems with language, enlightened Daoists can use language as well as anyone.[45] This also entails that they make choices in choosing words, and this entails a choice in action.

Both Laozi and Zhuangzi advocated purposeful behavior—the enlightened simply are using the Way to achieve those particular ends. Their yielding actions of *wu-wei* are guided by the Way, but the enlightened choose which actions to carry out. This means we are a causal part of reality even when the Way is working through us. To use the analogy to gravity again: while gravity constrains our actions, it does not determine what acts we choose to carry out in its field. So too the sage is no longer unintentionally defying the Way, as the unenlightened are, but works with it; nevertheless, the sage still must act and choose which actions to take. Similarly, the sage must choose how to implement the Way's compassion or Great Humaneness in his actions. Such freedom is all that is necessary to presuppose the possibility of morality as part of human life within the Way.[46]

However, the forgetting of all rules and evaluative categories raises another issue: is not some evaluation of alternative courses of conduct necessary to be moral? How can just letting the Way be be moral? Whatever values from the Way one has internalized, does not moral agency presuppose the ability to consider alternatives? Is not some reflection necessary? How else can the moral "ought" or "should" have any meaning? However, if one has internalized an other-regarding concern, it is not at all obvious that this reflection is always required. We would need the ability to decide how best to help others and the discussion in the last paragraph suggests the enlightened have that ability, but it is not obvious that we would need anything else. Just because the enlightened are not following a set of rules nor judging in terms of some cultural standards does not mean that they are not other-regarding—it only means that they have completely internalized a sense of other-regardingness and other-regarding virtues and values. We do not need a sense of moral "ought" to be moral if it is a natural part of our makeup. Our actions will be spontaneously moral even if we have "forgotten" the rules of proper conduct of a culture or, indeed, all conceptualizing. (More on this in Chapter 13.)

The enlightened do not need to be able to question the values they internalized—as Zhaungzi said of shoes, if we are truly comfortable with them, we will not be aware of them at all. "Forgetting" then becomes merely another word for "internalized completely." To Daoists, we could not adopt a moral point of view unless we had created the categories of "right" and "wrong" (i.e., unless we see something to contrast with morality), and thus the objective is to get beyond this distinction, making the moral point of view impossible to adopt. But if the enlightened see only morality and so have no such category, that does not mean that their actions will not appear moral to someone still stuck outside the enlightened perspective. In sum, simply because the enlightened do not follow a concept has no bearing on whether they are in fact moral or not.

Are the Way's Values Moral?

Thus, there is no presuppositional problem for the Daoists concerning agency. Nor are there any issues concerning the reality of a moral agent or persons to be moral about. So back to the first moral question: are the Way's values moral? The Daoist Way is not a propertyless underlying reality like Shankara's *ātman/brahman*, nor is it a personal creator god with intentions. Instead, it is a reality that, while underlying all of the world, is also guiding phenomena in the world. Part of its features are the values noted above—impartiality, emptiness, tranquility, even-mindedness, and taking a yielding position and so acting without assertion (Z 6, 13). Many scholars argue that these values must be amoral and thus that Daoists cannot be moral. That is, the Way's impartiality means total indifference, and thus Daoists must reject other-regardingness altogether. Any interactions with nature or people that are free of concepts will suffice. Any occupation will do. The Way operates as well in a robber as in anyone (Z 29). The enlightened are, as Robert Eno says, just as likely to carve up people as oxen—as the *samurai* so well illustrated.[47] Thus, moral quietism and indifference are the only attitudes compatible with their way of life.[48] In the words of Herrlee Creel: "Morally, Taoist philosophy is completely indifferent. All things are relative. 'Right' and 'wrong' are just words which we may apply to the same thing, depending upon which partial viewpoint we see it from. . . . From the transcendent standpoint of the *tao* all such things are irrelevant."[49] The enlightened are thus beyond good and evil. As Creel see things, an enlightened Daoist on a whim "might destroy a city and massacre its inhabitants with the concentrated fury of a typhoon, and feel no more qualms of conscience than the majestic sun that shines upon the scene of desolation after the storm. After all, both life and death, begetting and destruction, are parts of the harmonious order of the universe, which is good because it exists and because it is itself."[50]

However, this position fails because it omits the fact that other-regarding values are ascribed to the Way: either compassion (D 8, 31, 67) or Great Humaneness (Z 2, 12). Both Laozi and Zhuangzi said frustratingly little on these concepts, but the idea seems to be that the Way is naturally giving of itself.[51] It sustains everything like a mother (D 3, 25, 34), or is like water, nourishing all and not competing (D 8). The Way of Heaven is to benefit others and not to injure others (D 81). It is long-lasting because it does not live for itself (D 7). Its impartiality is not indifference but an evenness that is beneficial to all. Thus, it benefits both good and bad people (D 62); it does not despise the greedy or the low (Z 17). This does not mean that all actions are in conformity with the Way but only that the Way does not judge: the Way does not despise the robber (Z 29), but we cannot conclude from this that any self-assertive action—as an act of robbing or killing for one's own benefit must be—is in conformity with the Way.[52] There is no reason to believe the harmful acts that Eno and Creel think are compatible with Daoist values would not in fact be seen by Daoists as assertive acts out of keeping with the Way. The nonassertive *yin*-actions of *wu-wei* are, according to both Laozi and Zhuangzi, always the correct course of action. Once practicing *wu-wei*, how could they even form the notion of butchering people or of destroying a city (unless it somehow would benefit all)? They would not form the idea to do any act for a selfish reason—the compassion or Great Humaneness of the Way would prevail. Nor, as discussed above, would the enlightened be acting for no reason or purpose or objective.

The Way is impartially beneficial to all, and the sage, who reflects the actions of the Way, therefore is also impartially beneficial to all. Thus, the untrammeled man will not harm others, but he will also not make a show of his humaneness or charity (Z 17). The enlightened will be naturally compassionate or humane, free of the confines of concepts or of the need to follow rules. They will assist in the self-becoming (*ziran*) of all beings through non-self-assertive action (*wu-wei*). Far from renouncing the world or withdrawing from society, they are skillfully engaged at all times in helping others and do not abandon any of them (D 27). They use all they have in helping others (D 81). That is, we only truly help if we stop imposing our personal interests and desires on others and instead engage in yielding action. In that way, the sage achieves great deeds (D 23, 27, 63). Embracing the one, the sage is a model to all under heaven; he is not self-absorbed and so shines forth (D 22). He engages in beneficial activity on all levels of society (D 54). Certainly nothing in the texts suggests that being free from rule-following gives them license for immoral action, as Creel and Eno suggest.[53] Thus, the conclusion has to be that for Daoists the Way has moral attributes and therefore that anyone to the extent they are following the Way is engaged in moral actions.

Are Daoists Moral?

This leaves the second moral question: are the Daoists following the Way out of an other-regarding concern? Or are they taking the yielding position only because a retreating *yin*-action is always the best way to attain their own long, stress-free life, with any benefit to others being merely a fortuitous by-product of their selfish quest?

An argument can be made that the sage adopts the Way's values only out of self-concern. That is, the sage is only concerned with his own long life, and he adopts these values only because they result in the type of yielding action that helps him attain his own goal. Daoist ethics are exclusively a matter of an individual's own inner self-transformation to achieve an inner equanimity toward outward events.[54] For both Laozi and Zhuangzi, other-impinging acts may be necessary, considering we are part of a web of social relationships, but their focus is only on the actor's own self-development. Laozi may have advocated political reform, but Zhuangzi's position represents the position for philosophical Daoists in general. Since Laozi had a political program, he (and indeed even Zhuangzi) did influence some later rebels (mostly from the lower classes and political outcastes) who resisted foreign invasion or who rose up against a ruler who they believed was misruling. But it was the Confucians and the "religious Daoists" (*daojiao*) who were the real political reformers and revolutionaries in Chinese history.[55] Those most heavily influenced by the philosophical Daoists (e.g., Chan Buddhists) merely accepted whatever government or social structures happened to be in place. While the Confucians worked at the serious task of helping society through unselfish duty, the Daoists were off leisurely drinking, too drunk to be assertive. The skills of Zhuangzi's artisans are a matter of techniques only for their own welfare—no values regarding other-impinging conduct are involved.

However, the texts have nothing directly on the issue of a sage's reasons for adopting this way of life. The self-centered ethos of the Theravāda texts is certainly absent, but there is no direct evidence of an other-regarding intent either. But nothing states or even suggests that long life is a sage's only concern—indeed, even that goal is more presupposed than explicitly advocated. The *Daodejing* does state that the sage is free of personal desires (D 27) but also that being without desires is the way to gain the things one desires (D 7, 28, 48, 66, 67). The more a sage does for others, the more he gains for himself (D 81). This suggests that both ends—his own and benefits for others—are accomplished by the same acts, and thus that he makes no real sacrifice by his yielding actions. This then still leaves open the issue of whether other-regardingness is also a motive.

Nevertheless, there is a focus on other people, absent in Advaita Vedānta and Theravāda Buddhism, that makes it hard not to conclude that a genuine concern for others is one component to this tradition. This is especially evident in Laozi's work. Daoists were shaped by the prevailing concerns of their culture. Laozi reacted by proposing an alternative way of governing; this shows a concern for others, since he could simply have withdrawn from society. Zhuangzi reacted with an indifference to government, but his writings do not evidence a preoccupation with only his own salvation. The characterization of the Way as selflessly giving to benefit others is the strongest evidence for concluding that the sage, who mirrors the Way, is other-regarding. Granted, the sage's happiness does not depend on the welfare of others, and he is not commended to cultivate a perspective free of a sense of self and of conceptualizations in general in order to help others. But again there is nothing suggesting a preoccupation only with one's own welfare (as with the Theravādins), and the fundamental reality is characterized as other-regarding (unlike Advaita and Theravāda Buddhism). Thus, the least forced conclusion is that the interests of others constitute a fundamental feature of the world and thus that the sage has, in mirroring the Way, an other-regarding concern as part of his intentions.

In sum, it is reasonable to conclude that philosophical Daoists are moral. The enlightened, mirroring the selfless giving of the Way, do not live for themselves but benefit all beings (D 7, 8). The sage-ruler's *yin*-actions transform society in a way that Daoists believe is beneficial to all. Daoism is light on both concrete action-guides and examples of what to do.[56] Its ethos of acting through a yielding, nonassertive position only provides so much practical guidance in concrete moral dilemmas. But the enlightened have internalized the Way's point of view. They are at one with an inner self-giving potency (*de*) (D 38). The enlightened's inner clarity (*ming*) or the "light of heaven" (*tian*) guides their nonassertive actions (Z 2). They no longer look for the "good" thing to do. Dwelling beyond any category like "morality," freed from the mental constraints of evaluations and rule-following, the enlightened engage in an outpouring of beneficial action (D 19). The natural expression of their character is the caring and supportiveness of the Way. This conclusion may reflect a Western category, and if we were enlightened we would not even be aware of the category, but the texts support this judgment.

Notes

1. Later thinkers labeled this "philosophical Daoism" (*daojia*) in contrast with "religious Daoism" (*daojiao*). Whether the two early Daoist texts constituted a single "school" is doubtful. They also shared little more with "religious Daoism" than a name and some terminology. Religious Daoism involved an attempt to manipulate the Way in a quest for immortality that is the opposite of *wu-wei* discussed below (H. Creel 1970, p. 11). Later, "philosophical" and religious Daoism and Daoist yoga all merged into one tradition.

2. More so than any other texts discussed in this book, the translation of the *Daodejing* (abbreviated "D") is very much an interpretation. But there are limits. See Isabelle Robinet, "The Diverse Interpretations of the *Laozi*," in Kjellberg and Ivanhoe 1996, pp. 127-59. The translations relied upon here will be Waley 1954, Chan 1963, and Mair 1990. Watson 1968, Graham 1981, and Mair 1994 are the sources for the *Zhuangzi* (abbreviated "Z"). Citations will be to chapters.

3. "*Dao*" means path or road, but it has an ontological and cosmological dimension that a code of ethics such as the Jewish *halakhah* (whose name also derives from "to walk") does not. It is a structure to the universe and not only a guide for conduct.

4. In early Chinese thought, deceased ancestors play a role in the religious life, but there is relatively little concern with one's own destiny. There is also comparatively little on the metaphysical issues related to the person, but a person is thought to consist of three parts: the physical (*po*), the life-breath (*qi*), and the part that goes to heaven (*hun*). Whether people are innately good or not is more of an issue for these philosophers.

5. This is not to deny that there is a transcendental dimension to Confucianism—the role of humanity in nourishing "heaven and earth"—but only that this is not Confucius' central concern. Confucians also ground humaneness (*ren*) in the Way.

6. "*Ren*" is often translated as "benevolence" or "loving kindness," but the term is neutral on the issue of other-regardingness.

7. "*Yi*" is often translated "morality," but it has nothing to do with a sense of concern for others for their own sake ("other-regardingness").

8. It is sometimes said that Confucius was enlightened at age seventy in the same way as Daoists: they had merely reached the same point by different paths. But since Confucius' ideal state of mind involved the cultural rules and names that the Daoists reject (with a possible qualification from Zhuangzi noted below), he was "enlightened" into a different enlightened state than that of the Daoists. That is, Daoist unlearning is not a matter of

internalizing Confucian learning in a different manner; at least some central values and beliefs are diametrically opposed.

9. The Outer Chapters of the *Zhuangzi* suggest that Daoists could still adopt these rituals, but with a difference in the attitude in how they fulfill them (Z 10). See note 43.

10. Cua 1980, p. 13. On the complementary thesis, also see Cua 1977.

11. See Chen 1973; but also see Mair 1990, p. 111.

12. Under classical Chinese thought, we only have so much life-energy (*qi*), and the more we expend striving against the currents, the less we have to use for extending our life.

13. Whether Zhuangzi believed in life after death is not clear—he may have believed we simply return to the sources from which all emerge, with parts reemerging in other beings and thus there being no individual personal survival. Laozi also is not clear but more probably shared the classical Chinese view of life after death. He did say we only suffer because we have bodies (D 13), but this does not necessarily imply that he accepted a disembodied life after death. He also advocated accepting the inevitability of death and the return to the root (D 16).

14. H. Creel 1970, pp. 4-6, 43-47.

15. One way to reconcile the idea of two Ways, one nameable and one unnameable, is one as the root of the other. Another way is that they are in fact the same Way seen two ways: through language and not through language. As the unnameable, the Way creates the totality (heaven and the earth); but seen as nameable, it creates the same reality seen through language (the myriad of different phenomenal things). The Daoists' problem with language will be discussed below.

16. Commentators often see in Daoism the idea of a self-balancing rhythm to the things of the world—i.e., when one thing increases, another decreases, and thus there is a zero-sum to changes in the world. But philosophical Daoism is not holistic in the sense of emphasizing the whole of reality or organically interrelated parts within a cosmic whole. More important to Laozi and especially to Zhuangzi is the individuality of things operating with the Way. There is also the danger of reading in the *Yijing*'s metaphysics of cyclical changes into the idea of *yin-yang* in philosophical Daoism. For Laozi, the *yin* is always to be emphasized over the *yang*.

17. While the concept of *ziran* is prominent in Zhuangzi's work, it only occurs four times in the *Daodejing* (17, 23, 25, 64), and it is not clear that it always means "self-so."

18. "*De*" is usually translated "virtue" in the sense of "capacity," as in "The virtue of this pen is that it writes smoothly." But this translation might also suggest an ethical sense, and thus the moral issue would unknowingly be begged by a translation. In the Inner Chapters of the *Zhuangzi*, *de* does refer to virtue in the ethical sense and is not connected with the Way as its potency (Z 4, 5; see also D 63). However, in the *Laozi de* usually refers to a potency in all things in reality—their natural power that can affect others—and is not a matter of the moral character in people. It is the Way operating in each thing, human or nonhuman (D 21, 51). The Outer Chapters of the *Zhuangzi* carries on the connection to the Way (Z 8, 9, 16, 20). It is the source of effective action (Z 12).

19. The Daoists do not address the question of how and why we, unlike the rest of reality, could fall out of step with the Way. Where did our Confucian consciousness come from? That is, conceptualizing and reasoning are part of the human way—Laozi and Zhuangzi, after all, could think and write—so why do we also have the ability to misinterpret these processes and construct a false world, thereby falling out of step with our way? Why do we have to decultivate ourselves at all to be in sync with the Way?

20. That is, the constant Way is deemed "inexpressible" because once we label it we make it into a thing among other things—but, Daoists say, the Way is not one thing in the universe. As mentioned in Chapter 3, if we reject the theory that language must mirror reality, the paradox disappears: words may be finite and discrete, but that does not mean that the reality referred to is.

21. Another problem is translating the Chinese. For example, does *Daodejing* 19 refer to reducing a "sense of self" (*si*) or to reducing "selfishness"?

22. It is tempting to suggest that Laozi is getting in touch with the unnameable Way and Zhuangzi with the nameable ways. But all that needs to be said is that we can get in touch with the Way and live accordingly.

23. See Roth 1999 for this interpretation. *Daodejing* 12 (about sense-objects confusing the senses and thus the sage attends to his belly and not his eyes) is often taken to be about mystical cultivation, but a more likely interpretation is that the chapter is a condemnation of riches.

24. There is notably less in Daoism on becoming desireless and passionless (free of joy and sorrow) than in most mystical traditions. Although becoming free of desires is necessary to conform to the Way for both Laozi and Zhuangzi, it is not discussed much as part of the mystical techniques.

25. Translating "forgetting oneself" as "forgetting the self" is too metaphysical a reading of this idea: it brings in the issue of whether there is an entity called the "self." Zhuangzi and Laozi did not make absence of a sense of self the central feature in mystical cultivation, although Laozi did say that one who dies is not lost but has a long life (D 33), which may refer to the loss of a sense of self.

26. Zhuangzi at first reacted emotionally to the death of his wife but then responded by violating the Confucian standards of mourning to show the inappropriateness of the emotional reaction (Z 18).

27. Graham 1981, p. 6.

28. The Daoist texts do not emphasize detachment from the personal fruit of one's actions as did the *Bhagavad-gītā*.

29. Reversion into the Way (i.e., returning to the source) should not be confused with the reversal of the *yin-yang* cycle of the *Yijing*. In the latter, attaining one extreme always leads to the opposite extreme, while in Daoism the *yin* is emphasized over the *yang*.

30. The Daoists were not the only theorists to utilize the concept of *wu-wei* in connection with ruling. Other schools in different fashions also saw an orderly society as a manifestation of the Way; all thought that what they advocated was "natural action" reflected reality and was not anything artificial. Even the *Analects* refer to the idea (XV.4), although that chapter may not be by Confucius but be a later addition: all the ruler did was reverently sit facing south, the ritually required direction; he took no further action and thus ruled without interference. (The word "*Wu-wei*" was inscribed above the emperor's throne.) But the role ascribed even there to ritual shows precisely the social artificiality that Daoists reject as contrary to the Way. Hanfeizi and the Legalists (who may have predated Zhuangzi) also invoked *wu-wei*. They saw the ruler, like the Way, as the still, empty center of the state. But the state was to be run by active ministers, an extreme number of laws, and generous rewards and severe punishments. In principle, the country would be ruled effortlessly under an impersonal system of law. The isolated ruler could be inactive because the state would be running automatically like a machine under the tight control of an elaborate administrative system. But such an order-dominated regime is the extreme opposite of Laozi's view of ruling through the innate *yin*-action of the Way.

31. H. Creel 1970, pp. 54-55. Both Laozi and Zhuangzi are said to have been low-level civil servants for a time.

32. Some scholars see the *Daodejing* simply as a political treatise and not a mystical one. And the earliest extant text places the chapters on *de*—the manifestations of the Way—before the chapters giving a more general discussion of the Way. But even if the text is about governing, the *mystical* means of ruling by *wu-wei* remains central.

33. This connects to the general discussion above about names. Of course, if there were no laws against murder, then no "murder" would occur, but that does not mean there would be no unjustified intentional killing—just the label would be removed.

34. Some scholars call governing through *wu-wei* "anarchy," but they must concede that it is not "anarchy" in any traditional Western sense of literally no government. See, e.g., J. Clark 1983. Laozi saw the state as a natural institution; it only has to be free of coercion. Daoist government is governing by a type of "ungoverning"—through noncoercion the people spontaneously conform to the natural patterns of the Way. To speak of this in terms of the Western understanding of "anarchy" is misleading. Laozi did not advocate the anarchy of an absence of government but argued for a form of government (natural government by the Way) that needs an enlightened Daoist sage to make it work. (If the ruler's *de* has a magical power that transforms people, then his necessity in maintaining government is also needed.) In short, the Western notion of "anarchy" misses the role of the power of the Way.

35. The Confucian theory of how Confucius would change society is that the charisma of his inner power (*de*) would effect change through his example of proper cultivation and performance of the *li* rules (e.g., *Analects* XII.19). Unlike the Daoist ruler who is a valley, the Confucian ruler is the Pole Star that attracts homage (*Analects* II.1) and emulation from the others. The people then develop themselves. No coercion is needed (hence *wu-wei*), but no magical force is involved either—the power of the exemplar is enough.

36. Waley 1956, pp. 69-70.

37. There is the danger again of trying to read in the cyclical changes of the *Yijing* here—i.e., the Way is a mixture of good and bad, *yin* and *yang*, that goes in cycles, and so we should not try to force the Way by eliminating one but should emphasize one when the other is in decline. For Laozi, *yin*-action is always the way to go.

38. Chan 1963, p. 107.

39. *Daodejing* 67 lists three virtues: compassion (which leads to courage), frugality (which leads to generosity), and daring not to be ahead in the world (which leads to becoming a leader).

40. E.g., Lau 1963, H. Creel 1970, Graham 1981. See also the essays in Kjellberg and Ivanhoe 1996. It should also be added that Zhuangzi is not a radical skeptic about beliefs, nor is he being "antirational" or "anti-intellectual" in using reason to show that reasoning cannot establish that one point of view is absolute or otherwise uniquely grounded in reality.

41. A. C. Graham argued that Zhuangzi bridged the is-ought gap since the enlightened do not make judgments but simply spontaneously "respond with awareness" to a situation (Graham 1981, pp. 13-14; 1983). But if the Way has particular values grounded in it, the value-fact gap returns. The enlightened may have internalized those values so completely that they do not have to reflect on alternatives, but this does not mean that their actions follow from a value-neutral factual description of a situation. The Way has both factual and valuational components, and we cannot deduce claims about one from claims about the other. The separate value-component (the compassion or Great Humaneness of the Way) is still needed for the Daoist to know how to act. In sum, the Way is not value-neutral but has values, and so the is-ought issue does not actually arise.

42. Cua 1977, p. 313.

43. The Outer Chapters state that the sage does not renounce the world, and his actions may conform to a society's standards in a way in keeping with the Way (i.e., with detachment): the enlightened accords with humaneness but does not set great store by it; he draws close to appropriate behavior (*yi*) but does not labor over it; he responds to the demands of the rules of proper conduct (*li*) and does not shun them; he disposes of affairs and makes no excuses (Z 10). Zhuangzi accepted two conventions without reservation: service to one's parents (which is rooted in a love that "cannot be dispelled from the heart" and thus accords fully with the Way) and the service of a minister to his ruler (which we must accept as inevitable and thus learn to "roam free inside the cage") (Graham 1981, p. 13). But Zhuangzi's reaction to his wife's death (violating the Confucian rules of conduct) may be more in keeping with the Daoist spirit toward rituals (Z 18).

44. Rosemont 1988, p. 61. Rosemont points out that none of the cluster of terms related to ethics and morality—"autonomy," "choice," "duty," "rights," "ought," and so forth—are found in classical Chinese.

45. As discussed, the enlightened in Daoism are said to be totally free of concepts, having "forgotten" all distinctions. For example, in perceptions the enlightened would see a continuum of colors and not cut the continuum up into five distinct categories (one possible reading of D 12). The same would apply to values. But how being literally free of all concepts can be reconciled with the fact that Laozi and Zhuangzi could talk and write is not clear. Daoists may have to accept the Mahāyāna Buddhist position that the enlightened do not "course in signs," i.e., they can use language but do not project the linguistic distinctions onto reality, which would make an artificial world of multiple distinct entities that reflects only our conventions.

46. Contra Danto 1987, p. 118, on the will.

47. Eno 1996, p. 142.

48. See Graham 1981 for a defense of the amorality position.

49. H. Creel 1970, pp. 3-4.

50. Herrlee G. Creel, *Chinese Thought from Confucius to Mao-Tse-Tung* (Chicago: University of Chicago Press, 1953), p. 112.

51. Philip Ivanhoe sees the Way in Zhuangzi's thought as benign (Ivanhoe 1996). This is meant in the traditional sense of "kind" or "gentle," not the medical sense of "not malignant."

52. Putting some of his teaching in the mouth of a vicious robber leading an army of nine thousand men does present a problem (Z 29). (This is not part of the Inner Chapters that Zhuangzi most likely wrote.) But such brigands are somewhat ambiguous in Chinese history: some were more Robin Hood-type figures who opposed the government and aided the poor rather than stealing only for themselves. Much of the rest of that chapter is an attack against fame, greed, and power.

53. The problem of the robber was addressed in the previous note.

54. See Cua 1977.

55. Later nonphilosophical Daoist sects also participated in social works. Their monasteries fed orphans and the poor, cared for the sick, helped with public projects (e.g., roads), and were retreats for public officials. These Daoists also participated at court.

56. As noted earlier in note 43, the Outer Chapters of the *Zhuangzi* suggest that one could still adopt the action-guides of one's culture (in his case, Confucian) and be a Daoist—the difference is in the attitude in how we fulfill them (Z 10).

12

Christianity

Western Theistic Belief-Claims

When we turn from Daoism to Western theism, the religious framework changes radically. Basic to the Abrahamic traditions is the belief-claim that there is a god with the nature of a person who created and sustains our universe and who has laid down a code of ethics for us to follow. Thus, our reality is dependent for its existence on the creative transcendent reality. Some theists—especially millenarians and ascetics—are as "otherworldly" and "world-denying" as Hindus and Buddhists are accused of being. To them God is not the supreme reality but in the final analysis the only reality, and thus the focus of our lives should be exclusively upon him: the world without God is unreal and therefore has no value at all. And even if the world is in some sense real, it is still an abode of sin only to be endured and passed beyond—at best, it is merely a testing ground for our soul and of no value in itself. But most theists see the world as real and as essentially good and valuable precisely because it is God's creation (Gen. 1:31). Thus, everything that exists is good simply because God created it. (Evil is seen, following Augustine, as not really existing at all but as the absence of something good; at most, the only thing that exists without God is self-will.) This allows a concern for worldly matters not present in the Indian traditions discussed earlier. Suffering also becomes valued differently: it is not something to be escaped but is part of God's creation, which is good, and thus has a purpose (and hence value) in his plan—e.g., it trains us to endure and proves that we have passed God's test (Rom. 5:3-5), or for mystics it may awaken us to the fact that we are not the central reality in the scheme of things.

Moreover, the god of theism is seen, not as a deistic reality, but as a personal reality concerned with his creation—in particular with human beings—and somehow affected by our acts of obedience or disobedience. He can love us because we are real and distinct from him. Human history becomes a venue in which God acts; the idea of progress in transforming society in this world toward

God's will thus also achieves prominence. Each person is a distinct creation set off from God and each other. Thus, the orthodox in all theistic traditions criticize any allegation of a mystical union of "substances." There is no literal loss of a self even in the afterlife since we always remain a distinct creation of God. Ascetics have a very negative evaluation of the body, but for most theists each person is also part of this world, not just a disembodied soul that will return to its true state when we die. Moreover, although some early Christians accepted the belief in a series of rebirths, the standard belief is that our eternal fate is determined by our actions in this one life. Thus, a major error in this life can prove eternally fatal, not merely lead to one or more bad rebirths in an indefinite series. The commands set forth by God establish the standard. "Sin" is "missing the mark," being out of step with God's commands. Our fundamental error is a matter of our will, not our lack of knowledge (as with Advaita Vedānta and Buddhism). For mystics, the error is retaining any vestige of self-will—i.e., rebelling by asserting our own self-interest rather than God's—and thus not totally conforming our will to God's. As Ruusbroec put it, we do not belong to ourselves but to God and so should renounce self-will for God's. (He added that not all good people respond to God's movement by renouncing themselves but remain caught up in outward multiplicity and not inward simplicity.)

For theists in general, salvation need not involve attaining a mystical inner transformation of our character aligning our will with God's—we need not be "perfect" since the level of our inner life does not determine God's saving action—but it still involves overcoming the misalignment of ourselves with God's plan for us by conforming our actions to God's commands. Christians debate the relation of "faith" to "works" (e.g., Rom. 5 versus James 2:17-18), but all agree that no belief or amount of good deeds can force salvation: only a voluntary act of God—"grace"—secures a person's salvation. In the state of grace, in the words of Paul, "it is no longer I who lives but Christ who lives in me" (Gal. 2:20). God works in the person, inspiring both the will and action, for his own chosen purpose (Phil. 2:13). For Christians, this state is necessarily expressed in good deeds toward others. The basic religious virtues for Christians to exhibit are faith, hope, and love, cultivated in a community sharing God's grace.

Theism and Morality

It is usually assumed that theism and morality are compatible—indeed, many argue that theism is the only way to ground the moral point of view. But as discussed in Chapter 3 it is not at all obvious that this is the case. One problem is that God lays down the law and it is our duty to obey it, regardless of whether the law is moral. God is wholly beyond our understanding and thus we cannot know what is the right thing to do except through his revelation. If we decide to obey his commands only if we judge them to be moral, we are denying his absoluteness (since there is then some standard outside of him by which we judge him)—morality would become our idol. In addition, if God's commands were necessarily moral, we would not need revelation (since we could know moral truths through reason); but theists insist that God's plan is not knowable to the natural mind. God's treatment of Job shows that we cannot fathom his plans. (The story also raises the issue of whether our suffering and other concerns in this world are a major concern to God.) God may be "beyond good and evil"—he is "good" in the nonmoral sense of being the source of our existence (and hence is a value to us), but this does not entail that he is necessarily *morally* good (having an other-regarding concern for his creation).

In any case, our duty is simply to obey. "Sin" is not a moral concept defined in terms of other-regardingness, since one can be disobedient without harming others; rather it is a religious concept concerning our obedience to God's commands. No distinction is drawn between "religious" laws (concerning rituals) and "ethical" laws (concerning other-impinging conduct) in religious codes. We act in a certain way because that is the way we were told to act, not because following the commands necessarily leads to helping others. And we are judged by whether our actions are obedient to God's will, not by whether we are other-regarding. In short, we should do something simply "because it is God's will" and not because it is moral. Moreover, we may obey only because it is in our own self-interest to do so. Obeying God may become simply a matter of reward and punishment—literally heaven or hell—and genuine concern for the welfare of others may not enter the picture. When Jesus told the rich young ruler to give his money to the poor, the only concern set forth was with the man's attachments, not with helping the poor (Mark 10:17-22; Matt. 19:16-22; Luke 18:18-23). Even Mother Teresa of Calcutta can say that the reason she dedicated her life to helping the poorest of the poor was only to secure her place in heaven—if she saw everyone she helped as Christ, did she treat them as real persons in their own right?[1] In sum, when giving is done only out of a sense of religious obligation, it is not other-regarding.

It is also not obvious that being moral is even a prerequisite to being saved. Salvation is a matter of an unmerited gift—grace. Jesus forgiving the thief on the cross (Luke 23:39-43) illustrates the problem: all the thief's previous actions were irrelevant—his last minute faith alone mattered. That Paul's letters show interest only in Jesus' death and resurrection, and not in his teachings or miracles, also suggests that this event is all that matters—our fate depends on our faith, not on our moral actions or lack of them. The role of grace also brings up an issue that has troubled many Christians and the Mu'tazilites of Islam: *predestination*. Has God foreordained our fate and so no action we could possibly take can do anything about it? Whether the grace of God is bestowed upon us in no way depends on what we do—it is unearned, undeserved, and in the end totally arbitrary. (This is also the basis for the moral problem connected to miracles: why would God intervene in the natural order to help one person and not someone else in need and equally deserving? Are we then responsible for the lack of a miracle to cure us due to something we did?) Why God created the world in the first place is a hard question to answer in any case, but if our fate is predestined the issue becomes intensified: why are going through all this suffering if God has foreordained the outcome already? Predestination also negates a presupposition of morality: if God determines in advance what will happen, we do not have the autonomy—"free will," as Augustine dubbed it—to do otherwise. But to many theists our freedom would deny God's omnipotence and omniscience about the future. (The possibility of fatalism here—God's will is always done no matter what we do—is also a moral ground to reject theism.)

These issues show that theism is not necessarily moral. But theism can also be compatible with a moral concern for others—if God permits freedom of the will and if a genuine concern on our part for the welfare of others is part of God's plan. Christians purport their religion to be an instance of this, although their bloody history of wars, torture and inquisitions, anti-Semitism, racism, imperial colonialism, and other acts of social injustices and intolerance does not make this claim obvious. (It is also hard to reconcile the idea of a loving ground of being with the fact that, according to the orthodox since Augustine, the vast majority of humanity will be consigned to the torments of hell for eternity. Why even create a world if that is so?) There may be no independent, binding moral absoluteness—according to theists, the only obligation comes from God—but this does not mean we cannot also be genuinely other-regarding. As discussed in Chapter 3, one can have more than one motive at the same time, and one can thus be both religious and moral at the same time. Thus, Mother Teresa need not ultimately have been merely selfish in working to alleviate the suffering of the poor—she may well have had a genuine concern for the people she helped even if these actions were required for her to get to heaven.

An Ethos of Love

What separates Christianity from the other religions of the world is the role of the Christ: the creator god incarnated himself in the person of Jesus of Nazareth, took all the sins of everyone upon himself, and through his suffering and death reconciled humanity to himself, as evidenced by his resurrection. Jesus appeared to have been a wonder-worker and healer/exorcist who expected the impending supernatural arrival of the Kingdom of God (as did Paul) in which God's will would come to pass and replace the worldly kingdom of the Roman occupiers (Mark 1:15, 9:1; Matt. 16:28, 24:34-35; Lk. 9:27; Rom. 13:11-12; 1 Cor. 7:29; 1 Thess. 4:15). Many of his world-renouncing ethical teachings—e.g., giving up all of one's possessions (Luke 14:33; see also 1 John 2:15), renouncing one's family (Matt. 10:37; Luke 14:26), marriage as only a concession (1 Cor. 7:1-5)—appear appropriate only if such an apocalypse is in fact imminent. Once it became apparent that the coming of God's kingdom was not at hand, Christians adapted to the Greco-Roman ethics of their time. (The more mystical Gospel of John also appeared after the early apocalyptic fever faded.) Whether Jesus intended a political revolution is a matter of debate, but it must be agreed that the early Christians did not call for a political restructuring of the Roman Empire (e.g., Mark 12:17; Rom. 13), and their economic restructuring was confined to their own community. The Christians were mostly pacifists and nonconformists prior to Christianity becoming the state religion under Emperor Constantine. After that, their central symbol—the cross—became a symbol even of military conquest. Western civilization, as historians often note, reflects more of Greco-Roman culture than the Christianity of the New Testament. In effect, Rome reformed Christianity at least as much as vice versa.[2]

But Christians retained as central to their ethics the notion of love for others (*agapē/caritas*), sometimes limited to actions only among themselves but often also directed toward others. In the West, the conception of God was evolving from a savage tribal overlord to a self-emptying (*kenosis*) reality who expresses his loving concern for all of his creation through self-sacrifice. Unlike God, we are not divine by nature, but we become divine by doing what God does—constant acts of selfless love. Forgiveness is part of this love (1 Cor. 13:7). A forgiver knows someone has done something wrong but dismisses that wrong and still accepts the person.

Jesus summed up his ethics and the Jewish law in two commands: love God with all your heart and mind, and love your neighbor as yourself (Mark 12:29-31; Matt. 22:37-40; Luke 10:27-28; 1 John 4:20). God is love (1 John 4:16), demonstrated most fully in the sacrifice of Jesus, and we mirror his acts of love for us by acts of self-sacrificing love for others. We enter the Kingdom of God not by calling Jesus "Lord" but by doing God's will (Matt. 7:21). In short, we are judged by whether we acted out of love. Thus, one need not be a mystic to be saved, but unrestricted love shows that our will is aligned with God's. We should feed the hungry and thirsty, clothe the naked, take in the homeless, and visit the sick and imprisoned (Matt. 25:35-6). We should visit the fatherless and widows in their affliction and keep ourselves untarnished by the world (James 1:27). Most importantly, this love is extended to all people. This includes turning the other cheek (Matt. 5:38-42), loving your enemies and doing good to those who hate you (Matt. 5:44; Luke 6:27), and accepting social outcastes (e.g., John 4:5-42), as the parable of the Good Samaritan illustrates (Luke 10:29-37).[3]

Trying to derive specific action-guides from, for example, the humility of the Sermon on the Mount (Matt. 5:1-12) is not simple, nor is it clear how much of Jesus' ethics can be qualified as too apocalyptic in nature to be serviceable in any other setting.[4] Moreover, the general idea of helping the poor and the sick was nothing new in Jewish culture. What was revolutionary was the approach of freely going the extra mile, giving your coat as well as your shirt with no expectation of any benefit for oneself in return, extended even to strangers and enemies (Matt. 5:38-41). Thus, an active involvement with others and their welfare is integral to the Christian way of life. When Jesus says, "Anything you did for one of my brothers here, however humble, you did for me" (Matt. 25.40), one might think of the Buddha's very similar remark to his monks (VP I.302), but the import is totally different: Jesus' remark is a natural expression of his underlying ethos, while the Buddha's is an *ad hoc* precept to correct an egregious instance of the monks' selfishness. There is a focus in Jesus' teachings on the other person that is absent in Theravāda Buddhism. Indeed, the ethics of going the extra mile is a total giving of oneself, revealing a greater concern about another than oneself.

Thus, this is an ethos of total self-giving love, because reality is grounded in other-centered love. That is, Christians exhibit this love because that is the active love that God has in creating and sustaining his creation. God is love, and whoever abides in love abides in God (1 John 4:16). Paul summarized this unconditional self-giving love: "Love is patient and kind; love is not jealous or boastful; it is not arrogant or rude. Love does not insist on its own way; it is not irritable or resentful; it does not rejoice at wrong, but rejoices in the right. Love bears all things, believes all things, hopes all things, endures all things. Love never ends" (1 Cor. 13:4-8). Love cannot wrong a neighbor (Rom. 13:10). Without love, all action is in vain. One overcomes evil with good: if your enemy is hungry, feed him; if he is thirsty, give him drink (Rom. 12:17-21). Such love is the fruit of the Spirit of God possessing us, along with joy, peace, patience, kindness, goodness, fidelity, gentleness, and self-control; no law deals with such things (Gal. 5:22-23). Faith, hope, and love endure, and the greatest of these is love (1 Cor. 13:13).

The whole of the law governing other-impinging action is summed up by the command to love your neighbor as yourself (Mark 12:29-31; Matt. 5:44; Matt. 22:37-40; Luke 10:27-28; John 13:34; Rom. 13:10; Gal. 5:14-15). How exactly the idea of ". . . as yourself" is to figure in one's reasoning depends on the status of love for oneself.[5] If one's own self-love is the necessary starting point, then how we treat others depends on how we would want others to treat us in that situation, although specifying exactly how this works without paradox or moral problems is not as simple as it sounds. Garth Hallett identifies six options: self-preference, parity of self and others, other-preference, self-subordination, self-forgetfulness, and denial of all self-interest.[6] Søren Kierkegaard presented an argument that being a Christian demands absolute impartiality—no preference for one's own family or friends, let alone oneself.[7] The saying about the rain falling on the just and the unjust (Matt. 5:45) and the parable of the vineyard owner paying all the workers the same regardless of the amount of work they did (Matt. 20:1-16) do suggest God's impartial generosity toward all. Some theologians remove any apocalyptic demand for a radical other-regardingness from the command. For example, under one contemporary interpretation the command does not require putting the good of others above one's own—it ends up being the rather bland middle-class American commonsense idea that we should care for our own family and respect and support others in their care of theirs.[8] However, under all traditional interpretations the interests of others—including one's enemies—cannot be slighted but make an undeniable demand upon us. Sacrifice on our part is required.

Christian love requires action, not just emotion. But *agapē* by itself does not entail any particular code of conduct.[9] It is more an inner disposition animating loving action rather than a specific set of rules to follow, and there have been different ways Christians have tried to make it operative. No specific code of conduct has been universally accepted by Christians, and competing philosophies of ethics have been suggested (e.g., utilitarianism). But by the Middle Ages charity had became established as the central way Christians implemented *agapē*. Such giving without expecting reciprocating gifts from the recipients included hospitality to strangers, but much of the charity focused on the material needs of the poor and needy within the Christian community and on donations to the leaders—it was a matter of mutual assistance rather than genuine self-sacrifice.[10] The idea of "neighbors" was thus often restricted to other Christians and not extended further to enemies or other groups (see Heb. 13:1). But in principle, Christian love is not in-group in scope but extends to everyone.

Medieval Mysticism

Christian mystics from the medieval period in Western Europe will be the focus here, especially from the later period and in particular Meister Eckhart. This period was chosen because, in the words of Reginald White, "Perhaps in no era, save that of the apostles, have men so striven to live the Christian life at its highest excellence."[11] Mysticism in this era was called "contemplation," and those who dedicated their lives to it were among the "the religious." Not all were monastics taking vows of poverty, chastity, and obedience within an institution developed to end attachments, but the religious were seeking perfection in the Christian way of life. During this period, there was a movement of the religious out of the cloistered life into the world. There was also what has been called the discovery of the individual.[12] And with that, there was a turn to focusing on individual experience, with mystical experiences seen as God's self-disclosures.

As theists, these mystics were committed to the theistic belief that each person is an indestructible creation of God. This shaped their view of mystical experiences. Mystical selflessness was interpreted in terms of the loss of self-will or an infusion of knowledge, not in terms of the "union" of substances or natures—all sense of self or the personal will have melted away during the mystical experience, but the reality of the self is not ultimately denied.[13] That is, being lost in the moment of a depth-mystical experience means there is no space to be aware of the self, but that does not mean that it no longer exists. "I and my Father are one" applies to Jesus, not to the rest of us. Any mystical experience does not change our ontological relation to the ground of reality (the creator). To these mystics, since God creates and sustains all of reality, there is something in us that is identical in some way to God's being, but our personhood and individuality as a creature is never absorbed into the creator. (Thus, under this view, God does not create a second substance *ex nihilo*—God's substance is our substance.) To Eckhart, our being and God's is the same, but God *is* being while we remain created beings and have no being at all apart from God's gift. As Jan van Ruusbroec put it, never does a creature become so holy that it loses its status as a created being and become God. God remains a loving, personal reality in some way distinct from his creation. Thus, the orthodox tolerated no form of pantheism in the literal sense that the world is God: God supplies the being to the world, but he remained distinct as a creator. At most, one becomes united in spirit with Christ (1 Cor. 6:17).

Early medieval Christian mysticism, under the influence of Neoplatonism, was mostly centered on gaining a knowledge beyond our natural knowledge, but the later Middle Ages saw a resurgence of Augustinian "love" mysticism. That is, most mystics of this period saw the mystical union in terms of a marriage of two entities, the beloved and the lover, the bride (the soul) and bridegroom (God or Christ). It is by love alone, not a transformation in knowing, that one reaches God. Love here is a matter the merging of *eros*, not the self-giving love of *agapē*.[14] Sexual symbolism from kissing to marriage was common.[15] The biblical Song of Songs became the source of analogy for expressing the "ecstacy" of this merging.[16] As also occurred in Jewish and Islamic mysticism, God became a reality to be loved rather than an object of fear and awe. But love still requires a duality of two beings—even if it is overcome in a union, there is no identity of lover and beloved.

Love-mystics thus see a mystical union of wills, not substances. That is, in the enlightened state, there is no self-will but only God's will. Thus, the most important indication of enlightenment in this tradition is the absence of any *self-will*, defined in the *Theologia Germanica* as all strivings opposed to God: the "poor in spirit" have reduced the self to nothing and do not claim anything in a proprietary sense—not life, being, power, knowledge, deeds, or goodness. The proprietary urge vanishes, and one wills, desires, loves, and intends nothing but God, the eternal goodness. As Ruusbroec says, one acts with pure intentions intent only on God and other things in relation to God, not any self-interest. By surrendering the will, we become detached from our creaturehood. As should be true of all Christians, for the enlightened "it is no longer I who lives but Christ who lives in me" (Gal. 2:20). Sin is reduced simply to self-will—to desire other than what God does. As the *Theologia Germanica* put it, it is "selfdom"—resistance or disobedience to God by asserting one's own interests. Prayers are not prayers of petition for any particular benefit for oneself or others but prayers that "thy will be done on earth as in heaven" (Matt. 6:10). The will is "perfect" when it has no special reference and is cut loose from the self; then it is adapted and transformed into God's will.[17] For all medieval mystics, obedience to the rules of one's order freed one from making decisions or any personal will. Thus, true obedience is having no will of one's own. (As William Blake said, "There can be no Good Will. Will is always Evil.") One comes to love God more than oneself, and one's will is totally aligned with God's. Any sense of self-will keeps us from heaven. If at the moment of death, we still have a personal will, we will go to hell—for, as Teresa of Ávila said, "nothing burns in hell but self-will."[18]

The way to the transformation of one's will is traditionally divided into a threefold hierarchy adapted from the Neoplatonic path: purification, illumination, and perfection.[19] All the steps are focused on an inward journey. During purification, we are active in an inner cleansing of the soul—burning the soul of all impurities (i.e., stripping the soul of all self-will). This involves all types of renunciation. Some mystics such as Francis of Assisi stressed material poverty, but all mystics stressed poverty of the spirit. That is, "poverty" was not seen in terms of only external possessions but also of all internal things related to any self-will. (Mystics who emphasized knowledge over love spoke in terms of a self-emptying of all knowledge—an "unknowing" or "learned ignorance"—so that God's presence can enter.) It is total renunciation of all self-interest. Setting one's desires on any created thing is sinful—what does it matter if one gains the whole world and yet loses one's soul (Luke 9:25)? Thus, any wanting itself reveals a poverty.

This purging leads to asceticism, or the "active life" as it is called in medieval mysticism. (It is important to note that the "active life" here does not mean a moral engagement with the world but the ascetic *renunciation* of the world.)[20] This may involve detachment to lessen desires and also mortification, thereby reversing all normal desires. Love of the world is the cause of our inner suffering, and so renunciation of the world is the first step to the true love of God. This can lead to a total rejection of the world as an enemy of the soul: only things that are eternal are valued, and all things temporal are rejected. Few known mystics adopted the extreme mortifications that Henry Suso undertook for ten years, but inner renunciation and detachment is necessary. (Even Suso concluded that inner detachment and self-forgetting was what was needed, not self-torture.) Eckhart emphasized that the path to God is not tied to any particular way and that a way itself may become an attachment—we may gain the way and not God. Ascetics may end up treating suffering as perfection in itself and thus suffer simply for the sake of suffering. They concentrate on human effort and the performance of specific exercises. But for mystics it is the inner attachments that are central, not outward mortifications of the body. Thus, some may not have deemed even celibacy as necessary—only detachment is indispensable. Nevertheless, these Christian mystics usually valued suffering as a means to perfection—indeed, Eckhart called it the swiftest means to perfection—since it removes attachment to this world. Thus, suffering is not something to be escaped but accepted, just as everything else is accepted, with gratitude and humility. The more suffering that is endured, the more the sufferer shows he or she loves God.[21] Julian of Norwich, with her bloody visions, went so far as to see the biblical passage that "it is not I but Christ who lives in me" in terms of Jesus' suffering on the cross. Some mystics also suffered the stigmata. All were gladly willing to suffer damnation or to remain suffering in this world for eternity if that was God's will.

Part of the work of purification is the removal of vices and the cultivation of virtues. Chief toward cultivating inner poverty is *humility*. "Blessed are the poor in spirit" (Matt. 5:3). One must become like a child (Matt. 18:1-4). To these mystics, "humility" is not meekness in the face of the problems of life or the modern idea of a sense of modesty about one's accomplishments. Rather, it is seeing one's place in the scheme of things as a creature of God—a true knowledge of oneself and one's relation to God, free of self-assertion. It is realizing that nothing comes from the self but only from God: without God, we can do nothing and are nothing. Ruusbroec made humility—the "interior bowing of the heart and mind before the transcendent majesty of God"—the foundation and mother of other virtues of the mystical life (except charity and righteousness): obedience, renunciation of one's own will and opinion, patience, meekness, kindness, compassion (sympathy, pity), generosity of heart, zeal, moderation and sobriety, and purity. It is emptying oneself and humbling oneself in obedience to God (see Phil. 2:7-8). This can lead even to hating the self because it keeps us separate from God. But all pride is simply self-deception. It is the first of the seven "mortal sins," and the others are also all forms of egoism, and so all must be overcome. As the early-modern mystic William Law put it, covetousness, pride, envy, and wrath are simply different names for the restless workings of the will and desire. Humility thus forms a purgation of all self-will. Patience, which is evidence of conforming to God's will, was also highly valued. The classical Greek virtues of prudence, justice, courage, and temperance were still considered cardinal virtues in Christianity, applying to everyone regardless of whatever other virtues may be necessary to each person's particular life. But those virtues were also devalued in favor of the divinely "infused" religious values of faith, hope, and love, acquired in passive meditation.[22] Through cultivating these virtues, one aligns one's will with God's. And if one finally has a truly good will, one will not lack love, humility, or any other virtue.[23] But practicing the virtues cannot abolish self-will—no action can. As the *Theologia Germanica* states, practicing the virtues does not bring about the union of one's will with God's but is only preparation.

Purification of the soul leads to illumination, i.e., flashes of God's self-disclosure. This stage of the path involves a new level of purgation, and God becomes active. The mystic remains in passive contemplation, cultivating the inward vision of God. This is intermixed with "dark nights" in which the mystic does not seem to make progress in meditation; the meditator suffers but God remains active in purging the senses and the spirit. God alone is also active in his self-disclosures—purification only prepares the way. Some love-mystics call these intense feeling of God's presence "raptures." Visions, levitation, and other paranormal events are also alleged to occur. The mystic is being transformed into God's love. The will and intellect are becoming more aligned with God's, preparing the way for the birth of Christ in the soul.

The culmination of the path is the "unitive life"—in Ruusbroec's term, the "God-seeing life"—in which all sense of individual self-will is destroyed. There is an inner transformation of the total person—not just actions or beliefs but one's emotions and dispositions. Knowledge-mystics emphasize the transformation of our knowledge, while love-mystics emphasize the change in our wills; but for all there is a permanent transformation of our inner state and thus our character. Love permeates the participatory knowledge of the enlightening experience—love and knowledge of God are one, as Gregory of Nyssa, Bernard of Clairvaux, and others said. While the path has both active and passive phases, the enlightenment-experience is passive: it is an infusion of God that the mystic cannot control—a type of "mystical grace" is needed. That is, we cannot force ourselves by any action we undertake to have no self-will; it either occurs or it does not, but when all self-will is eliminated, the infusion occurs automatically. As Eckhart put it, if the mind is truly disinterested, God is compelled to come into it, just as the sun must pour in when the air is clear and pure.[24] Reality, as it were, abhors a spiritual vacuum—if we completely empty one type of will, the other immediately flows in.

Christian mystics emphasize the permanent change of the enlightened state, not any particular experience leading to it.[25] What is valued is the resulting enlightened state of mindfulness (the ecstasy or "rapture" with the senses), not any depth-experiences (or heights of "raptures" involving the abstention from the bodily senses) or any other temporary experiences.[26] Empty of oneself, one is "resting in God." In this state, one abides constantly in the unmediated presence of the divine ground of reality. There is a permanent fusion — a "marriage"of wills, not of substance, like (to use an image of John of the Cross) sunlight penetrating a clear crystal or (to use an image from Paul used by Eckhart) a mirror reflecting God's splendor (2 Cor. 3:18).[27] (But, to use another image from Bernard and John of the Cross, an iron heated red hot by a fire will become indistinguishable from the glow of the fire and thus might mistake itself for the fire, but the distinction of creator and created is never in fact lost.) In the spiritual marriage, the beloved is totally transformed by the lover. Divine attributes are infused into our being, and our will participates in God's. The result, mystics say, is the standard harvest of the spirit: love, joy, serenity, patience, kindness, goodness, fidelity, gentleness, and self-control (Gal. 5:22). But is a burst of other-regarding activity also a product?

Medieval Mysticism and Morality

It is not self-evident that these Christian mystics are moral. First, these mystics typically adopted the world-denying stance of early Christianity. God is the only reality of concern, and so all worldly concerns can be forgotten. If they are renouncing the world and focusing only on God, how can they be genuinely concerned with other people and thus be moral? We are not to love the world at all (1 John 2:15). We are in this world but not of it, and we cannot serve two masters. Does not a moral concern for creatures make people something to value other than God, and is that not a sin? Are not all things temporal to be rejected? Is not Richard Rolle right when he said to despise the world and seek nothing here but God? When faced with a choice, should we not always choose the greater good—here, God—over anything worldly? God becomes the only good to be valued—indeed, nothing created can be described as "good" (see Luke 18:19).

Second, most known medieval mystics did not flee the vanity of the world (although at least some, including Rolle and Ruusbroec, did become hermits for extended periods), but they did become monastics and focused on their own private inner states—the world, along with the flesh and the Devil, was the monastics' enemy. Most did not get married but followed Jesus' precept of renouncing one's own family in favor of God (Mark 8:34; Luke 14:26). The focus was on what was most beneficial to themselves—their own inner life—not actions toward others. They suffered for themselves, not others. The Kingdom of God is a mystical reality *within* each of us, not a social reality *among* all of us (Luke 17:21), and so only the personal cultivation of contemplation mattered. Any other-impinging acts mystics undertook were only to help themselves toward some type of immediate communion with God. We need to love others to get to heaven, but mystics did no more than use them for their own ends. People are reduced to nothing more than creations of God having no value, not ends in themselves with their own intrinsic value. When Thomas Aquinas said "What we love in our neighbor is God alone," this means that we will not genuinely care about the neighbor at all—all that the mystics see wherever they look is God, not a real person. Moreover, as the author of the *Cloud of Unknowing* put it, one loves God for himself alone and others because it is God's law: what God wills is all that counts—there is no idea of an independent moral concern for others. In the four degrees of love Bernard of Clairvaux outlined, not is one to love a neighbor for the neighbor's sake.[28] At best, mystics love others for God's sake, not for the other person's sake. In sum, the way the mystics chose to fulfill the first commandment (to love God) in fact required rejecting the second (to love our neighbor), and thus they are not moral.

But the interconnection of the two basic commandments changes this assessment. Christians cannot genuinely fulfill the second commandment unless they treat others as fully real and genuinely love others through actions. People are made in the "image of God" (Gen. 1:26). Whatever that may mean, Christian mystics are participating in God's relation to his creatures only when they love others for their own sake, not merely as creatures we must love to please God. They must treat people as end in themselves, not as objects merely to be used for their own benefit. Only then are they participating in the creator's loving activity to sustain his creation. In short, they must be other-regarding. Outside of any depth-experience in which the mystic is lost in the transcendental reality, there is the state of mindfulness in which God's love informs the actions of the mystic, and the resulting actions are love for others. In short, loving one's neighbor is what bursts forth from the enlightened state in a Christian framework. Thus, one can love God with all of one's heart—be focused on God—and express this love through actions toward others as ends in themselves. One is not merely serving God but manifesting his love for the world. Thus, the eternal and the temporal are combined through love for one's neighbor. In effect, the two commandments are interlocked: the first one has a value-component that entails the second—one cannot love God and hate one's brother (1 John 4:19-21). Or in Catherine of Siena's words, love of God and love of one's neighbor are the same thing.[29]

Selflessness and the Presuppositions of Morality

There is also no presuppositional problem here concerning whether there is a reality to be concerned about. Other people are real: God may be the source of all reality, but his creation is also real and valuable precisely because it is his creation.[30] And since God loves his creation, we can too. God is treating his creation, including the people, as real, and so can we. When mystics say that what they love in their neighbor is "the God in him," there is the danger that the mystics will love only God and discount the created person totally. However, within the Christian ethos and worldview it makes more sense to conclude that mystics are not treating the person as unreal but only claiming that each person is a creation of God and that each should be loved equally and disinterestedly. The world is not to be despised, as the doctrine of God's incarnation affirms. Indeed, the *Theologia Germanica* goes so far as to state creation is not just good but a paradise. In sum, the ultimate value of each person's individuality is affirmed.

The surrender of the will to a loving force presents no more of a presuppositional problem than did the problem with the *dao* discussed in the last chapter. Purged of self-will and inwardly still, the mystic's will is totally replaced with God's. This can mean that we accomplish nothing; only God does. As Ruusbroec put it, the mystic does exterior works "as if he was not even performing them." This can be interpreted as a total determinism of our actions by God and thus that there is no role for the mystic's will. We are simply the instrument through which God acts and accomplishes whatever he wants. (The mystical antinomians appear to have had this belief-claim.) However, the standard view appears to be that God's love informs the mystic's will and yet the mystic must still choose how to act. There is no loss of self-control with the loss of self-interest. According to the *Theologia Germanica* there is a free and unfettered will that is not self-will but is a will nonetheless—if there were no will, God could not be known, loved, and praised. The unfettered will has no restrictions but unerringly senses what to do. As with the *dao*, God's will can be likened to gravity: while we act in conformity to gravity, it does not determine what acts we choose to carry out.[31] Similarly, mystics who align their will with God's still have to choose how to implement God's love for their neighbors. The question to be asked, according to the *Theologia Germanica*, is: would a given act or omission be possible or fitting if God were abiding in man? They still have personal agency (as the mere fact that they choose what to write indicates), and each mystic becomes a co-divinity with God through loving acts. One is in a "working union" with God, performing external works through the strength God imparts.[32]

Mystical selflessness does present a problem in applying the second commandment: how do you love your neighbor "as yourself" if you have no sense of self? This leads to the charge that mysticism is incompatible with Christian ethics. Following Augustine, early-medieval mystics accepted self-love as a natural endowment from God and thus as inevitable. But by the later medieval period any role for oneself was denied. Eckhart could on the one hand assert the need for self-love and immediately turn around and say that we should not seek self-interest and that all creatures are pure nothing.[32] Apparently he saw only complete impartiality in self-love: "If you love yourself, you love all men as yourself. As long as you love one single person less than yourself, you have never really loved yourself; [that is,] unless you love all men as yourself, loving all men in one man, and that man is God and man."[33] Thus, the denial of self-will is different but compatible with treating your neighbor as yourself (i.e., impartiality). Love for one's own person is no longer a possible standard for determining how to love others. If one is to love God more than oneself, or even to despise oneself, how can there be any place for self-concern? (Despite arguing that one's love of God required hating oneself, their values kept any of these mystics from ever concluding that, since all people are the same creations of God as we, we should also hate them.) Indeed, for many mystics, love for others went beyond even any impartiality in which they counted themselves as one among equals—no regard for their own welfare, spiritual or worldly, mattered (see John 12:24-25).

Contemplation and the Active Life

Even if selflessness could not be easily reconciled with Christian theory, self-denial as a practical matter meant a totally self-giving devotion to helping others. If forced to choose between the "active life" of helping others (not asceticism) and the "contemplative life" of meditation, most mystics of this period valued the former. Following Augustine, most mystics believed no Christian was ever exempt from an active life of charity and good works. The laity may occasionally engage in contemplation, but the problem arose for the monastics and hermits whose lives were dedicated to it. A popular allegory from the period was the story of Martha and Mary (Luke 10:38-42): Martha represented the active life, Mary the contemplative, and Mary chose the better part. Some mystics (e.g., Bernard of Clairvaux) argued that Mary may have chosen the better part but she had already performed her tasks first. Thus, for those mystics the centrality of good works in the enlightened contemplative way of life was secured. Some English mystics, such as Richard Rolle, favored the contemplative over the active life for the mystics, arguing that the life of ordinary virtues is for the laity while the religious life of full contemplative concentration is incompatible with the constant demand for action.[34] But the majority opinion was to condemn any "spiritual gluttony," as John of the Cross called it, that favored concentrating on personal experiences over concern for others. To Eckhart, delighting in "great experiences" is a matter of self-will.

The vast majority of known mystics saw the ideal life as a combination of both the active and the contemplative. Ruusbroec argued for the integration of action and contemplation, of activity and receptivity, in the "comprehensive (*ghemeyne*) life" and attacked anyone who would devote themselves to the latter while ignoring the former. The enlightened life is not a "mixed" life (with distinct periods of meditation not influencing the periods when mystics "descended" from the heights of mystical ecstasy) but is a "unified" life in which contemplation informed active service for others. That is, mystics continued to meditate in the enlightened life, and thus there would be periods of contemplation without outward activity, but there would also be periods of action in which they acted within the constant awareness of God's presence. In sum, the periods of meditation inform the mystics' mindful "contemplation in action."

"Resting in God's love" becomes the wellspring generating loving action toward others.[35] Ruusbroec spoke of the "restlessness of love." Love cannot be idle but must act: the Spirit of God within the mystics moves them toward just and wise outward activity. It is a rhythm of two movements: God drawing us in and breathing us out in acts of love. Thus, the more contemplative Catherine of Siena became, the more active she said she became. In the enlightened state, there is the inner stillness of habitually "resting" inwardly in God (and thus being neutral to all that happens), but one can simultaneously engage outwardly in work for others. Love, says Ruusbroec, is both at rest and active at the same time: one receives both God inwardly and corporeal images through the senses, and one is inwardly blissful and outwardly active—inwardly the heart is empty and blissful and outwardly works are free of images and self-centeredness.[36] In sum, the offspring of the marriage of the mystic's will with God's are both an inner detachment and loving actions for others. From John of the Cross: unlike genuine experiences of God, "the Devil's visions produce spiritual dryness in one's communications with God and an inclination to self-esteem"—such experiences do not cause love of God and humility. In this way, the fruit of meditation—moral action in the service of others—becomes the test of whether the Christian mystic is enlightened or not. (But John also warned that those who act without first going through a contemplative stage will accomplish little good or may even do harm. Eckhart similarly warned that action without contemplation in God is meaningless.)

The active life is modeled on the ways of God as manifested in the life of Jesus, since Jesus was the "image of the invisible God" (Col. 1:15). This was the *imitatio dei*, not in the sense of participation in the sacraments (although most mystics treated these as also necessary), but in the sense of living a life of God's love. This was the "Christian constant" throughout the Middle Ages.[37] One is to be generous, tenderhearted, and forgiving as God forgave us—one is to live in love as Christ loved us and gave himself as a sacrifice (Eph. 4:32-5:2). But unlike many Christians whose interest in Jesus is limited to the events reconciling people to God (his death and resurrection), the mystics focus on his teachings and actions toward other people and his suffering. In their uncompromising *imitatio Christi*, Christian virtues—in particular humility but above all love—become internalized on the path. (Hope does not appear to have played a significant role in their thought.) Mystics "took up the cross" of the Christ life by surrendering the self. In the words of Thomas à Kempis, one is "to learn perfect self-surrender, and to accept My will without argument or complaint." This leads to a life of renunciation and poverty but also to a life of love toward the poor and needy. "Good" becomes simply what conforms to God's will, and "evil" any act of self-will, regardless of an act's result.

One no longer lives one's life as one's own but as God's. One no longer seeks one's own good but God's. Some Christians may be "hirelings" working for a reward or fear of punishment, but the enlightened are the "friends" or even "sons" detached from all personal concerns of reward or punishment. To the author of the *Theologia Germanica*, to love for a reward is a "false love." As Teresa said, "If I love God or a neighbor for the sake of heaven, send me to hell." As in other mystical traditions, we paradoxically obtain what is best for ourselves by renouncing self-interest. Other-regardingness, not any self-interest, is all that remains as they give themselves over to helping others in complete impartiality. One no longer desires or hates anything but is completely disinterested. One loves (i.e., gives oneself) without a sense of possessiveness. No one is despised or favored. Thus, one's love is now a disinterested love promoting the welfare of all equally. The English author of the *Cloud of Unknowing* agreed: charity sometimes demands that mystics come down from the heights of contemplation to do work, and during the work of contemplation everyone is equally dear. He added the paradox of helping others by forgetting them: the enlightened mystic does not deny the humanity or individuality of anyone but merely has no special regard for anyone in particular—all are equally a brother or sister, and no one is an enemy. The warmth of one's love reaches out to all. One does not judge but forgives in a life of joyful helping.

Prior to enlightenment, part of the purgation stage according to Bernard consisted of good works and practicing the virtues of the Christian tradition of the time. Ruusbroec concurred: even during the early stages of contemplation, the soul cannot enjoy permanent rest without going out into creation and performing works. Since other-regardingness is ingrained into the way of life, it is safe to conclude that the mystics were moral at that stage. (As with the traditions dealt with earlier, the philosophical issue of morality is not discussed in these writings.) They followed the general Christian ethics and the rules of their monastic order. Some may have been active in reforming the vigor of discipline within their order, but none saw any need to revise the general ethics of their day. Instead, most, like the majority of Jewish and Islamic mystics, were not interested in such reform, and this had the effect making them ethically conservative.[38] A difference lies in how the mystics fulfilled the ethics but not in any items in the codes of ethics themselves.

In the enlightened state, one no longer has any self-will, and thus, in Augustine's phrase, one can "love [God], and do what you will." (That this can lead to antinomianism is discussed below.) No particular list of rules is necessary for this.[39] The possibility of acting selfishly has evaporated, and acts of love flow from the mystics spontaneously and automatically. How do they know how to act? Have the enlightened mystics received some information from God? Or do they now simply know God's will by having practiced virtues based on Jesus' teachings? Or have they merely internalized the Christian precepts that informed their training? In any case, conformity to a code of conduct, including monastic vows, would not be of utmost importance.[40] Imitating God's love fulfills any commands (Matt. 22:37-40; Rom. 13:10). Thus, acting out of humility and love is what is essential. They are being the type of person Christians consider that God wants them to be, not doing anything unusual. Their actions may differ from those of the unenlightened who were following the precepts of their time and place but only because they are applying the standard Christian values in an uncompromising way, much as had the early Christians expecting the imminent end of the world.

Most importantly for the issue at hand, there is no question that in the enlightened state the mystics are other-regarding. That is, they now are not simply deciding to perform helpful acts but are totally other-regarding persons—their dispositions could not let them do otherwise. Jesus' first commandment entails the second, and this can only be done if one is genuinely other-regarding. These mystics could not merely use others for their own religious advancement.[41] Any union with God's will logically means one cannot be selfishly preoccupied with advancing one's own private holiness while the rest of the world looks after themselves.[42] Because the ground of being is all-loving, mystics must mirror it in their lives. Thus, not just good acts but love for others is woven into the fabric of the enlightened Christian mystic's way of life. A purity of motive, not just of action, is needed to be "perfect," to participate in the very ground of reality.

Meister Eckhart and Living "Without a Why"

Johannes Eckhart, the German Dominican friar-preacher, may seem like an odd choice as a mystic to focus on, considering the fact that if he had lived another week or so the papers excommunicating him would have arrived from Rome. But he does reveal how monistic metaphysics can ground a moral way of life.[43] He, like the more trinitarian Ruusbroec whom he influenced, was a knowledge-mystic rather than a love-mystic. Metaphysics derived from Neoplatonism plays a greater role than love and will in his thought.[44] Central to his metaphysics is the distinction between God (*gott*) and the Godhead (*gottheit*). The former is the personal god of theism that creates and acts, but the latter is the "God beyond God"—the silent, inactive abyss or ground (*grunt*), the source of our being.[45] Indeed, apart from the Godhead creatures are "pure nothingness."[46] This is not to deny that we exist but only to emphasize that we have no existence apart from the source—i.e., without the Godhead, we would cease to exist. All of existence, including God, ultimately emanates—"boils up" (*ebullitio*)—from the Godhead and returns to it. God, as the first reality emanated, creates all that follows and is the same being (*esse*) of all that is created. That is, the beingness the Godhead provides is identical in all of reality—God's isness (*istigkeit*) is our isness, and God is no more real than we are. But individuals do not lose their individuality: God (beingness) dwells only in the soul's innermost part—God the creator never absorbs the "spark" or "uncreated light" in each creature in a mystical union, nor is one creature identical to another. Thus, all being is one, but we retain individuality.[47] This means there is something more to us than just our being. Our individuality is in some sense also real, even if the Godhead could withdraw our being and we would cease. People remain distinct creatures, and hence there is a reality about which we can be morally concerned. The enlightened see creatures as "pure and noble" in the light of God (being), but neither creaturehood nor individuality is denied. The realness of the emanations thus avoids Advaita Vedānta's presuppositional problem.

For Eckhart, there is no other reality for us to be united to in a mystical experience—there is only being and its source. In a mysticism centered on the Godhead, rectifying our knowing is the focus.[48] There is no reality to love, nor will theistic devotional practice get us to the core. Instead, the means is a process of emptying—"unknowing" (*unwizzen*)—of all the content of our mind to become receptive to an infusion of mystical knowledge. The mind must be emptied of all ideas and images (*bilde*), including all sense of self, and detached from all emotions.[49] In short, the soul must be "stripped naked" of all multiplicity. Freed from our everyday mind, we achieve a radical inner simplicity and stillness—a "desert" or "poverty"—beyond all conceptual categories and desires. Through such "inner poverty," the "poor" (in spirit) knows and wills nothing. To be full of things is to be empty of God, and to be full of God is to be empty of things. So Eckhart prayed for "God that he may rid me of God"—i.e., to free the mind of all ideas of "God" in order to get into the uncreated isness beyond all mental images. Thus, this is part of the meditative process to free the mind of idols so that experiences can occur and is not a denial of God—Eckhart is, after all, praying to God. Nor does this mean that God cannot be characterized outside of the mystical experience: Eckhart, like most Christian mystics of the time, said God is love. We need to learn to penetrate the shell of all things (the images) and find the kernel of beingness at its core that is beyond the reach of understanding—in that darkness, God shines. In this central silence, no idea may enter, and the soul neither thinks nor acts. To be aware of knowing God is to know about God and the self—to be thinking in terms of entities—not to have the direct experience of the isness.

But, while we are completely passive, God is compelled to act: there is the "birth of the Son" (*geburt*) in the soul. That is, the birth of Christ is not just an historical event that occurred once two thousand years ago to overcome original sin but is an inner event that occurs throughout time in us all. Thus, we are all the begotten sons and daughters of God. Nothing ontologically changes with this birth in our soul—substantively, we have the same isness we always have had—but our awareness is transformed as we become aware of the eternal dimension to all things. Eckhart listed six stages of the "inner and new man": (1) haltingly trying to live according to the example of good and holy people; (2) observing the exemplars but also contemplating God; (3) constrained by love and zeal, losing the desire to do wrong and instead being led into joy, sweetness, and blessedness; (4) growing and becoming more rooted in love and in God; (5) living in peace in being, i.e., reposing silently in the overflowing riches of supreme and ineffable wisdom; and (6) the rest and blessedness of becoming free of all images and attaining complete oblivion of our transient life and being transformed into the image of God and thus becoming God's child.[50] We then have an immediate awareness of God (being) unblocked by any image. But Eckhart pushed even further: the soul must break through even the soul's own image into the divine source that is the Godhead beyond God. Here, through mystical knowledge one perceives the ground where God, the experiencer, and all else have one source.

Mystical experiences do not save the person but are only a tool for fulfilling the commands to love God fully and to love one another. Mystics may have forgotten all creatures (including themselves) during mystical depth-experiences, but in the enlightened state after such experiences sensations and conceptual differentiations return. They then become aware of their contemplation—"knows and perceives that he contemplates, perceives, and loves God." That is, in the natural order of things, once one is aware of one's own mystical awareness, there is a "going out and a return to the starting point." Eckhart's biblical citation for this is the allegorical interpretation of the "noble man" who leaves his home to go to a far country (contemplation), obtains a kingdom (enlightenment), and then returns home (now in the enlightened state) (Luke 19:12). In this enlightened state, the constant awareness of God (being) penetrates and permeates our dispositions and intentions—we are "shaped through and through with the shape of God." For Eckhart, to whomever God is ever present has the Kingdom of God within them. God's presence shines through the enlightened without effort, resulting in loving actions toward others. Thus, an inner stillness is incorporated into a life of outer action. In sum, the best and loftiest life is to be silent, without interposing any ideas, and to let God speak and act through us. One lives a life *in* God *without* God (i.e., without the concept "God" interfering).

This enlightened state is thus not a state of inaction. Central to Eckhart's thought is that the fruit of contemplation is loving action toward others—the soul is no longer a virgin but a wife that bears fruit in moral action. In the enlightened state, one no longer has a personal will but only God's: God loves and thus so do we—God and we are one in loving. These passages summarize Eckhart's view on concern for the differentiated "creaturehood" level:

> We ought to get over amusing ourselves with such raptures for the sake of that better love, and to accomplish through loving service what men most need spiritually, socially, or physically. As I have often said, if a person were in such a rapturous state as St. Paul once entered [2 Cor. 12:1-6], and he knew of a sick man who wanted a cup of soup, it would be far better to withdraw from the rapture for love's sake and serve

him who is in need.

> [N]o person in this life may reach the point at which he can be excused from outward service. Even if he is given to a life of contemplation, still he cannot refrain from going out and taking an active part in life. . . . No man may have virtues without using them as time and occasion require. Thus, those who are given to the life of contemplation and avoid activities deceive themselves and are on the wrong track. I say that the contemplative person should indeed avoid even the thought of deeds to be done during the period of his contemplation but afterwards he should get busy. . . .

> If a person withdraws into himself . . . [and] finds that he has no urge to get back to work or responsible activity, then he should break loose and get to work of some kind, mental or physical. . . . Not that one should give up, neglect or forget his inner life for a moment, but he must learn to work in it, with it and out of it, so that the unity of his soul may break out into his activities and his activities shall lead him back to that unity. In this way one is taught to work as a free man should. . . . If, however, the outward life interferes with the inner, then follow the inner; but if the two can go together, that is best of all and then man is working together with God.

> For what we plant in the soil of contemplation we shall reap in the harvest of action and thus the purpose of contemplation is achieved.[51]

This places charitable work squarely at the center of this mystical way of life. According to Eckhart, performing good deeds is both a necessary prerequisite to attaining the enlightened life and integral to the enlightened state itself. Eckhart himself certainly exemplified the active life as a well-traveled teacher, preacher, writer, counselor, and administrator.

Since Eckhart noted that during contemplation one should not even think of doing works, there are passages in his work suggesting inaction—e.g., "focus on what we ought to *be* rather than what we ought to *do*," "the exterior act adds nothing to the goodness of the interior work," "the spark in the soul has nothing to do with any actions," "our works do not greatly matter to God but only our intention and our love," "do not be attracted to external things," "seek nothing in this world but God," "if anything from outside moves you to work, the works are really all dead."[52] As noted below, some of his other remarks may have encouraged antinomians. But, as in the passages just quoted, it is clear that activity is an essential part of the enlightened life. Mary (contemplation) and Martha (action) are united in this state. (In his sermon on them, Eckhart portrayed *Martha* as spiritually more mature: her life integrated contemplation with action, while Mary was still on the path. Under this interpretation, Mary may have chosen the "better part" in choosing the contemplative life, but she still chose only a part of the ideal life.) Hence, it makes sense to see those passages as relating to attaining the state where loving action is spontaneous. Thus, when he said, "It does not matter so much what we may do," he added "What matters is the ground on which the works are built" and that "[w]e ought to do everything we can to be good."[53] That is, he was simply focusing on the inner aspect of a person in the enlightened state and is not denying the need for exterior action: if the "interior man" is aligned with God, works of the "exterior man" will be just, and the latter part did not need further comment.

Eckhart emphasized *detachment* (*abegescheidenheit*) from creatures. It is higher than love because God must give himself over to the disinterested. The completely dispassionate heart is most receptive to the inflowing of God. To be detached is to be inwardly unmoved by anything: even-minded in the face of all the joy and sorrow caused by the passing things of this world, totally disinterested in oneself and others (not loving oneself or one's family more than others or one's own happiness more than that of others), and totally empty of all things created.[54] All sorrow comes from partiality in one's loving and from holding something dear that is perishable.[55] Thus, detachment overcomes sorrow. The detached receive all things alike from God. They are dead to the world—nothing created can move them. They love God and could as easily give up the whole world as give up an egg. They have penetrated all images and reached their being. One is detached from all creatures and loves God alone, only for his own sake. But one has also broken through all images and hence loves God as he is—a nongod, nonperson, and nonentity but simply the One beyond all duality.

But being interested in "neither this nor that" is completely consistent with loving action: as with "detached action" in the *Bhagavad-gītā*, it is about being emotionally even-minded to the consequences of action to oneself, not about its effect on others. With this inner calm, one can act for all people—the "outer man" works while the "inner man" remains unmoved by whatever occurs. In short, detachment is simply the emotional counterpart to radically impartial action. (To Ruusbroec, living without self-will means that one lives without preferences regarding things to be done or left undone.) One is no longer more attached to one person than any other. Indeed, Eckhart claimed detachment brings us closest to God since God has always acted disinterestedly toward all, beginning with creation. Such detachment involves desiring nothing, neither loving nor hating the world or persons, but letting things be (*gelâzenheit*) without clutching or self-assertion. It remains an inner attitude—relinquishing all sense of ownership and attachment (*eigenschaft*) even of one's own acts—and does not entail the external renunciation of anything or any resignation concerning the results of actions. It involves accepting things free of all emotional response. And, with all self-assertion lost, nothing is used as a means to our own ends. In short, it is letting God be God in us.

Detachment does not involve moral indifference or inaction but rather a non-self-assertive way of acting in which one completely "forgets" oneself. One still acts but does not control or use people for one's own ends. It would be impossible for people living in God's loving presence to do evil "even if God commanded it" because they can seek their own advantage in nothing but act solely for loving-kindness.[56] The soul dwells in a condition beyond the necessity of virtues, where goodness as a whole comes naturally to her—i.e., the soul has transcended all necessity for cultivating virtues because they now flow from her being.[57] External acts of virtue were instituted so that the outer person might be directed to God, and that is no longer necessary.[58] One receives virtues in the ground of the soul where the soul and God are one in their beingness.[59] When one performs works of virtue without having to prepare one's will or having any intention but is acting virtuously for virtue's sake, one has perfected virtue.[60] With Christian virtues internalized, the soul is passive and God acts through us. This unites the contemplative and active lives: we can act while maintaining an inner calm, a still center to whatever activity occurs. One remains active but without the sense that the deeds are one's own. "It is the Father dwelling in me doing his own work" (John 14:10; see also John 3:21).

He whom Eckhart calls the "just man" (*iustus*)—or the "good," "noble," "humble," "inner," or "poor" man—does not seek or desire anything. He, like God, is just because he gives each person his or her due. Justice (*iustitia*), in effect, merely reflects detachment in action. Thus, the pursuit of justice is so imperative that if God were not just, the just would not give a fig for God.[61] But God is just, and thus justice is born in us with the birth of the son in our soul. The just person has been informed by, and transformed into, justice.[62] If we are just, all our works will be just. By removing all personal desires, one can lead a fully active life without losing the interior silence, the still hinge around which the door turns. All works are undertaken with the same disinterested frame of mind. Nothing is done for hope of heaven, fear of hell, or any other personal desire—as Eckhart said, the soul has no business deals with truth. (Those who love God because of what they can get for it are treating God as they would a cow.)[63] Attempts at good works do not move God's detachment. Nor can the detached soul pray, since prayer is to ask for something but the soul has no will but God's. At some points Eckhart said that the will is united with God's and at other points that self-will, being a form of creaturehood, does not really exist apart from being (and thus there is no self-will to annihilate or to burn in hell and no union of wills since we have no will to unite to God's). In either case, one no longer acts out of self-interest, nor even tries to do God's will, but God's will occurs spontaneously. One may be in a state where one is no longer aware of a self acting—being aware only of God or the world—but that does not mean the self is not there. Since God cannot but will what is good, one whose will is untouched by all created things now acts only in love. In short, love is simply the will reintegrated into Truth.[64] One can now drop external restraints, including disciplines bound by religious vows.

In this state, one lives "without a why" (*sunder warumbe*), i.e., without a personal purpose and without planning. Thus, one is like God, who also acts without a why: God is not moved to perform any deed by anything else than his own goodness; in particular, our deeds do not move him to give us anything or to do anything for us.[65] If someone asks why you are doing something, the only possible reply is "I do it because I do it."[66] No other motive (which would be personal) is involved. You live only to live and do not know why.[67] God's love is now acting through us, and self-giving love has no "why."[68] There is no further goal but living from one's nature. (As Ruusbroec put it, this is a "wayless state."

But as with the Daoist *wu-wei*, the actions are not truly purposeless or aimless: only the absence of personal motivation is the point.) Just as one loves God for the sake of loving God, so too one does all of one's work without calculation just for the sake of working—self-giving love is automatic. Those who seek something in their works or who work because of a "why" are hirelings, not the just persons who have God working in them.[69] But the Christian values framing the enlightened way of life have an other-regarding component, and thus living with no will but God's is a moral way of life. In sum, Eckhart is asserting that the enlightened perform acts of love only out of the ground of being with no other motive. To the author of the *Theologia Germanica*, living without a why means living for no personal ends and for no other reason except to fulfill the eternal Will: the inner man is immovable and has no independent will; the outer man moves and fulfills the duties and obligations ordained by God. It is a selfless life of purely detached action for others.

The transcendence of God presents the problem of how any term used for created things—such as "morally good"— could be ascribed to such a reality. How then can God be praised as morally good? Only if God is a type of reality that can be concerned with other beings can he be moral, but this would mean that God does not transcend all attributes of creatures. (Aquinas' analogical method for understanding language about God also requires that God's goodness be of the same type as human goodness: if God's goodness were radically different in kind from our conception of "goodness," the process of analogy cannot work.) Eckhart reveals the problem when he said that "God is not good; I am good" (reversing Mark 10:18, Luke 18:19). God is not good and to call God "good" is like calling white "black."[70] He may have said this to accent the degree of God's goodness or to attribute goodness only to the One beyond multiplicity (the Godhead).[71] Nevertheless, Eckhart did not discount all creaturely values: all goodness flows from God's overflowing goodness.[72] God plays and laughs in good deeds.[73] Good is that which shares itself; hence, a hermit is neither good nor evil; but God shares most of all.[74] Thus, a good man, born of goodness and living in God, enters into the attributes of the divine nature and so is good.[75] A man's being and ground, from which his works derive their goodness, is good when his intention is wholly directed to God—if we cling to God, God and all virtues cling to us.[76]

In sum, creaturehood may be nothing apart from God, and thus there is nothing to be of value apart from God, but a mystic can be concerned with the reality behind the images because creation is a product of God and hence good. Our substance may be from only one source, but our distinct creaturehood remains a reality. It is not to be treated in any negative way as with Advaita Vedānta's illusionism. Eckhart focuses more on the inner attitude than the externals of the actions, but this is only because that is where the source of goodness lies. Loving, selfless actions arise out of that source, and there is no question of inaction in this way of life. For Eckhart, to be fully is to love as God loves.[77]

The Question of Social Action

For these mystics, Christian charity involved both the spiritual and temporal needs of one's neighbor—both teaching, preaching, and counseling and also giving a cup of soup to the poor, the sick, and the outcaste. The belief that the world and people are real and valuable creations of God makes our this-worldly needs a more central concern in Christianity than in the Indian traditions discussed in earlier chapters. But this-worldly aid was usually expressed in face-to-face activities. Because of the mystics' concern with the inner life, there was no call to reform social structures and institutions on a societywide basis by enlisting groups or governmental powers. This is not to say that mystics saw themselves as isolated individuals rather than social beings: even if mystical experiences occur only to individuals, these mystics saw their ways of life within the context of a community.[78] But social reformers think in societywide terms, while these mystics saw only the individuals in front of them. Some larger projects did occur—such as Teresa of Ávila setting up charities and Catherine of Genoa, a hospital—but even these still focused concern on the neighbor at hand and not on reforming society as a whole. Johann Tauler staying in Strasbourg to help the sick and dying during the plague is representative. And, it should be noted, when these mystics did take positions on larger social and political issues did arise, they tended to be conservative, supporting the status quo—in particular the pope and other ecclesiastical institutions—against efforts at reform.[79] However, it must also be noted that this led to activities we would consider morally questionable today. Bernard of Clairvaux is usually considered the first inquisitor. Teresa also supported the Inquisition. And Bernard and Catherine of Siena were strong supporters of the Crusades—in fact, militancy of the religious was a major contributing factor in these armies for Christ going to war to win back Jerusalem from the Muslims. Indeed, there were religious military orders—the Knights Templar, Knights Hospitalers, and Knights of St. John.

More typically, however, the mystics focused on only one person at a time. The Kingdom of God reigns within each person individually. In the words of the *Theologia Germanica*, the Kingdom of God is living without self-will or the urge to possess; instead, it is abiding in the ground of being. There is no sense that the Kingdom of God could be brought about by social changes. That Kingdom is not merely the world free of social injustice but something entirely different—a state in which God's will prevails on earth—and for that, a personal inner transformation of individuals, not new social structures, is needed. Seldom is heard among these medieval mystics the prophetic voices of the ancient Israelite prophets or modern social reformers. Catherine of Siena, with her talks to the rich and powerful, was one of a few exceptions. Although the world is deemed good, there is no duty to transform the world but only to help one's neighbor. Nonmystical Christians may focus on political reform or social justice, but these mystics focused on simpler and more direct acts of charity.

Even in monasteries and nunneries, the focus was on individuals and not social action. These cloistered communities did create groups that had to be administered and thus had a social dimension. Some mystics, like Bernard, took on greater administrative roles within their order or the church. But each monk or nun was working on his or her own inner life individually. The image of monks silently tending the fields—their work as mindful contemplation—represents that communal/individual situation. The monastics' relation to the wider Christian community also involved immediate personal interaction. There was some reciprocal giving between the community and the monastery, as with the Buddhists: the laity gave material support, and the religious gave teaching and counseling. (Ironically, through their own work and the gifts they received, including vast tracts of land, many of these communities of men and women who renounced possessions became places of affluence and luxury. This, along with lax practices and losing sight of the purpose of the practices, created an almost constant call for monastic reform.) But the central Christian ethos of love also made charitable acts by the religious—e.g., dispensing food and shelter to the needy—a more prevalent activity than in Theravāda Buddhism. How involved with the outside world the monks were varied from order to order—the Franciscan and Dominican friars being the most active. (Monasteries in the Eastern Orthodox tradition were more ascetic, more isolated, and less active in this regard.) But the charitable activity remained focused on the immediate needs of the people and not on attempts to restructure society in ways that might benefit the poor and hungry more generally.

One effect of this focus on individuals was that mystics gave mystical interpretations to nonmystical biblical passages that could well have been used to advocate social activism. Indeed, Eckhart transformed the central historical event of Christianity—the "birth of the Son"—into a mystical event occurring in persons throughout time. He also interiorized potentially political passages. For example, Jesus' cleansing of the temple of money changers (Matt. 21:12-13)—an event full of possible political and economic reverberations—becomes simply a symbolic statement of Jesus entering the soul of an individual. Eckhart's sermon on the passage discusses only emptying oneself for a mystical experience, not economics or society.[80] It is treated no differently than other biblical events—i.e., mystically. The Kingdom of God becomes, not a social reality among us, but a state of a person—an inner state free of the sense of self for each person individually.[81] His understanding of justice (iustitia) is similarly nonsocial. It relates only to inner detachment. As discussed above, "justice" becomes a state of feeling impartially the same about everything that happens—nothing is desired from God, nor does one go beyond oneself to get something.[82] It has nothing to do with the social relationships among people or an end to social injustice. Indeed, it is a sign of "inward infirmity that any person should be glad or sad about the passing things of the world."[83] Social concerns would fall within the category of the "merely terrestrial and transient" to be avoided in favor of love for the "eternal realities" neutral to all outward matters.[84] To seek anything temporal or to work for a "why" runs counter to the enlightened way of living.

The medieval mystics may, of course, have influenced social and religious reformers.[86] And, like everyone else, mystics were aware and reacted to the social conditions of their time and place.[87] But the point is that any such effect on social reform was not their intention—the mystics' reaction was a way of life devoted to the inward transformation of a person. Eckhart may have been articulating a new religiosity, bringing monastic inner religiosity to the people in the growing towns, but his focus was still on the inner life of the individual. However, his writings and daring rhetoric may well have been misinterpreted by the people who heard him directly or indirectly. Matthew Fox suggests that Eckhart's listeners may have interpreted his phrase "I pray God to rid me of God" in terms of ridding themselves of any God (and hence any institution) supporting an unjust situation.[88] That might well have happened, but the context of Eckhart's remark makes it clear that he wanted to be rid of the concept "God" in order that God might enter him inwardly[89]—i.e., the mind must be emptied of all sensory and conceptual content, including the image "God." Eckhart was discussing the breakthrough to the Godhead beyond God, not works among people. Similarly with "poverty": Eckhart was concerned with an "inner poverty" in which the "poor in spirit" wills, knows, and wants nothing. While accepting external monastic poverty, he was concerned here with giving up a sense of self through detachment rather than in giving up possessions—external poverty without detachment leads nowhere, and the latter does not need the former.[90] In sum, the poor in spirit inherit the Kingdom of God (Matt. 5:3), and to Eckhart the Kingdom of God is something internal; thus, only inner poverty is needed. It was a change in attitude, not in property.[91] For the same reason, inner penitence is preferred to exterior works such as fasting and going barefoot.[92] His claim that we are all "aristocrats" might have influenced Anabaptists or other reformers, but Eckhart made it clear that "within us is the aristocrat."[93] "All people are equally noble with regard to their nature."[94] It is a matter of our being and knowledge, not our social status. Neither an endorsement of the status quo nor a call for social change is being advocated. Our inner "nobility" exists and remains constant regardless of what happens to our outward circumstances. Nothing external can in principle affect it.[95]

In short, Eckhart's response to the social injustices and materialism of his day was to transform concepts of poverty and nobility inwardly. No change in the social structure was sought. It certainly would require a major misinterpretation if Thomas Müntzer and John of Leyden were to use his or Johann Tauler's writings to justify their horrendous violence. As Carl Kelley says, Eckhart cannot be counted among those who insist the faithful must before all else be agents for healing social injustice.[96] Bernard McGinn adds that Eckhart's writings show no interest in the politics of the day and surprisingly little on the social or economic conditions; he was far from being an advocate of social revolution, and his teachings regarding inner transformation have no direct relation to anyone's social or economic status.[97] To interpret Eckhart's teaching as a call for social reform is to misunderstand him completely—it is comparable to altering and externalizing his advice that for God we ought to strip the soul bare (of all sensory and conceptual content) by walking around naked.

In sum, the individual inner transformations always remained central, not reforming societywide structures. Again, this is not to say that these mystics were not concerned with the material needs of the people around them but only that their other-regardingness was expressed in interpersonal actions of a more restricted scope. Still, the most important conclusion for the issue at hand remains that these Christians were moral: the mystic's inner transformation was connected to loving his or her neighbor through other-regarding, disinterested, compassionate action.

Antinomianism

The basic idea of antinomianism is that the elect are free of any legal, social, moral, or religious obligations—they are "above the law" in every sense. Orthodox enlightened mystics may believe they are "beyond good and evil" in the sense of no longer having to consult a list of rules or virtues since their wills are now fully aligned with God's. The enlightened thus have transcended the rules and virtues, but antinomians go one step further: they *repudiate* any rules and virtues as no longer being applicable to the enlightened way of life. No act is rejected as sinful. Whatever acts the elect do are by definition "pure" and free of sin. This leads antinomians to ignore or even intentionally to go against the social norms.[98] Christian antinomians frequently cited New Testament passages: "to the pure all things are pure" (Titus 1:15); "nothing is impure in itself" (Rom. 14:14); "sin has no dominion over you, and you are no longer under the law" (Rom. 6:14); "where the Spirit of the Lord is, there is liberty" (2 Cor. 3:17); "whoever is born of God does not sin . . . [and] cannot be a sinner" (1 John 3:9); "no one who dwells in Christ is a sinner" (1 John 3:6). Augustine's precept "love [God], and do what you will" was also certainly adoptable. Apparently a form of antinomianism existed even in the early Christian community: some intentionally continued to sin so that their grace would then be that much greater (Rom. 6:1).[99] The orthodox, starting with Paul, condemned this understanding of "freedom from sin" as heresy.[100]

Not all antinomians were mystics, but many were "enthusiasts" who placed all importance on experiences for their own sake and denied the need for any outward actions or Christian rituals. They were routinely accused of holding the belief that the world is merely a manifestation of God and ultimately only God is real. For if God alone is real, nothing in our world matters, so we can do whatever we want. But classical theistic metaphysics can easily lead to this antinomian conclusion: everything is from God, and thus all things are good and nothing is bad. The Devil is not really evil because he is one of God's creations and thus part of his plan. Or, if everything is the product of God, nothing we can possibly do is wrong. Or, if God is in the final analysis the only real agent, nothing that happens is not his will. Thus, whatever happens is his will—all events are predestined or occur out of necessity. Antinomians in the Rhineland area may well also have been inspired by Eckhart. Many of his remarks fit right in: "all creatures are pure for the soul to enjoy, for it enjoys all creatures in God and God in all creatures"; "if something were not God's will it would not come to pass"; "the spark in the soul has no truck with action, will or anything"; "when a person has a true spiritual experience, he may boldly drop external disciplines"; "if I sorrow for the harm done to external things, that is a true sign that I love external things"; "the kind of work we do does not make us holy but we make it holy"; "if it is God's will that we have sinned, we should not wish not to have sinned"; "the man who has attained complete detachment is so carried into eternity that no transient thing can move him"; "the exterior act adds nothing to the goodness of the interior act."

Prominent among the mystical antinomians were the Brothers (and Sisters) of the Free Spirit.[100] This was not an organized sect but rather individual mystics and informal groups within a general movement.[101] Central to their beliefs is the possibility of deification in this life. That is, through breaking self-will and meditation (including sitting still and trying to become emptied), the soul can become permanently identical to God in substance and will. In short, one becomes indistinguishable from God. Purged of self-will and desire, one is then incapable of sinning. Prior to this enlightenment, the "gross" soul must conform to social and religious rules, but upon deification the "free spirit" has no such restrictions. One thus attains a state of sinlessness beyond grace and thus beyond the need for the church's rituals, priests, the scriptures, or even Christ. Since God is "beyond good and evil" or any other value-characterization, so are the enlightened. Thus, no ethical injunctions apply to the enlightened life. And since the "Christ life" meant an obligation to keep external rules, the Free Spirits rejected it. Hell does not exist—God is all there is, and we return to him at death—and thus there is no punishment to be feared. They had no remorse or consideration for others in whatever they did.

Being in a "perfected" state, the Free Spirit is incapable of sinning, just as God is, and can do anything, just as God can. They would not consider themselves immoral since they had no self-will—saying, "I do anything I want," would have no meaning since there is no "I." Everything the enlightened do is attributed to God. One no longer acts at all, but God alone acts through him (see Matt. 10:20; Gal. 2:20). The Free Spirits were so in tune with God's will that they could grant their bodies whatever was pleasing to the bodies. Whatever nature required was from God, and thus whatever the body requires they may do. When on trial, Johann Hartmann of Ossmannstedt stated that he could take whatever property he wanted and kill anyone who was not a Free Spirit who tried to stop him; he even volunteered that a Free Spirit could have sex with his sister or mother anywhere, even on the altar. Such remarks led to the general impression among church leaders that the Free Spirits were constantly indulging their senses in a scandalous libertinism. But whether they treated their proclamations merely as theory (or only to shock) or actually practiced them is not clear; there are no records of any of them having been arrested for a secular crime.[102] Most of their own writings suggest that they were highly ascetic in pursuit of perfection—they renounced property and spent most of their time working on their inner life in self-emptying contemplation.[103] But an "active life" was no longer necessary—hence, the charge of passivity and moral quietism. Indeed, their greatest sin may have been one of indifference and inaction (and offending the leaders in power).

Closer to the orthodox positions was another movement of the time often confused with the Free Spirits: the laywomen in Northern Europe known as the Beguines and the laymen known as the Beghards. They were antischolastic and anti-intellectual and stressed contemplative prayer and visionary experiences, but they did not approach the antinomianism of the Free Spirits. For them, the rest in God of the "annihilated soul" (i.e., one in whom God's will has replaced self-will) is not disturbed by works. But they did not believe any of their deeds could violate the Christian codes of ethics. The enlightened are beyond any concern with virtues, but the virtues are nevertheless ingrained in the soul—the only difference is that it is now God, not the soul, who works through the person and carries out good works that minister to the neighbor's needs. Thus, there was no antinomian repudiation of Christian ethics. Their text *The Mirror of Simple Souls* does state that the annihilated soul can grant to nature whatever it desires, but to quote the author, Marguerite Porete of Hainault, the soul is so well-ordered that "nature does not demand anything prohibited." This defense, however, did not stop the inquisitors in Paris from burning her to death for heresy.[104]

One postmedieval movement needs a brief mention if for no other reason than its name—Quietism. The Quietists—Miguel de Molinos, Madame Jeanne-Marie Guyon, Archbishop François de Fénelon, and their followers—were love-mystics for whom the highest state was a "pure love" of God and thus one of "holy indifference" to one's own fate and to everything that is not God.[105] Like other theists, they aimed for a state free of all self-will, replaced by a total receptivity to an infusion by God. They are inwardly empty even of virtues. Thus, they emphasized quiet contemplation and passivity over not only more active forms of meditation but outward actions and the Christian rituals. Once the enlightened state is attained, one can do neither immoral nor moral acts on one's own initiative (since there is no longer any self-will)—God controls what is done. Any role for personal agency was denied: they are literally passive, and God is performing actions through their bodies. They are in effect no more than puppets. God alone is acting, but he is immutable, and so he has no desires about what occurs in this realm. Thus, the Quietists let whatever happens happen. Orthodox mystics could defend the quietistic state as one in which the soul does nothing but in which God works totally disinterested charity toward others through the mystic—inwardly there is a silent state, but outwardly there is still an active moral one.[106] But to Quietists whatever the body did came directly from God, not them. So they could follow any bodily desires because these do not come from them. Moreover, the ultimate objective seems to have been to remain continually in a state of quiet and indifferent contemplation, leading to a total lack of action, let alone moral actions toward others. Fénelon tried to defend Quietism against the charge of inaction (and was an active and effective administrator). But Molinos drew the wrath of church leaders when he ended up leading a life of sexual excess with his women followers. He explained this as being the result of acts by the Devil that he did not need to resist since they did not affect but in fact only deepened his inner quiet and thus were sinless and even purifying to the truly inward Christian. Guyon's clumsy writings also did not help convince others of their position.

Eckhart, Ruusbroec, the "Friend of God" who wrote the *Theologia Germanica*, and Tauler all attacked the antinomianism of their time as "a false light," "false freedom of the spirit," or "false emptiness." From Eckhart on living "without a why":

> Now some people say, "If I possess God and God's love, I can do anything I want." They do not understand these words correctly. As long as you can do anything against God and his commandments, you do not have the love of God, although you may fool the world [into thinking] you have it. The person who is established in God's will and God's love finds it delightful to do all things that are pleasing to God and to avoid doing those that are against God. . . . [It is impossible] for a person who is in God's will to do something against virtue.[107]

To the author of the *Theologia Germanica*, the Free Spirits' case was one of "spiritual pride"—thinking they were free of a sense of self when in fact they were not. To Ruusbroec, the Free Spirits had a form of "natural mysticism" in which they had emptied themselves of everything including self-will but had not been infused with the grace of God nor had they filled the void with works of virtue. To them, the highest holiness is following one's own nature without restraint, living in a state of emptiness satisfying every inclination of spirit and body. Elsewhere Ruusbroec took a more mainstream understanding: the Free Spirits in fact had not yet completely emptied themselves of sense of "I"—they have turned inward and feel nothing but the bareness and simplicity of their own being, which they mistake for God, but they are still operating with some self-will when they give the body whatever it desires. John of the Cross also inveighed against mystical antinomians who believed they reached a state where they no longer had a need for the Christian sacraments or for performing good works. The orthodox mystics of course saw an essential role for Christian rituals and official doctrines—and outward moral activity toward their neighbors. The inner transformation of enlightenment that carries over into action is what is central to Christian mysticism, not any mystical experiences. God the creator is always active, and thus so are the enlightened. Their activity is self-giving love, not license to do whatever they will.

Antinomians in Christianity are not like left-handed Tāntrikas who use immoral means to break attachments and thus attain enlightenment—here it is a case of "to the pure all is pure." But why did this antinomianism appear in a theism of love? (It is worth noting that Indian Tantrism also has a strong theistic element, even if the ultimate metaphysics is monistic.) Granted, there are passages in the New Testament and in the writings of other mystics that can be interpreted as permitting one to be beyond any law. But why did some theistic mystics conclude that immoral acts were implicitly permitted when other mystics did not? It cannot be simply, as is often suggested, that Neoplatonic metaphysics dictate this response, since more orthodox mystics (such as Eckhart) shared the beliefs at the same time and were moral, while the antinomians were among the love-mystics. Indeed, theism appears more conducive to antinomianism than monism. (Antinomian movements also developed in both the Jewish and Islamic mystical traditions.[108] In India, the nontheistic Advaitins never saw such implications entailed by their metaphysics, although as discussed in Chapter 5 they had trouble justifying any actions.) Why did some theistic mystics hold scrupulously to the orthodox values, while others took the same metaphysics and concluded that they were free of both sin and virtue and could commit any act? To Augustine, "love [God], and do what you will" meant that one's actions would necessarily be loving. Why did others think this meant self-indulgence was perfectly acceptable? This leads many theists to be suspicious of all mysticism. But how is it that some mystics stress the importance of inwardness without denying the orthodox value-system or the value of actions, while others took the same doctrine down an antinomian path?

Whatever answers social scientists might develop, the important philosophical point is that we cannot deduce values from beliefs. Something else is at work in the adoption of values. Theists may not want to admit that antinomianism is one option implicit within theistic beliefs or that theism and love-mysticism are amoral. (Of course, "orthodox" mystics by definition in any tradition will say the same.) And the orthodox in any tradition can point out that only a very small number, if any, of its participants actually indulged themselves. But the fact remains that the antinomians cited orthodox doctrines for all their points and considered themselves Christians. The question remains how they could do this and yet reach antinomian conclusions. To say that they misunderstood the Bible and Eckhart cannot explain it all—their ideas and values still had to come from somewhere. This means that valuing morality does not come from mystical experiences or the basic Christian doctrines. The Christian mystical antinomian practices appear to be as "logical" a conclusion from the doctrine that all that happens is God's will as advocating moral action.[109] Antinomianism is not a product of mysticism *per se*, since other mystics condemn it. Determining "heresy" from "orthodoxy" turns on grounds other than the mystical experiences themselves. (That all this suggests that mystical experiences themselves are value-neutral or nonmoral will be relevant for the discussion in the next chapter.) More generally, valuing the experiences themselves over a total way of life or engaging in immoral actions does appear to be one option for those who radically concentrate on the inner life. In short, all of this raises the issue of where basic values exactly come from.

Conclusion

Mysticism is one way to keep a religion from being reduced simply to a matter of tradition. It places the transcendent squarely within the religious life. As Augustine saw it, we are Janus-faced, facing both this world and the transcendent, living both in time and in eternity. Plotinus used the image of amphibians for the same point. To the orthodox, outward action is essential, but so is the inner dimension—what is needed is an active life arising from a deeper source within us. With mysticism, one "rests" in God, and love of one's neighbor becomes an expression of one's whole character, not merely a matter of rule-following or gaining a reward. Instead of the isolated act of charity, one lives one's life only for other people. Indeed, these mystics can be seen as simply living the Christian ethics of their day from the deepest level of their being. Prior to enlightenment, Christian mystics may need to be commanded to love, but after enlightenment loving one's neighbor comes naturally and spontaneously. The often-voiced claim that what is unique about Christian ethics is that the life of Jesus has proven a problem for ordinary practitioners but not for these mystics. They imitated Jesus' life, and they interiorized the death and resurrection of Jesus in terms of dying to self-will and being filled with the god of love. They also interiorized the apocalyptic teachings and thus lived the life commanded in the New Testament to the fullest. Thus, it is no coincidence that most known mystics were canonized.[110]

Church leaders in the West may always have been suspicious of mystics, with their emphasis on the inner life and comparatively little on the alleged historical self-sacrifice of Jesus, but mystics were not in fact anti-institutional.[111] Normally they were quite conservative in matters of ethics. Both the path and the enlightened state are shaped by the Christian framework. Salvation is a matter of the two love commandments, and so the enlightened state is restricted by them. The mystics did not rely upon their experiences as a source of authority, and even if they gave the Bible an allegorical interpretation that interiorized stories, their belief-claims were solidly Christian: an all-loving god is the source of our reality, other people are real, and thus self-emptying love of others reflects ultimate reality. Mystics in Christianity (and also in Judaism and Islam) may have grounded the loving god in an impersonal Godhead in some ways similar to *brahman/ātman*, but a loving god remains the creator of this real realm and the source of its values. Love becomes firmly grounded in the fabric of reality: the force at the center of reality is selfless love for another.[112]

The end result of Christian mysticism of this period is to have one's character thoroughly infused with God's self-emptying love for others. All actions are given a transcendental dimension, but the test of a genuine experience of God is whether the "fruit" is loving actions toward others. Since the world and people are considered real, a deep involvement with this world is required, and other-regardingness can be manifested in a concern for the "this-worldly" well-being of persons. Since the world is real, such active charity is not considered an attachment or product of delusion. The experience of God may have been initially sought only out of love of God or only for self-interest (i.e., one's own reward in heaven by loving God), but the result is a love for others, not a self-absorbed love of one's own spiritual achievement or welfare. Similarly, with action: one gives a cup of soup simply because the recipient needs it, not to build up treasures in heaven. One loves others because God first loved us (1 John 4:19). The mystics' love of God is expressed in love of their neighbors; in their effect, the two loves are the same. They empty themselves of all self-will and are filled by God's love for others. In William Johnston's phrase, they must resonate with the suffering of the poor, the afflicted, and the distressed.[113] Their actions are not frantic "do-gooding" but action infused with inward quiet, spontaneously poured out from the awareness of the divine love that they beheld in their contemplation.[114]

This ethos of self-giving love for one's neighbor—and one's enemies—is what is distinctive of Christian mysticism. The list of precepts accepted by Christians is not unique to Christianity, but the attitude of going the extra mile for another is, and the medieval mystics adopted that attitude. They retained living the self-giving life of Christ without compromise long after eschatological fervor had left Christianity as a whole.

For the issues at hand, the conclusion must be that these mystics are moral: on the path a genuine concern for others mixes with self-concern, and in the enlightened state the mystics' love is completely other-regarding, since no self-interest is involved. The Christian god, and thus the mystics, is morally good because he is self-emptying love for others. In internalizing the point of view of God, the mystics' selflessness is necessarily expressed in loving actions toward others—the "living flame of love," in John of Cross' phrase. The second commandment solidifies an orientation toward others at the core of this tradition, unlike in Advaita Vedānta and Theravāda Buddhism. In short, the "active life" of other-impinging actions energized by an other-regardingness is central. Christians only become "perfect" in the context of serving others. Virtues focused on others become important. Thus, far from conflicting with Christianity, these mystics embody a very moral expression of it.

That the verdict on Christian mystics is that the orthodox mystics are moral cannot be too surprising since the very concept of morality developed in Christian culture. Indeed, love of one's neighbor arose as the fundamental ethical principle in Judaism and Christianity, not in classical Greek thought or other traditions. Thus, that ethos would shape their ways of life. But, as the previous chapters showed, mystics in non-Western traditions can also be other-regarding and hence moral. Nevertheless, the point is still worth noting that, contrary to what many Christians suppose, mystical experiences and mystical ways of life need not introduce a conflict with a moral stance within Christian ethics.

Notes

1. One of Mother Teresa's helpers said after holding a dying person for three hours that she felt such joy, as if she had held Jesus for three hours. Her reaction seems so self-centered as to raise questions. While her act no doubt was a comfort to the dying person, one can still ask why she was doing it and whether she was really treating the person as a full human being. The same can be asked of many apparent acts of charity. Was Francis of Assisi kissing a leper to comfort him or only to get over his own disgust at the sight of lepers?

2. In the words of Beach and Niebuhr (1973, p. 140): "After the age of apocalyptic expectation and persecution had passed, the Christian church had settled down into a relatively assured status as the official religion of the empire. It had, in a sense, gained the world but at the price of its own soul. Or so it appeared to a few men who saw in the worldly accommodations and laxities of the church an utter betrayal of the commands of its founder. The church had become so secularized that the behavior of Christians seemed hardly distinguishable from that of nonbelievers." (The medieval mystics' reaction came later.)

3. Whether the command to love is simply a command to act certain ways or to have the *inner disposition* connected to love—hence, act-religion versus agent-religion—is not clear. Is sin, in short, a matter of will or of act alone? The stories of the rich young ruler (Mark 10:17-22; Matt. 19:16-22; Luke 18:18-23) and the widow's mite (Mark 12:41-44), the claims that one who hates is as guilty as one who kills (Matt. 5:21-22) and that the thought of lust is the same as the act of adultery (Matt. 5:27-28), and that nothing from the outside but only from the inside defiles us (Mark 7:17-23; Matt. 15:19-20) all suggest that the focus is on character—being "pure in heart"—and not on acts alone. Similarly, we are to love our enemies, not to convert them (as may be the case in Daoism) but because we are to be compassionate, as God is, to the unkind and wicked (Luke 6:35-36)—thus, we do it to be perfect ourselves. (This raises the whole issue of whether this ethics of caring is for a Christian's own self-directed transformation or is carried out out of genuinely other-regarding concern.) But it is hard to see how one can command an inner disposition. How can compassion be enjoined as a duty? Requiring actions is one thing, but requiring someone to act out of love—"Be a *cheerful* giver!"—is another.

4. An ethics consisting of a general ethos of love, an exemplar to follow, parables, and a few other general illustrations would seem to negate the requirement of a set of specific rules (but see Mark 19:18-22). The Golden Rule without substantive values of what values should be applied to others does not offer much guidance in actions in concrete situations; there is also an issue of whether it effectively states a truly radical ethics of self-giving. Nor is it clear why any ritual rules would be needed (but contrast Mark 7:1-23 with Matt. 5:17-20), or at least it should be that they can be broken if necessary to help others (see Mark 2:23-3:6).

5. Contrast Outka 1972 (who sees self-love as irreducible) with Nygren 1969 (who saw human beings as channels through which God's self-giving love flows to others). Paul in Phillipians 2:4—"You must look to each other's interest and not merely to your own"—can be interpreted as endorsing the necessity of some self-interest.

6. Hallett 1989.

7. Kierkegaard 1962. He presented a strong religious but *nonmystical* argument for absolute impartiality.

8. Don S. Browning, "Altruism and Christian Love," *Zygon* 27 (December 1992): pp. 434-35.

9. See Frankena 1973, pp. 57-58.

10. See Bird 1982, pp. 156-60.

11. White 1981, p. 92. This is not to deny that there are extensive corruption within the church at the time. Indeed, part of the reason mystics turned to inner devotion was the fact that they saw so much hypocrisy in the external acts of priests.

12. See Colin Morris, *The Discovery of the Individual, 1050-1200* (Toronto: University of Toronto Press, 1987).

13. See Grace Jantzen, "'Where Two Are to Become One': Mysticism and Monism," in *The Philosophy in Christianity*, ed. Godfrey Vesey (Cambridge: Cambridge University Press, 1989), pp. 147-166. Some antinomians spoke of a "union" of substances. They modified the traditional image of the soul being heated to a glow by the transforming power of God's love to the image of the iron *becoming* the fire itself.

14. Even the Neoplatonist Plotinus saw mystical experience in terms of love (*Enneads* VI.9.9). See Hadot 1993, pp. 48-63. But for Plotinus kindness is a spontaneous result of the recognition of our rational desire for the Good, not of other-regardingness: since we want the Good, we are favorably disposed to its products—the creatures of this world—but not to treating them as ends in themselves (as morality requires) (Gerson 1994, p. 190).

15. The terminology used is often sensual—"perceiving," "touching," "embracing," "penetrating"—but the mystical experiences are still not seen in terms of two objects becoming one.

16. "Ecstasy" in medieval Christian mysticism is meant in the classic sense of going "out of oneself" (and thus having no sense of self), not in the modern sense of exuberance or exaltation.

17. Meister Eckhart in Blakney 1941, p. 13.

18. This lack of self-interest is why "Pascal's wager," which involves calculations of self-interest for accepting belief, seems so peculiar from a mystical point of view.

19. See Dupré 1981.

20. Another possible source of misunderstanding is that "works" in this period did not always refer to moral action but to fasting, prayers, and the sacraments.

21. Catherine of Siena in Petry 1957, p. 277.

22. Plotinus also distinguished these "civic" virtues, which order desires related to the body and the interrelations with others, from the higher "purificatory" (*katharseis*) virtues for separating the soul from the body and thus leading to the One, which is beyond all virtues (*Enneads* I.2.4, I.8.6). The person possessing the higher virtues no longer lives the life of a "good" man—i.e., one governed only by the civic virtues—and is indifferent to many concerns arising out of such a life (*Enneads* I.2.7, I.4.7-15). For him, virtues are merely a way to attain our desired end (since the One is beyond all virtues).

23. Meister Eckhart in Blakney 1941, p. 13.

24. Ibid., p. 84. As Eckhart put it, the function of grace is to transform and reconvey the soul to God, but we should learn to take grace and divine goodness without asking.

25. The issue of whether the enlightened can backslide—"I do not do what I want, but I do the very things I hate" (Rom. 7:15)—or whether the transformation of the enlightened state is permanent and thus precludes this will not be addressed here.

26. For the distinction of raptures "with the senses" and "without the senses," and the valuing of the former over the latter, see, for example, Richard Rolle in Petry 1957, p. 210. The senses and affections are "purified" but not abolished in the former (p. 212).

27. Some Christians (especially in the Eastern Orthodox tradition and also the antinomians) refer to this enlightenment as "deification" (*theiosis*), i.e., the transformation of a person into a finite likeness of God. But under the orthodox Christian view one is not literally made a god or made one with God. It is the will or soul that is deified. At most, the

person is returned to his or her original condition as a creature of God free of self-will. Thus, the common mystical analogy of a drop of water poured into a vat of wine is not really applicable.

28. Petry 1957, pp. 60-65.

29. It must be noted, however, that in *early* Christianity the first commandment was in effect interpreted to mean the exclusion of the second: love of God led to excluding love of creatures and the abandonment of society by mystics.

30. It might be asked how God can love this world when he knows he created it and can end its existence. If we are not "real," how can God love us any more than we could truly love the characters we created in a novel? But if at least our suffering is genuinely real, there is some reality here to be concerned with and thus other-regardingness is possible.

31. The idea that a theistic god who would intervene to help some parts of his creation over others limits the analogy of gravity. Only if God is totally impartial would the analogy help illuminate the situation.

32. Kieckhefer 1978a.

33. E.g., McGinn 1986, pp. 249-50. It is worth noting that in this sermon Eckhart refers to loving "fellow *Christians* as oneself," not everyone.

34. McGinn 1986, p. 268.

35. See Kieckhefer 1978b; Baker 1999.

36. The *Theologia Germanica* says that if we want to be obedient, serene, and submissive to God, we must also be obedient, serene, and submissive to the world around us. This is to be done in a spirit of "compassionate yielding" and not of "busyness." The soul does this in silence, resting in its ground and in an inner suffering empathy enabling it to bear all and to suffer with everyone.

37. Ruusbroec also distinguishes this from the actions of the unenlightened: external activity of "natural love" resembles "true charity" as closely as two hairs on the same head, but the inward *intention* is totally different—intending God versus self-seeking.

38. The imitation of God—"to walk in the ways of the Lord"—also figured prominently in the Jewish mysticism of this period. Thus, even without an incarnated exemplar, mystics could try to replicate God's compassion through actions toward others.

39. Kabbalists and Hasidic Jews were also very conservative in matters of *halakhah*, helping that become standard in Judaism. Most Sūfīs were also scrupulous in matters of religious law (*sharī'a*), although there was also a strong antinomian stream in the tradition. For the Sūfīs, the rules of proper conduct (*ābāb*) applied to all ordinary Muslims and to Sūfīs on the path. The majority opinion (as finalized by al-Ghazālī) was that the rules also applied to the enlightened.

40. If there is a set of precepts, there is no universalizability problem: the precepts would hold for all people equally. A logical problem arises in advocating the principle "seek only the good of others." If you want everyone to seek only the good of all other people, this means that others will end up looking out for your good too (if they do not converge on only some people to help). But Christians can advocate, without being immoral, that people should seek the good of others and yet still accept that one effect will be that some benefit may also accrue to themselves.

41. Beach and Neibuhr 1973, p. 182. The same holds in Eastern Orthodox mysticism.

42. Oliver O'Donovan (1980) argues that Augustine reduced neighbor-love to an instrument for one's own salvation—others were used (*uti*) for the practitioner's own religious good. But this argument has been shown to be based on misunderstanding the concept of "*uti*" (Baer 1996).

43. Jantzen 1985, p. 322.

44. See Chittick 1993 for how monistic metaphysics in Islam can also ground morality.

45. Eckhart, being a knowledge-mystic, stressed the intellect alone as the *imago dei* (see, e.g., Colledge and McGinn 1981, p. 211). He did attempt to bring both strands of the contemplative life together by placing the will within the intellect. (Ruusbroec spoke of "loving knowledge.") For most Christian mystics love leads to true knowledge, but for Eckhart, knowledge contains love, and knowledge is better than love in the contemplative process because it is disinterested and peels off all coverings and "runs naked to God, until it touches him and grasps him."

46. A similarity is often drawn to Advaita Vedānta's distinction between *saguna* and *nirguna brahman*, but the ideas are different. To Shankara, *saguna* and *nirguna brahman* are two forms of the same thing, while Eckhart has a Neoplatonic emanationist metaphysics that distinguishes the Godhead and God and does not deny the reality of creatures. But Eckhart also used terms to describe the Godhead reminiscent of Daoism: the abyss, the river, the soil out of which all things emanate. He is also often mistaken for a pantheist, but in his system the Godhead is beyond the natural universe and the source of its being. God and his creatures share a common beingness but remain distinct.

47. This may seem reminiscent of Buddhism but the point is different: Eckhart's focus is on the transcendental source, not on the problem of our conceptions or the lack of substance to things.

48. Kieckhefer 1978a, p. 216. Eckhart said the three different persons of God were not identical in the Godhead, although they are one in the unity of being. Similarly, all persons remain distinct. In his Defense he also stated that no one is Jesus Christ or saved by anyone but Jesus Christ.

49. Eckhart adopted from Neoplatonism the idea that the "intellect" is a power of the mind distinct from reason (intelligence). It is the power by which we see the ground of the soul. Only it can reach God because God is beyond our power to reason and our senses. In sum, it is what in our mental anatomy permits the depth-mystical experience to occur.

50. Part of this involves freeing perception from conceptualizations ("images"). But part is also a Neoplatonic-influenced metaphysics of emanation in which the reality pours itself out into its "image" or "form." The point from the last paragraph can be restated as saying that the "image" too has some reality, even though the image is filled by the reality of what is reflected and nothing else. Thus, the objective is to get beyond the image and back to the reality reflected.

51. Colledge and McGinn 1981, pp. 241-42.

52. Blakney 1941, pp. 14, 238, 36-37, 111, respectively.

53. E.g., Colledge and McGinn 1981, pp. 265-66.

54. Ibid., pp. 250-51.

55. Ibid., pp. 285-94.

56. Ibid., p. 214.

57. Blakney 1941, p. 193.

58. McGinn 1986, p. 278; Kelley 1973, p. 218.

59. Blakney 1941, p. 115.

60. McGinn 1986, p. 278; Kelley 1973, p. 218.

61. Colledge and McGinn 1981, p. 277. Becoming virtuous requires detachment: to become rich in virtues, one must become poor in all things (ibid., p. 281).

62. Ibid., p. 186.

63. Ibid., pp. 126, 154, 296.

64. Ibid., p. 278.

65. Kelley 1973, p. 243.

66. Colledge and McGinn 1981, pp. 183-84, 228, 270; McGinn 1986, p. 307. It may be suggested that since God has no purpose for creation (since he works without a "why"), creation is just his play (*līlā*), as with Shankara's *brahman*. But Eckhart's point is that God has no "why or wherefore" outside or apart from himself (McGinn 1986, p. 120). That is, God is complete in himself and is not constrained by anything else—Daoists would say he is "self-so" (*zizan*).

67. Blakney 1941, p. 127.

68. Ibid., p. 180. This may be likened to *karmayoga* or *wu-wei*. Eckhart here seems to be emphasizing being without a personal will and the lack of calculation of personal consequences and is not addressing the issue of whether God has some purpose to the world or to our actions.

69. Colledge and McGinn 1981, p. 59.

70. Ibid., p. 296.

71. Ibid., p. 80; McGinn 1986, p. 257. The *Theologia Germanica* states the problem more traditionally: nothing worthy of the term "good" belongs to man—it belongs only to the Eternal. The problem of the incommensurability of worldly and transcendent values remains the same.

72. See McGinn 1986, p. 161.

73. Colledge and McGinn 1981, p. 189.

74. Blakney 1941, p. 143.

75. McGinn 1986, p. 257.

76. Colledge and McGinn 1981, p. 228.

77. Ibid., p. 251.

78. Kelley 1973, p. 217.

79. Our religious salvation may, like mystical experiences, also be an individual phenomenon. The idea of individual salvation is firmly planted in Western Christianity and in these mystics' writings, but in Eastern Orthodoxy a tradition of communal salvation of the whole church is stronger—each individual is "a member of one another." (The same seems true of Judaism.) A saying among the Russian Orthodox is "one can be damned alone but saved only with others" (H. Smith 1991, p. 354).

80. A Protestant-like substitution of immediate personal experiences of God in the place of religious authorities was not part of the agenda of at least the orthodox mystics of this period. Experiences were not cited to justify any aspect of their way of life, and the authority of ecclesiastical institutions was not questioned. Even Eckhart, when accused of heresy, denied any disloyalty to his church. Heresy, he said, was a matter of will and not of the reason, and he never meant to defy his church but was ready to recant anything judged heretical. (Most scholars today believe he was fairly orthodox in his views, once we get passed some of his daring rhetoric.)

81. Blakney 1941, pp. 156-60; M. Fox 1980a, pp. 450-55; McGinn 1986, pp. 239-43.

82. Blakney 1941, pp. 11, 129-32.

83. Ibid., pp. 179, 182.

84. Ibid., p. 71.

85. M. Fox 1980a, pp. 209, 418. See also Colledge and McGinn 1981, pp. 280-85, on interior and exterior works.

86. See R. H. Jones 1932; Cohn 1970; Ozment 1973; Greeley 1974; Fox 1980b. The possible historical effects are open to debate. Did Eckhart side politically with the peasants to whom he preached in calling them all "aristocrats," or was he offering a politically conservative alternative that would keep them in line (i.e., they were already aristocrats and so did not need to reform society)?

87. This can be true without reducing mystical experiences merely to a reflection of the mystic's social situation. An economic explanation of why a particular mystic had a particular view or was particularly influential or why mysticism flourished or declined at a particular time cannot eliminate the possibility that mystical experiences still may involve genuine insights into reality. Similarly, Eckhart may have represented the growing individualism of his age and have attempted to free the religious life from institutions and to center it in individuals (R. W. Southern, *Western Society and the Church in the Middle Ages* [New York: Penguin, 1970], pp. 301-4). But this fact cannot explain away any experiences involved. See generally R. H. Jones 2000, Chapter 8.

88. M. Fox 1980b, p. 557.

89. Blakney 1941, p. 231; M. Fox 1980a, pp. 217-18.

90. Blakney 1941, p. 189. When Eckhart said "Whoever wants to receive everything must also renounce everything" (Colledge and McGinn 1981, p. 281), there is no ambiguity that he might mean obtaining all material things, as with the Upanishads—the only objective is obtaining God.

91. Conversely, worldly success may be a sign of divine election in the numinous strand of theistic religiosity but not in the mystical.

92. Colledge and McGinn 1981, p. 265.

93. M. Fox 1980a, pp. 510-18; M. Fox 1980b, p. 550.

94. M. Fox 1980a, p. 199.

95. Ibid., pp. 463, 464, 472, 495.

96. Kelley 1973, p. 82; see also Kieckhefer 1978, p. 183.

97. Bernard McGinn, quoted in Forman 1991, p. 33.

98. There have been, of course, false mystics in all ages and religions who claim to be religious but are not and are only claiming it for some less than spiritual purpose. Antinomians do not fall into that group if they are sincere in their beliefs.

99. The church father Irenaeus also criticized those Gnostics who believed that one can only be saved by passing through every action. Sin became the way to salvation. See Jonas 1963, p. 274.

100. Plotinus also condemned the Gnostics who placed all value on knowledge and none on virtues (*Enneads* II.9.15). For Gnostics, laws do not apply to the soul and so all is permitted. Indeed, intentional violations of ethical precepts was considered a value. See Jonas 1963. For Plotinus, the inner transformation brought about by inner purifications and virtues is what leads to the One (*Enneads* VI.7.36). This shows that Neoplatonists could condemn others on moral grounds, and that all forms of Neoplatonism are not antinomian.

101. See Leff 1967; Cohn 1970, pp. 148-86; Lerner 1972; McLaughlin 1973. Antinomianism was not unique to mystical religiosity, but the mystical brand might have been more severe.

102. Leff 1967, p. 310; Lerner 1972, p. 178.

103. Cohn (1970) is of the opinion that these actions may have occurred. Lerner (1972, pp. 179-80) is doubtful that they were at least the standard practice of these poor ascetics.

104. Lerner 1972, pp. 239-40.

105. Ruusbroec was even willing to see antinomians burned at the stake to save the community.

106. The writings of John of the Cross may have been one source of the Quietists' inspiration. In his *Spiritual Canticle*, he wrote of a state beyond the active and contemplative life where one should not be occupied with outward acts since they might interfere with the abiding love of God. This passage may not be by John, but that is irrelevant to its possible influence on the Quietists. They may also have misinterpreted other passages from John on

the "idle tranquility of the soul."

107. In Islam, antinomians advanced such a defense. With the annihilation of any sense of self, no rules or principles applied in their enlightened state of being. They are beyond the norms applying to the masses, but all their acts proceed from love. That is because it is none but God who acts through them: God is pure love, and from pure love only pure love emanates. Thus, the only norm to which they adhere is love. See Aminrazavi 1995, pp. 22-23.

108. McGinn 1986, p. 288.

109. See Scholem 1971; Aminrazavi 1995. See also Sharot 1983; Hardy 1988.

110. Both McLaughlin (1973) and Sharot (1983) conclude that antinomianism is one course of action implicit within mystical theism. As Eleanor McLaughlin says, "The heresy of the Free Spirit thus is seen not as a perversion of medieval Catholic mysticism, but as a latent possibility within that kind of search for Christian perfection." (1973, p. 51).

111. Dupré 1981, p. 56.

112. Eckhart insisted on a role for the church sacraments. See Blakney 1941, pp. 30-31.

113. Again, not all Christian mystics were as active as others. Rolle and Ruusbroec became hermits for major portions of their lives. The risk in making generalizations about any tradition is that we obviously only know of those mystics who left some kind of effect through teaching, training, or writings—we do not know what percent of the mystics became hermits. In early Christianity, many mystics did renounce the world (and other people) and headed for the desert. But the Christian standard for the medieval period was not to wander off into the forest but to be an active mystic. The modern mystic Thomas Merton expressed the Christian attitude during an experience he had one day while standing on a street corner in the city near his monastery: "I was suddenly overwhelmed with the realization that I loved all those people, that they were mine and I theirs, that we could not be alien to one another even though we were total strangers. It was like waking from a dream of separateness, of spurious self-isolation in a special world, the world of renunciation and supposed holiness. The whole illusion of a separate holy existence is a dream" (quoted in Horne 1983, p. 86). (Note that the dream he awoke from is the opposite of the Buddha's—to the Christian, it was obvious that other people are central and that we must be socially engaged.)

114. Johnston 1998, p. 268.

115. White 1981, p. 180.

Part III

Analysis

13

Mystical Experiences and Morality

From the chapters in Part II, one can see that there is no one simple relation of mysticism to morality. The terrain of mysticism and morality is a good deal more complex than is indicated by the stereotype of the peace-loving, celibate, mystic sitting serenely in self-absorbed meditation. The specific factual and ethical beliefs of particular traditions must be considered. The self-cultivation that is the central objective on all paths to enlightenment presents a problem, but morality can be part of that cultivation. Mystics can be moral (clear examples being the Buddha, Mahāyāna Bodhisattvas, and orthodox medieval Christians) or immoral (as with the Tāntrikas). Or they can be nonmoral, valuing their own quest for enlightenment above all else but still not harming others with their other-impinging actions (as with the Theravādins). Mystics' beliefs can lead to inaction (as with the enlightened ideal in Jainism and as the chief option under Advaita), but not all mystics embrace the passivity and moral quietism of "holy indifference" toward others—instead, they may be very active. Their actions need not be nonviolent but may in fact appear to the unenlightened to be very harmful (as with Arjuna's actions in the *Bhagavad-gītā*'s war). Mystics can be indifferent to the entire natural realm (as in Advaita) or concerned with society (as with the *Bhagavad-gītā* and political Daoism). Moral mystics may be concerned with this-worldly, material well-being (as in Christianity) or with escaping this realm entirely (as with the enlightened Bodhisattvas). Essentially the same worldview can ground both a nonmoral ethos and a moral one (as in Buddhism). A conflict with morality may be a matter of values (as in Theravāda Buddhism and Advaita) or of the factual presuppositions of morality (as in Advaita).[1]

This variety of relations raises the issues of whether mysticism or mystical experiences in fact have any particular impact on morality at all. First consider mystical experiences. Does either type of mystical experience—the depth-mystical experience or mindfulness—contribute anything to morality? Or are they morally neutral? During a sitting exercise or other passive form of meditation or during a depth-mystical experience one is not capable of interpersonal action of any sort and thus obviously cannot act in a moral way, but do the experiences have a value-component—moral or otherwise—informing a mystical way of life outside those experiences? If not, what is the role of mystical experiences when a mystic adopts the ethics of a way of life?

Are Mystical Experiences the Source of Morality?

It is often argued mystical experiences have positive moral implications. Walter Stace presented the classic mystical theory of morality. Mystical experiences are the empirical, if not logical, justification of moral values because they are the part of the human experience out of which moral feelings flow.[2] That is, the separate-ness of individual selves produces the egoism that is the source of conflict, grasping, aggressiveness, selfishness, hatred, cruelty, malice, and other forms of evil; and this separateness is abolished in the mystical consciousness in which all distinctions are annulled.[3] Love and sympathy result from the incipient and partial breaking down of the barriers that the sense of separate selves has erected; when this breakdown is complete, it leads to the sense of the identity of "I" and "you"—thus, love is a dim groping toward the disappearance of individuality in the Universal Self that is part of the essence of mysticism.[4] Feelings of love and compassion are components, or necessary and immediate accompaniments, of mystical experiences. This is in fact the *only* source from which love flows into the world.[5] Obviously not every human being is moral, but some faint mystical sense is latent in all people (and perhaps animals) that influences their feelings without their knowing or understanding it; without this sense, there could be no such thing as love or even kindly feeling in human life, and life would be a wholly unmiti-gated Hobbesian war of all against all, for there is no rival nonmystical source of morality.[6]

   The idea that breaking down a sense of self-centeredness in a mystical experi-ence leads to a sense of sympathy is certainly plausible. But whether this is the origin of our sense of morality is another issue. Finding the origin of morality is difficult. Consider another theory of the origin of the feeling of concern for others: sociobiology. Sociobiologists argue that organisms sometimes engage in genetic "altruism"—i.e., behavior that increases the likelihood of the survival of another organism having some of one's own genes even when that decreases one's own likelihood of survival.[7] Nature thus is not just "red, in tooth and claw" but also has an "altruistic" component. There is, however, a major problem with this as a theory of morality: even if biology does dictate actions for the survival of our genes, these actions do not involve morality in any literal sense of the word. We must first ignore the fact that genes cannot think and thus cannot consider other organisms' interests. And, even if we focus on only the effects of actions, we still must realize that such "altruistic" actions involve "selfishly" conserving one's own genes present in related members of the same species or at most only a reciprocity benefitting oneself and others. In sum, one's self-interest remains central at the genetic level. Sociobiologists try to explain human behavior as an evolutionary product of selfish genes on a cultural level, but morality remains a distinctly higher-level phenomenon involving genuine concern for others for their own sake. Sociobiologists offer no explanation of human-level concern for others when people help genetically unrelated strangers with no hope of reciprocity other than to say that such people are misusing our genetic-ingrained sense of selfish "altruism." (Sociobiologists do admit that human beings have a freedom of will that can go against the genes' commands; this in effect admits that a level of reality other than the genetic must also be at work.) Certainly, the impartiality of mystical selflessness conflicts with the control of any selfish gene.

Thus, sociobiology fails here. Another alternative is that the moral sense is innate in human beings. Evidence of this is that babies begin to cry when they hear other crying babies. This empathy occurs even when they are only a few days old, and thus well before they learn to speak and before they reach the "mine, mine, mine!" stage in which they develop a sense of an independent self.[8] The same holds later for wanting to share. This suggests that sympathy and a sense of connectedness are innate in human beings, being both prelinguistic and preenculturation in origin. Stace would reply that these reactions are the product of the latent mystical consciousness in all of us. But any theory that must invoke the idea of "latency" is suspect as an explanation since no empirical evidence can even in principle falsify it—i.e., no amount of selfish behavior could possibly count against it—and it is hard to see what findings on human origins could verify it. More importantly, there is no reason to think *mystical* consciousness, either in the form of depth-mystical experiences or mindfulness, is the underlying basis for these states in babies. That is, there is no reason to suspect that the sympathetic state of young babies is in any way related to the state adults attain in overcoming a sense of self in mystical experiences. If a moral sense arises later in life—e.g., in the parent/child relation, or simply out of the social need of people living together to find some way everyone could survive and prosper—again there is no reason to believe mystical consciousness has anything to do with it.

If some such sociological theory is at all plausible for the origin of morality, then Stace's appeal to mystical consciousness as the historical origin loses credibility. And even if mystical experiences are the origin of our sense of concern for others, problems still exist. Most basic is that no one needs to be a mystic to be moral. Other-regardingness does not require that we abolish all self-centeredness with a mystical experience. (Of course, Stace would appeal to his "latency" theory, and the problem remains that there is no way either to eliminate or prove that possibility.) William Wainwright would add that mystical experiences may be the fountainhead of moral truths in the sense that without these experiences these truths would never have occurred to anyone, but once discovered we need not be mystics to discern their truth.[9] One can be concerned with the welfare of others without any feeling of love arising from the experienced sense of selflessness within a cosmic whole or of identity to one underlying reality. The nonmystical—including the nonreligious—can adopt a moral stance based on no more than our common humanity or the fact that all sentient beings suffer. Leo Tolstoy, upon witnessing an execution, said he needed no more to conclude that nothing could ever convince him that killing a human was right—he said that he understood, not with his mind, but with his whole being that it was wrong. Some hunters after watching an animal dying have reached a similar conclusion concerning hunting. So too the ideas of impartiality need not be based on any experience but only on philosophical reasoning about ethics. Those who see ethics as a matter purely for reason and not feelings may be correct. The development of moral maturity from childhood to adulthood is often said to involve becoming less and less self-centered and adopting more and more inclusive points of view—no mystical experience is needed for that to occur. This can be extended to humanity as a whole through thought alone. One can adopt on purely intellectual grounds a form of utilitarianism in which one values the majority—only actions that are believed to create greater good for the greater number would then be justified. In China, Mozi's "universal love" is not based on any experience but on the belief that the radical impartiality of treating all people equally reflects the actions of Heaven.

Even if we restrict attention just to mystics, problems still arise. First, not everyone who has had a mystical experience is moral. Agehananda Bharati is correct in asserting that mystical experiences need not change a person—a person who was evil, antisocial, selfish, and self-indulgent before the experience may remain so.[10] An isolated experience of selflessness may not change a person's negative psychological characteristics but only increase his or her sense of self-importance and pride. In short, the experience of oneness need not alter one's view of the world or one's character. Robert Zaehner also points out that a connection between mystical consciousness and loving action is not inevitable.[11] A momentary experience of "cosmic consciousness" will not necessarily make one a saint, either religious or moral. As Paul Tillich noted, religious saints are persons through whom the ground of being is transparent but are not necessarily models of moral perfection.[12] Being a mystical genius may require a change in character in a way that greatness in other fields does not (e.g., the musical genius of Mozart), but an active moral life need not be part of it. Nor does mastering breathing techniques or other mindfulness exercises have any bearing on one's values. Breaking down the sense of self may lead to release from inhibitions and thus to the libertine indulgence of desires under the guise of God's will, as in the antinomian traditions, or to giving oneself over totally to an immoral political cause such as Nazism. In short, a mystical experience of selflessness need not make one moral. The only definite effect one can predict from a mystical experience is an inner sense of joy and fulfillment—not necessarily other-regardingness. This strongly suggests the source of moral action does not appear to lie in these experiences.

In sum, one becomes a saint for reasons other than mystical experiences. The moral mystics Stace cited are all instances of mystics who cultivated a moral way of life as part of their training on the path to the enlightened state or otherwise developed in moral traditions. (And it must be remembered that mystical training also need not be moral: the self-restraints of Theravāda Buddhist self-cultivation result in no harm to others, but the motive for following them is not other-regardingness but only one's own spiritual self-development. We cannot advance on any mystical path by acting selfishly at the expense of others, but we may be indifferent to the suffering of others, as illustrated by the Theravāda monks who ignored the suffering of their fellow monks.) The enlightened have the inner transformation of the whole person that mystics deem central, not isolated exotic experiences. The role of a way of life's beliefs and values in this transformation will be discussed in the next chapter.

Stace conceded that not all mystics are moral but insisted that the "ideal" and "complete" mystical experience is necessarily moral.[13] Perhaps we can dismiss mystical teachers who exploit or mistreat their followers or otherwise act selfishly as being unenlightened (i.e., as not having successfully overcome all sense of self). Nevertheless, the fact remains that some major mystics, such as Shankara, have adopted clearly *nonmoral* values and factual beliefs that conflict with morality and that justify only indifference. If love is given in the depth-mystical experience, why did Shankara not emphasize it? His nonmorality is especially telling since he was at least indirectly influenced by the moral Mahāyāna Buddhism through his teacher. Thus, while mystical experiences may be compatible with morality and may even be seen by some mystics as the source of their moral concern, one still cannot argue that the experiences are necessarily moral when the belief-claims and value-claims of some major mystics do not justify a life of service for others.[14] Obviously, Stace risks arguing in a circle here—i.e., making morality a criterion for what counts as the highest or best mystical experience, and then concluding that in its essence mysticism contains the love that is the ultimate motivation for all good deeds.[15]

William Barnard also argues that becoming loving and compassionate is the normal result of a mystical experience and that those who are not moral have distorted the basic insight of love.[16] He argues that the enlightened typically do not feel that they have license to murder babies (although he must deal with the antinomians) and thus that morality is the normal product of mystical experiences. However, he does not differentiate the "nonmoral" from the "immoral," grouping them together under the heading of "amoral." This permits him to cite the general lack of antinomian "anything goes" indulgence as evidence that the "true" mystical experience is moral (since being moral would be the only alternative). But the real issue is not whether the enlightened are only rarely immoral but the possibility of the enlightened being *nonmoral* and simply indifferent to the suffering of others. Nonmorality may involve a benign neglect rather than harmful action. Barnard does not consider it; since he groups it with immoral action, he thinks that ruling out immoral action as the norm rules this out too. But we cannot argue that just because one extreme is wrong ("Immorality is the norm in mysticism") that the other extreme must be right ("Morality is the norm in mysticism") when there is a third possibility—aligning one's life with reality and being indifferent to the welfare of others. The enlightened may not evil in the sense of harming others for personal gain (since all sense of self is ended), but they may still not be concerned with the suffering of others. The beliefs and values advocated by Shankara are a prime instance of this third possibility. It is difficult to argue that mystical experiences are pregnant with moral action in light of that, and certainly Barnard cannot cite the general lack of immoral excesses to rule the third option out. Indifference is perfectly consistent with a sense of senselessness; it is hard to argue that it must be an aberration or distortion.

Of course, mystics may have *nonmystical* experiences that give them a sense that the ground of reality is moral, but it is hard to argue that mystics such as Shankara are not having the "fullest" *mystical* experiences. The state of mindfulness may be influenced by such nonmystical experiences, but if the depth-mystical experience is free of all content as at least some major mystics of all traditions (including Christians such as Eckhart) assert, then the explanation of why some mystics are moral, some nonmoral, and some immoral must lie outside these experiences. Mystical experiences themselves must then be neutral on this issue. (Thus, the fact that "love-mysticism" entered the Abrahamic traditions after "knowledge-mysticism" is the result of new interpretations and new factors in the religious traditions, not a new mystical experience being discovered.) Certainly the sudden shock of an isolated experience of pure selflessness need not make one concerned with others. As discussed below, mystical selflessness can be combined with a moral point of view; it would then have the effect of leading to a more energetic and comprehensive moral life. Thus, if one sets out on a long strenuous life of training to become more loving, then a mystical experience will no doubt be seen in those terms and make one more loving. But mystical experiences are not imbued with the moral point of view and thus cannot make an indifferent experiencer moral. Someone with no inclination to be compassionate before the experience will not magically be made compassionate. Therefore, there is no reason to think that compassion is the real base state of enlightenment and that other reactions are distortions. Any change of character will come from previous training or other experiences, not the mystical experiences themselves.

A second general problem with the theory that mystical experiences are the source of morality is that, even if mystics did discover sympathy or an interconnectedness with others or any other sense of concern for others, there is still the issue of whether morality can be based on that experience. The issue of whether morality is based on an emotion (such as love) was discussed in Chapter 2, but in any case morality does require action. Theravāda Buddhists stop with a feeling of sympathy in their meditative exercises—these experiences do not compel them to actual compassionate *action* helping others. Thus, one can have sympathy resulting from experiences of selflessness without any resulting action, and morality requires the latter.

In sum, it is hard to argue, in light of the data from mystics around the world, that love is necessarily given in mystical experiences and thus that these experiences "justify" morality. An implosion of the ground of reality does not necessarily lead to an explosion of moral action. Mystical experiences may be a strong impetus for moral action (as argued below) and may in fact be the historical source of morality as Stace argued, but they neither compel nor justify morality.

Are Mystical Experiences Incompatible with Morality?

Arthur Danto presents a version of the opposite claim from Stace's—that mystical experiences are in fact logically incompatible with being moral.[17] He does not distinguish "mystical experiences" from "mysticism" but focuses on the way traditional Asian mystical *factual beliefs* might conflict with the presuppositions of morality (or "application conditions," as he calls them). He is not arguing that the Asian factual beliefs are false or that they cannot evolve in the modern era—his is only the logical point that if they are true then morality is rendered inoperative. When we see the rope is not a snake, what to do about the snake is rendered groundless; so too if we see reality according to these Asian traditions, morality is no longer a possible concern. Thus, we cannot adopt the classical Asian factual beliefs and be moral. Two presuppositions in particular are a problem: the need for a moral agent and the need for an object toward which one can act morally.

Advaita Vedānta does exemplify Danto's position. Its factual belief of *brahman/ātman* being the only reality closes the "space" necessary for the moral concern of one real person for another real person to operate. What is real is actually unaffectable and only one—thus, how can we be concerned with another? Even though actions are apparently possible, the realm of differentiations is reduced to a realm of illusion, and along with it so is moral concern for other parts of the illusion. However, the other traditions discussed in Part II do not adopt a nondualistic metaphysics *cum* illusionism, and none support Danto's claim. During a depth-mystical experience and some forms of meditation, a practitioner does not act and thus obviously cannot act morally. But *after* these experiences, sensory and conceptual differentiations return, and it is in this state that factual beliefs interpreting the significance of those experiences are adopted. Not all transcendent grounding reduces everything in the world—including us—to a monism. It is possible to have a "divine spark" and still be a reality toward whether morality is possible. And the metaphysics of the traditions considered here other than Advaita Vedānta all grant sufficient reality to the parts of the realm of differentiations to provide for the possibility of morality.

Consider mystical selflessness. It may be objected that if there is no independent center of reflection and agency—no "self" or "soul"—then morality is impossible. That is, morality requires a sense of identity and agency, but mystics experience selflessness. Our ego is seen as a social creation that does not correspond to anything real.[18] The "self" is not "abolished" (since there was none to begin with), but the true reality of mental life is seen for what it is—a centerless activity. The issue is thus whether moral reflection and agency needs a center of agency. To Buddhists, there are feelings, consciousness, and so forth, but no additional entity or substance unifying the elements into a distinct being—no "self." That is, Buddhists accept all the consciousness, perceptions, motives, and feelings associated with agency, even though they reject an "I" in addition to the "bundle of different perceptions," to use David Hume's phrase. There is a "selfless person"—no "thinker" but still the "thought." However, the need for additional distinct, self-existent entity in this mix to be the controlling "agent" for moral responsibility is not clear. What would it do that the other elements do not already do? Certainly reductive materialists in the West today can accept agency without a center (a "self") that controls the mix.[19] All that morality requires is a mental capacity to choose—to think, to will, and to act accordingly—it does not entail a commitment to any particular type of metaphysical entity. And of the Asian mystical traditions covered here, only Advaitins are committed to a belief-claim that conflicts with that.[20]

This also bears on the inverse problem: whether there is a reality toward which moral concern is possible. Buddhists believe there are realities that suffer and can be directed toward the end of a chain of rebirths even though they deny any substance or center to a "person." Even if there is no "I" who suffers, there is the suffering associated with the configuration of elements constituting the "person." William Wainwright asks how can we be compassionate toward impersonal objects?[21] But why there needs to be a permanent core to a person to be compassionate to this configuration of elements is not clear. The Buddhists are not denying there is a reality there but only that there is a permanent, eternal reality to our unreflective idea of a "person." A "person" is "unreal" only in the technical sense that there is nothing permanent to us—no enduring, separate, independent center to our mental and physical configuration. The configuration of impersonal elements constituting a "person" is constantly changing and void of permanent parts but continues like a rope through time made only of overlapping parts, with no single strand running the full length. The "person" (again, there is no permanent entity corresponding to the term) suffers and is entrapped in a chain of rebirths, and the chain can come to an end. In no way do Buddhist mystics reduce people to "things" in any morally negative sense—the reality "has" all the interests and feelings we must take into consideration to be moral. Why we must adopt a metaphysics of some additional separate, substantive, self-contained element called a "soul" or "self" to be moral is not clear. Mystics may see our concepts as not corresponding to some separate, permanent object in reality, but this does not dissolve all reality into one featureless blob—the flux of reality still contains distinguishable eddies, and our conventional terms are still useful in identifying the differentiations as long we do not project them onto reality, thereby creating a false world of disconnected objects. In sum, there is an appropriate reality for our moral concern—a configuration "personal" in nature, even if there are no persons.

Danto also raises an issue not related to the presuppositions of morality but to the emotions associated with morality: how can mystical even-mindedness be compatible with compassion or any other concern with others? But this objection has problems. First, being detached in circumstances where others are emotional may in fact be morally more desirable, even if one's actions then come across as almost machinelike. If one is being attacked by a charging tiger, one's reactions may well be better if one is free of fear and other emotions that muddle one's mind. Even-mindedness does not mean that one will not react nor try to save oneself but only that one sees what is there and can then react accordingly. The same applies to moral decision-making. Second, even-mindedness may lead to a radically impartial other-regardingness, even if partiality toward one's own family or friends seems necessary to us. Third, even-mindedness relates only to the mystic's reaction to the possible effect of an action on him- or herself, not to the impact on others. They are being even-minded to their own pain and pleasure—not to the effect of their actions on others. Being *disinterested* in the consequences of one's actions for oneself does not mean being *uninterested* in the consequences for others. There would be an inward emotional passivity and quiet of dispassion, but this does not necessarily mean "quietism" in the sense of the absence of moral action.[22] Thus, one can be detached (concerning an action's effect on oneself) and compassionate (toward others) at the same time—indeed, it can be argued the former is valuable to be truly other-regarding.

Danto also raises the prospect that mystical values are incompatible with moral ones.[23] That is, the evaluative priorities for mystics always relate to escaping the chain of rebirths or whatever is the soteriological goal of a particular tradition, not to moral concerns for others. In short, the mystics' transcendental values always take priority over morality. The goal of life for mystics therefore must conflict with morality. The mystical experience revalues everything: the mystic's world is so different from ours that our principles do not apply. All the distinctions we make in the "dream" are no longer of concern. We still see the rope as a snake and worry about what to do with the snake, while the enlightened mystic sees it is really just a rope and thus the unenlightened's concerns evaporate. One cannot even speak of a moral dimension to mysticism because the very possibility of ordering mystical transcendental values with unenlightened ones is destroyed.

Danto is correct in pointing out the supremacy of mystical values in a mystic's way of life, but moral values may nevertheless be part of those mystical values. For moral mystics, the fundamental reality is a compassionate self-emptying reality. For the medieval Christian mystics, morality is built into the ground of reality. For Bodhisattvas, morality is at least built into the path and life of supreme *bodhi*. In Daoism, impartiality and compassion or Great Humaneness are part of the Way. None of their values are antithetical to morality, and morality becomes necessary both on the path and in the enlightened life of such mystics. More generally, just because the ground of reality is involved in mysticism does not mean that morality may not be the supreme value or that nonmoral values must trump it. In short, nothing about being the ground of reality rules morality out as a supreme value. The transcendent reality may be moral—morality would then be a necessary part of a life reflecting that reality. Thus, far from mysticism being necessarily antithetical to morality, morality can become a mystical value in a mystical ways of life and mystics reflect it in their lives.

In sum, none of the points Danto raises show that mystical experiences are necessarily in conflict with morality. Mystics' beliefs, valued emotions, and ethical values are not necessarily in conflict with morality. However, this discussion does raise the importance of the role of elements outside of the mystical experiences themselves in the factual beliefs and value-systems of mystical ways of life. That issue will be the topic for the next chapter, but first some other issues related to mystical experiences and the enlightened state must be explored.

The Mystical Enlightened State and Morality

Nonmystics may approach the freedom of mystical selflessness. For example, terminally ill patients who have accepted their impending death sometimes feel a freedom in letting go of their previous concerns: they no longer have a self-image to maintain, nothing to crave and so no desires, no fear of what might happen, no needs, and nothing to lose. They are calm or even full of joy, accepting who they are and what is about to happen. Sometimes they have a heightened appreciation of life and a new focus on the present. Sometimes they have a greater appreciation and acceptance or tolerance of others. Often they have a greater sensitivity to the suffering of others. But this state, as with mystical experiences, can also lead to feeling that there is no need to *do* anything. For mystics, all sense of "I" as an isolated reality divided off from the rest of reality is gone, along with the resulting mental suffering and conflict from having a sense of "I" to be defended and enhanced. They too have lost the fear of death. There is no longer an attempt to appropriate reality for an illusory ego, to grasp, to strive, or to possess. Indeed, there can be no attachments if we think there is nothing "real" (distinct and self-existing) and possessable for a nonexistent "I."

The enlightened state must be differentiated from any depth-mystical experience, since sensory and conceptual content is present in the mind in the former and not in the latter. In simplest terms, it is the state of awareness when one is free of the sense of self. If the depth-mystical experience is involved, the sense of everyday self is replaced by the permanent inflowing of the ground of the true self or of all of reality. Concepts return but the categories they differentiate are not reified into distinct entities. In the enlightened state, mystical selflessness affects the person cognitively, dispositionally, and evaluatively. The changes may be quite subtle, if one has been practicing within a tradition for years. But one is now free of seeing reality in terms of "I" and "mine," and one sees things as they really are (as defined by one's tradition's belief-system). Being disinterested, the mind becomes a mirror reflecting reality without distortion, accepting whatever is presented without interpretation or judgment, seeking and retaining nothing. Nothing real changes with the loss of individualness (since the "I" was never part of reality), but the "suchness" of reality comes through. One's view of oneself, others, and the world is transformed: the world is now seen to be free of realities self-existent entities that can be twisted for one's own advantage. With a changed view, a moral mystic's previous self-centered disposition is transformed into a Reality-centered concern for others. For them, what results when we are not clinging to a sense of self and trying to force reality to comply to our wishes are loving actions reflecting fundamental reality. The energies previously devoted to personal desires are now reoriented toward helping others. One sees reality objectively (i.e., free of self-oriented desires), and, with one's view of reality corrected, one knows what will truly help others and how to implement it (as defined by one's tradition). Reflecting reality, the enlightened expand their circle of concern toward an impartial concern for all. This can lead to a "ruthless compassion," like the love of a parent knowing what is best for a child, even if the child does not understand why.

The emotional reaction to an action's effect on oneself is even-mindedness. It is detachment from all personal desires and motives but not from intentionality. There is no hope or fear, no love or hate, no personal attachment to any outcome, no anger or stress, and no personal desire for any particular outcome. One is dispassionate to success and failure, pleasure and pain. One has no fear of death, nor any desire for it. No person is emotionally more valuable than another, including oneself. The question "Why me?" in reaction to adversity is seen to have no answer because it is a faulty question with no ground in reality—both because there is no "I" to reality and because all of reality is impartial ("Why not me?"). The enlightened live completely in the present moment, free of expectations or concerns about the past or future. Obviously we can only live in the present, but the point is the mystics' lack of thoughts about the past and present—their attention is fully in the present. (This would explain the mystics' relative lack of interest in *hope*, since hope is oriented toward the future.) They are content with whatever occurs. The enlightened still have physical suffering but are unperturbed by them.

Such detachment affects the enlightened's actions. One does not like or dislike what one does—one just does it. The fullness of reality is freed from the artificiality we normally impose on it, and the resulting actions seem natural. One sees one's own actions as a disinterested spectator would, as if from a third-person's point of view—i.e., not as one's own but as any other events in the world. To them, reality is simply working through them, since there is no "I" and thus no actor. Thus, the action appears self-caused. One focuses on doing the act itself and forgets all other emotional concerns and drives. Everything that comes one's way is accepted without liking or disliking—everything is accepted like a gift, without judgment. This leads to acceptance and simply "letting things be" rather than twisting them to one's own advantage. One is emotionally detached from all parts of the world. Such emotional detachment creates a coldness to one's response and actions. But this lack of any preferences based on self-interest results in a radical impartiality in one's actions—indeed, total impartiality is simply complete detachment in action. This does not mean the enlightened treat every sentient being exactly the same way; instead, they act appropriately to each individual's needs. Nor does it mean they cannot predict the outcome of their actions or are indifferent to its impact on others. However, detachment does produce an inner calm that leads to a clarity of mind enabling them to see reality as it is when they are not twisting it for their own advantage and to act accordingly (as defined by their tradition).

Mystical selflessness thus more generally affects *how* one is moral. For the moral mystic, reposing in the transcendent generates a flood of activity, but it also affects how one holds one's beliefs and values. One may subscribe to the same belief-claims and value-claims as before enlightenment, but the mystical experience itself gives a certainty to one's beliefs and values—one no longer has simply heard that water will quench thirst but has actually drank the water. One sees that one's worldview is true of everything and acts accordingly. The values one subscribes to have been transmuted by a pervading sense of impartiality, treating all people alike regardless of family relation or social status. One has a greater sensitivity to the suffering of others and a greater ability to work in a way that addresses their real problems (as defined by one's tradition). All attempts at imposing an unenlightened will on others—indeed, all self-assertion—have disappeared, and one acts with complete detachment. Indeed, from this perspective, only the enlightened can successfully help others—the unenlightened are without real power because they are living in a false world created by their own ideas and desires. The virtues that the enlightened now manifest include patience, tolerance, forgiveness, gentleness, and modesty. The virtue of charity is also transformed: one no longer acts for reward or fear of punishment but gives completely of oneself to help others for no personal gain. The result is a radical altruism arising out of a clear awareness of what one deems real and important.

How then do enlightened actions differ from unenlightened ones? The actions may differ greatly, since there are no restrictions imposed on the enlightened. Or, despite any profound enlightenment-experiences, the actions may in fact differ very little from those before enlightenment, since the mystics may have been cultivating certain actions and attitudes for years.[24] The only difference in that case would be the inner transformation of the dispositions driving the actions—even-mindedness (detachment)—resulting in a greater efficiency in the act's performance. The mystics have changed who they *are*, not what they *do*. (It is significant that mystical knowledge is often equated with "being" but not with "doing.") There is the effortlessness of simply "being" rather than consciously "doing." Old habits are broken, and thus one's actions are fresh. Their actions now conform to the ethical laws of the universe (as their tradition defines them), with no ego causing friction. Mystics no longer have a mixture of motives or any unenlightened selfishness driving their actions, and thus they can act more effectively. There is no longer a constant defensive self-concern.[25] The lack of a sense of shame, guilt, or even conscience—since these are predicated on a sense of self—also contributes to this effortlessness. They have stopped pushing or even thinking and are now moving through the world without deliberating, weighing alternatives, or making any conscious effort. They have none of the hesitancy, indecision, and lack of confidence associated with reaching a decision through reasoning. Their actions might be better described as passive *reactions* since the mystics do not initiate new actions but only respond to the situation. In that regard they would be like athletes who are masters of their game—they do not have to think but just react.[26] (Players' actions too are not smooth and easy when they think about what they are doing. As Yogi Berra says, "How can you think and hit at the same time?")

Thus, after perhaps years of strenuously cultivating simplicity, mystics acquire a spontaneity to their actions. Such spontaneity differs from impulsiveness in that there is no sense of self and thus the actor does not initiate the action but only reacts to the situation. They act quickly, with an economy of motion.[27] They are no longer forcing their actions to fit a rule.[28] They have no need to follow a command, and thus no conscious rule-following is involved. Even any awareness of rules, ethical concepts, or a sense of self mediates between reality and the action, and with the introduction of such mediacy one is not responding to what is really there. That is, the introduction of "I" and factual and evaluative images creates an artificiality that distorts what is real and thus adversely affects our actions. The false sense that there is an "I" interferes with the flow of what is real. Instead, the enlightened live effortlessly as each moment arises without applying concepts or evaluations to reality.

Free of our illusions and whims, the enlightened respond simply to what is before them without personal attachments interfering. In their state of mindfulness, they do not try to manipulate what is there. They are not inactive but interact with the rest of reality in accord with the way things are deemed to be and thus are fulfilling a natural role or are as noninvasive as possible. This does not mean the mystics do not have a *purpose* to their actions—literally "living without a why"—but only that no personal (and hence selfish) motives or conscious reflection on what to do is involved. Now they react with a purity of purpose and their actions are not muddled by emotion, the false sense of "I," or images of what should be done. From their point of view, they simply embody the true nature of things. The attention is more focused, not scattered by a mixture of considerations, and in surrendering to the act their reaction is quicker. With a singleness of purpose, they now concentrate on the acts themselves without having to consider the consequences for themselves or whether they are doing the right thing. They may simply be fulfilling their previous social role, as with the *Bhagavad-gītā*, or otherwise quietly living unnoticed. The focus would not be on *what* they do but *how* they do it, since the question of what to do has already been answered for them by their religious code or sense of compassion.[29] Thus, their behavior may not be noticeably different from that of others in their society—or they may be the "holy fool" who seems totally out of step with society. But they would be rejoicing in things as they are, unattached and unconcerned with the results of their actions.

Mystical selflessness thus does not determine whether one is moral or not and what actions are to be carried out. But it does affect the inner life—how one acts and thus how one is moral, if one is moral. The *Crest-Jewel of Discrimination*, a popular Advaita text wrongly ascribed to Shankara, sums up the variety of ways the enlightened may appear and act:

> The knower of Atman does not identify himself with his body. He rests within it, as if within a carriage. If people provide him with comforts and luxuries, he enjoys them and plays with them like a child. He bears no outward mark of a holy man. He remains quite unattached to the things of the world. He may wear costly clothing, or none. He may be dressed in deer or tiger skin or clothed in pure knowledge. He may seem like a madman, or like a child, or sometimes like an unclean spirit. Thus, he wanders the earth. The man of contemplation walks alone. He lives desireless amidst the objects of desire. The Atman is his eternal satisfaction. He sees the Atman present in all things. Sometimes he appears to be a fool, sometimes a wise man. Sometimes he seems splendid as a king, sometimes feeble-minded. Sometimes he is calm and silent. Sometimes he draws men to him, as a python attracts its prey. Sometimes people honor him greatly, sometimes they insult him. Sometimes they ignore him. That is how the illumined soul lives, always absorbed in the highest bliss. He has no riches, yet he is always contented. He is helpless, yet of mighty power. He enjoys nothing, yet is continually rejoicing. He has no equal, yet he sees all men as his equals. He acts, yet is not bound by his action. He reaps the fruit of past actions, yet is unaffected by them. He has a body, but does not identify himself with it. . . . The knower of Brahman, who lives in freedom from body-consciousness, is never touched by pleasure or pain, good or evil. If a man identified himself with the gross and subtle coverings within which he dwells, he will experience pleasure and pain, good or evil. But nothing is either good or evil to the contemplative sage, because he has realized the Atman and his bonds have fallen from him. . . . He neither directs his senses toward external objects nor does he withdraw them. He stands like an on-looker, unconcerned. He does not desire the reward of his actions, for he is intoxicated by the Atman—that nectar of pure joy.[30]

"Beyond Good and Evil"

That the enlightened are free of concepts distinguishing "good" from "evil" leads to the claim that they are "beyond good and evil" and thus cannot be moral. As Seng-can, the Third Patriarch of Zen Buddhism, extolled his listeners, "Be not concerned with right and wrong—the conflict between right and wrong is the sickness of the mind." Just as nature in itself is not "beautiful" or "ugly"—these are only our judgments from our point of view—so too nothing in itself is "good" or "evil." "Good" and "evil" are merely products of the unenlightened mind, reflecting our unenlightened interests—in particular, those of our personal will. That is, morality is tied to a sense of self, and without that sense morality cannot function. At best, morality is consigned to the path to enlightenment—since thinking about the welfare of others helps to lessen one's own sense of self—but it is jettisoned along with all other unenlightened baggage by the enlightened. The enlightened are free of all such restrictions and are free to do whatever they want. No course of action is binding. They are beyond all sanctions and all authorities. They are truly autonomous. Antinomian behavior is only to be expected. Even if the enlightened happen to choose only to do good, their mystical experiences render morality a concern only for the unenlightened—the enlightened have transcended it. The enlightened pass no judgments because there are no judgments to be made—all other-related values are rendered utterly groundless. Mystics self-indulgently focus simply on the task they are doing without any goal and without regard to the consequences to others. Thus, mystical ways of life can only be described as nonmoral, since they can have no moral dimension.

This conclusion, however, does not follow from the enlightened's freedom from conceptual categories. In their enlightened state, they are no longer consciously applying these values. They are not reacting to a label they themselves have created for a situation. There is no longer a question of "ought" or "duty." Moral mystics are now incapable of committing a selfish act and can only act with other-regardingness. They no longer ponder alternatives of what is good or bad or to review rules and then decide how to act. (This will be qualified in the next section.) They see what will help, even if they are not thinking, "This is good." Value-distinctions are not reified into objective entities in the world, but the enlightened are still operating implicitly with the values, thus allowing their responses to be spontaneous and effortless. The mystics' dispositions have been transformed, and so rule-following to adjust their behavior or to keep negative actions in check is no longer needed. Moral mystics now are in a state of awareness from which they spontaneously express their compassion.

However, this simply means the enlightened are "beyond good and evil" only in the sense that they are beyond all rule-following, as any expert in the virtues would be. Consciously following a rule would mean that one is not yet enlightened—it would indicate decisions based upon dichotomizing the situation into unreal entities. What has changed is what they are: they now *are* moral to their core; they do not simply decide to *do* some moral acts. It is a mode of being, and in that state the mystics are exempt from observing ethical precepts—the only ethical norm to which moral mystics adhere is love.[31] But in Augustine's phrase, the moral enlightened mystics can "love [God], and do what you will"—any resulting acts will always be moral. They have reached the spirit behind the letter of the rules and no longer need the letter. The enlightened may be moral but not "moralistic" in the sense of clumsily trying to follow the letter but not the spirit of a precept, nor "legalistic" in the sense of putting rule-following or duties above other-regardingness. In sum, enlightened moral mystics are beyond ethics (in the sense of needing to consult a set of norms before acting), but they are not beyond morality (in the sense of not being other-regarding).

To be moral, one does not have to consider consciously what is right. Normally the mystics' behavior will automatically conform to the precepts of their tradition. But if an exception to a rule is needed in order to be other-regarding, they will violate the rule. (Thus, they may not always appear ethical to us.) They are "unprincipled" in the sense of not needing to review principles but not in the morally objectionable sense. They are not choosing a good and rejecting an evil but abandoning the categories altogether when a greater good has taken over. To put the point paradoxically: they have "a morality beyond morality"—Zhuangzi's "Great Humaneness" beyond "humaneness." As with all concepts, the enlightened have overcome the duality of distinct entities that our value concepts create, and they now see what is really there. Other-regardingness is still the master value in their lives. That is the goodness beyond our judgments of "good" or "evil" underlying a moral life. In sum, they are in a state that transcends the rules but not morality.

Critics of the possibility of mystics being moral, however, point to another sense of the phrase "beyond good and evil." They may concede the enlightened have no personal will and thus the thought of acting for personal gain could not enter their mind, but they point out that the enlightened do not have to adopt moral values. They also point to Arjuna's enlightened action in the *Bhagavad-gītā*—the killing in a war that looks exactly like unenlightened killing, except that is may be more efficient. The inner attitude is all that matters to the mystics, not the actions themselves, and so any acts will do. No act is *per se* bad. The natural response is the immoral action of the libertines and antinomians who claim that ultimate reality, in either a theistic or nontheistic form, is beyond the attributes of our realm and thus is beyond good and evil; therefore, they too are beyond good and evil and so can adopt any action in this realm, no matter what its consequences are to others. No ethical injunctions can apply to the liberated life, and the enlightened may casually violate moral standards or be indifferent to the suffering of others. What a character does in a "dream" is inconsequential, and so no actions matter. All values from this point of view are merely arbitrary cultural conventions having no grounding in reality. We have been fooled by social forces into thinking value-judgments are somehow necessary and part of reality, but mystics see them for what they are—contingent and arbitrary. Thus, mystics are "beyond good and evil" in a value-sense—even if they happen to choose to be moral—since they can do anything.

The main problem with this position that it is hard to see how a truly selfless person could lead a life of real license—a life driven by hedonistic impulses—let alone after years of mystical training. How selfish would even the enlightened Free Spirits' natural impulses then be? The objection, however, does highlight the fact discussed earlier that the mystical experiences do not carry any moral values with them and that mystics thus must adopt other-regardingness if they are to be moral. The objection also points to another issue: is the ground of reality moral in some sense, or are moral values simply a matter of our realm? One position noted above is that ultimate reality must be beyond all our categories—by definition, what gives us being is "wholly other" and thus cannot be characterized by properties from what it creates. Ultimate reality is "not this, not that"—our concepts simply do not apply. But saying ultimate reality is neither "good" nor "evil" is like saying it is neither "blue" nor "nonblue" (i.e., some color other than blue): it is colorless and thus beyond all our color-terms, and the same applies to our value-terms. Moral "good" and "evil" are matters for this world only—the ground of reality is beyond the dichotomy. Saying it is morally "good" is in effect imposing restrictions on the transcendent. Nothing of the ground's values, if any, can be inferred from our realm, and conversely any values related to the experience of that reality are irrelevant to the interactions between beings within this realm. In short, there is a complete incommensurability between our values and the transcendent's, if it has any. (The opposite position is that God is infinite and so includes all possibilities. That is, we can ascribe properties to God but must include *all* properties since the transcendent is infinite. Therefore, to include only one side of any dichotomy—here, being moral rather than also immoral—is a restriction. Thus, the way opposite to the *via negativa* presents the same problem.)

Similarly, mystics or nonmystics who take the whole of this realm to be the sum total of reality can claim, following a form of Spinozean metaphysics, that reality just *is* and is not morally "good" or "evil"—all value-judgments represent the points of view of fragments of the whole (what is good or bad *for them*), and such judgments cannot apply to the whole. From the point of view of reality, the only thing actually "evil" is the human evil of acting selfishly and thus going against the grain of reality. If we saw reality as it truly is, we would have no sense of self and thus would not act selfishly. All of reality is in fact one interlocking whole; all the parts are real and therefore "good." Within the whole, no parts in fact can be separated and labeled "good" or "bad." What appears as "evil" to us only represents our limited, self-centered point of view. Nature just is. Poisonous snakes do not do anything "evil"—they are just doing what is natural. "Natural disasters" are simply the same forces at work in nature that made us in the first place. The bubonic plague from our point of view is something terrible that we should eradicate, but from the point of view of the bacteria it was just a matter of thriving. From the point of view of the whole, neither perspective has any priority. Hence, labeling any phenomenon but self-will "evil" is ultimately a matter of our own ignorance. There are no fixed values to reality—all values reflect self-centered points of view. As Tāntrikas would say, the energy that is nature is indifferent—we make up the values.[32] Pleasure and pain just are; they are not "good" or "bad." Our sense of moral "good and evil" is just another duality we have to overcome to see reality as it truly is. If we must make a value-judgment, we should accept whatever happens as "good" (if we value this realm) or as illusion or suffering (if we do not value this realm). But either way is arbitrary since reality is value-neutral.

Any ground to our reality can be called "good" in a nonmoral sense in that it supplies our reality—i.e., it is good for us that it exists or else we would not. Thus, it is intrinsically valuable to us. But *moral* goodness does not necessarily follow:

if the transcendent is a personal being that created us just to watch us suffer, it is certainly not morally good.[33] And considering all the sources of suffering in this realm (not to mention the immoral acts attributed to God in theistic texts), it is far from obvious that the transcendent is morally good, as atheists discussing the problem of evil are quick to point out. This leaves moral mystics with a problem: how to ground their moral ways of life in the transcendent. Their basic dilemma is that they want to argue that the transcendent reality is beyond all dichotomies, and yet, being moral, they want to weight one half of the value-dichotomy—love, compassion, goodness—over the other. They want to ground other-regardingness in the Godhead while still arguing that the Godhead is beyond human values.[34] In short, our values do not apply and yet ultimate reality is not value-free.[35] Thus, for theists to give up their will and to be filled by God's will is moral only if the latter is moral, and moral mystics cannot argue simply that existing is good (*esse qua esse bonum est*) in a moral sense—they still have to get to other-regardingness. The same holds for the nontheistic Mahāyāna Buddhists. Theists in the numinous/devotional strand of religiosity might argue that the transcendent has revealed commands or a purpose for this realm, but mystics have to rely upon mystical experiences. They are presented with the problem that Advaitins and others have depth-mystical experiences and yet advocate a nonmoral way of life. Others may argue that the transcendent has a type of moral goodness that is unlike ours—the "morality beyond morality" of the enlightened state grounded in a moral goodness beyond what we label "morally good" in the transcendent. They could follow the Daoists' argument that the dichotomy of "good" and "evil" comes into play only after goodness has declined: when all was good, we had no concept for "good"—only when a contrast appeared did the concepts arise. But they would then have to admit that the category of "goodness" does apply to the transcendent. The same is true if they argue for an analogy between our moral goodness and the transcendent's à la Thomas Aquinas.

In any case, these dilemmas show the difficulties mystics have when they argue both that reality is a loving presence or absolute goodness and that all conceptual dichotomies, including "good" and "evil," do not apply to what is real. But in the end mystics do not say that reality is value-neutral or that values are merely human conventions—they make evaluations of the nature of reality (e.g., all is suffering and thus to be escaped) and differentiate what practices are productive (and hence valuable) from those that are unproductive in leading to enlightenment or in helping others. At most, it appears that moral enlightened mystics, as noted earlier, are "beyond good and evil" only in the morally innocuous sense that they are beyond considering any moral rules and categories. All their interpersonal actions are other-regarding.

But a philosophical issue arises for those who cannot but act morally. It is the inverse of the Daoist observation. Since all the actions of the enlightened moral mystic are automatically moral, can the concept of "moral" even apply? Freedom to do otherwise is a presupposition of morality, and the enlightened have given that up. That is, if these mystics cannot choose but to act morally, do they really earn the epithet "moral" since they have no temptation to perform otherwise? As F. H. Bradley put it:

> Morality does involve a contradiction; it does tell you to realize that which can never be realized, and which, if realized, does efface itself as such. No one ever was or could be perfectly moral; and, if he were, he would be moral no longer. Where there is no imperfection there is no ought, [and] where there is no ought there is no morality.[36]

If the enlightened cannot possibly commit an *immoral* act, then they cannot possibly *choose* a *moral* one and so should not be given credit as "moral."[37] By having chosen the purely moral road, these mystics have no option to do otherwise, and thus the concept of "morality" no longer applies. Nevertheless, if they are aware of nonmoral options and still have freedom of choice but simply always happen to choose the moral, this problem does not arise. And, as discussed below, the enlightened may well still face choices. However, even if enlightened moral mystics are beyond the dichotomy of "good" and "evil" and thus beyond the category of "morality," the important point is that they are completely other-regarding.

Mystical Decision-Making

The spontaneity of actions and the idea of being "beyond good and evil" present a further issue: does not morality require reflecting on alternative courses of action and making decisions on how to act? How can mystics be moral if they do not distinguish "good" from "evil" and simply respond in the present without motive or without any categories for reflection? How can freedom from concepts, rules, calculation, and all decisions be compatible with a moral life?

The response to this is that the enlightened mystic's decision-making reflects that of any expert. For most of our activities, we do not consult lists of what we should do. Acting without thinking is the norm. We do not normally think about the process of walking when walking—we just do it. We speak without reviewing vocabulary or rules of grammar and usually only notice them when we make a mistake. Experts at a game like chess do not calculate their next move—they "see" what to do. Master pianists do not merely push down the keys in time but make music. The same holds in the moral life. People seldom make moral judgments—if asked, we can reflect on why we did something, but normally we simply act. Hubert and Stuart Dreyfus, in reviewing the "phenomenology of skillful coping," note that principles figure only in the early stage of ethical development. Higher stages involve spontaneous intuitions, and the highest form of ethical comportment consists of being able to stay involved, to gain more information, and to refine one's intuitions. The experts do not reason or solve problems. Their expertise is also not easily communicated—masters respond to philosophical questions with banalities. They do not act with deliberation but see intuitively and act spontaneously and naturally.[38] It seems reasonable to conclude that enlightened mystics also have a predisposition on how to respond in most situations and thus can do so without thinking and with immediacy and effortlessness. What precisely a moral mystic will do cannot be predicted in advance, but love or compassion will automatically lead only to acts that help. "What should I do?" is no longer asked—being free of self-interest, the enlightened will see what to do. As the Dreyfuses say of moral experts, caring does not entail any one particular way of acting—one does spontaneously whatever the situation requires.[39]

It is important to emphasize that the enlightened live in a state structured by their beliefs and values. Mystical freedom is not anarchy. The enlightened live completely in the present in one sense but are not stuck in a free-floating chaos—their structuring still guides them. Their actions are not blind—they normally do not drink poison rather than water and would step out of the way of a speeding truck. Their actions have intentions—Ding the Daoist cook did not flail away aimlessly with a carving knife but had an objective to accomplish, and he accomplished his purpose effortlessly. Seeing reality with images interposed may not be part of this state, but purposes still operate. Mystics do not act with animal impulses or conditioned reflexes but with a cultivated intuitive response. They can use language, even if they do not divide reality by means of linguistic categories. And they have values, even if they do not think in terms of "good" and "evil." As discussed above, they are emotionally even-minded but not blind to the outcome of their actions on others. They do not treat dogs and human beings alike but react in a way that is appropriate for each being. Similarly, they do not treat all human beings alike but treat each person individually, as, with the Buddha adjusting his teaching to the capacity of his listeners. In sum, even if the mystics do not normally deliberate, they still act deliberately.

However, even though mystics can see intuitively how to act in most situations, they may well encounter novel situations where their intuitions will not guide them and they then will have to deliberate. Moral experts when faced with a novel situation have to resort to abstract principles.[40] For moral mystics, the underlying other-regarding ethos will not be in question, but they too will have to have recourse to their religious ethics in determining what to do, whether their religious ethics is a detailed code or only very general norms. But even a tradition's religious ethics may not be enough as new problems arise. The rules do not dictate a precise move in every instance. Knowing the rules of chess do not explain a master's move.[41] The enlightened will do something to help that is selfless, but what precisely they will do may not be predictable. Problems obviously will arise only in hard cases—anything easy would not be a moral dilemma.

Conversely, dilemmas for them may not be dilemmas to the unenlightened. Consider the situation of a wild animal about to attack a baby.[42] Would a mystic intervene and kill the animal or let the animal continue its hunt for food? Either intervening or letting nature takes its course leads to a death. It is easy for the unenlightened with our beliefs and values—we, of course, favor human beings and so would save the baby. Arjuna too, following the warrior's *dharma*, would intervene to save a human life. Most moral mystics may think human beings are more advanced on the path to enlightenment and thus more worthy of help. However, not all mystics may show such anthropocentric partiality and instead may simply watch as events take their natural course (or let the *karma* of both beings takes its course). But whatever a mystic does, the point is that simply removing him- or herself from the picture by being selfless is not enough: some implicit value (favoring nature or human beings) becomes operative, and the mystic must decide what to do. Once the mystic has resolved this dilemma, he or she will have a new norm for the future. This situation would no longer be a crisis for the mystic after having had to deal with it once, but new dilemmas may still be out there, and once again merely saying "give up self-will, and the right answer will automatically emerge" will be wrong. The mystic will again be forced with a choice and all the mental difficulties that accompanies it (minus the presence of self-serving options and emotions).

Moreover, because they then must choose, mystics are liable to make mistakes. Unless they become literally omniscient—i.e., see from the transcendent's point of view and foresee all consequences of an act—they will be limited by human limitations on their ability to understand. Having paranormal powers to read others' minds may help to avoid mistakes in judgment. But their perspective on foreseeable consequences may be very short-sighted, even if they have the long-term interests of others, since they are focused only on the situation before them. They may well not hit upon the best action. Whatever actions they take will be "good" in that the acts will not be selfish—in that sense, it does not matter what they do because at least some other-regarding action will follow. But their actions will not necessarily be the most helpful actions possible since their internalized framework of beliefs and values may not in fact reflect reality. All the certainty and confidence accompanying a mystical experience does not mean their particular understanding of the experience or their worldview is correct. Thus, the possibility of negative consequences in the future cannot be ruled out.

Thus, mystics still have choices among nonselfish options in at least some crucial instances. If they were omniscient, they would know every consequence of their actions and there would be no decisions—their actions would always be dictated by their value of other-regardingness to the best possible outcome. However, if they are omniscient, their actions would be spontaneous but would be those of a mindless automaton, even if an other-regarding one. That would not be freedom *of* the will but freedom *from* the will.[43] (Again, we could not morally commend persons who have no choice in their actions, even if those actions are always other-regarding. But here other-regarding action would be a freely chosen restriction.) However, that there may still be moral crises for the enlightened, even when they have given up their will to God or the Way, means that decisions still may need to be made, and this means the mystic's mind is still involved. An act of "will" is in some way still necessary.

In the end, enlightened mystical moral decision-making is not all that different from that of nonmystics—the absence of a sense of self (and thus the option of selfish conduct) is what makes it seem strange. Like other ethical experts, the enlightened will not be reflecting on how to act but instead will be acting spontaneously. Only in situations that are ethically novel compared to those they have previously encountered will they have to reflect. But they have the ability to deliberate, and thus if morality is a matter of choices and reflection, then enlightened mystics too can be moral.[44]

Conclusion

William Wainwright argues that, while there is no "logical or epistemic connections" between mystical consciousness and morality, mysticism is compatible with morality.[45] That conclusion is correct. Mystical experiences do not have as much impact on morality, at least in the sense of any necessary connection, as is often supposed. One need not be a mystic to be moral nor vice versa. Instead, mystical experiences are compatible with a great variety of beliefs and both moral and nonmoral value-systems. Thus, mystical experiences cannot be said logically to ground in the structure of reality our sense of morality. They are morally neutral, as Agehananda Bharati asserts, in that isolated mystical experiences will not change an immoral and self-indulgent or antisocial person into a moral one—the depth-mystical experience is a mode of consciousness that has no moral value or implication.[46] But outside a depth-mystical experience—in particular, in the enlightened state—mystical selflessness is compatible with morality. However, while mystics thus are necessarily less *self*-oriented, they need not be *other*-oriented. Instead, they may be simply indifferent. The concern for others comes from outside the mystical experiences, as do the specifics on how to help others.

But the fact remains that mystics can adopt the moral point of view and the resulting mystical ways of life are then moral. Indeed, morality and mysticism are natural allies, since each leads away from a sense of self-centeredness—that the world does not revolve around oneself is both a moral and a mystical insight. Mysticism does involve the inner transformation of a person—depositions and cognition—away from self-centeredness to Reality-centeredness. Thus, while mystical cultivation is focused around the self-development necessary for enlightenment, it can easily fit into a moral point of view since the latter orients a person away from self-assertion and self-interest in both one's concerns and actions. Hence, the paradox: one helps oneself by forgetting oneself and helping others. Both on the path to enlightenment and in the enlightened state, a moral concern is the natural result if one's belief-framework involves believing the world and people are both fundamentally real and valuable. Otherwise, one's ethics is simply a matter of self-restraints and abstentions that do no harm to others but are not driven by other-regardingness, as in Theravāda Buddhism. And if morality is inculcated on the path, it most likely (but not necessarily) will become an internalized part of the enlightened way of life. The bottom line, however, is that mystical values are oriented around enlightenment, not moral concern for others, and thus the two sets of values are logically independent.

But the state of mystical *selflessness* does have moral implications for mystics who have adopted a moral way of life.[47] Immorality requires selfishness and hence some sense of an independent existence. So too the Christian antinomians who simply follow where their body leads show no concern for others who are used. But one can also enhance morality by removing the sense of self. Mystical selflessness and detachment can lead to a greater impartiality and a greater focus on the concerns of the person one encounters. The lack of indecision over what to do also leads to an effortlessness and spontaneity of moral action. In short, the contribution of mystical experiences to ethics is that they can transform the person and thus how one acts. It can make being moral easier and more encompassing for those mystics who adopt a moral point of view. Indeed, it can lead to a life of purely selfless service. In sum, mystical experiences can deepen one's moral commitment.

But, again, mystical experiences will only get us to selflessness—for that space to be positively filled with other-regardingness another step is required. Christians routinely claim that the mystical experiences Christians have are superior to those of others because they are moral and that the test of a genuine mystical experience is whether it bears fruit in good works.[48] But, if mystics are correct, the depth-mystical experiences are free of all diversified content and thus can have no value-content. Thus, the mindfulness state must be informed by the tradition's beliefs and values that mystics bring to it. In sum, morality can inform a way of life, but the moral sense still must come from a source independent of the mystical dimension of the mystic's state. Thus, whether Christians or other theists can claim a distinctive and superior "moral mystical experience" is open to doubt. (It should also be remembered that some medieval Christian mystics supported activities of dubious morality such as the Inquisition and the Crusades.) Similarly, trying to judge one mystical experience or way of life as authentic or as superior to another based on whether it produces moral mystics may appeal to modern Westerners but is normative and based on criteria outside of the experiences themselves.

Notes

1. If the presuppositional problem concerning persons discussed in Chapter 6 cannot be overcome, then the *Bhagavad-gītā* is an instance of a nonmoral otherworldly value-system. If compassion (*ci*) does not figure as prominently in Daoism as argued here, then Daoism is a case of a nonmoral this-worldly value-system.

2. Stace 1960, p. 323.

3. Ibid., p. 324.

4. Ibid., p. 329.

5. Ibid., p. 327.

6. Ibid., pp. 324-25. Stace also pointed out that not all mystics revel in their own experiences but some are great workers in the world (ibid., pp. 334-35).

7. Sober and Wilson 1998; E. Wilson 1978, pp. 155-75, and E. Wilson 1998.

8. James Q. Wilson, *The Moral Sense* (New York: Free Press, 1993), pp. 42-47, 123-36.

9. Wainwright 1976, p. 35; 1981, p. 231.

10. Bharati 1976, p. 53; also see Storr 1996 and W. Wilson 2000 for examples of narcissistic gurus, not all of whom were mystics, who declared themselves to be "perfect masters" beyond good and evil. There also appears to be no necessary correlation of moral character and yogic feats—paranormal meditative feats (such as lowering one's heartbeat) in no way depends on the overall character of the practitioner. Nor are other types of religious experiences necessarily transformative—Wordsworth's ego did not decrease after his theophanies, and Byron's experiences led only to his enjoyment of creation.

11. Zaehner 1972, 1974a, 1974b, 1974c.

12. Paul Tillich, *Systematic Theology*, vol. 1 (Chicago: University of Chicago Press, 1951), p. 121. Gandhi's family life illustrates the problem: that he was a less-than-perfect father, to say the least, shows that not all his actions were morally perfect. Or consider the contemporary Buddhist Chogyam Trungpa Rinpoche. His followers have no problem with his open drunkenness and sexual exploitation of followers. They consider him "deeply realized" and see no incompatibility of the two sides of his life.

13. Stace 1960, pp. 340-41. Stace made a distinction between "introvertive" and "extrovertive" experiences but tended to see only one "ideal" mystical belief-claim—breaking down the barrier of "I" and "you" into one whole.

14. Nontheists can account for theists' postexperiential sense of having been aware of a benign being or of a loving ground to reality by an appeal to a mystic's tradition—i.e., the sense that everything is all right or that things are the way they should be is simply the experience of the bald beingness of reality that is interpreted theistically after the experience.

15. Stace 1960, p. 341. Also see the quotation from Dasgupta note 47 below.

16. William Barnard, "Debating the Mystical as Ethical: A Response" in Barnard and Kripal 2002, pp. 78-90.

17. Danto 1987. Elsewhere he speaks more broadly of simply "mysticism" as if mysticism anywhere, not just in the Asian traditions he examines, must conflict with morality (Danto 1976).

18. Many sociologists argue that the self is merely social in origin—a product of our interaction with other people. Many philosophers see it as a by-product of language—we posit a reality to correspond to the word "I." But not all sociologists and philosophers deny the real existence of a self for these reasons. Many psychologists accept the self as something real independent of culture and point to experiments that suggest a sense of self (self-actualization, self-awareness) in infants and animals. If such a self (ego) is indeed part of the structure of reality, mystics would then have to treat it as any other part of the differentiated realm.

19. E.g., Daniel Dennett, *Consciousness Explained* (Boston: Little, Brown, 1991). He also tries to defend a form of free will. See his *Elbow Room: The Varieties of Free Will Worth Wanting* (Cambridge, Mass.: MIT Press, 1984).

20. As Danto notes (1987, p. 17), the will and freedom of the will are not major issues in traditional Asian philosophy. As discussed in Chapter 6, the doctrine of *karma* is not deterministic but gives those within its sanction the free will to choose actions. Predestina-

tion in Western theism is a far greater problem to free will than anything in the Asian traditions discussed here: predestination denies that any creature could have free will or control, since that would be contrary to God's absolute power.

21. Wainwright 1976, p. 31; 1981, pp. 211-12.

22. Enlightened mystics are "apathetic" in the traditional sense of *apatheia*, i.e., free of the control of the passions (and hence the vices of greed, anger, sadness, and so forth). But this is not to be confused with the modern of "apathy" as the lack of interest in events.

23. Danto 1976, pp. 42-45.

24. As noted above in Chapter 3, the preparatory activity itself cannot enlighten the mystic—the inner transformation to selflessness cannot be forced by any amount of actions.

25. Hick 1999, p. 7.

26. Mystical action is sometimes likened to play, since the focus is on the action itself as an end in itself. The idea of reality as Īshvara's play (*līlā*) also is often mentioned in this connection. But this focus on the act itself should not be taken to mean that mystics have not internalized beliefs, values, and objectives or that their actions are necessarily devoid of concern for others.

27. This can be approached in our ordinary life with the role of internalized beliefs and values also at work. Christmas Humphreys gives the example of two men who, while walking down the street in conversation, notice that another man walking in front of them has dropped his umbrella. One of them, without breaking the conversation, stoops and picks it up as he reaches it and hands it to the third man who had paused to recover it. There are polite words of thanks and the two men, almost without breaking stride, continue on their way. There is no deliberation or plan, no motive or thought—the time and place and the means were there and not only was there no consideration of a result but probably no memory of the event having taken place (Humphreys 1960, p. 167). (Notice that implicit beliefs and a plan are at work here, even though there is no deliberation: a choice to help and what to do—the man could have ignored the umbrella.)

28. Nor are they looking for ways to get around rules, as did, for example, the archbishop of Mainz during the Christian Reformation who went into battle with a mace in order to avoid the consequences of "he who lives by the sword shall die by the sword." He killed nine people. That that would conflict with Christian precepts did not bother him since it was for a cause that he justified on religious grounds. (Many premodern Christian armies did not fight each other in the period of Thursday through Sunday or on Christian holy days in order to honor their savior's suffering—and went back to the bloodshed the next day.)

29. Mystics do this without asking themselves whether their way of life is moral or not. But it should be noted that, contrary to many New Age advocates, merely being in an "altered state of consciousness" does not mean that a person can do only good acts—i.e., that it is impossible to misuse the power tapped by selflessness. Our word "assassins" comes from "hashish"—assassins were Muslims who ingested hashish before practicing their form of political action on Christian crusaders. Our word "berserk" comes from the Norse berserkers who ingested hallucinogens before going on rampages. This suggests once again that certain values do not come from inner mental states themselves but must be adopted into a way of life.

30. Swami Prabhavananda and Christopher Isherwood, trans., *Shankara's Crest-Jewel of Discrimination* (New York: New American Library, 1970), pp. 111-13.

31. Aminrazavi 1995, p. 25 (speaking of Sūfīs).

32. To use a medieval Indian example, many demons are said to have earned their demonic powers by performing good deeds in their previous lives. To us, this may seem like "good" can make "evil," but from the point of view of reality our distinctions do not apply.

It is like the jinn of Arabic lore who manifest their power for whoever controls them, regardless of their morality.

33. It can also be argued that theists focus only on what is good for human beings and ignore what is bad in concluding that creation is good. Christians who thank God for surviving a tornado and yet do not blame him for permitting the tornado to occur in the first place (and letting it kill others) are manifesting this partial point of view.

34. Mystics would not endorse the way John Hick suggests—that the Real manifests complementary impersonal and personal faces (or nonmoral and moral ones). See Hick 1989, pp. 338-39. Mystics in each tradition argue that their own position is better in some way than the other systems they are aware of, and thus they would not be willing to concede that any other position is merely a *complement* to their system. They certainly are not likely to concede it on such an important point of values as morality versus nonmorality.

35. Some moral virtues, such as courage, may only apply in this realm where there is at least apparent duality, not to any transcendental ground.

36. F. H. Bradley, *Ethical Studies*, 2nd ed. (London: Oxford University Press, 1927), p. 234.

37. See Underwood 1974, p. 65 (concluding that the enlightened-in-life are nonmoral).

38. Dreyfus and Dreyfus 1992. Also see Deutsch 1992 on "creative morality."

39. Ibid., p. 128.

40. Dreyfus and Dreyfus 1992, p. 122.

41. Ibid.

42. See W. King 1964, p. 136.

43. New Age advocates of mysticism sometimes claim that "freedom of the will is only for the unenlightened" without realizing the consequence that this means a presupposition of morality is negated for the enlightened.

44. If morality requires correct knowledge of reality, then we have the metaphysical issue of who in fact has the correct account, and that issue will not be discussed here. Having the correct knowledge of the nature of reality would lead to the most effective actions, but it seems obvious that we still can be other-regarding—and thus moral—even if we are mistaken about the true nature of things. In sum, being concerned with the welfare of others does not require a perfect worldview or complete factual knowledge.

45. Wainwright 1981, pp. 218, 224-26. But he also sees that mysticism and morality may have "significant psychological or social connections."

46. Bharati 1976, pp. 74-75.

47. One study shows that those who belong to a "quest" type of religion (such as mysticism) are *not* more likely to help others than are those who are in religion only out of self-concern rather than concern for others (i.e., only to show themselves to others and to themselves as being good, kind, and caring). But when questers do help, they are more likely to be responsive to the expressed needs of the person seeking help than are those concerned only with looking good. (Whether the quester's help is done out of genuine other-regardingness, rather than merely a sense of duty, required more research.) There also is evidence that the quest type is associated with *reduced* feelings of sympathy and compassion. But questers are also more likely to be tolerant and sensitive to the needs of others; the self-concerned in religion are more likely to be prejudiced. Batson, Schoenrade, and Ventis 1993.

48. E.g., Matt. 7:15-20. See Hick 1989, pp. 223-36; 1999, 163-70. Many non-Christian scholars also argue that a mystical experience or a mystical way of life that is not expressed in moral action is not "authentic," "real," "final," "complete," "true," or "genuine." To quote one instance, S. N. Dasgupta states "There can be no true mysticism without real moral

greatness" (*Hindu Mysticism* [New York: Frederick Ungar, 1927], p. viii). Any experience that increases a sense of an individual self or selfishness would not be a mystical experience, but any ethical criterion of a "true" mystical experience may be difficult since the possibility of indifference appears just as real.

14

Mystical Ways of Life and Morality

One conclusion from the last chapter is that the mystics' experiences do not determine the factual beliefs and values of their ways of life. Instead, factors outside those experiences become very important in the ways of life they adopt. This leads to questions about the relation of morality to the factual beliefs and values of those ways of life. The role of belief-claims in the mystics' ways of life extends beyond the issue of the presuppositions of morality to the more specific factual beliefs grounding values within a way of life. But the place to start is with the question of whether factual beliefs, even those associated with mystical ways of life, require morality.

Does "Mystical Metaphysics" Require Morality?

A distinction must be made between mystical experiences and the factual beliefs and values associated with them. Scholars often speak of a generic "mystical metaphysics" grounding morality in terms of the metaphysics of absolute oneness (resulting from an experience of being identical to the total cosmos) or of an interconnected wholeness (resulting from the experience of realizing that one is only a part integrated into one whole). First, it must be noted that there is no one "mystical metaphysics"—there are dualisms, nondualisms, and different theistic and nontheistic transcendent grounds to reality. Second, the "mystical oneness" of depth-mysticism does not involve a sense that one is the same as anything else in the phenomenal realm but only that there is a common source to everything or that we all share the same underlying being. Moreover, even if a metaphysics of oneness or interconnection were necessary to morality, one can still adopt it for reasons other than having a mystical experience. (Thus, Stace's position again becomes irrelevant.) For example, Parmenides accepted a metaphysics of oneness for reasons unconnected to these experiences. Ludwig Wittgenstein's early work presented a selfless view of reality based only on philosophical considerations.[1]

So too we do not need to be mystical or even religious to see that we are all products of one universe and thus ought to help others since we are all in the same boat and life is a struggle. This can produce a stronger tie to other people than any transcendental command. Realizing something as simple as the fact that each baby is born through the efforts of two other people and cannot survive long without the help of others can lead to the rejection of egoism—we can see that we need others and that no man is an island. So too we do not need a mystical state of conscious-ness or any meditative feat to adopt a metaphysics of the interconnectedness of all things. Human beings and everything else on earth are, after all, all made of the same stuff—the refuse from exploding stars. All life on earth has evolved from the same root DNA, and thus all human beings, plants, and animals are related. We can readily accept on grounds of ordinary experience and science that there are no independent entities (including selves) to reality—instead, all of nature is one flowing state in which all things have evolved and nothing is totally independent of its connections to other things. All the parts are born, grow, and die, but the whole continues. The self is integrated into the rest of nature and not self-existent, just as a tree is dependent on the earth, water, and sunlight but is still different from them—each part makes a unique contribution to the whole but is not independent of the rest. The world can thus be seen as free of selves in the sense that there is no independently existing self or other entity. The sense of a self separate from every-thing else is merely an illusion generated by our brain. We can then see our role in this world as a moral one in which we enhance the smooth interaction of parts by acting morally or even selflessly rather than selfishly manipulating other parts of the whole for the advantage of our little segment. Such a purely naturalistic metaphysics could ground a radically impartial concern for all other persons or all of reality, i.e., all beings are of equal worth and there would no reason to favor oneself or people important to us over others, or indeed people over other beings. In sum, morality can be seen as a perfectly natural response to naturalism, with selfishness being seen as totally out of step with the interconnected whole. Theistic ethics would then seem literally "unnatural," since the idea that we should be concerned with others has to be imposed upon us from a transcendental source.

However, even a sense of oneness or connectedness does not necessitate the moral conclusion. A metaphysics of absolute oneness in fact negates the space necessary to make love or any other concern for another possible: love presupposes a duality of one who loves and one who is loved. Thus, this metaphysics conflicts with morality—there is no other person to help. The discussion of the Upanishads in Chapter 4 showed that this metaphysics can lead to the idea that it is impossible to "kill" people in this realm, since we cannot actually affect what is truly real. This doctrine did not lead to immoral behavior or antinomianism in Advaita (contra Robert Zaehner) but to an indifference to everything in this realm. Only in the theistic traditions that treat God alone as real has this led to the antinomian conclusion (although Tantrism combines both theistic and nontheistic elements). In addition, feeling an overwhelming presence of an all-encompassing love does not necessarily lead to an active life of loving others—one could just as easily rest basking in the love, concluding that this realm is not real and that since our own suffering is no longer important then neither is anyone else's. (Also remember that Christians who saw the ground of reality as loving supported crusades and inquisitions—the ground had one value, but how it was manifested in the world by Christians was not always in ways we would now deem moral.) Stace dismissed such illusionism as an unnecessary component of mysticism, contrasting it with Christian realism.[2] But such a metaphysics appears as a natural correlate of a metaphysics of mystical oneness as a realism for our realm.

A metaphysics of an interconnective wholeness fares a little better. One may be moral with such a view: the parts are real and are not isolated monads that cannot be affected by our actions (as with the *Bhagavad-gītā*'s Sāmkhya-Yoga metaphystics), and the reality of the parts permits concern for the other parts. But just because we are connected does not have any moral consequences. It is not inconsistent to try to manipulate other parts for the advantage of our part. That is, even if the parts are impermanent and without substance, we can try to manipulate the configuration of parts that still produces effects to help only ourselves. There may be severe limits to how far we can twist reality for our particular little fragment's advantage, but nothing about the factual claim of a whole rules out all such effects. We can even accept that every act within our social or global whole or even the universe as a whole can have eventual repercussions within the whole and thus affect all other parts without concluding that we must be moral.[3] A value-choice still must be made.

Moreover, the claim "I should treat you as myself because you *are* myself" does not follow from a metaphysics of wholeness any more than from a metaphysics of absolute oneness: one part of the whole can damage another part without damaging itself, even if the parts are interconnected. Killing another does not mean we are harming ourselves. Indeed, one part may have to harm another part to maintain itself, just as we would amputate a cancerous limb to save the body. Conversely, if the belief in not harming any other part of the whole (from *ahimsā*) did follow from the metaphysical belief, then we could not eat anything, or, at best, we would be restricted to the diet of noncultivated products that the Jainas recommend. But if we are free to use crops to maintain ourselves, it is not clear that drawing the line of what one can kill at any point is required by a metaphysics of wholeness. How advocates of that view could value sentient life or life in general over inanimate objects is also not clear, since all are equal parts of the same world. They would also have to explain the millions upon millions of years of evolution that produced animals eating animals and such effects harmful to us as disease-causing viruses—that is nature as it is, free from our unenlightened self-centered point of view. Our ecological environment is one whole that reveals not just cooperation and beneficial symbiotic interrelations but also violence and competition. In short, life does not appear to be as precious as advocates of holism assert. Thus, we cannot read love off of nature very easily even if everything forms one whole. Holists may believe the ground of being breathes a love of everything and thus that the better value is to work helping the other parts of reality than to be selfish, but that value-judgment is not deducible from the belief-claim of interaction of the parts of the world and is in fact far from obvious from nature.

It should also be noted in this regard that the Golden Rule is harder to reconcile with a sense of selflessness and wholeness than Stace and others realize: treating others as *I* want *myself* to be treated involves the unenlightened self-centered point of view, i.e., projecting what I see as my own interests rather than looking out for the interests of the whole. Seeing everything as a part of myself or in fact as myself makes the self-interest condemned in mysticism central to how we would decide how to act. Instead, we should see reality free of selves. (Even the consciousness of Advaita is not a "self.") Equally important, that I should not harm you because I would thereby be harming myself is not a *moral* motive but only "enlightened" self-interest. In sum, the self-centeredness necessary to make the Golden Rule work conflicts with a mystical sense of selflessness.

A metaphysics of wholeness can also lead to total indifference. If all individuality within the whole is obliterated, then there are no other parts to help. Just because there is no substance differentiating us into separate, independent realities does not mean we must be concerned with the rest of reality. We can just as easily conclude that we should let everything proceed without our interference, paying no special attention to ourselves, our group, human beings, or even sentient beings—any self-assertion or any attempt to help one part over another would be going against the flow of reality. From the point of view of the whole, any changes are zero-sum, and so there is no reason to act. Thus, there is no reason to help one part over another. Nor are there separate realities we can be concerned about even if we wanted—we are all just different piles of the same elements of matter in one interconnected whole. This can lead to a nihilism usually ascribed to philosophical naturalists. (The same nihilism can follow from the factual claim that all of reality is sacred, as Christian antinomians demonstrated.) The whole is real and is what it is, and nothing we can do affects its well-being. Our acts are irrelevant. Being indifferent in such circumstances is more in step with reality than being concerned with other parts.

The belief that the world is the creation of a perfect, compassionate God can also lead to indifference in a similar way. That is, everything is perfect as is and need not be changed; so no action helping others should be undertaken. Even an experience of the ground of the world as the creation of a loving being need not change this: everything is perfect because it is the product of love, and so we should not try to change anything, no more how much it seems to be "evil." Moreover, the temporary suffering we suffer here, no matter how bad, will be nothing compared to the infinite joy we will experience for eternity; and so the suffering of others can be ignored. Thus, another type of experience is required to move us compassionately not to leave everything as it is and also to determine the nature of the "good" we are to achieve.

Similarly, the lack of independent selves does not help. It would certainly follow that if we believe we are all parts of one whole and have no independent self to maintain, then we could not rationally act selfishly (i.e., act to enhance what we know is a nonexistent ego). But then again, as pointed out in earlier chapters, it would be equally true that there are no *other selves* to help. Preferring another's welfare over one's own is as much tied to a sense of "selves" as egoism and thus is as unenlightened. In short, if there are no realities to be selfish about, then there also are no realities to help either. Conversely, if there are indeed parts to help, then there also are other parts to be "selfish" about—again moral concern does not follow. If hate and greed are impossible because these emotions presuppose an ego and there is none, then it is just as true that love and compassion are impossible because these reactions presuppose *other* egos and there are none. Thus, neither morality nor selfishness reflects reality as it is, free of selves; only a nonmoral value-system would.

It would be silly to argue that people prior to the twentieth century who held a Newtonian worldview of independent, isolated entities operating mechanically on each other clearly could not have been moral and that morality only became justified with the adoption of the interconnective holism of modern subatomic physics. There obviously still will be people that could be helped or hurt by our actions.[4] Only if the world is made of Leibnizian unaffectable monads would concern for others be irrational. (Thus, the other extreme of metaphysics from Advaita's oneness is also incompatible with morality.) But with anything short of that, we can cooperate and need not be antagonistic, clinging to our separateness, just because we are separate. Being moral or immoral is not tied to factual beliefs in that way. Immorality is indeed tied to selfishness, but that selfishness, as just discussed, can still be grounded in a holistic worldview. We not need delve into metaphysics to be selfish—we do not need to be committed to the belief-claim of an eternal "self" to act "selfishly." And we can be concerned with others even if we accept the existence of selves. That Buddhists argue murder is impossible because there is no "self" and the *Bhagavad-gītā* argues the same precisely because there *is* an eternal "self" should reveal that the arguments are not based on metaphysics. That the latter justifies a war and other apparent "killing" in our world also reveals more of the problem.

In sum, to be moral we need to feel *concern* for others, not *one* with them. The moral value does not necessarily follow from the metaphysics, and thus adopting a metaphysics of oneness or wholeness will not by itself get us to morality. A value-choice remains.

Factual Beliefs, Values, and Morality

There is no simple one-to-one correlation of beliefs and values. Mystics may have essentially the same factual beliefs and yet differ with regard to morality (e.g.,

Hīnayāna versus Mahāyāna Buddhism). Or they may have different metaphysical systems but have essentially the same ethics (as with the classical philosophical schools of Hinduism.)[5] There may be different justifications for the same values (as with Mozi's nonmystical justification of universal love). Religions may continue to maintain the same ethical code when their belief-claims change. Thus, mystics may differ on how the world is constructed rather than values, or the other way around. All this means that an ethos cannot be deduced from a worldview or vice versa.[6] In short, we cannot deduce an enlightened "ought" from the enlightened "is" or vice versa.[7] Thus, it is one error to suppose that all mystical traditions must have only one value-system, but so is the opposite extreme—that differences in metaphysics requires differences in value-systems. Mystical enlightenment may rule out any selfish action, but mystical factual beliefs do not entail one set of values or one course of action: what one does about the rope when one sees it is not a snake is not determined solely by seeing the rope correctly. Moral mystics may still differ on the best way to help others; thus, specific norms are not deducible from a basic ethos of morality but will depend on the factual beliefs the mystics adopt. Moreover, there can be a major shift with mystical enlightenment in one's factual point of view and yet the mystics may still adhere to their preenlightened values and action-guides. Hence, one's actions may not show one's new beliefs.

In sum, different beliefs can be the factual bases for the same action-guides and different action-guides can have the same factual bases, and so we cannot say an action-guide presupposes a factual belief. Thus, a practice is not justified in the sense of being logically entailed by a basic belief on the nature of reality or of a person. But the factual beliefs can still be said to "justify" a value or action-guide in the looser sense that they express the practitioners' belief that their action-guides are grounded in reality. In short, the beliefs "ground" action-guides without logically "justifying" them. The sense of reality imbuing mystical experiences solidifies the mystics' sense that their beliefs and values reflect reality and that they are related to our *summum bonum*. Thus, classical mystics, being value-realists, believe their worldview or specific belief-claims anchor and explain why their values are supreme (e.g., our moral practices are justified because the transcendental reality is moral), and they see this to be so based on experience, even if they do not always rely upon their own mystical experiences for formal justification of their beliefs. There is a circularity here: mystics act in keeping with reality, but they define what is accepted as fundamental "reality." As Clifford Geertz says of the relation between a worldview and ethos for traditional societies in general, the worldview is believed because the ethos that grows out of it is felt to be authoritative, while the ethos is justified because the worldview upon which it rests is held to be true—from inside the circle of faith, the factual beliefs and values appear as a simple fact.[8] To the practitioner, each mirrors the other: the worldview is merely the theory validating the ethos, and the ethos is merely the practical consequence of the worldview.

Beyond its presuppositions, morality does not depend further upon a specific ontology. As discussed in the last section, an Advaita-like nonduality or an extreme monadism would preclude morality, but beyond that one can be moral, immoral, or nonmoral with the same ontology. Values and ethics remain autonomous from factual claims. However, one's factual beliefs do set the horizon of one's actions. Not all metaphysical beliefs directly affect our actions, but belief-claims on the nature of a person, the general nature of reality, expectations at death, and the goals of life affect our actions now. One only lives in the world as one knows it—one acts according to the way the world "really is," as defined by one's beliefs. Belief-claims also rule out some actions as possible options. For mystics, selfish action is ruled out because they do not believe their ego is an element of reality: they cannot attach any importance to one pile of matter—their own body—just because they are aware of subjectivity through it when they know all consciousness is one or that nature is interconnected or whatever is really the case as defined by their tradition. (Even antinomians can be seen as selfless: they are merely letting their bodies go.) In this way, religious behavior is logically dependent upon religious ideas.[9] Such ideas set the context of one's actions. They set up what seems "reasonable," "obvious," or "appropriate." They determine what needs correcting and what is the best type of help (e.g., teaching related to getting out of the chain of rebirths versus providing material aid in this life). If we accept rebirth, we will not treat this life as unique or as determining our eternal destiny but will be concerned with the whole future chain. The Buddhist monk killing the robber for his own good or Gandhi's advice to Jews in World War II—to accept their murder calmly as the result of their own past *karma*, thereby scoring a moral victory over the Nazis—shows concern for the victims only if we reject the belief that this one life is all that matters and instead accept belief in a future life or a chain of rebirths in which one's past and present actions will have repercussions. Determining the moral status of an action thus requires consulting the beliefs the actor holds.

Mystical experiences are not tied to specific worldviews or value-systems, nor do they determine particular factual beliefs or values in any simple manner. Indeed, what separates Western and Indian religion is not the role of mystical experiences so much as the role of such nonmystical factual beliefs as rebirth and *karma*. This leads to the issue of what role these experiences play in devising mystics' beliefs and values. On one extreme are the postmodern constructivists following Steven Katz who believe all experiences have an intentional content and thus the depth-mystical experiences, contrary to the mystics' own claims, must have some conceptual content and structure. That content and structure is supplied solely from the mystic's existing tradition. Thus, depth-mystical experiences cannot contribute anything at any point to the actual beliefs or values that mystics adopt.[10] The religious beliefs that mystics bring to their experiences are not merely one component to their experiences but the *only* cognitive component. Meditation does not involve a deconditioning of a culture's framework permitting fresher cognitive experiences but simply helps the meditator fully to internalize the culture's beliefs and values. Enlightenment is merely the final internalization of a religion's beliefs and values through long training—the culmination of long periods of intense study, practice, and commitment to specific beliefs and values. The substance of any religious experience is reduced to nonexperiential factors from a mystic's culture. The belief-framework brought to the experience controls the experience entirely; it constitutes the experience's complete cognitive content. Religious experiences thus are not potential sources of any fresh cognitive input for a system of belief but merely an intense feeling of previous beliefs. Mystical experiences become, in the words of Robert Gimello, "simply the psychosomatic enhancement of religious beliefs and values."[11] Even if mystical experiences can be said to be experiences of reality in some sense, they are completely shaped by previous beliefs—all cognitive claims come from the belief-system, not any experience of reality.

Constructivists are correct in pointing out that there is no one abstract "mystical" value-system or worldview but instead a variety of mystical systems, often within the same religious tradition. Mystics do bring their cultural beliefs and values to their experiences, which influences their understanding of their own experiences. Whether one's factual beliefs and values are active *during* the depth-mystical experience itself or only influence the understanding *after* the experience needs not be addressed here. Either way, it appears that depth-mystical experiences do not determine one set of beliefs or values. Nevertheless, there also appears to be some substance to these experiences independent of a mystic's belief- and value-system. The mystical experience gives a sense of the direct experience of ultimate reality and of oneness, although these are interpreted differently after the mystics' return to differentiated consciousness. It also gives the experiencer a sense of *selflessness*—that the ego is not part of the fundamental structure of reality. It also affects what is valuable to us since what is experienced is seen as being of utmost significance to us (if it transforms one's life and is not an isolated experience). But this sense of selflessness does not merely reinforce previous beliefs and values: it expands one's sense of connectedness and thus the scope and significance of one's values. Thereby it alters one's views and values. Mindfulness may also involve an insight into the nature of reality that is directly relevant to ethics, although this state is structured differently in different mystical ways of life. (Such effects only apply to mystics whose lives are transformed by the experience or who lead a mystical way of life—as noted in the last chapter, an isolated mystical experience need not have that effect, and the person may remain as selfish as before the experience or otherwise unchanged. In that case, the experiencer does not see the experience as having any cognitive or evaluative import.)

Mystical selflessness, in short, is given different expressions depending on factors outside the mystical experiences themselves, but this does not mean that mystical experiences may not be cognitive and must be reduced to cultural factors. The sense of selflessness fixes limits to value-systems: one cannot behave selfishly if one sees reality as free of egos. Detached from egoistic concerns, one may still, however, not be moral but be nonmoral (e.g., indifferent or inactive), and anti-nomian indulgence—letting the body have its way—cannot be ruled out either.[12]

Mystics may react like the skeptic Pyrrho who, when he saw his teacher fall into a swamp, simply ignored him and walked on by. Selflessness is a shift from self-centeredness to Reality-centeredness (to use John Hick's phrase), not to other-regardingness as morality requires. One must still choose to be concerned with the rest of our realm. And if mystics do find significance to the rest of our realm, an impartial concern for all is the natural consequence: compassion—not pity but a sympathetic concern for others without attention to ourselves—is the basic non-self-centered disposition toward others. Thus, the selflessness of the mindfulness state can be filled with other-regardingness but need not be.

Thus, mystical experiences, even for the enlightened, are neutral with respect to morality and immorality. This means that a Christian mystic who concludes that "God is love" must be bringing that value to his or her enlightened state—the value is not the product of mystical selflessness. So where does the value of love come from? The answer is not as straightforward as constructivists believe. Mystics are no doubt shaped by the value-system of the tradition in which they practice, but mystical selflessness is also part of the experiential background shaping the tradition's value-system. To say that mystical experiences merely deepen previously held beliefs is wrong. Mystics both reflect their culture and affect it.[13] Ethics are not built by abstract intellectual reflection on what ought to be but also on the sense of what is real, and the mystical sense that reality is selfless and impartial thereby enters the picture. Mystical experiences thus can shape values even if they are not the source of other-regarding concern—in particular, if the mystics adopt a concern for others, mystical selflessness leads toward valuing greater compassion and greater impartiality as reflecting the fundamental reality. Hence, mystical experiences can neither be discounted as one possible influence on ethics nor given exclusive weight.[14]

Thus, the norms adopted within a tradition for the unenlightened, and brought to the enlightened state by later mystics, may have been affected previously by mystical experiences. The experience of a greater egoless reality expands the mystics' field of experiences and provides a new perspective on both the world and ethical norms. It leads to greater impartiality in implementing other-regarding concern. Thus, mystics may be ethical innovators in their traditions in expanding other-regardingness. What Gershom Scholem said of mystics in general can be applied to values: mystics are rooted in their tradition but they transcend it, widen it, and even outgrow it; they speak the language of the tradition but at the same time deeply transform it, giving old terms a new meaning and producing new ones; there is a dialectic of traditional terms the mystics must use and the new experience they have undergone.[15]

But again the important point is that the sense of moral concern comes from outside a mystical experience itself. (As discussed in the last chapter, the alternative—that moral mystics experience a reality nonmoral mystics do not—is ruled out by the assumption that the depth-mystical experience is indeed empty of all content.) If a mystic is to express the mystical selflessness morally, that value must be brought into a mystical way of life—mystical experiences themselves do not provide it. A mystical experience is morally neutral in that sense. The moral values that are exhibited by Mahāyāna Bodhisattvas, Christian contemplatives, and other mystics come from their traditions. When a new tradition arises, such as the Buddha's, one must still look for the source of moral concern in other influences—the initial enlightenment-experience is it. But, again, mystical experiences influence those traditions through mystical selflessness, and thus the picture is not as neat as advocates and critics of "mystical ethics" usually see it. Nevertheless, a moral concern for others cannot be said to be a necessary component of a mystical experience or way of life. So too moral critiques of earlier traditions (as perhaps with Mahāyāna Buddhism) do not come from simply having more mystical experiences—the innovation must come from other sources.[16]

The Role of Beliefs and Values in Mystical Decision-Making

How do moral mystics know what to do? To the enlightened, "Love God and do what you will" leads to a spontaneous flow of compassion. To them, their actions are a natural expression of reality. It will seem to be the action counterpart of what Krishnamurti called "choiceless awareness." But although it may seem choiceless, specific beliefs and values will have to be operating implicitly in what acts they choose. Most acts of compassion may be cross-cultural—we see someone fall down and we stop to help the person up. But above the simplest level, how we choose to help will depend on the factual beliefs and values we have internalized as the nature of reality. One needs concepts to structure perceptions—to focus attention on what is important—and the same holds for actions. Selflessness does not entail other-regardingness or any particular course of action expressing it. For the latter, we need specific belief-claims. Consider one vital issue again: whether there is a chain of rebirths. If we accept this belief, we may deem the best help not to be material but a form of religious teaching leading to the end of the long future of suffering that we will have to endure as long as we remain in the chain of rebirths. On the other hand, those who accept this world as valuable and this one life as supremely important will focus on material aid as well as religious aid. Thus, Christians are concerned with the problem of meaning for all but concentrate on material aid to the poor and the sick, while Buddhists spend as much time with the rich and privileged since the suffering associated with existence is just as great for them. An instance of the difference is the contrast between how Jesus and the Buddha dealt with people grieving over a dead person. Jesus worked a miracle with Lazarus, but when a woman stricken with grief brought the dead body of her child to the Buddha and asked him to raise him from the dead he asked her first to bring him a handful of mustard seeds from any family in the village where no one had died. She went from house to house until she finally realized that everyone has suffered a death. She then became a nun. Within the Buddha's framework of belief, that was the sort of help she really needed.

The mind of the enlightened may appear to them to mirror only what is there, but specific beliefs and values are nevertheless at work. The enlightened normally would not reflect on their belief-commitments—or perhaps even be aware of them—but such commitments would be shaping their actions. In the enlightened state, the mystics will have completely internalized a framework of belief, i.e., the framework is fixed in the mind on an unconscious level and thus will control their cognitive and dispositional structures. Normally there is no longer a need for an inner debate on what to do. There is a certainty to their frame of reference acquired, not through habit or practicing a virtue over and over again, but through the certainty the experience of selflessness provides. That allows them to respond without deliberation. As Peter Berger says of anyone thoroughly socialized, he "can conduct himself 'spontaneously', because the firmly internalized cognitive and emotive structures make it unnecessary or even impossible to reflect upon alternative possibilities of conduct."[17] One is freed from the disturbances of having to consider ideas, and one's attention thereby becomes concentrated on the action at hand. Thus, one can now respond spontaneously. The self-centered beliefs and habits previously propelling actions have vanished, but other motivations have replaced them—for the moral mystic, other-regardingness and the beliefs and values of a particular tradition. Arjuna saw his social role as part of the natural order of things; a Bodhisattva does not.[18] In short, if we become selfless, all of us will not necessarily do the same thing. How mystics know what they will do will depend on factors outside of the mystical experiences themselves. In this way, mystical wisdom is a type of practical knowledge—the application of beliefs and values to real situations—that depends on factors from both the experiences and the tradition in which a particular mystic lives.

Mystics may reject the internalization thesis, believing instead that there is an objective point of view provided in their mystical experiences—that they are freed from the past habits controlling their view of reality and their actions, and that they now see things as they really are and respond anew to that. They see their values as rooted in the very structure of reality itself. However, the comparative study of mystical ways of life presents a problem. To mystics the goal of the mystical way of life may seem to be the abolition of all philosophies and codes of conduct, but the variations in belief-systems suggest that these systems return in a strong form as the enlightened mystic's internalized framework. Whether or not the depth-mystical experience is free of all intentionality and conceptualizations and whether the mindfulness state frees us from many socially created distinctions, the enlightened still speak a specific language that reflects a differentiated awareness. They have to adopt a set of belief- and value-claims—mystical experiences and meditative techniques themselves do not entail any specific set of precepts. Thus, it is one thing to say that becoming selfless and detached is a necessary prerequisite to seeing reality as it really is and another to say that being selfless would lead all people to the same view of reality and set of values. Free of all desires, mystics still have to choose to help others if they are to be moral. If we ask a mystic "why are you doing that?" he or she will reply in the only way possible: "I do it because I do it."[19] That is, they are free of personal desires, but that does not mean we cannot determine their internalized beliefs and values by observing how they choose to act in different situations and by examining their writings. What to them seems like "no nature" is more like an acquired "second nature." These beliefs and values, while shaped by mystical experiences, also have nonmystical roots. A Christian mystic knows "God's will," not from his or her mystical experiences, but from the Christian tradition (which, as discussed above, is shaped by previous experiences of mystical selflessness).

Religious Codes of Ethics and the Question of Universals

One other issue deserves comment before closing. How do mystical experiences affect the religious codes that mystics adhere to? As discussed above, the ethical codes that mystics adopt develop in a context to which mystics have contributed the experience of selflessness. Enlightened mystics also are exemplars of selfless and humble conduct, thereby representing ethical ideals for the rest of their tradition. But is the effect of mystical experiences limited only to mystics expanding their impartiality and thus their scope and intensity of concern? Or do mystical experiences affect the specific *content* of the codes themselves?

Classical mystics did little to change traditional ethical codes. Mystics were usually quite conservative about adhering to the existing code rather than changing it, although some mystics were willing to suspend even a fundamental rule if other-regardingness requires it, as the example of the Bodhisattvas indicated. (Monastic codes are geared toward the path to enlightenment and away from the world of ordinary affairs. That would limit the effect of monastic precepts on the general life of the laity, although they may still have some impact.) The presence of mystics can effect some changes in a tradition's code, as when the wandering ascetics were institutionalized within the general Hindu way of life as later stages of life. In this way, mysticism can introduce some innovations within a tradition, but all in all it would have a limited impact on specific codes.

Since enlightened mystics typically use whatever code they were trained in to guide their actions, "mystical ethics" may be quite simple and mundane. The enlightened need some values (as discussed above), and moral mystics can adopt the codes of any major religion (since these can all be followed with an other-regarding motive, although such a motive is not necessary). Thus, the codes at hand can be utilized, and mystics have no need to challenge them. (Mystics' acceptance of any *political* system in power does present a moral issue, as discussed in the next chapter.) That they are value-realists also means that they would tend to accept the codes in which they have been trained as reflecting the ethical law of the universe, and thus they would tend not to question them. Again, mystical selflessness affects how they interpret and implement the code, but this means they do not require new precepts.

In the end, "mystical ethics" is more a matter of basic values than detailed codes, and this limits a mystical experience's impact on existing codes. The ethos—the underlying mystical values affecting how a code is understood and implemented—remains more important than the code itself. For example, Hīnayāna and Mahāyāna Buddhists utilize basically the same code of conduct (the *shīla*) while living nonmoral and moral lives respectively: for the former it is the basic code for self-restraint, while for the latter it is the basic code for an other-regarding life. Similarly, the enlightened and unenlightened in all traditions have the same values in one sense, but the internalization in the enlightened state transforms how the enlightened live those values. Selflessness manifested morally or nonmorally is what is central to mystical freedom, not the specifics of what a tradition deems important actions.[20]

One consequence is that there are many ways to express selflessness and, contrary to a popular claim, there is no reason to think that mystics would advocate one "universal ethics." Virtues, like precepts, also vary in different cultures and ages. Even if humility is a value in all mystical traditions, it is still open to question whether the inner state of a humble person is the same in all traditions, since it depends on the person's beliefs concerning our relation to the transcendent. And even if the inner state is the same, the various traditions set the context of what constitutes a proper act, and thus the acts will vary. This is true of all other religious virtues.[21] The traditions do not concur on one set of values or on one course of actions toward others. Factual beliefs again enter into the picture. The courses of action in fact conflict, not merely differ (e.g., Arjuna's warrior code versus Jainism's *ahimsā*). Even where compassion is central there are problems: Christians and Mahāyāna Buddhists may both advocate compassionate action, but the actions will vary significantly at times because of their difference on the value of this-worldly welfare. It is only on an abstract level that all forms of compassion converge into one category. In short, "compassion" only in the abstract is cross-cultural—how it is expressed depends on the specifics of the various beliefs and value-systems, and these differ. Similarly, all traditions have terms for detached action—*niskāma-karma, wu-wei, abegescheidenheit*—but the resulting actions vary according to cultural beliefs and values. Detachment may be common to all mystics, but their actions are not the same. In the *Bhagavad-gītā*, detachment leads to effortlessly fulfilling class duties but not so in Daoism. For Buddhists, certain occupations accepted by Hindus involve violations of their basic code of conduct and so are condemned. Also, the grim way of the warrior in the *Bhagavad-gītā* and Laozi's discussion of defensive warfare should lay to rest the notion that all mystics endorse pacifism and nonviolence. Their inner nonviolence and calm must be distinguished from their outer actions. In sum, constructing abstract categories may be of great importance to scholars for understanding, but it is the concrete ways of life that are actually lived, and that makes the differences in these ways of life more significant than any abstract commonality.

Anthropologists may find that most people around the world follow basically the same code of conduct. Societies have produced similar codes of conduct (at least for conduct within their own society): rules against murder, stealing (if the society recognizes private property), lying, sexual aggression, and so forth. Certain minimal rules of noninterference with others are probably necessary for any society to sustain itself. These may not be motivated by other-regardingness, since they are a matter of controlling people from interfering with other people and do not necessarily embody an other-regarding concern but only a self-regarding concern for one's own preservation. (That codes of conduct may protect only members within a group also should not be forgotten. Mystics, being conservative in matters of ethics, may also endorse in-group ethics rather than universalize the precepts by extending them to all people or even to all beings.) But any commonality to all societies on basic ethical precepts will come from nonmystical sources, both because they will be based on worldly concerns and because mystics are willing to suspend even basic precepts for mystical development and for helping others.[22]

Mystics' concern with self-cultivation on the path and their uncompromising standards lead to extremes beyond general social norms. Consider the idea of "not killing." Most Westerners limit the scope to human beings, but Buddhists, Hindus, and Jainas extend it to all sentient life—and Jainas carry it to truly extraordinary extremes. The Hindu class system creates gradations in the wrongness of different killings (e.g., killing a Brahmin versus killing an outcaste, or killing a cow versus killing a snake) and requires killing in such situations as a *dharma*-required battle. (Of course, the factual beliefs of the Upanishads and the *Bhagavad-gītā* make it impossible to *kill* even if it appears to the unenlightened that that is what is happening.) That mystics interiorize some external rules only further complicates the situation. For example, Sūfīs see the concept of "holy war" (*jihād*) as involving only an inner conflict going on within all of us and not referring to an external war. That Bodhisattvas may kill to *help* the victim or may violate any other precept in the name of other-regardingness also further complicates the picture. Similarly, the Christians' torture of heretics for their own good during the Inquisition—the inquisitors reasoning that a few hours of torture on earth may save them from an eternity of suffering in hell—raises the issue of what constitutes "love."

Thus, different traditions understand "Thou shall not kill" in very different ways, even if their codes may read the same, depending on different factual beliefs. Of course, we can always find commonality by abstracting away enough detail. But once we get into the details of the actual lived ways of life any superficial convergence is lost. Any "agreement" is so abstract as to be insignificant.[23] The same problem also arises with the Golden Rule as a guide for helping others. That rule is a matter of form, not substance: it is about *how* to implement values (using what you think is best for yourself as the model) and not the substantive issue of *what values* to implement (what interests are best). Even if all religions have some version of it, it is more significant that what constitutes helping will depend on the differing cultural beliefs and values than the obvious point that what we would want done to us should be our guide.

To try to lower all precepts against killing to a lowest common denominator would offend everyone who extends it to a greater scope and who believes their particular precept reflects the way reality truly is. This makes it very difficult to argue that mystics see an "innate moral law of the universe" that can be reflected in anything other than their own specific code of conduct. There is no one standard of "good" common to all the traditions. The total ways of life and goals of life in different mystical traditions vary greatly, and it is these that set the context within which any precepts are understood by the practitioners. And valuations of the world, human history, life, and even having a body differ from tradition to tradition.

Mystical experiences are not tied to one set of factual beliefs, values, goal, way of life, or course of action. Thus, such experiences cannot answer any questions related to how different cultures devise their codes of conduct, nor do they adjudicate between them. The one abiding mystical value is *selflessness*, but that can be expressed in different ways. Just as the one moral point of view can be expressed differently, so too selflessness is a value that does not entail any more specific action-guides. How selflessness is embodied depends on factors outside the experiences themselves. Thus, different belief- and value-systems will have different ideas of just what actions are required. Mystics are more interested in developing detachment and selflessness than in the specifics of a code. It is a matter of changing a person, not just his or her actions. Thus, character development and virtues are central, not what precepts are followed—the "how," not the "what," is important. As Joseph Dan says of writers on Jewish ethics, the concern is not so much with the problem of what should be done in certain circumstances (the *halakhah* answers that) as why one should follow the ethical demands.[24] Any code that will sustain self-restraint will do. Mystics can then focus on the inner side of the code (what motivates compliance), not the outer (what precepts would be best). Following the code then becomes an exercise in selflessness.

Conclusion

In sum, the moral issue of mysticism comes not just from mystical experiences themselves but from mystical ways of life as a whole. The problem shifts from trying to study mystical experiences alone or trying to treat mysticism in the abstract (i.e., treat all mystical ways of life as necessarily having certain universal belief-claims or ethics or having one stance on morality) to examining the beliefs and values of specific mystical ways of life, as was done in Part II.

Mystics see their values as objective features of reality, but the comparative study of mysticism leads to a different result: not only do mystical experiences not ground the moral sense (as discussed in the last chapter), they are not the source of any specifics for an ethical code and thus do not contribute any solution to the question of relativism arising from the diversity of social codes of conduct.[25] Mystical experiences are compatible with a great variety of moral and nonmoral value-systems. Thus, these experiences cannot be said logically to ground either our sense of morality or any particular code in the structure of reality.

Mystics live by the same rules as do nonmystics in their tradition unless they are monastics. Only the difference in inner motivation separates "mystical ethics" from the ethics of other members of a tradition. Mystical enlightenment changes the mystics' dispositions but not the code followed and perhaps not their actions. Thus, the vertical dimension of mystical transcendence primarily interacts with the horizontal dimension of ethics through the inner dimension of how the mystic follows the code, not in the creation of new codes.

Notes

1. See McGuinness 1966. It should be noted that Wittgenstein's view could lead to indifference in the hands of a mystic—as he said for purely philosophical reasons, *how* the world is a matter of indifference to a reality above it.

2. Stace 1960, p. 325.

3. Just because a whole is involved does not answer the question of morality. Nazi soldiers, in giving themselves over to their cause, may have felt like nodes in an interwoven web, but whether that whole was moral is another issue.

4. The issue of which comes first, actions or worldviews—whether a worldview causes us to act a certain way or whether our actions cause us to adopt the worldview that we then use to justify our actions—is a social or psychological issue that will not be entered into here. According to the psychologist Jerome Bruner, we can act our way to a way of believing or vice versa, but either way we tend to construe our acts as following from the reality of our experience.

5. Jhingran 1989, p. 137.

6. The religious may fabricate a worldview to fit their ethics perfectly—e.g., God as a caring mother to mirror an ethics of caring. Thus, it would appear that the ethics are deducible from the metaphysics. But one can still acknowledge a caring creator and not respond by helping others. In short, even here the ethics are not necessitated by the metaphysical beliefs. Moreover, no specific ethics will be derivable but can vary (as discussed below).

7. The fact-value dualism does not mean that factual beliefs do not play a vital role in how we live but only that we cannot deduce a value from a fact. The "is-ought" fallacy is limited in range to the latter point. How we decide to live reflects both how we see the world and the values we choose—one simply cannot be derived from the other.

8. Clifford Geertz, *Islam Observed: Religious Development in Morocco and Indonesia* (Chicago: University of Chicago, 1971), p. 97. Religious symbols, as Geertz notes, link the worldview and ethos—thus, "*dharma*" and "*dao*" have both factual and evaluative dimensions. Religious conceptions are therefore their own justification—they glow with their own authority (p. 17).

9. Spiro 1982, p. 5. Sociologists who believe economics alone is what really drives us can accept this. As Max Weber said, ideas do not directly govern actions—material and ideal economic interests do—but "world images" determine the tracks along which action is pushed by these interests. Thus, religious factual beliefs can still enter the picture.

10. For discussions of the epistemological issues in the constructivism controversy, see Steven Katz, ed., *Mysticism and Philosophical Analysis* (New York: Oxford University Press, 1978); Robert K. C. Forman, ed., *The Problem of Pure Consciousness: Mysticism and Philosophy* (New York: Oxford University Press, 1990); R. H. Jones 1993, pp. 8-11, 19-46; Robert K. C. Forman, ed., *The Innate Capacity: Mysticism, Psychology, and Philosophy* (New York: Oxford University Press, 1998); Robert K. C. Forman, *Mysticism, Mind, Consciousness* (Albany: State University of New York Press, 1999); R. H. Jones 2000, pp. 276-79.

11. Robert M. Gimello, "Mysticism in its Contexts," in *Mysticism and Religious Traditions*, ed. Steven T. Katz (New York: Oxford University Press, 1978), p. 85.

12. Contra S. Katz 1983, p. 188; also see S. Katz 1992a, 1992b.

13. Mystics' influence on a tradition's doctrines varies between traditions (e.g., more influence in Buddhism than Christianity) and within traditions (e.g., more influence in Eastern Orthodox Christianity than in Protestantism). Mystics may also have an influence in defining the orthodoxy of a tradition without influencing how the nonmystics of that tradition actually practice their faith (e.g., Western Christian orthodoxy and ideals were deeply influenced by mystics, but today Western Christianity is very unmystical in practice).

14. On the interaction of experience and doctrine, see R. H. Jones 1993, Chapter 1.

15. Scholem 1967, pp. 9, 13.

16. The same holds for metaphysics: mystical selflessness does not dictate one worldview or ontology. This matter will not be discussed here.

17. Berger 1970, p. 375.

18. This point assumes there is no "objective" framework—no perspective-free perspective—but only the perspective provided by a particular training. There may be one way reality truly is—i.e., we may be able to construct one set of concepts and laws mirroring the structure of reality—or some way to decide between competing mystical ontological claims. But such epistemological issues will be bracketed here.

19. Meister Eckhart in Blakney 1941, p. 127.

20. That is, selflessness is the real underlying value. Thus, it can be argued that in Christianity one is judged, not by the acts one does, but by whether one acted out of selfless love or not. Or, the doctrine of *karma* can be interpreted to mean that we are karmically damaged whenever we act selfishly, regardless of the code of conduct we happen to be following.

21. See Yearley 1990.

22. Another type of problem is illustrated by the *Theologia Germanica* when it says that where there is no self-will there is nothing owned, i.e., no private property. Without private property, there can be no theft, since that is defined in terms of taking someone else's property. Thus, the factual basis for the ethical precept would be removed and the precept rendered groundless. (The Upanishads do the same for killing.) This does not mean mystics may not take what we consider private property (as with, for example, a Bodhisattva taking the ill-gotten gains of a king), but it wreaks havoc with the idea of mystics conforming to social rules.

23. On the issue of universals in religious codes and whether there is the possibility of a "global ethic," see Donovan 1986; Hick 1989, pp. 316-40; S. King 1995 and 1998, and Küng 1996. One basic problem is whether any "thin" code of conduct can even be

meaningfully abstracted from the "thick" cultural context that sets the meaning and intention of a practice. Another is whether values from one tradition will determine what people see as universal: is any precept above a tautology—"You should not kill whom you should not kill"—going to be a precept reflecting only a particular tradition and thus be normative?

24. Dan 1996, p. 86.

25. On mysticism and relativism, see R. H. Jones 1993, Chapter 3, pp. 73-77.

15

The Lack of Social Action

One point that stands out in the classical mystical traditions covered in Part II is the general lack of social action. It should also be noted that, if anything, the historical record is skewed in favor of social activism: we only know of mystics who left some impact on society through teaching, works, or writings; those mystics who did not leave such a trace were obviously not interested in social reform or at least were not effective. Also note that there is an ambiguity with the word "social" that leads to confusion about whether mystics are "social" or not: mystics' actions are, of course, "social" in the sense of being interpersonal and in the sense that mystics live and act within a community, but they are not "social" in the sense of focusing on corporate action or societywide structures. It is only action in the latter sense—i.e., *group action or social reform*—that will be considered "social" here, not all interactions between people.[1] That is, "social action" is not simply the opposite of selfish action—other-regarding action is—but is interpersonal action revealing an interest in reforming structures in society as a whole or cooperating in groups to help others. It is that type of action that is noticeably lacking in the mystics' actions and writings. Laozi's concern for reordering government is the one exception. The *Bhagavad-gītā* sees the enlightened state in terms of fulfilling a social role to maintain society, but it does not foresee, let alone advocate, any social reform. More generally for the rest of Indian philosophy, the art of ruling and other social concerns are not topics of religious interest.

This is not to say that the other mystics were all asocial hermits fleeing the world or that they were selfishly concerned with their own salvation but only that their other-regardingness (if they were moral) was expressed in interactions of the face-to-face type, such as teaching a person or ministering to the material needs of the people they encounter. There may be stages on the path or periods in the enlightened state in which mystics withdraw from any interactions for meditative exercises, but the moral mystics return to the world. Even when this-worldly concerns predominate in the type of help offered, still there is little sharing of power or interest in transforming social institutions. Even among monastics or other mystical groups, there are few group actions for projects to help others or to transform social institutions outside their own. It is not so much that mystics consider and dismiss corporate work or social reform as simply not consider it in the first place. Indeed, seeing social action as a necessary part of morality is only a modern idea.

Why are individual acts of help valued over institutional action? Other strands of religiosity are more socially active (as discussed below). Why, from a mystic's point of view, could not others also be helped by fixing society, i.e., reorganizing social structures along lines that would materially help others or make social conditions more conducive to enlightenment? Why cannot their impartial love of all people be manifested in social-level actions? Is there something in mystical experiences or in mystical value-systems or belief-claims that screens out group action or social structures and instead focuses attention solely on individual interactions? Or is the lack of interest in social, economic, and political institutions simply a reflection of cultural values and beliefs from the premodern period?

The lack of social action is not to deny that the presence of mystics in a society may have an effect on social structures. The Buddhist monk's assassination of the Tibetan king mentioned in Chapter 8 would be a concrete instance of an effect of a political nature. More generally, mystical religiosity may affect the values of a society and thereby affect the economic and social structures of the larger community. The moral status of the mystics' acts may be judged in terms of this effect, although we may differ on whether to consider only the immediate effect or wider and longer-lasting effects on society. But the moral status of the mystics themselves cannot be judged by effects alone since their intention is also relevant, and that may be focused on something else, such as the karmic destiny of the Tibetan king. Nor is this to deny that certain social conditions may be needed for mystical religiosity to flourish—mysticism is a social phenomenon and thus needs social support (teachers, students, patrons) as much as any other. But the question remains why classical mystics apparently showed no interest in social structures.

The Fundamental Mystical Problem of Life

The principal reason classical mystics have little interest in social action is that their experiences produce an overwhelming sense that another dimension to reality is more real than our world and thus our true welfare lies in that dimension. Our problems of living will be solved only in terms of the transcendent. This perspective devalues our world and lessens any concern for its social institutions since even religious institutions are organized to deal with this-worldly aspects of problems and thus draw attention away from the transcendent. The overwhelming reality of the transcendent renders concern with rearranging the parts of our world less than vitally important—indeed, it tends to push such concern toward complete valuelessness. To put it bluntly, the transcendent renders this-worldly matters not worthy of our attention. To the moral mystic, all that matters in this realm are the individual, real persons. It is not that mystics are concerned with nature rather than society—rather, the concern is with the *beingness* of all things, not with the differentiations within the world. Neither the depth-mystical experience nor mindfulness changes anything except our perspective; nothing within the world needs to be changed but only seen properly. This is not just the case with Advaita Vedānta's illusionism: in moral traditions such as Mahāyāna Buddhism and Christianity, the fundamental mystical problem is related to the fact *that* we exist, not to *what* we are socially. Whether everything is equally unreal (as with Buddhism) or equally good (because it is God's creation), only the fundamental problem remains central. From the mystical point of view, adjusting the structures of our artificial world—in short, all social concerns—is valueless. Improving the conditions in Shankara's "dream" realm appears silly. Even running the "dream world" would be of no interest. Thus, taking social concerns seriously—even to help others—only reveals our lack of knowledge of what is fundamentally real.

In sum, our real suffering will not be corrected by any social changes. It is often noted that mystics need not flee society since the suffering they confront is just as real in a cave or the desert. But the flip side is not often noted: there is also no point in reordering society, since that would not address the mystical problem either. Mystical freedom is unrelated to what structures are in place in a society. Mystics remain emotionally detached, undisturbed by any social conditions but instead dispassionate, and thus not inclined to do anything about them. Needless to say, if they have the joy and inner peace that all beings are good or that everything is all right as it already is (since everything is a product of the transcendent), they will have little impetus to change anything. In the enlightened state, they are letting things be, responding to what is in front of them without imposing personal beliefs or values—this would foreclose any interest in what is not immediately there, such as general social structures. The best help one can give to those not on the mystical path is material aid, but their real welfare would be addressed by religious teaching. Each person must walk the path to enlightenment him- or herself. Other-regardingness in this situation is best manifested in helping the person in front of us—whether it is giving them a cup of soup or religious teachings. In short, compassion remains individualistic, not social. Even political acts such as the monk killing the Tibetan king are motivated only by concern for the immediate recipients (here, concern for the welfare in future lives of the king and his victims). The Bodhisattva Vimalakīrti's actions in society become more representative of moral mystical action than Laozi's sage-ruler's.

This lack of social action cuts across the cultural lines. It is as true in the West as in Asia. Thus, it is not simply the product of Asian belief-claims but is consistent with other factual beliefs. In India, the beliefs in *karma* and rebirth screen out the idea of social reform: everyone has gotten the physical and social circumstances in this life that they deserve from their own actions in past lives, and no one can help them out of suffering but themselves. *Karma* is nature's justice at work, and thus we do not need to try to remedy or correct anything ourselves. There is no need to reorganize society in any way—indeed, redistributing wealth or any other reform of social conditions would be *interfering* with karmic justice. At best, it is merely changing the field in which *karma* operates and thus is of little importance. Social projects to help others certainly would not flourish in such an atmosphere. In fact, Christians account for a little over 2 percent of India's population but for over a third of its hospitals and rural health care facilities. But such social aid is more likely the product of a nonmystical strand of religiosity informing Christianity than its mystics. Christian mystics more typically see this realm simply as a training ground for the soul—this factual belief can lead to a moral concern for others but not to any desire to reform social structures. Thus, theistic mystics need not differ from nontheistic mystics on this point. The mystical values and goals preclude granting full value to this realm, and thus social action drops by the wayside.

The problem in each case is that the physical welfare and even the personal survival that society enhances are not major mystical values. Not all mystics hated having a body, as Plotinus did, but few valued a long life, as the Daoists did. A certain minimal physical health is, of course, needed to maintain the mystical quest; so mystics are concerned with the physical conditions for maintaining the body and also sociopsychological conditions supporting them on the path. But the lack of social protest suggests that mystics found that each classical society provided the social and psychological conditions needed for the mystical quest. Mystics, that is, could find the personal freedom, material support from the populace for their simple ways of life, and the psychological dignity needed to pursue their quest. Conditions in societies could in principle be so harsh that human life is not sustainable, let alone a quest of a relatively small number of people for enlightenment. But each of the classical societies had a place in its social order for mystics and provided the minimal physical and psychological security they needed for the quest. To mystics that is all that could possibly matter in our realm, and so no reform of social structure was needed. This does not mean that they envisioned a society in which every member was a monk or beggar and where there would be no householders generating and distributing material goods; it only means that the social conditions for such householders were not a subject of their concern.

Face-to-face interpersonal action is adaptable to virtually any political circumstances. Thus, these mystics did not try to reform the politics of their culture. Nor did they endorse the status quo, nor were they anarchists or utopians who envision a perfect society (Laozi being an exception), nor were they simply waiting until social ills got so bad that societies would explode and a more mystic-friendly society would emerge—all such stances would be as political as trying to reform a society. These issues were simply screened out of their concerns. Classical mystics could accept the society at hand as they accept its language: just as language is part of the differentiated realm but need not be abolished, so too are social institutions. Mystics can operate with detachment regardless of the social structures in their culture. The phenomena of our realm merely have to be seen correctly. Social structures that seem unjust to us (e.g., social status being fixed by birth) are irrelevant to our real suffering. Arjuna found enlightenment within his social system in conforming to his social role, not in reforming the system in order to help others—indeed, the idea of social change could not occur in the *Bhagavad-gītā*'s mystical approach as long as a king was fulfilling his *dharma*. In sum, focusing attention on reforming society would misdirect our energy.

The mystical solution to the problems of life is an inner transformation of a person to mystical selflessness and detachment. Jean-Jacques Rousseau made the famous remark, "Men are born free and yet are everywhere in chains." Mystics would modify it: "Men are born free and yet are everywhere in *conceptual and emotional* chains." Social reform means wanting to alter the sensory realm, but for classical mystics everything phenomenal remains the same—only our knowledge and dispositions for action need correcting. No amount of this-worldly fulfillment or comfort can bring about that change, and thus social reform is irrelevant. Certainly the idea that worldly success is a sign of divine election is not a product of the mystical strand of religiosity. The only change on a societal scale conceivably of importance is the transformation of every single person's cognitive and emotional structures, but the focus of mystics' attention remains on the individual.[2] Of course, a possible consequence of the mystical inner transformation of everyone within society is that the roots of social problems may well end, but that is not the focus of concern. Krishnamurti was a modern mystic who was appalled by the social conditions in India, but he responded in the traditional mystical fashion: for him, social reform could not answer the fundamental problem but could only scratch its surface—until the nature of man was changed radically, all other change was useless and irrelevant.[3] Outward conditions merely reflect our inner states. For example, to end war we would have to end the war within us (anger, hatred, lust for power).[4] Until that happens, we will be dealing only with symptoms and not the causes, and thus war will not end.

In sum, under classical mystics' view, we would need to change human beings along mystical lines to change society. But the important point is that mystics are interested in the inner transformation of persons, not any cumulative social effects on our world.[5] Any social change is neither necessary nor sufficient to bring about what is really needed and hence is not a concern. Again, this does not mean that all mystics are selfishly concerned with only their own experiences or salvation and cannot be bothered with other people's problems, but it does mean that even moral classical mystics are not out to make social changes. When a radical inner transformation is required to end suffering, aiding one person at a time in his or her own transformation may be the best that can be done.

Religious Social Reform

It is also important that each religious tradition as a whole be distinguished, here as elsewhere, from the beliefs and practices of mystics within that tradition. Mystical selflessness pushes mystics toward social indifference, but the religious traditions in which mystics develop will be the product of more influences than just mystical experiences. Different streams of religiosity merge in forming any religious tradition. The mystical strand will influence doctrines but will never be the only source and in fact may not be the major source of beliefs and practices. (Plotinus' Neoplatonism is a mystical way of life without other strands of religiosity; thus, it is no surprise that it has no political or social philosophy.)[6] Most members of any given religion, being unenlightened, may take the social realm as an important focus of attention. Indeed, that in most cultures and eras the religious leaders were among the political leaders, reflecting a unity of "church" and "state" within one order, reveals that the religious normally have a great interest in the social realm.

Mystics, of course, may have an effect on those in their religious tradition who are interested in social reform. Mystics as exemplars of their tradition may inspire the nonmystics to a more impartial or selfless application of their own nonmystical ideas, such as social reform. In addition, mystics still on the path to enlightenment may see value in social reform since they still have unenlightened beliefs (although there is the danger in any social reform that the unenlightened will simply be imposing their self-will under the guise of social justice). Moreover, others within a tradition who have had isolated mystical experiences may also believe greater social reform is worth pursuing. There would, however, be limits to how much mystics' lives of voluntary simplicity can be a model for reforming society as a whole—one could not expect, for example, monastic poverty to be expanded to the abolition of all private property in a society, to say nothing of celibacy. Social reforms within a religious group may also have a limited impact on society in general. For example, Buddhists and the devotional theists of medieval India—the *bhakti*—in theory rejected caste distinctions within their religious groups, but this had little impact on their society at large.

Laozi, reflecting his Chinese cultural interests, had a political program, and thus one would expect that those in Chinese history who were influenced by his work would be more likely to protest political and social problems. And religious Daoists (as opposed to the philosophical ones) did indeed do that. Buddhism, on the other hand, proved itself very adaptable to different sociopolitical conditions, which one would expect if mysticism heavily influenced it. In the twentieth century, Buddhists supported socialism in Burma, capitalism and a monarchy in Thailand, and communism in China and Laos.[7] Western religions that accept this realm as real (albeit dependent upon a greater underlying reality) are more likely to have social reformers than are Asian traditions such as Advaita that dismiss this realm as valueless or unreal. When Christianity entered the mainstream of Roman culture it moved from an in-group ethic to add political and societywide dimensions to its way of life.[8] Thus, some mystics in the Western traditions, reflecting their religion, would be more likely to see social reform as valuable, even if most confine easing suffering to face-to-face interactions. People who have "ecstatic" experiences may well value our realm enough to engage in political protest and to form movements of revolt, but enlightened mystics and those among the unenlightened who are seriously cultivating a mystical way of life are less likely to do so.[9] Such indifference to social reform would obviously have the conservative effect of reenforcing the social status quo, thereby helping the ruling classes, even if that is not the mystics' intent.

It might be argued that conditions in our realm could be altered to make the path to enlightenment easier for a greater number of people; thus, rather than direct attention toward helping a few with their inner transformation, mystics should try the type of help in which a large number of people are each helped a little in their material conditions. If, for example, poverty and war were ended, greed and hatred might be reduced and more people would make greater progress on their path to enlightenment. Or, since individual self-interest is at the center of capitalism, installing socialism might weaken self-centeredness. Or, if we believed a long series of rebirths await us all, we might want to improve the conditions of everyone—e.g., whites in America might be inclined to improve race relations because they would realize that they or loved ones may be reborn as blacks.

But social work also presents the danger that the worker may get caught up in our realm. We may lose the transcendent dimension in thinking that reforming this realm will help bring about enlightenment. There is also the problem of knowing what would be best for a large number of people or how to help some while not hurting others—by definition, the unenlightened will not have the correct view of reality and thus not know how best to help. (What would count as helping would also depend on one's factual beliefs and thus may well vary from tradition to tradition—e.g., Buddhists are more likely than Christians to set up hospitals for birds.) Economic prosperity would allow more people to spend more time on their spiritual life, but Buddhist teachers have pointed out the danger of making people so comfortable that they, like the gods in the heavens, will not be inclined to seek enlightenment. And there is no reason to believe that most people would become interested in pursuing a mystical way of life; most would focus instead on new types of material well-being that would only further solidify the hold of this realm. Mysticism was a more influential strand of religiosity when social and economic conditions were worse precisely because its aim is to escape this world. It is no coincidence that a high point of mysticism in the West was at the time of the Black Death and the Hundred Years War. When conditions improve, people focus more on improving their own conditions in this world.

Thus, social help may not do much mystical good and may do damage by making us too comfortable. It is a matter of dealing with the symptoms of suffering and not the root causes (desire and the lack of knowledge of the fundamental nature of reality). But again the more basic problem is that we would have to take seriously a realm that mystics do not take to be fully real. To mystics, it is better to devote our energies to the inner transformation needed to become enlightened, whatever the social conditions.

The Problem with Politics

Mystics would have another problem with politics even if they take this realm as real. Politics deals with maintaining and changing the broad social structures of a society, and mystics may be aware of the difference between the way their society is and a way that would be more conducive for others to gain enlightenment. Concern for others could be manifested, for example, in justice in constructing and applying laws.[10] But the classical mystical approach would be to change one person at a time, and changing social conditions by transforming individuals one at a time would prove difficult at best. A more likely route would be working directly on the level of social structures, not changing all individuals first who would then alter the laws. That would require using such social mechanisms as laws and could only be done with the aid of nonmystics. Thus, to bring about social-level change in this manner, mystics would have to combine forces with the unenlightened, who do not see reality as it truly is.

Moreover, politics is a matter of power struggles. The inherent deception, ruthlessness, and general Machiavellian nature of politics presents a major problem for mystics who insist on honesty in all forms.[11] Enlightened mystics, in dealing only with the person in front of them and not thinking about others, would also be inclined to see things in terms of black and white, not shades of grey. Their precepts for inner change are in terms like "Do not kill," not "Kill as few as is reasonably possible to achieve your objective." The enlightened would also have trouble making political compromises with the unenlightened when they believe the unenlightened are living in a world of delusion. Those who believe they know the truth about the status of our realm would not take our unenlightened interests seriously—trying to compromise with characters in a dream would not occur to someone who is awake. The unenlightened majority will be defining what is "good" for the society, not the enlightened. As noted, what the unenlightened want—more material comfort, security, and so forth—may seem so unimportant that even trying to adjust society in such a way that enlightenment may be a little easier for the many will not be worth doing—it may even be counterproductive by making the unenlightened too comfortable. To mystics, for example, democracy may be seen as increasing divisiveness and tension in a society and thus as being antimystical. The inability to compromise may seem overly rigid to the unenlightened, but it is the result of a sense of absolute truth. (That it may lead in the end to having little effect will be discussed below concerning Gandhi.)

Another problem is that the political order inherently involves coercion rather than persuasion by teaching, actions, or example. Laws or any rewards and punishments on a societywide scale are an attempt to constrain behavior, and thus to manipulate others, even if it is for their own good. Laws are not freely adopted restrictions on one's own behavior, as with mystics adopting a monastic code. Mystics commend simplifying our lives, but there is no point in forcing others to conform by law. Laws at most will bring about a change in behavior by enforcing an ethical code through civil authorities, but they will not do much toward altering a person's inner disposition. Laws cannot require that we act out of humility or love, no matter how they constrain our actions. Adopting precepts for one's own behavior is the first step on the mystical path toward changing dispositions and beliefs, but requiring others not so inclined to act a certain way will not change their inner disposition; they will simply minimally comply or will look for ways around the regulation. In short, we cannot transform a person from the outside. Laws against racist practices in America and untouchability in India are examples of the problem. From the mystical point of view, laws are a form of violence, of imposing one's views on others. (Also note that since laws cannot control the motive for compliance, they cannot force the governed to have an inner motive of other-regarding concern. Thus, whether we can make society more *moral* by enacting laws to increase justice is also an issue.)

In sum, laws or other political manipulations are not effective in bringing about the inner transformation of concern to mystics. Such force is ineffective or even harmful to the mystical quest, since striving for any particular result shows attachment. The unenlightened may conform their actions to the laws for reasons totally unrelated to mystical selflessness, and thus the laws would have no effect at all on their mystical development. Moreover, changing laws without changing the inner nature of persons would mean that the same self-centered desires would persist in a society. A corollary of this is that any political change without an inner transformation of the people would be temporary. Thus, any revolution that does not change the inner person will be transitory, as the Russians' failed seventy-year experiment with communism demonstrates. No long-term help toward ending suffering will result from diverting energy from the mystical enterprise to such changes.

Another problem is broader: all institutions ossify, and so no matter how good the mystics' intentions, inevitably the unenlightened majority will take over. (Consider Thomas Jefferson's remark about the need for a revolution in every generation.) Groups are natural even among mystics. Monasteries and other communal groups can be very useful for a mystic's personal cultivation. They can provide teaching of doctrines, training in techniques, and evaluations of experiences. They can also make simplified living easier, both through simpler lifestyles and the abolition of private property. Obedience can lessen the ego by having one's decisions made by others. But institutionalization can kill the original driving spirit. This applies as much to religious institutions as to secular ones, as the constant need to create new Christian monastic orders and reform old ones in the Middle Ages indicates. Franciscans went from the ideal of Francis's poverty within a few generations to a prosperous institution. And when religious and secular orders combine, as is the case in traditional societies, the problem is only aggravated.

Power corrupts as much in religion as elsewhere. Thus, institutions even within mysticism may become obstacles. Once again mystics may conclude it is better to engage in face-to-face actions than to devote energy to institutions. (This has not stopped all mystics from being concerned with forming and reforming institutions. Even Shankara set up monastic orders for individuals to work toward their own enlightenment.)

The history of any religion shows a problem with institutions. The West has been shaped more by Greco-Roman values than Jesus' eschatological religion. It is a history of violence and intolerance—as Blaise Pascal said, "Men never do evil so completely and cheerfully as when they do it from religious conviction." Christianity has been the legitimating force for many totalitarian regimes. Christian scriptures have been used to justify all sorts of social practices that were later judged to be unjust. But there is also another problem: its scriptures have been used to justify *both sides* in social disputes—capitalism and socialism, slavery and abolition, polygamy and monogamy, each side in wars, and so on.[12] Today we can add civil rights, capital punishment, nuclear disarmament, and all issues in medical ethics. In such circumstances, it is hard to find one abiding "social ethic" in Christianity.[13] Our social values instead come from sources other than religious doctrines, and this raises the issue of whether religious leaders are just rationalizing their actions really based on other values by claiming, "God is on their side."[14] Why mystics would want to take sides on any political issue present in their culture at that moment is not clear, especially if they reject the entire social realm as not an ultimate reality. In particular, the modern form of tribalism—nationalism—must seem to classical mystics to be an artificial creation that has no basis in reality. It is a form of self-love that can only strengthen attachments by fixing an idol in the mind that interferes with seeing reality as it truly is.

Another problem is that mystical precepts are first-person forms of advice on what you should do, not laws telling other people what they can or cannot do. The mystics' response to a dilemma such as whether to have an abortion is that we should empty ourselves of all sense of self, and the answer will appear (as directed by their beliefs and values). Laws, from this perspective, are acts by a group of people telling *other people* what they can or cannot do. There is also an issue of the interactions between others. What should we do if we see another person being attacked? The precept "turn the other cheek" addresses what we should do when *we* are attacked—some religious people would willingly die rather than fight back—but the precept does not tell us what to do if we see *someone else* being attacked. That introduces a problem of third-person interests that does not arise on a path of mystical self-cultivation. Similarly, expanding "love your enemies" into a law or national foreign policy requires third-person considerations not given in face-to-face interactions. This means politics produces a new level of concerns to the realm of nescience that would move mystics further away from their concern.

All of this leads to the conclusion that any political reform will not solve the fundamental problem of life as mystics see it. Not only is this realm not finally real, social engineering by means of laws will not address our most fundamental suffering. Rearranging the structures of an artificial world only directs attention away from where it should be—on the transcendent. Any social reform without an inner spiritual reform is valueless and makes social reform an end in itself and thus an attachment. As the saying goes, mystics may have first to step into the mud (of the realm of nescience) to help pull someone out of the mud; but this is best limited to helping individuals, not to getting mired in the additional level of political action. In social reform, one must think in more abstract terms of long-range goals, weigh the welfare of different groups, and make other judgments based on utilitarian or other considerations—all in contrast to acting immediately and spontaneously, as with mystical action.

In short, politics introduces a level of problems alien to classical mysticism. Even if a mystic were not to dismiss moral concerns as a reflection of our unenlightened point of view, still politics present a different level of action and thus a new problem. It is not that the realm of morality is cut off from the realm of politics: each involves interpersonal actions, and all interpersonal actions may well have political consequences. So too political beliefs (such as the divine right of kings) may be part of the background beliefs internalized by mystics out of which they act. But mystics focus only on the immediate interaction at hand and thus restrict their considerations to face-to-face situations.

Social Virtues

Virtues that involve the social level illustrate the problems just discussed. Consider "justice." To most mystics, justice is a matter of the next life (through remedies from God or *karma*), not "social justice" within this realm. Granted, a radical impartiality governs mystics' actions, and thus to the extent such impartiality is equated with "social justice" there is no problem. But once impartiality is extended beyond individual face-to-face actions problems arise. Firstly, mystics would have no interest in, for example, equality before the law for the disenfranchised or the just distribution of material goods or equal opportunity for worldly success, since nothing on the social level addresses the fundamental misalignment with reality that we all suffer. From a mystical point of view, any redistribution of wealth or other adjustments without changing the dispositions of the people will leave the world basically as it is. Eckhart's reaction to the conditions of his time discussed in Chapter 12 would be typical of mystics' responses. Secondly, mystics would not accept any attempt to treat religious ethics solely as a matter of social ethics—e.g., substituting social justice for individual acts of compassion to those in need. Social action moves people further from the transcendent dimension of action by focusing only on the social level. Certainly the idea of loving humanity in general but not caring for the person in front of them would be the opposite of the mystics' approach to action. Thirdly, the suffering of concern to mystics applies to everyone—the "oppressors" need as much help as the "oppressed," and rearranging portions of our world would not help either party with their real problem. The Buddha would counsel the rich as well as the poor without arguing for change in the social conditions. He intervened on the battlefield but expressed only concern for the people involved, not the politics of the conflict. In general, mystics are tolerant of all, not judging anyone but accepting them as they are. This may lead to acts that we would consider unjust, such as letting a murderer go rather than letting others kill him (as with Āryadeva) since their unenlightened reactions would only protract their own suffering and further the cycle of violence. In sum, one would not expect to find concepts related to "social justice" in religious traditions heavily influenced by mysticism. And indeed, the Asian traditions discussed in Part II do not have any such concepts. The concepts are Western, and the fight for justice is found in Abrahamic religions.

The same applies to "just wars." The concept has roots going back to the Roman Cicero but was adopted by Christians after Christianity became Rome's official religion. (Previously military duty was considered incompatible with being a Christian; those expecting an imminent apocalypse would certainly have no reason to fight.) Augustine, who was mystically minded, developed the classic defense. Noting that the Old Testament has God repeatedly waging wars, he concluded wars are a means of judgment commanded by God—indeed, to Augustine wars against heretics were acts of *charity*. He tried to reconcile Jesus' more pacifist statements by interiorizing the ideas of loving one's neighbor and not resisting evil, i.e., applying them only to attitudes, not actions, thereby enabling Christian soldiers to practice them.[15] (He nevertheless inconsistently required absolute nonviolence in personal relationships, even denying the right to self-defense). Thus, as with the *Bhagavad-gītā*, inner peace need not be reflected in outer peace. Thomas Aquinas, another mystically minded thinker, also distinguished the person and the state, claiming that Jesus' remark "Those who live by the sword shall die by the sword" did not apply to official public acts. Thus, the military was accepted as a legitimate vocation in Christianity.

That a religion would adopt a "just war" concept is not surprising—some Buddhists advanced the idea and even Jainas permit wars as an exception to *ahimsā*. (Needless to say, religious authorities routinely declare wars to be "just," since the religious authorities are those accepted by the civil authorities.) But that mystics or those heavily influenced by them would be instrumental in the adoption is surprising. Not that all mystics are nonviolent or oppose war—the *Bhagavad-gītā* makes *dharma*-required wars an integral part of its way of life and Laozi accepted the inevitability of wars. (Many Hindus ended up restricting *ahimsā*, like Augustine on love, to personal, not governmental, actions.) Some Christian mystics supported the Crusades. However, the usual mystical response concerns what the individual soldier should do. The Quaker George Fox's advice is typical: if a soldier's conscience does not bother him, he is not ready to give up the sword.[16] It is not the mystical point of view to think in political terms of which wars are or are not justified or how much violence should be used to counter other violence—even whether force should be used to protect the innocent is the sort of third-person issue not central to mystical ways of life. In the *Bhagavad-gītā*, whether the war is justified is not Arjuna's concern but Krishna's; the rules of war were devised by others in the *dharma* texts; Arjuna's dilemma is not over those matters but is solely over whether to fulfill his duty or not. More generally, mystics probably would not consider which side might be more in the right in a given conflict, since wars involve hatred on a huge scale. (The effect again would be conservative—not to oppose their rulers' choice.) War may instead be seen as the opportunity for compassionate action to both sides. But the Abrahamic religions with their belief-claims about the reality of the world dominated by nonmystics' beliefs do make "just war" doctrines appear a natural accommodation to the world. And those Christians heavily influenced by mystics have ended up being quite fanatical in their violence.[17]

Another problem is the question of human rights, i.e., rights we all have simply by reason of our being human. The concept of "human rights" is a modern Western one, arising from the modern idea of each individual as being entitled to respect and dignity. It is often pointed out that classical cultures, both Western (including Greece) and Eastern, have no concept remotely connected to such rights. The idea is foreign to the *Bhagavad-gītā*, even with its concept of class duties for a functioning society, and the *Daodejing*. It is not that these traditions favor society over the individual but that the entire issue of rights as human beings does not arise. Scholars may argue that some rights are entailed by religious doctrines or practices (e.g., the right of all to get out of the realm of suffering or to choose a path to enlightenment, or the equality of all people before God, or impartiality requiring equality before the law), but the fact remains that the traditions do not think in terms of individuals' *social* rights within this world. If people in general in these cultures did not think in these terms, then it is not surprising that their mystics did not either. But more importantly, nothing in the idea of mystical selflessness would lead one to suspect that human rights would be relevant. Indeed, demanding rights would be an instance of unenlightened self-assertiveness and thus run counter to mysticism. The mystical freedom of enlightenment is simply not relatable to our freedoms in society. The only freedom relevant is the freedom to choose our actions (in order to make possible control of our future course), and that is not a "social right" but a personal ability. Thus, any focus on the rights of individuals or communities misdirects our energies.[18]

Mystical and Prophetic Religiosity

The mystics' lack of interest in social reform points to the validity of the commonly drawn distinction between "mystical" and "prophetic" religiosity. Prophets are part of the devotional strand of religiosity. They too allegedly have experiences of the transcendent, but theirs is an encounter with a distinct transcendent reality, not an inner realization of the ground of reality—i.e., not a mystical experience empty of content but a revelation filled with God's plans or commands for us. Of interest here is that prophets call for reforms of society to help the poor and oppressed and to remedy other social injustices, while mystics are even-minded to whatever occurs and indifferent to social conditions and thus to reform.[19] As Bertrand Russell noted, in mysticism there is the "absence of indignation or protest" but "acceptance with joy."[20] Prophets focus on social change in the world—redeeming the world—while mystics focus on inner change. This is not to say that mystics are necessarily asocial or immoral (as demonstrated in Part II) but only that prophets have another type of experience resulting in a different orientation to the world.[21]

Of course, the same person may have both types of religious experience. As Richard Woods notes, we cannot know what was going on in the minds of Isaiah or Muhammad or other prophets.[22] Prophets may well also have mystical experiences that they fit into a framework dominated by their revelatory experiences, and such experiences of selflessness may well affect their social activity. But the difference in how mystics and prophets weigh mystical and revelatory experiences comes down to which experience seems more powerful or significant to them. The Western belief-claim that this world is the creation of God becomes significant here. It permits a prophetic concern with the world and communal responsibility that is nearly absent in traditions that attach less reality to the world. Combining this belief-claim and the greater prominence given revelations in the West, one would expect more prophets in Western traditions. This is not to say that there have not been people classifiable as "prophets" in other traditions (e.g., the Buddhist Nichiren) but only that they are rarer. No religious tradition is purely "mystical" or purely "prophetic" but is a mixture of different strands of religiosity. A social conscience, however, has always been prominent throughout the Abrahamic traditions. Beginning with the Jewish prophet Amos, prophets have called for people to establish justice throughout the land or be destroyed by the wrath of God.[23] The changing course of human events—for which Westerners devised the concept "history"—becomes an arena for the work of God. It is, in John Calvin's phrase, the "theater of God's glory." Social "progress," another nonmystical modern idea, becomes important. But mystics give greater weight to mystical experiences. To them, our ultimate happiness lies outside of history. In India the factual belief-claim of the cycle of ages also blunts any call for progress in the social realm: we live in the dark age (kali-yuga), and nothing we can do will stop the further decline of the world. There is no hope for social improvement—the world-age will continue to decline until a new cycle begins. Karma will control our destiny; thus, all that can be done is an individual effort for improvement of his or her own karmic fate.

There have been, however, mystics in medieval Christianity who can also be classified as prophets—Birgitta of Sweden, Hildegarde of Bingen, and Catherine of Siena. Islam, with its greater emphasis on social justice than in Christianity, has also produced prophetic mystics starting with Wasil ibn Ata. This points again to the centrality of doctrines and values in any mystic's total way of life arising outside of his or her mystical experiences. Mystical experiences inform the ways of life, but they are never the total experiential base, and a mystic's tradition provides how these experiences are understood and will affect the significance the mystic attached to them. Mystical selflessness can inform a call for justice—indeed, the sense of radical impartiality could help a reformer. The sense of being in touch with the source of reality given in mystical experiences could also help energize a reformer.

But the basic problem remains that social reform requires taking the social realm as the arena in which our most important aims are developed. In addition, the more passive character of mysticism contrasts with the aggressiveness of the prophets. Neither the depth-mystical experience nor mindfulness provides an impetus motivating social action, and thus cultivating a full mystical way of life leads away from social action. In short, it is hard to provoke the "holy anger" of prophets with mystical detachment. Again, this does not mean we cannot have both types of experiences, but we must leave one point of view to adopt the other. Hence, there is no natural connection between the two—the more mystical one's bent of mind, the less one will be prophetic, and vice versa. Thus, one would expect mystical prophets to be rare. Conversely, when mysticism declines in a Western tradition (as with Protestantism), one would expect greater emphasis on reforming the world and less on an inner attainment of the transcendent realm. In sum, the overall actions and teachings of mystics suggest that the mystics' contribution to the development of the ethics of even a prophetic tradition lies in the inner development of individuals rather than in reforming group-level structures.

Modern Mystics

The conclusion for classical mystics is that the moral mystics express their compassion mainly in individual acts of charity, leaving untouched the structural evils of society.[24] One explanation is, as John Hick notes, a universal blindness to such social issues shared by all people prior to the modern sociological consciousness.[25] The economic and political institutions already in place in a society were accepted as ordained by God or as fixed as the laws of nature; they were unquestioned, and the issue of reform thus would not arise. As Hick notes, it would be anachronistic to look for doctrines of human rights or political or economic liberation in the "age of faith" when political power and responsibility were beyond the horizon of all except those at the top of the social hierarchy.[26] Social and economic stagnation was the norm. Only in the modern era did people begin to see the possibility of working on our realm to lessen suffering. (When Jefferson put "the pursuit of happiness" in the Declaration of Independence, it was a new idea—prior to that, people accepted that they would have to suffer through the "vale of tears" for their postmortem reward.) Thus, classical mystics could not be expected to see a remedy that others in their culture could not see, and we cannot project our modern political and social concerns back upon them. Modern reform movements, with roots in the prophetic strand of the Abrahamic religions and the secular humanistic thought of ancient Greek origin revived in the modern era, introduce a new perspective—an awareness that structural changes to the social realm may redress social evils and thus help others. Technological change also allows us to provide aid not only for the people we happen to encounter: modern communications can make us intimately aware of the suffering throughout the world, and modern technology makes it possible to deliver aid to the other side of the world. Thus, today we can see people globally in a way not possible before and in a way that brings social structures and more types of group action into the picture.

This change in social perspective and the societywide or global scope of work can affect mysticism. After all, mysticism, like all cultural phenomena, can evolve through interaction with other elements of culture. And there are figures in the modern world—from the Dalai Lama to the Ayatollah Khomeini—who are mystics and yet politically active. The field may be expanded to include people from Dag Hammarskjöld to the fundamentalist Jews in Israel who are asserting their political presence. In India, Neo-Vedāntins, claiming an Advaita heritage, have introduced socially active missions that help the lower castes, the poor, and the sick.[27] As Vivekānda put it, we should "worship Shiva in the poor, the sick, and the feeble." By their own admission, Neo-Vedāntins have been heavily influenced by Western and Christian ideas. Rāmakrishna, a product of a Westernized Indian middle class, is an example. Discussing the value of medical work he says: "Hospitals, dispensaries, and all such things are unreal. God alone is real. . . . Why should we forget him and destroy ourselves in too many activities? After realizing him, one may, through his grace, become his instruments in building many hospitals and dispensaries."[28] (Why God would want us to build "unreal" things is not clear, but this shows the problem of mixing Advaita metaphysics and Western social ethics. In addition, note that personal cultivation is still central—if the end of mysticism is just to build more hospitals, it is not clear why one should bother with mysticism in the first place.) There are also modern mystics who take a more traditional approach to inner change and rejecting sociopolitical reform as a means of helping others (e.g., Krishnamurti). But people in the West who now take up meditation without adopting a full mystical way of life often become more involved with others.[29]

Two things should be noted about this change in modern times. First, it points once again to the fact that mystics are influenced by factors other than mystical experiences. Mystical experiences may be the most powerful or important experiences, but they are not the only experiences or only factors in determining a way of life. The factual belief of the world as a real arena in which people's lot can be improved and the value of social reform do not come from mystical experiences but from beliefs and values coming from other sources. Any modern evolution of mysticism incorporating social reform as a value will have to come from sources outside of meditation and mystical experiences themselves. (But the difficulty of accepting both the modern worldview that the world is fully real and adopting a classical mysticism will be the central issue of the next chapter.) Second, the lack of social action in classical mysticism is more than just the product of classical social beliefs—there remains the tension between the mystic's call for the personal development of inner stillness and the prophetic call to social reform. Mystical selflessness and each individual's experience of the ground of reality still remain central to a mystical way of life, and they are not fostered through social reform. Thus, one can still expect few social reformers among mystics even today.

Reinventing the Wheel of *Dharma*

Many Buddhists in the twentieth century became much more active with Western-type social projects in many Asian countries, both Theravādin and Mahāyānist, although most Buddhists remained more traditional. There was some shift from traditional forms of almsgiving to supporting schools, hospitals, and other public projects. Some Buddhists worked on "Buddhist economics" in the form of socialism and other ways to combat poverty, pollution, and other social ills. Some monks and laity became more politically active, e.g., those in Sōka Gakkai (one of the New Religions of Japan) or the Zen monks of Vietnam in the 1960s who carried on its monks' traditional opposition to foreign invaders (sometimes immolating themselves to bring attention to their country's suffering). Zen leaders also supported Japanese militarism and Zen monks helped to prepare Japanese soldiers for World War II.[30] A monk in Sri Lanka assassinated a politician in 1956, and monks now participate in the politics (and the religious violence) of that island nation. The Buddhist "just war" doctrine returned in the Thai fight against communists: one monk concluded (although many others disagreed) that it was not demeritorious to kill communists by arguing that such killing did not constitute murder "because whoever destroys the nation, the religion, the monarchy, such bestial types are not complete persons. Thus, we must intend not to kill people but to kill the Devil (Mara); this is the duty of all Thai."[31]

Some Western-oriented Buddhists have acknowledged the social and political indifference of traditional Buddhism. Buddhists have traditionally adopted the existing social and political structures of whatever society they entered (e.g., accepting the right of kings). Buddhism, like religions everywhere, was used to legitimate the classes in power.[32] But these modern thinkers are now rejecting this conservatism and are attempting to create a "socially-engaged Buddhism."[33] They emphasize the Buddha's few discourses addressed to laity's worldly needs (e.g., A III.29, IV.56; D III.180) and to kings (e.g., D I.59; I.175). The Mādyamika philosopher Nāgārjuna also gave advice to kings in his *Jewel Garland of Royal Counsels.*[34] The Mauryan King Asoka who practiced some form of Buddhism after conducting a bloody war is also taken as an exemplar of Buddhist politics. He instituted policies reflecting Buddhist values (e.g., nonviolence to people and animals and compassionate worldly actions in such matters as medicine). He was, however, an anomaly in Buddhist history, with only few imitators in over two thousand years.[35] He was also disillusioned with the effects of his reforms on his society, and his reforms did not survive his death intact (e.g., Brahmanic animal sacrifices soon returned). But he did expand Buddhism's social impact, especially in the area of nonviolence (e.g., some later kings abolished executions).[36]

Based on this history, the new thinkers are attempting to develop a form of Buddhism that will address Western interests in freedom, justice, wealth and poverty, human rights, and the environment.[37] For instance, Christopher Ives has given a complete rereading of Zen Buddhism along these lines.[38] However, the entire enterprise of creating a socially-engaged Buddhism is questionable. Religions certainly do evolve, and there are issues today that the religious did not have to face in premodern times that they can address today. But this does not mean Buddhism can be adopted to all new issues. Supposedly, socially-engaged Buddhism is "latent" in the Buddhist tradition but has been "inhibited in premodern Asian settings."[39] However, finding any doctrinal support for this claim is difficult. Claiming that Westerners after more than two millennia have discovered the "essence" of Buddhism free of all cultural accretions in a few peripheral passages from the Pāli canon (some of questionable authenticity) is absurd. This distorts Buddhism more than the typical Western exposition of Buddhism as a religion of only a few religious virtuosi. First, Buddhists have never been "disengaged" from society: the monks, nuns, and laity all interact with others—it was simply a different type of engagement with a different goal than these theorists want. The Buddha and the Bodhisattvas are exemplars of moral conduct toward others, although Buddhism is an "individual transcendentalism," as Robert Thurman says.[40] Second, how do we get from Buddhism's face-to-face, individualistic approach to answers for social issues? Institutional issues were not merely unaddressed by traditional Buddhists, no answers to them are entailed by the individualist approach.[41] They are an entirely new set of issues, and the individualist approach has no straightforward bearing on them. Earlier Buddhists (with a very few exceptions) did not address the latter because these problems were irrelevant to our fundamental suffering (*dukkha*). Suffering cannot be remedied by social and political action but only by escaping the chain of rebirths.[42] Political indifference was a straightforward consequence of this mystical religiosity.

In principle, the idea of changing social and political conditions so that a large number of people can overcome a little of their self-centeredness, greed, hatred, anger, or aggression can be a concern of mystics. Thus, mysticism can influence social reformers. The tension, however, between the mystical and prophetic stances was discussed above. Indeed, the socially-engaged Buddhists reflect this by completely abandoning the traditional transcendental orientation in favor of reforming the world toward social freedom for all and the improvement of social conditions. They differ from most social reformers in that they accept the idea that changing social structures without changing people's inner attitudes will not produce a permanent improvement.[43] But they are no longer interested in the transcendental dimension at all. They are not trying to make social conditions more conducive to mystical enlightenment for a greater number of people but making the social world an end in itself. *Nirvāna* is not different from this world (*samsāra*), so all we should do is make this world better. This approach misses the entire thrust of Buddhism's soteriological goal of getting out of the realm of suffering. Buddhists were not out to save the world or at best to save it by ending it one person at a time through the mystical inner transformation of each individual. The Buddha was not tempted to be a world-monarch (*cakkavatti*) since the world held nothing of value. The socially-engaged Buddhists concede both that they are not addressing the problem the Buddha addressed and that social reform will not bring about mystical enlightenment. They admit they are doing something else. There is a fundamental reorientation away from enlightenment to worldly matters that reflects their Western background more than Buddhism. Switching the focus from enlightenment to improvement of social conditions—"from a transmundane (*lokuttara*) to a mundane (*lokiya*) definition of liberation"[44]—is not merely to deal with issues previously unaddressed by Buddhists but radically to reorient Buddhism to the point that it is questionable whether it can be called "Buddhism" at all.

In sum, these thinkers are not giving "new readings to ancient Dharma" but creating something new—something modern and Western in foundation and outlook, no doubt with a Buddhist influence, but not a form of Buddhism. Or perhaps it should be seen as the final version of Buddhism for our dark age (*kali-yuga*): the Buddha said the purity of his doctrine would decline, and perhaps the switch "from a highly personal and other-worldly notion of liberation to a social, economic, this-worldly liberation"[45] is the end of the line.

Mahatma Gandhi

For a modern mystic who attempted to apply personal ethics to social-scale situations consider Mohandas Gandhi. He tried to show how the New Testament's "love your neighbor" and "turn the other check" could be applied politically and not just between individuals. Gandhi was a Hindu, but the influences for his social actions were not primarily Hindu. He accepted Advaita metaphysics (although he was a theist) as a basis for the claim that all life is one, but the influence from Hinduism on social matters was minimal. He defended most of the traditional religious Hindu system, including inherited class distinctions, but his stress on the equality of all people caused him to reject "untouchability." He learned of devotional love from the *bhakti* tradition from his mother. As a young man in England he read the *Bhagavad-gītā*, but later he gave it a symbolic interpretation, interiorizing the war as an allegory of the inner struggle we all go through; nevertheless, the text remained important to him for the rest of his life. His major non-Hindu influences were Jaina and Buddhist on nonviolence (*ahimsā*), the Sermon on the Mount, and such modern figures as Henry David Thoreau on civil disobedience, Leo Tolstoy, and John Ruskin. It should also be noted that he was not very impressed with the Christians he encountered. The personal and collective humiliations of Indians in British South Africa convinced him of the need for political action.

But Gandhi was a mystic. For him, God was ultimate reality, and all his efforts were directed toward attaining his release (*moksha*) through "reducing himself to zero." After the birth of his third child, he adopted a life of renunciation and self-restraint in all matters (*brahmacaryā*); that included celibacy as a shield against temptation, but it also comprised control of all the senses in thought, word, and deed. This personal self-rule (*svarāj*) was necessary truly to practice nonviolence. His highly ascetic form of mysticism was also the religious basis for his political activity. He had to purify himself continuously if he was to attempt to purify others—he was out to enlighten himself but through a means that focused on the help that would result for others. Indeed, his entire inner discipline was to prepare himself for the service of others. He reinterpreted the Indian concept of austerity (*tapas*) to mean self-suffering, even joyfully suffering death, for the sake of others. (Death, he said, held no terror for those who believed in a living God; he tried to turn even a massacre into a day of thanksgiving and joy.) Thus, his yoga was one of service to others, not just inward meditation. Fasting and intense prayer preceded his acts of civil disobedience, and he maintained his disciplines during them. This was a form of *karma-yoga* in that he held that self-purification could be attained only through doing one's duty without any attachment to the fruits of one's actions. But most important is that his devotion to God (Reality) was manifested in political and economic activity—his way to God was through social action for others.

The importance of nonviolence (*ahimsā*) to his social efforts cannot be over-emphasized. Gandhi saw nonviolence as the "universal *dharma*" (*sādhārana-dharma*). He said that "nonviolence is the law of our species as violence is the law of the brute," and that everyone will respond to it. But it was not just a tool to attain political ends—it was a fundamental principle of reality. He, however, was never as radical as enlightened Jainas in applying this to the personal level, arguing that we cannot be completely free of killing in our personal or social lives no matter what we do. He accepted exceptions to nonviolence (e.g., killing a suffering calf to end its suffering)—most importantly, if one is forced to choose between violence and cowardice in the defense of the innocent or doing something that would degrade one's dignity or self-respect, one must choose violence. But on the scale of a society as a whole and on the level of corporate action, nonviolence is absolute. Any war of self-defense is rejected. A country should not resist invasion but accept annihilation rather than fight. Even any violence as a means to a legitimate end is rejected: one's attitude is what has to be changed, and this would not occur if even a little violence was acceptable.

However, for Gandhi nonviolence is not merely the passive avoidance of harm but an active means to political change. Gandhi's nonviolence is filled with positive action: compassion in thought, words, and deeds toward one's enemies. It is not passive submission to a tyrant's will but suffering with the aim of an inner conversion of one's enemies. This was central to his experiments in "grasping Reality/Truth" (satyāgraha). Inwardly, this meant discipline and selfless devotion to duty; the idea is to attain an even-mindedness to friend and foe and to all that happens. Outwardly are acts of total, nonviolent noncooperation. His own acts included boycotts (including English courts and schools), strikes, nonpayment of taxes, the march to the sea to make salt, imprisonment, abandoning Western medicine and technology, abandoning English clothing and the English language, and general self-sufficiency. Satyāgraha is not surrender or capitulation or cowardice. It is a weapon only of the strong and the brave—one must be willing to lay down one's life, to stand quietly before cannons and be blown to bits.

The theory behind satyāgraha is that satya is a power that can accomplish something—it is literally the "power of truth" to move the hearts of others.[46] The objective is to help the oppressor as much as the victim—the power of reality will work an inner change within the oppressor. (Entailed by this are the beliefs that humans are basically good and can be converted.) This can only be done by converting them inwardly, not just embarrassing people in the court of public opinion. Nor is changing the laws enough—that would be a form of external coercion. Violence only begets violence, and thus an inner transformation of the aggressor is needed. Anything less would only be suppressing violence temporally. Thus, one should give material goods to thieves—eventually they will have a change of heart and give up their ways. Gandhi's advice to Jews in World War II was to accept their fate nonviolently in order to convert the Nazis. The oppressor is bound to turn away from evil if enough victims continue to suffer long enough. To accomplish this, however, the satyāgrahin needs an infinite capacity for suffering and patience. His or her intention must remain pure: one never acts for one's own gain, but only for others. But given a just cause, the capacity for endless suffering, and the total avoidance of violence, Gandhi was confident that victory was certain in the long run. (Gandhi did, however, have doubts about many of his followers. He realized that an unarmed army of trained satyāgrahins would be needed to effect social change, but he had to call off some actions because of their violence.) But he was sure this way was grounded in reality (satya). Indeed, according to Gandhi a belief in God was needed to be a satyāgrahin, since God (Reality) would bring the victory—the satyāgrahin's role was but to suffer patiently. For his part, Gandhi said he was willing to suffer for the sake of others for a thousand years.

This religious foundation became more prominent in his later years. He believed no positive change would be permanent unless he acted for pure motives and changed the hearts and minds of others. But his uncompromising stance ended up limiting his political impact. In South Africa, he helped the Indians gain more self-respect, but there was no political changes. In India, he did accomplish some changes, but more through embarrassing the British than through the inner transformation he sought. His lack of a role in the final settlement that granted India its independence reveals the problem. He had been instrumental in the Indian National Congress gaining power, but he left the organization when Jawaharlal Nehru agreed to fight for England in World War II in exchange for India's independence after the war. For Gandhi, nonviolence was not merely an expedient means to an end but a fundamental principle, and he would not compromise it. He founded a religious community, not a political party. He was out to transform both Indians and the British, not exchange one unenlightened government for another. In sum, he was trying to lead an entire country to *moksha*.[47] He did want to free India from modernity and return to a self-sufficiency on a village scale, but his goal was to change persons—self-rule (*svarāj*) on a personal scale (personal self-control, self-respect, and nonviolence), not just self-rule for India. Only that would bring about a permanent positive change. In the end, this left him out of the picture when the final political solution for India's independence was worked out.

It can be argued that Gandhi's nonviolent resistance actually slowed down the process of India's independence by helping to control violence and thus making the conditions easier for the British. The counterargument is that he helped independence by keeping the opposition mainly nonviolent—otherwise, British policy would have prevented them from giving in to the violence and letting India go. (It can also be argued that such action needed a particular cultural setting: it would only work in a liberal culture such as England or America—if Gandhi had tried it in a French or German colony, he would have been unceremoniously killed.) But it is more likely that the same deal involving World War II would have been worked out even if Gandhi had never conducted his political activity: Indian opposition to English rule existed long before Gandhi and England could not have fought the war and ruled a resisting India at the same time, and so they had to work out a deal.

However, Gandhi realized that his influence was waning rapidly by the end of his life—he said shortly before his death, "Everyone is eager to garland my photos, but nobody wants to follow my advice."[48] His fasting to quell the intense rioting after the announcement of the independence plan partitioning the subcontinent was ignored—and his violent death at the hands of Hindu fundamentalists who opposed the division of the subcontinent only accented his lack of success.[49] He had some disciples (notably the land reformer Vinoba Bhave) and has influenced some people outside of India (notably Martin Luther King, Jr.). However, in India he had little lasting social influence, as the continuing violence between religious groups indicates. Now he is just a historical figure.

Gandhi may have shown the limitations to social change through mysticism: if social actions did not work in British India, they probably would have limited effect elsewhere. In addition, he may have shown the indispensability of a charismatic leader in any attempt of mystical social action. It also must be admitted that the combination of influences that created a new nonviolent form of social action introduced something new to mysticism. It does not reflect classical Hinduism—indeed, Hindus accused Gandhi of distorting their tradition by his social concern.[50] It is a product of the modern era, both in its social focus and in its use of multiple Western and Eastern sources.

However, none of that changes the fact that his mysticism had a strong political component. His yoga was not merely a form of "contemplation in action" but "contemplation in social action." This keeps his yoga from fitting neatly into categories of either "this-worldly" or "otherworldly" since there was a focus on both this-worldly action and the transcendent. But this yoga was clearly moral, although he was also looking out for his own salvation: he was concerned with helping both the victims of oppression and also the oppressors by changing their hearts and minds. His "experiments with Truth/Reality" may not have proven that nonviolence is in fact a fundamental law of human existence or that suffering can melt the heart of aggressors, but the mysticism of it all is undeniable.

Is Mysticism Necessarily Individualistic?

Even with Gandhi's social action the individual remained central, whether it was a victim or an oppressor: changing the social conditions was necessary and required group action, but his ultimate objective was to change souls, not just to create new social and political structures. He also stressed that each participant in a mass *satyāgraha* action must maintain his or her own individual responsibility and not relinquish his or her will to the group. The action was very much to be an aggregate of individuals working out their own salvation individually, and not one unified selfless unit in motion. In fact, one point that follows from the above discussions is that classical mystics are individualistic in the sense of emphasizing personal interactions over group actions. But this does not entail two contemporary senses of "individualism"—the modern liberal belief that the freedom of the individual is paramount (and thus that we each ought to be able to do whatever we want as long as we do not interfere with others) or the modern tendency to isolate mystical experiences from ways of life and to emphasize esoteric experiences.

It also makes sense to infer that classical mystics would be individualistic in the socio-scientific sense of explaining social phenomena as a collection of individual interactions. These mystics do not address this issue, but the belief-claims of the various traditions entail that conclusion. Individualism in this sense is that all social phenomena can be explained as the additive result of individual interactions, and all social concepts can be translated without remainder into individual ones.[51] The opposite—social holism—sees reality as having a level of social structure above individuals that somehow constrains our actions; thus, society cannot be reduced to the sum of individuals, and social wholes cannot be explained solely by the actions of individuals. More extreme holists see the "individual" as merely an abstraction from the concrete web of interactions constituting the true reality, thereby raising the issue of what reality individuals could contribute to the whole and hence whether they are real at all. But the basic issue is: is society merely a collection of individuals, or is it something more, a reality in its own right?

An individualist need not deny there are any social phenomena—one has only to claim that social phenomena can be *explained* in individualist terms. Thus, the existence of mystical groups (monasteries and so forth) does not entail holism—the community's actions need only be explainable in terms of the sum of the individuals' actions. Similarly, mystics can work within society and still see society as merely an aggregate of individuals to interact with. The *Bhagavad-gītā* does recognize social structures, but they are the creation of Krishna—what is ultimately real is only the ground of reality and perhaps individuals. People are not reduced to a social role. Our social role is merely a mask we temporarily put on, and there is no sense that society is a distinct level of reality. One may think that Daoists would be more holistic than individualistic in their thinking (since the Chinese emphasize the social), but again nothing suggests that. The issue was not explicitly addressed, but their writings emphasize only the acts of individuals and entail that people are not reducible to Confucian roles. Western mystics would be more likely to affirm the existence of social phenomena (reflecting their more realistic view of the phenomenal world) than most Asian mystics, but nothing in their writings or actions suggests that social structures are real and influence our lives. With such a view, the idea of working on "social structures" becomes meaningless. (How realistic mystics' explanations of social phenomena are is another matter: for example, are wars merely the cumulative reflection of individuals' inner violence and fear? Without an inner transformation, can social ills still not be cured?)

Thus, society is reduced to a pile of individuals—a "nonsociety" of people. But mystics can accept that our ego is socially created, although they may affirm a transcendental self in addition to that personality. Western mystics and Sāmkhya-Yogins may accept such a self, but another branch of individualists maintain that part of what constitutes us is our interactions with others. This may seem to jibe better with the Buddhist no-self doctrine, but the no-self doctrine and the Advaita denial of any individual selves do not entail social holism, i.e., that social structures in fact constitute the ego's reality. In Advaita Vedānta, everything in the social world is dismissed as unreal. Buddhists come close to denying that there in fact are any social phenomena at all, i.e., that all alleged social phenomena are only the accumulation of individual ones. The Buddhist ontology of empty "elements of experiences" (*dharma*s) constituting a person and everything else phenomenal is an individualistic ontology. There are no social elements to reality, and even the "self" is constituted by parts with no abiding core. On the ontological issue, in most subtraditions our interactions with others are not emphasized but only the impermanence of the parts and the lack of any abiding whole. That is, not only do Buddhists deny a social level, they deny any "individuals" too—only parts exist. (The interconnected whole of Indra's web in the *Avatamsaka Sūtra* is arguably an exception, but it is not the standard Buddhist ontology.) An individualism thus is the appropriate conclusion for Buddhism. Even "socially-engaged Buddhism" theorists admit that traditionally Buddhists see society as "no more than the aggregate of the individuals composing it."[52] Nothing about a social whole constitutes what is real. Each karmic stream of becoming—each "person"—is conditioned by other elements and empty of anything permanent. Thus, each karmic stream is constituted by conditioned parts, but it has its own course. Each stream interacts with other such streams, but the streams are not constituted by other streams nor responsible for them. There is no role for social wholes in this view—society is simply the sum of all the individual karmic streams. In the *Bhagavad-gītā* and the other Indian traditions discussed in Part II, such karmic individualism also prevails.[53] The traditions tried to temper the harshness of this with "merit transfer" and "group *karma*," but the inherent individualism of the basic doctrine was always the prevailing belief.

It is only natural that mysticism, with its focus on personal inner experiences, should be individualist in nature. It is an instance of what William Inge called the hardness of all ancient ethics—that no one can do anything for anyone else.[54] Everyone must travel the mystical path for themselves and do their own mystical cultivation. Everyone must have their own experiences and are responsible only for themselves. Any "social realities" would not fit in this picture—it is a matter only of individuals and the transcendent reality. Community is not the way to connect to the transcendent. This does not mean that there are no mystical groups or that mystical experiences cannot occur in a group setting, nor is it to deny that there is a social dimension to mystical ways of life. But it does mean that in this strand of religiosity the center of the way of life is each person ultimately working out his or her own salvation alone.

Conclusion

From the above, one can see that there are reasons mystics typically do not participate in social reform nor are very effective when they do. The problem is more than just the premodern belief that the realm of change cannot be improved: mystics are focused on the eternal and are not concerned with the things of this world outside of that context. Inner reform is central and cannot be replaced by social reform. It is not so much that the world cannot be repaired as that it is not worth bothering with at all. No amount of social or technological change will correct the problems of living that mystics find central. In addition, we cannot derive social answers from the mystical solution. Social-level answers cannot be deduced from individualistic precepts. Mystical freedom—freedom from attachments and thus not wanting or needing anything—simply does not relate to social and economic freedoms. Mystical concepts of "right" and "wrong" cannot be translated into social concepts of justice or equality. Mystical selflessness cannot be an impetus to changing social conditions in such circumstances. External forms of reform attempt to dominate and manipulate and thus cannot be effective in producing an inner change. Liberals see humans as changeable by changing social structures; thus, solutions to our problems lie on the social level. Mystics see the opposite: only through an inward change can any outward changes be effected, and, they would add, with the inward change the outward changes are no longer needed. Society cannot make people virtuous no matter how much it regulates actions. Thus, devoting energy to reorganizing social institutions is a waste of time. Accepting society as it is therefore is the norm for these mystics, not restructuring it (as with Laozi).

Again, this does not mean all mystics are selfishly focused only on their own lives—many mystics have been great workers—but only that their help is limited to beings immediately in front of them and that help on the mystical path is vital. (Nor is it the case, as is often asserted, that mystics bifurcate responsibility: they handle the inner life and leave social problems for others to deal with. This claim misses both the comprehensive nature of a mystical way of life and that mystics advance what they think is the total solution to the fundamental problem of life.) To the unenlightened, this will look like mystics are leaving the world to the unjust and thus that they are neglecting their social responsibility—indeed, mystics look like they are trying to escape reality. Similarly, the mystics' idea that the final cure to all human ills lies inwardly in the experience of the ground of reality may look incredibly unrealistic to the nonreligious. But mystics have not set out to cure social ills but to help individuals, and for this only a radical inward change is worth devoting energy toward.

In principle, mystics can adopt social reform—mystical experiences do not entail other-regardingness but that can be opted for, and similarly social action can be opted for. But for social action be adopted into the mystical life, mystics must adopt the belief-claim that our realm is more than just the stage on which we individually develop our religious career. (If this world is accepted as real, one can still accept that human society is incurable—a tenet of traditional Christianity—and yet act on a social scale to ease the suffering present in the world to the extent possible.) Without such a realism, social problems are at most just opportunities for the soteriological development of oneself and others. The sociological cause for such a new belief may be that in modern times we now believe that social and natural conditions can be improved and thus that the suffering of many people can be alleviated by group action; this belief also gives us hope about the future of our realm. Other beliefs are also necessary. For example, if we think people are inherently "sinful," we would be more inclined to see a need for institutions to educate and control people and thus to think in terms of social structures; on the other hand, if we think people are inherently good, we would not see the need for such institutions and would focus on individual development.

However, the mystical inward focus still makes the idea of social-level reform very hard to advocate. The type of action that is appropriate for the mystical quest is still face-to-face, and the social scale they see as useful for this is at best their immediate community. Switching to larger-scale action or social-level reform would change their focus dramatically—material needs can be dealt with by social action but not the inner transformation that will permanently end our suffering. There is also the possibility that people will get caught up in the temporal and will turn away from the transcendental reality. Moreover, it is safe to assume that physical conditions and social injustices were much harsher in premodern societies than they are today, and yet mystics at the time did not believe the conditions had to be changed. If the mystical quest did not appear to classical mystics to be incompatible with social conditions then, why would they want social change today when conditions are no doubt better? Any further improvement would be irrelevant from their point of view (and may make people too comfortable to focus on anything but material satisfaction), and nonmystics would no doubt not be particularly interested in reform simply to improve conditions for the quest for enlightenment.

It is also important to remember that valuing the social realm would have to come from outside the mystical experiences. If mystical experiences give any ontological values, it is that there is another dimension to reality than the one we normally experience, that that reality is more real and the source of this realm, and thus that that dimension must be valued supremely. The prophetic strand of religiosity accepts that the natural realm is not fully real but dependent upon a transcendent reality and still takes this realm seriously as a reality. The mystical stance attaches reality primarily if not exclusively to the transcendent, and this makes the notion that the world is of value in its own right very difficult to connect to mysticism. Only if values from outside mystical experiences dominate in a mystical tradition will social reform even be considered. But even in "world-affirming" cultures, moral mystics most often express other-regarding concern only in face-to-face actions. The strong effect of mystical experiences is that the mystic's task is to live in the world as it is, not to alter it.

Notes

1. If mystics have paranormal powers to radiate love or otherwise affect people during meditation, that would be a type of social action (since it affects everyone and not just the people they personally encounter), even if it does not affect social structures. Bodhisattvas creation of Buddha-fields, which have ideal conditions for attaining Buddhahood, can also be seen as a type of social action since people will be comforted and the aim is to help their religious advancement toward enlightenment.

2. Even in Judaism, where there is a strong emphasis on society, Hasidics emphasized personal religious redemption rather than the redemption of the nation or cosmos as a whole. They deemphasized restoration (*tiqqun*), the process by which messianic redemption is

enhanced by the collective efforts of the Jewish people as a whole, in preference to personal communion with God (*devequt*, "cleaving"), a process by which individuals uplift their souls into contact with the divine powers. Joseph Dan, "Hasidism: An Overview," *The Encyclopedia of Religion*, vol. 6, ed. Mircea Eliade (New York: Macmillan, 1987), p. 207. Other Kabbalist mystics within Judaism are more interested in "repairing" the world through social ethics. There is also the notion of a "national salvation"—i.e., every Jew will be rewarded, when the redemption of the nation of Israel is reached, by sharing in the collective salvation and not just by a personal reward from God (Dan 1996, pp. 101-2). Also, the ideal for a Hasidic mystic is to help his community individually. When the mystics has reached his highest goal, he is confronted with the Buddha's choice of whether to remain hidden from the world or to become active in society, and the orthodox view is for the just man (the Zaddik) to "step down a little" from the highest form of communion with God in order to be nearer to his community (Scholem 1967, pp. 18-20).

3. Mary Lutyens, *Krishnamurti: The Years of Fulfilment* (New York: Farrar, Straus & Giroux, 1983), p. 42.

4. Ibid., pp. 40-53, 56-57.

5. It may also be the case that those who focus on virtues and character-reconstruction are more likely to focus on instances of individual interaction than those who advocate rule-following. The latter may be more interested in social reform since they think more abstractly in terms of the actions of everyone.

6. Plotinus did engage in helping others as, for example, a guardian of orphans. He also asked the Roman emperor to restore a ruined city for philosophers to rule by Plato's laws—"Platonopolis." But, if it had occurred, it would have been more like a monastery than a model for general social reform. In general, he advised his students to stay out of the political arena.

7. Harvey 2000, p. 118.

8. Early Christians did not see the political conquest of the world as their mandate. Once Christianity became the official religion of Rome, aspirations changed. But there have always been Christians who have separated themselves from the world (i.e., withdrawn from society at large) rather than try to reform it or who have restricted trying to change things by converting individuals and not by restructuring the laws of the land. (Some fundamentalists in America today advocate returning to this withdrawal.) There is also the danger that even the prophetically religious can get caught up in worldly matters of politics and lose their transcendental focus.

9. World-rejection and a lack of social concern can also occur in the devotional strand of religiosity. J. C. Ghosh writes of Vaishnavism in Bengal in the seventeenth and eighteendth centuries: "For two centuries the Bengali people sang, danced, and passed out in ecstatic trance while the world around them remained sunk in ignorance and misery."

10. All mystics can utilize the social abstentions necessary for maintaining any society—not killing without a socially accepted justification, not stealing, and so forth—for purposes of self-cultivation since these are a matter of not interfering with others. Social justice, however, would require positive acts toward others that only moral mystics could endorse.

11. See Scharfstein 1995 on politics throughout history.

12. Paul's claim that in Christ there is no slave or free (Gal. 3:28) is not a call for social reform by freeing the slaves. Elsewhere he exhorts slaves to obey their masters (Col. 3:22; Eph. 6:5; 1 Tim. 6:1-2; see also 1 Pet. 2:18-20). The point, to which mystics would agree, is that the slaves' social status is irrelevant to their being saved, just as it does not matter if one is male or female (Gal. 3:28). Similarly, Christians apparently began with communal

ownership (Acts 4:32-35) and groups have periodically attempted it (e.g., the Hutterites), although Christianity is now more closely tied to capitalism.

13. See Ernst Troeltsch, *The Social Teaching of the Christian Churches* (London: George Allen & Unwin, 1931) and *Religion in History* (Edinburgh: T. & T. Clark, 1991). Twentieth-century Christian theologians have disagreed with Troeltsch and have claimed that there is in fact a social ethic, although they differ among themselves as to what exactly it is.

14. Theistic mystics, as with the *Bhagavad-gītā*, may accept the social order of their society as ordained by God. This would obviously have a conservative effect: there would be no impetus to reject what God has instituted. At best, theists of the classical period would see a right to remove a king who is violating the system but not to question "the divine right of kings." Only under the influence of secular modern culture has this changed.

15. Augustine also interiorized Christian love as an inner attitude regardless of the act. Thus, love was separated from law. External actions could then be judged by civil authorities in terms of justice and laws regardless of the actor's inner Christian attitude.

16. Evelyn Underhill advanced a similar combination of mystical detachment and military service, thereby permitting participation in World War I. See Horne 1983, pp. 79-84.

17. See Greeley 1974 on Thomas Müntzer and John Bockelson of Leyden. Today religious violence is accelerating. See Juergensmeyer 2000.

18. It would be a mistake to conclude that because Buddhists and others do not believe in selves (egos) that therefore they would reject individual rights—i.e., asserting human rights would mean they believe in a self. As discussed in Chapters 8 and 9, the metaphysics of the nature of the self does not entail one moral position, and the same applies here.

19. See Nygren 1969 for a Protestant condemnation of mystics for not being prophetic (or moral).

20. Bertrand Russell, *Mysticism and Logic* (Garden City: Doubleday, 1957), 10. His definition of "mysticism" is restricted just to feelings, but his comment still applies.

21. That some religious persons can be prophetic does not mean that others have not been politically conservative. Thus, religion can function as either a force for change or for the status quo in different circumstances.

22. See Woods 1996.

23. Micah 6:8 states that what is good and what is required of us is "to do justice, to love kindness, and to walk humbly with your God."

24. Hick 1989, pp. 304-5, 338.

25. Ibid., p. 338.

26. Ibid., p. 305. To say that mystics knew they could not change social structures and so turned inwardly (Hick 1999, p. 178) assumes that they thought social change would have been relevant if only they could have effected it. It is being argued here that that is wrong.

27. See Fort 1998, pp. 172-81, for the question of whether Western-style social work can really be grounded in Advaita metaphysics. Trying to see social reform as present in classical Indian thought is to distort it through modern and Western glasses. Similarly, trying to use Eckhart to make a modern "socially-engaged Christian mysticism," as Matthew Fox (1980a, 1980b) seems to be doing, is also an anachronistic error.

28. Quoted in Geoffrey Parrinder, *Mysticism in the World's Religions* (New York: Oxford University Press, 1976), p. 41.

29. See Kipnis 1994. The extent to which Kipnis means actual "social reform" rather than "personal interaction" with others when he refers to "social action" is not clear. The sensitivity, cooperation, and caring he mentions in connection with the yoga students can be

more easily manifested in face-to-face interactions.

30. See Victoria 1997. Some Zen leaders in Japan made World War II look like a "holy war" for Zen.

31. Quoted in Ives 1992, p. 142.

32. One exception was the messianic groups connected to the Bodhisattva Maitreya: some followers believed in Maitreya's imminent return and his establishment of a new social order. These Buddhists became connected with anticolonial revolutionary groups.

33. The term comes from the Vietnamese Zen monk Thich Nhat Hanh (1967).

34. See R. Thurman 1983, 1992.

35. Stanley Tambiah could cite only a few kings in Thailand who claimed to be a Bo-dhisatta or a Dhamma-king (1976, pp. 96-97) and many of these of course did it only for self-serving reasons (p. 226).

36. Buddhism always had a limited impact in India—its emphasis on celibacy for monks and nuns and allowing anyone in effect to enter the sannyāsin stage of life limited its appeal.

37. Christopher Queen concedes that the spirit and substance of anything like a socially-engaged Buddhism first manifested itself only in the nineteenth century in Sri Lanka (1996, p. 20). This was after Western influence, in particular Christianity—indeed, this form of Sri Lankan Buddhism is called "Protestant Buddhism." See Gombrich 1988, pp. 172-97.

38. Ives 1992; see also Aitken 1984. Ives recognizes Zen's traditional conservative stance toward social structures (p. 66), but it is not, as he claims, just the result of a division of intellectual labor leaving social matters to Confucianism (p. 101). The focus on indi-viduals' spiritual development and enlightenment (which Ives also acknowledges) makes social matters irrelevant to mystics, even if a full religious way of life for the general Zen Buddhists included a Confucian-influenced social dimension.

39. Kenneth Kraft, "Introduction," in Eppesteiner 1988, p. xiii.

40. R. Thurman 1983, 1992. Gary Synder notes the individualist nature of Buddhism as a practical system of meditation, and admits that "[i]nstitutional Buddhism has been conspicuously ready to accept or ignore the inequalities and tyrannies of whatever political system it found itself under" (in Eppesteiner 1988, pp. 82-83).

41. For example, such doctrines as "skillful means" that permit enlightened Bodhisat-tvas even to kill are limited to the religious context of helping individuals and cannot be invoked to justify social actions by the unenlightened to help others for other purposes.

42. In principle, socially-engaged Buddhists could take the individualistic approach traditional to mysticism to solving social problems—i.e., if we transform each person, society will no longer have wars, oppression, and so forth. But the fact remains that this would have to turn mysticism around: the focus would no longer be on a transcendent reality but on using mystical techniques merely as means to end social problems.

43. Kenneth Kraft in Kraft 1992, p. 12; Ives 1992, pp. 134-35.

44. Christopher Queen, "Introduction," in Queen and King 1996, p. 11.

45. Ibid., p. 10.

46. In the term "satya" truth and reality are not distinguished. And its power as reality means that it can influence others and nature (e.g., tapas can have a purifying influence on those on whose behalf it is undertaken).

47. Gandhi was interested in reforming Indian society in many areas—education, sani-tation, and a sense of community. He was not interested in gifts to the poor but in creating jobs and a viable small-scale economy. But Gandhi's economics may not have been practical on a national scale. The quip made during his life was that it cost a fortune to keep him in a loincloth.

48. Krishnamurti said much the same about his followers. He said that even in India there was not a single person who had listened to him and had taken him seriously enough to actually undergo an inner change. The problem with adopting a full mystical way of life in a world deemed real will be discussed in the next chapter.

49. Gandhi disliked the title "Mahatma" because he thought only those who were socially effective truly deserved it.

50. See John Bowker, *Problems of Suffering in Religions of the World* (New York: Cambridge University Press, 1970), pp. 234-36. Rabīndranāth Tagore accused Gandhi of being too socially active and overly concerned with the material needs of the poor without giving sufficient consideration to the spiritual emancipation that must accompany the material. Ibid. Gandhi's concern with the spiritual emancipation was greater than Tagore's remark acknowledges, but Tagore is correct in that Gandhi's was not a traditional form of mysticism.

51. On individualism versus holism in the explanations of social phenomena, see R. H. Jones 2000, pp. 212-17.

52. K. Jones 1989, p. 202; see also R. Thurman 1983, 1992.

53. See Jhingran 1989, pp. 140-41.

54. Cited in Rist 1967, pp. 153, 260.

16

What Can Mysticism Contribute to Morality Today?

The basic conclusions on the relation of mysticism and morality were reached in the prior chapters of Part III: mysticism has less logical relevance for morality, either positively or negatively, than is often supposed. Mystical experiences do overcome a sense of self, but a positive, active other-regarding concern still has to be supplied from other sources. Mystics thus need not be moral. On the other hand, mystical experiences do not conflict with the presuppositions of morality, and thus mystics may adopt moral values. But even if there is no logical connection between mysticism and morality, mystical selflessness can reinforce a moral point of view, and such mystics as the Buddha and the Bodhisattvas are in fact paradigms of a moral life. Mystical experiences can push one toward more impartiality and make other-regarding conduct more central in one's life. Thus, if a mystic chooses to be moral, the experiences can make him or her more morally active toward others.

Since ethical values come from sources outside of the mystical experiences themselves, mystical value-systems are basically the same as those of the religious traditions within which a particular mystic practices (but which classical mystics in turn have influenced). Mysticism's only contribution to values is the experience of selflessness—ethical codes remain independent of mystical experiences. This limits any contribution mystical ways of life may make to solving ethical dilemmas today. There is no one set of mystical virtues or precepts—no "mystical ethics"—to contribute to the discussion. Mystics can be exemplars of moral conduct, and the study of the belief- and value-systems of different cultures can expose hidden assumptions of our systems and widen our perspective on possible solutions. But if mystics simply contribute classical religious ethical codes, the question is: what value do mystical ways of life or mystical experiences have for ethics today? Are they no more than the serious application of the religious solutions of a particular tradition, or does mysticism offer its own contribution?

But before addressing that question it must be reiterated that a moral concern cannot be derived from mystical experiences. One can remain selfish after the experiences. The selflessness of mystical enlightenment also does not entail other-regardingness—the mystic is then *Reality*-centered and not necessarily *other*-centered. Moral action thus cannot be the test of the true quality of a mystical experience. Morality remains a separate issue—to be moral, a mystic must choose to reject inaction or indifference to others. Those such as Robert Zaehner who see mysticism without morality as "dangerous" have a point. If morality is not adopted as a value, the overwhelming importance of the transcendent dimension can negate all other values and lead to an antinomianism that uses and may harm others or to an indifference and disengagement from the world. Mystical experiences can direct us away from the world as easily as it can ground us in it. Conversely, left-handed Tāntrikas show how mystics can be very "this-worldly" but not other-regarding in exploiting the energies of the universe.

Mystical Selflessness and Morality

The principal impact of mysticism on morality today is that it enables us to go beyond an ordinary moral concern to a selfless concern for all. There is a shift in point of view away from all self-centeredness. Self-will or its cognitive base (a sense of separateness and self-sufficiency) comes to be seen as the cause of all dissonance with reality. Realizing that there is no ego to enhance becomes the cognitive ground out of which one operates. Each thought, word, and deed has an effect. Emotional states connected to self-will and self-love—pride, hatred, envy, anger, jealousy, and so forth—become targets. Virtues that lessen a sense of self are valued—e.g., kindness, honesty, patience, generosity, gentleness, forgiveness, tolerance, and in particular humility in the sense of seeing one's true place in the scheme of selfless things.[1] Value-concepts and rules do not stand between the mystic and reality; at best, rule-following is the first step on the path for a practitioner—since rules that restrict actions that might harm others are also valuable in lessening a sense of one's individual importance—but no more.

For the moral mystic, all personal desires must be ended, including any desire for a reward for one's actions. Paradoxically, one's own spiritual well-being is promoted by forgetting oneself and giving oneself over fully to the welfare of others. As with morality among nonmystics, one's attitudes and behavior gradually shift from self-centered concern to concern with wider and wider circles—family, friends, one's own community, all people. Indeed, mystical selflessness may lead to a less anthropocentric view of reality that embraces all beings as worthy of concern. But in any case the moral mystic goes beyond our normal moral concern by becoming selfless: it is a radical impartiality that goes beyond even complete impartiality (i.e., attaching no more importance to oneself than to any others) to denying any value to oneself. One no longer has any self-image to maintain, no personal desires, no fears—the result is a complete self-denying love of others.

In the enlightened state, radical selflessness is not an idea adopted for intellectual reasons but paradoxically becomes what one is. Virtues are then grounded in one's knowledge of the fundamental nature of reality. Mystical experiences are part of this—providing a sense of reality, certitude, and selflessness—but so are the beliefs and values from the religious tradition the mystic belongs to. A moral mysticism is not merely about cultivating depth-mystical experiences but requires engaging the world morally. One becomes a selfless person only through cultivating a complete mystical way of life, not in isolated experiences. Nor will meditation alone inculcate the virtues and beliefs necessary for that. Meditation may help break down our tendency to reify concepts into self-existent entities or help to internalize a new framework of values and beliefs, but it is important to remember that values and beliefs are not given there—meditation is not tied to any particular way of life or set of belief-claims. It can begin to give a sense of selflessness and to energize oneself to whatever actions one chooses. It can also aid in calming the mind and focusing attention. This helps one's efficiency and spontaneity outside of meditation. However, all aspects of one's life become important in a mystical way of life.

Mystical detachment must be seen in light of this selflessness: it is not lack of concern but lack of personal attachments and desires. It is not a passive withdrawal from the world but reattachment to reality. To renounce and hate the world would be a form of reverse attachment, and mystics would still have to explain why the world is here to be renounced. All objects of desires are neutralized—one is no longer attached to this or that—but their reality cannot be denied. The change is simply that all personal desire has disappeared, not anything affecting what is really there. We now see everything from a third-person point of view: in a Copernican-like revolution, reality and not the self is once again the center of everything. One no longer sees one's life and actions as one's own—it is simply selfless reality at work. With our sense of self abrogated, the source of reality now fills the vacuum. Mystics now act from the source, not from a false sense of their own reality. They no longer have personal desires in their actions, but they still act. All acts become like volunteer work, selflessly done for no reward and only to help others. Their actions are now spontaneous, since they are free of deliberation and motivation.[2] With the false sense of self no longer causing friction, one's action conforms to what is perceived as the ethical law of the universe as easily as one's action conforms to the law of gravity.

The result of the selflessness in a moral mystical way of life is, in the words of Evelyn Underhill, not a selfish, otherworldly calm but renewed vitality—the flowers of the contemplative life are practical energies that help mystics to enter social life more completely.[3] Compassionate action becomes the expression of what one is. One is no longer imposing self-centered desires (self-will) through actions. All actions become works for other (equally selfless) beings rather than attempts to twist reality to meet the needs of an illusory independently existing individual self. Through mystical experiences one has recovered something lost, and, having tapped into the underlying source of being, one is now working with the energies of the universe to help others. The need to act compassionately no longer requires explaining but is a natural product of one's state in the world. All of one's actions will be moral in that none will be to harm another for one's own benefit and that one will be actively helping others even if one's factual beliefs turn out to be wrong.

In sum, mystical inwardness can be combined with moral action. If so, a life of self-giving action is seen as reflecting the ground of reality. Paradoxically, compassion becomes a self-denying but self-giving love for all. The resulting actions will be completely impartial. One, again paradoxically, helps people by forgetting them and treating all people equally. All people (or in fact all beings) are fundamentally alike. One has no loved ones or enemies. The resulting actions mirror those of the overflowing source. The transcendent, to use an image from various traditions (e.g., BSB II.3.42; Matt. 5:45-46), is like sunlight or rain in that it gives to all without discrimination, and thus the mystic's compassion is also without distinctions, giving to each person what that person needs. In a type of religious deism, the source can be seen as loving in the sense that it is continuously giving itself over to produce and sustain the natural realm despite the problems of natural evil.[4] That is, a deistic source, unlike a theistic one, is a self-giving power that does not intervene in the natural order to perform miracles or answer prayers to help particular persons with their personal (self-centered) concerns.[5] Nothing in the comparative study of mystical experiences suggests the underlying source would be more concerned with one part of reality than another (although theistic mystics will be influenced in their understanding of their mystical experiences by other considerations)—the simple joy of existence is more central to the experience.

Mystical Action in a Real World

To understand the resulting actions when morality and mysticism are combined, it first must be remembered that mysticism is not merely intellectually conceiving ourselves in a cosmic context or having a profound sense of oneness or seeing our actions as having a transcendental dimension. As discussed in Chapter 13, naturalists can argue on philosophical grounds alone that we are all parts of one interconnected naturalistic whole and thus that we would be more in tune with reality if we were less self-centered and less manipulative of others. Similarly, naturalists can argue for animal rights, a greater sharing of our wealth, and a simpler life on purely utilitarian grounds.[6] It is not such ideas that drives mystics. Instead, experiencing the source must be the fount of action. For this a transformation of the center of one's character is required, not merely the adoption of new ideas or new actions. The important intellectual shift in worldview is no longer to see people as distinct objects but as other manifestations of the underlying ground of reality (or at least free of the empirical egos); the only change in ethos is to a more thorough morality; the only new actions may be more actions involving helping others. But the most important change is that one's actions seem to be informed by the depth of reality. One has a sense of contact with the source while one acts. One then no longer acts simply from the surface-distinctions the mind produces; this removes hesitancy and produces more spontaneous and effortless actions. Thus, contemplation comes to inform one's actions. Mindfulness lets us see the differentiated surface-world as free of self-existent objects, and the depth-mystical experience lets one become aware of the common source of everything.

When combined with a moral commitment, the mystic will see love as the power of the universe. One's life then becomes an expression of the power tapped into by mystical experiences. This means that human beings realize our fullest state by being constantly engaged in self-emptying acts grounded in an awareness of our source, not in seeking our own happiness alone. Realizing both the "vertical" dimension of being and the "horizontal" dimension of becoming, one remains inwardly calm, grounded in the source of the world, while still remaining outwardly active—paradoxically, one acts while "reposing" unmoved and still in the source. Thus, the impact is not only on one's inner life in general but on the inner dimension to one's actions. One's consciousness is no longer cut off from the source, but yet one remains active in the world of diversity. All actions, however mundane, become meaningful. One "lives constantly in the presence of the divine" through one's actions. Rooted in the transcendent, mystics become the action of the transcendent in the realm of change, treating all they encounter with moral concern. The resulting actions may seem unspectacular to an observer—no more than simply no longer being selfish and instead acting according to the values of one's religious tradition. But the actions reflect the self-giving source of being and conform to the ethical laws of the universe (as defined by a religious tradition). In Jalāl al-Dīn Rūmī's words, one will be "the shadow of God on earth."

The Basic Problem

However, there is a basic problem for any mystic today with the above position: how can any classical mystical way of life be adopted in a world now deemed fully real? Under the modern worldview our world has to be accepted as fundamentally important, even if it is dependent on some underlying source—"real enough," even if dependent, that we must take it as an end in itself.[7] It has value in itself and not only as the creation of something else. The only purpose of the world cannot be just to get us out of it and to return to our original state. But under all traditional forms of mysticism, the world ultimately has no meaning or value in itself. It is just a veil hiding true reality. It has no reason to be other than for our testing or development—the world is merely a stage from which we return to the uncreated source.[8] We are pilgrims, and this world is not our real home. As Jan van

Ruusbroeck put it, the focus of living—the focus of the created life—is not this world but our eternal life. Buddhists think they know the suffering involved in this world well enough that they are not interested in the ontological issues related to whether it is real—they just want to get out. The objective in all the classical mystical ways of life is to get out of this world or to lead a life in conformity to God's will or the Way until we die. Our purpose is not to be part of this world—not to reproduce genes as sociobiologists thinks or anything else worldly in nature. We are not to develop human nature—in the words of Katherine Hepburn's character in *The African Queen*, "Human nature is what we were put here to rise above." We are to know and love God and to free ourselves from the world. The problem is not mitigated by seeing this life as one in an indefinite series of rebirths as long as the objective is oriented away from this world: if we are simply going from life to life with the ultimate goal of getting out of this world, the world can be ignored.[9]

Thus, any realism about the world rejects a fundamental premise of all classical mystical worldviews—that in the final analysis the source of the world or the self alone is real or of value and that our goal is only to return to it.[10] But mystics have a problem. To use Plato's analogy: the enlightened prisoner returning to the cave has ended all illusions and sees things correctly, but unless the world is real and valuable he has no explanation for why there are unenlightened prisoners or a cave. And with the world accepted as real, other-regarding concern cannot be manifested only by trying to get others out of this realm. Instead, this means mystics must take the suffering in this world seriously and not merely expect some future paradise that will make going through this life seem worth while. For a moral mystic, this means that working to ease the suffering of others here and now becomes a moral imperative.

This position obviously reflects the modern Western belief-claim and is problematic for all classical mysticism.[11] This switch of both factual beliefs and values changes our entire orientation to the world. Scientists have revealed a complex and intricate universe of extraordinary dimensions, with billions of galaxies, billions of years old, with a fascinating history and diversity of life. The fact that it existed for billions and billions of years without any conscious life is enough to dispute any claim that the universe is just a staging ground for us to return to our true state unless one wants to accept a wasteful creator of truly cosmic proportions. In light of evolution, it is also hard to maintain that each of us is a special creation of God or even that human beings in general are specially created (even if there are biological structures to reality guiding the universe to life and consciousness).[12] And once we have passed through this education, it is very hard to put the genie back in the bottle and treat the unfolding world of time as no more than the "dream" realm of some other reality, even if we do not know the purpose of this world. Indeed, many scholars argue that we are no longer able to experience the world the way the premodern religious did—as an appearance of another reality. The modern view is too thoroughly ingrained in our consciousness.

This means that the reality of this world is now irrevocably embedded in our view of reality, and thus no matter how powerful the depth-mystical experience is it has to be interpreted giving full reality to the world. In sum, mystics today must provide an interpretation giving full significance both to the transcendental ground and to this realm if mysticism is to be acceptable. (That Theravādins today are now more likely to participate in social action and that some monks are undertaking the Bodhisattva vow shows that morality—through the influence of Mahāyāna Buddhism, Christianity, and modern secular thought—is also harder to ignore even in classical forms of mysticism. The social concern of Neo-Vedānta is another such indication.)[13] The problem for any future mystical ways of life, in other words, is how to reinject the world into a transcendent reality without denying its full reality.

The Case Against Mystical Values

But before showing how such an interpretation is possible, the fact must be discussed that a realism about the world raises the fundamental issue of whether mystical values should even be taken seriously. If we take the world as real, it is not obvious that their values can apply. Does not mysticism end what is human about us? The starting point of the modern point of view is that we are not pilgrims alien to this world but a natural part of this world. So how can our destiny lie in solitude, in Plotinus' words "the flight of the alone to the alone"? We are not born human but become human only through interactions with others. Babies cannot survive long without help from others, and without physical contact with others they fail to thrive. They also quickly develop empathy for others. How can mystics deny that being a social being is a part of reality in the final analysis? At a minimum, are they not trying to return us to a prehuman animal state? As the Daoists best illustrate, to mystics culture is basically a veneer to be removed—we need to be desocialized to see reality as it truly is. But that Daoists concede some society is needed only shows that mystics do not understand all of reality. In short, mystics deny the full reality that a human being can develop. Mindfulness in an extreme form would make us live in the present moment with no orientation—no memory of the past and no plans or goals for the future. We would be "living in the moment" but totally unconnected to the past or future. This would certainly be less than human. With no memory, we would have no fear or hate, but we would also not have the type of love that makes us human. It may be easy to live in the present moment if we do not care whether we live or die, but we have evolved to survive. Our brain has developed through millions of years to support a mind that can remember the past and imagine future scenarios—removing the memory and conceptual portions of the mind might reveal something of reality, but it also eliminates something real. Classical mystics cannot explain that power of the mind—or indeed why "nescience" should exist at all.

To dismiss all the psychological aspects developed in light of our social nature is to fundamentally misconceive reality. And even ignoring that point, mystical selflessness conflicts with the fact that a self is part of the makeup of reality. There may not be a permanent, self-contained entity called the "self," but there is a configuration that has agency and free will. That causal power cannot be escaped. Persons are an irreducible part of the world. Babies quickly acquire this function. If we lost our sense of self we would not be in contact with a greater reality but psychotic. Each person contributes something unique to the whole, and any mysticism that denies this must be rejected. The value most naturally connected to the self is selfishness, and thus mystical selflessness flies in the face of reality. A Nietzschean will-to-power is more natural than mystical values emphasizing the passive and yielding. Even sociobiological "altruism" is based on a genetic-level "selfishness." On the human level, most ethical theorists (including Christians) think a healthy sense of self is necessary to being moral: we need a rational self-interest or a self-love to see how to help others. Indeed, those mystics who freely choose their own self-absorbed quest for enlightenment above any concern for others are acting more humanly than people who place the welfare of strangers over their own.

History certainly does not suggest that selfless love is the basis of reality. Indeed, the religious admit as much when, in order to salvage the idea that "the universe is good," they insist that there must be a life after death to compensate for the suffering and injustices of this life.[14] Human beings are beset with stillbirths, birth defects, lethal diseases, and plagues.[15] Biological evolution is based on a struggle, with animals eating plants and other animals. Moreover, in the words of David Hull, evolution is haphazard, cruel, "rife with happenstance, contingency, incredible waste, death, pain, and horror"—all evidencing the careless indifference of an almost diabolical god.[16] The human species is particularly aggressive and cruel. We and some social insects are the only species that form armies that fight to the death. Only human beings prey on their own species. Only human beings torture. Human history is one of hatred, greed, and violence. And the last century was the most vicious of them all.[17] Some mystics claim to experience an all-encompassing reality of love that makes all life precious—nevertheless, it still would be hard to explain how that reality could possibly be the source of a realm where life is worth so little. Any bliss mystics experience confirms, not that they are conscious of the transcendental ground of reality, but only that their minds are functioning completely out of touch with reality. In fact, they have not escaped the human condition. Our lot is one of struggle, and any happiness we find will be very temporary and found only in interactions with others.[18]

The values that mystical selflessness engenders also do not help in our situation. Even when mystics accept a moral concern, they still treat people as if we do not really belong here—they do not treat us as fully human. They can live at peace in the world, free from the bother of pains and strive, only by a self-induced, artificial stupor that also kills emotions. Freed from love and hate, their inward calm removes all human qualities from them. One lives "as if one is already dead," and inwardly the mystics are. Their serenity and detachment produces a coldness to their actions that does not reflect any humanity. Undisturbed by success or failure, their resulting actions are machinelike in their efficiency, but this does not mean that the mystics are more in touch with reality. Moreover, if the *Bhagavad-gītā* is any indication, achieving inner peace is not necessarily reflected in outer peace and thus is not a way to end war. Emotions reflect something in reality (and fulfill a need for survival) that the dispassionate miss. Partiality for one's family members may be a product of evolution that enhances survival. There is something wrong with Angela of Foligno who was grateful for the death of her family because it released her from an attachment. Similarly, mystics such as Plotinus who hate having a body or ascetics who torture their body must be out of sync with reality—how could that be the end we are to achieve if our bodies are real? We are both mind and body, as the Tāntrikas make clear, and we cannot deny the reality of either. Indeed, Sāmkya-Yogins make most of the mind part of the material order. Even if mystics achieve a serenity from experiencing the ground of reality, they still have bodies and are still part of this world. They are detached not only from emotions but from reality.

Moreover, to be moral may require an impartiality (i.e., presenting ethics so the "who" does not matter) that is in tension with our normal responses, but totally overcoming partiality with the radical impartiality of mystical selflessness does not reflect how reality operates in this realm. For example, expressing a universal compassion for everyone indiscriminately—completely random generosity without a thought of reciprocity or a sense of community—is not a fundamental principle of life in the world. There is a need for cooperation, and partiality is part of what makes that work; thus, partiality is part of the value-structure of reality. Similarly, it is not clear how treating one's children the same as all other people, even if one loves everyone, reflects reality more than being attached to some and not others. Even on the mystics' own terms there is a self-contradiction with mystical impartiality: if one completely discounts oneself while treating others as real, one would be making a "discrimination" (since one is actually as real as anyone and so must be treated equally); indeed, there is a type of reverse attachment in the total devaluation of oneself. Not being moved by love or hate may reveal an aspect of reality we normally miss, but that does not mean it reveals the complete picture. Even-mindedness and detachment need not lead to squashing all of the inner emotional life, but replacing a full life with only virtues from the less testosterone-filled side of things—empathy, patience, and so forth—cannot claim to be more in keeping with the way we really are but only to be a one-sided approach. Moreover, losing all personal desires leads to a life of celibacy, and that obviously cannot be the foundation of this world. Why must we overcome our nature? Why are our needs, desires, and even senses considered a barrier between us and what is real? That the world exists at all must mean that desire reflects something of reality (as Tāntrikas realize) and has a role to play in it—ending desires misses that. In short, detachment at best reveals something we otherwise miss, but it too misses the fullness of reality.

The commitment to the reality of this world means that this world must be valued as an end in itself. Even if the world is in fact the product of some transcendental source, it has some "purpose" or "meaning," and we are not an evolutionary accident of a purposeless universe. The world may be a stage to a further existence, but it is also real in its own right. Mystics cannot retreat from this world and devalue all things or all desires. Realism also entails that we are a natural part of this world and should be perfectly at home in it—we are "of the world" and not just "in" it. Thus, any answer to "Why are we here?" must involve more than the idea of escaping this world and returning to our "true" state in another realm. That is, the transcendent did not create this world or people merely to have us return to it, and this world is not just a training ground to get back to where we started. Something must be wrong if the only goal of this world is to get out of it. Why create something if the end result is simply the same as the beginning? Reality would then be only a pointless, painful play. Any related claim—e.g., predestination or that we are suffering through this "vale of tears" to a foreordained conclusion—that would render the world or us less than fully real must also be rejected.

Thus, any claim by mystics that the only end of life is contemplation misses the fullness of reality—the "good life" is not just a matter of returning to the source but a full life contributing to our world.[19] Classical mystics who see the depth-mystical experience as overwhelming in importance reject this realism, but they have to explain why this world exists at all. Why this world exists may remain a mystery to naturalists too, but classical mystics make it a twofold enigma: why anything exists (i.e., why the ultimately real source exists) and why it then generates an illusory realm. The purpose of the world may also remain unknown, but if we accept this realm as fully real we can no longer accept that the universe is the meaningless play of the transcendent, and any pessimism toward life in this world cannot result in denying its final reality.

Interpreting Mystical Experiences and Accepting a Real World

All of these objections have to be taken seriously, and if mysticism is to be taken seriously it must be shown that mystical values are applicable in the real world. Classical mystics reject the natural realm as either unreal or as not significant enough when compared to its transcendental source to care about. Their experience of the source is extremely powerful and in the context of a way of life transforms the experiencer.[20] However, it must be realized that no experience—no matter how powerful—carries its own interpretation. After the depth-mystical experience, mystics return to a state where they have to understand what has occurred. If mystics are correct, the basic ontological implication of the depth-mystical state of consciousness is that mystics have indeed been aware of a reality having profound ontological significance for our world: it is an infusion by the source that blows away the ego as an irreducible reality. It can overwhelm all other types of experiences in its cognitive importance, leading to the dismissal of everything else experienced as unreal (as with Shankara). But it is also open to other interpretations. For example, Sāmkhya-Yogins take it to be the experience of our true self (*purusha*) distinct from matter—thereby, the material realm (*prakriti*) remains equally fully real (even though the goal is to separate the self from the material).

Nevertheless, whatever interpretation is applied, the important point is that mystical experiences must be understood outside the depth-mystical state of consciousness and must be weighed against other experiences—the experiences themselves do not entail the rejection of the world and ordinary states of consciousness as unreal. It is one thing to claim, "There is a source to this world" and something quite different to claim, "There is nothing but the source." The Advaitic interpretation is not given in the experience itself and is merely one possible interpretation. That Shankara appealed to revealed scripture (albeit heavily interpreted) for the correct understanding of experiences is an admission that the correct understanding is not given in the depth-mystical experience itself. Any such decision is based on factors outside the mystical experiences themselves. There is no simple empiricism even in mysticism. Experiences constrain our worldview, but there is an irreducible human element of reasoning in creating it. In the end, we all choose (in our ordinary state of mind) how to weigh our various experiences, based on values and considerations outside any one type of experience. (This points once again to the reality of this world.)

Many who claim mysticism is incompatible with morality are actually arguing about only one classical interpretation of mystical oneness—Advaita Vedānta's. The depth-mystical experience can be accepted as an awareness of the ground of being without reducing all of reality to that underlying reality. Similarly, those scholars are wrong who argue that the multiplicity of the sensory realm is always more compelling than mystical oneness and so the mystical experiences must be rejected as possible insights.[21] They are correct that the world of multiplicity and ordinary states of consciousness cannot be eliminated and thus in the final analysis real, but mystical experiences may nevertheless be an insight into reality, even if one common interpretation is deficient. In short, the problem is not mystical experiences *per se*, but the factual beliefs of classical mystical traditions.

If a mystic accepts the reality of the natural world, anything like the Advaitic interpretation must be rejected. (It should also be noted again that Shankara's own practices contradicted his theory.) The world is fully real in the sense that, although it may be dependent in some way on a transcendental source, it is now part of the ultimate makeup of reality.[22] Advaitins are no doubt correct in arguing that what is permanent, changeless, and eternal is real, but they are wrong in thinking this entails that other things cannot also be real. The changeless may be experienced in the depth-mystical experience, but our other experiences are not "sublatable"—as even Shankara realized, in the enlightened state the other experiences remain. Shankara cannot explain why the "optical illusion" remains after enlightenment. In our world, there may not be anything "real" in the Advaitic sense, but at least those things within our world that have causal power are not "illusory" or "nonexistent" in any meaningful sense; they cannot be dismissed but must be dealt with and thus are "real" in any legitimate sense of the word. In sum, the phenomena of our world may be dependent, but their reality cannot be denied.[23] The analogy of the dream is helpful for our understanding how this world may be dependent upon another reality, but the fact remains that the "dream" is part of reality even if it is not the "dreamer"—it may have a derivative reality (and hence "less real" in that sense), but the dreaming itself is also part of what exists. The world thus is "real enough" that we must take it with complete seriousness, even though it has no reality apart from its source. Why the world is here—for theists why God created the world, or for Shankara why the unenlightened world exists at all—may be a mystery, but it is here now and must be treated as part of reality.

Most importantly, nothing rules out both accepting the depth-mystical experience as an awareness of the source of being and accepting the full reality of life and our natural world. Thus, adopting the modern worldview need not require the denial that mystical experiences occur or even that they are cognitive. As discussed in the next section, we can interpret mystical experiences as a cognitive insight into the depth of reality and still affirm the full reality of the natural world and ordinary states of consciousness. Thus, the problem for a moral mysticism is not mystical experiences *per se* but only the belief-claims of classical worldviews in which the world is deemed less than fully real. A mysticism can in principle be "world-affirming," "life-affirming," and "optimistic" while still affirming the ontological priority of the transcendent source. It can also accept all the factual presuppositions of morality—in particular, we must have free will and there must be other "persons" (i.e., some reality toward which a moral concern is possible).[24] Thus, no mysticism would be acceptable in which our world melts into a featureless blob, either by all of our world being no more than a manifestation of the transcendental ground that will ultimately be absorbed back or by all structures within our world being ultimately unreal. Moral mystics most naturally believe that reality is not value-neutral and that morality is a value ingrained in the structure of reality—e.g., that love is rooted in the transcendent source itself, and thus the source of being is also the source of value. But such moral realism is not needed for a mystic to be moral—all that is required is that morality is a possible value in this world.[25]

Mystical Experiences as Cognitive in a Real World

To see how it is possible to interpret mystical experiences as insights into reality and yet to accept the natural world as fully real, consider this possibility: science provides insights into the various structures of the natural world, and mystical experiences provide insights into the source of the world (depth-mystical experience) and the beingness of the world (mindfulness).[26] This position reflects a nonmystical point of view, since it gives weight to a nonmystical approach to the world, but it shows one way that mystical insights can be integrated into a nonmystical point of view. The two approaches remain distinct ways of knowing: mystics are interested in the changeless beingness outside of time, while scientists are only interested in understanding the causes of the changes within the world of time. For mystics only the "now" of immediate, lived experience matters; but to scientists there is no "now" in the description of reality, only the before-and-after stream of the causal relation of events. Thus, both the analytic mind and the meditative mind reveal aspects of reality but different aspects and so both are needed.[27] Mindfulness involves seeing the differentiated world but the focus is on the beingness or "suchness" of reality rather than the differentiations that normally control our thoughts, actions, and perceptions. Freed of greed and other emotions and freed of our habitual conceptual responses, mystics see the natural world "as it really is." In the enlightened state, knowledge, memories, language, and concepts in general are not destroyed, but the mindful mind is now free of all projections of reified entities and thus free of all attachments to our own artificial creations. Nevertheless, the structures of the differentiated realm are real, even though mindfulness does not lead to new scientific insights into them (since it does not focus the mind on the differentiations).

The problem of classical mysticism can be restated in those terms: classical mystics see the analytical mind as only a source of delusion and the meditative mind as the only source of insight and thus only the latter is worth developing. The meditative mind does not supplement the analytical. Instead, there is no place in the mystics' schemes for the analytical mind—mystics want to replace it entirely, not to accept that both functions of the mind are part of what we really are. The alternative to the classical mystical views is that the point of view of the beingness of reality is not the only source of insights—focusing on the structures also reveals something irreducible about reality. Both beingness and the structures are real. Even if we could see the differentiated world totally free of structures, that does not mean the structures are not real any more than focusing on the structures means that they exist outside of the world of being. Structures remain causal forces and part of the makeup of reality; thus, focusing our awareness on them in the scientific approach does not mean we are deluded. The "survival consciousness" or "instrumental mind" supported by a brain that has evolved for our particular nodes in the web of life to survive in this world reveals something real. But if mysticism is in fact cognitive, the brain has also evolved for the still mind to produce insights into reality and thus it is also needed. In sum, both the still mind and the imaginative mind are needed for a full life, since each supplies something the other misses.

Thus, if mysticism is cognitive and the world is real, accepting either dimension—the source of being or the structured natural world—alone as real is a mistake. This means accepting the source alone as real is as much a mistake as accepting the natural world alone as real. If we focus on being alone, everything blissfully seems "perfect" as it is (since it is rooted equally in the same source of being), and we have no reason to avoid danger or to mend a broken leg or to eradicate AIDS—everything is what it is, there is no value in changing things or trying to alleviate suffering, and we should just let things be. But we cannot reduce our situation to one dimension. There may be no lasting sources of pleasure in this world, but we cannot renounce our home. Any bliss from "clinging to the Void" is as one-sided as denying the source of being and living only in the surface-dimension. Even if our lives were dedicated solely to acts of compassion, we would not have achieved the highest life possible as long as we remained in the surface-dimension alone. We live at once in both the realm of the eternal and of time—the "now" of experience and the continuum of change. Through mysticism, we can live with full awareness in the present, but this does not mean that the past and future are not also part of reality. In short, we live in two environments: the natural world through which life is evolving and the reality upon which the world depends. Both the white light of the source and the colors of the rainbow are part of the totality of reality and thus completely real. Both must be accepted and valued, and the two cannot be reduced to one order. As Plotinus said, we are amphibians living in two realms at once,[28] and the mystery remains of how that is so.

The same mystery applies to persons.[29] We are beings at home in this world, not alien "spiritual beings" having a "human experience" while waiting to return to our real home. The vertical and horizontal dimensions are both present in us—something in us is deathless and uncreated, and yet we are also active agents in the realm of the differentiated. Both dimensions are legitimate sources of concern, and we cannot ignore our nonspiritual dimension. We have no being apart from the source (and thus are "nothing" in that sense), but we still have a causal presence in the natural world (and thus are real parts of the structured realm). All the known structures in the universe from matter to consciousness converge in us. We cannot obliterate this causal "lower self" and remain in only the "higher self" of being—both are irreducible parts of reality.[30] Indeed, the combination of structures constituting personhood may be a fundamental category of reality. Even if the causal self has no permanent core among surface-phenomena or is dependent in some way on the rest of the web of the differentiated world, we still are nodes with causal force in the web: we are not constituted by our interconnections to the web but contribute to the whole through our actions. We may be inherently social beings, and our personalities may be largely socially constructed, but we are still nodes of agency too and that must be given its due. Experiencing reality free of a personal point of view may reveal something that is missed otherwise, but to deny that we also are real as agents in the web of reality is as distortive as losing all sense of the source of being and identifying ourselves with our bodies.

Our will may be aligned with the will of the transcendent (as defined by the mystic's particular religious tradition), but it cannot be replaced by the latter—personal consciousness may just be waves on a deep ocean, but the waves are nevertheless a feature of reality. Personal consciousness has evolved and is as real as the rest of reality. If we lose all sense of self—become literally selfless, with no control over our actions, and thus are lived by the source—we are distorting reality since we are part of the realm of becoming. To deny oneself for the sake of others distorts reality as much as egoism does. We can become selfless in a value-sense, if not an ontological one, by eliminating any self-value and completely replacing it with other-regardingness for other people, all life, or all of the natural world—emptying ourselves of all self-will and being filled by "the will of God." But again that would not reflect the fact that we too exist and are causally active in this realm—it is still "Love God, and do what *you will*."

Mystical Selflessness and the Real World

Thus, mystical experiences can be reconciled with accepting the world of becoming as real and accepting people as causal agents: the experiences can be limited to insights into the source of being and need not be taken as overwhelming other types of insight. A greater problem, however, arises when we try to accept both selflessness as a value and values associated with life in the natural world. The discontinuity of the dimensions to reality also applies to values: mystical values relate to the source of being and not to the values necessary to living in the natural world. Trying to reconcile both sets of values into one set to live by is difficult. Science and mysticism can be seen as supplementary ways of knowing in one total worldview, but mystical selflessness competes with the values of the natural world. We cannot simply tack mystical selflessness onto our everyday value-system. Total selflessness may reflect the ground of reality totally giving itself over for benefit of all, but it cannot reflect being a real part within this world where self-interest is necessary to survive. Our "created nature" cannot be gotten around. Thus, the selfless source cannot be the basis for living a full life in this world.

But how can mystics not only give recognition but value to the realm of "appearances"? To mystics, the overwhelming power of the source of being makes it of supreme value to us. It is in fact not the highest good in a hierarchy but the *only* good: it dwarfs all other values to the point that mystics cannot even treat the two sets of values as important enough to be integrated into one value-system that would somehow give equal weight to both the source and the natural world. In particular, we must accept a self as fully real (since there is agency and free will, and thus a "self" has causal effect), but the mystical value is to lessen the assertion of that self as much as possible, either in terms of value or as an ontologically distinct entity. Not all self-assertion is selfishness, but mystics would not advocate anything that would enhance a sense of ego. But how can mystics then treat any role for personal desires or self-will as anything but an error? So too the radical impartiality of mystical selflessness cannot be readily reconciled with human existence evolving through partiality and desires—the need for family or others for our survival means that partiality is a legitimate value in this world. Impartiality may permit the highest manifestation of a particular type of love, but it is too impersonal and indeed inhuman since it does not reflect the personhood present in reality. It also leads to an indifference to one's own life and death and thus conflicts with the self-interest (both individual and social) necessary for our survival throughout evolution. In short, once the natural world is taken as an end in itself, total selflessness becomes a very problematic value. The view *sub specie aeternitatis* may reveal something of reality but of necessity not all of it. The point of view of our partiality reflects other features of reality.

Similarly, how can mystics accept the natural world and society as areas of concern? Their focus would be on the beingness of things and not on the structures of the world, on the "now" and not on the processes of temporal change. The beingness experienced in the eternal "now" makes, in Tennyson's words, "death [seem] an almost laughable impossibility"—how then can mystics be concerned with the temporal realm at all? There is no sense of history or progress within our world or hope for the future. For mystics there would still need to be some mystical reason for why we should transform this world. No concern for social reform beyond anything needed for our minimal survival would be a mystical value. The individualism of this strand of religiosity would not aid any sense of community or cooperation for the common good. Overcoming a sense of self is not automatically replaced with a social sense; that must come from other sources.

In addition, personal detachment produces an acceptance of things as benign as they are that still remains hard to integrate into a prophetic call for action: tension remains between the mystical focus on beingness, with the resulting pull toward quiet acceptance, and the prophetic call to reform the differentiated realm—between the joy or serenity of experiencing being and a greater concern for the suffering of others in this realm. Mysticism remains a matter of observing rather than altering. Moreover, how effective any personal action resulting from this inner transformation can be in bringing about social change in a world of unenlightened people remains an issue: the focus of the latter would still be only on the surface-changes and not with rooting ourselves in the source—the person is not changed but only actions.[31] From a mystical point of view, that is a matter of dealing with symptoms and not the real causes. There is also the danger that mystics would be drawn up into the struggles of the social realm and away from the root of the world's beingness, resulting in a superficial focus on regulating actions alone on both the interpersonal- and group-levels. That is, by focusing on the details needed for social change, mystics may get caught up in the surface-world alone and not act from the source of our being—mystics would have to step back from our immediate action (and hence the source) and think about how to end suffering on a societywide or even global scale.

However, social concern is not impossible for a mystic who treats the world as real and valuable in itself, even if focusing on the ground of being and on the structures of the social realm pulls our attention in different directions. A contribution mysticism can make to the social problems of today is advocacy of a simpler life—a life not caught up solely in all the minutiae of the surface-realm but one grounded in depth of reality. Attention can be focused on reforming social institutions, since they are part of the real world and affect our well-being. Thus, social values should be part of the value-system of a way of life that takes this world as real and valuable. But changing the surface alone will still not suffice to rectify our lives. Mystical selflessness only provides the broadest outline of change—less self-centeredness and thus less attachment and grasping in all its forms, more generosity and less competitiveness, more concern with suffering, the equality of all people, tolerance, and so forth—and not the details of how actually to restructure society. In sum, we cannot deduce social-level solutions from mystics' individualistic ethics. Mystics would have to formulate social-level solutions, with the accompanying danger of getting totally caught up in the "horizontal" level.

Nevertheless, concerns alien to classical mysticism—the material needs of the world's population (food, shelter, education, medicine, and so forth), human rights and other social-level concerns, the exploitation and pollution of the rest of nature—become legitimate once the world is deemed fully real.[32] Political, economic, and environmental problems exist today on a global scale that did not exist before modern times simply by the sheer number of people now alive. If such problems had been raised in premodern times, classical mystics would have dismissed them as concerns only of the prisoners in the cave. But today, even under classical mystical ways of life, such problems might be considered mystical concerns on the analogy of the body: classical mystics do not love their bodies but realize that they have to take care of them in order to continue their quest for enlightenment. As the *Questions of King Milinda* (73-74) puts it: monks care for their wounds not because they love them but because they must. So too mystics today may have to care for the world's natural and social wounds if mystical quests are to continue. (But note once again that classical mystics who reject any realism connected to the world can have no explanation of why they have bodies or today why the world could have such problems.)

That mystics can reject this world shows that solutions to our social problems today cannot come solely from mystical selflessness—they must adopt values not given in mystical experiences. Inner peace and outer peace are two different things, as the *Bhagavad-gītā* illustrates. And because mystics can achieve an inner calm without necessarily changing their outer acts (except to do them more effortlessly), another level of the mind must work at finding solutions to these problems. A focus on a social level other than face-to-face interactions is also needed. Merely changing the surface-structures without changing the persons may not bring lasting relief from war or our other problems, but neither does an inner change alone. Rerooting ourselves in the source is only part of the solution. Values such as compassion must also become part of our life and inform our actions, and we must also adopt a social-level concern.

Mystical Selflessness and Ethical Codes

A problem for a modern mystical morality related to the last point should be noted before returning to the problem of mystical values. Moral mystics cannot simply "be compassionate" or "love and do what they will"—they need some specific directions on how to act to implement that compassion. And that is where factual beliefs and ethical codes enter the picture. Selflessness in a real world entails one general standard: "Do not value yourself more than one among equals." You should not devalue oneself totally (as classical mystics tend to do) since you are also a real part of the world, but you should not assert your interests as more than one among equals. This standard pulls toward radical impartiality in the application of any precept and hence to the universality necessary to be moral. Thus, selflessness offers us a type of guidance for our everyday problems, but we cannot deduce more specific precepts from it on how positively to help others. How do mystics know what the natural ethical laws are? Such laws cannot be revealed by an experience that is empty of all content—thus, the depth-mystical experience cannot be the source of new ethical precepts. Detached mindfulness also does not appear to add any values but selflessness. In sum, selflessness is the only value from the mystery of the source of reality, and the values we need to operate in the world of becoming (including moral ones such as compassion) cannot be deduced from that.

How then do we know what actions will help or are the best if there is no one set of "mystical ethics" to consult? Every enlightened mystic may think the ethical beliefs of his or her religious tradition reflect the true order of reality and are not social creations. Indeed, probably everyone thinks that of their own religious beliefs or obviously they would change them. However, the problem is that there is no one core of ethical precepts common to all traditions (as discussed in Chapter 14). A certain minimal set of precepts may be necessary for any society to survive—do not kill without justification, do not interfere with private property without justification, do not lie without justification, and so forth. But what constitutes "justification" and the scope of application both differ from tradition to tradition. There is commonality only on an abstract level, and beyond these minimal restraints on behavior there is no agreement at all. Thus, mystical experiences will not contribute to resolving any pluralism or relativism of values by grounding one set of ethical precepts in the structure of reality—its only "objective" value is general selflessness. Any resolution of any relativism will have to come from other sources.

Two aspects of the problem are worth noting. The first relates to factual beliefs and values. For example, if we accept a life after death, we will not be as insistent on the value of this one life—in a real world, we must take this life seriously, but we will also look to the benefit to one's total existence. More generally, any precept like "act to create greater good in the world" will depend on the total worldview the mystics adopts. But no one set of factual beliefs are shared by all mystical traditions. Similarly with values: how far do we expand moral concern? Impartiality would require including all human beings (and not just one's own group), but do we all include all sentient animals or all life? Accepting this world as real does not compel only one choice, and mystical morality will differ according to the answer a mystical tradition chooses.

A second problem with this is that we cannot make exceptionless rules. For the moral mystic, compassion is the overriding value, and no rule of conduct can capture that and thus none is absolute. No list of rules will resolve every dilemma since no act is selfless *per se* in every circumstance; only acting for selfish reasons is wrong. This lies behind the adage that we are judged by whether we acted out of love, not by the particular acts we do. It leads to the position that we do not need concrete rules at all—the general standard of not acting selfishly but compassionately will suffice.[33] However, we would still need some guidance in concrete dilemmas. Meditation or other spiritual exercises alone will not help. Specific factual beliefs and values would have to be part of the consideration. In short, making selflessness operational would still require something more concrete. Conversely, this presents a basic problem for mystics: the only value given by mystical experiences is selflessness, and hence finding any basic moral order in the structure of reality will remain beyond these experiences. Thus, "aligning our lives in accord with the way reality really is" in the end is not a matter of mystical experiences alone, even if mystical selflessness makes such alignment possible.

How much help the classical ethical codes of the world's religious traditions can offer for new problems arising today is open to question.[34] Ethics evolve over time, as our knowledge and values change. What virtues are deemed central change, as do the ethical rules within religious traditions. The possibility of moral progress cannot be ruled out as we learn more about how to live with others. But in the idea of "moral progress," the concepts of "morality" and "ethics" again must be distinguished. "Moral progress" proper is the idea that more people will come to act morally more often. "Ethical progress" is the reform of ethical norms or laws along the lines of some set of values (e.g., that slavery and torture are now generally seen to be wrong). Mystical selflessness can contribute to the former and could affect the latter by suggesting we should accept wider and wider circles of people as equals.

In sum, mystical selflessness has at best only a limited contribution to make to specific precepts. It would pull toward constructing precepts that reflect selflessly helping others and universalizing any concern to all people or all beings. In addition, when we take this world to be fully real and valuable, reforming social institutions or focusing on rights and justice may be given more importance than in classical mysticism. But mysticism's main contribution would lie in the inner dimension of action—how any precepts are carried out—since mysticism is a matter of inner development.

Mystical Selflessness and Self-Interest

But the basic dilemma for a moral mysticism remains reconciling mystical self-lessness with the belief that we are part of a world that is in the final analysis real and not illusory and thus of value in itself. As discussed above, the person as a causal agent remains a part of reality, and mystics cannot reflect the reality of the differentiated world by becoming completely self-emptying—the source of being may be that way, but mystics have to reflect both the source and the reality of being in the world. Thus, a life exclusively of other-regarding actions would not reflect all of reality. Simply put: if we only radiate love for others with no concern for ourselves, we will not survive long in this world, and that shows we are not taking this world seriously. But all selfishness (i.e., treating people and the rest of reality as merely resources to be used for our own advantage) must be ruled out. Thus, a middle path between total selflessness and selfishness is needed if this world is taken as real and valuable. This leaves some partiality and self-interest (and hence attachments and desires) as part of any way of life since they are necessary to life in the world. That is, a wholly other-centered life is not a human life and is not reality-centered, if the world is indeed real.[35] Some self-assertion is necessary, and thus we cannot reflect only the selfless underlying source of reality in our lives—more is involved to reality, and we must reflect that assertiveness too. Each person, including every mystic, is an equal part of reality. Each being has the right to have his or her interests advanced. Going beyond this and asserting one's own welfare at others' expense when they have morally legitimate claims is what is unacceptable. However, determining how much assertiveness is acceptable remains the problem.

But self-assertiveness can incorporate a central mystical insight: selfish acts go against the grain, and therefore we suffer when we act selfishly and our lives will then be ultimately unsatisfying. Natural drives within us become "deadly sins" when selfishness takes over. In short, what needs to be removed is viewing reality from a self-centered point of view. From the mystics' point of view, the evils of asserting a self over others—greed, hatred, aggression, and so on, and the accompanying dissatisfaction and suffering—are dependent on the false sense of an ego set off from the rest of reality and trying to twist other things to its advantage rather than seeing all beings as equally the products of the one underlying source. The enlightened life is one focused on being rather than on having and consuming, accepting rather than controlling, giving rather than acquiring. Self-preservation is still a value but not the only value in the mix. Harming another being for personal reasons is not an issue for classical mystics, but if the world is considered real and valuable the issue arises of when it is legitimate to harm other people or other beings for self-preservation in order that one may continue to contribute to reality.

Moreover, it is hard to see how from a mystical point of view even human beings could be given a privileged place as the center of reality, since everything is grounded equally in the same source. Everything is intrinsically valuable as is—life and death do not matter. Indeed, why life should even be considered precious is not clear, since all of reality—animate and inanimate—share the same beingness, and for mystics only beingness matters. But if we treat the world as real, life is indeed different since more types of *structures* are at work in living bodies; conscious life have even more structures, and self-conscious beings have the most complex interaction of structures. Human beings thereby become more valuable and more worth preserving than inanimate objects. The way this world is set up, however, nothing can survive without harming other life. From eating plants and animals to bacteria dying in our bodies during digestion, everyday we kill, both indirectly and directly. If everything is perfect as is, why fight plagues? Or consider vegetarianism. Should we be vegetarians who eat only plant life that has not been killed or cultivated? We are evolved meat-eaters, and nothing separates animal from nonanimal life in the scheme of being in that all are equally real products of the same source; thus vegetarians cannot make a moral argument for their cause without a nonmystical appeal to the structures of reality. Or, should we never kill another human? If each person is infinitely valuable, we cannot kill one person even to save a thousand. Theists may also add that killing would be interfering with God's purpose for that person. All self-defense, defense of loved ones, or defense of innocent third parties would be prohibited. Mystics who reject the ultimate significance of this world would have no trouble with that, but if life in the world has significance such absoluteness should not prevail. We live in a society of many types of beings and we have no reason to treat all of reality as being here only to serve human beings, but absolute nonviolence toward animals and other human beings is hard to reconcile with the way reality is set up. Also add to this the violence in inanimate nature—volcanos, earthquakes, tornados, hurricanes. Aggression and violence apparently are a vital part of the interconnectedness of nature.[36] Thus, modern mystics cannot have it both ways—that the human "way" is a natural part of the world and yet that we must be essentially different by asserting no self-interest.

A Truncated Mysticism

The basic problem of combining mysticism and a full realism about the world of multiplicity is how to maintain awareness of both reality's "vertical" dimension of being and "horizontal" dimension of structures without getting caught up in one and forgetting the other. Both beingness and structures are real, and we need to recognize both. We can live mindfully in the "now" in the sense of focusing single-mindedly on the task immediately at hand, free of distractions and fully concentrated; but we cannot still be fully human if we live immersed in the "now" with a mind "empty" of differentiations, simply responding without knowledge or purpose, without regard to the consequences of our actions or the future. (This problem would arise only for extreme forms of mindfulness devoid of all conceptualizations. Normally, the enlightened appear to be aware of the consequences of their actions, and moral mystics are concerned with the effects on others—in effect, this is accepting the world as real.) We cannot engage the real world free of attachment, free of desire, nor without at times some thought to the future. A modern mystic will need a life concerned with both the waves and the ocean depth, and not caught up in the waves alone as most people are. One is fully human only when one has awareness of the source but one's life is geared toward the dependent realm. Both the inner stillness of mind from the vertical dimension and the outer activity of the horizontal dimension are necessary to live the fullest human life in light of all of reality. Contrary to classical mystics, our lives are not just a matter of *being* but also of *doing*—"resting" in the source of being and still active in the realm of becoming. But the need for action becomes completely natural when the world is accepted as real and we are accepted as part of it—the enlightened Jaina ideal of nonaction looks totally out of step with how reality actually is. Bringing in a commitment to morality means that it would only be with other-regarding interactions with other people that our life is complete. A balanced moral life values both dimensions and thus involves cultivating both awareness of being and an active life of self-giving—compassion is seen as the basic value of the source, but some self-interest is also needed to live in the realm of becoming and thus is needed if we take this realm seriously.

This rejects the classical monastic life dedicated solely to cultivating one part of what is human. The "great souls" are not examples of human perfection. If our world is deemed real and valuable, such a one-sided approach would miss part of what it is to be human, and mystics should not devote a large portion of their life to only one side of our nature. Working with others would be integral to a way of life even in the unenlightened state since it connects to something real. Conversely, a life spent as a hermit or in a monastery without teaching or otherwise helping would have to be judged selfish, even if the mystic is operating with a nonmoral value-system.[37] In addition, such a life would only develop one aspect of the complete human life. Moreover, the belief-claim problem for classical mystics also remains: the objective of their life is to escape the world. Even Bodhisattvas, who voluntarily remain in this realm to help others, have the objective of getting everyone out of here. Naturalists can uproot Buddhist practices and action-guides from their traditional framework and make compassion and mindfulness a matter of the "horizontal" dimension alone (grounding them in the interconnection of all of reality or our mutual need for others). But without a focus on beingness it would not be a form of mysticism, let alone Buddhism. In the lay life of classical mystical traditions such as Zen, there is also the danger that one may compartmentalize the mystical from ordinary life rather than fully integrate the two into a "contemplative life" of action, with mindfulness informing all aspects of life. (More Westerners meditate and go on retreats today but often only for the beneficial "secular" effects—lessening stress and other health benefits—and perhaps to be a little more mindful in the rest of their lives. This may make our lives more satisfying, but this is not a matter of adopting a mystical way of life or of cultivating alleged mystical insights into reality.) There is also the problem that the laity in all traditional mystical traditions are in principle committed to a classical belief-framework and goal that does not give full weight to the reality of the natural world. The Hindu solution of relegating the mystical to later stages of life does accommodate both the world and the transcendent, but it also shares the problem of the classical belief-claim and goal; it also leads to a bifurcated life in which one can ignore part of reality at each stage of life rather than to a life integrating the transcendent and the natural at each stage. Of the classical traditions covered in this book, the this-worldly and life-affirming Daoists come closest to a possible modern balance.

But this means a modern mystic will be left with a mysticism that is truncated when compared to a full classical mystical way of life since weight must also be given to the natural world. Mystics would have to focus on both the source and this world as equally real and valuable, and that will separate them from classical mystics. Classical mystics focus on beingness with as little attention as possible to the structures of our realm (and with no explanation for why this world should exist at all). Their only objective is to empty the mind of all content of the world. For them, all selfhood vanishes—one is fully real only when the "person" within the realm of diversity is annihilated. To them, we are spiritual amphibians who at any given time have to look one way or the other rather than in a state of mindfulness integrating one into the other, thereby living in both realms at once and treating both as real and valuable. Mystics who would now accept the world as real and valuable in itself would live in the constant awareness that the world is grounded in a transcendent reality but still is equally real. And that is the problem: total self-renunciation does not reflect all of our two-natured reality. Even moral classical mystics may seem to have an otherworldly air about them because they focus on the transcendent and on the otherworldly soteriological needs of other people, not on the full reality of the people they encounter: if they treat others only as manifesta-tions of the source of being and not as real in themselves, they can still be other-regarding but are not treating the full reality in them.

However, for those who accept the world as fully real and valuable in itself the situation is different. Changes in social conditions may bring about a new interest in mysticism that will cause a collective rebirth from our spiritual dark age, but a concern for social problems will have to be part of any new mystical way of life. (Whether mystical selflessness is a practical way to bring about social change or whether enough people will become interested in mysticism to make a difference on a social scale is another issue.)[38] We may integrate more awareness of the vertical dimension into our lives, thereby producing a life of less self-centeredness, but life in the world is still real and requires some self-assertiveness. We may meditate or temporally withdraw from society to focus on beingness and to lessen a sense of self, thereby enhancing a moral life. Some may ignore the centrality of getting out of the realm of suffering in Buddhism and reduce it to a matter of psychology. Or we may try to induce isolated mystical experiences as ends in themselves. But we cannot adopt a full classical mystical way of life with its entailed beliefs and still give full weight to the natural world. To do the latter means moving away from the focus exclusively on the vertical dimension of being and into concerns for the horizontal dimension, including some self-interested ones.

There may always be a few people in any society who will take up a classical mystical way of life and devote their lives completely to focusing on being to the exclusion of the other dimension of reality. But classical Christian mystics adopt eschatological values interpreted on an individual scale, and something analogous happens with classical mystics of other traditions. Their life may be one of joyful self-giving, living every day as if it is their last. But these people are not of this world—they are one-dimensional. Such mystics will remain exemplars of religious ideals for others to admire or even strive toward, but their perspective limits the impact their values can have on anyone who does not see the world as ultimately valueless. Any realism requires a focus also on the natural world. As long as the mystery of the existence of this realm remains—a mystery that is likely to last as long as we do—we cannot adopt a full-blown mystical way of life without admitting that we are foregoing part of what is in the final analysis real in the world and part of what it is to be human.

Notes

1. Hans Blumenberg puts the very definition of modernity in terms of "self-assertion." See his *The Legitimation of Modernity* (Cambridge, Mass.: MIT Press, 1982), p. 138. He is not contrasting it with mystical humility, but nevertheless classical mystics would readily agree. (More generally, the mystical denial of self-assertion makes mystics appear irrational and immoral—i.e., quietistic—under the modern view.)

2. As discussed in Chapter 13, the mystic has internalized beliefs and values but may have to deliberate in situations where the internalized framework does not readily supply an answer.

3. Underhill 1915, p. ix.

4. If the transcendent source were literally ineffable, it could not be of any significance to our lives beyond being the source—it could not be the source of value and could not provide any basis for morality nor offer any other guidance because it would have no properties. To the moral mystic, a caring, nurturing love or absolute goodness appears as an attribute of the reality enveloping our world. For Mahāyāna Buddhists, the role of the Bodhisattva Avalokiteshvara makes compassion a cosmic principle. For theists, the underlying energy of the universe is love. It is the power that "shakes the universe" (Johnston 1978, p. 172). For the Muslim Jalāl al-Dīn Rūmī, love is the astrolabe of the transcendent. Richard Bucke is a more recent theistic example. His "cosmic consciousness" showed him that this world is not composed of dead matter governed by unconscious laws but is a living presence whose foundation is love; everyone and everything has eternal life; God is the universe and the universe is God, and no evil could ever enter into it; and the

happiness of everyone in the long run is absolutely certain (*Cosmic Consciousness* [New York: Dutton, 1969], pp. 17-18). But, as noted above, whether the self-giving transcendental ground can be characterized as moral in the sense of evincing an other-regarding concern for parts of this realm is open to question if the natural realm is accepted as real. A simpler deistic source would not satisfy theists—even if it somehow programmed in a moral structure to the universe—since they want a source that responds in this realm to people's needs. Other types of religious experiences would have to be the experiential ground for such a theism.

5. Most mystical traditions accept that paranormal powers exist within the natural order. Thus, it is claimed that a moral mystic could help others by tapping into this energy. For example, the Transcendental Meditation way to world peace is through collective meditation (since the government of each country merely reflects the cumulative consciousness of its individual citizens). That is, their claim is that the group dynamics of TM consciousness can neutralize the turbulence in the "world consciousness" and that world peace will ensue.

6. Singer 1993a, 1993b; also see Unger 1996. Peter Singer and Peter Unger, who operate within a strictly nonreligious naturalistic framework, present a significant challenge for Christians under the Good Samaritan principle concerning how they too should act.

7. This position rejects the claim that all "true religion is essentially otherworldly" (Radhakrishnan 1940, p. 75). Mysticism does deal with a dimension of reality not seen if we live focused solely on the world of multiplicity, but it need not be "other-worldly" in the sense of being concerned only with the transcendent or life after death. It should be noted that the devotional strand of religiosity can also be a source of world-rejection: God the creator can be given so much reality that the world once again is not considered real enough to be worthy of our attention. Indeed, valuing the universe as an end in itself (e.g., showing a concern for the environment) becomes a form of idolatry. Thus, different theisms that combine both strands can readily produce followers who reject this world.

8. Mystical experiences may supply a sense that the world is meaningful or at least that everything is all right as it is, but these experiences do not provide an exact answer to the question of what is the meaning to the world—different religions do that. As John Hick says, the religious are "cosmic optimists" (Hick 1989, pp. 56-69; 1999, pp. 47-73). This may just reflect something in our brain that makes us look for reasons and causes, but the religious have a sense that there is a "purpose" or point to all of this, perhaps not in a teleological sense but in the sense that there is some reason for all of this and the suffering we go through. Religions supply the frameworks that make life meaningful. See Chapter 3.

9. Mysticism does not have the dualism of the numinous strand of religiosity (with a creator totally set off from its creation) since the transcendent is open to direct experience, and according to theistic mystics the world shares the same being as the transcendent reality. But the question here is of the focus: must it exclusively be on the transcendent reality?

10. The issue also arises in other strands of religiosity. For example, Paul said that Christians are fixed on the eternal, not on the temporal that passes away (2 Cor. 4:18). We are "strangers and exiles on the earth" (Heb. 11:13). This can easily lead to focusing only on our postmortem fate in heaven or hell and to not taking the world seriously.

11. Under the naturalist worldview, any dependence on a transcendental reality—creation, manifestation, emanation—is, along with all transcendental realities, also rejected. If naturalists accept that mystical experiences occur, they would interpret them as at best an insight into the natural world.

12. This is not to say that theists have not stopped trying to restore a special place for human beings within the scientific view of reality. The Anthropic Principle is a current example. Theists point to the truly amazing "fine-tuning" of physical forces that permits the

highly improbable outcome of human life arising on earth and conclude that nature knew we were coming. (The various "multiple worlds" hypotheses advanced by naturalists that would neutralize the seeming improbability are generally dismissed by theists.) To them, this means that all of reality was planned for us, although at best it can only mean that human beings are as natural a part of the universe as stars and trees and that any particular being or type of beings were not planned in advance.

13. Shri Aurobindo is a modern Indian who, with Western influences, began to take the world seriously. Even popularists have begun to see the problem with classical mysticism. See the dialogue of Andrew Cohen and Ken Wilbur, "The Evolution of Enlightenment," *What is Enlightenment?* (Spring-Summer 2002): pp. 38-49, 136-41.

14. See Hick 1999, pp. 241-42.

15. See John Stuart Mill's essay "Nature" in *Three Essays on Religion* (responding to Alexander Pope's claim that "whatever is, is right") for a description of nature as a realm of violence, hideous death, and cruelty, totally devoid of any mercy, justice, peace, or harmony.

16. David Hull, "The God of the Galapagos," *Nature* 352 (8 August 1992), p.486.

17. For a truly depressing history, see Jonathan Glover, *Humanity: A Moral History of the Twentieth Century* (New Haven, Conn.: Yale University Press, 2000). Religion is also playing a major role in this violence. See Juergensmeyer 2000 on the disturbing connection of religion and violence today.

18. One common religious explanation of human suffering is that God allows children to die and makes the innocent suffer (as with Job) so that the rest of us will know that this world is not the ultimate reality. If so, God is not obviously moral (since God would be harming innocent people), and it would also mean that human suffering does not count for much in the ultimate scheme of things.

19. Plotinus dismissed concern for the "lower self" as pointless sentimentalism—only the return to the One mattered. We exist only as a movement toward the One (*Enneads* VI.9.9). But, like Shankara's, his own practice contradicted his theory. For example, he showed concern for the worldly needs of the orphans in his care (Rist 1967, pp. 163-64).

20. That the experience can transform the experiencer does not guarantee that the experiencer is in contact with the source of the natural realm. The experience may have a powerful effect on a person even if it results merely from the mind malfunctioning when it is active but is totally empty of all content. All such epistemological issues will not be addressed here.

21. Proudfoot 1976.

22. Assuming that our universe is in fact the product of an underlying source, how can a contingent reality be considered part of the ultimate makeup of reality? Our universe did not have to exist, but now that it does it is an irrefutable part of reality. It cannot now be removed from the history of what has been real and it is currently fully real.

23. Emergent realities can be ontologically dependent upon another reality and yet structurally still irreducibly real. For example, antireductionists argue that the mind is such a reality, even if it needs the physical level (the brain or body) as a base. See R. H. Jones 2000 for a discussion of these issues.

24. Mystics devalue what the unenlightened value in light of a reality of higher value. Classical mysticism is negative or "world-denying" only in the sense of denying what the unenlightened take to be real, not in denying that something is ultimately real and supremely valuable. It is reality-affirming and also optimistic in that each way of life offers a way out of our suffering. It is "escapism" only in that mystics want to escape an illusory world for the real one.

25. The transcendent is "good" in a nonmoral sense in that it is the active, self-emptying source of our realm, but problems with the transcendent being seen as loving (and hence *morally* good) were noted above. Thus, in the end, determining whether the transcendent is moral will depend on nonmystical sources.

26. See R. H. Jones 1986, pp. 214-18, for a discussion of a possible reconciliation.

27. Thus, mysticism is not "practical" in the sense of dealing with the "horizontal" problems of life, but if mystical experiences are cognitive mysticism is essential for seeing the total context in which we live. That is, it can expand the experiential base in which we live our life to encompass the total ontological environment in which we actually live, thereby affecting our values and how we treat others.

28. *Enneads* IV.8.4.

29. See Evans 1993 on human beings.

30. Many Hindu philosophers see this as the reason one cannot be "enlightened in life." As Huston Smith puts it, enlightenment is only an ideal in this life because our "mortal coils" are too tight. But the problem for all classical mystics again is why this would be the case unless this realm is real in the final analysis.

31. Enlightened mystics also may never be numerous. In Tibet, with a population of between three and four million people 20 percent of whom were ordained monks or nuns, it is said that only about thirty people in the twentieth century attained enlightenment. Jean-François Revel and Matthieu Ricard, *The Monk and the Philosopher* (New York: Schocken Books, 1999), p. 51. If we have to wait for enlightened mystics to be a social force, it may be a long wait.

32. Morality is defined in terms of "other-regardingness." It may be extendable to a concern for animals (i.e., they are the type of beings toward which other-regardingness is possible because they are conscious or they suffer), but can it be extended to plants and the rest of nature? Is nature the type of reality toward which other-regardingness is legitimate, or is a concern for nature merely self-serving for us? In short, can the environment have moral rights? In any case, mystical selflessness can be extended to all of reality, even if it is not a *moral* concern.

33. See Deutsch 1992 for a version of this.

34. See Rolston 1987 for a discussion of this issue in connection with the environment.

35. See Tillich 1963 on self-transcendence and self-centeredness in ethics.

36. Camouflage and other forms of deception are common in animals and plants, both to survive predators and to capture food. Thus, not only is violence ingrained in the structure of reality, but "lying" seems to be a natural virtue.

37. Monastics who live solely on the charity of others have a moral problem: granted, they may provide teaching and the opportunity for charitable giving in exchange, but they have merely shifted the burden of a desire-driven life onto others. It is like eating meat others have killed and not thinking that one is involved in the process of killing animals. As long as monastics live in this world, they too are caught up in its processes, and they have to accept that reality.

38. Some scholars assert that mystical experiences are actually quite common. Some would add that there are more near-death experiences (since more people are now being revived with the advance of medical technology) and other types of paranormal experiences. And yet these and mystical experiences have not had a great social effect in the modern world. If they are indeed common, this points to the fact that factors outside the experiences themselves determine their social impact. One would be hard pressed to argue that social conditions today are more conducive to a mystical revolution rather than to an increase in interest in our material condition and away from any transcendental focus.

Selected Bibliography

Adams, Robert M. "A Modified Divine Command Theory of Ethical Wrongness." Pp. 318-47 in *Religion and Morality: A Collection of Essays*, edited by Gene Outka and John P. Reeder, Jr. Garden City, N.Y.: Anchor, 1973.

Aitken, Robert. *The Mind of Clover: Essays in Zen Buddhist Ethics*. San Francisco: North Point Press, 1984.

Alexander, Edwin. "Review of Danto's *Mysticism and Morality*." *Journal of Indian Philosophy* 4 (September-December 1976): pp. 135-54.

Allinson, Robert E. "The Confucian Golden Rule: A Negative Formulation." *Journal of Chinese Philosophy* 12 (September 1985): pp. 305-15.

———. "Having Your Cake and Eating it, Too: Evaluation and Trans-Evaluation in Chuang Tzu and Nietzsche." *Journal of Chinese Philosophy* 13 (December 1986): pp. 429-43.

———. "The Golden Rule as the Core Value in Confucianism and Christianity: Ethical Similarities and Differences." *Asian Philosophy* 2, no. 2 (1992): pp. 173-85.

———. "Moral Values and the Daoist Sage in the *Dao De Jing*." Pp. 156-68 in *Morals and Society in Asian Philosophy*, edited by Brian Carr. Richmond, Surrey: Curzon, 1996.

Ames, Roger T. *The Art of Rulership: A Study in Ancient Chinese Political Thought*. Honolulu: University of Hawaii Press, 1983.

Aminrazavi, Mehdi. "Antinomian Tradition in Islamic Mysticism." *Bulletin of the Henry Martyn Institute of Islamic Studies* 14 (January-June 1995): pp. 17-24.

An, Ok-Sun. *Compassion and Benevolence: A Comparative Study of Early Buddhist and Classical Confucian Ethics*. New York: Peter Lang, 1998.

Angel, Leonard. *Enlightenment East and West*. Albany: State University of New York Press, 1994.

Anscombe, Elizabeth. "Modern Moral Philosophy." *Philosophy* 33 (January 1958): pp. 1-19.

Aronson, Harvey B. "The Relationship of the Karmic to the Nirvanic in Theravāda Buddhism." *Journal of Religious Ethics* 7 (Spring 1979): pp. 28-36.

———. *Love and Sympathy in Theravāda Buddhism*. Delhi: Motilal Banarsidass, 1980a.

———. "Motivations to Social Action in Theravada Buddhism: Uses and Abuses of Traditional Doctrines." Pp. 1-12 in *Studies in History of Buddhism*, edited by A. K. Narain. Delhi: B. R. Publishing, 1980b.

Awn, Peter J. "The Ethical Concerns of Classical Sufism." *Journal of Religious Ethics* 11 (Fall 1983): pp. 240-63.

Baer, Helmut David. "The Fruit of Charity: Using the Neighbor in *De doctrina christiana*." *Journal of Religious Ethics* 24 (Fall 1996): pp. 47-64.

Baker, Denise N. "The Active and Contemplative Lives in Rolle, the *Cloud*-Author, and Hilton." Pp. 85-102 in *The Medieval Mystical Tradition in England, Ireland, and Wales*, edited by Marion Glasscoe. Rochester, N.Y.: D. S. Brewer, 1999.

Barnard, G. William, and Jeffrey J. Kripal, eds. *Crossing Boundaries: Essays on the Ethical Status of Mysticism*. New York: Seven Bridges Press, 2002.

Barnhart, Michael, ed. *Varieties of Ethical Reflection: New Directions for Ethics in a Global Context*. Lanham, Md.: Lexington Books, 2002.

Barnsley, John H. *The Social Reality of Ethics: The Comparative Analysis of Moral Codes*. Boston: Routledge and Kegan Paul, 1972.

Bartholomeusz, Tessa. "In Defense of Dharma: Just-War Ideology in Buddhist Sri Lanka." *Journal of Buddhist Ethics* 6 (1999): pp. 1-11.

Basham, A. L. "Asoka and Buddhism: A Re-Examination." *Journal of the International Association of Buddhist Studies* 5 (1982): pp. 131-43.

Batson, C. Daniel, Patricia Schoenrade, and W. Larry Ventis. "Concern for Others or Self-Concern?" Pp. 331-64 in their *Religion and the Individual*, 2nd ed. New York: Oxford University Press, 1993.

Bastow, David. "Buddhist Ethics." *Religious Studies* 5 (December 1969): pp. 195-206.

Bauer, Nancy F. "Advaita Vedānta and Contemporary Western Ethics." *Philosophy East and West* 37 (January 1987): pp. 36-50.

Beach, Waldo, and H. Richard Niebuhr, eds. *Christian Ethics: Sources of the Living Tradition*, 2nd ed. New York: Ronald Press, 1973.

Becker, Carl B. "Buddhist Views of Suicide and Euthanasia." *Philosophy East and West* 40 (October 1990): pp. 543-56.

Berger, Peter L. "Identity as a Problem in the Sociology of Knowledge." Pp. 373-84 In *The Sociology of Knowledge: A Reader*, edited by James E. Curtis and John W. Petras. New York: Praeger, 1970.

Bergson, Henri. *The Two Sources of Morality and Religion*. Translated by R. Ashley Audra and Cloudesley Brereton, with W. Horsfall Carter. New York: Henry Holt, 1935.

Bharati, Agehananda. *The Light at the Center: Context and Pretext of Modern Mysticism*. Santa Barbara, Calif.: Ross-Erikson, 1976.

———. *Tantric Traditions*, rev. ed. Delhi: Hindustan Publishing, 1993.

Bhārgava, Dayānanda. *Jaina Ethics*. Delhi: Motilal Banarsidass, 1968.

Bhattacharya, Abheda Nanda. *Dharma-Adharma and Morality in* Mahabharata. Delhi: S. S. Publishers, 1992.

Bird, Frederick B. "Paradigms and Parameters for the Comparative Study of Religious and Ideological Ethics." *Journal of Religious Ethics* 9 (Fall 1981): pp. 157-85.

———. "A Comparative Study of the Work of Charity in Christianity and Judaism." *Journal of Religious Ethics* 10 (Spring 1982): pp. 144-69.

———. "How Do Religions Affect Moralities? A Comparative Analysis." *Social Compass* 37, no. 3 (1990): pp. 291-314.

Blakney, Raymond Bernard, trans. *Meister Eckhart*. New York: Harper & Row, 1941.

Bleich, J. David. "Is There an Ethic Beyond Halaklah?" Pp. 527-46 in *Studies in Jewish Philosophy: Collected Essays of the Academy for Jewish Philosophy, 1980-1985*, edited by Norbert M. Samuelson. Lanham, Md.: University Press of America, 1987.

Bloom, Irene, J. Paul Martin, and Wayne L. Proudfoot, eds. *Religious Diversity and Human Rights*. New York: Columbia University Press, 1996.

Boyd, Richard N. "How to be a Moral Realist." Pp. 297-356 in *Contemporary Materialism: A Reader*, edited by Paul K. Moser and J. D. Trout. New York: Routledge, 1995.

Brandt, Richard B. *Hopi Ethics: A Theoretical Analysis*. Chicago: University of Chicago Press, 1954.

Brear, A. D. "The Nature and Status of Moral Behavior in Zen Buddhist Tradition." *Philosophy East and West* 24 (October 1974): pp. 429-41.

Brockington, John. *Hinduism and Christianity*. New York: St. Martin's Press, 1992.

van Buitenen, J. A. B. "*Dharma* and *Moksa*." *Philosophy East and West* 7 (April-July 1957): 33-40.

Bstan-'dzin-rgya-mtsho (XIV Dalai Lama). *Ethics for the New Millennium*. New York: Riverhead Books, 1999.

Butler, Dom Cuthbert. *Western Mysticism: The Teaching of Saints Augustine, Gregory and Bernard on Contemplation and the Contemplative Life*. New York: Dutton, 1923.

Carman, John B. "The Ethics of the Auspicious: Western Encounter with Hindu Values." Pp. 167-83 in *Foundations of Ethics*, edited by Leroy S. Rouner. Notre Dame, Ind.: University of Notre Dame Press, 1983.

Carter, John Ross. "Beyond 'Beyond Good and Evil.'" Pp. 89-103 in his *On Understanding Buddhists: Essays on the Theravāda Tradition in Sri Lanka*. Albany: State University of New York Press, 1993.

——. "Reflections on Social and Political Ideals in Buddhist Philosophy." Pp. 360-69 in *A Companion to World Philosophies*, edited by Eliot Deutsch and Ron Bontekoe. Malden, Mass.: Blackwell, 1999.

Carter, John Ross, and Mahinda Palihawadana, trans. *The Dhammapada*. New York: Oxford University Press, 1987.

Carter, Robert E. *Encounter with Enlightenment: A Study of Japanese Ethics*. Albany: State University of New York Press, 2001.

Chan, Wing-Tsit, trans. *The Way of Lao Tzu*. New York: Paragon House, 1963.

Chappell, David W. "Searching for a Mahāyāna Social Ethic." *Journal of Religious Ethics* 24 (Fall 1996): 351-75.

Chapple, Christopher Key. *Nonviolence to Animals, Earth, and Self in Asian Traditions*. Albany: State University of New York Press, 1993.

Chatterjee, D. "Karma and Liberation in Sankara's Advaita Vedanta." Pp. 158-69 in *Perspectives on Vedānta: Essays in Honor of Professor P. T. Raju*, edited by S. S. Rama Rao Pappu. Boston: E. J. Brill, 1988.

Chen, Ellen Marie. "Is There a Doctrine of Physical Immortality in the *Tao Te Ching?*" *History of Religions* 12 (February 1973): pp. 231-49.

——, trans. *The Tao Te Ching*. New York: Paragon House, 1989.

Childress, James F. "Methodological Issues in Comparative Religious Ethics." *Journal of Religious Ethics* 7 (Spring 1979): pp. 1-10.

Ching, Julia. *Mysticism and Kingship in China: The Heart of Chinese Wisdom*. Cambridge: Cambridge University Press, 1997.

Chittick, William C. "Ethical Standards and the Vision of Oneness: The Case of Ibn al-'Arabî." Pp. 361-76 in *Mystics of the Book: Themes, Topics, and Typologies*, edited by R. A. Herrera. New York: Peter Lang, 1993.

Clark, Henry. *The Ethical Mysticism of Albert Schweitzer: A Study of the Sources and Significance of Schweitzer's Philosophy of Civilization*. Boston: Beacon Press, 1962.

Clark, John P. "On Taoism and Politics." *Journal of Chinese Philosophy* 10 (1983): pp. 65-88.

Cobb, John B., Jr. "Incommensurability: Can Comparative Religious Ethics Help?" *Buddhist-Christian Studies* 16 (1996): pp. 39-45.

Cohn, Norman. *The Pursuit of the Millennium: Revolutionary Millenarians and Mystical Anarchists of the Middle Ages*, rev. ed. New York: Oxford University Press, 1970.

Colledge, Edmund, and J. C. Marler, "'Poverty of the Will': Russbroec, Eckhart and *The Mirror of Simple Souls*." Pp. 14-47 in *Jan van Ruusbroec: The Sources, Content, and Sequels of his Mysticism*, edited by P. Mommaers and N. de Paepe. Leuven, Belgium: Leuven University Press, 1984.

Colledge, Edmund, and Bernard McGinn, trans. and eds. *Meister Eckhart: The Essential Sermons, Commentaries, Treatises, and Defense*. New York: Paulist Press, 1981.

Conze, Edward, trans. *Buddhist Wisdom Books*. London: George Allen & Unwin, 1958.

——. *The Perfection of Wisdom in Eight Thousand Lines & Its Verse Summary*. Berkeley: Four Seasons Foundation, 1973.

Cook, Francis Dojun. *How to Raise an Ox: Zen Practice as Taught in Zen Master Dōgen's Shōbōgenzō*. Los Angeles: Center Publications, 1978.

Cottingham, John. "Ethics and Impartiality." *Philosophical Studies* 43 (January 1983): pp. 83-99.

——. "The Ethics of Self-Concern." *Ethics* 101 (July 1991): pp. 798-817.

Cousins, Lance S. "Ethical Standards in World Religions: Buddhism." *Expository Times* 85 (January 1974): pp. 100-4.

Coward, Harold G., Julius J. Lipner, and Katherine K. Young. *Hindu Ethics: Purity, Abortion, and Euthanasia*. Albany: State University of New York Press, 1989.

Crawford, S. Cromwell. *The Evolution of Hindu Ethical Ideals*, 2nd ed. Honolulu: University of Hawaii Press, 1982.

——, ed. *World Religions and Global Ethics*. New York: Paragon House, 1989.

Creel, Austin B. "*Dharma* as an Ethical Category Relating to Freedom and Responsibility." *Philosophy East and West* 22 (April 1972): pp. 155-68.

——. "The Reexamination of *Dharma* in Hindu Ethics." *Philosophy East and West* 25 (April 1975): pp. 161-73.

——. "Studies of Hindu Ethics: A Bibliographic Introduction." *Religious Studies Review* 2 (January 1976): pp. 26-33.

——. *Dharma in Hindu Ethics*. Calcutta: Firma KLM, 1977a.

——. "The Modern Study of Hindu Ethics." *International Philosophical Quarterly* 17 (December 1977b): pp. 445-54.

Creel, Herrlee G. *What is Taoism? And Other Studies in Chinese Cultural History*. Chicago: University of Chicago Press, 1970.

Csikszentmihalyi, Mark, and Philip J. Ivanhoe, ed. *Religious and Philosophical Aspects of the* Laozi. Albany: State University of New York Press, 1999.

Cua, Antonio S. "Forgetting Morality: Reflections on a Theme in *Chuang tzu*." *Journal of Chinese Philosophy* 4 (September 1977): pp. 305-28.

——. *Dimensions of Moral Creativity: Paradigms, Principles, and Ideals*. University Park: Pennsylvania State University Press, 1978.

——. "Chinese Moral Vision, Responsive Agency, and Factual Beliefs." *Journal of Chinese Philosophy* 7 (March 1980): pp. 3-26.

——. "Reflections on Moral Theory and Understanding Moral Traditions." Pp. 280-93 in *Interpreting Across Boundaries: New Essays in Comparative Philosophy*, edited by

Gerald James Larson and Eliot Deutsch. Princeton, N.J.: Princeton University Press, 1988.

——. "Reasonable Challenges and Preconditions of Adjudication." Pp. 279-98 in *Culture and Modernity: East-West Philosophic Perspectives*, edited by Eliot Deutsch. Honolulu: University of Hawaii Press, 1991.

Dan, Joseph. *Jewish Mysticism and Jewish Ethics*, 2nd ed. Northvale, N.J.: Jason Aronson, 1996.

Danto, Arthur C. "Role and Rule in Oriental Thought: Some Metareflections on *Dharma* and *Li*." *Philosophy East and West* 22 (April 1972): pp. 213-20.

——. "Ethical Theory and Mystical Experience: A Response to Professors Proudfoot and Wainwright." *Journal of Religious Ethics* 4 (Spring 1976): pp. 37-46

——. *Mysticism and Morality: Oriental Thought and Moral Philosophy*, 2nd ed. New York: Columbia University Press, 1987.

Dasgupta, Surama. *Development of Moral Philosophy in India*. New York: Frederick Ungar, 1965.

Dayal, Har. *The Bodhisattva Doctrine in Buddhist Sanskrit Literature*. Delhi: Motilal Banarsidass, 1970.

DeNicola, Daniel R. "Supererogation: Artistry in Action." Pp. 149-64 in *Foundations of Ethics*, edited by Leroy S. Rouner. Notre Dame, Ind.: University of Notre Dame Press, 1983.

Deussen, Paul. *The Philosophy of the Upanishads*. New York: Dover Publications, 1966.

Deutsch, Eliot. *The Bhagavad Gītā*. New York: Holt, Rinehart, and Winston, 1968.

——. *Advaita Vedānta: A Philosophical Reconstruction*. Honolulu: East-West Center, 1969.

——. "A Creative Morality" and "Creative Anarchism." Pp. 179-219 in his *Creative Being: The Crafting of Person and World*. Honolulu: University of Hawaii Press, 1992.

Dillon, John M. "An Ethic for the Late Antique Sage." Pp. 315-35 in *The Cambridge Companion to Plotinus*, edited by Lloyd P. Gerson. Cambridge: Cambridge University Press, 1996.

Donovan, Peter. "Do Different Religions Share Moral Common Ground?" *Religious Studies* 22 (September-December 1986): pp. 367-75.

Dreyfus, Georges. "Meditation as Ethical Activity." *Journal of Buddhist Ethics* 2 (1995): pp. 1-17.

Dreyfus, Hubert L. and Stuart E. Dreyfus. "What is Moral Maturity? Towards a Phenomenology of Ethical Expertise." Pp. 111-31 in *Revisioning Philosophy*, edited by James Ogilvy. Albany: State University of New York, 1992.

Dupré, Louis. *The Other Dimension: The Search for the Meaning of Religious Attitudes*. Garden City, N.Y.: Doubleday, 1972.

——. "Beyond Self-Achievement." Pp. 31-41 in his *Transcendent Selfhood: The Loss and Rediscovery of the Inner Life*. New York: Seabury, 1976.

——. *The Deeper Life: An Introduction to Christian Mysticism*. New York: Crossroad, 1981.

——. *The Common Life: The Origins of Trinitarian Mysticism and its Development by Jan Ruusbroec*. New York: Crossroad, 1984.

——. "The Christian Experience of Mystical Union." *Journal of Religion* 69 (January 1989): pp. 1-13.

Edgerton, Franklin. "The Upanishads: What Do They Seek and Why?" *Journal of the American Oriental Society* 49 (1929): pp. 97-121.

——. "Dominant Ideas in the Formation of Indian Culture." *Journal of the American Oriental Society* 62 (September 1942): pp. 151-56.

——, trans. *The Bhagavad Gītā*. Cambridge: Harvard University Press, 1944.

——. "The Upanishads and the Fundamental Doctrines of Later Hindu Thought." Pp. 28-34 in his *The Beginnings of Indian Philosophy*. Cambridge, Mass.: Harvard University Press, 1965.

Endo, Toshiichi. *Dāna: The Development of its Concept and Practice*. Colombo: Gunasena, 1987.

Eno, Robert. "Cook Ding's Dao and the Limits of Philosophy." Pp. 127-51 in *Essays on Skepticism, Relativism, and Ethics in the* Zhuangzi, edited by Paul Kjellberg and Philip J. Ivanhoe. Albany: State University of New York Press, 1996.

Eppsteiner, Fred, ed. *The Path of Compassion: Writings on Socially Engaged Buddhism*. Berkeley, Calif.: Parallax Press, 1988.

Evans, Donald. "Mysticism Humanism and Morality." Pp. 171-95 in his *Spirituality and Human Nature*. Albany: State University of New York Press, 1993.

Fakhry, Majid. *Ethical Theories in Islam*. New York: E. J. Brill, 1991.

Falk, Ze'ev W. *Religious Law and Ethics: Studies in Biblical and Rabbinical Theonomy*. Jerusalem: Mesharim, 1991.

Feuerstein, Georg. *Holy Madness: The Shock Tactics and Radical Teachings of Crazy-Wise Adepts, Holy Fools, and Rascal Gurus*. New York: Paragon, 1991.

——. *Tantra: The Path of Ecstasy*. Boston: Shambhala, 1998.

Flood, Gavin D. "Making Moral Decisions." Pp. 30-55 in *Themes and Issues in Hinduism*, edited by Paul Bowen. London: Cassell, 1998.

Foot, Philipa. *Virtues and Vices, and Other Essays in Moral Philosophy*. Oxford: Blackwell, 1978.

Forman, Robert K. C. *Meister Eckhart: Mystic as Theologian*. Rockport, Mass.: Element, 1991.

Fort, Andrew O. "Knowing Brahman While Embodied: Śankara on Jīvanmukti." *Journal of Indian Philosophy* 19 (September 1991): pp. 369-89.

——. *Jīvanmukti in Transformation: Embodied Liberation in Advaita and Neo-Vedanta*. Albany: State University of New York Press, 1998.

Fort, Andrew O., and Patricia Y. Mumme, eds. *Living Liberation in Hindu Thought*. Albany: State University of New York Press, 1996.

Fox, Douglas A. "Zen and Ethics: Dōgen's Synthesis." *Philosophy East and West* 21 (January 1971): pp. 33-41.

Fox, Matthew. *Breakthrough: Meister Eckhart's Creation Spirituality, in New Translation*. Garden City, N.Y.: Doubleday, 1980a.

——. "Meister Eckhart and Karl Marx: The Mystic as Political Theologian." Pp. 541-63 in *Understanding Mysticism*, edited by Richard Woods. Garden City, N.Y.: Image Books, 1980b.

Frankena, William K. *Ethics*, 2nd ed. Englewood Cliffs: Prentice-Hall, 1973.

——. *Thinking About Morality*. Ann Arbor: University of Michigan Press, 1980.

——. "Relations of Morality and Religion." Pp. 400-403 in *The Westminster Dictionary of Christian Ethics*, edited by James F. Childress and John Macquarrie. Philadelphia: Westminster Press, 1986.

Freund, Richard A. "Jewish Ethics and Jewish Mysticism." Pp. 182-99 in his *Understanding Jewish Ethics: Major Themes and Thinkers*, vol. 2. San Francisco: EMText, 1993.

Furtado, Vincent Gabriel. *Classical Sāmkhya Ethics: A Study of the Ethical Perspectives of Īśvarakrsna's Sāmkhyakārikās*. Würzburg, Germany: Echter, 1992.

Gandhi, Mahatma. *An Autobiography, or The Story of My Experiments with Truth*. Translated by Mahadev Desai. Washington: Public Affairs Press, 1954.

Garner, Richard. *Beyond Morality*. Philadelphia: Temple University Press, 1994.

Gerson, Lloyd P. "Conquering Virtue." Pp. 185-202 in his *Plotinus*. London: Routledge, 1994.

Ghose, Sisirkumar. *Mystics and Society: A Point of View*. Bombay: Asia Publishing House, 1968.

Gombrich, Richard F. *Theravada Buddhism: A Social History from Ancient Benares to Modern Colombo*. New York: Routledge and Kegan Paul, 1988.

———. *Buddhist Precept and Practice: Traditional Buddhism in the Rural Highlands of Ceylon*, 2nd ed. Delhi: Motilal Banarsidass, 1991.

Gómez, Luis O. "Emptiness and Moral Perfection." *Philosophy East and West* 23 (September 1973): pp. 361-73.

Goodwin, William F. "Ethics and Value in Indian Philosophy." *Philosophy East and West* 4 (September 1955): pp. 321-44.

———. "Mysticism and Ethics: An Examination of Radhakrishnan's Reply to Schweitzer's Critique of Indian Thought." *Ethics* 67 (October 1956): pp. 25-41.

Graham, A. C., trans. *Chuang-tzŭ: The Seven Inner Chapters and Other Writings from the Book of Chuang-tzŭ*. London: George Allen & Unwin, 1981.

———. "Taoist Spontaneity and the Dichotomy of 'Is' and 'Ought.'" Pp. 3-23 in *Experimental Essays on Chuang-Tzu*, edited by Victor H. Mair. Honolulu: University of Hawaii Press, 1983.

Greeley, Andrew M. "Ecstatic Politics." Pp. 98-111 in his *Ecstasy: A Way of Knowing*. Englewood Cliffs, N.J.: Prentice-Hall, 1974.

Green, Ronald M. "Jewish Ethics and the Virtue of Humility." *Journal of Religious Ethics* 1 (Fall 1973): pp. 53-63.

———. *Religious Reason*. New York: Oxford University Press, 1978.

———. "Morality and Religion." Pp. 92-106 in *The Encyclopedia of Religion*, vol. 10, edited by Mircea Eliade. New York: Macmillan, 1987.

———. *Religion and Moral Reason: A New Method for Comparative Study*. New York: Oxford University Press, 1988.

Green, Ronald M., and Charles H. Reynolds. "Cosmogony and the 'Question of Ethics.'" *Journal of Religious Ethics* 14 (Spring 1986): pp. 139-56.

Gudmunsen, Chris. "Ethics Get in the Way: A Reply to David Bastow." *Religious Studies* 8 (December 1971): pp. 311-18.

Guroian, Vigen. "Notes Toward an Eastern Orthodox Ethic." *Journal of Religious Ethics* 9 (Fall 1981): pp. 228-44.

Hadot, Pierre. *Plotinus, or, The Simplicity of Vision*. Translated by Michael Chase. Chicago: University of Chicago, 1993.

Halberstam, Joshua. "Supererogation in Jewish *Halakhah* and Islamic *Shari'a*." Pp. 85-98 in *Studies in Islamic and Judaic Traditions*, edited by William M. Brinner and Stephen D. Ricks. Atlanta, Ga.: Scholars Press, 1986.

Hallett, Garth L. *Christian Neighbor-Love*. Washington, D.C.: Georgetown University Press, 1989.

Hardy, Friedhelm. "The Esoteric Traditions and Antinomian Movements." Pp. 649-59 in *The World's Religions*, edited by Stewart Sutherland, J. Leslie Houlden, Peter Clarke, and Friedhelm Hardy. Boston: G. K. Hall, 1988.

Harris, Charles E., Jr. "Can *Agape* Be Universalized?" *Journal of Religious Ethics* 6 (Spring 1978): pp. 19-31.

Harvey, Peter. "Criteria for Judging the Unwholesomeness of Actions in the Texts of Theravāda Buddhism." *Journal of Buddhist Ethics* 2 (1995): pp. 1-8.

——. *An Introduction to Buddhist Ethics.* New York: Cambridge University Press, 2000.

Hawley, John Stratton, ed. *Saints and Virtues.* Berkeley: University of California Press, 1987.

Herman, E. "Quietism." Pp. 533-38 in the *Encyclopedia of Religion and Ethics*, vol. 10, edited by James Hastings. New York: Charles Scribner's Sons, n.d.

Hick, John. *An Interpretation of Religion: Human Responses to the Transcendent.* New Haven, Conn.: Yale University Press, 1989.

——. *The Fifth Dimension.* Boston: Oneworld Publications, 1999.

Hindery, Roderick. "Exploring Comparative Religious Ethics." *Journal of Ecumenical Studies* 10 (Summer 1973): pp. 552-74.

——. *Comparative Ethics in Hindu and Buddhist Traditions.* Delhi: Motilal Banarsidass, 1978.

Hiriyanna, Mysore. *Indian Conceptions of Values.* Mysore, India: Kavyalaya Publishers, 1975.

Hoffman, Bengt, trans. *The Theologia Germanica of Martin Luther.* New York: Paulist Press, 1980.

Holm, Jean with John Bowker, ed. *Making Moral Decisions.* London: Pinter, 1994.

Hopkins, Edward W. *The Ethics of India.* New Haven, Conn.: Yale University Press, 1924.

Hopkins, Jeffrey, trans. *Compassion in Tibetan Buddhism.* Valois, N.Y.: Gabriel/Snow Lion, 1980.

——. *Buddhist Advice for Living and Liberation: Nāgārjuna's Precious Garland.* Ithaca, N.Y.: Snow Lion Publications, 1998.

——. *Cultivating Compassion: A Buddhist Perspective.* New York: Broadway Books, 2001.

Horne, James R. "Saintliness and Moral Perfection." *Religious Studies* 27 (December 1981): pp. 463-71.

——. *The Moral Mystic.* Waterloo, Canada: Wilfrid Laurier University Press, 1983.

Horner, I. B. *The Early Buddhist Theory of Man Perfected.* London: Williams and Norgate, 1939.

Hourani, George F. *Reason and Tradition in Islamic Ethics.* Cambridge: Cambridge University Press, 1985.

Hume, Robert Ernest, trans. *The Thirteen Principal Upanishads*, 2nd ed. New York: Oxford University Press, 1931.

Humphreys, Christmas. *The Way of Action: A Working Philosophy for Western Life.* New York: Macmillan, 1960.

——. "Divine Law, Human Justice." *Parabola* 1, no. 2 (1976): pp. 62-67.

Hunnex, Milton D. "Mysticism and Ethics: Radhakrishnan and Schweitzer." *Philosophy East and West* 8 (October 1958): pp. 121-36.

Ingalls, Daniel H. H. "Śankara on the Question: Whose is Avidyā?" *Philosophy East and West* 3 (January 1953): pp. 69-72.

——. "*Dharma* and *Moksa*." *Philosophy East and West* 7 (April-July 1957): pp. 41-48.

Ivanhoe, Philip J. "Was Zhuangzi a Relativist?" Pp. 196-214 in *Essays on Skepticism, Relativism, and Ethics in the* Zhuangzi, edited by Paul Kjellberg and Philip J. Ivanhoe. Albany: State University of New York Press, 1996.

——. "The Concept of *de* ('Virtue') in the *Laozi*." Pp. 239-57 in *Religious and Philosophical Aspects of the* Laozi, edited by Mark Csikszentmihalyi and Philip J. Ivanhoe. Albany: State University of New York Press, 1999.

Ives, Christopher. *Zen Awakening and Society.* Honolulu: University of Hawaii Press, 1992.

Jacobs, Louis. "The Relationship Between Religion and Ethics in Jewish Thought." Pp. 155-172 in *Religion and Morality: A Collection of Essays*, edited by Gene Outka and John P. Reeder, Jr. Garden City, N.Y.: Anchor, 1973.

Jaini, Padmanabh S. *The Jaina Path of Purification*. Berkeley: University of California Press, 1979.

James, William. *The Varieties of Religious Experiences*. New York: New American Library, 1958.

Jantzen, Grace M. "Ethics and Mysticism: Friends or Foes?" *Netherlands Theologisch Tijdschrift* 39 (1985): pp. 314-26.

Jhingran, Saral. *Aspects of Hindu Morality*. Delhi: Motilal Banarsidass, 1989.

Johnston, William. "The Intuitive Approach to Morality." Pp. 101-117 in his *The Still Point: Reflections on Zen and Christian Mysticism*. New York: Fordham University Press, 1970.

———. *The Inner Eye of Love: Mysticism and Religion*. New York: Harper & Row, 1978.

———. *Mystical Theology: The Science of Love*. Maryknoll: Orbis Books, 1998.

Jonas, Hans. "Gnostic Morality." Pp. 270-81 in his *The Gnostic Religion: The Message of the Alien God and the Beginnings of Christianity*, 2nd ed. Boston: Beacon Press, 1963.

Jones, Ken. *The Social Face of Buddhism: An Approach to Political and Social Activism*. London: Wisdom Publications, 1989.

Jones, Richard H. *Science and Mysticism: A Comparative Study of Western Natural Science, Theravāda Buddhism, and Advaita Vedānta*. Lewisburg, Pa.: Bucknell University Press, 1986.

———. *Mysticism Examined: Philosophical Inquiries into Mysticism*. Albany: State University of New York Press, 1993.

———. *Reductionism: Analysis and the Fullness of Reality*. Lewisburg, Pa.: Bucknell University Press, 2000.

Jones, Rufus M. *Mysticism and Democracy in the English Commonwealth*. Cambridge, Mass.: Harvard University Press, 1932.

———. *The Flowering of Mysticism: The Friends of God in the Fourteenth Century*. New York: Macmillan, 1939.

Juergensmeyer, Mark. "Doing Ethics in a Plural World." Pp. 187-201 in *Theology and Bioethics: Exploring the Foundations and Frontiers*, edited by Earl E. Shelp. Boston: D. Reidel, 1985.

———. *Terror in the Mind of God: The Global Rise of Religious Violence*. Berkeley: University of California Press, 2000.

Kalupahana, David J. *Ethics in Early Buddhism*. Honolulu: University of Hawaii Press, 1995.

Kattackal, Jacob. *Religion and Ethics in Advaita*. Kerala, India: C.M.S. Press Kottayam, 1982.

Katz, Nathan. *Buddhist Images of Human Perfection*. Delhi: Motilal Banarsidass, 1982.

Katz, Steven T. "Ethics and Mysticism." Pp. 184-202 in *Foundations of Ethics*, edited by Leroy S. Rouner. Notre Dame, Ind.: University of Notre Dame Press, 1983.

———. "Ethics and Mysticism in Eastern Mystical Traditions." *Religious Studies* 28 (June 1992a): pp. 253-67.

———. "Ethics and Mysticism in Western Mystical Traditions." *Religious Studies* 28 (September 1992b): pp. 407-23.

Kelley, Carl F. *Meister Eckhart on Divine Knowledge*. New Haven: Yale University Press, 1973.

Keown, Damien. *The Nature of Buddhist Ethics*. New York: St. Martin's Press, 1992.

——. "Buddhism and Suicide: The Case of Channa." *Journal of Buddhist Ethics* 3 (1995a): pp. 1-15.

——. "Christian Ethics in the Light of Buddhist Ethics." *Expository Times* 106 (Fall 1995b): pp. 132-37.

——. "Karma, Character, and Consequentialism." *Journal of Religious Ethics* 24 (Fall 1996): pp. 329-50.

Kieckhefer, Richard. "Meister Eckhart's Conception of Union with God." *Harvard Theological Review* 71 (1978): pp. 203-25.

——. "Mysticism and Social Consciousness in the Fourteenth Century." *Revue de L'Universite D'Ottawa/University of Ottawa Quarterly* 48 (July-September 1978): pp. 179-86.

——. *Repression of Heresy in Medieval Germany*. Philadelphia: University of Pennsylvania Press, 1979.

——. *Unquiet Souls: Fourteenth-Century Saints and Their Religious Milieu*. Chicago: University of Chicago Press, 1984.

Kieckhefer, Richard, and George D. Bond, eds. *Sainthood: Its Manifestations in World Religions*. Berkeley: University of California Press, 1988.

Kierkegaard, Søren. *Works of Love: Some Christian Reflections in the Form of Discourses*. Translated by Howard and Edna Hong. New York: Harper, 1962.

——. *Fear and Trembling*. Edited and translated by Howard V. Hong and Edna H. Hong. Princeton, N.J.: Princeton University Press, 1983.

Kim, Hee-Jinn. *Dōgen Kigen, Mystical Realist*. Tucson: University of Arizona Press, 1975.

King, Sallie B. "It's a Long Way to a Global Ethic: A Response to Leonard Swidler." *Buddhist-Christian Studies* 15 (1995): pp. 213-19.

——. "A Global Ethic in the Light of Comparative Religious Ethics." Pp. 114-140 in *Explorations in Global Ethics*, edited by Sumner B. Twiss and Bruce Grelle. Boulder, Colo.: Westview Press, 1998.

King, Winston Lee. *Buddhism and Christianity: Some Bridges of Understanding*. Philadelphia: Westminster Press, 1962.

——. *In the Hope of Nibbana: An Essay on Theravada Buddhist Ethics*. LaSalle, Ill.: Open Court, 1964.

——. *Theravāda Meditation: The Buddhist Transformation of Yoga*. University Park: Pennsylvania State University Press, 1980.

——. "Buddhist Self-World Theory and Buddhist Ethics." *The Eastern Buddhist* 22 (Autumn 1989a): pp. 14-26.

——. "Motivated Goodness and Unmotivated Perfection in Buddhist Ethics." *Anglican Theological Review* 71 (Spring 1989b): pp. 143-52.

——. "Is There a Buddhist Ethic for the Modern World?" *The Eastern Buddhist* 25 (Autumn 1992): pp. 1-13.

——. *Zen and the Way of the Sword: Arming the Samurai Psyche*. New York: Oxford University Press, 1993.

——. "Engaged Buddhism: Past, Present, Future." *The Eastern Buddhist* 27 (Autumn 1994): pp. 14-29.

Kipnis, Andrew B. "Yogic Meditation and Social Responsibility." *Buddhist-Christian Studies* 14 (1994): 111-25.

Kitagawa, Joseph M. "Buddhism and Social Change: An Historical Perspective." Pp. 84-101 in *Buddhist Studies in Honour of Walpola Rahula*, edited by Somaratna Balasooriya, et al. London: Gordon Fraser, 1980.

Kjellberg, Paul and Philip J. Ivanhoe, eds. *Essays on Skepticism, Relativism, and Ethics in the* Zhuangzi. Albany: State University of New York Press, 1996.

Kloppenborg, Ria. *The Paccekabuddha: A Buddhist Ascetic.* Leiden, Holland: E. J. Brill, 1974.

Knox, Ronald A. *Enthusiasm: A Chapter in the History of Religion, with Special Reference to the XVII and XVIII Centuries.* New York: Oxford University Press, 1950.

Koestler, Arthur. *The Lotus and the Robot.* New York: Macmillan, 1960.

Kraft, Kenneth, ed. *Inner Peace, World Peace: Essays on Buddhism and Nonviolence.* Albany: State University of New York Press, 1992.

Kripal, Jeffrey J. *Kalī's Child: The Mystical and Erotic in the Life and Teachings of Ramakrishna,* 2nd ed. Chicago: University of Chicago Press, 1998.

——. *Roads of Excess, Palaces of Wisdom: Eroticism & Reflexivity in the Study of Mysticism.* Chicago: University of Chicago Press, 2001.

Kristiansen, Roald E. "Ethics and Emptiness." *Japanese Religions* 16 (July 1991): pp. 14-31.

Küng, Hans, ed. *Yes to a Global Ethic.* New York: Continuum, 1996.

Kupperman, Joel J. "The Supra-Moral in Religious Ethics: The Case of Buddhism." *Journal of Religious Ethics* 1 (Spring 1973): pp. 65-71.

——. "The Supra-Moral in Chinese Ethics." *Journal of Chinese Philosophy* 1 (June 1974): pp. 153-60.

——. "Tradition and Moral Progress." Pp. 313-28 in *Culture and Modernity: East-West Philosophic Perspectives,* edited by Eliot Deutsch. Honolulu: University of Hawaii Press, 1991.

——. *Character.* New York: Oxford University Press, 1991.

——. *Learning from Asian Philosophy.* New York: Oxford University Press, 1999.

Kuppuswamy, B. *Dharma and Society: A Study in Social Values.* Delhi: Macmillan, 1977.

Kvastad, Nils Bjørn. "Ethics." Pp. 165-201 in his *Problems of Mysticism.* Oslo: Scintilla Press, 1980.

Ladd, John. *The Structure of a Moral Code.* Cambridge, Mass.: Harvard University Press, 1957.

Larson, Gerald J. "The *Trimūrti* of *Dharma* in Indian Thought: Paradox or Contradiction?" *Philosophy East and West* 22 (April 1972): pp. 145-53.

Lau, D. C. *Lao Tzu: Tao Te Ching.* New York: Penguin Books, 1963.

Leff, Gordon. "The Heresy of the Free Spirit." Pp. 308-407 in his *Heresy in the Later Middle Ages: The Relation of Heterodoxy to Dissent c. 1250-c.1450,* vol. 1. New York: Barnes & Noble, 1967.

Lerner, Robert E. *The Heresy of the Free Spirit in the Late Middle Ages.* Berkeley: University of California Press, 1972.

Leslie, John. *Value and Existence.* Totowa, N.J.: Rowman and Littlefield, 1979.

Levine, Michael P. "Deep Structure and the Comparative Philosophy of Religion." *Religious Studies* 28 (September 1992): pp. 387-99.

——. "Holism and Comparative Religious Ethics." *Method & Theory in the Study of Religion* 7 (1995): pp. 131-62.

Li, Huiren. "Some Notes on the Ethics of Mystical Militancy." *Insight: A Journal of World Religions* 2 (1977): pp. 37-46.

Lipner, Julius. *Hindus: Their Religious Beliefs and Practices.* New York: Routledge, 1994.

——, ed. *The Fruits of Our Desiring: An Enquiry into the Ethics of the Bhagavadgita for Our Times.* Calgary: Bayeux Arts, 1997.

Little, David. "Comparative Religious Ethics." Pp. 216-45 in *The Study of Religion in Colleges and Universities*, edited by Paul Ramsey and John Wilson. Princeton, N.J.: Princeton University Press, 1970.

———. "Max Weber and the Comparative Study of Religious Ethics." *Journal of Religious Ethics* 2 (Fall 1974): pp. 5-40.

———. "The Present State of the Study of Comparative Religious Ethics." *Journal of Religious Ethics* 9 (Spring 1981): pp. 210-27.

Little, David, and Sumner B. Twiss, Jr. "Basic Terms in the Study of Religious Ethics." Pp. 35-77 in *Religion and Morality: A Collection of Essays*, edited by Gene Outka and John P. Reeder, Jr. Garden City, N.Y.: Anchor, 1973.

———. *Comparative Religious Ethics: A New Method*. New York: Harper & Row, 1978.

Lovin, Robin W., and Frank E. Reynolds, eds. *Cosmogony and Ethical Order: New Studies in Comparative Ethics*. Chicago: University of Chicago Press, 1985.

MacIntyre, Alaisdair. *After Virtue: A Study in Moral Theory*, 2nd ed. Notre Dame, Ind.: University of Notre Dame Press, 1984.

———. *Whose Justice? Which Rationality?* London: Duckworth, 1995.

Macy, Joanna Rogers. "Dependent Co-Arising: The Distinctiveness of Buddhist Ethics." *Journal of Religious Ethics* 7 (Spring 1979): pp. 38-52.

———. "Mutual Morality." Pp. 193-213 in her *Mutual Causality in Buddhism and General Systems Theory: The Dharma of Natural Systems*. Albany: State University of New York Press, 1991.

Madan, T. N. *Non-Renunciation: Themes and Interpretations of Hindu Culture*. New York: Oxford University Press, 1987.

Mahadevan, T. M. P. "The Basis of Social, Ethical, and Spiritual Values in Indian Philosophy." Pp. 317-35 in *Essays in East-West Philosophy: An Attempt at World Philosophical Synthesis*, edited by Charles A. Moore. Honolulu: University of Hawaii Press, 1951.

Mair, Victor H., trans. *Tao Te Ching: The Classic Book of Integrity and the Way*. New York: Bantam Books, 1990.

———, trans. *Wandering on the Way: Early Taoist Tales and Parables of Chuang Tzu*. Honolulu: University of Hawaii Press, 1994.

Marcaurelle, Roger. *Freedom Through Inner Renunciation: Śankara's Philosophy in a New Light*. Albany: State University of New York, 2000.

Maritain, Jacques. "Action and Contemplation." Pp. 170-93 in his *Scholasticism and Politics*. New York: Macmillan, 1940.

Masson, Joseph. "Positions et Problems d'une 'Morale' Theravada." *Studia Missionalia* 27 (1978): 135-38.

Masunaga, Reihō, trans. *A Primer of Sōtō Zen: A Translation of Dōgen's* Shōbōgenzō Zuimonki. Honolulu: East-West Center Press, 1971.

Mathur, D. C. "The Concept of Action in the *Bhagavad Gita*." *Philosophy and Phenomenological Research* 35 (March 1974): pp. 34-43.

Matics, Marion L., trans. *Entering the Path of Enlightenment: the Bodhicaryāvatāra of the Buddhist Poet Śāntideva*. New York: Macmillan, 1970.

Matilal, Bimal Krishna, ed. *Moral Dilemmas in the Mahābhārata*. Delhi: Motilal Banarsidass, 1989.

Mayeda, Sengaku. "Sankara's View of Ethics." Pp. 192-207 in *Philosophy East and West: Essays in Honour of Dr. T. M. P. Mahadevan*, edited by H. D. Lewis. Bombay: Blackie & Son, 1976.

——, trans. *A Thousand Teachings: The Upadeśasāhasrī of Śankara*. Tokyo: University of Tokyo Press, 1979.

McGinn, Bernard, ed. *Meister Eckhart: Teacher and Preacher*. New York: Paulist Press, 1986.

McGuinness, B. F. "The Mysticism of the '*Tractatus*.'" *Philosophical Review* 75 (July 1966): pp. 305-28.

McKenzie, John. *Hindu Ethics: A Historical and Critical Essay*. London: Oxford University Press, 1922.

McLaughlin, Eleanor. "The Heresy of the Free Spirit and Late Medieval Mysticism." Pp. 37-54 in *Medieval and Renaissance Spirituality* (*Medievalia et Humanistica* no. 4), edited by Paul Maurice Clogan. Denton: North Texas State University Press, 1973.

Merton, Thomas. *Contemplation in a World of Action*. Garden City, N.Y.: Doubleday, 1973.

Mikkelson, Douglas K. "Who is Arguing About the Cat? Moral Action and Enlightenment According to Dōgen." *Philosophy East and West* 47 (July 1997): pp. 383-97.

Misra, G. S. P. *Development of Buddhist Ethics*. New Delhi: Munshiram Manoharlal, 1984.

Moore, Charles A. "Metaphysics and Ethics in East and West." Pp. 398-424 in *Essays in East-West Philosophy: An Attempt at World Philosophical Synthesis*, edited by Charles A. Moore. Honolulu: University of Hawaii Press, 1951.

——. "Radhakrishnan's Metaphysics and Ethics." Pp. 281-313 in *The Philosophy of Sarvepalli Radhakrishnan*, edited by Paul A. Schilpp. New York: Tudor Publishing, 1952.

Munro, Donald J., ed. *Individualism and Holism: Studies in Confucian and Taoist Values*. Ann Arbor: University of Michigan Press, 1985.

Nagel, Thomas. *The Possibility of Altruism*. Oxford: Clarendon Press, 1970.

Neelakantan, K. N. Elayath. *The Ethics of Śankara*. Kerala, India: University of Calicut, 1990.

Neville, Robert Cummings, ed. *The Human Condition*. Albany: State University of New York, 2001.

Nhat Hanh, Thich. *Vietnam: Lotus in a Sea of Fire*. New York: Hill and Wang, 1967.

Nietzsche, Friedrich. *Beyond Good and Evil*. Translated by Walter Kaufmann. New York: Vintage Books, 1966.

——. *On the Genealogy of Morals*. Translated by Walter Kaufmann and R. J. Hollingdale. New York: Vintage Books, 1967.

Nuovo, Victor. "Two Cheers for Moral Religion: An Essay Review." *Journal of the American Academy of Religion* 48, no. 1 (1980): pp. 97-109.

Nygren, Anders. *Agape and Eros*. Translated by Philip S. Watson. New York: Harper & Row, 1969.

O'Donovan, Oliver. *The Problem of Self-Love in St. Augustine*. New Haven, Conn.: Yale University Press, 1980.

O'Flaherty, Wendy Doniger. *Karma and Rebirth in Classical Indian Traditions*. Berkeley: University of California Press, 1980.

O'Flaherty, Wendy and J. Duncan Derrett. *The Concept of Duty in South Asia*. New Delhi: Vikas Publishing House, 1978.

O'Flaherty, Wendy and Brian K. Smith, trans. *The Laws of Manu*. New York: Penguin Books, 1991.

Olivelle, Patrick. *The Āśrama System: The History and Hermeneutics of a Religious Institution*. New York: Oxford University Press, 1993.

——, trans. *Upanisads*. New York: Oxford University Press, 1996.

Otto, Rudolf. *Mysticism East and West: A Comparative Analysis of the Nature of Mysticism*. Translated by Bertha L. Bracey and Richenda C. Payne. New York: Macmillan, 1932.

Outka, Gene. *Agape: An Ethical Analysis*. New Haven, Conn.: Yale University Press, 1972.

Outka, Gene and John P. Reeder, Jr., eds. *Religion and Morality: A Collection of Essays*. Garden City, N.Y.: Anchor, 1973.

Ozment, Steven E. *Mysticism and Dissent: Religious Ideology and Social Protest in the Sixteenth Century*. New Haven, Conn.: Yale University Press, 1973.

Palmer, David. "Masao Abe, Zen Buddhism, and Social Ethics." *Journal of Buddhist Ethics* 4 (1997): pp. 1-12.

Pandeya, R. C. "Jivanmukta and Social Concerns." *Indian Philosophical Annual* 2 (1966): pp. 119-24.

Pappu, S. S. Rama Rao. "Detachment and Moral Agency in the Bhagavad Gita." Pp. 148-57 in *Perspectives on Vedanta: Essays in Honor of Professor P. T. Raju*, edited by S. S. Rama Rao Pappu. New York: E. J. Brill, 1988.

Passmore, John. *The Perfectibility of Man*. London: Duckworth, 1970.

Peacock, James L. "Mystics and Merchants in Fourteenth Century Germany: A Speculative Reconstruction of Their Psychological Bond and its Implications for Social Change." *Journal for the Scientific Study of Religion* 8 (Spring 1969): pp. 47-59.

Perrett, Roy W. "Egoism, Altruism and Intentionalism in Buddhist Ethics." *Journal of Indian Philosophy* 15 (March 1987): pp. 71-85.

——. *Hindu Ethics: A Philosophical Study*. Honolulu: University of Hawaii Press, 1998.

Petry, Ray C. "Social Responsibility and the Late Medieval Mystics." *Church History* 21 (March 1952): pp. 3-19.

——, ed. *Late Medieval Mysticism*. Philadelphia: Westminster Press, 1957.

Porete, Marguerite. *The Mirror of Simple Souls*. Translated by Ellen L. Babinsky. Mahwah, N. J.: Paulist Press, 1993.

Potter, Karl H. *Presuppositions of India's Philosophies*. Englewood Cliffs, N.J.: Prentice-Hall, 963.

——, ed. *Advaita Vedānta Up to Śamkara and His Pupils*. Princeton, N.J.: Princeton University Press, 1981.

Prebish, Charles S. ed. *Buddhist Monastic Discipline: The Sanskrit Prātimoksa Sūtras of the Mahāsāmghikas and Mūlasarvāstivādins*. University Park: Pennsylvania State University Press, 1975.

——. "Text and Traditions in the Study of Buddhist Ethics." *Pacific World* 9 (Fall 1993): pp. 49-68.

Proudfoot, Wayne. "Mysticism, the Numinous, and the Moral." *Journal of Religious Ethics* 4 (Spring 1976): pp. 3-28.

Putnam, Hilary. "The French Revolution and the Holocaust: Can Ethics be Ahistorical?" Pp. 299-312 in *Culture and Modernity: East-West Philosophical Perspectives*, edited by Eliot Deutsch. Honolulu: University of Hawaii, 1991.

Pye, Michael. *Skilful Means: A Concept in Mahayana Buddhism*. London: Duckworth, 1978.

Queen, Christopher S., and Sallie B. King, eds. *Engaged Buddhism: Buddhist Liberation Movements in Asia*. Albany: State University of New York Press, 1996.

Quinn, Philip L. *Divine Commands and Moral Requirements*. Oxford: Clarendon Press, 1978.

Radhakrishnan, Sarvepalli. "The Ethics of the Upanisads." Pp. 207-30 in his *Indian Philosophy*, vol. 1. London: George Allen & Unwin, 1948a.

——. "The Ethics of Samkara." Pp. 612-34 in his *Indian Philosophy*, vol. 2. London: George Allen & Unwin, 1948b.

——. "Mysticism and Ethics in Hindu Thought." Pp. 58-114 in his *Eastern Religions and Western Thought*, 2nd ed. London: Oxford University Press, 1951.

Rahman, Fazlur. "Some Key Ethical Concepts of the Qur'an." *Journal of Religious Ethics* 11 (Fall 1983): pp. 170-85.

Raju, P. T. "The Epics and the Ethical Codes." Pp. 210-18 in his *The Philosophical Traditions of India*. Pittsburgh: University of Pittsburgh Press, 1972.

Reat, Noble Ross. "Theravada Buddhism and Morality: Objections and Corrections." *Journal of the American Academy of Religion* 48 (Fall 1980): pp. 433-40.

Reichenbach, Bruce R. *The Law of Karma: A Philosophical Study*. Honolulu: University of Hawaii Press, 1990.

Reynolds, Frank E. "The Two Wheels of Dhamma: A Study of Early Buddhism." Pp. 6-30 in *The Two Wheels of Dhamma: Essays on the Theravada Tradition in India and Ceylon*, edited by Gananath Obeyesekere, Frank Reynolds, and Bardwell L. Smith. Chambersburg, PA: American Academy of Religion, 1972.

——. "Four Modes of Theravāda Action." *Journal of Religious Ethics* 7 (Spring 1979): pp. 12-26.

——. "Contrasting Modes of Action: A Comparative Study of Buddhist and Christian Ethics." *History of Religions* 20, no. 1-2 (1980): pp. 128-46.

Reynolds, Frank E., and Robert Campany. "Buddhist Ethics." Pp. 498-504 in *The Encyclopedia of Religion*, vol. 2, edited by Mircea Eliade. New York: Macmillan, 1975.

Rist, J. M. "The Self and Others." Pp. 153-68 in his *Plotinus: The Road to Reality*. Cambridge: Cambridge University Press, 1967.

Rolston, Holmes. "Can the East Help the West to Value Nature?" *Philosophy East and West* 37 (April 1987): pp. 172-90.

Rosemont, Henry, Jr. "Against Relativism." Pp. 36-70 in *Interpreting Across Boundaries: New Essays in Comparative Philosophy*, edited by Gerald James Larson and Eliot Deutsch. Princeton, N.J.: Princeton University Press, 1988.

——. "Is There a Primordial Tradition in Ethics?" Pp. 234-50 in *Fragments of Infinity: Essays in Religion and Philosophy*, edited by Arvind Sharma. New York: Avery, 1991.

Rost, H. T. D. *The Golden Rule: A Universal Ethic*. Oxford: George Ronald, 1986.

Roth, Harold D. "The *Laozi* in the Context of Early Daoist Mystical Praxis." Pp. 59-96 in *Religious and Philosophical Aspects of the* Laozi, edited by Mark Csikszentmihalyi and Philip J. Ivanhoe. Albany: State University of New York Press, 1999.

Ruf, Henry L. "Moral Problems and Religious Mysteries: A Cross-Cultural Perspective." *Dialogue & Alliance* 1 (Fall 1987): pp. 77-92.

Runzo, Joseph, and Nancy M. Martin, eds. *Ethics in the World Religions*. Oxford: Oneworld Publications, 2001.

Ruse, Michael. "Evolutionary Ethics." Pp. 93-112 in *Biology, Ethics, and the Origins of Life*, edited by Holmes Rolston III. Boston: Jones and Barlett, 1995.

Ruusbroec, John (Jan van). *The Spiritual Espousals and Other Works*. Translated by James A. Wiseman. Mahwah, N.J.: Paulist Press, 1985.

Saddhatissa, Hammalaiva. *Buddhist Ethics: Essence of Buddhism*. New York: George Braziller, 1971.

Sathaye, S. G. *Moral Choice and Early Hindu Thought*. Bombay: Jaico Publishing, 1970.

Sayre-McCord, Geoffrey, ed. *Essays on Moral Realism*. Ithaca, N.Y.: Cornell University Press, 1988.

Scharfstein, Ben-Ami. *Amoral Politics: The Persistent Truth of Machiavellism*. Albany: State University of New York Press, 1995.

Schatz-Uffenheimer, Rivka. *Hasidism as Mysticism: Quietistic Elements in Eighteenth Century Hasidic Thought*. Translated by Jonathan Chipman. Princeton, N.J.: Princeton University Press, 1993.

Scholem, Gershom G. "Mysticism and Society." *Diogenes* 58 (Summer 1967): pp. 1-24.

———. "Redemption Through Sin." Pp. 78-141 in his *The Messianic Idea in Judaism and Other Essays on Jewish Spirituality*. New York: Schocken Books, 1971.

Schwartz, Benjamin I. *The World of Thought in Ancient China*. Cambridge, Mass.: Harvard University Press, 1985.

Schweitzer, Albert. *Christianity and the Religions of the World*. Translated by Johanna Powers. New York: H. Holt, 1939.

———. *Indian Thought and Its Development*. Translated by C. E. B. Russell. New York: H. Holt, 1936.

Seneviratne, H. L. "Samgha and Society." Pp. 40-47 in *The Encyclopedia of Religion*, vol. 13, edited by Mircea Eliade. New York: Macmillan, 1975.

Sharot, Stephen. "The Sacredness of Sin: Antinomianism and Models of Man." *Religion* 13 (January 1983): pp. 37-54.

Singer, Peter, ed. *A Companion to Ethics*. Oxford: Blackwell, 1991.

———. *How Are We to Live? Ethics in an Age of Self-Interest*. Melbourne: Text Publishing, 1993a.

———. *Practical Ethics*, 2nd ed. New York: Cambridge University Press, 1993b.

Sizemore, Russell F., and Donald K. Swearer, eds. *Ethics, Wealth, and Salvation: A Study in Buddhist Social Ethics*. Columbia, S.C.: University of South Carolina Press, 1990.

Slingerland, Edward. "Effortless Action: The Chinese Spiritual Ideal of Wu-wei." *Journal of the American Academy of Religion* 68 (June 2000): pp. 293-328.

Slote, Michael. *From Morality to Virtue*. New York: Oxford University Press, 1992.

———. "Virtue Ethics." Pp. 175-238 in Marcia W. Baron, Philip Pettit, and Michael Slote, *Three Methods of Ethics: A Debate*. Oxford: Blackwell, 1997.

Smart, Ninian. "Moral Discourse and Religion." Pp. 179-96 in his *Reasons and Faiths: An Investigation of Religious Discourse, Christian and Non-Christian*. London: Routledge & Kegan Paul, 1958.

———. "God, Bliss, and Morality." Pp. 11-24 in his *Concept and Empathy: Essays in the Study of Religion*. New York: New York University Press, 1986.

———. "Living Liberation: Jivanmukti and Nirvana." Pp. 89-97 in his *Concept and Empathy: Essays in the Study of Religion*. New York: New York University Press, 1986.

Smith, Huston. *The World's Religions: Our Great Wisdom Traditions*. San Francisco: Harper, 1991.

Smurl, James F. *Religious Ethics: A Systems Approach*. Englewood Cliffs, N.J.: Prentice-Hall, 1972.

———. "Cross-Cultural Comparisons in Ethics: A Critical Response to Sally Wang." *Journal of Religious Ethics* 4 (Spring 1976): pp. 47-56.

Sober, Elliot, and David Sloan Wilson. *Unto Others: The Evolution and Psychology of Unselfish Behavior*. Cambridge, Mass.: Harvard University Press, 1998.

Spero, Shubert. *Morality, Halakha, and the Jewish Tradition*. New York: Ktav Publishing House, 1983.

Spiro, Melford E. *Buddhism and Society: A Great Tradition and Its Burmese Vicissitudes*, 2nd ed. Berkeley: University of California Press, 1982.

Staal, Frits. "Review of Danto's *Mysticism and Morality*." *Journal of Philosophy* 71 (28 March 1974): pp. 174-81.

Stace, Walter T. *Mysticism and Philosophy*. Philadelphia: Lippincott, 1960.

Stack, George J. "Nietzsche's Antinomianism." *Nietzsche-Studien* 20 (1991): pp. 109-33.

Stark, Rodney. "Gods, Rituals, and the Moral Order." *Journal for the Scientific Study of Religion* 40 (December 2001): pp. 619-36.

Statman, Daniel, ed. *Virtue Ethics*. Edinburgh: Edinburgh University Press, 1997.

Stauffer, Lee. "Is an Ethical Theory Possible Within Zen Buddhism?" *Southwest Philosophical Studies* 11 (Spring 1989): pp. 80-84.

Stoeber, Micheal. *Evil and the Mystics' God: Towards a Mystical Theodicy*. Houndmills, England: Macmillan, 1992.

Storr, Anthony. *Feet of Clay—Saints, Sinners, and Madmen: A Study of Gurus*. New York: Free Press, 1996.

Stout, Jeffrey. "Weber's Progency, Once Removed." *Religious Studies Review* 6 (October 1980): pp. 289-95.

——. "Toward a Genealogy of Morals." Pp. 201-227 in his *The Flight from Authority: Religion, Morality, and the Quest for Autonomy*. Notre Dame, Ind.: University of Notre Dame Press, 1981.

——. "Holism and Comparative Ethics: A Response to Little." *Journal of Religious Ethics* 11 (Fall 1983): pp. 301-16.

——. "Religion and Morality." Pp. 109-23 in his *Ethics After Babel: The Languages of Morals and Their Discontents*. Boston: Beacon Press, 1988.

——. "Commitments and Traditions in the Study of Religious Ethics." *Journal of Religious Ethics* 25 (1997 Supplement): pp. 23-56.

Strong, John S. *The Legend of King Aśoka: A Study and Translation of the Aśokāvadāna*. Princeton: Princeton University Press, 1983.

Suzuki, Daisetz Teitaro. "Ethics and Zen Buddhism." Pp. 606-15 in *Moral Principles of Action: Man's Ethical Imperative*, edited by Ruth Nanda Anshen. New York: Harper & Row, 1952.

——. *Mysticism: Christian and Buddhist*. New York: Harper & Row, 1957.

——. "Basic Thoughts Underlying Eastern Ethical and Social Practices." Pp. 428-47 in *The Status of the Individual in East and West*, edited by Charles A. Moore. Honolulu: University of Hawaii Press, 1968.

——. *Zen and Japanese Culture*. Princeton, N.J.: Princeton University Press, 1970.

Swearer, Donald K. "Nirvana, No-Self, and Comparative Religious Ethics." *Religious Studies Review* 6 (October 1980): pp. 301-6.

——. *The Buddhist World of Southeast Asia*. Albany: State University of New York Press, 1995.

——. "Buddhist Virtue, Voluntary Poverty, and Extensive Benevolence." *Journal of Religious Ethics* 26 (Spring 1998): 71-103.

—— and Patrick G. Henry. *For the Sake of the World: The Spirit of Buddhist and Christian Monasticism*. Minneapolis, Minn.: Fortress Press, 1989.

Tachibana, Shundō. *The Ethics of Buddhism*. London: Oxford University Press, 1926.

Tambiah, Stanley. *World Conqueror and World Renouncer: A Study of Buddhism and Polity in Thailand Against a Historical Background*. Cambridge: Cambridge University Press, 1976.

——. *Buddhism Betrayed? Religion, Politics, and Violence in Sri Lanka*. Chicago: University of Chicago Press, 1992.

Tatz, Mark, trans. *Asanga's Chapter on Ethics with the Commentary of Tsong-Kha-Pa: The Basic Path to Awakening, the Complete Bodhisattva.* Lewiston, N.Y.: Edwin Mellen Press, 1986.

Taylor, Richard. *Virtue Ethics: An Introduction.* Amherst, N.Y.: Prometheus Books, 2002.

Thakur, Shivesh Chandra. *Christian and Hindu Ethics.* London: George Allen & Unwin, 1969.

Thurman, Howard. "Mysticism and Ethics." *Journal of Religious Thought* 27, Supplement (1970): pp. 23-30.

———. "Mysticism and Social Change." *Spiritual Frontiers* 4 (1972): pp. 229-35.

Thurman, Robert A. F., trans. *The Holy Teaching of Vimalakīrti: A Mahāyāna Scripture.* University Park: Pennsylvania State University Press, 1976.

———. "The Emptiness That is Compassion: An Essay on Buddhist Ethics." *Religious Traditions* 4 (October-November 1981): pp. 11-34.

———. "Guidelines for Buddhist Social Activism Based on Nāgārjuna's *Jewel Garland of Royal Counsels*." *The Eastern Buddhist* 16 (Spring 1983): pp. 19-51.

———. "The Politics of Enlightenment." *Tricycle: The Buddhist Review* 2 (Fall 1992): 28-33.

Tiles, J.R. *Moral Measures: An Introduction to Ethics West and East.* New York: Routledge, 2000.

Tillich, Paul. "Vertical and Horizontal Thinking." *The American Scholar* 15 (Winter 1945-1946): pp. 102-5.

———. *Morality and Beyond.* New York: Harper & Row, 1963.

Underhill, Evelyn. *Mysticism: A Study in the Nature and Development of Man's Spiritual Consciousness.* New York: E. P. Dutton, 1911.

———. *Practical Mysticism.* New York: E. P. Dutton, 1915.

Underwood, Frederic B. "Notes on Conscience in Indian Tradition." *Journal of Chinese Philosophy* 2 (March 1974): pp. 59-65.

———. "Aspects of Justice in Ancient India." *Journal of Chinese Philosophy* 5 (September 1978): pp. 271-85.

Unger, Peter. *Living High and Letting Die: Our Illusion of Innocence.* New York: Oxford University Press, 1996.

Upadhyaya, K. N. *Early Buddhism and the Bhagavad Gita.* Delhi: Motilal Banarsidass, 1971.

Urmson, J. O. "Saints and Heroes." Pp. 198-216 in *Essays in Moral Philosophy*, edited by Abraham I. Melden. Seattle: University of Washington Press, 1958.

Victoria, Brian. *Zen at War.* New York: Weatherhill, 1997.

Wahba, Mourad. "The Concept of the Good in Islamic Philosophy." Pp. 484-92 in *A Companion to World Philosophies*, edited by Eliot Deutsch and Ron Bontekoe. Malden, Mass.: Blackwell, 1999.

Wainwright, William J. "Mysticism and Morality." *Journal of Religious Ethics* 4 (Spring 1976): pp. 29-36.

———. "Mysticism and Morality." Pp. 198-231 in his *Mysticism: A Study of its Nature, Cognitive Value, and Moral Implications.* Madison: University of Wisconsin Press, 1981.

Waley, Arthur. *The Way and its Power.* London: George Allen & Unwin, 1934.

———. *Three Ways of Thought in Ancient China.* Garden City, N.Y.: Doubleday, 1956.

Wallace, Vesna A., and B. Alan Wallace, trans. *A Guide to the Bodhisattva Way of Life by Śāntideva.* Ithaca, N.Y.: Snow Lion Publications, 1997.

Wang, Sally A. "Can Man Go Beyond Ethics? The System of Padmasambhava." *Journal of Religious Ethics* 3 (Spring-Summer 1975): pp. 141-55.

Warriar, A. G. Krishna. "Advaitic Ethics—A Re-Examination." Pp. 499-508 in *Sanskrit and Indological Studies: Dr. V. Raghavan Felicitation Volume*, edited by R. N. Dandekar, et al. Delhi: Motilal Barnarsidass, 1975.

Watson, Burton, trans. *The Complete Works of Chuang Tzu*. New York: Columbia University Press, 1968.

Wattles, Jeffrey. "Levels of Meaning in the Golden Rule." *Journal of Religious Ethics* 15 (Spring 1987): pp. 106-29.

——. *The Golden Rule*. New York: Oxford University Press, 1996.

Wayman, Alex. *The Buddhist Tantras: Light on Indo-Tibetan Esotericism*. New York: Samuel Weiser, 1973.

——. *Ethics of Tibet: Bodhisattva Section of Tsong-Kha-Pa's Lam Rim Chen Mo*. Albany: State University of New York Press, 1991.

Weber, Max. "Religious Ethics, the World Order, and Culture." Pp. 207-22 in his *The Sociology of Religion*, translated by Ephraim Fischoff. Boston: Beacon Press, 1963.

Weiss, Raymond L. *Maimonides' Ethics: The Encounter of Philosophic and Religious Morality*. Chicago: University of Chicago Press, 1991.

White, Reginald E. O. *Christian Ethics: The Historical Development*. Atlanta, Ga.: John Knox Press, 1981.

Whitehill, James. "Is There a Zen Ethic?" *The Eastern Buddhist* 20 (Spring 1987): pp. 9-33.

——. "Buddhist Ethics in Western Context: The Virtues Approach." *Journal of Buddhist Ethics* 1 (1994): pp. 1-15.

Williams, Bernard. *Ethics and the Limits of Philosophy*. Cambridge, Mass.: Harvard University Press, 1985.

Williams, Paul. *Altruism and Reality: Studies in the Philosophy of the Bodhicaryāvatāra*. Surrey, England: Curzon, 1998.

Wilson, Colin. *Rogue Messiahs: Tales of Self-Proclaimed Saviors*. Charlottesville, Va.: Hampton Roads, 2000.

Wilson, Edward O. *On Human Nature*. Cambridge, Mass.: Harvard University Press, 1978.

——. "The Biological Basis of Morality." *The Atlantic Monthly* 281 (April 1998): pp. 53-70.

Wilson, Joe Bransford. "The Monk as Bodhisattva: A Tibetan Integration of Buddhist Moral Points of View." *Journal of Religious Ethics* 24 (Fall 1996): pp. 377-402.

Wiltshire, Martin G. "The 'Suicide' Problem in the Pāli Canon." *Journal of the International Association of Buddhist Studies* 6 (1983): pp. 124-40.

Wolf, Susan. "Moral Saints." *Journal of Philosophy* 79 (August 1982): pp. 419-39.

——. "Morality and Partiality." *Philosophical Perspectives* 6 (1992): 243-59.

Woods, Richard. "Mysticism and Social Action." Pp. 159-73 in his *Mysterion: An Approach to Mystical Spirituality*. Chicago: Thomas More Press, 1981.

——. "Mysticism and Social Action: The Mystic's Calling, Development and Social Activity." *Journal of Consciousness Studies* 3, no. 2 (1996): pp. 158-71.

Yandell, Keith E. "On Classifying Indian Ethical Systems." *Journal of the Indian Council of Philosophical Research* 2 (1985): pp. 61-66.

Yearley, Lee H. "The Perfected Person in the Radical *Chuang-tzu*." Pp. 125-39 in *Experimental Essays on Chuang-Tzu*, edited by Victor H. Mair. Honolulu: University of Hawaii Press, 1983.

——. *Mencius and Aquinas: Theories of Virtue and Conceptions of Courage*. Albany: State University of New York Press, 1990.

——. "Selves, Virtues, Odd Genres, and Alien Guides: An Approach to Religious Ethics." *Journal of Religious Ethics* 25 Supplement (1997): pp. 127-55.

Zaehner, Robert C. *Hindu and Muslim Mysticism*. New York: Schocken Books, 1969.

——. "Beyond Good and Evil." Pp. 136-71 in his *Zen, Drugs, and Mysticism*. London: Collins, 1972.

——, trans. *The Bhagavad-Gita*. New York: Oxford University Press, 1973.

——. "Mason, Murder, and Mysticism." *Encounter* 42 (April 1974a): pp. 50-58.

——. "Mysticism Without Love." *Religious Studies* 10 (June 1974b): pp. 257-64.

——. *Our Savage God: The Perverse Use of Eastern Thought*. New York: Sheed and Ward, 1974c.

Index

About the Author

Richard H. Jones holds a Ph.D. from Columbia University in the history and philosophy of religion and an A.B. from Brown University in religious studies. He also a J.D. from the University of California at Berkeley and practices law in New York City where he lives. He is the author of *Science and Mysticism* (Bucknell University Press), *Mysticism Examined* (State University of New York Press), *Reductionism* (Bucknell University Press), and numerous philosophy of religion and law review articles.